HANDBOOK ON TEACHING AND LEARNING FOR SUSTAINABLE DEVELOPMENT

Handbook on Teaching and Learning for Sustainable Development

Edited by

Walter Leal Filho

Professor and Head of the Research and Transfer Centre 'Sustainable Development and Climate Change Management', Hamburg University of Applied Sciences, Germany and Professor of Environment and Technology, Department of Natural Sciences, Manchester Metropolitan University, UK

Amanda Lange Salvia

Research Associate, Graduate Program in Civil and Environmental Engineering, University of Passo Fundo, Brazil

Fernanda Frankenberger

Professor of the Business School, Pontifical Catholic University PUCPR and Universidade Positivo – UP, Brazil

 Edward Elgar
PUBLISHING

Cheltenham, UK • Northampton, MA, USA

Published by
Edward Elgar Publishing Limited
The Lypiatts
15 Lansdown Road
Cheltenham
Glos GL50 2JA
UK

Edward Elgar Publishing, Inc.
William Pratt House
9 Dewey Court
Northampton
Massachusetts 01060
USA

Paperback edition 2022

A catalogue record for this book
is available from the British Library

Library of Congress Control Number: 2021936628

This book is available electronically in the **Elgar**online
Geography, Planning and Tourism subject collection
http://dx.doi.org/10.4337/9781839104657

ISBN 978 1 83910 464 0 (cased)
ISBN 978 1 83910 465 7 (eBook)
ISBN 978 1 0353 0906 1 (paperback)

Typeset by Servis Filmsetting Ltd, Stockport, Cheshire

Printed and bound by CPI Group (UK) Ltd, Croydon, CR0 4YY

Contents

Contributors

Jessica K. Abbonizio, Monash University, Australia

María Fernanda Acosta Altamirano, National University of Education (UNAE), Ecuador and Université Côte d'Azur, France

Cahyono Agus, Universitas Gadjah Mada, Indonesia

Francesca Allievi, JAMK University of Applied Sciences, Finland and Barilla Center for Food & Nutrition Foundation, Italy

María Alló, Universidade da Coruña, Spain

Bruno Neves Amado, Federal University of Rio de Janeiro, Brazil

Erika Gabriela Araujo Pérez, National University of Education (UNAE), Ecuador

Katherine Cilae Benedict, Colégio Pedro II, Brazil

María Olga Bernaldo, European University of Madrid, Spain

Joannette J. (Annette) Bos, Monash University, Australia

Gert-Olof Boström, Umeå University, Sweden

Diane Boyd, Liverpool John Moores University, UK

Sharon Bramwell-Lalor, The University of the West Indies, Jamaica

Pita Asih Bekti Cahyanti, Universitas Indonesia, Indonesia

Bento Cavadas, Polytechnic Institute of Santarém, Portugal

Sharon Coen, University of Salford, UK

Loraine D. Cook, The University of the West Indies, Jamaica

Marina Alves Novaes e Cruz, Colégio Pedro II and Universidade Federal do Rio de Janeiro, Brazil

Everton Cummings, The University of the West Indies, Jamaica

Ann Dale, Royal Roads University, Canada

Monica Dantas, Concordia University, Canada

Javiera Eskuche, Universidad de La Frontera, Chile

Therese Ferguson, The University of the West Indies, Jamaica

Ana Fernández, Canterbury Christ Church University, UK

Gonzalo Fernández-Sánchez, European University of Madrid, Spain

Sergio Luiz Braga França, Fluminense Federal University, Brazil

Fernanda Frankenberger, Pontifical Catholic University and Universidade Positivo, Brazil

Anke Franz, Canterbury Christ Church University, UK

Leonardo Esteves de Freitas, Fundação Oswaldo Cruz and Universidade Federal do Rio de Janeiro, Brazil

Carmen Gago-Cortés, Universidade da Coruña, Spain

Edmundo Gallo, Fundação Oswaldo Cruz, São Paulo State University, Brazil, Coimbra University, Portugal and Antióquia University, Colombia

Esther García-González, Universidad de Cádiz, Spain

Genilson Geraldo, Federal University of Santa Catarina (UFSC), Brazil

Sherif Goubran, The American University in Cairo, Egypt

Paula Guarda-Saavedra, Universidad de La Frontera and Universidad Católica del Maule, Chile

Nur Aini Iswati Hasanah, Directorate General of Water Resources, Ministry of Public Works and Housing, Indonesia

Susie S.Y. Ho, Monash University, Australia

Ian Hocking, Canterbury Christ Church University, UK

João Luiz de Moraes Hoeffel, UNIFAAT University Center – Sustainability and Cultural Studies Center (NESC/UNIFAAT), Brazil

Carol Hordatt Gentles, The University of the West Indies, Jamaica

Jean Hugé, Open University of the Netherlands, the Netherlands

R. Bruce Hull, Virginia Tech University, USA

Dzintra Iliško, Institute of Humanities and Societal Sciences, Latvia

Usha Iyer-Raniga, RMIT University, Australia

Aqmal Nur Jihad, Universitas Gadjah Mada, Indonesia

Rocío Jiménez-Fontana, Universidad de Cádiz, Spain

Karishma Kashyap, RMIT University, Australia

Hock Lye Koh, Sunway University, Malaysia

Walter Leal Filho, Hamburg University of Applied Sciences, Germany and Manchester Metropolitan University, UK

Hilary Leighton, Royal Roads University, Canada

Gilson Brito Alves Lima, Fluminense Federal University, Brazil

Elisabete Linhares, Polytechnic Institute of Santarém, Portugal

Ángeles Longarela-Ares, Universidade da Coruña, Spain

Nicholas Van-Erven Ludolf, Fluminense Federal University, Brazil

Claudia Mac-lean, University of Magallanes, Chile

Cecilia Maria Marafelli, Colégio Pedro II, Brazil

Ana Claudia Campuzano Martinez, Colégio Pedro II and Universidade Federal do Rio de Janeiro, Brazil

Sonia Massari, Roma Tre University, Italy and ISIA Design School, Italy

Naomi McLeod, Liverpool John Moores University, UK

Marcelo Jasmim Meiriño, Fluminense Federal University, Brazil

Michael Mortimer, Virginia Tech University, USA

Estefanía Mourelle, Universidade da Coruña, Spain

Antonio Navarrete, Universidad de Cádiz, Spain

Dennis Nigbur, Canterbury Christ Church University, UK

Michael-Anne Noble, Royal Roads University, Canada

Isabella Arlochi de Oliveira, Federal University of Rio de Janeiro, Brazil

Daniel Otto, University of Duisburg-Essen, Germany

Stathi Paxinos, Monash University, Australia

Marli Dias de Souza Pinto, Federal University of Santa Catarina (UFSC), Brazil

Sinikka Pöllänen, University of Eastern Finland, Finland

Rudi W. Pretorius, University of South Africa, South Africa

Osvaldo Luiz Gonçalves Quelhas, Fluminense Federal University, Brazil

Francesca Recanati, Barilla Center for Food & Nutrition Foundation, Italy

David P. Robertson, Virginia Tech University, USA

Carmel Roofe, The University of the West Indies, Jamaica

Maria Inês Rocha de Sá, Colégio Pedro II, Brazil

Amanda Lange Salvia, University of Passo Fundo, Brazil

Luan Santos, Federal University of Rio de Janeiro, Brazil

Sonia Regina da Cal Seixas, State University of Campinas, Brazil

Elizabeth Sidiropoulos, Victoria University, Melbourne, Australia

Victória Fernandes da Silva, Federal University of Rio de Janeiro, Brazil

Wendy Stubbs, Monash University, Australia

Muhammad Sulaiman, Universitas Gadjah Mada, Indonesia

Suratman, Universitas Gadjah Mada, Indonesia

Aldrin E. Sweeney, The University of the West Indies, Jamaica

Verónica Gabriela Tacuri Albarracín, National University of Education (UNAE), Ecuador

Su Yean Teh, Universiti Sains Malaysia, Malaysia

Canute Thompson, The University of the West Indies, Jamaica

Niina Väänänen, University of Eastern Finland, Finland

Rodrigo Vargas-Gaete, Universidad de La Frontera, Chile

Madhavi Venkatesan, Northeastern University, USA

Isabella Villanueva, University of Chile, Chile

Nadra Wagdy, PME MTL – Centre-Est, Canada

Diana Watts, Johns Hopkins University, USA

Katarina Winka, Umeå University, Sweden

Katarzyna Wolanik Boström, Umeå University, Sweden

Luís Perez Zotes, Fluminense Federal University, Brazil

Preface

Education can play a key role in pursuing and in implementing sustainable development. When duly deployed, teaching methods not only serve the purpose of informing students about matters related to sustainable development – be it at school or at university level – but may also empower learners to adopt behaviours and actions that may lead to more sustainable lifestyles and to a sustainable future.

It is widely known among educators and practitioners, that among the many challenges to realise the goal of implementing sustainable development, teaching education has been and still is, one of the major areas to tackle. Indeed, there is a pressing need to strengthen and adapt the institutional framework of pre-service and in-service teacher training, especially at the regional and national levels, so that teaching programmes can better relate to sustainability issues. This need has been highlighted for many years now. Paradoxically, despite the number of recommendations and suggestions made outlining the need to pursue sustainable development in teaching, little progress has been achieved.

This state of affairs suggests that specialist publications are needed in order to move things forward in a more systematic way. One of these basic needs is to acknowledge that it is necessary to address the fragmented nature of the handling of sustainability issues at formal education programmes as a whole, and in teacher education in particular.

Improvements are needed not only in respect of ways to cater for handling sustainability issues in the curriculum, but also on how to approach and promote issues related to sustainable development at multiple levels (e.g., at the community and family level) with a focus on the interplays and interlinkages. Also, the development of flexible teaching methods capable of incorporating environmental, economic, societal and cultural elements, is greatly needed.

It is against this background that this book has been produced. It is a truly interdisciplinary publication, useful to teaching staff and scholars on the one hand, but also to members of governmental agencies on the other, as well as to all those undertaking research and/or executing teaching projects focusing on sustainability from across the world. The book is structured around two parts. Part I, Teaching Practices, comprises chapters dealing with learning processes and methods, as well as curriculum-related issues. It also relates to the UN Sustainable Development Goals, and teachers' training. Part II, Innovation and New Technologies, comprises chapters on pedagogical approaches, case studies, interdisciplinary initiatives and chapters that describe the use of technological approaches and tools to foster sustainability learning.

We thank the authors and reviewers for their contribution. We hope that the contributions in this *Handbook* will provide timely support towards the implementation of teaching initiatives on sustainable development, and will foster the global efforts towards promoting sustainable development practices across schools and universities.

Walter Leal Filho, Amanda Lange Salvia and Fernanda Frankenberger
Winter 2020–21

Introduction to the *Handbook on Teaching and Learning for Sustainable Development*
Walter Leal Filho and Amanda Lange Salvia

The present *Handbook on Teaching and Learning for Sustainable Development* offers a wide range of perspectives, and a comprehensive overview of innovative teaching methods and innovative approaches (e.g., technological, non-technological, social and governance) that show how sustainability teaching may be practised. It contributes to a further understanding of:

- the role of sustainable development in different teaching realities;
- the contribution of sustainable development to citizenship;
- future perspectives in the curriculum;
- the means to reorient education for a sustainable future;
- the various challenges in implementing the principles of sustainable development in practice.

In this context, the contributions of the authors play a key role and outline the many ramifications of a broader understanding of sustainability.

PART I   TEACHING PRACTICES

In Chapter 1, María Olga Bernaldo and Gonzalo Fernández-Sánchez describe how the acquisition of skills related to the field of sustainability from universities may be considered one of the most significant challenges of higher education institutions (HEIs). They describe the work undertaken at the European University of Madrid (EU), a private Spanish university. Results obtained in the last three years from an international volunteer programme are evaluated from two perspectives: (1) service: analysing the perspectives of the local population concerning what objectively has been done in their community and how much it has subjectively impacted their lives; and (2) learning: studying the experience of students who have been working in this programme, assessing the acquisition of skills and values from their education in sustainable development.

In Chapter 2, Marli Dias de Souza Pinto and Genilson Geraldo discuss the inclusion of the discipline of 'informational sustainability' in graduate programmes, as a way of placing information science in the context of the dimensions of sustainable development. Informational sustainability is evidenced as an informational mechanism of access, dissemination and use of sustainable information, aiming at institutionalization, organization and awareness of the information society, with a goal to provide a present quality of life without compromising that of future generations. This methodology may allow students to obtain information about the context of sustainable development and

1

provide informational support for global objectives through participation in seminars, socialization of readings and discussion of the topic, and through the development of scientific studies.

In Chapter 3, Diane Boyd and Naomi McLeod demonstrate the transformative power of reflexive teaching approaches and creative hermeneutics with final year undergraduate students in a university in the United Kingdom. Initially, whilst they demonstrated knowledge of environmental aspects, there was a distinct lack of understanding of political and socio-cultural influences in the form of relational ethics (praxeology). Students were not making interconnections between the three pillars of sustainability (namely political-economical, environmental and socio-cultural) as an embodied, natural, instinctive phenomenon. Creating a relaxed collaborative, open environment was important for encouraging the students to engage reflexively.

In Chapter 4, Elisabete Linhares and Bento Cavadas discuss the fact that oceans are experiencing a reduction in biodiversity due to both overexploitation and various forms of pollution – that is, plastic waste – and that raising the awareness of higher education students about this environmental problem is important. They report on an educational resource entitled 'Bad Plastics – Oceans Free of Plastic'. The resource was structured on the 7E teaching model and focused on UNESCO's Sustainable Development Goal 14 – Life Below Water.

In Chapter 5, focusing on sustainable higher education institutions promoting a holistic approach, Usha Iyer-Raniga and Karishma Kashyap use secondary literature to focus on campus awareness about sustainability through all functions of a higher education institution. The chapter draws on relevant gaps in the literature and suggests a holistic approach be adopted by HEIs in terms of managing indoor and outdoor spaces on campus while also using such institutions to push the boundaries for green building and green campus performance practices. A leadership model is suggested that brings a commitment to education and demonstrating these on campus where possible, while also engaging internal and external stakeholders in the process.

In Chapter 6, Claudia Mac-lean, Isabella Villanueva and Jean Hugé investigate the scope of student-led actions at higher education institutions in Latin America. The University Students Sustainability Congress student initiative at the University of Chile is presented as an in-depth case study followed by an explorative review of four student-led sustainability initiatives at universities in Argentina, Bolivia, Mexico and Peru. The chapter concludes by indicating that higher education institutions show a medium to high level of student involvement in the process of transformation towards sustainability. Additionally, the dominant activities are outreach oriented and their scope can be at the university or at the city level.

In Chapter 7, aiming to identify the main variables associated with recycling behaviour and motivations for waste separation of students at Universidad de La Frontera in Chile, Rodrigo Vargas-Gaete, Paula Guarda-Saavedra and Javiera Eskuche collect and analyse descriptive, behaviour and motivational variables through an online survey. It was identified that students over 21 years of age, who have resided in rural environments and regularly practise physical activity, were the most likely to carry out waste separation for recycling. Environmental education was considered the highest motivation factor to separate waste to recycle, probably linked with increased information/education. The authors indicate how local empirical evidence could support recycling promotion plans.

In Chapter 8, Niina Väänänen and Sinikka Pöllänen present some examples of how to teach sustainability through craft in a Finnish context in light of recent theories of sustainable craft and the United Nations Sustainable Development Goals of Agenda 2030. Craft refers to a standard school subject in which learning by doing has been the distinctive feature of the implementation of the core curriculum since the school system was established in Finland. In crafts, sustainability begins from materials and environment but can ultimately turn into a holistic understanding of crafting as a lifestyle and a viable alternative for a sustainable future.

In Chapter 9, Carmel Roofe, Therese Ferguson, Carol Hordatt Gentles, Sharon Bramwell-Lalor, Loraine D. Cook, Aldrin E. Sweeney, Canute Thompson and Everton Cummings undertook a collaborative action research project to infuse education for sustainable development (ESD) into the courses of the University of the West Indies (Jamaica). Qualitative data in the form of self-reflections along with action plans for infusion were analysed. Self-critique and openness to new ideas, creation of opportunities for students' feedback, flexible application of the process and collaboration with colleagues were presented as four key strategies for infusing ESD. The findings offer a useful platform that other universities can learn from as they seek to infuse ESD into courses and programmes.

In Chapter 10, R. Bruce Hull, David P. Robertson and Michael Mortimer argue that leadership competencies should be included in the education of sustainability professionals, since advancing any of the Sustainable Development Goals requires mobilizing and influencing people. By focusing on leadership for wicked situations, the authors describe a programme that teaches these leadership skills to inspire sustainability professionals using a hybrid of in-person and online pedagogies that include self-guided reflection, problem-based learning, transdisciplinarity and peer-to-peer learning.

In Chapter 11, based on more than two decades of analysis of processes of urbanization and industrialization with deep socio-environmental reflections, Sonia Regina da Cal Seixas and João Luiz de Moraes Hoeffel address the implications of this with regard to violence and the mental health of the population of specific regions in the state of São Paulo, Brazil. This chapter presents how the Sustainable Development Goals of the 2030 Agenda are present in the analyses that aim to improve both socio-environmental and life quality of the population of these study areas, especially concerning mental health and violence reduction.

In Chapter 12, Luan Santos, Victória Fernandes da Silva, Isabella Arlochi de Oliveira and Bruno Neves Amado analyse the Federal University of Rio de Janeiro (UFRJ), Macaé campus, as a case study for developing sustainable extension projects in engineering courses, especially in the context of the Sustainable Development Goals and the 2030 Agenda. Such projects represent a great potential in environmental and sustainable issues and in the internalization of the SDGs at UFRJ. The results mapped some gaps and proposed some actions to better align the assessed projects with the SDGs, inspiring new attitudes both within the university environment and beyond that sphere.

In Chapter 13, Marina Alves Novaes e Cruz, Ana Claudia Campuzano Martinez, Cecilia Maria Marafelli, Katherine Cilae Benedict, Maria Inês Rocha de Sá, Leonardo Esteves de Freitas and Edmundo Gallo present a Brazilian project that is expected to be developed over the next four years in partnership with the Universidade Federal Fluminense, Fundação Oswaldo Cruz, local government and the Forum of Traditional

Communities. The project relates to the training of about 30 teachers from public schools located in *caiçara* communities, in the coastal region of Paraty, Brazil, aiming to strengthen the way of life of these groups and favour processes of adaptation to climatic change. The first part of the training encompasses teachers' awareness, socio-cultural diagnoses of schools and communities diagnosis and the theoretical basis of a differentiated educational proposal.

In Chapter 14, Diana Watts discusses the challenge of engaging environmental science graduate-level students to examine sustainable business as a more dynamic interplay involving business, government and civil society. The chapter describes integrative course projects that serve to challenge key assumptions and encourage reformulation of basic premises preparing environmental students to become co-collaborators in developing future sustainable solutions.

PART II   INNOVATION AND NEW TECHNOLOGIES

In Chapter 15, based on the aspirations of the United Nations Decade of Education for Sustainable Development (DESD 2005–14) and on the need for an educational paradigm shift to integrate socio-cultural and economic dimensions with ethical and aesthetical values, Hock Lye Koh and Su Yean Teh provide critical reflections and useful suggestions on innovations in curriculum and pedagogy. These innovations are considered essential to education for sustainable development in achieving the UN Sustainable Development Goals. Sustainably solving global issues such as climate change, acute water shortages and rapid loss of biodiversity is supported by pedagogy through living examples and experiences at the local, regional and international levels.

In Chapter 16, Daniel Otto draws on the pedagogical approach of digital storytelling – a combination of the ancient tradition of storytelling and the use of digital media – to present the benefits of open educational resources (OER) in an international university teaching project about climate change. The chapter argues that digital storytelling is even more powerful as well as sustainable if implemented in conjunction with concepts related to OER and open pedagogy. A re-examination of the case study through the lens of OER-enabled pedagogy reveals that it secures the students' recognition as the creators of their stories and that their products are made publicly available, ensuring further use and carrying value to others.

In Chapter 17, Wendy Stubbs, Susie S.Y. Ho, Jessica K. Abbonizio, Stathi Paxinos and Joannette J. (Annette) Bos argue that traditional monodisciplinary educational approaches do not adequately prepare students to develop innovative solutions to address the Sustainable Development Goals, as sustainability demands knowledge, skills and perspectives from different disciplines, industries and cultures. To address this, a multidisciplinary team of educators from Monash University, Australia, co-designed an integrated sustainability course to prepare students to address the complex issues underlying the SDGs, drawing upon the Research Skills Development framework. The chapter describes the collaborative model used to design and develop the Master of Environment and Sustainability course and concludes with personal reflections from academics and students.

In Chapter 18, Elizabeth Sidiropoulos demonstrates a novel application of an augmented Learning Activities Survey instrument to assess sustainability education in higher education. Using an online post-test survey administered to students undertaking introductory sustainability education units at two Australian universities, the chapter provides insights on key influences, experiences and types of learning outcomes. The main influences on transformative learning were indicated as personal support, educational resources/activities enabling independent research, engaging in reflection and trying new roles. The use of an augmented Learning Activities Survey instrument has been suggested as a useful first step to evaluate sustainability education in higher education.

In Chapter 19, based on the need to take time in building the concept of environment so that educators can access the concept of sustainability and of the Sustainable Development Goals, Rocío Jiménez-Fontana, Esther García-González and Antonio Navarrete present an educational process developed over 11 years as part of the Andalusian Interuniversity Master's Degree in Environmental Education. The chapter examines to what extent SDGs are present in the prospective environmental teachers' conceptions about the environment, and how this varies throughout the process. Even though the goals are present from the beginning, the results indicate increased richness and representativeness in approaching the SDGs towards the end of the process. Additionally, the results indicate that the greatest increase at the end corresponds to the SDGs comprising economic sustainable development in combination with social and natural aspects.

In Chapter 20, Osvaldo Luiz Gonçalves Quelhas, Sergio Luiz Braga França, Marcelo Jasmim Meiriño, Gilson Brito Alves Lima, Luís Perez Zotes and Nicholas Van-Erven Ludolf present a case study of the Post-graduation Program in Management Systems (PPSIG) at Fluminense Federal University, in Rio de Janeiro, Brazil. The PPSIG database was investigated through a data mining process to analyse its performance and results, including scientific production, technical reports, research projects, teaching activities, official documents, among others. The promotion of interdisciplinary courses, social actions, internationalization and interinstitutional integration are indicated as contributors to the promotion of education for sustainable development, qualifying the programme for the implementation of sustainability in the region.

In Chapter 21, Gert-Olof Boström, Katarina Winka and Katarzyna Wolanik Boström present two different cases from Umeå School of Business, Economics and Statistics, Sweden, to discuss the potential of extra-curricular activities (ECAs) in providing opportunities for a multidimensional learning experience in education for sustainable development. The cases suggest that ECAs can serve as a source of deeper interest by offering an up-to-date, nuanced knowledge of sustainability practices in research, work life and society at large, in addition to motivating students to think critically and creatively about the practices they are going to encounter in their future work life.

In Chapter 22, Sonia Massari, Francesca Allievi and Francesca Recanati investigate the principles needed to develop a new pedagogy for sustainability, accounting for the role of empathy. The teaching approach is developed through the use of the Food Sustainability Index (FSI) as an educational tool for teaching food sustainability in higher education settings, taking into consideration a systematic approach and the complexity of food sustainability issues. The chapter describes two experiments based on the use of the tool at the Bachelor and Master degree levels. Based on these experiments, an educational model to foster the empathic process for sustainability teaching in higher education is presented.

In Chapter 23, Madhavi Venkatesan highlights how the teaching of economics can enable the tangibility of the discipline, considering the importance of how teaching is provided and how freedom is given to question and critically assess the social construction of the economic framework. The chapter establishes the opportunity for the economics discipline to foster sustainability and promote its adoption through addressing the role of conscious consumption and responsible participation in consumer, investor and government decision making. The role of culture in sustainability and the relationship between economic measurement and cultural convergence, resource utilization and climate change are also discussed.

In Chapter 24, Dzintra Iliško reinforces the role of universities in creating spaces to envision sustainable futures and the need to change students' lifestyles and habits to involve them in the process of imagining sustainable futures and allowing experiential and applied learning modes. Based on the importance of viewing sustainability as a multidimensional issue involving multiple actors and allowing the space for profound agreements and respectful disagreements among all of them, the author presents initiatives undertaken in the regional university by engaging students in the process of changing their perspectives and identifying core values in a sensemaking mode towards more sustainable futures.

In Chapter 25, Cahyono Agus, Nur Aini Iswati Hasanah, Aqmal Nur Jihad, Pita Asih Bekti Cahyanti, Muhammad Sulaiman and Suratman discuss the initiative and strategy taken by Universitas Gadjah Mada in planning and developing a sustainable campus. The Sustainable Blue Campus works as a programme to implement education for sustainable development and the Sustainable Development Goals and promote both academic and non-academic atmospheres to support the integrated education, research and community service processes. Principles of win–win solutions, co-creation, co-finance, flexibility and sustainability are integrated and a network collaboration between the university and the regional government, industry, community and professional associations is proposed.

In Chapter 26, Rudi W. Pretorius critically reflects on the value and challenges of interdisciplinary settings in higher education as intellectual spaces for sustainability learning. The chapter uses the undergraduate curricula of 19 geography departments at universities in South Africa (2016–17) and feedback from interviews and focus groups conducted at a selection of these departments. The chapter presents the trends towards interdisciplinarity in undergraduate geography curricula in South Africa and discusses the need for a balance in the undergraduate geography curricula regarding aspects such as the discipline's integrity, vocational requirements and twenty-first-century sustainability challenges.

In Chapter 27, Michael-Anne Noble, Hilary Leighton and Ann Dale address prevailing dualisms between humans and nature and subject and object through a curriculum designed to invite students to step into experiential outdoor spaces with time enough to develop an affective connection to the place and a greater conscious awareness of belonging. Through the development of critical knowledge and practices related to ecosystem structure and function, biodiversity and sustainability, examples from Royal Roads University faculty illuminate how natural and social sciences, when choreographed together for learning, are critical to establishing a primary motive of 'relatedness' as it pertains to an indissoluble unity between people and place. The chapter suggests that while moving from nature as a mere backdrop to co-implicating themselves in a continual process of being in place, students deepen their identification with place and might develop willingness to protect what has become part of their own sense of identity.

In Chapter 28, Monica Dantas, Sherif Goubran and Nadra Wagdy investigate the evolution of sustainability-related projects and initiatives at universities, moving beyond simple participation formats to include innovative collaborative and communal forms, claiming varied levels of contribution to community building and resilience, and narrowing the knowledge-to-action gap. The chapter uses Season Jars, a student-led project at Concordia University (Montreal, Quebec), to examine how innovative approaches to education combined with the innate interdisciplinary of food can provide innovative experiential learning platforms for sustainable development. The significance of the shifting roles of organizers and participants in building capacity for transformative action within participatory learning environments is discussed and a universal framework that can be replicated in other universities has been proposed.

In Chapter 29, María Fernanda Acosta Altamirano, Verónica Gabriela Tacuri Albarracín and Erika Gabriela Araujo Pérez explore and gather information regarding the agricultural and festival calendar of the rural parish San Andrés Taday located within the province of Cañar, Ecuador, and the methodology they used to get this information. Ancestral knowledge is transmitted over generations through the Agrofest calendar, which seeks to implement and harvest family orchards for self-consumption while balancing agricultural activities and caring for the environment. In research by the National University of Education to reconstruct and recognize the 'Agricultural and festive calendar', information on the oral ancestral knowledge of people has been compiled through participatory workshops with families that own the orchards. This experience reflects the importance of building an educational establishment focused on the dialogue between knowledge and the preservation of the environment.

In Chapter 30, María Alló, Carmen Gago-Cortés, Ángeles Longarela-Ares and Estefanía Mourelle present a pioneer project carried out by the Universidade da Coruña, Spain, to incorporate sustainable development in the criteria of future professionals. The sustainability and Big Data massive open online course (MOOC) emerged as a space to raise awareness and promote sustainability in the environmental, social and economic dimensions. The MOOC is presented as a project for exploring new educational tools, as well as serving as a means to publicize and increase the visibility of sustainable development.

In Chapter 31, after summarizing previous research on the social psychology of sustainability, Dennis Nigbur, Ana Fernández, Sharon Coen, Anke Franz and Ian Hocking report on a survey of 118 university staff measuring attitudes, social norms, perceived control, self-identity and intentions relating to office waste recycling, energy saving and transport choice. The chapter discusses how universities can cultivate sustainability through norms and self-identities.

In the final chapter, Chapter 32, Walter Leal Filho provides an overview of some of the challenges seen in sustainable development teaching and outlines ways to maximize its impacts, including students' engagement, variety of methods and balanced global–local focus. After several cases exploring strategies and tools to successfully contribute to sustainability teaching, this chapter calls attention to the need to unlock the transformative power of the teaching process and therefore better engage learners and promote a positive effect on their own lives, both personal and professional.

In summary, the contributions provided in this *Handbook* offer an overview of the many ways in which sustainability can be integrated into both institutional practice and in all areas of the curriculum, in particular into cross-curriculum themes such as citizenship, health and consumer education. The experience and knowledge shared by the authors means that some advice may be provided to those interesting in developing or deploying new teaching and learning strategies, which may foster the cause of embedding sustainable development as a core part of teaching and learning processes.

PART I

TEACHING PRACTICES

1. International service-learning as a driver for sustainability competencies development

María Olga Bernaldo and Gonzalo Fernández-Sánchez

1. INTRODUCTION

Sustainable development (SD) is fundamental to every human activity, and in the field of education it is considered essential (United Nations Educational, Scientific and Cultural Organization [UNESCO], 2009). The interrelationship between education for sustainable development (ESD) and SD was understood even before they were formally defined, as early as 1972 in the Stockholm Declaration. Future decision makers will be those who are currently being trained in higher education institutions (HEIs). The literature reflects an important consensus on the important role HEIs have in achieving SD and establishing initiatives that generate sustainable livelihoods, a future for young people and the transformation of behaviours and practices (Mochizuki and Fadeeva, 2008; UNESCO, 2009; Yasin and Rahman, 2011).

Some authors consider ESD as a new paradigm: a social metamorphosis capable of restoring the balance between the social, economic and political systems using holistic strategies that place the natural environment in the foreground. Currently, the social, economic and political systems are part of the problem because they promote individualistic patterns as well as certain behaviour and consumption patterns (e.g., Wade, 2008). Pavlova (2009) proposes that ESD becomes a new paradigm in the curricula to respond to social needs. The Education Network for Sustainable Development defines ESD as 'the process of acquiring the knowledge, skills and attitudes necessary to build local and global societies that are fair, equitable and live within the environmental limits of our planet, both now as in the future' (Environmental Association for Universities and Colleges, 2013, p. 7).

Although many HEIs have begun their journey towards ESD, programmes are far from being fully implemented (Hanover Research, 2011; Waas, Verbruggen and Wright, 2010; Wright and Wilton, 2012). The conceptual complexity of SD, difficulty of implementing new concepts in the university environment and inertia for change (Ferrer-Balas et al., 2010; Jones, Selby and Sterling, 2010; Lozano, 2012) hinder ESD's integration into university activities and curricula. Indeed, only 15 universities out of more than 14 000 worldwide publish sustainability reports (Lozano, 2010).

According to Lee, Barker and Mouasher (2013), it is necessary to integrate ESD in all aspects of university life. This includes education, campus operations, community outreach, evaluation and reports, institutional frameworks and research (Lidgren, Rodhe and Huisingh, 2006; Lozano, 2010; Fernández-Sanchez et al., 2014a). The main objective of a university towards ESD is to be a proactive agent by introducing the student and the entire university community to an educational process that facilitates a personal transformation and offers a different view of the world (Ortega, 2014). In this process, learning, teaching, practical applications and different social needs must be linked (Aguilera et al., 2010).

The skills, knowledge, habits, attitudes, aptitudes and values of SD are considered the main drivers for achieving ESD in HEIs (Murga-Menoyo, 2015). A consensus in the literature regards a set of key sustainability competencies based on critical thinking and systems thinking as well as communication and collaboration skills (Tarrant and Thiele, 2015, 2016; UNESCO, 2017).

The identification of competencies, however, is of no benefit for ESD unless students are given the capacity for their development. Murga-Menoyo (2015) explains the importance of identifying elements or components that interact with each other, which can be competing. When interacting, these elements lead to capabilities that will generate these factors or competencies. Observation of indicators (behaviours) allows for inferring of the existence of corresponding capacities. For these capacities to be useful in ESD, the development of competencies should be coordinated. Table 1.1 summarizes Murga-Menoyo's explication.

The qualitative systematic review of competencies in SD carried out by Muñoz et al. (2017) concludes that three competing axes are present: (1) knowing; (2) knowing how to do; and (3) knowing how to be present. Yet according to Muñoz et al., the axis of 'knowing how to live together' needs to be explicitly added to contribute to the development of alliances and value the interdependence of people, communities and cultures.

The Association for the Advancement of Sustainability in Higher Education (AASHE, 2012) evaluated 1777 publications related to ESD, a small number of which focused on the pedagogy of skills development. In the literature reviewed, there is a lack of studies on how to acquire sustainability competencies. Studies reviewed consisted chiefly of proposals on which competencies should be developed, the degree of acquisition, and methods for how to achieve competence. Research lacked empirical results on different improvements from diverse strategies for the acquisition of ESD skills. Only a few attempts are seen in the body of literature, such as analysing the integration of competencies in a specific curriculum (Lambrechts et al., 2013) or evaluating the acquisition of sustainability competencies qualitatively through surveys and interviews based on student comments (Barth, 2007; Staniskis and Katiliute, 2016; Steinemann, 2003). Murga-Menoyo (2015) established a basic competency matrix that identified the key indicators of each competency and the skills required to acquire them.

The initial tendency to respond to these challenges was the formal inclusion of SD competencies in university curricula through the development of theoretical projects and problem-based learning or the inclusion of new SD courses (e.g., Lehmann et al., 2008; Segalas, Ferrer-Balas and Mulder, 2009; Steinemann, 2003). A significant opportunity exists, however, to contribute to the development of such curricula through informal activities outside of class or by combining formal and informal learning processes.

There are several approaches in this regard, such as student internships in communities, companies and governments (Brundiers, Wiek and Redman, 2009), collaboration of students with neighbouring industries, businesses setting an example through their own management practices, serving as technical experts or acting as leaders in regional sustainability plans (Adomssent, 2013; Staniskis and Katiliute, 2016). To acquire SD skills, Lehmann et al. (2008) and Haan (2006) affirm the importance of academic exchanges and internships with local companies, international collaborations with other universities and work on case studies.

Service-learning (SL) can be considered as an integrated approach to formal and informal learning. SL is defined as 'a form of learning in which students participate in

Table 1.1   Basic matrix of competencies for sustainability

Competencies (UNESCO, 2014, p. 12)	Components[a]	Capacity
Critical analysis	Critical thinking Ethical commitment Intellectual commitment	To understand that knowledge is incomplete and subjective To understand that every system (conceptual, socioeconomic, etc.) presents dysfunctions that can be identified and corrected To recognize social and economic dysfunctions that oppose SD To propose alternatives for improvement
Systemic reflection	Relational thinking Holistic thinking Feeling of belonging to the community of life	To understand reality, physical and social, as a dynamic system of interrelated factors at global and local levels To understand the interrelationships between values, attitudes, social uses and lifestyles, and customs To look deeply into the causes of phenomena, facts and problems To understand the human being as an ecodependent being
Collaborative decision making	Argumentative skills Participatory skills Democratic commitment and universal human rights	To put skills to work collaboratively in diverse groups To recognize the right of people to participate in all issues that affect them and the processes of SD (endogenous processes)
Sense of responsibility towards present and future generations	Ethical commitment Social commitment Anticipatory thinking Synchronous and diachronic thinking Universal, synchronous, diachronic and differentiated responsibility Compassion	To understand the effects that individual behaviours have, in the medium and long term, on social uses and customs and, through them, on human collectives from the community and others To understand the consequences of individual behaviours and groups on the biological conditions necessary for life, present and future To care for intra- and intergenerational relationships with equity and justice To contribute to change for sustainability, adopting alternatives to unfair and unsustainable lifestyles

Note: a. The elements of the 'components' column, in one measure or another, are within the different competencies. They have been assigned to one or the other considering the significance of their specific weight in each case.

Source: Based on Murga-Menoyo (2015).

community service as part of the academic work of the course' (Lisman, 1998, cited by Hall et al., 2004, p. 37), where the voluntary service to the community and the learning of knowledge, skills and values are combined, establishing a close connection of the service and learning in a single activity (Martínez et al., 2008). In a more global approach, international service-learning (ISL) can contribute to the development of essential sustainability competencies. ISL has developed in different contexts (e.g., Bamber and Pike, 2013; Kiely, 2005) but has not been directly associated with ESD, although the concepts are related. Battistoni, Longo and Jayanandhan (2009) and Hall et al. (2004) stated that universities cannot escape global and local problems such as poverty, human development, health and safety, education, water and sanitation, local economy, rural development or the strength of local institutions. In light of these challenges, the conceptual framework of ESD and ISL converge to achieve the same objectives: to develop social and environmental sustainability in practice for a targeted area in which the current state is improved in a real, measurable way (Aramburuzabala, Cerrillo and Tello, 2015). Following Bamber and Pike (2013), ISL seeks to combine student learning with service for a more just and sustainable society, according to its definition:

> ISL is a form of ecological commitment with aesthetic, moral and spiritual dimensions that is promulgated through the participation with the lives and 'worlds' of those who live in different countries and that allows ethical reflection, improves personal effectiveness and seeks to engender a more just and sustainable society. (Bamber and Pike, 2013, p. 536)

Currently, by focusing on students, research on SL tends to neglect the real impact on local communities (Kiely, 2005). As proposed by Hall et al. (2004), the SL approach is understood as service and learning objectives of equal weight. For this reason, this study incorporates the analysis of local achievements and their social importance for the community. Wiek et al. (2015) establishes three future challenges for research on ESD: (1) how to develop key sustainability competencies synergistically; (2) how to develop these competencies for real projects in actual contexts with future professional applicability; and (3) how complexity, stakeholders, location and other elements impact the acquisition of skills. Faced with these three challenges, linking ESD and ISL would serve as a guideline for the acquisition of sustainability competencies in real and complex environments in different locations. Analysing the impact on the local population where an intervention has occurred, including Muñoz et al.'s (2017) axis of 'knowing how to live together', will contribute to the development of partnerships and value the interdependence of people, communities and cultures.

1.1   Objectives and Scope

The objective of this study is the analysis of the importance of ISL as a useful strategy in the new ESD paradigm in HEIs. The starting hypothesis is that ISL can contribute to the development of sustainability competencies in a synergistic way through the integration of formal and informal learning. Formal learning would be included in the regulated education system and informal learning through an alternative extension of formal learning by proposals organized, in this case, within an international cooperation programme.

The main aims of this study are to: (1) apply ISL in a case study with a formal and informal learning approach; (2) evaluate from an ISL approach the achievements of the service (local impact and subjective impact from a local point of view) and learning (acquisition of skills in volunteer students).

2.   METHODOLOGY

The methodology proposed in this study is based on the ESD paradigm, the importance of competencies for SD and the way to develop these competencies by establishing links between ISL and ESD.

Based on a proposal by Brundiers et al. (2009), a volunteer student could follow the path outlined in Figure 1.1 where in the first and second year the student acquires theoretical knowledge from formal learning with an approach to the real world through practical classes on actual cases. In the third and fourth year, these students will apply the knowledge acquired in solving real problems in real contexts by participating in its implementation, combining formal and informal learning.

This method is the approach that has been applied at the European University (EU) of Madrid, Spain. The EU has a volunteer programme that has been carried out since 2009 for conducting ISL. In this programme, students from every year are incorporated into the ISL programme with the objective that the first- and second-year students make their first participation in the real world. Third- and fourth-year students participate in the resolution of real problems by completing and implementing final degree projects, thereby applying the knowledge acquired in the classroom through formal learning to practical cases within the scope of informal learning. In this project, the Brundiers model has been taken into account in terms of participation in the real world and in the capstone (object of the study to be published) and not so much in the integration of curricular sustainability and ESD in the degree.

The first project was carried out in Ethiopia with the design and construction of basic

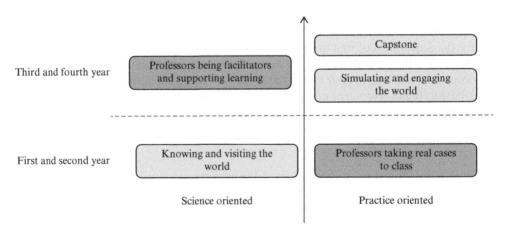

Source: Based on Brundiers et al. (2009).

Figure 1.1   Model for sustainability competencies development through international cooperation learning opportunity

infrastructure identified as a priority for local society (construction of dams, implementation of water distribution networks, irrigation and sanitation) and the performance of work related to health in the environment of orphanages (studies of diseases, deformities, medication and health system). This project involved disciplines of civil engineering, physiotherapy, pharmacy and medicine. It was funded and supported by the Spanish Agency for Development Cooperation (AECID) and the University of Addis Ababa. Within this framework, professors decided to incorporate students of the project through a volunteer programme where students develop microprojects or final bachelor's or master's degree projects in real contexts. For the Ethiopia project, a total of seven end-of-degree projects or master's thesis projects were carried out in different disciplines (e.g., physiotherapy, information and communications engineering and civil engineering). Subsequently, five civil engineering students travelled to Guatemala to conduct a study on water distribution systems in the city of Tecpan to analyse different alternatives that would guarantee the supply of drinking water to the population. In Guatemala, two final degree projects were carried out.

In 2013, a new volunteer programme began in collaboration with the Cerro Verde Foundation (FCV). The project focused on a small village, Cerro Verde, in the Choluteca region, Honduras. The project was conducted from 2013 to 2016 and was selected as an ISL case study to achieve the first objective of this work: the application of formal classroom knowledge through informal learning in a specific environment.

The Cerro Verde study was carried out at the request of the FCV who, knowing the work carried out by the EU in Ethiopia and Guatemala, decided to establish a collaboration agreement to generate synergies between the needs of the local population and the EU's expert knowledge. The EU offered experience in the domain of international cooperation projects as well as technical expertise to solve problems and fulfil requirements of the local projects.

The village of Cerro Verde is in Southern Honduras – one of the most depressed areas of the country, without water or electricity. For some years, locals have suffered a severe drought that decimated crops and forced part of the population to emigrate to the United States and Europe. In this context, this project planned to collect data before and after the intervention through surveys and interviews with the local population to address the impact and perception of the project in the area. The researchers conducted a survey in 79 of the 96 inhabited houses in the village based on three fundamental areas, water, electricity and housing:

- Water: usual forms of water storage, quantities of water consumed per day, where it was obtained, the existence of latrines, the state of natural sources and the distance of each house to the water points.
- Electricity: determine the existence of solar panels or any type of batteries, distance from the street to the entrance of the house, number of bedrooms, initial state for the installation of conventional electrical energy.
- Housing: analysis of the type of enclosure, construction materials, roof, soil structure, number of occupants, size of the house, place of the kitchen and existence of a fireplace. Figure 1.2 shows the state of one of the houses in the village before the intervention, with plastic in areas where there should be adobe branches and aluminium where there should be some other type of coating.

Figure 1.2   House with plastic and aluminium plate

In addition, the survey analysed data related to road access to the area, education, demography, economy, work, safety, health and hygiene, community, nutrition, transportation, technology and well-being.

In the village of Cerro Verde, there are 426 inhabitants (146 are adult men, 127 adult women and 153 children). There are 103 buildings. There are 100 houses, of which there are 99 numbered houses, 96 of which are inhabited and three of which are uninhabited (house 19 – lives in Spain; house 17 – lives in the United States; and house 18b – used by the FCV). There is one unnumbered house. The other three buildings are: building 36 – cooperative; building 37 – church; building 49 – school.

Surveys were conducted in 79 households, or 81.44 per cent. A sample of more than 80 per cent indicates that the data obtained can be reliable, since it fits almost the entire population. The survey was divided into the following blocks: living space, demography, economy and work, education, safety, health and hygiene, water, electricity, community, nutrition, transportation, technology and well-being.

For the student learning goal of the project, the skills of EU students within the Curriculum Sustainability Plan 2012–16 related to SD were analysed to compare students' acquisition of skills obtained after the intervention in the volunteer programme. This analysis was executed through surveys and interviews. For this, eight competencies were selected, five of them taken from a study carried out by Fernández et al. (2014b) on the competency model in the civil engineering degree: critical thinking, problem solving, decision making, work in multidisciplinary teams and adaptation to change. The other three are linked to the experience gained from the years of volunteering with students in

Ethiopia and Guatemala: responsibility, time management and communication skills. Eighteen students of civil engineering, building engineering, industrial engineering, information and communications engineering (ICE) and medicine were involved.

2.1 Description of Practical Experience

As mentioned above, the EU volunteer programme in collaboration with FCV began in 2013 in Cerro Verde. The objectives of the FCV in the village are to provide electricity, drinking water and sanitation as well as promoting education for children and adults to provide better living conditions for the local population. The overarching objective of the project is to develop a sustainable village model that can be replicated in different villages in line with the philosophy of AECID. Lessons learned and knowledge from previous projects in Ethiopia and Guatemala were integrated into the project.

Between 2013 and 2016, 18 students of civil engineering, building engineering, industrial engineering, ICE and medicine were involved in the programme. Before travelling to the area, students were required to complete training on international development cooperation and a previous study to gather information about the area. Pre-deployment studies identified and analysed needs and main objectives of the FCV and the village, considering data relevant to the country, region, work areas, regulations and more. Teachers and students were then placed in the area for three weeks to generate maps and collect necessary on-site data related to local needs while working on the development and implementation of the projects. Before leaving the village, students generated reports of the tasks performed during the stay.

Note that to promote and favour coexistence and an intercultural approach, both students and teachers live with the local population in their homes, sharing their day-to-day routines. The houses have a latrine, but no shower. Students and teachers had to fill a small container with water to use in their daily toilet. Water is limited, so it is key to be efficient in its use. The electricity supply is, of course, poor and limited to a few places that use solar panels.

3.   RESULTS AND DISCUSSION

3.1   Objective Results in the Village for Service-learning

Work completed during the three years of the project has had a significant impact on the village of Cerro Verde. In 2013, students and teachers from the EU made a topographic map of the area and held interviews with the inhabitants of the village. In addition, researchers completed questionnaires on the three areas mentioned above – water, electricity and housing – and other relevant data for the analysis of the area.

The data obtained facilitated establishing the needs of the inhabitants and their priorities. The population obtained water from a natural source called 'La Joya', which they had channelled by gravity in a rudimentary way, generating numerous losses. The sourced water had no treatment to guarantee it was potable. The volume of water from the natural source was absolutely insufficient for the needs of the village, which meant that the population had to look for alternative water supply points in dry periods, forcing

Figure 1.3   Water filtration system

them to travel long distances. The small amount of water favours the transport of solid particles through such precarious distribution networks. As shown in Figure 1.3, this situation forced people to filter water.

Cerro Verde also had no electricity. Only a few houses had solar panels (Figure 1.4) that allowed them to charge batteries to illuminate a light bulb. The remainder of the population depended on the solidarity of the neighbours for power. The recharging of mobile phone batteries is crucial because many family members work away or even abroad, so the phones are their only way to maintain family ties.

The access to the town is through a steep dirt road that has already caused numerous accidents, especially after heavy rains. This type of precipitation generates furrows so deep in the ground and rockfall that prevents the passage of vehicles. When this happens, the town is incommunicado to road traffic until the government repairs it. The inhabitants can only access other populations on foot. These repairs can take months and are never final, which causes the situation to recur every time it rains torrentially.

For education, in 2013 the solitary school had a small classroom for kindergarten (children up to five years old) with a teacher paid by a local donor and two classrooms for all children in six grades, from first to sixth, with two teachers. Children aged six to 11 were divided into two classes.

Over the past three years, some of these issues have been resolved:

Figure 1.4   Solar panels

- Two successful water wells have been drilled, one of which is reserved for future use in anticipation of possible population growth. The other well, currently in use, feeds a water tank where it is chlorinated and from which it is distributed to each house in the village through a distribution network, thus ensuring water potability throughout the route. Figure 1.5 displays a test pump and Figure 1.6 shows the installation of the water supply network.
- A part of the electricity grid has been built. This project has benefited 60 per cent of the population and it is expected that by 2020 the extension of this network will be completed.
- The access road to the village has been repaired, reducing the time spent accessing the area, avoiding worrying isolation and minimizing the number of accidents.
- Finally, regarding education, an additional classroom has been built in the old facilities and three additional classrooms and a dining room were constructed on a new nearby plot. Younger students now have three classes from the first to the sixth year (six to 12 years old) with three teachers. And those in seventh, eighth

Figure 1.5   Test pumping

and nineth grade have three new classrooms with three teachers, according to the conditions established by the Honduran Ministry of Education. In addition, the school has separate bathrooms for boys and girls, drinking water and a septic tank. The school's extension affects not only school attendance in Cerro Verde but also children in small nearby towns that until now simply had no chance of attending school.

A schematic summary of the objective impact on the village is shown in Figure 1.7.

Project tasks were developed with the participation of the local population, where work groups coordinated work performed (e.g., wells, ditches for the installation of the water supply network, installation of the pipe network and the bases of the light posts). Also, the local population housed and maintained the university students.

Furthermore, adult training courses were provided in Cerro Verde. A line of collaboration was established between the FCV and the Food and Agriculture Organization of the United Nations (FAO) to improve crops and food habits. The goal of the collaboration was to optimize agricultural systems while preserving the use of traditional methods and introducing improvements in performance with less water. Courses in the trades, such as plumbing, masonry, sewing and crafts, were held to improve the employability of locals.

These improvements and the expansion of the school allow children to study until they

Figure 1.6   Citizen participation in the network installation

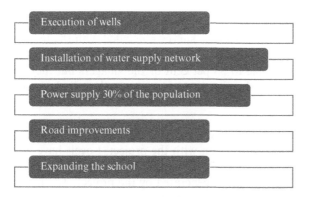

Figure 1.7   Work in the village

are 16 without leaving the village, which allows them to combine household chores with studies and avoid having to leave school early. Adults now benefit from a water supply network and the possibility to connect to the electricity grid; therefore, they have been encouraged to establish small businesses, including a new corn grain mill and basic supply stores, which they call grocery stores.

3.2   Results from Surveys and Interviews in the Village

The last survey, conducted in July 2015, allowed us to evaluate the population's perception of the impact of the project. The interviews and surveys can be summarized as follows:

- Most houses are made of adobe and tree branches. Roofs are made of plastic sheets or metal tiles and floors are almost always made of clay. The houses do not have bathrooms.
- A total of 96 people (24 per cent of the population) work for others. In 15 per cent of households, women obtain money by selling basic products while simultaneously caring for their home and family.
- Only 11.3 per cent of respondents can save money, which corresponds to those families who have one or more family members working abroad.
- Although the educational level in the town is low, many have studied at least until the sixth year. Participating in continuing studies involves walking to the nearest larger town, at least one hour. In general, everyone agrees that studying is relevant, and they recognize the significance of the opportunity for their children to attend school as much as possible. Textbooks are a common good and are shared among students. The literacy rate is 67 per cent of the population.
- An initial diagnosis in the healthcare centre is free; however, travel, medications, tests and treatments have a major cost that most of the population cannot afford. Respiratory problems afflict 33 per cent of the populace. The lack of chimneys for cooking is identified as probable cause. In addition, 66 per cent of waste is burned within the town.
- The basic food is corn pancakes. Sixty-eight per cent of the population eats, almost exclusively, these pancakes.
- The arrival of the water distribution network to all households is considered a vital change in their lives. The survey coincided with the installation of the water distribution network; therefore, the population had not had enough time to enjoy it.
- Electricity is available to 33 per cent of the villagers but they are still reluctant to turn on a light bulb when it gets dark or plug in the cell phone battery. Some people bought a TV.

As shown, there is still a lot of work to do. The interviews with the villagers reflect an apparent general public satisfaction with the project. Locals have improved their living standards to some extent. About 70 per cent of the population interviewed look forward to the development opportunities generated by the project. The new context favours its survival and development. Though recognizing the improvements made, approximately 30 per cent of the population have such an extreme lack of resources that they consider their situation irreversible.

The arrival of water and electricity has contributed to the establishment of a new 'pulpería' (small grocery store) in house 19 and a new mill for corn grain in house 26. With increased production, prices have decreased. In general, people believe that these improvements can reduce both internal migration to larger cities and external migration to other countries, promoting family reunification for those who had to emigrate in the

Table 1.2   Acquisition levels of competencies for SD

Competencies for SD	Volunteer Students		Non-volunteer Students	
	Average	Typical Deviation	Average	Typical Deviation
Critical thinking	4.2	0.7	4.0	0.6
Responsibility	4.4	0.7	3.9	0.9
Problem solving	4.3	0.7	4.1	0.6
Decision making	4.3	0.7	4.0	0.9
Time management	4.1	0.8	3.6	1.0
Adaptation to change	4.6	0.7	4.0	0.8
Teamwork	4.2	0.8	4.1	1.0
Communication skills	4.4	0.7	4.1	0.9

past. It may also happen that people who have been forced to emigrate now look to the future with new hope and genuinely consider returning home.

3.3   Results from Students' Survey

A survey was conducted with 40 respondents in 2015, nine of whom were volunteers who travelled to the village during the three years and 31 are non-volunteer students of similar grades (who have no experience in volunteering). The objective of the survey was to analyse the level of acquisition of competencies for SD. The skills assessed were the five defined as essential for graduates in an ESD context: critical thinking, problem solving, decision making, teamwork and adaptation to change (Fernández-Sanchez et al., 2014b). Three additional key competencies linked to the experience gained in the years of volunteering with students in Ethiopia and Guatemala were included: responsibility, time management and communication skills. Note that there was already a sustainability curriculum integrated into the EU degrees, so skills were developed in the classroom through project-based learning in at least one course per year.

The data obtained from these surveys indicate that the level of acquisition of these competencies with an international service and learning approach in a non-formal learning environment seems to be greater than that acquired in the classroom with formal teaching methodologies applied in the EU (Table 1.2).

As one student pointed out, 'such projects encourage personal growth'. Another student, who has travelled twice in the last two years, was so affected that he is now professionally engaged in development cooperation: 'My stay in cooperation projects has changed my life. It has affected my way of seeing life and has generated a significant change in my priorities and in the approach that I want to give to my professional career.' There are other students who have already completed their studies and who continue to collaborate with specific actions, such as technical advice or financial donations. Another student mentioned that:

[l]iving with the local population and collaborating with this cooperation project of the Cerro Verde Foundation has led me to get personally involved in donations that have allowed part of the expansion of the school. Waking up and seeing the faces of these children and the few

opportunities they have just to be born in this place has changed my perception of the important things in life.

Another student developed the water distribution and supply network as a final degree project, which was executed in 2015. One of his comments was that 'It is a great satisfaction to have had the opportunity to participate in a project to provide access to water I drink to a population and thus improve the standards of life and health with my final degree project and its final implementation.'

During the three years of the project, students from different disciplines participated, spending all of their time in the village, conducting interviews, designing and managing training in waste management and hygiene, playing with children and making 'gymkhanas' (public places) for garbage collection. According to their speciality, each student became more involved in some subjects than others. For instance, civil engineers participated mainly in topographic studies and hydraulic and sanitation projects. Medical students covered subjects related to health, investigating the most prevalent diseases and their causes, as well as the medical management system existing in the country and region. Building engineers analysed construction materials used and their availability, durability and efficiency, the stability of buildings, possible improvements and the properties of local materials. Telecommunications engineers designed different ways to monitor water quality.

Results indicate that volunteering and cooperation promote awareness and professional and personal development of the student. It is also an excellent way to acquire new knowledge and competencies while working to improve the lives of disadvantaged populations to solve real problems and needs.

4.   CONCLUSION

In a global context in which the mobility of international students is increasing (Rizvi, 2011), the strategy of HEIs focused on ESD can consider ISL as an interesting and powerful tool to develop competencies for SD, which can respond to some of the challenges proposed by Wiek et al. (2015) in the area of ESD research.

In this study, an ISL programme was applied in the EU in a similar way to other existing international experiences (e.g., Bamber and Pike, 2013; Kiely, 2005). However, in this case, the ISL approach has been analysed from two perspectives: the students' perspective and the local population's perspective. A remarkable improvement in the development of the perceived SD skills is shown when comparing volunteer and non-volunteer students. An average improvement of 8.5 per cent is achieved in all skills for sustainable development (SD) compared to non-volunteers. Qualitatively, the feelings and values of volunteer students are in the same direction as the findings of other authors with a deeper qualitative study (such as Bamber and Pike, 2013), changing the way students perceive the world and life.

When comparing these results with traditional methods, Ferreira, Lopez and Morais (2006) found that competencies such as teamwork, communication skills, the ability to adapt to changes, responsibility and ethical values are much more developed by participation in the project, followed by practical learning and theoretical classes. Following Barth et al. (2007), four elements can characterize the processes of voluntary learning for the acquisition of skills: (1) volunteering and individual responsibility; (2) ethically oriented learning in real-life situations; (3) involuntary but conscious learning; and (4) interdisciplinary collaboration. In this type of voluntary learning, sustainability competencies are promoted – mainly interdisciplinary collaboration, planning, implementation skills and motivation. The results of our study are also aligned with these findings, combining formal and informal learning.

This study has a limitation, which is not measuring the initial situation – a lesson learned for future applications. The surveys were carried out on the students' return, considering that the feedback survey was more positive, not during the activity, but when completed and everyone had returned. However, there was a problem of the non-response in some cases, given that for some students it was their last course and it was very difficult contact them on their return. Although the sample is small, we do not consider that the key to the study is in a quantitative statistical question, but we understand the study presented more from the anthropological-qualitative point of view. In this regard and considering the basic matrix of competencies for sustainability established by Murga-Menoyo (2015) in the field of volunteering, the development of the eight competencies used for the study is promoted:

- Critical thinking: the EU is one of the most expensive Spanish private universities; therefore, the profile of students and their environment is significantly different from the reality that is lived in the village. Through the vital experience of the student in this environment, the student generates a deep analysis of poverty, its origins and connection with SD.
- Troubleshooting: without water and light, any inhabitant not already habituated has a problem to solve. Students are accustomed to an Internet connection to gather technical information and connect with their loved ones. The shortage of electricity makes these options difficult. When a challenge is considered, a solution is sought from the means available, but when resources are scarce and the budget is low, ingenuity is required to solve any issues and, you also have to do it from the perspective of the SD so that when you leave others can find those spare parts that preserve the service. Adaptive and innovative skills for SD are required that are not obtained in a classroom yet are essential to reach the most appropriate solutions for a local context.
- Decision making: the student's project is the one that is going to be implemented and any errors or failures may significantly damage a vulnerable population. Each decision regarding the project design, types and quality of materials, implementation procedures, useful life and maintenance are key to the SD of the local population.
- Working in multidisciplinary teams: students work in interdisciplinary environments with inhabitants of the local population who are from another country. Locals may have work methodologies totally different from the students' a language that, although having the same roots, has semantic nuances that lead to misconceptions on many occasions. In this environment, the skills necessary to ensure that the work meets the original objectives set in the field of SD of the local population are fundamental.
- Adaptation to change: the change experienced by the student has already been

mentioned and it is significant. Students live in a village in Southern Honduras, with no water, electricity or Internet connection. The students stay in local houses with a population they do not know who have completely different customs, are in dire poverty and consume a diet of mostly corn cakes and beans. Note that the students in this context live in critical situations and slowly adapt to change. It is a favourable situation to reflect on the change of society towards sustainability and the importance of adopting alternatives to face the challenges of unsustainable lifestyles.

● Responsibility: students have a great responsibility because the proposed project is going to be implemented. Students must ensure the village attains the SD linked to their project, which depends on the technical rigor of the programme and its calculation.

● Time management: students are only in the area for three weeks. In that short time, they are required to adapt to the environment, analyse the needs of the population, study the possibilities to achieve the SD with the technical and economic means available and obtain all the data needed for the study.

● Communication skills: there is currently an important function – that is, knowing how to live. For this, it is essential to know how to communicate. The cultural shock that occurs is significant. Knowing how to communicate with the inhabitants of the village and with the members of the FCV is crucial for all aspects of the project.

From the local approach, objective and subjective improvements were achieved, including improvement of the perceived quality of life, expectation of further improvements in the medium term and new or adapted infrastructure (accessibility, education, energy supply, water and sanitary network). FCV achieved these results between 2013 and 2016 with the close cooperation of the EU. These projects received an award from the National Congress of Honduras in December 2015.

This study explicitly links ISL with ESD, since they are synergistic areas with similar primary objectives. Results indicate the great potential to enrich each other as an integral and global strategy for any university towards a more sustainable world. A global framework that considers local and regional SL will be necessary and also ISL, integrated into the ESD strategic framework in future research. In addition, more evidence is needed from qualitative studies of change in both local communities and universities. Future research is needed on the acquisition of skills from different approaches to prioritize and balance future curricula while preparing future professionals and decision makers to achieve sustainability and SD – a fairer world.

The impact of this international service and learning approach is not obvious. From one perspective, this project has been developed by the FCV. The added value given by the university, professors and students, is important but not necessary. The biggest challenge is that the experience for students is normally in the month of July, but the need for help and project planning is not just for that month but throughout the year. The value given to the local community and the FCV is important, but it is merely anecdotal considering the whole project. Service-learning in practice is more learning (as a live experience) than service. To balance the importance of the service, an important commitment would be needed to be deployed whenever necessary, which is not an easy task with real curricular programmes.

REFERENCES

Adomssent, M. (2013). Exploring universities' transformative potential for sustainability bound learning in changing landscapes of knowledge communication. *Journal of Cleaner Production*, 49, 11–24.

Aguilera, A., Mendoza, M., Racionero, S. and Soler, M. (2010). El papel de la universidad en CdA. *Revista Interuniversitaria de Formación del Profesorado*, 6(24,1), 45–56.

Aramburuzabala, P., Cerrillo, R. and Tello, I (2015). Service-learning: a methodological proposal for the introduction of curricular sustainability in the university. *Revista de Curriculum y Formación del Profesorado*, 19(1), 78–95.

Association for the Advancement of Sustainability in Higher Education (AASHE) (2012), *2012 Higher Education Sustainability Review*. Denver, CO: AASHE.

Bamber, P.M. and Pike, M.A. (2013). Towards an ethical ecology of international service learning. *Journal of Curriculum Studies*, 45(4), 535–59.

Barth, M., Godemann, J., Rieckmann, M. and Stoltenberg, U. (2007). Developing key competencies for sustainable development in higher education. *International Journal of Sustainability in Higher Education*, 8(4), 416–30.

Battistoni, R.M., Longo, N.V. and Jayanandhan, S.R. (2009). Acting locally in a flat world: global citizenship and the democratic practice of service-learning. *Journal of Higher Education Outreach and Engagement*, 13(2), 89–108.

Brundiers, K., Wiek, A. and Redman, C.L. (2010). Real-world learning opportunities in sustainability: from classroom into the real world. *International Journal of Sustainability in Higher Education*, 11(4), 308–24.

Environmental Association for Universities and Colleges (2013). *Embedding Sustainable Development in the Curriculum*. Accessed 11 February 2021 at https://www.sustainabilityexchange.ac.uk/files/embedding_sustainabilyt_in_the_curriculum_guide.pdf.

Fernández-Sanchez, G., Bernaldo, O., Castillejo, A. and Manzanero, A. (2014a). Education for sustainable development in higher education: state-of-the-art, barriers and challenges. *Higher Learning Research Communications*, 4(3), 3–11.

Fernández-Sanchez, G., Bernaldo, O., Castillejo, A. and Manzanero, A. (2014b). Proposal of a theoretical sustainability competence based model in a civil engineering degree. *Journal of Professional Issues in Engineering Education and Practice*, 141(2), https://doi.org/10.1061/(ASCE)EI.1943-5541.0000206.

Ferreira, A.J.D., Lopez, M.A.R. and Morais, J.P.F. (2006). Environmental management and audit schemes implementation as an educational tool for sustainability. *Journal of Cleaner Production*, 14, 973–82.

Ferrer-Balas, D., Lozano, R. and Huisingh, D. et al. (2010). Going beyond the rhetoric: system-wide changes in universities for sustainable societies. *Journal of Cleaner Production*, 18(7), 607–10.

Haan, G. (2006). The BLK '21' programme in Germany: a 'Gestaltungskompetenz'-based model for education for sustainable development. *Environmental Education Research*, 12(1), 19–32.

Hall, D., Hall, I., Cameron, A. and Green, P. (2004). Student volunteering and the active community: issues and opportunities for teaching and learning in sociology. *Learning and Teaching in Social Sciences*, 1(1), 33–50.

Hanover Research (HR) (2011). *Embedding Sustainability into University Curricula*. Washington, DC: HR.

Jones, P., Selby, D. and Sterling, S. (2010). *Sustainability Education: Perspectives and Practices Across Higher Education*. London: Earthscan.

Kiely, R. (2005). A transformative learning model for service-learning: a longitudinal case study. *Michigan Journal of Community Service Learning*, Fall, 5–22.

Lambrechts, W., Mula, I. and Ceulemans, K. et al. (2013). The integration of competencies for sustainable development in higher education: an analysis of bachelor programs in management. *Journal of Cleaner Production*, 48, 65–73.

Lee, K., Barker, M. and Mouasher, A. (2013). Is it even espoused? An exploratory study of commitment to sustainability as evidenced in vision, mission and graduate attribute statements in Australian universities. *Journal of Cleaner Production*, 48(1), 20–28.

Lehmann, M., Christensen, P., Du, X. and Thrane, M. (2008). Problem-oriented and project-based learning (POPBL) as an innovative learning strategy for sustainable development in engineering education. *European Journal of Engineering Education*, 33(3), 283–95.

Lidgren, A., Rodhe, H. and Huisingh, D. (2006). A systemic approach to incorporate sustainability into university courses and curricula. *Journal of Cleaner Production*, 14(9–11), 797–809.

Lozano, R. (2010). Diffusion of sustainable development in universities' curricula: an empirical example from Cardiff University. *Journal of Cleaner Production*, 18(7), 637–44.

Lozano, R. (2012). Organizational learning and creativity as means to foster sustainability in universities. In Global University Network for Innovation (ed.), *Higher Education in the World 4. Higher Education's Commitment to Sustainability: From Understanding to Action* (pp. 262–7). Basingstoke: Palgrave Macmillan.

Martínez, M., Tapia, M. and Naval, C. et al. (eds) (2008). *Aprendizaje Servicio y Responsabilidad Social de las Universidades*. Barcelona: Ediciones Octaedro y Fundació Jaume Bofill.

Mochizuki, Y. and Fadeeva, Z. (2008). Regional centres of expertise on education for sustainable development (RCEs): an overview. *International Journal of Sustainability in Higher Education*, 9(4), 369–81.

Murga-Menoyo, M.A. (2015). Competencias para el desarrollo sostenible: las capacidades, actitudes y valores meta de la educación en el marco de la Agenda global post-2015. *Foro de Educación*, 13(19), 55–83.

Muñoz, V.G., Sobrino Callejo, M.A., Benítez Sastre, L. and Coronado Marin, A. (2017). Revisión sistemática sobre competencias en desarrollo sostenible en educación superior. *Revista Iberoamericana de Educación*, 73, https://doi.org/10.35362/rie730289.

Ortega, M.L. (2014). Guide for collaboration between ONGD and university. ETEA Foundation for Development and Collaboration, ETEA-Loyola University, Andalucía.

Pavlova, M. (2009). Conceptualisation of technology education within the paradigm of sustainable development. *International Journal of Technology and Design Education*, 19(2), 109–32.

Rizvi, F. (2011). Theorizing student mobility in an era of globalization. *Teachers and Teaching: Theory and Practice*, 17(6), 693–701.

Tarrant, S.P. and Thiele, L.P. (2015). Environmental political theory's contribution to sustainability studies. In T. Gabrielson, C. Hall, J.M. Meyer and D. Schlosberg (eds), O*xford Handbook of Environmental Political Theory* (pp. 116–130). Oxford: Oxford University Press.

Tarrant, S.P. and Thiele, L.P. (2016). Practices makes pedagogy – John Dewey and skills-based sustainability education. *International Journal of Sustainability in Higher Education*, 17(1), 54–67.

Segalas, J., Ferrer-Balas, D. and Mulder, K.F. (2008). Conceptual maps: measuring learning processes of engineering students concerning sustainable development. *European Journal of Engineering Education*, 33(3), 297–306.

Staniskis, J.K. and Katiliute, E. (2016). Complex evaluation of sustainability in engineering education: case & analysis. *Journal of Cleaner Production*, 120, 13–20.

Steinemann, A. (2003). Implementing sustainable development through problem-based learning: pedagogy and practice. *Journal of Professional Issues in Engineering Education and Practice*, 129(4), 216–24.

United Nations Educational, Scientific and Cultural Organization (UNESCO) (2009). Education for sustainable development and climate change. *Policy Dialogue 4*. Accessed 11 March 2020 at http://unesdoc.unesco.org/images/0017/001791/179122e.pdf.

United Nations Educational, Scientific and Cultural Organization (UNESCO) (2014). *Roadmap for Implementing the Global Action Programme on Education for Sustainable Development*. Accessed 11 March 2020 at https://unesdoc.unesco.org/ark:/48223/pf0000230514.

United Nations Educational, Scientific and Cultural Organization (UNESCO) (2017). *Education for Sustainable Development Goals. Learning Objectives*. Accessed 11 March 2020 at https://www.developmenteducation.ie/app/uploads/2017/07/Sustainable-development-goals-learning-objectives-2017.pdf.

Waas, T., Verbruggen, A. and Wright, T. (2010). University research for sustainable development: definition and characteristics explored. *Journal of Cleaner Production*, 18(7), 629–36.

Wade, R. (2008). Education for sustainable development. *Policy and Practice*, 6, 30–49.

Wiek, A., Bernstein, M. and Foley, R. (2015). Operationalising competencies in higher education for sustainable development. In M. Barth, G. Michelsen, M. Rieckmann and I. Thomas (eds) (2015), *Handbook of Higher Education for Sustainable Development*. Abingdon: Routledge, pp. 241–60.

Wright, T.S.A. and Wilton. H. (2012). Facilities management directors' conceptualizations of sustainability in higher education. *Journal of Cleaner Production*, 31(1), 118–25.

Yasin, R.M. and Rahman, S. (2011). Problem oriented project based learning (POPBL) in promoting education for sustainable development. *Procedia – Social and Behavioural Sciences*, 15, 289–93.

2. Information science and informational sustainability: a discipline in construction
Marli Dias de Souza Pinto and Genilson Geraldo

1. INTRODUCTION

Information science, committed to the broad study of the properties and behavior of information, is constantly challenged, especially with the technological advances and resources of the Internet, which often change the relationships between the use of information and the research field itself. Responsible for optimizing access, organization, use and dissemination of information, information science focuses on scientific studies that offer informational mechanisms that encourage social, technological and economic development.

In the current scenario, with the sustainable development project put forward by the United Nations (UN) at the global level, the relevance of information science is justified as an area of knowledge with a prominent role in supporting and aligning actions and communicative aspects of integration, awareness and transformation of society in the pursuit of quality of life and the planet. The 2030 Agenda for Sustainable Development and the associated Sustainable Development Goals (SDGs) (United Nations, 2015a, 2015b) was developed (2013–15) in conjunction with governmental, non-governmental organizations and civil society from 193 countries. It is a new global model that aims to end poverty, promote prosperity and well-being for all, while protecting the environment and combatting climate change.

The universal scope of the 2030 Agenda for Sustainable Development is an ethical imperative, as stated by the former Deputy Secretary-General of the United Nations, Jan Eliasson (2012–16), who declared that 'They must be implemented by all segments of all societies, working together. No one should be left behind' (United Nations, 2015b). In this context, the International Federation of Library Associations and Institutions (IFLA), an international body representing the interests of the provision of library services, information science and other institutions linked to the Federation, recognized that it could support the 17 SDGs in their area of competence in the three dimensions of sustainability: environmental, economic and social.

To identify sustainable actions, surveys on knowledge of the SDGs were conducted in 2018 with Brazilian library managers. It was found that the managers and librarians participating in the research did not demonstrate knowledge on the subject. It was evident that the three dimensions were not known by those responsible for disseminating them in their information units, as defined by the IFLA. Based on the finding that the subject was not yet known to the vast majority of information professionals in the country, publications on the subject were sought in the international scenario. Studies on sustainable development and sustainable information in information science were recovered by the pioneering authors Spink (1999) and Nolin (2010), who pointed out the scarcity of works related to this theme.

The discussions presented by Spink (1999) and Nolin (2010) brought about motivation for the development of more research. Thus, a debate was brought to the agenda of the area of information science in Brazil, and authors Geraldo and Pinto (2019) presented an article entitled 'Pathways to information science and the Sustainable Development Goals of the 2030/UN Agenda' (Geraldo and Pinto, 2019). This article provides a quantitative and qualitative analysis of research spanning from 2008 to 2018. This analysis revealed the existence of a mere 53 articles on this theme in 16 journals of information science in Brazil.

With the evidence provided and before the IFLA's proposal for an International Advocacy Program (IAP) for the 2030 Agenda (IFLA, 2018), we aimed to assert the importance of creating the subject 'informational sustainability' within the postgraduate course on information science. The respective discipline was formulated in 2019 and, from the first semester of the academic year 2020, became part of the Thematic Axis: Information and Knowledge Management of the Graduate Program in Information Science at the Federal University of Santa Catarina (PGCIn/UFSC). The course was and is currently offered to master's and doctoral students in information science and its purpose goes beyond making the participants multipliers of a theme, to be an opportunity for reflection and discussion on the dimensions of sustainable development.

2.   THEORETICAL-CONCEPTUAL ASPECTS

This space was reserved to present the information science and SDGs of the UN 2030 Agenda, focusing on inserting informational sustainability as a discipline into the information science area with conceptual theoretical subsidies, in the search for the social approximation related to global goals.

2.1   Information Science

In Brazil, information science (CI) is part of the broad area of applied social sciences, with library and economics and archivology as sub-areas, according to the table of knowledge areas of the Coordination for the Improvement of Higher Education Personnel (CAPES; Ministério da Educação [Ministry of Education], 2014). CAPES is a foundation of the Ministry of Education (MEC), responsible for postgraduate programs, master's and doctoral degrees, in all states of the Federation (ibid.).

The study of information science began at the end of World War II, primarily due to the quantity of documents with significant value generated while there was no system to manage the growth in the volume of data. During this period, Vannevar Bush published an article entitled 'As we may think' in *The Atlantic*, in which he recommends that scientists focus their research on the challenge of making the stock of knowledge more accessible (Kripka, Viali and Lahm, 2016).

In 1968, Borko defined information science as a discipline that investigates the properties and behavior of information, the forces that govern information flow and the means of processing information to optimize access and use (Passarelli and da Silva, 2014). Supporting this issue, Costa, Leite and Tavares (2018, p. 17) emphasize that 'information science has studied, since its genesis, issues related to scientific communication as a central phenomenon of interest, since the discipline arose due to the concern of scientists, technologists and documentalists in the middle of the last century with information flows in science and technology'. In this context, information science emerges from two distinct panoramas: 'one that foresees, on the one hand, the generation and organization of information and, on the other, the transfer of information mediated by technology for its preservation and recovery' (Nhacuongue and Ferneda, 2015, p. 9). In his dissertation study on the subject, Santos (2012) confirms what Costa et al. (2018) postulate, that the beginning of information science arises from the use of information to access data. The Conference on Scientific Information, held at the Royal Society in 1948, and the Conference on Scientific Information held in Washington in 1958, are seen as the beginning of information science as an area of knowledge.

It should be noted that information science has always been part of the life of human beings, in the harmonious search between the production, sharing and use of information in society. In the same context, in which all fields of knowledge are nourished by information, information science is the one that has information as its object of study. In the article 'What is information science?', Araújo (2014, p. 2) points out that 'Any attempt to make a history of information science must necessarily go back in time to when humans began to produce material records of their knowledge – an action that is at the very origin of the formation of human culture.'

This area of knowledge, in the perspective of Saracevic (1996), focuses on procedures related to information and to make it present in many places in society. For this to happen, its procedures are defined by the organization and management of information, accompanied by information and communication technologies to assist in the processes of recovery, availability and access to information. It is important to highlight that all areas of knowledge have always been intrinsically linked to a multitude of information. Nowadays, social networks have enhanced communication, not limited to being only a means of relationship between users but also a source of information and a tool to mobilize and promote changes in society (Silva, 2016). The concept of information has been systematically developed by information science since its inception. Araújo (2011, p. 126, citing Capurro, 2003) states that information science:

> initially moved by a 'physical paradigm', it understood information only as a physical object, capable of being transmitted and recovered with mathematical precision. Then, from a 'cognitive paradigm', it started to consider, in order to define what information is, knowledge in the minds of producers and users. Finally, in more recent years, through a 'social paradigm', information has been understood as something defined and constructed by collectives of people in interaction.

In 2019, the authors Santos and Damian prepared an article entitled 'The popularization of information science before society and potential information professionals' and, to deepen the subject discussed here, the authors conclude that:

> it is believed that this type of analysis raises the level of reflections on the area and they assist in the constant maintenance of the information science to make it a recognized field in the popular scope. Furthermore, this type of approach contributes to the population's interest in researching this scientific field and understanding that its foundations help in the country's social, economic and intellectual development. (Santos and Damian, 2019, p. 182)

In this scenario, by understanding information science as an area that studies, manages and organizes ways of disseminating and using information, it can be used in the cause of sustainability, seeking to supply the organizational and informational needs of a sustainable society in line with global objectives such as the SDGs. The SDGs aim to understand the world in an interaction between humankind and the environment, seeking to predict and raise awareness of our attitudes in different dimensions (economical, environmental, institutional and social), through educational and informational means, within an ethical and conscious context of use of our natural resources, aiming at the well-being of all (Sachs, 2015). Taking these propositions into account in the context of the sustainability theme, it is believed that visibility and recognition of the role of information science is an important driver for the development and guarantee of information resources necessary to disseminate the knowledge and use of informational sustainability.

2.2   The UN 2030 Agenda Sustainable Development Goals

Sustainability is a contemporary challenge that is on the agenda for discussion and is reflected by all segments of human life because it proposes new directions and establishes new bases for development in all contexts and sectors of humanity. The term 'sustainable development' was first adopted and popularized in 1987 in the report of the United Nations World Commission on Environment and Development (WCED), widely known by the name of its president, Gro Harlem Brundtland (Sachs, 2015).

The Brundtland Commission created a classic definition of the concept of sustainable development: 'it is a development that meets the needs of the present without compromising the ability of future generations to meet their own needs' (WCED, 1987, p. 46). Over the following years, new strategies, actions and global agendas were developed by the UN in order to strengthen, raise awareness and achieve sustainable development on a global basis.

In September 2015, the heads of state and government and senior representatives, together with the United Nations, met in New York and made the decision to implement new global SDGs and adopted a historic decision on a set of universal and transformative objectives and goals that were comprehensive, far-reaching and people centered. The proposition of this agenda, widely discussed, aims to create conditions for sustainable, inclusive and economically sustained growth, shared prosperity and decent work for all, taking into account the different levels of development and national capacities.

The greatest objective of the UN, when embarking on this great mission collectively, is to make everyone aware that 'nobody can be left behind', as it recognizes the dignity of the human person as fundamental and wishes that the objectives and goals are met for all nations and peoples (United Nations, 2015b). The 2030 Agenda comprises 17 SDGs (United Nations, 2015a) and 169 universal goals that involve the whole world as well as developed and developing countries. They are integrated and indivisible and balance the three dimensions of sustainable development. These objectives and targets set by the UN are the result of more than two years of intensive public consultation and engagement with civil society and other stakeholders around the world, 'paying special attention to the voices of the poorest and most vulnerable' (United Nations, 2015b, p. 4). The 17 SDGs are listed below:

1. End poverty in all its forms everywhere.
2. End hunger, achieve food security and improved nutrition and promote sustainable agriculture.
3. Ensure healthy lives and promote well-being for all ages.
4. Ensure inclusive and equitable quality education and promote lifelong learning opportunities for all.
5. Achieve gender equality and empower all women and girls.
6. Ensure availability and sustainable management of water and sanitation for all.
7. Ensure access to affordable, reliable, sustainable and modern energy for all.
8. Promote sustained, inclusive and sustainable economic growth, full and productive employment and decent work for all.
9. Build resilient infrastructure, promote inclusive and sustainable industrialization and foster innovation.
10. Reduce inequality within and among countries.
11. Make cities and human settlements inclusive, safe, resilient and sustainable.
12. Ensure sustainable consumption and production patterns.
13. Take urgent action to combat climate change and its impacts.
14. Conserve and sustainably use the oceans, seas and marine resources for sustainable development.
15. Protect, restore and promote sustainable use of terrestrial ecosystems, sustainably manage forests, combat desertification, and halt and reverse land degradation and halt biodiversity loss.
16. Promote peaceful and inclusive societies for sustainable development, provide access to justice for all and build effective, accountable and inclusive institutions at all levels.
17. Strengthen the means of implementation and revitalize the global partnership for sustainable development.

These objectives seek to achieve the eradication of poverty, respect human rights and achieve gender equality and the empowerment of women and girls. According to the United Nations, these objectives and targets will stimulate action for the next 15 years (2015–30) in areas of crucial importance to humanity and the planet (United Nations, 2015b). IFLA, recognizing the importance of information professionals and associated movements, urged professionals worldwide to contribute their time, experience and financial resources to make the implementation of the SDGs possible. Through the strategic planning of the information units and, concomitantly, with the strengthening of the profession through associated entities, the Brazilian Federation of Associations of Librarians and Information Scientists (FEBAB) in Brazil assumed this commitment nationally – promoting actions, events and campaigns to intensify the IFLA objectives and, therefore, commit everyone to the objectives of the 2030 Agenda (IFLA, 2020). The primary factors that have driven organizations and libraries to adopt a different approach include the opening of the globalized market, the speed of information processing, the significant changes in people's information demands and the management of information and knowledge.

The Brazilian commitment to the SDGs was defined by Federal Decree No. 8.892/2016, which in Article 1 creates the National Commission for the Sustainable Development Goals with the purpose of internalizing, disseminating and making the process of implementing the 2030 Agenda transparent for sustainable development of the United Nations, supported by the Federative Republic of Brazil. The proposal is that these actions become a tool for governments and society to follow the progress achieved by the country in the implementation of the objectives and goals until 2030 (President of the Republic of Brazil, 2016). However, through Message No. 743, of 27 December 2019, the Presidency of the Republic of Brazil vetoed this commitment, as follows:

> By inserting as a guideline of the PPA 2020-2023 the pursuit of the goals of the United Nations Sustainable Development Goals, without disregarding the diplomatic and political importance of the United Nations Sustainable Development Goals, it ends up giving it, even contrary to its purely recommendatory nature, a degree of legal cogency and obligation, to the detriment of the dualistic procedure of internalizing international acts, which violates the provision of arts. 49, item I, and art. 84, item VIII, of the Federal Constitution. (Presidency of the Republic of Brazil, 2019)

The Civil Society Working Group for Agenda 2030 (Grupo de Trabalho da Sociedade Civil para a Agenda 2030, 2020) in Brazil, declared that the presidential veto is serious, as it indicates that the federal government has no interest in maintaining, let alone expanding, sustainable social and environmental policies. The Working Group further states that:

> To deny the relevance and pertinence of monitoring and evaluating the implementation of public policies in Brazil based on these objectives and goals is not only to go against an international agreement, but rather to the democratic process that allowed the construction of the 2030 Agenda. It also means neglecting the responsibility of the Republic's powers to inspect government spending in the light of the results that Brazilian society needs to see achieved over the next ten years. (ibid., p. 2)

However, the Presidency of the Republic of Brazil states that the UN resolution itself provides for the possibility for each country to decide on how to implement the Agenda in its territory, with no obligation to link the Agenda to the budget planning instrument (Presidency of the Republic, 2019). It is important to emphasize that the SDGs are relevant and consistent in the search for human dignity with sustainability, something that any government should prioritize. The veto represents more a denial of the principles of the 2030 Agenda and a lack of interest in implementing its content, than an apparent concern with Brazil's sovereignty.

2.3 Proposal for the Insertion of a Discipline on Informational Sustainability

Sustainability is not a recent discussion, but it has been intensified in recent years and has become a focal point for global discussion in which new ways of approaching problems and defining solutions are envisioned. New global agendas and public policies are essential to raise awareness and encourage the transition of society to a new socioenvironmental model. Sustainability is a choice for attitudinal transformation of society, organizations, communities and individuals, and this transformation is only possible if there is society involvement. Related this change in society, Vecchiatti (2004, p. 4) explains that the sustainability factor:

> is still very recent, especially in public policies. Its development can be an important factor in the period in which we live, as it is not restricted to a specific segment, but permeates various sections

of society; it deals with the creativity that transits between the new and the old and impels society to build a frame of reference in relation to its future.

The author emphasizes that sustainability and cultural policies in society are important because they are the tools of intervention and human approaches. Thus, in the current scenario, people need to interact in relation to resources of all kinds and the social issues involved, as it is a continuous process in the construction of a culture of quality, inclusion and preservation. By approaching informational sustainability by drawing a parallel with information science in the perspective of acting harmoniously, it is believed that it is possible to offer informational mechanisms for the contribution of a sustainable society.

In this perspective, pioneering international studies on the theme are highlighted, such as that presented by Spink (1999) under the title 'Information science in sustainable development and de-industrialization', which describes the various dimensions of the dichotomous views on sustainable development and discusses the emerging discourse on the possible implications and new challenges that are emerging for information science. Another study highlighted is 'Sustainable information and information science', by Jan Nolin (2010), in which Nolin points out that his theme comprises two distinct parts: (1) 'information for sustainable development'; and the (2) 'sustainable information development'. It also stresses that the articulation of sustainable information is important for information science and for related disciplines and research and concludes by suggesting the integration of sustainable information concepts in educational programs for information professionals (Nolin, 2010).

The proposition of the present study is to contribute to what belongs to the management and, in a persuasive way, to the dissemination and mediation of information, thus contributing to progress in the objective of forming conscious citizens and, consequently, a more egalitarian society (Girard and Pires, 2014). As Dutra, Pinto and Geraldo (2017) point out, through the use of information for sustainable development aligned with global objectives defended by Nolin (2010), the introduction of the SDGs theme in information science can be carried out through the services provided by libraries.

IFLA promotes the International Advocacy Program (IAP), aiming to empower, promote and support the role that libraries can play in the planning and implementation of the 2030 Agenda and the SDGs. Through the IAP, IFLA intends to establish a community of engaged professionals who will articulate significant opportunities to raise the profile and highlight the positive impact of librarians in achieving the SDGs (IFLA, 2018). It is worth highlighting how Patri (2011, p. 143) defines advocacy: 'it is the act of advocating, exercised by nonprofit organizations, when they defend their own interests, try to influence some aspect of society or when they appeal to individuals to change their behavior'.

According to the Canadian Association of Public Libraries (CAPL), advocacy is a planned, deliberate and sustained movement, with the central objective of raising awareness of a problem or problems, in which the advocacy action can be seen as a continuous process of actions, seeking the understanding of the individuals involved, created incrementally over a long period (CAPL, 2011). The Ohio Library Council (OLC), making the document called *Library Advocacy: A Handbook for Ohio Public Libraries* available to public library managers, explains that the advocacy movement in libraries must be linked to the general objectives of the library and the awareness program's ongoing public policy. To set up an effective advocacy campaign, you must have an action plan with a focal objective and support objectives, with a vision evidenced in an action plan for the defense of libraries, the professional librarian and the objectives of a prosperous life for the community (OLC, 2017).

In view of this, aligning the action plan and strategic objectives, IFLA sponsored, with the collaboration of several librarian associations from different countries, the International Advocacy Program, which, according to Ferrari (2017, p. 2), was 'a milestone that showed that libraries really have a leading role in society'. As a result, it provided opportunities and encouraged these associations to work with professionals and align the actions that should be taken for and with governments (Ferrari, 2017). Taking into account the 17 SDGs of the 2030 Agenda, IFLA presents examples of initiatives that can be made available in libraries, as described in Table 2.1 (opposite).

Table 2.1 shows the 17 SDGs, UN 2030 Agenda and the promotion of the implementation of SDGs in libraries, with a premeditated proactive character, capable of involving its community and the management of information units with a view to sustainability. For Silva et al. (2015, p. 473) the advocacy movement 'has grown and is increasingly valued within librarianship', with the objective of 'giving visibility to the services promoted by libraries, but also in their defense and in the valorization of the librarian's work'.

As an action to align sustainable development in line with the 2030 Agenda, IFLA understands that acting locally and organizing activities on the 2030 Agenda in its own institutions are the responsibility of librarians. For librarians involved in national advocacy activities, it proposes to help: (1) understand the UN 2030 Agenda process and IFLA's advocacy work; (2) understand how the UN 2030 Agenda will be implemented at the national level; (3) organize meetings with policy makers to demonstrate the contribution that libraries and access to information provide for national development and in all SDGs; (4) monitor the UN 2030 Agenda and the implementation of the SDGs; and (5) inform library users about the SDGs (IFLA, 2018).

3.   FINAL CONSIDERATIONS

The present study aimed to report on our experience in the elaboration of the informational sustainability discipline in graduate programs, as a way of inserting information science in the context of the dimensions of sustainable development and of what IFLA proposes in relation to the 2030 Agenda SDGs. The proposition of the syllabus and the methodology of the discipline comprises two parts, as pointed out by Nolin (2010): (1) information for sustainable development; and the (2) sustainable information development.

To think about a new social paradigm for information science, one must take informational sustainability into account together with the information dissemination mechanism, to generate knowledge about the premises of sustainable development and sustainability, and, at the same time, promote the visibility of information science and information professionals in alignment with global objectives. In Brazil, in the 1990s, the discussion in higher education institutions on sustainability dealt only with the environmental dimension, including teaching and research in areas of knowledge such as economics, administration, engineering and biological sciences. However, in the Brazilian scenario, a few years later it was found that the theme of sustainability is multidimensional and should be introduced and discussed within other areas of knowledge. In the last

Table 2.1   The 17 SDGs for libraries

Goal	Sustainable Development Goals	How Libraries Can Promote the Implementation of the 2030 Agenda (IFLA)
1	End poverty in all its forms everywhere	Libraries support this by providing public access to information and resources that generate opportunities to improve people's lives: training for building new skills needed for education and employment; information to support decision-making processes to combat poverty by governments, civil society and the business sector
2	End hunger, achieve food security and improved nutrition and promote sustainable agriculture	Agricultural research and data towards making crops more productive and sustainable; public access for farmers to networked resources such as local market prices, weather reports and new equipment
3	Ensure healthy lives and promote well-being for all	Research available at medical and hospital libraries that supports education and improves the medical practice of healthcare providers; public access to health and wellness information in public libraries to help make all people and families healthy
4	Ensure inclusive and equitable quality education and promote lifelong learning opportunities for all	Dedicated teams supporting early childhood education (continuing education); access to information and research for students around the world; inclusive spaces where costs are not a barrier to acquiring new knowledge and skills
5	Achieve gender equality and empower all women and girls	Safe and pleasant meeting spaces; programs and services designed to meet the needs of women and girls such as law and health; access to information and technologies that enable women to develop business skills
6 and 7	Ensure availability and sustainable management of water and sanitation for all Ensure access to affordable, reliable, sustainable and modern energy for all	Access to quality information on good practice to develop local water management and sanitation projects; free and safe access to electricity and lighting to read, study and work
8	Promote sustained, inclusive and sustainable economic growth, full and productive employment and decent work for all	Access to information and training to develop skills that people need to find better jobs, apply for them and succeed
9	Build resilient infrastructure, promote inclusive and sustainable industrialization and foster innovation	A large structure of public, specialized and university libraries with qualified professionals; pleasant and inclusive spaces; access to ICT, for example, with high-speed Internet
10	Reduce inequality within and among countries	Neutral and pleasant spaces for learning for all, including marginalized groups such as immigrants, refugees, minorities, indigenous peoples and people with disabilities; equitable access to information that promotes social, political and economic inclusion

Table 2.1   (continued)

Goal	Sustainable Development Goals	How Libraries Can Promote the Implementation of the 2030 Agenda (IFLA)
11	Make cities and human settlements inclusive, safe, resilient and sustainable	Reliable institutions dedicated to promoting inclusion and cultural exchange; documentation and conservation of cultural heritage for future generations
12–15	Ensure sustainable consumption and production patterns	A sustainable material exchange and circulation system that reduces waste generation; record history of coastal changes and land use; research and production of data needed for climate change policy making; widespread access to information needed to guide decision makers by local or national governments on topics such as hunting, fishing, land use and water management
	Take urgent action to combat climate change and its impacts	
	Conserve and sustainably use the oceans, seas and marine resources for sustainable development	
	Protect, restore and promote sustainable use of terrestrial ecosystems, sustainably manage forests, combat desertification, and halt and reverse land degradation and halt biodiversity loss	
16	Promote peaceful and inclusive societies for sustainable development, provide access to justice for all and build effective, accountable and inclusive institutions at all levels	Public access to information about government, civil society and other institutions; training in the skills necessary to understand and use this information; inclusive and politically neutral spaces for people to gather and organize
17	Strengthen the means of implementation and revitalize the global partnership for sustainable development	A network of community-based institutions that form local development plans

Source: IFLA (2018).

four years, in a tentative way, seven scientific articles published in Brazilian information science journals have specifically addressed sustainability actions in libraries, on reading and inclusion. Of these seven articles, two dealt directly with informational sustainability and sustainability paths in information science, written by the authors of this chapter.

In the Brazilian academic environment, in the area of information science and the sub-areas of librarianship, archivology and museology, it is evident that sustainability is not addressed exclusively, but superficially in other disciplines. Based on the studies carried out to write this chapter, it is recommended that higher education institutions that offer undergraduate and graduate courses in the area of information science and its sub-areas make the informational sustainability discipline available. This recommendation is made for two reasons: first because information science is interdisciplinary and responsible for information; and second, because it has social, technological and economic characteristics, thus being able to consolidate its scientific studies to offer informational mechanisms, so leading to a conscious and sustainable society.

There is a tendency in education aimed at sustainability to highlight the need for changes in individual attitudes and behaviors, to the detriment of changes that involve political, social and economic processes. Therefore, it is necessary to take into account, above all, that one of the objectives of education, dissemination and access to information, is to create responsible citizens who can adequately understand the problems faced by their societies and then act to help solve them. Promoting knowledge and access to information on sustainability and global objectives facilitates awareness and participation in socio-environmental issues, fostering the ability to think critically and allowing the acquisition of informational skills necessary to proactively seek possible solutions for society.

Finally, higher education institutions are expected to offer pedagogical proposals with curricular content on global social, environmental and economic problems, reverting to the importance of the role of human beings and their commitment to individual and collective actions in improving life and preserving the planet today and for future generations.

REFERENCES

Araújo, C.A.Á. (2011). Ciência da informação, biblioteconomia, arquivologia e museologia: relações institucionais e teóricas [Information science, librarianship, archivology and museology: institutional and theoretical relations]. *Encontros Bibli: Revista Eletrônica de Biblioteconomia e Ciência da Informação*, 16(31), 110–30.

Araújo, C.A.Á. (2014, January–April). O que é ciência da informação? [What is information science?]. *Informação & Informação*, 19(1), 1–30.

Canadian Association of Public Libraries (CAPL) (2011). *Library Advocacy Now! A Training Program for Public Library Staff and Trustees*. Accessed 14 September 2020 at http://cla.ca/wp-content/uploads/LibraryAdvocacyNow.pdf.

Capurro, R. (2003). Epistemologia e ciência da informação [Epistemology and information science]. Accessed 17 September 2020 at http://www.capurro.de/enancib_p.htm.

Costa, S.M.M., Leite, F.C.L. and Tavares, R.B. (eds) (2018). *Comunicação da informação, gestão da informação e gestão do conhecimento* [Information Communication, Information Management and Knowledge Management]. Brasília: IBICT.

Dutra, S.K.W., Pinto, M.D.S. and Geraldo, G. (2017, December). Agenda 2030: uma proposta de advocacy junto às bibliotecas universitárias públicas de Florianópolis [Agenda 2030: an advocacy proposal with the public university libraries in Florianopolis]. *Revista Brasileira de Biblioteconomia e Documentação*, 13(1), 2606–19.

Ferrari, A.C. (2017). Brazilian libraries and the Agenda 2030: actions to support compliance with ODS. In *Proceedings of the 83 IFLA WLIC 2017*, pp. 1–8. Accessed 14 September 2020 at http://library.ifla.org/1626/.

Geraldo, G. and Pinto, M.D.S. (2019, April–Jun). Percursos da ciência da informação e os objetivos do desenvolvimento sustentável da agenda 2030/ONU [Pathways to information science and the Sustainable Development Goals of the 2030/UN Agenda]. *Revista ACB: Biblioteconomia em Santa Catarina*, 24(2), 373–89.

Girard, C.D.T. and Pires, E.A.N. (2014, February). A sustentabilidade informacional e sua relação com a biblioteconomia no século [Information sustainability and its relationship with librarianship in the century]. In *Proceedings XVII Encontro Regional dos Estudantes de Biblioteconomia, Documentação, Ciência e Gestão da Informação*. Universidade Federal do Ceará Fortaleza. Accessed 3 February 2021 at http://repositorio.ufpa.br/jspui/bitstream/2011/9823/1/Artigo_SustentabilidadeInformacionalRelacao.pdf.

Grupo de Trabalho da Sociedade Civil para a Agenda 2030 (2020). Nota de preocupação sobre veto presidencial aos ODS no PPA 2020-2023 [Note of concern over presidential veto of ODS in PPA 2020–2030]. Accessed

3 February 2021 at https://gtagenda2030.org.br/2020/03/05/gt-agenda-2030-divulga-nota-de-preocupacao-sobre-veto-presidencial-aos-ods-no-ppa-2020-2023/.

International Federation of Library Associations and Institutions (IFLA) (2018). *The International Advocacy Program (IAP) 2017*. Accessed 14 September 2020 at https://www.ifla.org/ldp/iap.

International Federation of Library Associations and Institutions (IFLA) (2020). New partnerships, stronger voice: libraries engage in Brazil's 2030 Agenda. Accessed 27 February 2021 at https://www.ifla.org/node/93253.

Kripka, R.M.L., Viali, L. and Lahm, R.A. (2016). Contribuições de Vannevar Bush para a ciência e a tecnologia, especialmente ao hipertexto [Vannevar Bush's contributions to science and technology, especially to hypertext]. *Revista Conhecimento Online*, 8(2), 55–68.

Ministério da Educação [Ministry of Education], Coordenação de Aperfeiçoamento de Pessoal de Nível Superior (CAPES) (2014). Tabela de áreas do conhecimento [Table of knowledge areas]. Accessed 3 February 2021 at https://www.ufrb.edu.br/pibic/images/repositorio/pdfs/areas_de_conhecimento_capes.pdf.

Nolin, J. (2010). Sustainable information and information science. *Information Research*, 15(2), Article 431.

Nhacuongue, J.A. and Ferneda, E. (2015, April–June). O campo da ciência da informação: contribuições, desafios e perspectivas [The field of information science: contributions, challenges and perspectives]. *Perspectivas em Ciência da Informação*, 20(2), 3–18.

Ohio Library Council (OLC) (2017). *Library Advocacy: A Handbook for Ohio Public Libraries*. Government Relations Committee, OLC.

Passarelli, B. and da Silva, A.M. (2014). *E-infocomunicação estratégias e aplicações* [E-infocommunications Strategies and Applications]. São Paulo: Senac.

Patri, E.C. (2011). Relações governamentais, lobby e advocacy no contexto de public affairs [Government relations, lobbying and advocacy in the context of public affairs]. *Organicom*, 8(14). Accessed 3 February 2021 at https://www.revistas.usp.br/organicom/article/view/139089.

Presidency of the Republic of Brazil (2016). *Decreto 8.892, de 27 de outubro de 2016* [Decree 8.892 of 27 October 2016]. Accessed 3 February 2021 at https://www.in.gov.br/materia/-/asset_publisher/Kujrw0TZC2Mb/content/id/21293488/do1-2016-10-31-decreto-n-8-892-de-27-de-outubro-de-2016-21293421.

President of the Republic of Brazil (2019). Mensagem n° 743, de 27 de dezembro de 2019 [Message No. 743 of 27 December 2019]. Accessed 3 February 2021 at https://presrepublica.jusbrasil.com.br/legislacao/795189079/mensagem-743-19.

Sachs, J.D. (2015). *The Age of Sustainable Development*. New York: Columbia University Press.

Santos, A.P.L. dos (2012). *Relações interdisciplinares entre a ciência da informação e a biblioteconomia: limites e possibilidades* [Interdisciplinary relations between information science and librarian ship: limits and possibilities]. Master's dissertation, Universidade Federal Fluminense, Niterói.

Santos, B.R.P. and Damian, I.P.M. (2019, September–December). A popularização da ciência da informação perante a sociedade e potenciais profissionais da informação [The popularization of information science before society and potential information professionals]. *Ciência Informação*, 48(3), 173–83.

Saracevic, T. (1996, January–June). Ciência da informação: origem, evolução e relações. [Information science: origin, evolution and relationships]. *Revista Perspectivas em Ciência da Informação*, 1(1), 41–62.

Silva, A.S., Spudeit, D.F.A. and Duarte, E.J. et al. (2015). Associação Catarinense de bibliotecários: 40 anos de serviços prestados na defesa e valorização da biblioteconomia Catarinense [Santa Catarina Association of Librarians: 40 years of services rendered in the defense and valorization of the Santa Catarina Librarianship]. In *Proceedings of the 26 Congresso Brasileiro de Biblioteconomia e Documentação*, São Paulo: FEBAB, pp. 472–85.

Silva, P. (2016). De 'um para todos' a 'todos para todos': as mudanças socioculturais da cultura de massas à cultura digital [From 'one for all' to 'all for all': the sociocultural changes from mass culture to digital culture]. In M.L. Vilaça and E.V.F. Araujo (eds), *Tecnologia, Sociedade e Educação na Era Digital*. Rio de Janeiro: Unigranrio.

Spink, A. (1999). Information science in sustainable development and de-industrialization. *Information Research*, 5(1). Accessed 20 September 2020 at http://informationr.net/ir/5-1/paper65.html.

United Nations (2015a). *The 17 Sustainable Development Goals*. Accessed 3 February 2021 at https://sdgs.un.org/goals.

United Nations (2015b). *Transforming our World: The Agenda 2030 for Sustainable Development*. Accessed 3 February 2020 at https://sustainabledevelopment.un.org/content/documents/21252030%20Agenda%20for%20Sustainable%20Development%20web.pdf.

Vecchiatti, K. (2004).Três fases rumo ao desenvolvimento sustentável: do reducionismo à valorização da cultura. [Three phases towards sustainable development: from reductionism to culture appreciation]. *Perspectivas em Ciência da Informação*, 18(3), 90–95.

World Commission on Environment and Development (WCED) (1987). *Our Common Future*. Oxford: Oxford University Press.

3. Using an arts-based, flexible approach to evaluate students' interconnected learning of education for sustainability in early childhood
Diane Boyd and Naomi McLeod

1. INTRODUCTION

This chapter recognises the need for early childhood studies (ECS) degree students to be reflexive (QAA, 2014) in relation to appreciating the interconnected nature of education for sustainability (EfS), and in doing so advocates innovative new ways of teaching and learning (UNESCO, 2016). A narrative is presented that takes the reader through various stages (before, during and after) involving reflexive provocations that enabled students to make interconnections between the three pillars of EfS as an embodied, natural instinctive phenomenon. The chapter outlines the students' starting point (before), followed by provocations (during) that aimed to unsettle and disrupt the students' unconscious bias about key issues related to EfS. The creative hermeneutic evaluations provided insights into their new transformational appreciation of the interconnected nature of EfS (after).

At the start of a final year ECS degree module, called: 'Global Dimensions: Sustainable Futures Across Early Years', students at a university in the UK demonstrated some knowledge of environmental aspects related to sustainability. However, they were not making interconnections between the three pillars of sustainability (namely, political-economic, environmental and socio-cultural). There was a distinct lack of understanding and critical engagement in relation to political and socio-cultural influences in the form of neo-liberalism, marketization, sustainability and relational ethics. Thus, a rights-based approach that values and respects both human and non-human perspectives is advocated. In doing so, EfS needs to be valued as something that is right and ethical rather than a government initiative (Bourn et al., 2016), so it is not just about 'doing it' but rather an authentic choice. Our aim is for ECS students to be advocates who challenge anti-bias and inequalities and be proactive (QAA, 2014).

In preparing students as reflexive professionals that are committed to EfS, there was and still is a need for personal questioning. In this context, learning provocations were provided that unsettled students and prompted them to become aware of and question their own personal unconscious biases, attitudes and beliefs, thus developing an understanding about power imbalances. In this endeavour, the need for students to value different perspectives and lenses such as human and non-human (i.e., children, marginalised groups, the environment) was important.

There was also a need for students to be able to share their sensitive and personal biases without being judged (for example, the purpose of education and question dominant discourses). Therefore, a safe, trusting and unquestioning environment was essential (Leitch, 2006). An open, collaborative approach was adopted, which was supported by creating a relaxed atmosphere and the use of reflective journaling. This enabled students to engage with unconscious biases and emotions that influenced their interconnected understanding of early childhood care and education (ECCE) and EfS. This is explained later. Our focus was for students to engage reflexively through a series of international provocations so their thinking was disrupted and they developed a new appreciation of the interconnected nature of EfS.

2.   LITERATURE REVIEW

2.1   Education for Sustainability (EfS)

The foundations of EfS are the principles of critical reflection, empathy, agency, participation, empowerment and democratic practice, which are the bedrock of ECCE (Boyd, 2018). Davis (2015a, p. 18), however, argues that for education to truly be transformative it cannot be just 'more of the same', which resonates with Orr (1994, p. 83), who highlighted that education as it is (was) 'cannot be solved by the same kind of education that has helped create the problems'. Despite society being more aware through the media, there is little acknowledgement about the relevance of the Sustainable Development Goals (UNESCO, 2015) regarding pedagogical practices, nor do they feature in the English statutory Early Years Statutory Framework (Department for Education, 2017). As Huggins and Evans (2018) note, educators in ECCE are still not engaging in this debate and, consequently, not transforming their practice. As Wals and Peters (2017, p. 39) note, 'democracy is painfully slow', and therefore this chapter challenges higher education to recognise the need to value more creative and reflexive teaching approaches.

2.2   The Need for Reflexivity in the Context of EfS

The original concept of reflection comes from Aristotle over 2000 years ago, who was concerned with the philosophical understandings of epistemology (what knowledge is, how we develop it and understand ethics, and the notion that actions should be good and moral) (Aristotle, 1925). As Noddings (2003) identified, Aristotle was concerned with ethics and questioning aspects of everyday life and the evidence that supports thoughts and actions. This open form of reasoning is known as phronesis praxis or an intentional and committed action with moral intent. It is about behaving 'for the good of humankind in acts consciously and *collectively* performed to contribute to the good' (Kemmis, 2010, p. 419). By reflecting on collective and individual action and its consequences, Kemmis argues that this is 'how we learn *wisdom* and how we develop what Aristotle called *phronesis*'. For Aristotle, *phronesis praxis* was guided by a moral disposition to act truly and rightly; a concern to further human well-being and the good life.

In its basic form, critical reflection or reflexivity requires an internal personal awareness and self-examination of what is thought and done, which can then result in a conscious change (Bolton, 2010; McLeod, 2015; McLeod and Giardiello, 2019). It is an ongoing entangled fluid process involving the head, heart and will, and means becoming conscious of knowledge, which in turn facilitates multi-layered complex thought processes and connections with underpinning personal views, values, principles, assumptions and beliefs. This can open up new ways of seeing and offers insight into individuals' multiple identities and interpretations of situations (Smith, 2016). Put more simply, reflexivity offers insight into 'working out how our presence influences knowledge and actions' (Bolton, 2010, p. 7). Most essentially it is a willingness or readiness to question personal values, beliefs and assumptions so it is possible to examine their influence on actions (pedagogy practised) (McLeod, 2015; McLeod and Giardiello, 2019) and make appropriate changes (Derrida, 1999; Moon, 2008). Reflexivity, then, in relation to ECCE, and EfS, means having an awareness of issues of power and the need for reciprocal, respectful relationships. This leads to a more deliberate scrutinisation of values and assumptions, which can be done through viewing different 'lenses' (Brookfield, 2017). In a sense, this willingness to be open and question becomes an ongoing, fluid 'learning journey' of inter-relationships as part of professional development for empowering educators to see and do differently (Edwards, Gilroy and Hartley, 2002; McLeod, 2011; Reed and Canning, 2010).

2.3 Challenging Thinking Through Creativity in EfS

As noted by d'Orville (2019, p. 65), 'creativity is at the heart of sustainability, rooted in sustainable social, economic, environmental and cultural practices' and seeing the world through different complexities. Within the influential report, *Our Common Future* (World Commission on Environment and Development [WCED], 1987, p. 6), the Chairman, Brundtland, highlighted 'urgent but complex problems' that needed addressing to sustain our environment and the continuation of life. The report also advocated a lens that utilises interconnection, as the 'environment does not exist as a sphere separate from human actions, ambitions, and needs' (ibid., p. 7). Therefore, within the report, there was a recognition for the need for all citizens of the world to become effective decision makers and participants, with the burden resting on young people and those who will have influence upon them, in supporting change. Davis (2015a), however, cautions that children must not be burdened with these responsibilities, but challenges and encourages ECCE to become a site for ecological, societal and cultural agency. This idea of capable children, rich in experience and curiosity, also resonates with Maria Montessori, who argued that the 'foundations of man are laid down' in ECCE (Montessori, 2012, p. 3).

However, whilst Vare and Scott (2007) suggest that the future is 'unknown', Sandri (2013) states that it is the role of education to ensure that children can address these complex problems through challenging and creative pedagogical ways of learning. Rather than following predetermined educational pathways or a 'prophetic curriculum' (Cagliari et al., 2016) young people and children need the skills and capabilities to question, critique and be provoked. As Montessori (2012, p. 236) highlighted, decision making is a formation of character and that without a solid childhood that nurtures resilience, confidence and creativity, children are 'incapable of making a decision', which resonates with Boyd and Bath (2017) whose research with early childhood students noted them feeling lost and afraid when provided with a creative provocation. Consequently, Paniagua and Istance (2018) and the *Global Education Monitoring Report* (UNESCO, 2016) call for innovative new approaches to education to ensure both learners and their educators have the potential to initiate change through creativity and strong decision making. In doing so, Ziegler and Paniagua (2019, p 1) agree that innovative creative playful pedagogies 'can take root and scale, putting SDG 4 [UNESCO, 2015] within reach', which is the ultimate transformational aim of EfS. However, there is a note of caution, as such creative skills could just 'reflect norms of powerful social groups or countries' (UNESCO, 2016, p. 253) such as the dominant Anglo American minority world. As Nsamenang (2006) noted, this is the picture that tends to be represented in ECCE. The challenge of prioritising ECCE, specifically, 'in identifying and overcoming the barriers that deprive marginalised groups of the same learning opportunities as others' is crucial here (UNESCO, 2007, p. 67). This is reinforced by Mbebeb (2009, p. 23), who stated that 'entrepreneurial mindsets priming is a viable component of early childhood education through life skills orientation within the family' and challenging neo-liberal views of education. As a result, Boyd (2018) urges early childhood education to provide opportunities for complex issues of sustainability to be considered, however difficult or unsettling, rather than focusing on assessment and narrow learning outcomes. The higher education module as the focus for this chapter and its creative assessment was a direct result of the issues discussed above.

Similarly, Sandri (2013) argues that in the current climate of EfS, students need more than just knowledge and technical skills that are useless in dealing with the uncertainty of the future at a time of vast change. To respond to complex EfS matters such as social inequality or environmental issues, she calls for creative educational processes that involve students asking 'different' or 'better' questions that challenge the rules of the current paradigm (Cherry, 2005; UNESCO, 2016). As a result, new possibilities can be considered rather than 'the same kind of thinking that led to problems in the first place' (Wals, der Hoeven and Blanken, 2009, p. 9). This requires a shift from content learning to nurturing creative competencies by engaging with challenges of sustainability or professional contexts so students are empowered (Hager, 2006; Montessori, 2012; UNESCO, 2016). Such aptitudes involve experimental learning, engaging in critical thinking, developing imagination and empathy, evaluating, acting fairly and developing tolerance. This is very different from the teacher-directed 'reproductive' approach associated with many schools and universities (Montuori, 2012). Students are a result of their education history, which has focused on teacher-directed learning and outputs (Boyd and Bath, 2017; Lumsden, McBride-Wilding and Rose, 2010). Creating the conditions for connective EfS learning/or an environment that cultivates creativity is essential (McCormack and Boomer, 2007). In his reflection on the lack of effective preparation of graduates to address issues of sustainability (survival), Orr (1994) implies that the solution lies in a change in the way knowledge is defined and education is perceived. That is, a departure from courses focused on just the transmission of knowledge to spaces for pedagogical transformation that support transformative and transdisciplinary learning (Moore, 2005, cited in Leal Filho and Pace, 2019, p. 3). Montuori (2012) identifies the need for a pedagogy that opens up creative spaces, where the teacher encourages, facilitates and nudges students through social interactions that are unpredictable. The notion of provocations that are deeply unsettling for students or requiring 'both order and disorder' (p. 66) are advocated here in order to challenge values, beliefs and assumptions. As Schulz (2010) argues, 'to abandon certainty is to abandon our inner sensation that something just is' (p. 163). In this way, EfS requires challenging personal truths (values and beliefs), professional truths (processes and disciplinary traditions) and societal truths (social norms and dominant discourses of the world). Through uprooting, thinking shifts from what 'is' to what 'is possible' (Sandri, 2013). Once students have begun to question their own taken-for-granted certainties, they can then begin to explore divergent approaches to complex problems of sustainability.

2.4 Transformational Learning

Transformative learning, according to Mezirow (2000), is based on deep learning that goes beyond content knowledge acquisition and is a learning process that positions critical reflection as central. It involves emotional self-awareness and understanding, through true emancipation from sometimes unquestioning acceptance of life experience, to active engagement or questioning of how we know what we know. By being open to 'negotiat[ing] meanings, purposes and values critically, reflectively and rationally instead of passively accepting the social realities defined by others' (ibid., p. 3), transformative learning can lead to emancipation and greater autonomy in thinking. As Imel (1998) and Taylor (2007) consider, it is the creative process that is important, based on the use of dialogue devoted to searching for a truthful understanding and questioning the evidence that underpins knowledge. Similarly, Wilson, McCormack and Ives (2006) refer to 'taking self-responsibility for learning' (p. 90), which they consider key in the context of socio-cultural influences central to EfS. In this way, critical reflection can lead to the transformation of oppressing professional or socio-cultural and political customs (Jacobs and Murray, 2010). Given that transformative learning theory is based on engagement, consciousness, personal adjustment regarding new situations, emancipation and change (Kabakci, Odabasi and Kilicer, 2010), the theory (including emotions) provided an appropriate underpinning for our module and the needs of the students in the context of EfS.

3.   METHODS USED IN THE STUDY

3.1 An Emancipatory Theoretical Framework (During)

The module took Freire's (1994) theory of 'conscientisation'/critical social theory as its theoretical underpinning, an approach based on the principles of empowerment, social justice, emancipation and freedom. This involves questioning assumptions that have been taken for granted and raises awareness of new perspectives and personal actions that can lead to the transformation of oppressing professional customs (Jacobs and Murray, 2010; Mezirow, 1997, 2000). This informed the methodology that comprises the following:

- participatory action learning drawing on international rights-based provocations;
- reflective journaling using McLeod's reflexivity framework;
- the use of creative hermeneutic evaluation: students created an image that captured the essence of their new learning and haiku poems.

The intention of this project was to provoke the students using creative approaches to questioning, so they became aware of their own unconscious bias. A practical understanding of reflexivity using McLeod's practical framework (McLeod and Giardiello, 2019) was embedded as part of the module in relation to EfS.

3.2   Participatory Action Learning (During)

The most appropriate design for supporting conditions for change was a creative, participatory action learning approach (McIntosh, 2010) that is concerned with both the process and the end product (Leitch and Day, 2000), which in this case was an individual presentation that demonstrated how they had engaged reflexively in the workshop involving international provocations that disrupted their thinking. This was followed by an individual rationale by each student. It was about working *with* students to develop their ownership and understanding of their own situation, so otherness is valued (Mason, 2002). The emphasis was on the underpinning principles of action learning according to McCormack and Boomer (2007, p. 20) as follows:

- working with students' beliefs and values;
- 'working with' rather than 'doing to' students;
- valuing students as co-learners;
- placing an equal emphasis on action and process.

In the context of this study, creative learning is understood as the right for students to be engaged in playful, creative learning, so they express themselves and take responsibility for decision making about matters that are important for EfS (United Nations Convention on the Rights of the Child [UNCRC], 1989, Articles 12, 13 and 31). At the heart of this process is democratic co-constructive thinking and communication rather than a transmission of knowledge and skills (Malaguzzi, 1994; Rinaldi, 2006; Villen, 1993).

The 2018–19 cohort of final-year early childhood degree students that were studying this module was a small group of 11 students who were familiar with each other and the participating tutors. Over a period of five months, students were encouraged to engage reflexively with journal keeping in relation to interconnected sustainability through a series of international provocations. Hesterman (2018, p. 148) notes how provocations in higher education can help students to 'go beyond and extend' by critically reflecting on sensitive issues and questioning unconscious biases. In doing so, this resonates with both the *Global Education Monitoring Report* (UNESCO, 2016), which argues for newer approaches in education, and SDG 4 (UNESCO, 2015) on lifelong learning.

3.3   Examples of International Rights-based Provocations Included as Part of the Module (During)

Each of the following case studies were designed to 'unsettle' and provoke by asking encouraging questions and developing self-awareness about personal views, attitudes and beliefs and power imbalances:

- questioning what the purpose of education is;
- how children are viewed (i.e., in need and vulnerable or as capable, independent and creative agents of change);
- New Zealand (Mount Taranaki) granting the same rights to the environment as human rights (i.e., the rights of nature/valuing a bicentric lens and relational ethics/

ethno-ecology (the example of water having memories and trees talking/having feelings was used));
- ECCE in Palestine and an anti-bias approach/gender stereotyping;
- ECCE in Australia and colonialism/white privilege/nationalism and the need to appreciate indigenous culture;
- Te Whāriki, a New Zealand early childhood education curriculum, using a socio-cultural intergenerational learning lens;
- colonial barriers: fences, walls and borders – for example, white picket fences in Australia/the integrated primary school in Northern Ireland with a 30-foot peace wall around it/US Mexican border wall/Wales language barriers;
- a local community intergenerational EfS approach called 'Squash';
- examples of children's agency: Greta Thunberg/The Little Collector on the Wirral/Millennium Kids in Perth Australia;
- a critique of a Forest School in England/valuing nature/the process of learning rather than outcomes/the need to question neo-liberalism;
- democratic leadership through reflexivity;
- the need for a praxeological approach, so children and students as future early childhood educators are empowered.

This module was characterised by nurturing conscious steps to increase student participation in both the creative democratic learning sessions and in the assessment process, which resulted in a transformation of their mindsets, attitudes and a deeper understanding of EfS (Leal Filho and Pace, 2019).

3.4   Reflective Journaling (During)

McLeod, Karlsson Häikiö and Mårtensson (2019) and Mason (2002) identify how the use of reflective journaling can reveal to the writer things about a subject area and about themselves that were previously unknown. Likewise, Moon (2006, 2008) and Schön (1987) reinforce that the process of writing can increase the quality of reflection about practice and illuminate personal thoughts and ideas so new knowledge can be created. This is more meaningful when provocations are used within familiar contexts. In this way, Moon (2008) explains how reflective journaling through writing shifts from a description to a deep reflective account. It progresses from no questions (as a narrative) to the asking of questions and responding to questions, and is comparable with reflection-in-action (Schön, 1987). As an awareness of personal emotional influences is developed, there is an increasing ability to stand back and question from an alternative perspective (Moon, 2008). Reflective journaling can therefore support self-awareness (phronesis), a consciousness of other perspectives and new insights about power (politics) and what is ethically right as part of early childhood practice. Such reflexive visual research methods are crucial in the current climate of an increasing multicultural global society (Alpers, 2007; Fors and Bäckström, 2015) as they can be used to make non-verbal aspects of learning visible and generate new meanings (Karlsson Häikiö, 2018).

In the context of this research and this module, students documenting their feelings and biases and seeing through different lenses in relation to the different provocations was key in transforming their new understandings and appreciations of otherness. Students used

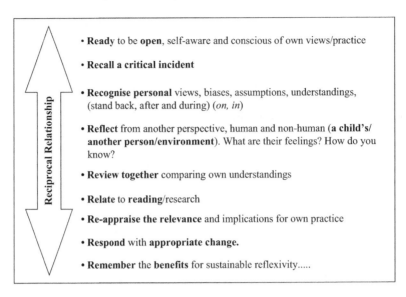

Source: McLeod (cited in McLeod and Giardiello, 2019, p. 226).

Figure 3.1   McLeod's reflexivity framework

McLeod's (McLeod and Giardiello, 2019) reflexivity framework headings to support this process (Figure 3.1). They were encouraged to make it meaningful to them – for example, doodling, drawings, mind-maps and images. These reflections demonstrated their new visible understandings of interconnected EfS relationships that emerged because of the provocations. As Titchen and McCormack (2010) note, this required a personal openness so it was possible to see differently and respond (Scharmer, 2009).

This framework was offered as a practical set of principles for applying critical reflection in a sustainable way. The students used this to record personal views and emotional responses about different aspects of the provocations that struck a chord with them, and how these disrupted or unsettled their thinking about their place in the world and the purpose of early childhood education. The reflexive provocational process is explained below:

- 'Critical incident' in this context became a provocation that students were encouraged to identify or recall as a particular incident of interest and recognise their personal view, bias, assumptions, experience and understandings.
- They were then encouraged to reflect from a different perspective and consider emotions, which became highly significant in the transformative nature as discussed later in the analysis.
- Students were secure enough in their relationships with each other and in the space that had been created to review together, so their thinking was disrupted and sometimes uncomfortable.
- Each provocation was informed by or related to reading/research, which empowered their thinking and authenticated it.

- This process then enabled students to reappraise the provocations in relation to their own social and cultural contexts (e.g., Northern Ireland [the 'troubles'], Wales [the 'Welsh Knot' language punishment], outdoors, the life of a caterpillar).
- Students were then able to respond with appropriate change in relation to EfS (demonstrated in their individual rationales at the end of the module).
- It was the combination of the above that made it relevant and sustainable so the students remembered for future pedagogical practice (link to SDG 4: 'Quality education for all'; UNESCO, 2015).

In this way, students explored concepts of quality and value that were personally important and included embodied emotions for them (McIntosh, 2010). This became possible through enlightenment (understanding self), through empowerment (courage to change self) and emancipation (becoming what we need to be) (McCormack and Boomer, 2007). This reflective aspect supported students' capacity to identify issues or problems in relation to their own ways of seeing EfS, which informed their assessed rationale at the end of the module.

It was the combination of the provocations, the trusting creative environment and the journal keeping that was at the heart of their transformational learning, so the students were empowered by recognising deeper embodied emotions.

3.5   The Use of Creative Hermeneutic Evaluation (After)

Hermeneutics as a methodology of interpreting or making oneself understood by others was appropriate in the context of this research. It offered a way of revealing or self-disclosing desires, feelings and thoughts in relation to other views (Urban, 2008). Altman and Taylor (1973) describe it as a peeling back of onion layers to reveal the inner. As Jupp (2006) identifies, creative hermeneutics is an interpretation of what is said or done understood from the inside against the backdrop of how one thinks and feels about the world in which they live. Sense is made of a situation or provocation by exploring underlying motives, feelings and rationales (Schutt, 2006). These principles of creative hermeneutic analysis were consistent with the open and engaging approach taken as part of this module and the evaluation of it. Simons and McCormack (2007) suggest using resources and processes that people are familiar with, such as using creative arts, which does not make assumptions about prior knowledge, but instead helps the participant (students) to convert their tacit knowledge (knowledge we know but cannot tell) into a different context. As Leitch (2006) identifies, creative approaches are necessary to reveal hidden unconscious emotion that language alone can restrict. In this case, the students created a 2D or 3D image accompanied by a poetic narrative or haiku.

The use of haiku as a kind of poetic narrative (more commonly known as a Japanese poetic form that consists of 17 syllables arranged in three lines containing five, seven and five syllables) enabled students to draw on personal experience, particularly emotions, as a creative means for supporting engagement in a cognitive critique. As Janchowski-Hartley et al. (2018, p. 908) note, the use of haiku poetry can convey a 'sense of play' and is the ideal tool 'for reframing complex topics'. It allowed for a deconstruction of different contexts and then a reconstruction based on new understandings because of engaging in the creative and reflexive journey as part of the module. Through the interplay of the hermeneutic 2D and 3D images and the narratives shared by each student, keywords and metaphors were identified and haiku-type poems were crafted to provide meaning to their experience (Titchen and McCormack, 2010, p. 551). As Luff (2018) advocates, there is a need for more arts-based interventions in early childhood EfS. O'Gorman (2014, 2015) likewise identifies creative approaches as having the potential for unleashing unconscious biases around controversial social problems, such as colonialism. Most recently, in relation to sustainability, d'Orville (2019, p. 69) notes how creativity and artistic expressions help to 'build better ways of living together in a world of increasingly diverse societies', resonating with the SDGs/Agenda 30 and in particular SDG 17, 'Partnerships for the goals' (UNESCO, 2015).

At the end of the module, the students were briefly reminded of the focus of each workshop and the key thinking around EfS that had arisen through open discussion. The creative reflective process evaluation that students engaged in is explained as follows:

1. Students were invited to create an image that captured the essence of their impressions of engaging in the module and their understanding/critical awareness of EfS in the context of international ECCE: before the module; during the module (and key provocations/critical incidents; and after the module. As McCormack and Boomer (2007) reinforce, it is capturing the essence of students' narratives that is important.
2. A selection of art materials was provided, such as clay, different coloured paper of various sizes, paints, glue, straws, stars, sticky coloured paper, string, pipe cleaners, coloured wooden sticks, sequins, pom-poms and felt-tip pens, so students had a good selection to choose from.
3. The students were allowed 30 minutes to select materials and create an image of their impressions/understandings of EfS in the context of international ECCE (before, during and after).
4. Once students had created their 2D/3D image, they were invited to pair up and share their narrative about their creative work while the other student listened and noted keywords. These highlighted the journeys experienced by the students (Titchen and McCormack, 2010) and their new appreciation of the interconnected nature of EfS.
5. Each student shared their 'before, during and after' words.
6. As students shared their creative explanation, the tutors (and authors) noted keywords and metaphors in the form of a poetic haiku and agreed it with each student.

4.   RESULTS

Below, Figures 3.2–3.12, are the pictures created by the students. Each is accompanied by the metaphorical haiku created together as a representation of each student's story.

Less value, assume
Respected interconnected
Being open minded

Figure 3.2   Student 1

Narrow minded
Complex thinking, creative
Still developing

Figure 3.3   Student 2

Divided, normal
Thinking, impact, grudges
Should be united

Figure 3.4   Student 3

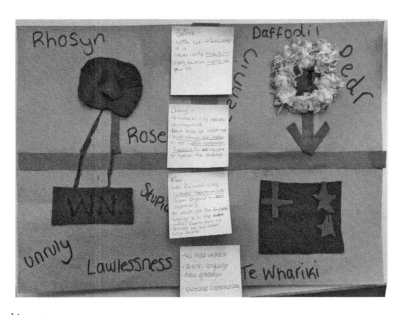

No real impact
Welsh language, now grateful
Culture, environments

Figure 3.5   Student 4

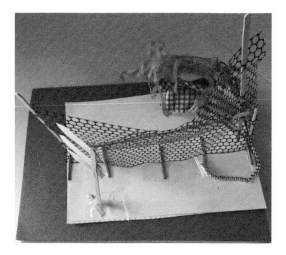

Segregated trauma
Stop, cut, break down fences
Justice, freedom, peace

Figure 3.6   Student 5

Environmental
The Three Pillars
Interconnectedness

Figure 3.7   Student 6

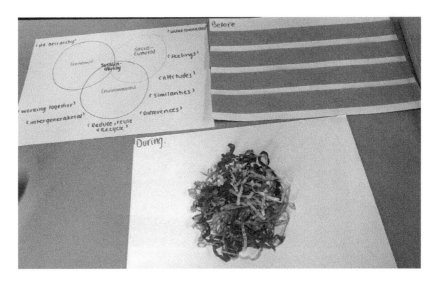

Willingness to change
Provoking challenge and thought
Transformative change

Figure 3.8   Student 7

Closed minded to all
Opened eyes, community
A new environment

Figure 3.9   Student 8

Basic environment
Power, nature imbalance
Welcoming people

Figure 3.10   Student 9

Impact, division
Norms challenged
Challenge reproduction

Figure 3.11   Student 10

Segregated fortress
Hierarchical, no rights
No separation now

Figure 3.12   Student 11

5.   DISCUSSION

As the students engaged reflexively through a series of international provocations, so their thinking was disrupted and they developed new appreciations of the interconnected nature of EfS. Drawing on the above haikus, insights into the process emerged that represent students' thinking about the nature of EfS before, during and after the module, which demonstrated how their engagement in the creative learning process supported their overall transformed socio-cultural and political-economic understanding of EfS. The haikus were a catalyst for their interconnected thinking, which enabled them to tap into their emotions, a process that would be described as 'metamorphic'.

Our next stage of the analysis process was to unpick the phrases from the haikus. In doing so, there is a focus on similarities and differences, so all the haikus are valued.

5.1   Haiku Analysis

Before
It became apparent how limited their understanding of the interconnected nature of EfS was by their chosen language. For example, 'closed', 'basic', 'less', 'no' and 'segregated'.

Additionally, the language was very negative and reflected their narrow view of sustainability, which had tended to be dominated by environmental thinking. Boyd (2018) raises this as a concern in terms of a lack of awareness of socio-cultural sustainability, which is and should be the foundation of early childhood.

While there is some evidence of their reflections on their understanding of EfS before the module, to some extent this new thinking is visible as a consequence of the reflexive process they have engaged in as part of the module (McLeod, 2019) and the safe, trusting environment (Leitch, 2006). For example, the use of words such as 'divided' and 'segregated' reflect an appreciation of the socio-cultural lens, was not visible at the beginning of the module. This indicates the beginnings of the metamorphic process the students engaged in.

During
The students' engagement in the creative, collaborative process as part of the module is visible in a similar way to that of the 100 languages of children described by Malaguzzi (1998). This values a process that is a democratic co-constructive way of learning that emphasises communication rather than a transmission of knowledge and skills (Rinaldi, 2006; Villen, 1993). As Boyd and Bath (2017) identify, engaging in creative learning processes enables students to 'discover new meanings' (p. 196), which is evident in the language used by students in their haikus. For example, using the words 'provoking', 'opened', 'respected', 'thinking' and 'challenged' demonstrates how their thinking is changing because the words are more positive and empathetic. This indicates an awareness of 'otherness' (Mason, 2002) that was facilitated by them developing an understanding of their own situation and how it might have impacted on others, which at times they described as painful and disturbing. For example, in relation to the provocations used as part of the workshops, one student uses the phrase, 'stop, cut, break down fences' in relation to colonialism in Northern Ireland. The safe, comfortable space as part of the workshops allowed students to share unconscious biases, which they found difficult but possible.

After
During the analysis, it was clear that the 'after' phrases reflected a new way of thinking about the interconnected sustainability of all three pillars (Davis, 2015a) and transformative pedagogical practice (Leal Filho and Pace, 2016). The provocations during the module and creative process of the haiku poems had allowed students to critically reflect openly and without judgement. For example, the words used were 'welcoming', 'transformative', 'united', 'freedom', 'new', and 'interconnectedness'. The changes that students identified involved a shift not only in thinking but also in practice. For example, the following haiku captures insight into one student's change in praxeological thinking and action as a result:

Willingness to change
Provoking challenge and thought
Transformative change

During the module, the student shared reservations about life in Northern Ireland and noted no desire to return there, mainly because of the violence between Catholics and Protestants and a helplessness in not being able to make a difference. However, because of the provocations, the creative collaborations, appropriate environment and reflexive engagement during the process, she shared during her presentation assessment that she had re-evaluated her position: 'If I don't do it, who will?' Here she demonstrates a heightened awareness of power (politics) alongside a sharpened consciousness of her values (ethics) and actions (praxis) as a result. As Wilson et al. (2006) note, self-responsibility is central to EfS in the context of socio-cultural influences.

At the heart of EfS within the current political climate, there is agreement with Pascal and Bertram (2012, 2018) who emphasised the need for educators to engage reflexively (phronesis). As a result, a more astute awareness about power (politics) alongside a sharpened focus of values (ethics) can be developed and a change in action (praxis) (Pascal and Bertram, 2012, 2018) can take place, as evident in the haikus. This mix of phronesis, praxis, ethics and power is referred to as 'praxeology', which collectively can enable an authentic worldview of modern early childhood and a transformational appreciation of the interconnected nature of EfS. Fundamentally, praxeological inquiry is about questioning 'how' and 'why' and is always situated within local contexts about real-world situations. However, Mitchell and Walinga (2017, p. 1875) caution that while a 'creative process is useful' in generating such new thinking, the actual problem, in this case the interconnected nature of sustainability 'cannot be solved with acts of creative thinking and creating alone'. The students needed to demonstrate how their interconnected thinking informed their shift in thinking and as a result their behaviours and actions. Student 7 noted above, has since returned to Northern Ireland, and is attempting to transform thinking in practice, which again highlights the small successes of this action research and how critical reflection can be sustainable, as noted by McLeod (McLeod and Giardiello, 2019).

6.   CONCLUSIONS AND OUTLOOK

This small-scale research project has shown that EfS should no longer be interpreted solely as an academic or transmissive subject, but as participatory, reflexive, creative lifelong learning process, (UNESCO, 2015), which involves all areas of society. Furthermore, EfS can lead to an informed and involved community with creative problem-solving skills and a commitment to engage in responsible individual and cooperative actions, which resonates with the aims of the European Commission (2014). These actions will help ensure an 'environmentally sound, socially just and economically prosperous future'. EfS has 'the potential to serve as a tool for building stronger bridges between the classroom and business, and between schools and communities' (Leal Filho and Pace, 2019, p. 5). As Paniagua and Istance (2018) highlight, there is a need for alternative ways for measuring outcomes that reflect the necessary skills of the twenty-first century. As Januchowski-Hartley et al. (2018) and Mitchell and Walinga (2017) urge, and as this research project demonstrates, there is a need for more creative arts-based innovative teaching methods in promoting sustainable topics and new learning. There is currently little evidence of this style of teaching using provocations where students engage in complex and sensitive topics that explore the inter-related nature of EfS, especially within early childhood EfS. As a result of this research, a follow-on, longitudinal survey involving the student participants will be evaluated in a further project to determine if and how their new thinking has been sustainable and in doing so determine the value of using creative and hermeneutics approaches in higher education and journaling as a means of sustaining reflexivity (Karlsson Häikiö, 2018). Given the SDG 4 (UNESCO, 2015) target to develop relevant creative skills, which echoes the 'creative playful pedagogies' noted by Ziegler and Paniagua (2019) earlier, this resonates with the module outcomes, and the need for ECE students and educators to engage in critical reflectivity and despite being uncomfortable, to 'remember the benefits' (McLeod and Giardiello, 2019, p. 39).

REFERENCES

Alpers, P. (2007). *Etnografiska metoder: Att förstå och förklara samtiden* [Ethnographic Methods: To Understand and Explain Contemporary Times]. Malmö: Liber.

Altman, I. and Taylor D. (1973). *Social Penetration: The Development of Interpersonal Relationships*. New York: Holt, Rinehart and Winston.

Aristotle (1925). *The Nicomachean Ethics*. Edited by D. Ross. Oxford: Oxford University Press.

Bolton, G. (2010). *Reflective Practice: Writing and Professional Development* (2nd ed.). London: SAGE Publications.

Bourn, D., Hunt, F., Blum, N. and Lawson, H. (2016). *Primary Education for Global Learning and Sustainability: CPRT Research Survey 5*. York, UK: Cambridge Primary Review Trust.

Boyd, D. (2018). Early childhood education for sustainability and the historical legacies of two pioneering giants. *International Journal of Early Years*, 38(2), 227–39.

Boyd, D. and Bath, C. (2017). Capturing student perspectives through a 'Reggio' lens. *International Journal of Teaching and Learning in Higher Education*, 29(2), 192–200.

Brookfield, S.D. (2017). *Becoming a Critically Reflective Teacher* (2nd ed.). San Francisco, CA: Jossey-Bass.

Cagliari, P., Castagnetti, M. and Giudici, C. et al. (2016). *Loris Malaguzzi and the Schools of Reggio Emilia: A Selection of His Writings and Speeches 1945-1993*. Abingdon: Routledge.

Cherry, N.L. (2005). Preparing for practice in an age of complexity. *Higher Education Research and Development*, 24(4) 309–20.

Davis, J. (2015a). *Young Children and the Environment: Early Education for Sustainability*. Melbourne: Cambridge University Press.

Davis, J. (2015b). What is early childhood education for sustainability and why does it matter? In J. Davis (ed.), *Young Children and the Environment: Early Education for Sustainability*. Melbourne: Cambridge University Press, pp. 7–27.

Department for Education (2017). *Statutory Framework for the Early Years Foundation Stage: Setting the Standards for Learning, Development and Care for Children from Birth to Five*. Runcorn, UK: Crown Publishers.

Derrida, J. (1999). *Adieu to Levinas*. Stanford, CA: Stanford University Press.

d'Orville, H. (2019, 12 October). The relationship between sustainability and creativity. *Cadmus: Promoting Leadership in Thought that Leads to Action*, 4(1), 65–73.

Edwards, A., Gilroy, P. and Hartley, D. (2002). *Rethinking Teacher Education: Collaborative Responses to Uncertainty*. London: RoutledgeFalmer.

European Commission (2014). *Final Report of the Expert Group 'Education for Entrepreneurship': Making Progress in Promoting Entrepreneurial Attitudes and Skills through Primary and Secondary Education*. Brussels: European Commission.

Fors, V. and Bäckström, Å. (2015). *Visuella metoder* [Visual Methods]. Lund: Studentlitteratur.

Freire, P. (1994). *Pedagogy of Hope*. New York: Continuum.

Hager, P. (2006). The nature and development of generic attributes. In P. Hager and S. Holland (eds), *Graduate Attributes, Learning and Employability*. Dordrecht: Springer, pp. 17–48.

Hesterman, S. (2018). Designing environmentally sustainable multimodal provocations for early learning environments. In V. Huggins and D. Evans (eds), *Early Childhood Education and Care for Sustainability: International Perspectives*. Abingdon: Routledge, pp. 137–52.

Huggins, V. and Evans, D. (2018). Introduction. In V. Huggins and D. Evans (eds), *Early Childhood Education and Care for Sustainability: International Perspectives*. Abingdon: Routledge. pp. 1–13.

Imel, S. (1998). Transformative learning in adulthood. *ERIC Digest No. 200*.

Jacobs, G. and Murray, M. (2010). Developing critical understanding by teaching action research to undergraduate psychology students. *Educational Action Research*, 18(3), 319–35.

Januchowski-Hartley, S.P., Sopinka, N. and Merkle, B.G. et al. (2018). Poetry as a creative practice to enhance engagement and learning in conservation science. *Bioscience*, 68(11), 905–11.

Jupp, V. (ed.) (2006). *The SAGE Dictionary of Social Research Methods*. London: SAGE Publications.

Kabakci, I., Odabasi, F. and Kilicer, K. (2010). Transformative learning-based mentoring for professional development of teacher educators in information and communication technologies: an approach for an emerging country. *Journal of Professional Development*, 36(1–2), 263–73.

Karlsson Häikiö, T. (2018). Förskolan som visuell kultur [Preschool as visual culture]. In M. Bendroth Karlsson, T. Karlsson Häikiö and L.O. Magnusson, *Skapande verksamhet i förskolan: Kreativt arbete med analoga och digitala redskap*. Lund: Studentlitteratur.

Kemmis, S. (2010). What is to be done? The place of action research. *Educational Action Research*, 18(4), 417–27.

Leal Filho, W. and Pace, P. (eds) (2016), *Teaching Education for Sustainable Development at University Level*. Hamburg: Springer.

Leal Filho, W. and Pace, P. (2019). *Sustainability and the Humanities*. Hamburg: Springer.

Leitch, R. (2006). Limitations of language: developing arts-based creative narrative in stories of teachers' identities. *Teachers and Teaching*, 12(5), 549–69.

Leitch, R. and C. Day (2000). Action research and reflective practice: towards a holistic view. *Educational Action Research*, 8(1), 179–93.

Luff, P. (2018). The place of expressive arts in early childhood education and care for sustainability. In V. Huggins and D. Evans (eds), *Early Childhood Education and Care for Sustainability: International Perspectives*. Abingdon: Routledge, pp. 40–51.

Lumsden, E., McBride-Wilding, H. and Rose, H. (2010). Collaborative practice in enhancing the first year experience in higher education. *Enhancing the Learner Experience in Higher Education*, 2(1), 12–24.

Malaguzzi, L. (1994). Listening to children. *Young Children*, 49(5), 55.

Malaguzzi, L. (1998). History, ideas and basic philosophy: an interview with Lella Gandini. In C. Edwards, L. Gandini and G. Forman (eds), *The Hundred Languages of Children. The Reggio Emilia Approach – Advanced Reflections*. London: Praeger, pp. 49–99.

Mason, J. (2002). *Researching Your Own Practice: The Discipline of Noticing*. London: RoutledgeFalmer.

Mbebeb, F. (2009). Developing productive life skills in children: priming entrepreneurial mind sets through socialisation in family occupations. *International Journal of Early Childhood*, 41(2), 23–34.

McCormack, B. and Boomer, C. (2007). *Creating the Conditions for Growth: Report on the Belfast City Hospital and the Royal Hospitals Collaborative Practice Development Programme*. Belfast: Belfast Health and Social Care Trust.

McIntosh, P. (2010). *Action Research and Reflective Practice: Creative and Visual Methods to Facilitate Reflection and Learning*. Abingdon: Routledge.

McLeod, N. (2011). Exploring Early Years educators' ownership of language and communication knowledge and skills: a review of key policy and initial reflections on *Every Child a Talker* and its implementation. *Education 3-13: International Journal of Primary, Elementary and Early Years Education*, 39(4), 429–45.

McLeod, N. (2015). Reflecting on reflection: improving teachers' readiness to facilitate participatory learning with young children. *Professional Development in Education*, 41(2), 254–72.

McLeod, N. and Giardiello, P. (eds) (2019). *Empowering Early Childhood Educators: International Pedagogies as Provocation*. Abingdon: Routledge.

McLeod, N., Karlsson Häikiö, T. and Mårtensson, P. (2019). Hope for the future: new possibilities for sustaining a reflexive approach. In N. McLeod and P. Giardiello (eds) (2019), *Empowering Early Childhood Educators: International Pedagogies as Provocation*. Abingdon: Routledge, pp. 222–43.

Mezirow, J. (1997). Transformative learning: theory to practice. In P. Cranton (ed.), *Transformative Learning in Action. Insights from Practice: New Directions for Adult and Continuing Education No. 74*. San Francisco, CA: Jossey-Bass, pp. 5–12.

Mezirow, J. (2000). Learning to think like an adult: core concepts of transformation theory. In J. Mezirow and Associates (eds), *Learning as Transformation: Critical Perspectives on a Theory in Progress*. San Francisco, CA: Jossey-Bass, pp. 3–33.

Mitchell, I.M. and Walinga, J. (2017). The creative imperative: the role of creativity, creative problem solving and insight as key drivers in sustainability. *Journal of Cleaner Production*, 140, 1872–84.

Montessori, M. (2012). *The Montessori Series Volume 17: The 1946 London Lectures*. Amsterdam: Montessori-Pierson Publishing.

Montuori, A. (2012). Creative inquiry: confronting the challenges of scholarship in the 21st century. *Futures*, 44, 64–70.

Moon, J. (2006). *Learning Journals: A Handbook for Reflective Practice and Professional Development*. Abingdon: Routledge.

Moon, J. (2008). *Critical Thinking: An Exploration of Theory and Practice*. Abingdon: Routledge.

Noddings, N. (2003). *Happiness and Education*. Cambridge, UK: Cambridge University Press.

Nsamenang, A.B. (2006). Cultures in early childhood care and education. Background paper for *EFA Global Monitoring Report 2007*. 2007/ED/EFA/MRT/PI/3UNESCO.

O'Gorman, L. (2014). The arts and education for sustainability: shaping student teachers' identities towards sustainability. In J. Davis and S. Elliott (eds), *Research in Early Childhood Education for Sustainability: International Perspectives and Provocations*. Abingdon: Routledge, pp. 266–79.

O'Gorman, L. (2015). Early learning for sustainability through the arts. In J. Davis (ed.), *Young Children and the Environment: Early Education for Sustainability*. Melbourne: Cambridge University Press, pp. 209–79.

Orr, D.W. (1994). *Earth in Mind: On Education, Environment and the Human Prospect*. Washington, DC: Island Press.

Paniagua, A. and Istance, D. (2018). *Teachers as Designers of Learning Environments: The Importance of Innovative Pedagogies*. Paris: OECD Publishing.

Pascal, C. and Bertram, T. (2012). Praxis, ethics and power: developing praxeology as a participatory paradigm for early childhood research. *European Early Childhood Education Research Journal*, 20(4), 477–92.

Pascal, C. and Bertram, T. (2018). Effective early learning: a praxeological and participatory approach to evaluating and improving quality in early childhood education. *Revista da FAEEBA*, 27(51), 105–20.

QAA (2014). *Subject Benchmark Statement: Early Childhood Studies*. Accessed 6 September 2020 at https://www.qaa.ac.uk/docs/qaa/subject-benchmark-statements/subject-benchmark-statement-early-childhood-studies.pdf?sfvrsn=7e35c881_8.

Reed, M. and Canning, N. (2010). *Reflective Practice in the Early Years*. London: SAGE Publications.

Rinaldi, C. (2006). *In Dialogue with Reggio Emilia: Listening, Researching and Learning*. Abingdon: Routledge.

Sandri, O. (2013). Exploring the role and value of creativity in education for sustainability. *Environmental Education Research*, 19(6), 765–78.

Scharmer, C.O. (2009). *Theory U: Leading from the Future as It Emerges*. San Francisco, CA: Berrett-Koehler Publishers.

Schön, D.A. (1987). *Educating the Reflective Practitioner Toward a New Design for Teaching*. San Francisco, CA: Jossey-Bass.

Schulz, K. (2010). *Being Wrong: Adventures in the Margin of Error*. New York: HarperCollins pp. 159–80.

Schutt, R.K. (2006). *Investigating the Social World: The Process and Practice of Research*. London: SAGE Publications.

Simons, H. and McCormack, B. (2007). Integrating arts-based inquiry in evaluation methodology: challenges and opportunities. *Qualitative Inquiry*, 13(2), 292–311.

Smith, J. (2016). Sailing through social LA GRRAACCEESS: tool for deconstructing and facilitating reflective and reflexive practice. *Reflective Practice*, 17(5), 570–82.

Taylor, A. (2012). Common worlds: reconceptualising inclusion in early childhood communities. *Contemporary Issues in Early Childhood*, 13(2), 108–19.

Titchen, A. and McCormack, B. (2010). Dancing with stones: critical creativity as methodology for human flourishing. *Educational Action Research*, 18(4), 531–54.

United Nations Convention on the Rights of the Child (UNCRC) (1989). *Convention on the Rights of the Child*. New York: United Nations.

United Nations Educational, Scientific and Cultural Organization (UNESCO) (2007). *Education for All Global Monitoring Report 2007: Strong Foundations: Early Childhood Care and Education*. Paris: UNESCO.

United Nations Educational, Scientific and Cultural Organization (UNESCO) (2015). Sustainable Development Goals. Accessed 6 January 2020 at http://www.un.org/sustainabledevelopment/sustainable-development-goals/.

United Nations Educational, Scientific and Cultural Organization (UNESCO) (2016). *Global Education Monitoring Report: Education for People and Planet: Creating Sustainable Futures for All*. Paris: UNESCO. Accessed 8 January 2020 at https://en.unesco.org/gem-report/report/2016/education-people-and-planet-creating-sustainable-futures-all.

Urban, M. (2008). Dealing with uncertainty: challenges and possibilities for the early childhood profession. *European Early Childhood Education Research Journal*, 16(2), 135–52.

Vare, P. and Scott, W. (2007). Learning for change: exploring the relationship between education and sustainable development. *Journal of Education for Sustainable Development*, 1(2), 191–8.

Villen, K. (1993). Pre-school education in Denmark. In T. David (ed.), *Educational Provision for Our Youngest Children: European Perspectives*. London: Paul Chapman, pp. 18–34.

Wals, A.E.J., der Hoeven, N. and Blanken, H. (2009). *The Acoustics of Social Learning: Designing Learning Processes that Contribute to a More Sustainable World*. Wageningen: Wageningen Academic Publishers.

Wals, A.E.J. and Peers, M.A. (2017). Flowers of resistance. In A. Konig and J. Ravetz (eds), *Sustainability Science: Key Issues*. Abingdon: Routledge, pp. 29–52.

Wilson, V., McCormack, B. and Ives, G. (2006). Re-generating the 'self' in learning: developing a culture of supportive learning in practice. *Learning in Health and Social Care*, 5(2), 90–105.

World Commission on Environment and Development (WCED) (1987). *Our Common Future*. Oxford: Oxford University Press.

Ziegler, L. and Paniagua, A. (2019, 19 September). How innovations in teaching and learning help education leapfrog. Accessed 7 January 2020 at https://www.brookings.edu/blog/education-plus-development/2019/09/19/how-innovations-in-teaching-and-learning-help-education-leapfrog/.

4. 'Bad Plastics – Oceans Free of Plastic': the role of education
Elisabete Linhares and Bento Cavadas

1. INTRODUCTION TO PLASTIC POLLUTION

Plastic is a breakthrough technology that offers many conveniences and has improved the quality of life of recent generations worldwide. It has many uses and countless benefits for consumer health and safety, including food and water packaging and food and energy conservation (Andrady and Neal, 2009). However, plastic is so widely used that its management has become a huge problem. In fact, some types of plastic are deposited in the oceans, many from land-based sources (Veiga et al., 2016). The authors designate these as 'bad plastics' for the aim of this study.

Although some researchers believe that plastic is not as great a threat to oceans as overfishing or climate change (e.g., Stafford and Jones, 2019; Steffen et al., 2015), the fact is that plastic waste is a serious problem in most of the world. Changing patterns of production and consumption as a result of economic development have led to a huge increase in plastic waste (Chow et al., 2017). The recovery rate of this waste remains very low and this is due to the low recycling value and lack of technological support for recycling; consequently, a major part of it is washed into the oceans (Chow et al., 2017), where it contaminates the food chain. According to Eriksen et al. (2014), there are more than 5 trillion plastic pieces, weighing 268 940 tons, floating in the different oceans. There is evidence that the Great Pacific Garbage Patch is rapidly accumulating plastic and comprises mostly megaplastics such as fishing nets (Lebreton et al., 2018). For example, in Portugal, the floating marine debris average density is 2.98 items/km^2 and contains about 752 740 items (Sá et al., 2016). According to one study, packaging and consumer products were abundant in rivers, and fishery and aquaculture items were predominant in the oceanic environment (Schwarz et al., 2019). The same type of plastic fragments were found in Portugal's oceans because cables and fishing lines were among the top ten floating marine debris items (Sá et al., 2016). In addition, Wilcox et al. (2016) pointed out that plastic litter is harmful to marine wildlife, mainly due to ingestion and entanglement.

A comprehensive study of the accumulation of different types of plastic litter in aquatic environments revealed that only larger and thick-walled plastic debris from low-density polymers are released into the ocean by rivers, while the larger fraction of plastic litter is likely to be retained in sediments on beaches (Schwarz et al., 2019). A study of plastic fragments on Brazilian beaches found that plastic represented 87.45 per cent of all materials sampled during the winter, and 85.24 per cent during the summer (Fernandino et al., 2016). Most of the sampled beaches in that study were extremely dirty in the winter and the summer, according to the Clean Coast Index (ibid.). Various polymer types (polyester, polyamide, polystyrene, polypropylene and polyethylene) were found in oceanic, freshwater and beach sediments, many in the form of microplastics (Schwarz et al.,

2019). Regarding the quantities and characteristics of microplastics in European beach sediment, Lots et al. (2017) found a substantial variability in concentration, ranging from 72 ± 24 to $1\,512 \pm 187$ microplastics per kg of dry sediment, as well as a high variability in sampling locations. The majority of microplastics were fibrous, smaller than 1 mm in size, blue/black in colour, and made of polyester, polyethylene and polypropylene.

It is known that single-use plastics (SUP) make up an average of 49 per cent of beach litter, with cigarette butts being the most littered item in all four European Regional Seas Areas (Seas at Risk, 2015). As a result, strong legislative and non-legislative strategies have been adopted to reduce marine pollution – that is, limiting single-use plastics (Schnurr et al., 2018; Xanthos and Walker, 2017). Tariffs and taxes on consumers have played an important role in the reduction of SUP, such as plastic bags (Schnurr et al., 2018). For example, the Portuguese plastic carrier bag tax, implemented in 2015, had effects on consumers' behaviour (Martinho, Balaia and Pires, 2018). Results showed a 61 per cent increase in the use of reusable plastic bags and a 74 per cent reduction of plastic bag consumption (ibid.). However, regarding plastic pollution awareness, the tax had no effect on the perception of the impact of plastic bags on health and the environment – namely, on oceans (ibid.). Therefore, these results seem to indicate that taxes are effective in reducing the use of SUP but have little effect on consumers' environmental consciousness.

These numbers show that marine plastic pollution is so complex that only a legally binding international instrument could help solve this problem at a global level (Dauvergne, 2018; Tessnow-von Wysocki and Billon, 2019) and avert the inefficient global governance of plastic from damaging the oceans (Dauvergne, 2018).

However, the above-mentioned measures could only be fully effective with formal, non-formal and informal educational efforts that prepare citizens to deal with plastic pollution. Education was called on to act against plastic pollution, as patent in the European Union 'Sea Change project' (European Union, 2015). This is one of the reasons why recommendations to further reduce SUP marine pollution include education and outreach to raise awareness of this problem and diminish consumption of plastic bags and microbeads at the source (Xanthos and Walker, 2017).

To cope with this situation, the United Nations (2015) 2030 Agenda for Sustainable Development and its associated Sustainable Development Goals (SDGs), and the United Nations Educational, Scientific and Cultural Organization (UNESCO, 2017) address this problem in multidisciplinary fields. A solution for marine litter is likely to be found in a transition towards more sustainable ways of production and consumption that are also promoted via the SDGs (Löhr et al., 2017).

The next section presents an overview of the educational approaches to plastic waste management and plastic pollution.

2.   ADDRESSING PLASTIC POLLUTION THROUGH EDUCATION FOR SUSTAINABLE DEVELOPMENT

The concept of education for sustainable development (ESD) has many connotations. For some authors 'education for sustainable development', 'sustainability education' and 'education for sustainability' mean the same thing (Besong and Holland, 2015). According to Leal Filho and Pace (2016a), many authors claim that 'what you call it' is not important if people share the same educational principles of ESD. However, for the purpose of this study, the authors were influenced by Longhurst (2014), who defined ESD as the 'process of equipping students with the knowledge and understanding, skills and attributes needed to work and live in a way that safeguards environmental, social and economic wellbeing, both in the present and for future generations' (Longhurst, 2014, p. 5).

The objective of ESD programmes is to prepare students for an uncertain future (Leal Filho and Pace, 2016a), and encourage students' participation in future causes; as Coyle (2010) stated, learners need challenges, action and opportunities based on real-life interactions with the outdoor environment to develop twenty-first-century skills. The case studies presented in the book *Teaching Education for Sustainable Development at University Level* (Leal Filho and Pace, 2016b) are good examples of efforts to adopt outdoor classes that involve going out into nature to approach sustainable development (SD) issues.

There seems to be a relation between high levels of education and environmentally responsible behaviour (Scott and Willits, 1994). Although circumstantial, there is evidence that environmental education programmes can lead to positive changes in students' awareness, skills, attention, intentions, and behaviour (Stern, Powell and Hill, 2014). Therefore, education in plastic waste management could greatly contribute to reducing plastic in the environment (Chow et al., 2017). Plastic pollution control via education, in addition to the research and development of alternative materials to plastic, and other actions, are imperative for immediate action to be taken to help reduce marine plastic pollution (Schnurr et al., 2018).

Institutions, educational systems and teachers all over the world are using different strategies to approach plastic waste management and plastic pollution. Cuba has successfully used art in primary schools to address environmental problems (Gutiérrez, Estupiñán and Díaz, 2014). In Brazil, some teachers use lectures and digital educational resources in elementary school to emphasize the importance of plastic recycling and reducing the use of plastic products (Mattos and Peres, 2010). Some initiatives focus on interventions directed at future teachers to raise their awareness about oceans' plastic pollution and the urgent need to reduce plastic consumption (Jaén, Esteve and Banos-González, 2019). German schools are adopting citizen science campaigns to do research on macro- and microplastics in German rivers (German Federal Ministry of Education and Research, n.d.). The UNESCO Bangkok Office (n.d.) is promoting The Plastic Initiative in schools to avert plastic pollution in the Asia-Pacific. Portugal is adapting the 7R approach – Rethink, Refuse, Reduce, Repair, Reintegrate, Recycle and Reuse in educational contexts to change students' attitudes and behaviour towards waste management, with a focus on plastic (Agência Portuguesa do Ambiente, 2017). Hong Kong has also focused on increasing the understanding of environmental matters via education about sustainability. A study conducted by Chow et al. (2017) with 61 primary school pupils (8–12 years old) from Hong Kong using different educational strategies such as direct teaching, hands-on teaching and simulation game-based teaching, showed that knowledge of the 3Rs (reduce, reuse and recycle), plastic waste problems and management increased significantly after the pupils had undergone one of the teaching strategies. They also found that the simulated game-based strategy was most effective. Concerning the difficulties, it seems that pupils take longer to change their behaviour if they already have inherent habits (Chow et al., 2017). Other setbacks for ESD in formal education can be, for example, time limitations, lack of human resources support and insufficient pupil engagement (So and Chow, 2018). This is an example of how changing people's behaviour so that they adopt sustainable practices is both a huge and a difficult goal of ESD.

It seems clear that approaches to plastic waste management have different results depending on the culture and traditions of the places where they are implemented. Some studies revealed a gender difference when referring to plastic and the environment (Aydinli and Avan, 2015). Male students in Turkish primary schools demonstrated positive attitudes towards waste recycling and reuse as an energy source, assessing these subjects from an economic angle, whereas female students gave more importance to environmental pollution and to cleaning workshops, perceiving this subject in a social manner (ibid.).

3. ACTIVISM FOR AN EDUCATION FOR SUSTAINABLE DEVELOPMENT

The solution for major environmental problems requires the active engagement of informed citizens (Linhares, 2016). Developing critical thinking skills in youngsters about social values is an education oriented towards socio-political action (Hodson, 2010), or activism. Activism has been defined in many ways, but Alsop and Bencze (2010) identified a common characteristic: the desire for personal, social, political, economic or environmental change. Researchers (Bencze and Alsop, 2009; Hodson, 2010) identified concrete forms of activism, such as boycotting, volunteering, petitioning or distributing flyers among the population.

It is fundamental to provide opportunities for citizens in general and to students to participate in action-oriented activities. The authors of this study are currently engaged in didactic practices that involve the participants in inquiry-based activities with an empowerment dimension, such as those that can be delivered through interactive scientific exhibitions.

In a study of pre-service teachers focused on the planning and implementation of activism initiatives, Linhares (2016) concluded those teachers developed: (1) more knowledge about the environmental issues addressed; (2) problem-solving and reasoning skills; and (3) communication skills for intervening in the community. Another study with 19 pre-service teachers who were planning a scientific exhibition for the community revealed a positive impact on the pre-service teachers' scientific knowledge and ability for action (Linhares and Reis, 2017). These results were concurrent with the ideas of Roth (2009), who concluded that, rather than using traditional educational practices, education with the above-mentioned characteristics increased the interest of youngsters in environmental problems. However, the students involved in scientific exhibitions reported some difficulties when working with their peers, as well as with time management (Linhares and Reis, 2017).

4. RESEARCH METHODOLOGY

The educational resource 'Bad Plastics – Oceans Free of Plastic' (Linhares and Cavadas, 2018) was elaborated under the project CreativeLab_Sci&Math (Cavadas et al., 2019) and followed an inquiry-based learning approach. The learning sequence of the resource was structured on the 7E teaching model, which consists of seven teaching moments: Engage,

Explain, Exchange, Explore, Elaborate, Evaluate, and Empower (Biological Sciences Curriculum Study [BSCS], 2006; Reis and Marques, 2016). The content of the resource was influenced by the UNESCO's SDG 14, 'Life below water', within the suggested topic 'Ocean pollutants: plastics, microbeads, sewage, nutrients and chemicals' (UNESCO, 2017, p. 39), whose specific learning objectives are: (1) cognitive learning: 'The learner understands the threats to ocean systems such as pollution and overfishing and recognizes and can explain the relative fragility of many ocean ecosystems, including coral reefs and hypoxic dead zones' (UNESCO, 2017, p. 38); (2) socio-emotional learning: 'The learner is able to show people the impact humanity is having on the oceans (biomass loss, acidification, pollution, etc.) and the value of clean healthy oceans' (ibid.).

The research design of this work is exploratory because it gathers preliminary information about the object of study (Ponte, 2006). This study took an interpretative approach (Coutinho, 2011) that is meant to identify the cognitive and socio-emotional learning of the participants. In this type of research, the goal is to identify the meaning of individual actions and social interactions from the perspective of the participants (Coutinho, 2011).

The participants consisted of 12 Portuguese students of higher education (S1–S12), between the ages of 18 and 53 (nine female and three male), enrolled in the first year of the environmental education and ecotourism course. The study was implemented within the context of the curricular unit of environment and geological heritage of that degree.

4.1   Implementation of the 'Bad Plastics' Educational Resource

The resource was implemented in four sessions and the students performed all the tasks as a group. In order to *engage* the students, they explored the causes and consequences of plastic pollution using digital educational resources, such as those used in the project Ocean Action (CIIMAR, n.d.) and the documentary *Troubled Waters* (Sylvestre and Dressen, n.d.). Next, in the *explain* phase, students used different online resources to research the subjects of ocean conservancy and plastic waste management. This task was followed by an *exchange* moment where each group shared and discussed with the other groups what they had learnt, using a digital canvas.

Then, in several *explore* moments, during an outdoor activity they identified, registered and collected plastics at a local beach, using the methodology proposed by Alkalay, Pasternak and Zask (2007). The recording of plastics and other collected waste was done using the Clean Swell application (Ocean Conservancy, n.d.), before quantitatively analysing the plastics in a laboratory and calculating the Clean Coast Index (CCI) (Alkalay et al., 2007). Students also observed microplastics collected in a sand sample at the beach using microscopes. Afterwards, in an *elaborate* moment, they studied the theme of microplastics and actions that can be implemented to reduce these particles in ecosystems, sharing with the other groups what they had learned. One of the last activities was the *evaluate* phase, where the students compared the knowledge they had acquired with their initial conceptions. They then wrote a self-reflection about what they had learned.

Finally, to *empower* the community, they planned and implemented an activism activity – an interactive scientific exhibition about ocean plastic pollution – to raise the awareness of primary school students about that issue. Each group of students contributed with one task. All tasks had a strong hands-on focus, as well as a minds-on emphasis, to develop the activism reasoning of primary school students about plastic pollution.

4.2 Methods of Data Collection

After the implementation of the 'Bad Plastics – Oceans Free of Plastic' resource and the activism activity (scientific exhibition) for primary school students, the participants were given a survey with five open questions. The first four questions were designed to identify what type of knowledge they had developed regarding the causes, consequences, global and individual solutions for the ocean plastic waste problem. The last question was focused on the activism activity and was designed to identify the potentialities and difficulties faced by the participants.

4.3 Data Analysis

The students' responses to the survey were subject to a content analysis. First, the analysis units were identified in each answer, and then they were organized into categories (Bardin, 2009). In the process of categorization, the participants' responses to the first four questions, an adaptation of the cognitive, affective and psychomotor dimensions and factors applied by Aydinli and Avan (2015) was used in an attitude scale to define the students' attitudes towards the environment, recycling, plastic and plastic waste (Avan et al., 2011). The final framework applied is presented in Table 4.1. The factor 'Knowing the hazardous effects of plastics' was subdivided into subfactors to convey the diversity of the students' answers (Table 4.2).

Table 4.1   Dimensions and factors of the attitude scale

Dimensions	Factors
Cognitive domain	Understanding the recycling and environmental problems
	Knowing the hazardous effects of plastics
	Evaluating plastics as an energy resource
Affective domain	Wishing to live in a clean environment:
	awareness
	citizenship
	law
	training
	Wishing to reuse, recycle and reduce plastics:
	reuse
	recycle
	reduce
	How scattered plastics affect us emotionally
	Worrying about the health effects of reused plastics
Psychomotor domain	Reducing and reusing plastics:
	reduce
	reuse
	Attending environment protection initiatives:
	active participation/intervention
	awareness/citizenship
	Using the recycling bin

Source: Adapted from Aydinli and Avan (2015).

Table 4.2   Types of hazardous effects of plastics related by the students

Factor	Subfactors	n
Knowing the hazardous effects of plastics	Reduction of biodiversity	10
	Microplastics accumulation	9
	Water pollution	8
	Ecosystem damage	4
	Human health damage	4
	Pollution of coastal regions	3

The last question was categorized according to an adaptation of the cognitive, affective and psychomotor dimensions and factors applied by Aydinli and Avan (2015), combined with the items of the framework for evaluating environmental education activities for sustainability proposed by Huerta, Colás and Valentí (2016). The resulting categories were organized into the dimensions 'benefits' and 'difficulties'. The 'benefits' of the affective domain were: experimenting with new sensations and learning to work collaboratively; those related to the psychomotor domain were: attending environmental protection initiatives; active participation. The 'difficulties' of the cognitive domain were: learning how to plan, implement and evaluate an environmental education activity, and those related with the affective domain were: learning to work collaboratively.

5.   RESULTS AND DISCUSSION

5.1   Learning About the Causes of Plastic Pollution

The answers to the question 'What have you learned about the causes of plastic pollution?' were organized into two main dimensions: cognitive ($n = 11$) and affective (n = 8). In the cognitive domain, two factors were identified: 'Understanding recycling, and environmental problems' ($n = 8$) and 'Evaluating plastics as an energy resource' ($n = 1$). Most students appeared to understand the problem and attributed the cause to human consumption: 'humans consume excessively' (S3); the use of plastic materials: 'The causes are related essentially to the excessive use of plastic materials' (S2); together with a lack of consideration: 'and little consciousness when it [plastic materials] is discarded' (S2). Only one student associated the problem with the use of plastic as an energy resource, highlighting its use as a raw material in various products: 'due to our modern lifestyle, plastic is used as raw material for a number of single-use objects, such as plastic bottles, diapers, ear swabs, cutlery, etc.' (S12). In fact, as this student pointed out, SUP is a major source of plastic pollution (Seas at Risk, 2015).

Regarding the affective domain, the factor 'Wishing to reduce, recycle and reuse plastics' emerged from the students' answers. This environmentally friendly behaviour is associated with the 7R approach (Agência Portuguesa do Ambiente, 2017), which is presently being implemented in schools in Portugal, so it would be expected that students refer to actions such as reduce ($n = 1$): 'to do everything so that their use becomes less and less' (S8); recycle ($n = 5$): 'direct waste to appropriate destinations, such as recycle bins' (S3); and reuse ($n = 2$).

5.2   Learning About the Consequences of Plastic Pollution

The consequences reported by the participants were classified in the dimension of 'cognitive domain', and under the heading 'Knowing the hazardous effects of plastics'. The different consequences they mentioned indicate good knowledge about the effects of the accumulation of plastics on marine ecosystems (Table 4.2).

Biodiversity loss was the most reported impact ($n = 10$), with emphasis on the death of marine animals in the food chain: 'plastic causes the death of living creatures in oceans, and of organisms that eat them because plastics are easily confused for food' (S2). Students acknowledged that animals can get stuck in fishing nets or have difficulty in moving from one place to another due to the presence of plastic in the water: 'Many whales, dolphins and turtles appear on beaches stuck in fishing nets or wrapped in plastic parts' (S11). In fact, much of the plastic in the oceans comprises the remains of fishing nets or fishing lines (Lebreton et al., 2018; Sá et al., 2016).

The problem related with the microplastics accumulation in the environment referred to by Lots et al. (2017) was a consequence of plastic pollution, and commonly showed up in students' answers ($n = 9$). They were familiar with how it entered the food chain, and had such far-reaching effects as actually harming human health: 'the problem with microplastics is that we cannot see them and they accumulate inside the body of marine animals, which are later ingested by people' (S3).

Water pollution by plastics and their toxicity is another problem that students were aware of ($n = 8$): 'plastics have numerous toxic elements that can be dissolved in water' (S8). The students also mentioned the problem of garbage patches and the huge concentrations of plastics in some parts of the oceans: 'The increasing waste, especially plastic in the oceans, often causes large concentrations of waste' (S3), forming a 'sea of plastic' (S8), such as the Great Pacific Garbage Patch composed of megaplastics like fishing nets (Lebreton et al., 2018).

Some students' reports addressed the damage that plastic accumulation in oceans can cause to the balance of ecosystems and to human health. For examples, concerning 'ecosystem damage' ($n = 4$), students' reported 'harm to marine ecosystems, due to an ecological imbalance [caused by plastics]' (S6). In terms of human health, some ($n = 4$) reported that plastics 'are going to harm human health' (S8).

Although less mentioned, the pollution of coastal regions appeared in some students' reflections ($n = 3$) due to the visual impact caused by the accumulation of plastics on beaches: 'it is very common to find beaches covered with plastics and other waste' (S11), and the subsequent 'degradation of coastal regions' (S6).

5.3   Learning About General Solutions for Plastic Pollution

Students' answers concerning the solutions for plastic pollution were framed in the 'affective domain'. In the factor 'Wishing to live in a clean environment', four subfactors were created to attend to the diversity of students' feedback: awareness ($n = 6$), citizenship ($n = 4$), law ($n = 3$) and training ($n = 1$). The factor 'Wishing to reuse, recycle and reduce plastics' was organized into three subfactors: recycle ($n = 6$), reduce ($n = 6$) and reuse ($n = 4$).

The key solution for plastic pollution for half of the students who participated in the study was education, and actions to raise the awareness of the population. They presented examples of those initiatives: 'The solution is to deliver a "green" message, educate and teach the population with creative initiatives. Explain what the alternatives are for plastic, and that there are economic gains if we reuse materials, use energy in an environmentally friendly way' (S5). Some students' answers were associated with good citizenship and the importance of individual actions that have collective benefits: 'people could collect plastics that they find in places where they do not belong' (S1) and 'not polluting beaches and helping to clean them' (S7).

In the same line of thought as Schnurr et al. (2018) and Xanthos and Walker (2017), some students mentioned legal actions to reduce the use of plastics: 'every country should have laws that penalize [plastics] usage' (S2), 'maybe the most important aspect is law and supervision (especially of companies) . . . with penalties for those who do not comply with the law' (S5). One student (S6) reported that the answer was to train professionals who could intervene and rehabilitate damaged marine ecosystems, and another (S10) said that countries can have a strong influence if they promoted activism against plastic pollution.

Students also expressed their wish to reuse plastics as solutions for plastic pollution: 'use of reusable products' (S10); recycle plastic: 'Transform the linearity of plastic consumption into a circular system, making plastic waste return to the chain as raw material for other objects' (S12); and to reduce plastic: 'it is necessary to reduce plastic consumption significantly, by not using straws, for example' (S8).

5.4   Individual Intervention About Plastic Pollution

The question about their personal intervention to diminish plastic pollution resulted in the categorization of the students' answers in the 'psychomotor domain' and factors 'Reducing and reusing plastics' ($n = 11$), 'Attending environment protection initiatives' ($n = 10$) and 'Using the recycling bin' ($n = 9$).

Regarding the reduction of plastics ($n = 6$), one student said that he was going to 'try to minimize the consumption of plastics' (S5). Regarding reusing ($n = 5$), another said that he tries to 'reuse plastics for something that might be useful for daily life' (S4).

Regarding environmental protection, many ($n = 8$) advocated actions related to the exercise of good citizenship: 'we can change behaviours to reduce their impact [plastics] on the environment' (S10), and to increase population awareness: 'actions to promote population awareness, like campaigns for cleaning beaches and coastal areas' (S6). With a focus on activism, some students considered that active participation was essential in projects that 'try to sensitize people to do the same' (S3) and 'to be an active member . . . passing the information on to other people' (S5).

Many students mentioned recycling bins ($n = 9$), as the right way to dispose of plastic waste and avoid ocean pollution: 'place my waste in the proper places' (S3) and 'stop polluting because there are proper places to dispose of waste' (S8).

5.5   A Scientific Exhibition as a Way of Empowerment

This section presents the benefits, difficulties and related subcategories mentioned by students after the implementation of a scientific exhibition (activism activity) for primary

Table 4.3   Benefits and difficulties for the students that participated in the scientific exhibition

Categories	Subcategories	*n*
Benefits	Experiment with new sensations	4
	Learn to work collaboratively	3
	Attend environment protection activities: active participation/intervention	1
Difficulties	Learn how to plan, implement and evaluate an environmental education activity for sustainability	12
	Learn to work collaboratively	4

school students. The benefits and difficulties were classified into the subcategories presented in Table 4.3.

Regarding the new sensations aroused by the interactive exhibition that involved contact with children, students admitted that 'it was worth it' (S3). Regarding the engagement of the public, they claimed that: 'the fact that this exhibition intended to be a dynamic experience rather than one of passive observation was very positive because I think it caused more impact' (S8). To accomplish this goal, the whole class had to collaborate: 'every student contributed in some way for the exhibition, with ideas, materials or mounting it' (S11). One of the major benefits was the children's empowerment: 'it was an enriching experience for the children and for us. I think that, in an entertaining way, we raised their awareness of the problem of plastic in the oceans and, thus, the goal of the exhibition was achieved' (S7). This kind of empowerment was also identified in the research of Linhares and Reis (2017).

Most of the difficulties reported were related to the planning, implementation and evaluation of an environmental education activity for sustainability, since this was the first experience for many of them. As in the study by Linhares and Reis (2017), time management presented some issues. Several students reported problems in managing their personal time in terms of the schedule for planning and implementing the scientific exhibition tasks: 'We had so many things to do that sometimes it seemed impossible . . . we really spent many hours in that room' (S3). The resources were also a problem because the students had trouble in obtaining materials for the tasks. Some students also reported that they had difficulty in the adaptation of the tasks for primary school students: 'We tried to adapt the exhibition tasks to the age of the children, and that originated some discussion in the class' (S3). Some students also mentioned communication and collaboration issues while working in a group, like those identified in the study by Linhares and Reis (2017).

However, their final thoughts expressed a sensation of achievement: 'I think all goals were accomplished' (S10); and that the time of exhibition should be prolonged so that it can be 'visited by more people, from schools or other spheres, because this work deserves to be disseminated!' (S8). The final balance is that this scientific exhibition contributed to the empowerment of the students who prepared it, helping them to become active citizens in the quest for solutions for the oceans' plastic pollution.

6. CONCLUSIONS

Shaping behaviours for sustainable practices is a huge goal of ESD, and the educational resource 'Bad Plastics – Oceans Free of Plastic' contributed towards that aim. In this study the students of higher education acquired the knowledge, skills and attitudes needed to work and function in a plastic-free environment and through their involvement in the 'Bad Plastics' tasks, raised their awareness about SDG 14: 'Life below water'. These tasks improved their cognitive learning, promoted their understanding of the threats to ocean systems, and expanded their knowledge of the consequences of and solutions to plastic pollution.

The students were aware of the huge influence of human behaviour and their excessive consumption and lack of consideration concerning the reduction, reuse and recycling of SUP. The resource's tasks also influenced their socio-emotional learning, raising their awareness of individual impact on plastic pollution, and the power of collaborative work to solve it. The scientific exhibition they organized had the double benefit of empowering both the students of higher education, who implemented tasks focused on plastic pollution, and the primary school students who attended the exhibition and actively participated in all the tasks.

The implementation of the educational resource 'Bad Plastics – Oceans Free of Plastic' presented circumstantial evidence, as shown in other studies (Stern et al., 2014), that environmental education programmes can lead to positive changes in students' knowledge, awareness, skills, and conceivably, in their behaviour. Therefore, the present study creates knowledge about how a didactic proposal structured according to the 7E teaching model and guided by collective activism can be used to explore SDG 14.

Similar approaches in the context of formal education can be adapted to other SDGs, helping to foment a greater interest on the part of students in environmental issues, and providing them with the necessary skills to intervene in society. Higher education institutions should also adopt practices oriented to educating and enabling conscientious citizens to address environmental problems. These practices help individuals to become active citizens and promote sustainability.

REFERENCES

Agência Portuguesa do Ambiente (2017), *Estratégia Nacional de Educação Ambiental 2020* [National Strategy of Environmental Education 2020], Lisboa: Agência Portuguesa do Ambiente.
Alkalay, Ronen, Galia Pasternak and Alon Zask (2007), 'Clean-Coast Index – a new approach for beach cleanliness assessment', *Ocean & Coastal Management*, **50**, 252–362.
Alsop, Steve and Lawrence Bencze (2010), 'Introduction to the Special Issue on Activism: SMT education in the claws of the hegemon', *Canadian Journal of Science, Mathematics, and Technology Education*, **10** (3), 177–96.
Andrady, Anthony L. and Mike A. Neal (2009), 'Applications and societal benefits of plastics', *Philosophical Transactions of the Royal Society*, **364**, 1977–84.
Avan, Çağri, Bahattin Aydinli, Fatma Bakar and Yunus Alboga (2011), 'Preparing attitude scale to define students' attitudes about environment, recycling, plastic and plastic waste', *International Electronic Journal of Environmental Education*, **1** (3), 179–91.
Aydinli, Bahattin and Çağri Avan (2015), 'Chemical dimensions of plastic wastes and their recycling in environmental education', *Journal of Educational and Social Research*, **5** (1), 37–42.
Bardin, Laurence (2009), *Análise de conteúdo*, Coimbra: Almedina.
Bencze, Lawrence and Steve Alsop (2009), 'A critical and creative inquiry into school science inquiry', in

Wolff-Michael Roth and Kenneth Tobin (eds), *World of Science Education: North America*, Rotterdam: Sense, pp. 27–47.

Besong, Frida and Charlotte Holland (2015), 'The Dispositions, Abilities and Behaviours (DAB) framework for profiling learners' sustainability competencies in higher education', *Journal of Teacher Education for Sustainability*, **17** (1), 5–22.

Biological Sciences Curriculum Study (BSCS) (2006), *The BSCS 5E Instructional Model: Origins and Effectiveness*, Colorado Springs, CO: BSCS.

Cavadas, Bento, Marisa Correia, Nelson Mestrinho and Raquel Santos (2019), 'CreativeLab_Sci&Math: work dynamics and pedagogical integration in science and mathematics', *Interacções*, **15** (50), 6–22.

Chow, Cheuk-Fai, Wing-Mui W. So, Tsz-Yan Cheung and Siu-Kit D. Yeung (2017), 'Plastic waste problem and education for plastic waste management', in Siu Cheung Kong, Cheuk Fai Chow and Tak Lam Wong et al. (eds), *Emerging Practices in Scholarship of Learning and Teaching in a Digital Era*, Singapore: Springer Nature Singapore, pp. 125–40.

CIIMAR (n.d.), 'Project Ocean Action', accessed 07 January 2020 at www.oceanaction.pt/.

Coutinho, Clara P. (2011), *Metodologia de Investigação em Ciências Sociais e Humanas: Teoria e Prática*, Coimbra: Almedina.

Coyle, Kevin J. (2010), *Back to School: Back Outside!*, Reston, VA: National Wildlife Federation.

Dauvergne, Peter (2018), 'Why is the global governance of plastic failing the oceans?', *Global Environmental Change*, **51**, 22–31.

Eriksen, Marcus, Laurent C.M. Lebreton and Henry S. Carson et al. (2014), 'Plastic pollution in the world's oceans: more than 5 trillion plastic pieces weighing over 250,000 tons afloat at sea', *PLoS ONE*, **9** (12), 1–15.

European Union (2015), 'Sea Change: Our ocean. Our health', accessed 22 December 2019 at www.seachange project.eu/.

Fernandino, Gerson, Carla I. Elliff and Iracema R. Silva et al. (2016), 'Plastic fragments as a major component of marine litter: a case study in Salvador, Bahia, Brazil', *Journal of Integrated Coastal Zone Management*, **16** (3), 281–7.

German Federal Ministry of Education and Research (n.d.), 'Plastics in the environment: plastic pirates', accessed 9 December 2019 at www.bmbf-plastik.de/en/plasticpirates.

Gutiérrez, Alberto Torres, C. Mavel Moré Estupiñán and Noevia Torres Díaz (2014), 'Environmental education in plastic elementary educational Cuban: positive and good practice experiences', *Avances en Supervisión Educativa*, **20**, 1–34.

Hodson, Derek (2010), 'Time for action: science education for an alternative future', *International Journal of Science Education*, **25** (6), 645–70.

Huerta, Rosa M. Medir, Raquel Heras Colás and Carla Magin Valentí, (2016), 'An evaluation framework for environmental education through sustainability activities', *Educación XXI*, **19** (1), 331–55.

Jaén, Mercedes, Patricia Esteve and Isabel Banos-González (2019), 'Los futuros maestros ante el problema de la contaminación de los mares por plásticos y el consumo', *Revista Eureka sobre Enseñanza y Divulgación de las Ciências*, **16** (1), Article 1501.

Leal Filho, Walter and Paul Pace (2016a), 'Teaching education for sustainable development: implications on learning programmes at higher education', in Walter Leal Filho and Paul Pace (eds), *Teaching Education for Sustainable Development at University Level*, Cham, Switzerland: Springer International Publishing, pp. 1–6.

Leal Filho, Walter and Paul Pace (2016b), *Teaching Education for Sustainable Development at University Level*, Cham, Switzerland: Springer International Publishing.

Lebreton, L., B. Slat and F. Ferrari et al. (2018), 'Evidence that the Great Pacific Garbage Patch is rapidly accumulating plastic', *Scientific Reports*, **8** (4666), 1–15.

Linhares, Elisabete (2016), 'Capacitar futuros professores para a ação: práticas interventivas que partem da discussão de problemáticas ambientais', *Da Investigação às Práticas*, **7** (2), 54–70.

Linhares, Elisabete and Bento Cavadas (2018), 'CreativeLab_Sci&Math | Bad Plastics – Oceanos Livres de Plástico: participar na mudança', accessed 07 January 2020 at www.casadasciencias.org/recurso/8684.

Linhares, Elisabete and Pedro Reis (2017), 'Interactive exhibition on climate geoengineering: empowering future teachers for sociopolitical action', *Sisyphus Journal of Education*, **5** (03), 85–106.

Löhr, Ansje, Heidi Savelli and Raoul Beunen et al. (2017), 'Solutions for global marine litter pollution', *Current Opinion in Environmental Sustainability*, **28**, 90–99.

Longhurst, James (2014), *Education for Sustainable Development: Guidance for UK Higher Education Providers*, Gloucester, UK: The Quality Assurance Agency for Higher Education.

Lots, Froukje A.E., Paul Behrens and Martina G. Vijver et al. (2017), 'A large-scale investigation of microplastic contamination: abundance and characteristics of microplastics in European beach sediment', *Marine Pollution Bulletin*, **123**, 219–26.

Martinho, Graça, Natacha Balaia and Ana Pires (2018), 'The Portuguese plastic carrier bag tax: the effects on consumers' behavior', *Waste Management*, **61**, 3–12.

Mattos, Nei Carlos Morais de and Paulo E.C. Peres (2010), 'Coletar e reconhecer o plástico: uma atitude em educação ambiental', *Revista Eletrônica em Gestão, Educação e Tecnologia Ambiental*, **1** (1), 1–12.

Ocean Conservancy (n.d.), 'About Clean Swell', accessed 07 January 2020 at www.oceanconservancy.org/trash-free-seas/international-coastal-cleanup/cleanswell/.

Ponte, João Pedro (2006), 'Estudos de caso em educação matemática', *Bolema*, **25**, 105–32.

Reis, Pedro and Ana R. Marques (2016), 'Investigação e inovação responsáveis em sala de aula: módulos de ensino IRRESISTIBLE', Lisbon: Instituto de Educação da Universidade de Lisboa.

Roth, Wolff-Michael (2009), 'On activism and teaching', *Journal for Activist Science & Technology Education*, **1** (2), 31–47.

Sá, Sara, Jorge Bastos-Santos and Hélder Araújo et al. (2016), 'Spatial distribution of floating marine debris in offshore continental Portuguese waters', *Marine Pollution Bulletin*, **104** (1–2), 269–78.

Schnurr, Riley E.J., Vanessa Alboiu and Meenakshi Chaudhary et al. (2018), 'Reducing marine pollution from single-use plastics (SUPs): a review', *Marine Pollution Bulletin*, **137**, 157–71.

Schwarz, Anna E., Tom N. Ligthart, Elise Boukris and Toon V. Harmelen (2019), 'Sources, transport, and accumulation of different types of plastic litter in aquatic environments: a review study', *Marine Pollution Bulletin*, **143**, 92–100.

Scott, David and Fern K. Willits (1994), 'Environmental attitudes and behavior: a Pennsylvania survey', *Environment and Behavior*, **26**, 239–60.

Seas at Risk (2015), *Single-use Plastics and the Marine Environment Leverage Points for Reducing Single-use Plastics*, Brussels: Seas at Risk.

So, Winnie Wing Mui and Stephen C.F. Chow (2018), 'Environmental education in primary schools: a case study with plastic resources and recycling', *Education*, **47** (6), 3–13.

Stafford, Richard and Peter J.S. Jones (2019), 'Viewpoint – ocean plastic pollution: a convenient but distracting truth?', *Marine Policy*, **103**, 877–91.

Steffen, Will, Katherine Richardson and Johan Rockström et al. (2015), 'Planetary boundaries: guiding human development in a changing planet', *Science*, **347** (6223), Article 1259855.

Stern, Marc J., Robert B. Powell and Dawn Hill (2014), 'Environmental education program evaluation in the new millennium: what do we measure and what have we learned?', *Environmental Education Research*, **20** (5), 581–611.

Sylvestre, Isabelle and Arnaud Dressen (n.d.), *Troubled Waters* [video], accessed 07 January 2020 at http://troubled-waters.net/index-EN.html.

Tessnow-von Wysocki, Ina and Phillippe Le Billon (2019), 'Plastics at sea: treaty design for a global solution to marine plastic pollution', *Environmental Science and Policy*, **100**, 94–104.

United Nations Educational, Scientific and Cultural Organization (UNESCO) (2017), *Education for Sustainable Development Goals: Learning Objectives*, Paris: UNESCO.

United Nations Educational, Scientific and Cultural Organization (UNESCO) Bangkok Office (n.d.), *The Plastic Initiative*, accessed 6 November 2020 at www.theplasticinitiative.org/.

United Nations (2015), *Transforming Our World: The 2030 Agenda for Sustainable Development*, New York: United Nations.

Veiga, Joana Mira, David Fleet and Susan Kinsey et al. (2016), *JRC Technical Report: Identifying Sources of Marine Litter: MSFD GES TG Marine Litter – Thematic Report*, Luxembourg: Publications Office of the European Union.

Wilcox, Chris, Nicholas J. Mallos and George H. Leonard et al. (2016), 'Using expert elicitation to estimate the impacts of plastic pollution on marine wildlife', *Marine Policy*, **65**, 107–14.

Xanthos, Dirk and Tony R. Walker (2017), 'International policies to reduce plastic marine pollution from single-use plastics (plastic bags and microbeads): a review', *Marine Pollution Bulletin*, **118**, 17–26.

5. Sustainable higher education institutions: promoting a holistic approach
Usha Iyer-Raniga and Karishma Kashyap

1. INTRODUCTION

Sustainability, including climate change has been recognised as a potential threat to our ecosystem; a realisation that is not new (Revkin, 2018). The last decade has seen the most progressive ideas and solutions available for climate change resilience, mitigation and adaptation (Holloway Houston Inc. [HHI], 2018; Pitt et al., 2009; Pramanik et al., 2019). Climate change impacts have been drastically elevated in the last two decades due to rapid globalisation and urbanisation, making the built environment sector one of its biggest contributors (International Energy Agency [IEA], 2019).

Buildings in general, being responsible for one-third of global greenhouse gas emissions, are also extremely vulnerable to climate change in terms of operations, health and performance (United Nations Environment Programme [UNEP] and IEA, 2017). As the impacts of climate change are mounting over the building sector, the role of design and construction has now, more than ever, put even greater pressure on sustainable practices in terms of building design, operations and end of life. While the building and construction sector has had to contend with sustainability issues in the past, now climate change and its associated impacts also need to be considered. As a result, the challenges faced are also greater.

To address the issue of climate change and adhering to national and international policies and guidelines for the building industry, a shift towards 'green' design and construction has called for more urgency in globally driven interests at governmental, institutional and community levels. Green buildings have a high potential for delivering significant cuts in greenhouse gas (GHG) emissions (Bourne et al., 2018; C40 Cities, 2019; Department of Environment, Land, Water and Planning [DELWP], 2017; Intergovernmental Panel on Climate Change [IPCC], 2014), acting as an effective means to combat climate change (World Green Building Council [WGBC], 2018) at no cost (Bourne et al., 2018; IPCC, 2014) whilst also being socially responsible (Chappell and Corps, 2009; Wang et al., 2013).

The terms green and sustainable are not interchangeable, as being green reflects the environmental movement in general (Prum, 2010; Rademacher, 2018), while sustainability is ultimately about ensuring that the needs and resources of current generations are met without compromising requirements for future generations (United Nations Educational, Scientific and Cultural Organization [UNESCO], 2014; World Commission on Environment and Development [WCED], 1987). This chapter, however, does not distinguish these concepts. It considers green synonymously with sustainability and issues associated with climate change. In this context, it highlights the impact of higher education institutions (HEIs) on the environment and their commitment to being sustainable.

The chapter begins with the method used for the research. A deep dive into the UN

Sustainable Development Goals (SDGs) as a backdrop to understanding where sustainable development practices in HEIs have headed follows. Next, potential opportunities for HEIs to engage with holistic sustainability outcomes are discussed. Student and staff awareness/understanding of sustainability issues, governance models to incorporate sustainable practices and sustainable campus operations are all considered before presenting the discussion and conclusions.

Over the course of the chapter, references are made to stakeholders of HEIs. Stakeholders are students, teaching and professional staff that support campus operations and student welfare, the community and the industry that benefits from ongoing research and engagement.

2.   METHOD

Secondary literature, largely through peer-reviewed academic publications, have been used as the main sources of information and knowledge in this research. Where appropriate, grey literature through credible websites such as the United Nations (UN) have been used. Using suitable keyword searches, broad fields were then determined to understand and establish the state of play with sustainability interactions and outcomes in HEIs. The main considerations were education for sustainability (EfS), curricular development and implementation for sustainability outcomes, sustainability policies and programmes in HEIs, sustainability initiatives and similar ideas fostering sustainability through demonstration or best practice in HEIs, student education, awareness and knowledge, staff development, governance models, sustainable building and campus operations.

Having the potential to demonstrate best practice, HEIs can lead by example due to their status and impact on society (Sustainable Development Solutions Network [SDSN] Australia/Pacific, 2017). HEIs by nature, perform different functions. The chapter discusses the key aspects of HEIs that need to be incorporated within the institutional system to achieve desired green campus and sustainability outcomes. The functional aspects have been broadly categorised into teaching and learning pedagogies; research, including theoretical and applied research; governance strategies; and campus operations.

Ramos et al. (2015) suggest a holistic approach to incorporate each aspect and principle guiding sustainability into HEIs but does not elucidate what comprises a holistic approach. If such a holistic approach were to be used, then what may this need to consider? The aim of this research is to therefore understand what an ideal best practice approach may be for HEIs to support overall sustainability outcomes. The analysis of the secondary literature is used to understand the gaps and seek appropriate solutions.

3.   EVOLUTION OF SUSTAINABLE DEVELOPMENT PRACTICES IN HEIs

Buildings in HEIs do not exist on their own; they are part of a precinct of buildings with spaces. The green building movement dates back to the mid-1970s, arising primarily after the Organization of the Petroleum Exporting Companies (OPEC) oil embargo of 1973 (Revkin, 2018) and out of the need to switch to better and more efficient alternatives to energy and environmentally friendly building practices (US Environmental Protection Agency [US EPA], 2016). More recently, there is a body of supporting literature demonstrating the building sector's commitment towards the principles of sustainability (Akadiri, Chinyio and Olomolaiye, 2012; HHI, 2014; IPCC, 2018; World Economic Forum [WEF], 2016). To support this shift and green building strategies, various green building standards, codes and rating systems have been developed, dating back formally to the early 1990s (Organisation for Economic Co-operation and Development [OECD], 2019). Research shows many successful examples of such green designs being translated into expected building performance functions in reality (demonstrated through reduced utility bills, for example) in the residential and commercial sectors (Akadiri et al., 2012; Bradshaw et al., 2005; Chappell and Corps, 2009; WGBC, 2018).

However, it is observed that within the institutional building sector, HEIs have not yet caught up with greening their buildings and campus operations (Grosseck, Tîru and Bran, 2019). Although the role of HEIs acting as drivers for initiating the change and leading by example demonstrates that sustainable practices have been discussed (Iyer-Raniga et al., 2016; SDSN Australia/Pacific, 2017), the literature specific to green buildings is also limited with respect to demonstrating sustainability efforts in HEIs holistically (Kahle et al., 2018; Porritt, 2012; SDSN Australia/Pacific, 2017; Wang et al., 2013). Almost no examples of such approaches and attendant successes are found in the literature. The next section examines the state of play of policies with respect to sustainability in HEIs.

4.   POLICIES AND SUSTAINABILITY IN HEIs

HEIs offer opportunities along several different fronts – education, scholarship, research and campus operations – providing better sustainability outcomes and playing a crucial role in shaping the sustainability abilities and capacities of the future pool of design and construction professionals (Matthias, 2013; Porritt, 2012; Wright and Horst, 2013). Adhering to various global declarations and sustainability policies and conforming to various international agreements and conventions, HEIs throughout the world have a role in driving sustainability efforts (Wright, 2002). Additionally, the declaration of the 'United Nations Decade of Education for Sustainable Development' (Velazquez, Munguia and Sanchez, 2005) that ended in 2015 also spurred HEIs to develop and implement education for sustainability and related awareness.

To acknowledge the research to date and address sustainability considerations led to the development of the Rio+20 Treaty on Higher Education in 2012 – a partnership between the Copernicus Alliance with the United Nations University Institute of Advanced Studies (UNUIAS) and the International Association of Universities (IAU) (Copernicus Alliance, 2015). The treaty, supported by over 100 signatories, represents the collective vision of these higher education stakeholders seeking to achieve sustainability outcomes through research and practice. Such initiatives demonstrate the commitment of HEIs towards those outcomes (Matthias, 2013; Porritt, 2012; Wright and Horst, 2013; Salvioni, Franzoni and Cassano, 2017).

Similar efforts can be observed globally through supporting student and other stakeholder engagements. For example, the Environmental Association for Universities and Colleges (EAUC) developed in the UK empowers UK and Irish educational institutions to be a global leader in sustainability and stimulate a change in society (EAUC, 2020; UNESCO, 2014); Association for the Advancement of Sustainability in Higher Education (AASHE) in North America (AASHE, 2018; UNESCO, 2014); and Australasian Campuses Towards Sustainability (ACTS) in Australasia (ACTS, 2017) are other examples of non-profit organisations aligning the HEI objectives with sustainability and the SDGs to advance sustainable practices in their respective institutions.

The SDGs (UN, 2020a) came into effect on 1 January 2016 and have a timeframe of delivery by 2030 following global efforts undertaken by various agencies worldwide, and discussions at various conferences leading to the start of its implementation on this day. Under the umbrella of the 'Future We Want', the SDGs, associated targets and indicators reinforce now, more than ever, the need for sustainable development practices to be incorporated by HEIs across all subject areas and campus operations (Findler et al., 2019). Global ranking systems such as *Times Higher Education* (THE) HEI Impact Rankings, developed in 2004, have also brought the rating metrics to the twenty-first century, in terms of capturing the impact of the HEIs adhering to the goals of the SDGs (THE, 2019). Such efforts led to HEIs taking a renewed interest in sustainability concepts.

When considering the built environment itself, relevant SDGs directly applicable are SDG 7 on affordable and clean energy, SDG 8 on decent work and economic growth, SDG 9 on industry, innovation and infrastructure, SDG 11 on sustainable cities and communities, SDG 12 on responsible consumption and production and SDG 13 on climate change (UN, 2020b). SDG 4 deals with quality education to ensure inclusive and equitable quality education and promote lifelong learning opportunities for all. From an HEI context, relevant targets and indicators focusing on education and educational environments are 4.3, 4.4, 4.7, 4.a–4.c, as presented in Table 5.1 (UN, 2020c). These targets include education and associated outcomes and also, where relevant, the physical setting that is used to deliver and engage in education. Table 5.1 provides the targets and indicators for SDG 4: Quality education.

The preamble to the SDGs state that sustainability is indivisible. This infers that a fragmented approach will not deliver sustainability outcomes. As indicated earlier, some authors have noted the importance of holistic approaches. Yet, there are still many challenges in holistic approaches to HEIs, explored in the next section.

5.   HEIs SHOWCASING HOLISTIC SUSTAINABILITY PRACTICES: WHERE ARE WE AT?

A sustainable HEI has the potential to demonstrate how a given principle of sustainable development can be translated into practical illustrations through improving the design, operations and management adhering to sustainability concepts on campuses (Leal Filho et al., 2018). HEIs incorporate human values into its users' lives to seek academic excellence and promote sustainability practices in teaching, research, community outreach and its operations (Leal Filho et al., 2019; Nejati and Nejati, 2013). Traditionally, HEIs tend to be core stakeholders for the building industry as they are one of the major property owners and developers (Porritt, 2012; SDSN Australia/Pacific, 2017).

Over the last decade, the role of HEIs has evolved from performing conventional research and education functions to serving as an innovation-promoting knowledge

Table 5.1 *Goal 4: 'Ensure inclusive and equitable quality education and promote lifelong learning opportunities for all': quality education, targets and indicators*

Goal No.	Goals and Targets from 2030 Agenda	Indicators
4.1	By 2030, ensure that all girls and boys complete free, equitable and quality primary and secondary education, leading to relevant and effective learning outcomes	4.1.1 Proportion of children and young people: (a) in grades 2/3; (b) at the end of primary; and (c) at the end of lower secondary achieving at least a minimum proficiency level in (i) reading and (ii) mathematics, by sex
4.2	By 2030, ensure that all girls and boys have access to quality early childhood development, care and pre-primary education so that they are ready for primary education	4.2.1 Proportion of children under five years of age who are developmentally on track in health, learning and psychosocial well-being, by sex
4.3	By 2030, ensure equal access for all women and men to affordable and quality technical, vocational and tertiary education, including university	4.2.2 Participation rate in organized learning (one year before the official primary entry age), by sex
4.4	By 2030, substantially increase the number of youth and adults who have relevant skills, including technical and vocational skills, for employment, decent jobs and entrepreneurship	4.4.1 Proportion of youth and adults with information and communications technology (ICT) skills, by type of skill
4.5	By 2030, eliminate gender disparities in education and ensure equal access to all levels of education and vocational training for the vulnerable, including persons with disabilities, indigenous peoples and children in vulnerable situations	4.5.1 Parity indices (female/male, rural/urban, bottom/top wealth quintile and others such as disability status, indigenous peoples and conflict-affected, as data become available) for all education indicators on this list that can be disaggregated
4.6	By 2030, ensure that all youth and a substantial proportion of adults, both men and women, achieve literacy and numeracy	4.6.1 Percentage of population in a given age group achieving at least a fixed level of proficiency in functional (a) literacy and (b) numeracy skills, by sex
4.7	By 2030, ensure that all learners acquire the knowledge and skills needed to promote sustainable development, including, among others, through education for sustainable development and sustainable lifestyles, human rights, gender equality, promotion of a culture of peace and non-violence, global citizenship and appreciation of cultural diversity and of culture's contribution to sustainable development	4.7.1 Extent to which (i) global citizenship education and (ii) education for sustainable development, including gender equality and human rights, are mainstreamed at all levels in: (a) national education policies, (b) curricula, (c) teacher education and (d) student assessment

Table 5.1   (continued)

Goal No.	Goals and Targets from 2030 Agenda	Indicators
4.a	Build and upgrade education facilities that are child, disability and gender sensitive and provide safe, non-violent, inclusive and effective learning environments for all	4.a.1 Proportion of schools with access to: (a) electricity; (b) the Internet for pedagogical purposes; (c) computers for pedagogical purposes; (d) adapted infrastructure and materials for students with disabilities; (e) basic drinking water; (f) single-sex basic sanitation facilities; and (g) basic handwashing facilities (as per the WASH indicator definitions)
4.b	By 2020, substantially expand globally the number of scholarships available to developing countries, in particular least developed countries, small island developing States and African countries, for enrolment in higher education, including vocational training and information and communications technology, technical, engineering and scientific programmes, in developed countries and other developing countries	4.b.1 Volume of official development assistance flows for scholarships by sector and type of study
4.c	By 2030, substantially increase the supply of qualified teachers, including through international cooperation for teacher training in developing countries, especially least developed countries and small island developing States	4.c.1 Proportion of teachers in: (a) pre-primary; (b) primary; (c) lower secondary; and (d) upper secondary education who have received at least the minimum organized teacher training (e.g. pedagogical training) pre-service or in-service required for teaching at the relevant level in a given country

Note: Direct quote from the UN website.

Source: UN (2020c).

hub (SDSN Australia/Pacific, 2017). HEIs nowadays are regarded as 'small cities' due to their extensive portfolio in relation to size, associated direct users of buildings and spaces, the direct and indirect impacts on society, and the environment as a result of the various activities and campus operations (Wang et al., 2013). Due to the large number of buildings that comprise HEIs, the size of their campus, the number of direct users and high resource consumption of buildings and associated services such as food and other activities on campus, HEIs have the potential to act as urban learning labs (ULLs) for a transition to low-carbon futures, whilst also leading the next generation of professionals in an appropriate direction with respect to sustainability and climate change (Iyer-Raniga et al., 2016).

HEIs play a role in dealing with issues of social, environmental and economic underpinnings for sustainability from both EfS and broader societal changes. Hence, they have the potential to become a significant contributor in the pursuit of sustainability initiatives. Through education, research and direct impact on the society, HEIs play a fundamental role in producing significant effects and addressing global challenges (Darling-Hammond et al., 2020). Demonstrating best practices through their actions by generating appropriate knowledge awareness and skills, and campus operations, HEIs can influence and multiply the current efforts of society to achieve sustainable development (Ralph and Stubbs, 2014). Previous studies undertaken with respect to sustainability in HEIs since the early 1990s (Grindsted, 2011; Wright, 2002) have supported some key domains that HEIs have been working on from the sustainability front, including the:

- ethical and moral responsibility of an HEI to contribute to its own level/s of engagement, be it local, regional and global sustainability;
- the need to communicate and engage with society to become models or exemplars of sustainability in their own local context or communities;
- encouraging sustainable physical operations of their buildings and assets;
- encouraging research related to sustainability;
- fostering overall ecological literacy; and
- the development of an interdisciplinary curriculum.

The identification of these themes and patterns assists in defining the key sustainable priorities for an HEI and the journey they need to embark upon to achieve these objectives (UN, 2019). These sustainability priorities provide a starting point for an exploration of the challenges to sustainability in HEIs (Findler et al., 2019). The next section considers student knowledge and awareness of sustainability.

6.   SUSTAINABILITY AND PROMOTING STUDENT AWARENESS FOR SUSTAINABILITY IN HEIs

Students form a key stakeholder group for an HEI, and it may be argued that HEIs exist for students. Learning is a key process guiding students to become aware of and develop understanding of any given topic (National Research Council [NRC], 2000). The learning capacities and awareness of sustainability concepts via education need to be strengthened. An interdisciplinary holistic insight and deep learning environment is relevant in relation to education for sustainability (Leal Filho et al., 2019; Warburton, 2003). Some studies have emphasised research in HEIs (Iyer-Raniga, Arcari and Wong, 2010; Wu et al., 2016), but, ultimately, a blend of research and teaching and learning processes has been found to be more productive (Darling-Hammond et al., 2020; Australian Government Productivity Commission, 1999), supporting transformative learning in HEIs (Iyer-Raniga and Andamon, 2016; Leal Filho et al., 2018).

Research on EfS has grown in visibility and significance worldwide, with a clear increase in relevant operations in HEIs (Grosseck et al., 2019; Tilbury, 2014; UN, 2019). HEIs are considered to influence the efforts and understanding of future professionals and leaders in all sectors through the provision of education. However, effective integration of EfS and mainstreaming it in teaching and learning priorities are still lacking

(Mader et al., 2014; Mulà et al., 2017). By exploring research on approaches adopted by HEIs to achieve sustainability through education, Salvioni et al. (2017) state that there is no specific approach that fits all operations. Hence, the adoption of a heterogeneous approach is required to achieve desired sustainability outcomes in an institution. Current research methodologies and teaching processes need to be modified to give the students an opportunity to apply sustainability principles and learn from attendant practices. Sustainability may be applied across diverse research paradigms (Sibbel, 2009).

Orr (1999) argued that the education process and content need a transformation and commented on the significance of ecological literacy, which is about developing environmental studies curricula in HEIs. He referred to educational facilities as 'institutions having potential leverage points for a transition to sustainability' (ibid., p. 84). Since then, this ideology has progressed further and several studies comment on the importance of incorporating sustainability concepts in education and enhancing student awareness and knowledge on sustainability (Iyer-Raniga et al., 2010; Leal Filho, 2019; Sibbel, 2009). Integrating sustainability concepts in the curriculum is an important requirement and has direct practical applications to enhance the learning process within HEIs (Sibbel, 2009). It is also important to engage industry, academics and the educational institution itself in the development of the curriculum to understand the key concepts to be taught and understood (Darling-Hammond et al., 2020; Zanko et al., 2011).

Concerns about the changing environmental conditions and associated problems have defined the patterns of environmental education and the manner in which it is promoted (Hudson, 2001; Leal Filho et al., 2018; Tilbury, 1995). The history of environmental education adopts an educational approach that focuses primarily on reducing the overall environmental impacts but recommends adapting the current teaching and learning processes to educate for sustainability (Hayles and Holdsworth, 2008). Synergy is required across every aspect of a higher educational campus operation, creating a 'learning for sustainability' environment to address sustainability comprehensively (Findler et al., 2019; Leal Filho et al., 2018; Ralph and Stubbs, 2014).

However, despite the considerable progress on education access and participation over the past years, the teaching and learning processes, student curriculum, capacities of academics and quality of performance are still lagging behind (UN, 2019). Rapid technological changes and sustainability targets present opportunities and challenges (Darling-Hammond et al., 2020). Efforts need to be refocused towards restructuring the current education curriculum for HEI students and improving learning for achieving sustainability outcomes. But students are not the only internal stakeholders in HEIs; staff are yet another group to be considered.

7.   STAFF DEVELOPMENT FOR IMPROVING STRATEGIES AND EDUCATION FOR SUSTAINABILITY

The current scenario of events occurring as a result of climate change has led to various policy-level efforts and interventions globally and locally, pushing HEIs to integrate sustainable practices throughout their campuses (Shawe et al., 2019). EfS has typically been considered as important from a curriculum perspective. It is also important to create more awareness and sensitivity towards ensuring holistic approaches to sustainability, including comfort of the users of HEI buildings, which in turn is expected to improve productivity of occupants of such buildings (Tilbury, 2014). However, the education system still lags in terms of concrete institutional, thematic, and methodological guidance that directs the teaching and learning process (Mader et al., 2014; Sibbel, 2009). Therefore, in addition to developing curricula incorporating sustainability education, efforts to build the capacities of academic staff are equally important (Sibbel, 2009). This is because unsustainable practices and thinking still exist in the current education system (Gibbs and O'Neil, 2015). Professional development of teaching staff must be considered, as they have the opportunity and the knowledge to modify and transform the curriculum and lead the next generation of students to understand and engage with global sustainability (Gibbs and O'Neil, 2015; Porritt, 2012; Sibbel, 2009).

It may well be that the majority of teaching staff and students (users) have a good overview of climate change and sustainability but are not very familiar with the concept and equipped with the knowledge of a sustainable HEI (Porritt, 2012; Shawe et al., 2019). Although, being aware of the issues, majority users are motivated to contribute towards building and campus sustainability, the current constraints in relation to lack of understanding and relevant approaches inhibits the required change. Support, guidance and appropriate engagement of the whole institution (at all stages pre- and post-construction) hence acts as the means to achieve the desired sustainability outcomes. Therefore, governance models also need to be considered. Not just the academic staff, but also non-academic staff need to be inculcated with sustainability knowledge and awareness so their behavioural practices will support governance models. The next section examines these models.

8. GOVERNANCE MODEL OF HEIs TO INCORPORATE SUSTAINABLE PRACTICES

HEIs are responsible for contributing to environmental pollution, leading to severe detrimental effects due to high energy and resource consumption at all stages throughout their lifecycle (Grosseck et al., 2019; Porritt, 2012). However, if appropriate organisational and technical measures are taken, these adverse impacts can be reduced considerably (Revkin, 2018). HEIs throughout the world are thriving to adopt best practices, target green building design and utilise green building assessment tools to measure their respective successes. This movement is primarily client driven and supported at both policy and industry levels (Salvioni et al., 2017).

Given the growing global pressures through international agreements such as the Paris agreement and aligned with pressures for sustainability rankings, increasing numbers of HEIs supporting the promotion and advancement of sustainability (UN, 2019). For example, since the 1980s after the energy crisis, yet again a wave of change was observed in the US HEIs. The change involved HEIs voluntarily opting for more energy-efficient and sustainable practices in their routine operations. Due to their early and constant efforts, the US HEIs have been leading the way through practice and innovation (Emmanuel and Adams, 2011; Salvioni et al., 2017).

Similar advancement can be observed in Australian HEIs (SDSN Australia/Pacific, 2017). A report by the Parliament of the Commonwealth of Australia (2007) recommended the importance of and guidelines for major industries, including HEIs, to incorporate a 'sustainability agenda' and green design in their governance structure. Therefore, appropriate governance and management practices are critical to make informed decisions and achieve holistic sustainability outcomes in an efficient manner.

The contribution of HEIs towards sustainability goals requires responsible leadership (Pitt et al., 2009) to promote research and demonstrate practical applications (US EPA, 2009; Wang et al., 2013), and considerable professional development of teaching staff to guide the students towards global sustainability efforts (Darling-Hammond et al., 2020; Ferreira, Ryan and Tilbury, 2006; Leal Filho et al., 2018). However, the literature states that, globally, HEIs lack the key ingredients to incorporate sustainability holistically, including internal leadership amongst stakeholders with decision-making power, quantifiable sustainability targets, an operational structure in relation to design and energy costs and communication between stakeholders – all this whilst also engaging students and staff in sustainability education (HHI, 2014; Pramanik et al., 2019; Ralph and Stubbs, 2014; Sibbel, 2009).

Studies show that increasing awareness and the potential of students to gain sustainability knowledge in HEIs, where green practices are being demonstrated and practised, is highly beneficial (Darling-Hammond et al., 2020; Kagawa, 2007; Leal Filho et al., 2018; Tuncer, 2008). Students these days are becoming increasingly aware of the issues of climate change due to increased carbon emissions and energy consumption and are concerned about the state of the planet they will inherit from the current generation (Gibbs and O'Neil, 2015; Mulà et al., 2017). Hence, an HEI's image due to its acquired green status is not only important from the perspective of governance but also from the perspective of the students. Due to increased awareness of global climatic issues, student perceptions and preferences are impacted by the sustainability initiatives adopted by HEIs (Lehtonen, Salonen and Cantell, 2018).

The literature supports attracting more highly qualified students to HEIs striving towards better design and practices and achieving green building standards and/or certifications (WGBC, 2018). Student respondents themselves have given higher satisfaction ratings based on the incorporation of sustainable features by an HEI, irrespective of their knowledge and familiarity with sustainability concepts. This is because students, in general, primarily prioritise sustainability with environmental benefits over economic or social outcomes (Kagawa, 2007; Sundermann and Fischer, 2019).

Delivery of green HEI buildings hence benefits both the HEI as well as the students. However, addressing sustainability as a concept and their understanding regarding their responsibility as building stakeholders still needs to be developed (Ngai et al., 2018; Revkin, 2018). The next section explores campus buildings and operations.

9. SUSTAINABLE BUILDING AND CAMPUS OPERATIONS

HEI campuses have been identified as opportunities for transforming learning and increasing the scope of research by becoming examples of sustainable campuses (Leal Filho et al., 2018). Promoting capacity-building and knowledge-sharing activities that allow transdisciplinary exchange of ideas, best practices and lessons learned across sectors, acts as a useful and beneficial resource for future projects. For example, a study by Shawe et al. (2019) examines 16 case studies (Irish and international) to compare the integration of on-campus sustainability practices. The study tests new ideas and technologies and reports on strengthening the knowledge transfer via accounting for the lessons learned. The study concluded that the integration of sustainable development into HEIs follows no single standardised approach, as the number of strategies outweighs the desired numbers of initiatives. It also concluded that to date most efforts are primarily restricted to enhancing campus actions, but not aiming to amplify the results through opportunities to support and enable outreach for the design and construction stakeholders.

There are examples in the literature that showcase high satisfaction rates of building occupants due to better design and management decisions for campus operations. For example, a study by Bluyssen et al. (2018) finds a 27 per cent reduction in headaches reported by staff and a 26 per cent improvement in student learning with improved access to daylight. The results demonstrate that improved lighting conditions, which is one of the key aspects of green buildings, is associated with enhanced user productivity – one of the expected green building outcomes.

From an overall built environment-centric focus, efficient practices such as resource consumption, waste management, building performance and the like are encouraged by incorporating EfS in HEIs (Bengtsson et al., 2018). Although some HEIs are transitioning towards adopting green design features and achieving green buildings on campus, the major thrust of the effort is still restricted to reducing the overall carbon footprint and gaining economic benefits (Brown and Cole, 2009; Brown, Dowlatabadi and Cole, 2009; Delzendeh et al., 2017; Wu et al., 2016). Studies by authors such as Tilbury (2014) embrace the shift towards EfS. Several guiding principles and models have been recommended, but the practical exploration of these theoretical explanations have not yet been translated to its full potential (Darling-Hammond et al., 2020).

10. DISCUSSION: GAPS AND SOLUTIONS

In previous sections, the evolution of sustainable development practices in HEIs, the potential of HEIs as hubs for showcasing sustainability practices, sustainability and student awareness in HEIs, sustainability curriculum development, governance models and sustainable campus operations have been presented. While the research has been quite comprehensive in demonstrating the potential of HEIs towards sustainability in their campuses, the various components and strategies discussed are often addressed in isolation. Table 5.2 captures the key themes arising from the various functions of HEIs.

In addition to these various functions is the changing political landscape such as the extinction rebellion where young students have demonstrated their concern for the environment. Also, ranking criteria of HEIs are increasingly being forced to consider the impact of sustainability and provide evidence of sustainability outcomes in their teaching, research, governance and physical assets, requiring a change in direction from the current siloed approach that has been undertaken to date. Lack of a clear approach to engaging with HEIs has led to various initiatives by organisations such as AASHE and ACTS.

Table 5.2   HEI and sustainability outputs/outcomes

Themes	HEI Domains	Outputs/Outcomes	Related SDG(s)
Sustainability research and education	Teaching and learning curriculum, scholarship of teaching, research	Building sustainability knowledge, fostering ecological literacy	4
Innovation promoting knowledge hub/ sustainable cities	Research, industry and community engagement	Finding solutions to global challenges and applied research outcomes	9, 11
Ethical and moral responsibility	Teaching, learning, research, governance, community and industry engagement	Responding to local, regional and global sustainability challenges	4, 16
Models/ demonstration of sustainability	Outreach and engagement, teaching, learning, research	Community interaction and engagement to embed sustainable solutions	9
Physical operations of buildings and campus	Property and building services, campus operations	Better buildings and resource efficient campus operations including savings as appropriate	6, 7, 9, 11, 12, 13
Student knowledge and awareness	Inter and transdisciplinary teaching and learning (supported by curricular knowledge), using campus as learning labs, engaging with industry and community	Theoretical and practical knowledge, work ready graduates, ecologically aware and responsible students	4
Staff development and engagement	Professional development/ knowledge about sustainability for teaching staff; awareness and engagement on sustainability issues for non-teaching staff	Knowledge and awareness of sustainability issues across all staff, engagement with industry and community as appropriate	3, 17
Sustainability policies and plans across all functions	Teaching and learning, research, engagement and governance (leadership)	Better knowledge, short and long-term sustainability outcomes engaging all stakeholders across all functions providing better sustainability outcomes for students, staff, buildings, campus operations	9, 17

10.1 A Holistic Approach Needs Strong and Committed Leadership

It can be seen in the preceding sections that there are no particular set of guidelines or disciplines overarching the teaching and learning processes for sustainability; the approaches need to be developed or modified as per the needs of the building users and the importance that the HEI governance places on sustainability outcomes across all its functions. Clearly, HEI campuses can be demonstrators of sustainability. As far as campus operations are concerned, considerations relevant for enhancing campus operations focus on internal and external stakeholder prioritisation and engagement, performance assessment, sustainability reporting and enhancing organisational capacity.

As described earlier, HEIs have the potential to provide evidence-based solutions and breakthroughs for the wider community. As can be observed from the preceding paragraphs, a holistic approach is certainly not the mainstream in HEIs. The focus has been fragmented on one or another aspect, such as demonstration of sustainability, sustainability and student awareness in HEIs, governance models and sustainable campus operations. What is currently required is to utilise the potential of HEIs to go beyond viewing them purely as buildings or a campus or a governance structure, and to create a difference by demonstrating impact on sustainable development outcomes through a holistic approach.

A noteworthy argument may be made, therefore, that only a holistic approach that incorporates *all* the themes of an HEI can potentially assist HEI leaders in the development of their sustainability model and strategy to mobilise and motivate the community to take practical steps towards building a sustainable campus. This begs the question then, as to what will constitute a holistic approach? And, what are the elements of an ideal approach to enhance the performance and longevity of sustainable HEIs across all considerations?

The idea of using a holistic approach itself is not new. But a holistic approach that can set up clear targets and outcomes as appropriate and delivers the outcomes by collaborating across all functions of the HEI needs a rethink. It requires strong and committed leadership. There is no one way or route to achieve sustainability outcomes across HEIs. Indeed, there may be no one best practice approach as there are many variables to be considered. The overall sustainability outcomes will need to be fit for purpose, across internal stakeholders – students, academics, professional and other relevant staff – external stakeholders – government, industry, civil societies and the community – and education that supports technical, ethical and moral values that espouse sustainability values in day-to-day life for both staff and students and is demonstrated through campus operations across various types of spaces and functions/uses on campus.

11. CONCLUSION

University campuses contain buildings and other spaces and are therefore subject to the same challenges facing the built environment. The current focus on achieving sustainability outcomes in HEIs is extremely fragmented. The SDGs state that sustainability is indivisible and therefore points to the need to support holistic outcomes. HEIs need to expand their functions to develop capacities through education to promote better sustainability outcomes, thereby creating better informed and capable future professionals. Research needs to progress further to showcase a paradigm shift within such institutions to serve as a vehicle for increasing awareness and engagement of students in sustainability practices. Bringing sustainability education into the classroom does not happen by chance. This requires committed leadership. Likewise, holistic sustainability outcomes across all functions of a university also needs forethought, planning and monitoring.

Currently, the teaching process requires building the professional capacities of the instructors/teachers and changing the current teaching approaches, including the subject matter as appropriate, in an integrated manner by the institutional structures of the HEI itself. Achieving campus sustainability through education can act as a remedy to address the current knowledge gap in HEIs, ensuring sustainable developmental outcomes for campuses as well. Effective learning approaches through education based on sustainability engages with the students and coaches them to be better aware of sustainability concepts and approaches beyond their campus lives. When this type of sustainability awareness is extended to professional staff, their increased capacities will support changes that endorse governance policies towards sustainability outcomes for HEIs.

Therefore, modification to existing approaches or new approaches needs guidance in order to be developed as a fit-for-purpose model, incorporating and demonstrating best industry practices across all functions of a HEI from a sustainability perspective. There cannot be one singular prescriptive model that covers best practice across education, research, governance and campus operations because each HEI needs to create its own goals based on its current transitional platform for sustainability outcomes. Aligning the sustainability drivers and engagement across all functions of an HEI needs a strong and committed leadership. It requires defining these outcomes and setting priorities based on the organisation's overall sustainability intent and desired impact.

The targets and indicators set by the SDGs provide an excellent platform from which to engage in the sustainability process. Five years into the launch of the SDGs, it is time for HEIs to start engaging urgently and seriously for sustainability outcomes. The SDGs themselves with their targets and indicators provide opportunities to create and monitor progress across all functions of HEIs. Tracking these at interim periods by setting up baselines or benchmarks supported by continual monitoring will ensure that sustainability outcomes stay on track and goals are met.

REFERENCES

Akadiri, P.O., Chinyio, E.A. and Olomolaiye, P.O. 2012. Design of a sustainable building: a conceptual framework for implementing sustainability in the building sector. *Buildings*, 2(2), 126–52.

Association for the Advancement of Sustainability in Higher Education (AASHE). 2018. History of AASHE. Accessed 29 January 2020 at https://www.aashe.org/about-us/aashe-history/.

Australasian Campuses Towards Sustainability (ACTS). 2017. ACTS initiatives. Accessed 20 November 2018 at https://www.acts.asn.au/.

Australian Government Productivity Commission. 1999. *The Environmental Performance of Commercial Buildings: Research Report*. Canberra: Commonwealth of Australia. Accessed June 2015 at https://www.pc.gov.au/inquiries/completed/building-performance/report/buildingperformance.pdf.

Bengtsson, S.E.L., Barakat, B. and Muttarak, R. et al. 2018. *The Role of Education in Enabling the Sustainable Development Agenda*. Abingdon: Routledge.

Bluyssen, P.M., Zhang, D. and Kurvers, S. et al. 2018. Self-reported health and comfort of school children in 54 classrooms of 21 Dutch school buildings. *Building and Environment*, 138, 106–23.

Bourne, G., Stock, A. and Steffen, W. et al. 2018. Australia's rising greenhouse gas emissions. Working paper. Climate Council of Australia Limited. Accessed 21 March 2019 at https://www.climatecouncil.org.au/wp-content/uploads/2018/06/CC_MVSA0143-Briefing-Paper-Australias-Rising-Emissions_V8-FA_Low-Res_Single-Pages3.pdf.

Bradshaw, C.P., Koth, C.W. and Bevans, K.B. et al. 2008. The impact of school-wide positive behavioral interventions and supports (PBIS) on the organizational health of elementary schools. *School Psychology Quarterly*, 23(4), 462–73.

Brown, Z. and Cole, R.J. 2009. Influence of occupants' knowledge on comfort expectations and behaviour. *Building Research and Information*, 37(3), 227–45.

Brown, Z., Dowlatabadi, H. and Cole, R. 2009. Feedback and adaptive behaviour in green buildings. *Intelligent Buildings International*, 1(4), 296–315.

C40 Cities. 2019. New research shows how urban consumption drives global emissions. Accessed 25 November 2019 at https://www.c40.org/press_releases/new-research-shows-how-urban-consumption-drives-global-emissions.

Chappell, T.W. and Corps, C. 2009. *High Performance Green Building: What's It Worth? Investigating the Market Value of High Performance Green Buildings*. Accessed 7 October 2019 at https://living-future.org/wp-content/uploads/2016/11/High_Performance_Green_Building.pdf.

Copernicus Alliance. 2015. Rio +20 Treaty on Higher Education. Accessed 26 January 2020 at https://www.copernicus-alliance.org/rio-20-treaty.

Darling-Hammond, L., Flook, L. and Cook-Havey, C. et al. 2020. Implications for educational practice of the science of learning and development. *Applied Developmental Science*, 24(2), 97–140.

Delzendeh, E., Wu, S., Lee, A. and Zhou, Y. 2017. The impact of occupants' behaviours on building energy analysis: a research review. *Renewable and Sustainable Energy Reviews*, 80, 1061–71.

Department of Environment, Land, Water and Planning (DELWP). 2017. *Energy Efficiency and Productivity Strategy*. Victoria State Government. Accessed 24 October 2018 at https://www.energy.vic.gov.au/__data/assets/pdf_file/0030/89292/Energy-Efficiency-and-Productivity-Strategy-Web.pdf.

Emmanuel, R. and Adams, J. 2011. College students' perceptions of campus sustainability. *International Journal of Sustainability in Higher Education*, 12(1), 79–82.

Environmental Association for Universities and Colleges (EAUC). 2020. Our governance. Accessed 29 January 2020 at https://www.eauc.org.uk/eauc_governance.

Ferreira, J., Ryan, L. and Tilbury, D. 2006. *Whole-School Approaches to Sustainability: A Review of Models for Professional Development in Pre-Service Teacher Education*. Australian Government Department of the Environment and Heritage and the Australian Research Institute in Education for Sustainability (ARIES). Accessed 2 April 2016 at http://aries.mq.edu.au/projects/preservice/files/TeacherEduDec06.pdf.

Findler, F., Schönherr, N., Lozano, R. and Stacherl, B. 2019. Assessing the impacts of higher education institutions on sustainable development: an analysis of tools and indicators. *Sustainability*, 11(1), 59, https://doi.org/10.1016/j.jclepro.2018.07.017.

Gibbs, D. and O'Neil, K. 2015. Building a green economy? Sustainability transitions in the UK building sector. *Geoforum*, 59, 133–41.

Grindsted, T. 2011. Sustainable universities – from declarations on sustainability in higher education to national law. *Environmental Economics*, 2(2), https://doi.org/10.2139/ssrn.2697465.

Grosseck, G., Tiru, L.G. and Bran, R.A. 2019. Education for sustainable development: evolution and perspectives: a bibliometric review of research, 1992–2018. *Sustainability*, 11(21), Article 6136.

Hayles, C. and Holdsworth, S. 2008. Curriculum change for sustainability. *Journal for Education in the Built Environment*, 3(1), 25–48.

Holloway Houston Inc. (HHI). 2014. Importance of construction industry in the economy and use of construction equipments. Accessed 23 July 2018 at https://www.hhilifting.com/importance-of-construction-industry-in-the-economy-and-use-of-construction-equipments/.

Hudson, S.J. 2001. Challenges for environmental education: issues and ideas for the 21st century: environmental education, a vital component of efforts to solve environmental problems, must stay relevant to the needs and interests of the community and yet constantly adapt to the rapidly changing social and technological landscape. *BioScience*, 51(4), 283–8.

Intergovernmental Panel on Climate Change (IPCC). 2014. *Climate Change 2014: Synthesis Report: Summary for Policymakers*. Geneva: IPCC.

Intergovernmental Panel on Climate Change (IPCC). 2018. Summary for policymakers, technical summary and frequently asked questions. In V. Masson-Delmotte, P. Zhai and H.-O. Pörtner et al. (eds), *Global Warming of 1.5°C. An IPCC Special Report on the impacts of global warming of 1.5°C above pre-industrial levels and related global greenhouse gas emission pathways, in the context of strengthening the global response to the threat of climate change, sustainable development, and efforts to eradicate poverty.* Accessed 3 February 2021 at https://www.ipcc.ch/sr15/.

International Energy Agency (IEA). 2019. *Global Status Report for Buildings and Construction 2019.* Paris: IEA. Accessed 1 March 2021 at https://www.iea.org/reports/global-status-report-for-buildings-and-construction-2019.

Iyer-Raniga, U. and Andamon, M.M. 2016. Transformative learning: innovating sustainability education in built environment. *International Journal of Sustainability in Higher Education,* 17(1), 105–22.

Iyer-Raniga, U., Arcari, P. and Wong, J.P.C. 2010. Education for sustainability in the built environment: what are students telling us? In C. Egbu (ed.), *Proceedings of 26th Annual ARCOM Conference, 6–8 September 2010, Leeds, UK,* pp. 1447–56.

Iyer-Raniga, U., Moore, T., Ridley, I. and Andamon, M.M. 2016. Aligning goals for sustainable outcomes: case study of a university building in Australia. In W. Leal Filho and L. Brandli (eds), *Engaging Stakeholders in Education for Sustainable Development at University Level.* Cham, Switzerland: Springer.

Kagawa, F. 2007. Dissonance in students' perceptions of sustainable development and sustainability: implications for curriculum change. *International Journal of Sustainability in Higher Education,* 8(3), 317–38.

Kahle, J., Risch, K., Wanke, A. and Lang, D.J. 2018. Strategic networking for sustainability: lessons learned from two case studies in higher education. *Sustainability,* 10(12), 1–24.

Leal Filho, W. 2019. *Encyclopedia of Sustainability in Higher Education.* Cham, Switzerland: Springer.

Leal Filho, W., Mifsud, M. and Molthan-Hill, P. et al. 2019. Climate change scepticism at universities: a global study. *Sustainability,* 11(10), 1–13.

Leal Filho, W., Raath, S. and Lazzarini et al. 2018. The role of transformation of learning and education for sustainability. *Journal of Cleaner Production,* 199, 286–95.

Lehtonen, A., Salonen, A.O. and Cantell, H. 2018. Climate change education: a new approach for a world of wicked problems. In J.W. Cook (ed.), *Sustainability, Human Well-Being, and the Future of Education.* Cham, Switzerland: Springer.

Mader, M., Tilbury, D., Dlouhá, J. and Benayas, J. (eds). 2014. *State of the Art Report: Mapping Opportunities for Developing Education for Sustainable Development Competences in the UE4SD Partner Countries.* University Educators for Sustainable Development. Accessed 10 March 2020 at file:///Users/dee/Downloads/UE4SD_State-of-the-art-report_2014.pdf.

Matthias, B. 2013. Many roads lead to sustainability: a process-oriented analysis of change in higher education. *International Journal of Sustainability in Higher Education,* 14(2), 160–75.

Mulà, I., Tilbury, D. and Ryan, A. et al. 2017. Catalysing change in higher education for sustainable development: a review of professional development initiatives for university educators. *International Journal of Sustainability in Higher Education,* 18(5), https://doi.org/10.1108/IJSHE-03-2017-0043.

National Research Council (NRC). 2000. *How People Learn: Brain, Mind, Experience, and School: Expanded Edition.* Washington, DC: National Academies Press.

Nejati, M. and Nejati, M. 2013. Assessment of sustainable university factors from the perspective of university students. *Journal of Cleaner Production,* 48, 101–7.

Ngai, E.W.T., Law, C.C.H. and Lo, C.W.H. et al. 2018. Business sustainability and corporate social responsibility: case studies of three gas operators in China. *International Journal of Production Research,* 56(1/2), 660–76.

Organisation for Economic Co-operation and Development (OECD). 2019. Australia needs to intensify efforts to meet its 2030 emissions goal. Accessed 30 October 2019 at https://www.oecd.org/australia/australia-needs-to-intensify-efforts-to-meet-its-2030-emissions-goal.htm.

Orr, D.W. 1999. *Ecological Literacy: Education and the Transition to a Postmodern World.* Albany, NY: State University of New York Press.

Pitt, M., Tucker, M., Riley, M. and Longden, J. 2009. Towards sustainable construction: promotion and best practices. *Construction Innovation,* 9(2), 201–24.

Parliament of the Commonwealth of Australia (PoA). 2007. *Sustainability for Survival: Creating a Climate for Change: Inquiry Into a Sustainability Charter.* Canberra: House of Representatives Standing Committee on Environment and Heritage, Commonwealth of Australia. Accessed 6 February 2021 at https://www.aph.gov.au/parliamentary_business/committees/house_of_representatives_committees?url=environ/charter/report.htm.

Porritt, J. 2012. Universities must lead the way on the sustainability agenda. *The Guardian,* 16 February. Accessed 21 March 2018 at https://www.theguardian.com/higher-education-network/blog/2012/feb/16/universities-lead-sustainability-agenda-porritt.

Pramanik, P.K.D., Mukherjee, B. and Pal, S. et al. 2019. Green smart building: requisites, architecture, challenges, and use cases. In A. Solanki and A. Nayyar (eds), *Green Building Management and Smart Automation.* Hershey, PA: IGI Global.

Prum, D.A. 2010. Green buildings, high performance buildings, and sustainable construction: does it really matter what we call them? *Villanova Environmental Law Journal,* 21(1), https://ssrn.com/abstract=1731688.

Rademacher, A. 2018. *Building Green: Environmental Architects and the Struggles for Sustainability in Mumbai.* Oakland, CA: University of California Press.

Ralph, M. and Stubbs, W. 2014. Integrating environmental sustainability into universities. *The International Journal of Higher Education and Educational Planning*, 67(1), 71–90.

Ramos, T.B., Caeiroa, S. and Van Hoof, B. et al. 2015. Experiences from the implementation of sustainable development in higher education institutions: environmental management for sustainable universities. *Journal of Cleaner Production*, 106, 3–10.

Revkin, A. 2018. Climate change first became news 30 years ago. Why haven't we fixed it? *National Geographic.* Accessed 17 December 2019 at https://www.nationalgeographic.com/magazine/2018/07/embark-essay-climate-change-pollution-revkin/.

Salvioni, D.M., Franzoni, S. and Cassano, R. 2017. Sustainability in the higher education system: an opportunity to improve quality and image. *Sustainability*, 9(6), 914–41.

Shawe, R., Horan, W., Moles, R. and O'Regan, B. 2019. Mapping of sustainability policies and initiatives in higher education institutes. *Environmental Science and Policy*, 99, 80–88.

Sibbel, A. 2009. Pathways towards sustainability through higher education. *International Journal of Sustainability in Higher Education*, 10(1), 68–82.

Sundermann, A. and Fischer, D. 2019. How does sustainability become professionally relevant? Exploring the role of sustainability conceptions in first year students. *Sustainability*, 11(19), 1–22.

Sustainable Development Solutions Network (SDSN) Australia/Pacific. 2017. *Getting Started with the SDGs in Universities: A Guide for Universities, Higher Education Institutions, and the Academic Sector.* Accessed 21 March 2018 at http://ap-unsdsn.org/wp-content/uploads/University-SDG-Guide_web.pdf.

Tilbury, D. 1995. Environmental education for sustainability: defining the new focus of environmental education in the 1990s. *Environmental Education Research*, 1(2), 195–212.

Tilbury, D. 2014. *Education for Sustainability in Higher Education (Final Draft). Report Commissioned by UNESCO ESD Secretariat to inform the 3rd Global DESD Report.* Accessed 1 March 2021 at https://www.researchgate.net/profile/Daniella_Tilbury/publication/324828998_Ten_Years_of_Education_for_Sustainability_in_Higher_Education_UNESCO_Commissioned_Report_for_the_Decade_in_Education_for_Sustainable_Development_DESD/links/5ae57ca9458515760ac08826/Ten-Years-of-Education-for-Sustainability-in-Higher-Education-UNESCO-Commissioned-Report-for-the-Decade-in-Education-for-Sustainable-Development-DESD.

Times Higher Education (THE). 2019. Impact rankings: FAQs. Accessed 26 January 2020 at https://www.timeshighereducation.com/world-university-rankings/university-impact-rankings-faqs.

Tuncer, G. 2008. University students' perception on sustainable development: a case study from Turkey. *International Research in Geographical and Environmental Education*, 17(3), 212–26.

United Nations (UN). 2019. *Annual SDG Accord Report: Progress Towards the Global Goals in the University and College Sector.* UN High-level Political Forum. Accessed 10 March 2020 https://sustainabledevelopment.un.org/content/documents/242552019_the_sdg_accord_un_high_political_forum_final_online_version_1.pdf.

United Nations (UN). 2020a. *Future We Want – Outcome Document.* Sustainable Development Goals Knowledge Platform. Accessed 5 March 2020 at https://sustainabledevelopment.un.org/index.php?menu=1298.

United Nations (UN). 2020b. *Take action for the Sustainable Development Goals.* Accessed 5 March 2020 at https://www.un.org/sustainabledevelopment/sustainable-development-goals/.

United Nations (UN). 2020c. *Goal 4: Ensure inclusive and equitable quality education and promote lifelong learning opportunities for all.* Accessed 5 March 2020 at https://sustainabledevelopment.un.org/sdg4.

United Nations Educational, Scientific and Cultural Organization (UNESCO). 2014. *Shaping the Future We Want: UN Decade of Education for Sustainable Development (2005-2014): Final Report.* Accessed 2 December 2019 at https://sustainabledevelopment.un.org/content/documents/1682Shaping%20the%20future%20we%20want.pdf.

United Nations Environment Programme (UNEP) and International Energy Agency (IEA). 2017. *Towards a Zero-emission, Efficient, and Resilient Buildings and Construction Sector: Global Status Report 2017.* Accessed 3 February 2021 at https://www.worldgbc.org/sites/default/filesUNEP%20188_GABC_en%20%20%28web%29.pdf.

US Environmental Protection Agency (EPA). 2009. Buildings and their impact on the environment: a statistical summary. Accessed 15 March 2015 at https://archive.epa.gov/greenbuilding/web/pdf/gbstats.pdf.

US Environmental Protection Agency (EPA). 2016. Definition of green building. Accessed 18 April 2017 at https://archive.epa.gov/greenbuilding/web/html/about.html.

Velazquez, L., Munguia, N. and Sanchez, M. 2005. Deterring sustainability in higher education institutions: an appraisal of the factors which influence sustainability in higher education institutions. *International Journal of Sustainability in Higher Education*, 6(4), 383–91.

Wang, Y., Shi, H. and Sun, M. et al. 2013. Moving towards an ecologically sound society? Starting from green universities and environmental higher education. *Journal of Cleaner Production*, 61, 1–5.

Warburton, K. 2003. Deep learning and education for sustainability. *International Journal of Sustainability in Higher Education*, 4(1), 44–56.

World Commission on Environment and Development (WCED). 1987. *Our Common Future*. Accessed 21 March 2018 at https://sustainabledevelopment.un.org/content/documents/5987our-common-future.pdf.

World Economic Forum (WEF). 2016. *Shaping the Future of Construction: A Breakthrough in Mindset and Technology. Industry Agenda*. Accessed 1 December 2019 at http://www3.weforum.org/docs/WEF_Shaping_the_Future_of_Construction_full_report__.pdf.

World Green Building Council (WGBC). 2018. About green building. Accessed 21 September 2019 at https://www.worldgbc.org/benefits-green-buildings.

Wright, T. 2002. Definitions and frameworks for environmental sustainability in higher education. *International Journal of Sustainability in Higher Education*, 3(3), 105–20.

Wright, T. and Horst, N. 2013. Exploring the ambiguity: what faculty leaders really think of sustainability in higher education. *International Journal of Sustainability in Higher Education*, 14(2), 209–27.

Wu, S.R., Greaves, M., Chen, J. and Grady, S.C. 2016. Green buildings need green occupants: a research framework through the lens of the theory of planned behaviour. *Architectural Science Review*, 60(1), 5–14.

Zanko, M., Papadopoulos, T. and Taylor, T. et al. 2011. Professional learning in the business curriculum: engaging industry, academics and students. *Asian Social Science*, 7(4), 61–8.

6. Student-led sustainability actions at Latin American universities: a case study from Chile
Claudia Mac-lean, Isabella Villanueva and Jean Hugé

1. INTRODUCTION

Transformational processes towards sustainability in higher education institutions (HEIs) are mostly ad hoc developments that grow over time, are characterised by a top-down and/ or bottom-up approach, and often depend at least in part on the actions of 'sustainability champions'. A commitment from the university's hierarchy seems to be fundamental (Hugé, Mac-lean and Vargas, 2018; Ramísio et al., 2019).

HEIs are facing the challenge of teaching students how to embrace the complex nature of sustainable development and how to become future agents of change (Sammalisto et al., 2016). As empirical evidence shows, student-led action and initiatives can contribute to addressing this challenge (Duram and Williams, 2015).

There is wide consensus that stakeholder engagement is a key principle for sustainability integration at HEIs to assure the process is supported by the whole HEI community (Drupp et al., 2012; Ramísio et al., 2019). Drupp et al. (2012) argue that student-led action 'facilitate change by acting as (1) institutional innovator, (2) "boundary agent", and (3) creator of social and institutional learning spaces' (p. 733), and that they should feel stimulated to utilise their abilities towards making changes that would allow sustainability to happen within universities.

Murray (2018) carried out a literature review regarding sustainability initiatives led by students and noted that behavioural change initiatives that focus on mitigating the environmental impacts of the participants' actions were the most common, followed by policy changes and targeted education actions. Murray (2018) identifies the main barriers and drivers faced by student initiatives. In terms of barriers, insufficient student involvement, difficulty in influencing organisational change and lack of funding are mentioned. Regarding drivers, collaboration with other student groups, university professors and external stakeholders, and promoting interdisciplinary approaches are considered key. Student initiatives have incorporated social media and technology, which has modernised their collective and personal developments to inform and also to share their processes and achievements (Kerr and Hart-Steffes, 2012).

So far, the potential of student-led initiatives in the transformational processes of HEIs towards sustainability has not yet been sufficiently documented in the scientific literature (as mentioned, for example, by Drupp et al., 2012). Such studies are especially scarce in Latin America. The relevance of such studies lies in the fact that students may have a fundamental role in these sustainability endeavours within HEIs. Improving the understanding of student motivations and actions will allow: (1) the HEI to internalise and incorporate student-led sustainability initiatives into their own sustainability strategies; (2) the HEI to increase the commitment of this key stakeholder category; (3) the students to use their student-led initiatives as leverage to catalyse organisation-wide institutional change; (4) to identify patterns and success stories which can be shared with other HEIs.

The institutional culture where these sustainability transformation dynamics occur is diverse. Transparency, motivated by a shared objective, and the presence of so-called 'sustainability champions' play an essential part in these sustainability transformational processes at HEIs (Bauer et al., 2018; Kolleck and Bormann, 2014; Shriberg, 2002). As students are in the process of being educated and trained, they do not have much work experience, and hence a close partnership with the university staff is key to gaining a better understanding of their own projects' potential and limitations (Spira, 2013).

The purpose of the present work is to explore the scope of student-led action at universities in Latin America. This is achieved, first, by presenting the case study of the Faculty of Physical and Mathematical Sciences at the University of Chile (hereafter, FPMS). This Chilean case study focuses on student initiatives in terms of their involvement and impact at the university level, the type and reach of projects and the individual motivations of students in engaging in such initiatives. We study barriers to change and issue recommendations for people involved in other student-led sustainability actions. Second, the Chilean case study is analysed in light of the experience of four student-led initiatives at HEIs in Argentina, Bolivia, Mexico and Peru, with the aim of identifying patterns and providing a comparative view on the topic.

Section 2 presents the methodology, section 3 provides insights regarding student-led action in sustainability issues in four Latin American HEIs, section 4 describes the Chilean case study and section 5 discusses the findings. Section 6 concludes.

2. METHODOLOGY

First, an explorative study of student-led sustainability initiatives at HEIs in Argentina, Bolivia, Mexico, and Peru was carried out, and second an in-depth case study was conducted. Regarding the case study, it was carried out with a student-led initiative at the FPMS named the University Students Sustainability Congress (hereafter, Congress). This methodological approach mainly consisted of a literature review combined with interviews to the former sustainability director of the FPMS and to the Congress initiative director. In this way, it was possible to explore and analyse both the university's background and institutional context, and the student-led action developments in detail in terms of members, origins, projects, barriers and drivers encountered, and key achievements, among others.

2.1 Explorative Study of Student-led Sustainability Initiatives in a Subset of Latin American HEIs

To explore the scope of student-led initiatives towards sustainability in a subset of Latin American HEIs, an online survey was conducted targeting key stakeholders involved in student-led initiatives in these four HEIs. An informal network of students from Latin America and the Caribbean involved in climate change and sustainability action was created at the Conference of the Parties (COP) 25 event in Madrid, Spain, in December 2019. To identify university student groups leading sustainability efforts at HEIs, this particular network was contacted to ask its members to either participate in the study themselves if suitable, and if not, to indicate existing student-led sustainability initiatives at universities in their respective countries that might be interested in contributing. The distributed questionnaire focused on the following topics:

- number of members of the student initiative;
- perceived degree of the involvement and participation of students in the transformational process towards sustainability of the university;
- student initiative main projects' description;
- student initiative activities' emphasis: teaching, research, campus operations, outreach, sustainable lifestyles, governance;
- student initiative activities' scope: university level, city level, national level, international level;
- main barriers encountered;
- primary drivers to joining or creating the initiative; and
- recommendations to other student groups.

Based on these questions, we aimed to shed light on the relation between the student-led action and the HEI in which they are based, on the number of students involved, on the scope of their activities, as well as on associated motivational aspects.

The surveys were administered to university students who were currently part of sustainability initiatives in Latin America, excluding Chile. The questionnaire responses of these key resource persons participating in student-led sustainability initiatives at universities in Argentina, Bolivia, Mexico and Peru were obtained via Google Forms. The data collection process was carried out from 17 to 22 January 2020. The list of student initiatives that took part in this work is shown in Table 6.1. Content analysis and simple statistical analysis were used to examine the results of the open-ended and closed-ended questions, respectively.

2.2   Case Study: University of Chile

Subsequently, the case study of the FPMS was developed. This HEI is the oldest and main public Chilean university, founded in 1842, and it is an institution where the role of students in sustainability integration within the university has been essential, which makes it a relevant case study to examine.

Methodologically, the institutional context at the FPMS was approached through a literature review on its organisational experience in the sustainability transformational process. This was accompanied by interviews with key actors inside the university community such as the former sustainability director.

In this context, one of the most recent and significant student-led actions at the FPMS has been the Congress initiative. When compared to other student groups working on sustainability matters at the university, its level of achievement has been acknowledged mainly due to student engagement and the scope of the more complex and various tasks led by these students. To collect the data of this particular student endeavour, the Congress initiative director was approached, and an in-depth interview was conducted regarding open-ended questions according to the following themes:

Table 6.1   Overview of student-led sustainability initiatives explored in this work

Student Initiative	Country	University	University Funding	University Number of Students	Reference
Environmental citizenship and climate change	Bolivia	Unidad Educativa Nuestra Señora del Pilar, Cochabamba, Bolivia	Private	No data found	–
Technological surveillance for biological sciences	Mexico	Universidad Nacional Autónoma México	Public	356 530	(UNAM, n.d.)
Ecology and common house care[a] programme	Peru	Interuniversity 'Association of Evangelical University Groups of Peru': Universidad Nacional Mayor de San Marcos, Universidad Nacional Agraria La Molina, Universidad César Vallejo de Piura, Universidad Continental de Huancayo, Universidad Nacional de Trujillo, Universidad Privada del Norte de Trujillo, among others	Private and Public	>200 000	(Universidad Nacional Mayor de San Marcos, n.d.) (Universidad César Vallejo, n.d.) (Universidad Nacional de Trujillo, n.d.) (Universidad Privada del Norte de Trujillo, n.d.)
Green FAUBA	Argentina	Universidad de Buenos Aires	Public	308 748	(UBA, n.d.)

Note: a. The 'common house' is the way in which Catholics refer to the Earth, thus, common house care means caring for the shared planet.

- number of members of the student initiative;
- initiative origins and evolution;
- description of the student initiative projects and scope;
- main barriers encountered;
- primary drivers to create the initiative;
- key achievements of the initiative;
- observed learning outcomes of the students participating in the initiative; and
- recommendations to other student groups.

By following this two-track approach, the study aims to broadly characterise the scope of student-led action at HEIs in Latin America, as a way of strengthening the understanding of the motivations and activities of students who are involved in sustainability action at universities.

3. EXPLORATION OF STUDENT-LED SUSTAINABILITY INITIATIVES IN LATIN AMERICA

The regional experience shows an average number of students participating in the initiatives of 18.75, with a minimum of 15 and a maximum of 30. Also, three out of four case studies indicate that students have a medium degree of involvement in the transformational process towards sustainability in their universities, while one initiative indicated that their level of involvement is high.

The reported general description of the student-led action has been analysed by identifying keywords and looking for patterns. The resulting synthesis is as follows:

- Environmental citizenship and climate change at the Unidad Educativa Nuestra Señora del Pilar, Cochabamba, Bolivia: this initiative focuses on waste management through an agro-ecological system, along with outreach initiatives in the neighbourhood, working on endemic species and environmental education.
- Technological surveillance for biological sciences at the Universidad Nacional Autónoma México: this endeavour reports to support start-ups or companies with a focus on the 2030 Agenda for Sustainable Development.
- Ecology and common house care programme at the interuniversity Association of Evangelical University Groups of Peru: this student-led sustainability initiative develops environmental education with evangelical students, linking ecology and religion. They also work with wider communities.
- Green FAUBA at the Universidad de Buenos Aires: this initiative works on the circular economy for waste management, university community awareness and environmental education.

The four case HEIs reported a total of ten specific projects that are categorised as shown in Figure 6.1. These categories have been defined based on the four dimensions of HEIs: teaching, research, campus operations and outreach (working with internal and external communities). Governance (policy changes) and sustainable lifestyles (behavioural change) criteria have been added following the main types of student-led initiatives found by Murray (2018).

Three out of four student-led sustainability initiatives have reported a city-level reach, and one a university scope. In terms of the main barriers encountered for the survival of their student-led action, these are lack of commitment of students and insufficient awareness of the university community. To a lesser extent, reference is made to lack of resources and time, disinterest of the HEIs' stakeholders and institutional bureaucracy. This is shown in Figure 6.2.

The lack of commitment from the HEIs' management bodies partly explains the lack of engagement of the students who are participating in the movements and initiatives.

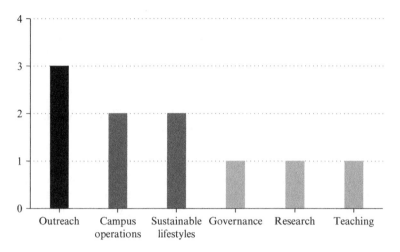

Figure 6.1   *Main project types of student-led sustainability initiatives (of a total of ten reported projects)*

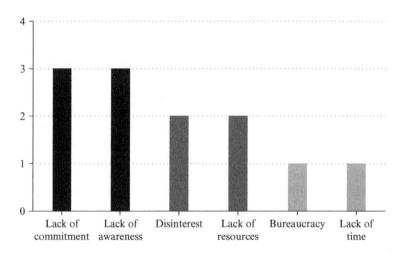

Figure 6.2   *Main barriers encountered by the student-led sustainability initiatives (number of times mentioned in the surveys out of a total of 12)*

Lack of awareness and/or disinterest within the institutional community (professors, non-academic staff and students not involved in the initiative) creates difficulties for student-led action, in terms of internal funding, institutional support and/or coalition building with other stakeholders.

The greater motivations declared by the interviewees to become part of these endeavours are to acquire new knowledge and skills, and the commitment itself of other young people who are part of these initiatives. Other incentives mentioned correspond to generating a positive impact, taking action in the socio-environmental crisis, becoming entrepreneurs and educating others.

Finally, recommendations provided to other student groups include: peer cooperation (three mentions), search for institutional support (two mentions), and generation of networks with external stakeholders (two mentions). Other notions that have been identified are teamwork, short- and long-term planning, and perseverance in the process.

4. THE CHILE CASE STUDY

The FPMS, in which the national case study is based, is one of the 14 faculties at the University of Chile. It hosts the School of Engineering (including mining, mechanical, chemical, industrial, electrical engineering). It has around 6000 students and 450 professors.

As has been previously suggested, student-led organisations have been key stakeholders in the transition from emergence to the formalisation phases of sustainability incorporation within the institution (Vargas, Mac-lean and Hugé, 2019). Bucchi, Jacques-Coper and Sánchez (2012) have documented the role of students in this organisation. This background has had a multiplier effect and has enabled several students' projects to flourish, one of the more recent and outstanding of them being the Congress initiative. Its level of advancement has been identified in comparison to other student-led actions at the university in terms of student involvement and the scope of the more complex tasks they have been able to lead.

The Congress beginnings relate to the conception and implementation of a student sustainability congress in the year 2016, and later turned into a non-governmental organisation (CEUS, n.d.). Its mission is to create a network that connects Chilean students and young professionals, who have a strong sustainability oriented profile and who are aiming to initiate their careers in sectors and positions associated with sustainable development. It currently has 51 members.

4.1 Institutional Context at the Faculty of Physical and Mathematical Sciences of the University of Chile

Rojas et al. (2017) describe the beginnings of the sustainability agenda at the FPMS of the University of Chile and identify three phases: (1) Oikos in 2005; (2) Sustainable Campus Commission in 2011; and (3) Office of Engineering for Sustainable Development in the year 2013. The work by Rojas et al. (2017) explains that Oikos was a student group that self-organised around the issue of waste management, implementing the first recycling system at the FPMS. Subsequently, after the realisation that sustainability matters at the university level required a wider lens, they engaged with the Sustainable Campus initiative. This entailed a participatory approach cross-cutting every dimension of the HEI. Thus, a request was presented to the Faculty Council to generate a Sustainable Campus Commission (second stage), which would be formed by non-academic staff, professors and students. Not long after, the availability of a full-time professional who would lead the planned projects and activities was requested. Subsequently, a sustainability director was hired and months after the Office of Engineering for Sustainable Development was established, which is a non-academic staff unit. The Office's vision is 'to promote and integrate a culture of engineering for sustainable development at the faculty, as an enhancing element of the training of the students' (Oficina de Ingeniería para la Sustentabilidad, n.d.).

A significant amount of the Office's endeavours were motivated by a Cleaner Production Agreement for universities deployed nationwide, which turned out to be a major driver and catalyst for Chilean HEIs to transition to sustainability integration in their institutions. The Cleaner Production Agreement was signed between the head of the universities involved and the Chilean government; thus, the authorities became more aware and committed. The mechanism demanded the accomplishment of 11 broader goals, which included at the same time several concrete actions to be executed. Some of these goals were to: develop a sustainability policy; promote sustainability related subjects in the curriculum; install recycling facilities on campus; and train professors and students (20 per cent) in sustainability. The FPMS has succeeded in the first stage of fulfilment of the agreement, along with other 13 universities (Agencia de Sustentabilidad y Cambio Climático, 2017), showing that this was a collective effort at the national level.

The FPMS transition towards sustainable development has been analysed under the social issue maturation framework by Vargas et al. (2019), a publication in which the following key milestones and accomplishments of the Office of Engineering for Sustainable Development are presented:

- sustainability policy design;
- sustainability award in sustainable construction category for the Beauchef 851 building because of its Leadership in Energy & Environmental Design (LEED) Gold Certification;
- realisation of energy audit;
- first calculation of the carbon footprint;
- design of a Minor in Engineering for Sustainability;
- implementation of the 'ReBeauchef' recycling system;
- development of a study on water management and efficiency;
- inauguration of the solar plant;
- organisation of two events to recycle e-waste;
- publication of the first sustainability newsletter;
- implementation of two work meetings on sustainability (with the campus community);
- design of an energy policy;
- implementation of a seminar about sustainability research in universities;
- compliance of the Cleaner Production Agreement;
- creation of a sustainable alumni network; and
- beginning of the sustainable hints/tips campaign. (Vargas et al., 2019, p. 447)

Thus, initially, the sustainability culture was relatively poor at the time of student group Oikos, and the sustainable development efforts were mostly student led. Reported lessons learned as part of strategy building towards a sustainable campus in the early stages of the maturation framework at the FPMS, in order to move from isolated actions to more advanced phases, are stated by Bucchi et al. (2012) as follows:

- learn from international experiences;
- incorporate the local mindset and habits into the projects;

- provide well-designed and robust initiatives to the authorities;
- work along with other university stakeholders to produce a shared perspective and plan;
- create alliances and collaborate for feedback and increased negotiating power; and
- produce a feasible plan that can be easily assessed.

After six years, when other non-student stakeholders joined, more members of the organisation could relate to sustainability principles and values, and developments became more tangible. Student initiatives then had the support from several professors, as the stakeholders' constellations had changed. At this point it has been almost entirely a bottom-up approach.

Due to their political pressures, the establishment of the internal sustainability governing body (Office of Engineering for Sustainable Development) by the authorities and the signing of the external commitment of the Cleaner Production Agreement were achieved. This significantly changed the inner dynamics and power structures in such a way that top-down measures were adopted, the authorities became involved in decision-making processes in sustainability-related projects and more resources were allocated.

Over the time period 2005–19, the sustainability culture and accomplishments were significantly upgraded for four main reasons: first, because of the existence of sustainability champions who joined forces in a bottom-up scheme; second due to the eventual and partial commitment of the authorities; third because of the implementation of a sustainability governing body placed high within the university hierarchy; and fourth due to the growing interest and awareness from professors, students and non-academic staff in sustainability topics.

4.2   The Congress Experience

The FPMS institutional sustainability path has been compatible with the emergence of various student-led action groups, and the Congress initiative has been particularly successful in terms of number of students actively participating and the wide range of activities organised.

Congress origins and transitional phases
In 2015, the Engineering Students Union's (CEI by its Spanish acronym) sustainability commission was created. With the creation of this commission, the position of 'sustainability delegate' was generated, whose main role was to represent students in front of the Office of Engineering for Sustainable Development and the Sustainable Campus Commission. The central CEI sustainability commission's tasks were the organisation of events to promote sustainability education and awareness, management of 'Sustainability Week', and coordination of the work of the 13 sustainability delegates coming from different careers/departments.

For the CEI 2016 team, one of the planned projects was the creation of a national sustainability student congress, which would bring undergraduates from various HEIs into a learning space. The student leader of the congress idea stated that her drive to conceive this project was, first, to share best practices being successfully implemented at the FPMS University of Chile, which had positioned itself as a frontrunner in Chile, and where students had been key change agents. Second, the need for a more interdisciplinary approach was identified, and this congress could provide opportunities to further collaborate beyond the engineering field. In terms of the motivation to join student-led action, the student leader of the congress idea has affirmed it to be to: 'do something different to only studying', 'complement my career with more applied aspects', and 'contribute to sustainable development in my future job'.

During 2016, the first University Student Sustainability Congress was organised by a group of eight students and led by the CEI sustainability delegates. The Congress focused on giving a sustainability perspective to engineering and science, and to broaden the concept of sustainability, which was mainly centred on ecology at that time. It was funded by a private company and the FPMS, and there were only 35 student attendees.

The organising team held weekly meetings; nevertheless, the inefficiency of the team was problematic. This was mainly due to inexperience and the inability to achieve some of the most imperative aspects (activities, presenters, sponsorships, etc.), and the small number of participants in the coordination efforts. Thus, one of the central learning outcomes of the first Congress experience was that it is indeed necessary to generate a larger team with previously defined tasks in a planning phase. Unfortunately, the first Congress did not achieve its goal of uniting students from universities in different geographical areas of the country and from different careers.

However, a second attempt of the Congress was pursued. As anticipated, the 2017 version had clear goals: to ameliorate the internal logistics, to increase the number of members of the organising team, and to invite a greater number of student attendees with more diverse backgrounds. An open meeting was held as an invitation to become part of the team and 20 students joined. This time, the Congress had 68 attendees from 13 HEIs.

By the end of 2017, a part of the team made the decision to create a non-governmental organisation (NGO). Its main objective would be to become a meeting point for students and young professionals interested in pursuing their careers in sustainability-related sectors. In March 2018, the NGO was officially founded and four guiding dimensions were defined: education, society, environment and sustainable development. The type of projects undertaken are closely related to environmental education, capacity building, networking and youth participation in public policy making.

During 2018, the NGO organised the third congress, entitled 'Chile and Its Natural Assets: A Look Into the Future'. It had 207 participants and it was held in three different universities. In addition to this emblematic endeavour, the following supplementary projects were executed – widening the scope of the activities that had been developed at the time:

- environmental education in schools with students coming from low-income families;
- internships with students to work on the creation of a park in the Petorca Valley; and
- internships that allowed three NGO members to travel to Haiti to contribute to the implementation of a solar energy system.

During 2019, the NGO began to move from the university realm towards broader

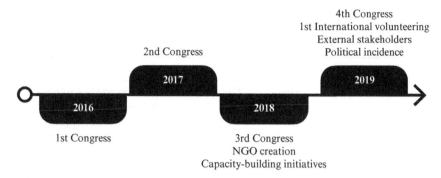

Figure 6.3   Congress initiative trajectory

society. The latter was accomplished by collaborating with larger and more experienced organisations. In such a way, novel challenges were pursued, such as:

- Cooperation in the implementation of the Social Summit for Climate Action, which was an alternative climate summit to the COP 25.
- Participation at the COP 25 in Spain.
- Creation of the Chilean Youth Climate Action Agenda. This process and corresponding final document aims to increase the political influence of young people on socio-environmental issues.

Finally, the Congress initiative trajectory is summarised in Figure 6.3.

Congress influence and recommendations
This subsection provides an overview regarding the Congress initiative impacts, barriers encountered for the student initiative to survive over time, and a three-step guide, which might be of help to other students in the implementation of their own activities. It has been stated in the present work that the number of participants, and the reach of the projects and accomplishments of the student-led action are suggested as metrics with which to measure the success of the student initiatives. Accordingly, the Congress had 53 members in its first year as an NGO and its main achievements are presented in Table 6.2. Participation in the Congress has had two main reported benefits for the students' profes-

Table 6.2   Congress main achievements

Achievement	Year	Reach
National Environmental Award by the Recyclápolis Foundation	2017	National level
Honourable mention of the Faculty of Physical and Mathematical Sciences at the University of Chile Award	2017	University level
Authorisation as an observer organisation at COP 25	2019	International level
Winners of the Volunteers Fund of the National Youth Institute	2019	National level

Table 6.3   Main competencies and concepts encouraged by the Congress initiative in its members

Competence	Concept	Mechanism/Activity
Interpersonal competence	Strengths, weaknesses, success, and failure in teams Concepts of leadership	The process of transforming the Congress into an NGO has enabled the acquisition of skills linked to this competence, due to the required leadership to achieve collaboration between different actors and the ability to negotiate, among others
Strategic competence	Instrumentalisation and alliances	The Congress initiative has deepened the ability to work with external stakeholders, where students not only communicate with peers but also with representatives of companies, other NGOs, governmental agencies, etc.

sional training. First, teamwork: the opportunity to participate in a diverse group of young people enhances the way in which students relate to their peers, which often does not occur in traditional courses. The work environment has allowed them to perform better as an individual, through the integration of sustainability values, gender equality and a strong sense of respect and responsibility. Second, career preparation: the contribution in the initiative facilitates and encourages students to learn about sustainability in more depth. This somehow shortens the distance students must advance towards developing their professional occupations in sustainable development-related sectors and positions.

If this particular experience is analysed under the five key sustainability competencies, as proposed by Wiek, Withycombe and Redman (2011), the leading concepts declared by the initiative's director that the Congress experience stimulates within its members are presented in Table 6.3. These are shown along with the internal mechanisms and/or activities of the student initiative that allow these learning processes to occur.

However, among the most difficult obstacles to overcome for the student initiative to survive over time has been the fundraising process, especially when the organisation was not officially documented. A second relevant reported difficulty is managing the timings and the coordination between the members, as tasks are voluntarily adopted by students and other commitments might be more relevant to them in a specific period of time. Finally, the inexperience of the student group has shown to be a significant barrier to delivering the expected outcomes on time to assure the performance of the committed tasks.

Certain recommendations can be made from the Congress experience, which might be of interest to other students interested in starting or already implementing sustainability student-led action. Thus, a brief three-step guide is proposed, as a tangible takeaway that might be transferable to different backgrounds:

1.   Create a common vision and mission for the endeavour. In view of this, design well-defined and unambiguous projects that should incorporate clear objectives, goals, activities and deadlines.
2.   Get to know your team and plan accordingly. Learn how to manage the internal

organisation of the participants in terms of time availability and capabilities, considering their simultaneous academic and personal commitments. Likewise, being aware of their expectations, knowledge, ideas and views is essential.

3.   Identify your key stakeholders. These actors can be placed both inside the institution (authorities, professors, non-academic staff) and/or outside the university (governmental agencies, NGOs, or others).

In addition, it is advisable to continuously reflect on what the benefits of the endeavour are, and to understand and work on both its strengths and weaknesses. At the same time, a robust communication plan will increasingly benefit your organisation.

5.   DISCUSSION

First, the size of the FPMS, in terms of number of students, compared with those of the regional case studies, is significantly inferior. Nevertheless, the number of the Congress initiative members is 2.7 times higher than the regional average.

Drupp et al. (2012) have emphasised the relevance of student commitment as a key principle in sustainability incorporation at universities. Accordingly, Latin American case studies included in the present work report a medium to high level of involvement in the process of transformation towards sustainability in their own institutions, while at the FPMS, evidence shows that student participation has been fundamental in such developments between the years 2005 and 2019. In fact, in that period of time at least seven student-led initiatives have flourished at the FPMS, in addition to the Congress initiative. These have worked on various aspects such as promoting bike use, internal community awareness, managing e-waste, reusing clothing, vegan food, and gardens.

Murray (2018) identifies that behavioural change initiatives were the leading type of activities implemented by student-led action, followed by policy changes and education. The regional evidence is well aligned with those findings as it incorporates sustainable lifestyles, governance and teaching. However, the leading aspect is outreach (collaborating with internal and/or external communities), as in the Congress experience.

It is worth mentioning that the scope of the Latin America case studies are either at the university or city level, while the Congress initiative has developed international projects. The number of student participants, the effective leadership, the scope of the projects developed and the alliances acquired might explain these accomplishments.

Murray (2018) identifies that in terms of barriers, insufficient student involvement, difficulty in influencing organisational change and lack of funding are crucial in student-led action. The regional case studies similarly report aspects of student engagement and insufficient resources, but lack of awareness appears to be one of the most important barriers faced. The Congress initiative also states lack of funding, and proposes new challenges like coordination difficulties and inexperience. In this regard, Spira (2013) shows that students need to form close partnerships with staff for the success of their own initiatives.

The primary drivers to create or join the student initiative, as declared by the interviewees both at the Latin American and national levels, are to develop skills and gain further knowledge, to be part of a committed group of young people and to become a change agent in sustainability issues.

In terms of recommendations made to other student groups, stakeholder engagement and project management are predominant elements found in all case studies included in the present study – the four regional and the Chilean case. Additionally, the Congress initiative experience explicitly mentions communication actions, which is to a certain extent coherent with the idea presented by Kerr and Hart-Steffes (2012) that young activists have incorporated social media into their collective and personal development.

Regarding the FPMS sustainability incorporation trajectory, it seems to be consistent with Ramísio et al.'s (2019) suggestion that balancing top-down and bottom-up approaches is appropriate. Also, the authorities' eventual commitment and the existence of sustainability champions relate to the findings of Hugé et al. (2018) about an at least implicit commitment from the university's hierarchy and the engagement of sustainability frontrunners as fundamental elements for success. Furthermore, the fact that the Office of Engineering for Sustainable Development was placed high in the organisational hierarchy is coherent with what has been described in the literature as the need to position a sustainability actor close to the university leaders (Mader, Scott and Abdul Tazak, 2013; Scott et al., 2012; Littledyke, Manolas and Littledyke, 2013, cited in Bauer, 2018).

6. CONCLUSIONS AND FINAL REMARKS

This study explored student-led sustainability initiatives at HEIs in Latin America, and focused on the Chilean experience of the Congress initiative. In general terms, the regional case studies have a medium to high level of involvement in the process of transformation towards sustainability in their own institutions. The leading type of activities implemented by student-led action are outreach oriented and, excluding the Congress initiative, their scope is either at the university or city level.

Lack of awareness within the institutional community (professors, non-academic staff and students not involved in the initiative) has been reported to be one of the most important barriers faced by student initiatives for the survival of their endeavour.

The FPMS development initially began bottom-up, with students as the primary actors. These 'sustainability champions' formed a small and active team, which led to the set-up of, for example, a sustainability commission, and the Congress organisations.

The university culture and its decision-making procedures have been fundamental in this transformational process towards sustainable development, enabling the implementation of specific projects and facilitating formal collaboration with professors. Thus, student-led sustainability initiatives have been integrated into the institutional structure of the FPMS.

Overall, the case studies we report in this work highlight that student-led sustainability action is more likely to emerge: (1) in institutions that reward and formally incorporate student actions; (2) if barriers such as lack of student involvement, insufficient resources, and coordination difficulties are overcome; and (3) if these student-led initiatives can gather support from both internal and external stakeholders. The lessons that we learned through this short explorative study may be valuable to inform student-led sustainability actions in HEIs worldwide.

REFERENCES

Agencia de Sustentabilidad y Cambio Climático. (2017). Estas son las 14 universidades más sustentables de Chile. Accessed 24 January 2020 at http://www.agenciasustentabilidad.cl/noticias/estas_son_las_14_universidades.

Bauer, M., Bormann, I. and Kummer, B. et al. (2018). Sustainability governance at universities: using a governance equalizer as a research heuristic. *Higher Education Policy*, 31(4), 491–511.

Bucchi, F., Jacques-Coper, M. and Sánchez, P. (2012). Towards a sustainable campus at Universidad de Chile: the key role of students in sustainable development at universities. In W. Leal Filho (ed.), *Sustainable Development at Universities: New Horizons* (pp. 845–56). Bern/Frankfurt: Peter Lang Scientific Publishers.

CEUS. (n.d.). Nuestra historia. Accessed 24 January at https://www.ceuschile.cl/sobre-nosotros/.

Drupp, M., Esguerra, A. and Keul, L. et al. (2012). Change from below – student initiatives for universities in sustainable development. In W. Leal Filho (ed.), *Sustainable Development at Universities: New Horizons* (pp. 733–42). Bern/Frankfurt: Peter Lang Scientific Publishers.

Duram, L.A. and Williams, L.L. (2015). Growing a student organic garden within the context of university sustainability initiatives. *International Journal of Sustainability in Higher Education*, 16(1), 3–15.

Hugé, J., Mac-lean, C. and Vargas, L. (2018). Maturation of sustainability in engineering faculties – from emerging issue to strategy? *Journal of Cleaner Production*, 172, 4277–85.

Kerr, K. and Hart-Steffes, J. (2012). Sustainability, student affairs, and students. *New Directions for Student Services*, 137, 7–17.

Kolleck, N. and Bormann, I. (2014). Analyzing trust in innovation networks: combining quantitative and qualitative techniques of social network analysis. *Zeitschrift für Erziehungswissenschaft*, 17, 9–27.

Littledyke, M., Manolas, E. and Littledyke, R.A. (2013). A systems approach to education for sustainability in higher education. *International Journal of Sustainability in Higher Education*, 14(4), 367–83.

Mader, C., Scott, G. and Abdul Razak, D. (2013). Effective change management, governance and policy for sustainability transformation in higher education. *Sustainability Accounting, Management and Policy Journal*, 4(3), 264–84.

Murray, J. (2018). Student-led action for sustainability in higher education: a literature review. *International Journal of Sustainability in Higher Education*, 19(6), 1095–110.

Oficina de Ingeniería para la Sustentabilidad (n.d.). Accessed 24 January 2020 at http://ingenieria.uchile.cl/oficina-de-ingenieria-para-la-sustentabilidad/quienes-somos/106318/oficina-de-ingenieria-para-la-sustentabilidad.

Ramísio, P.J., Pinto, L.M.C. and Gouveia, N. (2019). Sustainability strategy in higher education institutions: lessons learned from a nine-year case study. *Journal of Cleaner Production*, 222, 300–309.

Rojas, M., Mac-lean, C. and Morales, J. et al. (2017). Climate change education and literacy at the Faculty of Physical and Mathematical Sciences of the University of Chile. *International Journal of Global Warming*, 12(3–4), 347–65.

Sammalisto, K., Sundstrom, A. and von Haartman, R. et al. (2016). Learning about sustainability – what influences students' self-perceived sustainability actions after undergraduate education? *Sustainability*, 8(6), https://doi.org/10.3390/su8060510.

Scott, G., Tilbury, D., Sharp, L. and Deane, E. (2012). *Turnaround Leadership for Sustainability in Higher Education (Executive Summary 2012)*. University of West Sydney. Accessed 24 January 2020 at https://www.uws.edu.au/__data/assets/pdf_file/0018/411075/TLSHE_Final_Exec_Summary_HA_12_Nov_12_pdf_version.pdf.

Shriberg, M.P. (2002). Sustainability in U.S. higher education: organizational factors influencing campus environmental performance and leadership [Doctoral dissertation]. Accessed 28 January 2020 at http://citeseerx.ist.psu.edu/viewdoc/download?doi=10.1.1.333.2202&rep=rep1&type=pdf.

Spira, F. (2013). Driving the energy transition at Maastricht University? Analysing the transformative potential on energy efficiency of the student-driven and staff-supported Maastricht University Green Office (MSc dissertation). Accessed 28 January 2020 at http://rootability.com/wp-content/uploads/2013_Spira_GO-Maastricht-energy-efficiency.pdf.

Universidad de Buenos Aires (UBA). (n.d.). Accessed 24 January 2020 at http://www.uba.ar/comunicacion/noticia.php?id=3319.

Universidad César Vallejo. (n.d.). Accessed 24 January 2020 at https://estudiaperu.pe/universidades/ucv/.

Universidad Nacional Autónoma de México (UNAM). (n.d.). Accessed 24 January 2020 at http://www.estadistica.unam.mx/numeralia/.

Universidad Nacional de Trujillo. (n.d.). Accessed 24 January 2020 at https://estudiaperu.pe/universidades/unitru/.

Universidad Nacional Mayor de San Marcos. (n.d.). Accessed 24 January 2020 at https://www.unmsm.edu.pe/.

Universidad Privada del Norte de Trujillo. (n.d.). Accessed 24 January 2020 at https://www.laureate.net/es/school/universidad-privada-del-norte/.

Vargas, L., Mac-lean, C. and Hugé, J. (2019). The maturation process of incorporating sustainability in universities. *International Journal of Sustainability in Higher Education*, 20(3), 441–51.

Wiek, A., Withycombe, L. and Redman, C.L. (2011). Key competencies in sustainability: a reference framework for academic program development. *Sustainability Science*, 6(2), 203–18.

7. Understanding recycling behavior in the university: a case study from Southern Chile

Rodrigo Vargas-Gaete, Paula Guarda-Saavedra and Javiera Eskuche

1. INTRODUCTION

Solid waste generation by the modern consumer society has grown steadily in line with world population growth, as well as with the economic development of countries (Hernández-Berriel et al., 2016; Universidad de Chile, 2016). The generation of municipal solid waste (MSW) in Latin America increases at an estimated rate of ~5 percent per year, moving from 130 million tons produced in 2012, to 220 million tons projected by 2025 (Hoornweg and Bhada-Tata, 2012). The previous projection, which is based on empirical data, makes waste management crucial, considering the threat that such a volume of solid waste may represent for public health and thus for local and national governments.

On average, the most developed countries of the world, members of the Organisation for Economic Co-operation and Development (OECD), generate around 2.2 kg/capita/day (Universidad de Chile, 2016). In Chile (18 million population), solid waste generation is estimated at 1.2 kg/capita/day, totaling about 7.5–7.8 million tons of MSW waste per year (ibid.).

Recycling is one of the most powerful alternatives to regular unmanaged waste disposal; it promotes material savings by converting waste into new materials and objects, and moreover, it also helps in the reduction of greenhouse gas emissions by limiting the consumption of fresh raw materials (Geissdoerfer et al., 2017). Recycling is the third component of the 'Reduce, Reuse, and Recycle' waste management strategy. It can be oriented into a circular economy approach, in which resource use, waste production emissions and energy are minimized to create a closed system of positive interactions between the economy and the environment (Geissdoerfer et al., 2017; González et al., 2018). In Chile, it is estimated that ~85–95 percent of the total MSW ends up in landfills, and only 5–15 percent is destined for recycling, including organic waste composting (Comisión Nacional del Medioambiente [CONAMA], 2009; Vásquez, 2011). This contrasts with what happens, for example, in Germany, where about 62 percent of the total MSW is recycled, surpassing the European Union's target goal of recycling over 50 percent of MSW by 2020 (Fischer, 2013).

Since the 1970s, universities from around the globe have encouraged sustainability practices (Wright, 2002). This was first declared in 1972, at the United Nations Conference on the Human Environment held in Stockholm (United Nations, 1973). Here, special importance was given to higher education entities to act as spearheads on environmental practices, including efforts to improve waste management models, energy reduction and greener buildings (ibid.). In this scenario, the idea of promoting sustainability on university campuses emerged. Thus, each educational entity should promote, according to its capacity, a sustainable environment and/or the implementation of flexible models and policies to be used by the academic community (Velazquez et al., 2006). Currently, there is an international network representing over 80 universities from 30 countries that promotes commitment to sustainability and leadership in research that encourages best practices by universities and knowledge mobilization (i.e., the International Sustainable Campus Network [ISCN], 2018). In Chile there are 14 universities that currently participate in a national network of sustainability campuses called Red Campus Sustentable (RCS), which has similar objectives to the ISCN (Eskuche, 2019; RCS, 2019). Their concrete actions support four of the 17 Sustainable Development Goals: health and wellness, quality education, climate action and partnerships to achieve the goals (RCS, 2019).

The Universidad de La Frontera (UFRO) has been part of the national network of sustainability campuses since 2019 (Eskuche, 2019). Located in Temuco (~300 000 inhabitants), the main city of the Araucanía region located ~650 km south of Santiago de Chile, UFRO is the largest university in the Araucanía region, with six faculties and around 9000 students. Around 340 000 tons/year of MSW are generated in the Araucanía region, representing ~4.5 percent of the total national MSW of Chile. About 57 percent of the people of the Araucanía region declare that they separate waste for recycling, which is above the Chilean average (~50 percent; Browne et al., 2016). It is important to clarify that this does not mean that >50 percent of the waste is recycled, but how many people state that they separate at least some materials for recycling (Browne et al., 2016; CONAMA, 2009). At UFRO, there is an estimated total daily production of MSW that varies between 668 and 1065 kg, from which ~45 percent is classified as non-recyclable, ~42 percent corresponds to compostable organic waste, and about 13 percent to recyclable waste, like paper (~10 percent), plastics, glass and metal (~3 percent) (Sepulveda, 2019). Waste management on campus is the main concern of students, academics and workers of the university, followed by paper misuse (Riveros, 2019). Moreover, 636 out of 909 surveyed people from the university declared that they separate waste for recycling on a regular basis at home (i.e., 70 percent), and about 50 percent mention the use of recycling containers on campus (ibid.). Nevertheless, there is no official data quantifying current amounts of waste disposed for recycling at UFRO. Although several recycling campaigns have been implemented since the mid-1990s, most of them have not continued long term, given the lack of a coordinated support from the university, lack of funding and/or motivation of the people involved (Barra et al., 2017). What determines the motivation of someone to recycle in this scenario?

Individual behaviors dealing with waste separation can be of diverse origins, from aesthetic to economic motivations, associated with more personal altruistic beliefs, or external normative regulations (Moreno-Ávila and Rincón-Salazar, 2009). Individual beliefs on this matter can be influenced by the perception that each person has of the natural environment (Palavecinos et al., 2016). For instance, several works have identified that women usually show greater concern for the environment and more pro-environmental and ecological behaviors than men (Browne et al., 2016; Palavecinos et al., 2016). Understanding factors that influence people's ecological behavior, such as waste separation, is relevant information that can successfully orientate initiatives, campaigns and policies to foster recycling. Previous studies in the United States have identified recyclers as older and wealthier, living in households with fewer members, and more liberal in political orientation (Morgan and Hughes, 2006). In Europe, it has been identified that behavior patterns that lead to waste reduction are seldom socially oriented, and are very reliant on purely personal 'altruistic' attitudes (Cecere et al., 2014). In Chile, no study has focused on understanding which variables are common to people who recycle.

In this work, through a survey analysis, the main attributes of students who declared they separated solid waste for recycling on a regular basis were investigated. We sought to learn about ecological behaviors of students at UFRO. For this, two guiding questions were used: (1) Which variables are associated with waste separation for recycling by students at UFRO? (2) What are the main motivations for the practice of waste separation for recycling by students at UFRO? Based on these, the objective of this work was to characterize the main attributes of students who recycle solid waste in the university, unveiling variables that can favorably predict this behavior within the studied population. Thus, variables favorably associated with the separation of solid waste in UFRO students were considered, analyzing which motivations are identified for waste separation by students who declare they recycle. Finally, information and ideas to encourage solid waste separation in university students were considered, presenting this case study based on local empirical evidence, as an example to support recycling plans at a broader level.

2.   METHODS

2.1   The Survey Instrument

An online survey was designed and distributed to ascertain basic behavioral information on waste separation from students, using the mailing lists provided by UFRO. All participants agreed to participate in the investigation voluntarily, and each participant was assigned an ID to ensure protection of confidentiality and the anonymity of their data subject to the Declaration of Helsinki (World Medical Association [WMA], 2014). A total of 262 surveys were answered from which 261 were completed and processed through the QuestionPro platform, which was available for online responses for about one month (99.6 percent valid answers, December 2018; QuestionPro, 2018). The questionnaire was designed to create a correlational model investigation (*sensu* Palavecinos et al., 2016). Three sections were included: (a) sociodemographic data; (b) behavioral information; and (c) motivation/values related with waste separation (Table 7.1).

First, (a) sociodemographic data were considered: gender, age, ethnicity (i.e., belonging to an indigenous community or not), faculty (i.e., categorical data identifying one of the six faculties of the university), and student status (undergraduate/graduate student). Second, (b) behavioral information included questions dealing with: spiritual beliefs of the participants, the importance of being involved in social associations, regularly practicing physical activity (World Health Organization [WHO], 2010), and how closely connected they felt to rural/natural environments. Finally, each participant was asked if he or she separated waste for recycling on a regular basis (Table 7.1) – regular basis, is understood to mean that each person separates waste at least on a weekly basis (Browne et al., 2016). The survey we used to collect our data was peer reviewed by two professionals with experience in sustainability and sociological surveys, respectively. Moreover, a short validation process was performed with ten students.

Table 7.1   Description of the data obtained by the applied instrument

Data	Description (Alternatives)
(a) Sociodemographic data	
Gender	Female/Male/Other
Age	Years
Ethnic origin*	Indigenous origin/No indigenous origin
Student status	Undergraduate/Graduate
Faculty	Faculty of Agricultural and Forestry Sciences/ Faculty of Education, Social Sciences and Humanities/Faculty of Engineering and Sciences/Faculty of Legal and Business Sciences/ Faculty of Medicine/Faculty of Dentistry
(b) Behavioral information	
Select if you actively participate in any spiritual group*	Catholic/Protestant/Ethnic, Indigenous/Oriental/ Other/None
Select if you belong to some community participation organization*	None/Student organization/Neighborhood/ Sports/Ecological/Pastoral/Social/Other
Do you practice regular physical activity, (i.e., at least three times a week > 40 minutes each time)? (Adapted from WHO, 2010)	Yes/No
Select whether you have lived or resided temporarily (> three weeks) in a rural/ natural environment*	Yes/No
Do you separate waste for recycling at home on a regular basis? (Browne et al., 2016)	Yes/No

Note: Variables marked with an (*) were combined from several categories into a binary format to facilitate analysis (e.g., ethnic origin options included: Mapuche/Huilliche/Pehuenche and others, which were recategorized into: indigenous origin/no indigenous origin).

Moreover, to understand which motivations were related with waste separation, for the subset of students who declared they recycled ($n = 149$), a set of statements and questions dealing with (c) motivation/values related to waste separation were included. This was aimed at identifying pro-environmental conducts, understood as conscious human behaviors to protect, preserve and/or minimize the negative impact on the environment (Ones et al., 2015; Palavecinos et al., 2016; Table 7.2).

2.2   Data Analyses

The QuestionPro web-based software was used to explore and download the raw databases (QuestionPro, 2018). Sociodemographic and behavioral information of the participants was synthesized using percentages, and to create tables contrasting the information of students that either separate waste for recycling, or not. The information related to motivations/values of students who declared they practiced waste separation was conducted in a similar way. All statistical analyses were performed using R (R Development Core, 2018).

Table 7.2   Instrument to characterize motivations/values related to students that declared they practice waste separation (n = 149)

	Motivation/Value
I recycle because . . .	1. It is a habit, I learned it in my family and we all do it/We all do it in my group of friends
	2. I am interested in human sustainability and doing my bit
	3. I am concerned about the problem of waste and the future of the planet
	4. It is a way to activate the local economy
What motivates me to continue recycling is . . .	1. I like to contribute to the local economy
	2. I like to motivate more people to recycle
	3. Media campaigns
	4. I feel good about myself and that's enough for me
How can recycling be encouraged in the city (Temuco)?*	1. Incentives and outreach
	2. Penalties, fines to people that do not separate waste
	3. To implement a differentiated waste collection/More recycling points in the city
	4. To encourage recycled materials economy

Note: For the last question of this section (*), respondents could mark several answers.

To identify variables that were significantly related to the separation of waste for recycling, classification tree analyses were used (library 'party'; Hothorn, Hornik and Zeileis, 2012; R Development Core, 2018). This was possible because in the database waste separation was treated as a dichotomous (i.e., logistic) variable; either you separated (i.e., presence: 1) or not (i.e., absence: 0). Thus, it was possible to predict waste separation as a function of sociodemographic and/or behavioral variables (Table 7.1). At each step of the analysis, one explanatory variable was selected from all available variables based on the best separation of two homogeneous groups using a permutation test; this point was determined by a numerical value (threshold) of the explanatory variable (Hothorn et al., 2012). The minimum sum of weights considered in the analyses were ten participants for splitting, and seven participants for terminal nodes (ibid.).

3.   RESULTS

From the 261 students that participated in the survey, 149 (57 percent) declared they separated waste for recycling, while 112 (43 percent) stated that they did not perform any waste separation (Table 7.3). Considering the sociodemographic data, women separated more than men and three-quarters of graduate students declared they recycled, compared with only about half of undergraduates (Table 7.3). When looking at the behavioral information, people who mentioned that they have some rural/natural environment experience, as well as people that participated in associations/organizations and performed regular physical activity seemed to recycle more than those that did not have a relationship with rural places, nor participated in associations and/or doing exercise regularly (Table 7.3).

*Table 7.3   Description of the participants of the survey (*n = 261*)*

Variable	Separate Waste (%) (*n* = 149)	Not Separate Waste (%) (*n* = 112)	Total (%) (*n* = 261)
(a) Sociodemographic data			
Gender			
Female	109 (61%)	72 (39%)	181 (69%)
Male	39 (50%)	39 (50%)	78 (30%)
Other*	1 (50%)	1 (50%)	2 (1%)
Total	149 (57%)	112 (43%)	261 (100%)
Average age (± standard deviation)	22.3 ± 4.7	24.9 ± 6.3	23.7 ± 5.8
Ethnic origin			
Indigenous origin	28 (57%)	21 (43%)	49 (19%)
No indigenous origin	121 (57%)	91 (43%)	212 (81%)
Student status			
Undergraduate	116 (53%)	101 (47%)	217 (83%)
Graduate	33 (75%)	11 (25%)	44 (17%)
(b) Behavioral information			
Religion/Spirituality			
No	102 (56%)	81 (44%)	183 (70%)
Yes	47 (60%)	31 (40%)	78 (30%)
Participation in associations/organizations			
No	92 (54%)	77 (46%)	169 (65%)
Yes	57 (62%)	35 (38%)	92 (35%)
Rural/Natural environment experience			
No	36 (42%)	49 (58%)	85 (33%)
Yes	113 (64%)	63 (36%)	176 (77%)
Practice regular physical activity (exercise)			
No	51 (50%)	52 (50%)	103 (39%)
Yes	98 (62%)	60 (38%)	158 (61%)

Note: Information is presented from students who declared they did or did not separate waste for recycling.

The age of the participants was the most important predictor of waste separation, followed by rural/natural environment experience and exercise (Figure 7.1a). The highest probability (about 75 percent) for waste separation for recycling was for students older than 21 years old, who practice physical activity on a regular basis. When removing the age variable from the analyses, natural environment experience was significantly related with a higher probability for waste separation (~65 percent; Figure 7.1b).

Considering the motivations for recycling, most students that declared to separate waste for recycling (*n* = 149) mentioned that they did it because they felt good personally, or because they wanted to encourage more people to recycle (Figure 7.2a). Almost three-quarters of the people that separated waste identified their main motivation for recycling as their concern about the 'waste problem' and the 'future of the planet' (Figure 7.2b). To encourage recycling in the city, most people mentioned that the solution is to implement a differentiated waste collection and more recycling points (Figure 7.2c).

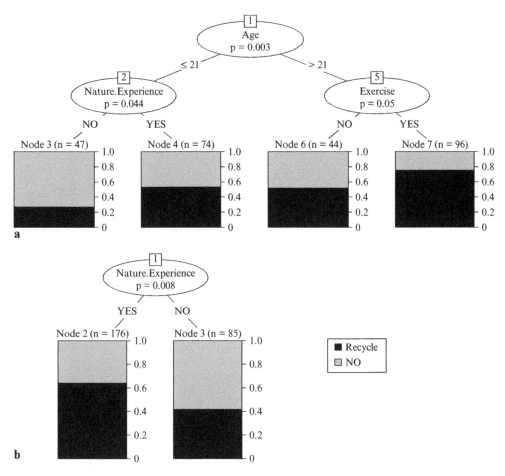

Figure 7.1 Classification tree analyses to predict the separation/no separation of waste by students of UFRO (n = 261), based on a conditional inference tree model. The encircled explanatory variables are those showing the strongest association with the response variable (i.e., separation of waste = Recycle; no separation of waste = NO). Values on lines connecting explanatory variables indicate splitting criteria; for example, the first split of Figure 7.1a separates students ≤ 21 years old (left side of the split) from those > 21 years old (right side of the split). Numbers in boxes above the explanatory variable indicate the node hierarchical number. P-values at each node represent the test of independence between the listed independent variable and the response variable. 'n = x' over terminal nodes indicates the number of persons classified in that node. The predicted waste separation is given by the terminal block representing the probability of waste separation (Recycle, dark part of the block) or no waste separation (NO, gray part of the block). Explanatory variables included were all sociodemographic and behavioral information from Table 7.1 (Figure 7.1a). For Figure 7.1b, the sociodemographic variable 'age' was not included

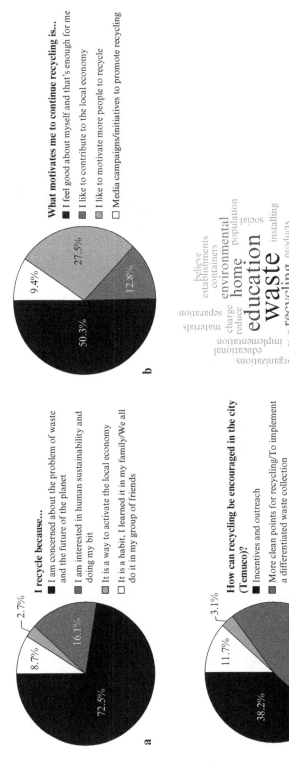

Figure 7.2 *Main motivations identified by students who declared they separated waste for recycling at UFRO (n = 149; see Table 7.2). The word cloud (Figure 7.2d) identifies the most repeated words when replying to 'How can recycling be encouraged in the city?' Those who answered 'Other' were able to write down their ideas. The larger the type size of the word, the most repeated among the received answers*

4.   DISCUSSION

4.1   Attributes of Students Who Separate Waste for Recycling at the University

Based on our survey, about 57 percent of the students at UFRO declared that they separate waste for recycling, which is quite concordant with the official data of Chile for the Araucanía region (Browne et al., 2016). This percentage is a little more conservative than what has been reported previously at UFRO, when including academics and administrative staff (~72 percent; Riveros, 2019). This makes sense considering that the age of the participants was the most important variable in predicting recycling, and most academics and workers of the university are older than 21 years (the significant threshold given by the analysis) (Figure 7.1a). Similarly, other studies in Chile have also reported that older people present more ecological behaviors than younger ones, independent of whether people live in rural or urban environments (Moyano-Díaz et al., 2017).

The rural/natural environment experience was also identified as one of the variables that increases the chances of recycling by students. This means that someone who has had a more direct connection with rural or natural environments is more likely to separate waste than someone associated with urban environments. This could be understood when considering that separating organic waste is traditionally done in rural places in Chile, for feeding the animals and/or composting for the orchard (Browne et al., 2016). In addition, other studies have identified that rural places manifest a higher connection with nature, associated with higher pro-environmental behaviors, positive emotions towards nature, and even happiness (Cuervo-Arango et al., 2013; Moyano-Díaz et al., 2017).

The third most important variable in predicting waste separation probability by students at the university was the regular practice of physical activity, which could be related with the more proactive behavior of those who recycle (WHO, 2010). Considering that many sports/exercises are performed in the outdoors, a higher pro-environmental behavior and positive emotions towards nature could also be expected for this group of people (Figure 7.2a; Cuervo-Arango et al., 2013).

Considering the motivations of people to recycle, almost three-quarters of the students that separate waste on a regular basis declared that they did it because they were concerned about waste as a problem (Figure 7.2a). This can be considered as altruistic behavior of the students, who assume responsibility for taking care of their environment, as they acknowledge there is a problem. Similarly, when studying reasons for waste separation in the United States, altruistic behaviors and recycling have been identified as associated with more educated people and of liberal political orientation (Morgan and Hughes, 2006). Nevertheless, personal satisfaction was identified as an important motivation for students to recycle (Figure 7.2b), which could be further analyzed by considering the motivational relationship that could be established among recycling and happiness (Cuervo-Arango et al., 2013).

The implementation of more recycling points and the development of a differentiated waste collection campaign in the city was identified as the most important idea to promote recycling (Figure 7.2c). This has been the trend in many European countries like Germany, which has implemented an effective recycling system since the 1990s (Fischer, 2013). Education seems to be the way to go to encourage waste separation for recycling.

This was one of the most repeated word on the answers students gave when asked about personal ideas to promote recycling in the city (Figure 7.2d).

5.   CONCLUSIONS

Waste separation for recycling in university students at UFRO (South Chile) was primarily influenced by the age of the students, their rural/natural environment experience, and the regular practice of physical activity. Further research could focus on differentiating whether age tends to influence students due an increased social awareness given the greater access to information/education, or the fact that the older the student, the more likely they are to live alone (i.e., away from their parents' house) and to implement recycling systems in their own homes. Considering rural/natural environmental experience influence over waste separation, it would be valuable to differentiate types of rural/natural environment experiences, rural areas, natural or green spaces, forests, and so on. Similarly, to examine the positive relationship found between waste separation and regular practice of physical activity would be important in understanding the possible interaction among exercise and natural environment experience, considering that several sports are practiced outdoors (i.e., rural/natural environments).

Considering the results of this study, the university should support environmental education in their curriculum, and the promotion of outdoor activities and support for regular physical activity (and/or exercise) that fosters contact with nature would be a good strategy to increase recycling.

This research provided us with empirical data at a local level that can contribute as guidance to promote environmental behaviors on a broader level. Similar approaches could be developed in a neighborhood or even a city with larger data analyses.

ACKNOWLEDGMENTS

Many thanks go to Javiera Cordova and Deyanira Cortez (Laboratorio de Biometría, Universidad de La Frontera) who helped us with data processing, and to Rebecca Todd (Brave Team, Temuco, Chile) for her help with proofreading of the manuscript, and to Alex Bosso (Núcleo Científico Tecnológico en Ciencias Sociales y Humanidades, Universidad de La Frontera) for his comments on previous versions of this work. The support of all volunteers of the SepaRRRemos students group has been key since 2016 to encouraging waste separation at Universidad de La Frontera. The continuous support of many colleagues of the Facultad de Ciencias Agropecuarias y Forestales of Universidad de La Frontera have contributed directly and indirectly to developing this manuscript, particularly Rodolfo Pihán, Ricardo González and Adison Altamirano. Last, but not least, we thank the labor of all the attendants who form part of the cleaning staff of the Universidad de La Frontera.

REFERENCES

Barra, V., Salas, N., Inaipil, F., Barrientos, M., Gonzalez, M.J. and Vargas-Gaete, R. (2017). SepaRRRemos: waste separation campaign; growing from a small faculty into the university. Paper presented at the Symposium on Sustainability in University Campuses (SSUC-2017), 17–19 September, Universidad de São Paulo, Brazil.

Browne, M., Ayala, C., Vega, M.J. and Marchant, C. (2016). *Encuesta nacional de medio ambiente y cambio climático 2016*. Accessed 4 March 2020 at http://portal.mma.gob.cl/wp-content/uploads/2018/01/Informe-Final_2016.pdf.

Cecere, G., Mancinelli, S. and Mazzanti, M. (2014). Waste prevention and social preferences: the role of intrinsic and extrinsic motivations. *Ecological Economics*, 107, 163–76.

Comisión Nacional del Medioambiente (CONAMA). (2009). *Plan de acción intersectorial: mesa intersectorial: 'Santiago Recicla': Región Metropolitana*. Accessed 9 October 2020 at http://metadatos.mma.gob.cl/sinia/C2520REC.pdf.

Cuervo-Arango, M.A., García, J.A. and Nuñez, T.S. (2013). Actitudes y comportamiento hacia el medio ambiente natural. Salud medioambiental y bienestar emocional. *Universitas Psychologica*, 12(3), 845–56.

Eskuche, J.L. (2019). Motivaciones, asociatividad y experiencia en la naturaleza vinculadas a la separación de residuos sólidos en una muestra de estudiantes de la Universidad de La Frontera. Master's degree study, Facultad de Ciencias Agropecuarias y Forestales, Universidad de La Frontera.

Fischer, C. (2013). Municipal waste management in Germany. Working paper for the European Environment Agency.

Geissdoerfer, M., Savaget, P., Bocken, N.M.P. and Hultink, E.J. (2017). The circular economy – a new sustainability paradigm? *Journal of Cleaner Production*, 143, 757–68.

González, J.M., Ovalle, M.J. and Salazar, M. (2018). La economía circular como respuesta alternativa a los desafíos de la alimentación: análisis de caso para la situación de Chile. *Revista Chilena de Relaciones Internacionales*, 2(2), 94–104.

Hernández-Berriel, M., Aguilar-Virgen, Q., Taboada-González, P., Lima-Morra, R., Eljaiek-Urzola, M., Márquez-Benavides, L. and Buenrostro-Delgado, O. (2017). Generación y composición de los residuos sólidos urbanos en América Latina y el Caribe. *Revista Internacional de Contaminación Ambiental*, 32, 11–22.

Hoornweg, D. and Bhada-Tata, P. (2012). What a waste: a global review of solid waste management. *Urban Development Series Knowledge Papers No. 15*. World Bank.

Hothorn, T., Hornik, K. and Zeileis, A. (2012). party: a laboratory for recursive partytioning. Accessed 16 December 2019 at https://cran.r-project.org/web/packages/party/vignettes/party.pdf.

International Sustainable Campus Network (ISCN). (2018). *Sustainable Development: Educating with Purpose*. Accessed 9 October 2020 at https://international-sustainable-campus-network.org/iscn-sustainable-campus-best-practices/.

Moreno-Ávila, O.L. and Rincón-Salazar, M.T. (2009). Nociones de basura y prácticas en el manejo de residuos sólidos en encerramientos residenciales. *PROSPECTIVA. Revista de Trabajo Social e Intervención Social*, 14, 299–332.

Morgan, F.W. and Hughes, M.V. (2006). Understanding recycling behavior in Kentucky: who recycles and why. *JOM: The Journal of the Minerals, Metals & Materials Society*, 58(8), 32–5.

Moyano-Díaz, E., Palomo-Vélez, G., Olivos, P. and Sepúlveda-Fuentes, J. (2017). Natural and urban environments determining environmental beliefs and behaviours, economic thought and happiness/Ambientes naturales y urbano determinan creencias y comportamientos ambientales, el pensamiento económico y la felicidad. *PsyEcology*, 8(1), 75–106.

Ones, D.S., Wiernik, B.M., Dilchert, S. and Klein, R. (2015). Pro-environmental behavior. In J.D. Wright (ed.), *International Encyclopedia of the Social & Behavioral Sciences* (pp. 82–8). Oxford: Elsevier.

Palavecinos, M., Amérigo, M., Ulloa, J.B. and Muñoz, J. (2016). Preocupación y conducta ecológica responsable en estudiantes universitarios: estudio comparativo entre estudiantes chilenos y españoles. *Psychosocial Intervention*, 25(3), 143–8.

QuestionPro. (2018). QuestionPro Online Survey Software. Accessed 16 December 2019 at https://www.questionpro.com/.

Red Campus Sustentable (RCS) (2019). *Memoria 2018-2019*. Accessed 3 March 2020 at https://redcampussustentable.cl.

R Development Core Team. (2018). The R Project for statistical computing. R Foundation. Accessed 16 December 2019 at http://www.R-project.org/.

Riveros, R. (2019). Un acercamiento a la sustentabilidad en las universidades: UFRO sustentable. Dirección de Análisis y Desarrollo Institucional, Universidad de La Frontera. Accessed 3 March 2020 at http://ima.ufro.cl/index.php/documentacion/.

Sepulveda, C. (2019). *Informe 2019: Caracterización de residuos sólidos de la Universidad de La Frontera, Campus Andrés Bello*. Santiago: UFRO.

United Nations (1973). *Report of the United Nations Conference on the Human Environment, Stockholm, 5-16 June 1972*. New York: UN.

Universidad de Chile. (2016). Sección 8.2: Evolución global de la calidad ambiental de los asentamientos humanos en las dos últimas décadas. In *Informe País: Estado del Medio Ambiente en Chile*. Centro de Análisis de Políticas Públicas, Instituto de Asuntos Públicos.

Vásquez, Ó.C. (2011). Gestión de los residuos sólidos municipales en la ciudad del Gran Santiago de Chile: desafíos y oportunidades. *Revista Internacional de Contaminación Ambiental*, 27(4), 347–55.

Velazquez, L., Munguia, N., Platt, A. and Taddei, J. (2006). Sustainable university: what can be the matter? *Journal of Cleaner Production*, 14(9–11), 810–19.

World Health Organization (WHO). (2010). *Global Recommendations on Physical Activity for Health*. Accessed 16 December 2019 at https://www.who.int/dietphysicalactivity/publications/9789241599979/en/.

World Medical Association (WMA). (2014). WMA Declaration of Helsinki: ethical principles for medical research involving human subjects. *The Journal of the American College of Dentists*, 81(3), https://doi.org/10.1001/jama.2013.281053.

Wright, T.S. (2002). Definitions and frameworks for environmental sustainability in higher education. *Higher Education Policy*, 15(2), 105–20.

8. Sustainability in Finnish craft education: United Nations Sustainable Development Goals of the 2030 Agenda as a frame for an overview

Niina Väänänen and Sinikka Pöllänen

1. INTRODUCTION TO SUSTAINABLE CRAFT IN FINNISH CRAFT EDUCATION

In Finland, for decades, sustainability has been one of the leading themes in the national core curriculum and also a distinctive feature of craft education (Finnish National Board of Education [FNBE], 2014). Participation, involvement and building a sustainable future are the transversal competence areas that are comprised of knowledge, skills, value and will (ibid.). Those transversal competence areas are the best link to understanding the significance of students' choices, lifestyles and actions, not only for themselves, but also for their communities, society and nature.

For years, craft education has played an important role in educating responsible consumers (Komiteamietintö, 1952) and citizens within a cultural context (Markkula, 2011) in the implementation of crafts as learning by doing. Today, the Finish curriculum in crafts outlines the holistic craft process and multi-materiality to be implemented through open themes, a holistic interdisciplinary approach and environment-based learning tasks. However, in reality, there are various practices within craft education because teachers in Finland have the autonomy to implement the curriculum. Regrettably, the new concept of multi-materiality has created confusion (Kokko, Kouhia and Kangas, 2020), leading to the question of how to implement craft education and, thereby, the potential of craft education as an arena and an environment for sustainable education has been left behind. In crafts, the concept of 'ecological handprint' (Biemer, Dixon and Blackburn, 2013), by focusing on the healing and building abilities of the hands, in contrast to a heavy footprint of carbon emissions, provides a lens for positive solutions, instead of focusing on the problems (Norton, 2015).

Learning, living and working in a changing world means changes in culture, production and consumption, which challenges us to redesign our educational content and practices to extend the boundaries of traditional learning but also to maintain the traditions and skills that have travelled with humanity for many millennia (Dissanayake, 1995). Sustainability is integrated into crafts through materials and the environment, but it can ultimately turn into holistic understanding of crafting as a lifestyle and co-crafting as a viable alternative for a sustainable future (Räisänen and Laamanen, 2014). Thereby, this chapter will describe the basic concepts in craft education in the Finnish basic core curriculum, and thereafter present some examples of how to teach sustainability through craft in light of recent theories of sustainable craft and the United Nations Sustainable

Development Goals (SDGs) of the 2030 Agenda (UN, 2015). The last section of this chapter presents practical solutions to integrate sustainability learning through crafts at different levels of education.

1.1 Craft Education in Finland

Finland has integrated crafts into general education as a school subject in its own right – separate, for example, from art and home economics since the Finnish school system was established in 1866 (Marjanen and Metsärinne, 2019). Internationally, Finnish craft education, unlike other countries, includes both design and technology education (Kokko et al., 2020). Craft education in Finland has responded to societal and individual needs through teaching practical and technical skills to create products for home living, and later to freely choose contents of crafts – that is, techniques or materials and those contents that support gender equity within the subject (ibid.). Today, the emphasis in craft education is on exploratory production, meaning that the aim is to explore different materials and methods and innovate during the creative hands-on process of seeing alternatives and combining perspectives across existing boundaries (FNBE, 2014).

Currently in Finland, craft is a single compulsory subject for all students in basic education emphasizing a holistic craft process, multi-materiality and participatory learning (ibid.). In the holistic craft process, the craftsperson is in charge of the ideas, the design, the preparation, and finally the assessment of the artefact and the production process, so that if some phase is omitted it becomes an ordinary craft (Kojonkoski-Rännäli, 1995). In the latter case, the maker manufactures the desired product by using a ready-made design and instructions (e.g., from 'how to' magazines) that contain the aesthetic or technical qualities of the artefact (Pöllänen, 2020). Because in ordinary craft the processes are divided, they do not develop the individual skills needed for a holistic process (Kojonkoski-Rännäli, 1995). It is important that this kind of model imitation should not be confused with traditional crafts that are usually based on making and repeating cultural shapes, patterns, motifs, and even values with the materials (Zhan et al., 2017). Traditional crafts as an embodiment of vernacular craft, refers to the cultural produce of a community, the things that are collectively made, spoken and performed (Ihatsu, 2002).

In Finnish craft education, the concept of multi-materiality combines design and technology as textile work and technical work (Lepistö and Lindfors, 2015) without dichotomies between them or between genders (Kokko et al., 2020). The mixed materials and visualization and making methods are appropriately selected based on what works best for the intended product (Pöllänen, 2020). Multi-materiality can be understood as a learning environment for creative, innovative and practical combination and experimentation of materials and techniques to ground the learning experiences for new ways of thinking and doing in a sustainable way (cf. Binkley et al., 2012).

1.2 Sustainable Craft

A vision of doing by hand constitutes a special way of knowing about oneself and about the world, shaped by the mental and concrete products of doing with any kind of material (Kojonkoski-Rännäli, 1995). Thereby, sustainable craft is based on consideration and reflection of product properties and effects of practice. Sustainable craft can be seen as

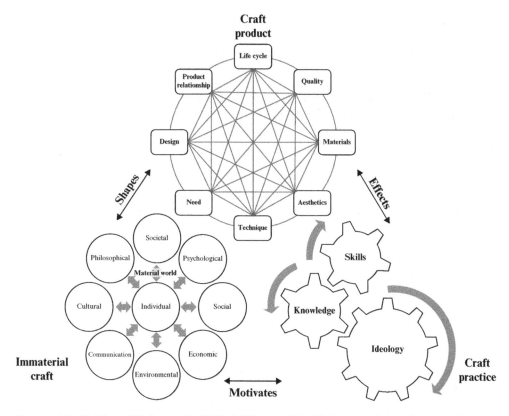

Craft
product

Source: Modified from Väänänen et al. (2017). © Väänänen 2017. With the permission of the copyright holder. Citable version originally published in *Craft Research*, 8(2), 2017, by Intellect Ltd.

Figure 8.1   System of sustainable craft

a holistic system of practice, products and immaterial craft that each have characteristics of their own but affect, shape and motivate each other in an intertwined system (Figure 8.1) (Väänänen et al., 2017). On a very basic level, sustainable craft is approached through the materials and the products' lifecycle (Räisänen and Laamanen, 2014). In an individual approach, the maker reflects on, for instance, how she or he can make things better or more efficient. After familiarizing themselves with methods and materials and gaining more practice, the approach becomes socio-cultural, as the maker learns about the effects on the environment at large (see Bayliss and Dillon, 2010; Väänänen et al., 2018). The approach depends on the level of commitment to the process – the more involved one is in the process, the more reflective is the dialogue with the environment as a whole (cf. Dillon, 2018; Novak, 2010; Räisänen and Laamanen, 2014).

Values attached to craft have extrinsic or intrinsic relationships to sustainability (Zhan and Walker, 2018). Extrinsic values are related to the environment and the economy – for instance, eco-friendly materials, production process, consumption, or increasing income. Intrinsic values are social, local-cultural and spiritual. These values connect with, for instance, social equality, community building, local distinctiveness and self-identified culture instead of cosmopolitan culture, and a spiritual sense of being and self-fulfilment through making. To realize these values, they are linked to skills and knowledge of materials, methods, or product lifecycle (Väänänen et al., 2017; Väänänen and Pöllänen, 2020).

2.　THE SUSTAINABLE DEVELOPMENT GOALS OF THE 2030 AGENDA THROUGH CRAFT

The 17 SDGs (UN, 2015) comprise a more detailed framework for sustainable development in general but also for craft to support the *tri*-vision of environment, economy and equity (World Commission on Environment and Development [WCED], 1987). The 17 goals with 169 targets can comprise issues of *people, planet, prosperity, peace* and *partnership* (UN, 2015, pp. 1–2). Sustainability means sustaining living conditions on planet Earth for present and future generations through cultural change (Ehrenfeld, 2014), education (Leal Filho, Manolas and Pace, 2015), and by safeguarding cultural traditions (Kokko, 2018; United Nations Educational, Scientific and Cultural Organization [UNESCO], 2003) or by renewing them (Nugraha, 2018).

Closely connected to sustainability, on a material level, are eco-friendly production methods and consumption patterns (Fry, 2009). The viewpoint has changed from single issues towards holistic thinking (Ceschin and Gaziulusoy, 2016; Salonen, 2019), which at the same time makes it more complex to realize (cf. Norton, 2015; Räisänen and Laamanen, 2014). A consortium of independent researchers (UN, 2019a, p. xxi) highlighted that there are six entry points that 'offer the most promise for achieving the desired transformations at the necessary scale and speed': human well-being and capabilities; sustainable and just economies; food systems and nutrition patterns; energy decarbonization with universal access; urban and peri-urban development; and global environmental commons. This helps in understanding the systemicity and complexity of the task more clearly (Ceschin and Gaziulusoy, 2016; Leal Filho et al., 2015). Therefore, social, economic and environmental issues can be viewed separately, but they need to be understood as connected for actions to take place (UN, 2019b).

Salonen (2019) explains that there are weak and strong responses to sustainability. Weak responses focus on desires, standards of living, on products and services, linear and market economies, fossil energy and consumer citizenship and individualism. Strong responses emphasize quality of life, human needs, local products and services, circular economy with true costs, clean energy, active citizenship and belonging. These dichotomies describe material and post-material worldviews, and suggest the need to move towards post-material quality-of life values. The 17 SDGs (UN, 2015) and targets are specific action points, and yet, they may seem too remote to understand on a concrete level. Thus, for instance, sustainable craft may serve as an arena in which to begin from something concrete, to understand the complexity, and reach the immaterial level (Väänänen, 2020). Consequently, this chapter views these 17 goals as themes through craft.

2.1　Participation Levels: People, Peace and Partnership

On the participation level, craft has traditionally been considered to reduce issues of poverty by creating employment (Thomas, 2006). Historically, craft has been a means of providing the basic necessities of life, providing shelter, food and jobs (Dillon, 2018). Even today, developing holistically from skills to know-how and shaping makers' attitudes and values (Kouhia, 2016; Väänänen et al., 2017), craft can be a viable source of income and entrepreneurship (Luckman, 2015). More widely, craft as an intention-based activity (Ihatsu, 2002) offers different kinds of well-being and has reported health benefits (e.g., Kouhia, 2016). Craft can be applied as a therapeutic action or used in rehabilitation (Pöllänen, 2009). The elements that enhance well-being have been connected to the raw materials, the artefacts, the sense of achievement, the possibilities for personal growth, the development of physical and cognitive skills, the control of one's body and feelings, and the social and cultural dimensions of craft. Thus, craft can be viewed from an individual perspective as providing well-being, empowering and recovering from stress (Pöllänen, 2015), but also can be used for healing from eco-catastrophes (Maidment et al., 2019).

In quality education, the emphasis is usually placed on literacy and numeracy education (UN, 2015) in order to counter problems such as poverty and equity, for example (Nussbaum, 2011). However, the role of crafts in education should be emphasized because of the developmental aspect of its aesthetics and understanding of quality (Kojonkoski-Rännäli, 1995), learning the basics of product lifecycle and traditions (Kokko and Räisänen, 2019; Räisänen and Laamanen, 2014) as well as embodied cognitions (Dillon, 2018; Huotilainen et al., 2018). Crafts also offer a hands-on learning experience incorporating the abstractions of cross-curricular learning – for example, mathematics and other STEM subjects (Kokko, Eronen and Sormunen, 2015). Today, in our complex future, crafts may provide opportunities for learning technological and computational skills, and logical and holistic thinking (Pöllänen and Pöllänen, 2019).

Gender equity in crafts has been a topic in Finnish craft education because of the historical gender-specific division of girls'/women's 'soft' materials and textile techniques and boys'/men's 'hard' materials and technical methods (Lepistö and Lindfors, 2015). This division was supported by the official national curriculum until 1985, when gender was not a criterion from which to choose among techniques and materials in crafts in basic education (Marjanen and Metsärinne, 2019). Today, craft is a compulsory multi-material school subject for all pupils in which learning is realized with various visual, material, technical and manufacturing projects (FNBE, 2014). However, there is still a potential danger in home-based craft production and entrepreneurship – that it may tie women to the home instead of seeking employment elsewhere (Luckman, 2015). Yet, at the same time, it may empower them to earn their own income, and gain control over time management and 'me time' (Pöllänen and Voutilainen, 2017) and break gender barriers in interdisciplinary or multicultural projects at school and adult education (Lappalainen, 2014).

Because sustainable development is a political issue, ensuring that the SDGs (UN, 2015) are met is a governmental responsibility (cf. Nussbaum, 2011), and policy making needs to support peace, justice and strong institutions. Sustainable craft may have the potential for holistic understanding, healing and intervention for a healthier future on personal, societal and cultural levels. To educate humankind (Dissanayake, 1995) and to develop our capabilities holistically we need to understand the complex systems and environments of which we are a part (Dillon, 2018; Huotilainen, 2019; Väänänen, 2020; cf. Nussbaum, 2011). Individually, taking into account the positive impacts of hands-on activities on the brain at all stages of life, it is important to ensure that craft education is included in formal education on national and local levels from early childhood to higher education (Huotilainen, 2019). Hands-on activities and interaction with materials may concretize responsibilities towards others and nature (Harrod, 2013) and, therefore, enhance a sense of balance (Pöllänen, 2015) and reduce inequalities between people, animals and nature. However, the appreciation of crafts still needs the support of institutions and policy because craft as a profession is sometimes undervalued and because of the rejection of cultural traditions (Kokko, 2018; UNESCO, 2003).

To realize all the SDGs there needs to be collaboration with multiple stakeholders, and the craft industry needs to utilize this collaboration for its business strategies (Väänänen and Pöllänen, 2020). Although the purpose of crafts in the Finnish education system has been to develop individual skills, within education for the twenty-first century (Binkley et al., 2012) a maker culture, co-design and co-crafting can harness the skills needed to work in collaboration with various visual, material, technical and manufacturing solutions (Härkki, Seitamaa-Hakkarainen and Hakkarainen, 2018) towards a partnership for the SDGs. Thus, crafts may offer an inclusive context for learning and social relationships in situations where the participants are at risk of isolation and discrimination (Lappalainen, 2014).

2.2   Action Points: Planet and Prosperity

Materials are indispensable for making. In craft processes, we interact with materials, natural or humanmade, from close by or shipped from far away, with techniques that transform the materials into function. These methods and materials are cultivated, harvested and extracted from nature. These processes in small-scale local craft production are in the maker's hands (Fletcher, 2008), but purchased in global markets, the maker cannot be certain that the methods used in collecting the materials are in accordance with the maker's values (Räisänen and Laamanen, 2014; Väänänen et al., 2017).

More widely, the manufacturing of craft materials poses a risk for life below water and life on land. First, water is needed for cultivating natural fibres; second, it is needed for the processes that modify those materials into a usable form (Fletcher, 2008). In regard to affordable and clean energy, craft processes and tools can be the most affordable and cleanest form of energy used to produce an item with traditional methods (Dissanayake, Perera and Wanniarachchi, 2017). However, legislation as well as education and infrastructure should be provided on self-sufficiency and maintenance to ensure that craft-based processes are not as pollutive as any other given production methods (cf. Le et al., 2016).

Craft industry in general and as an occupation can provide work and economic growth when it is based on freedom to choose (Nussbaum, 2011). This means that individuals are not forced to labour under poor working conditions or remuneration. The whole production chain should be as transparent as possible, detailing workforce used, the conditions, and the payment. Craft with consumer responsibility alone cannot make a change alone, but it can offer an alternative and a visionary path towards collaboration and innovations needed for the change (cf. Harrod, 2013; König, 2013).

Artisanal craft production as a form of local production offers an alternative for industry, innovation and infrastructure (Aakko, 2016; cf. Fletcher, 2008). On the other hand, mass-produced products are seen to compete in terms of quantity, time and price over quality or innovative traditions (e.g., Nugraha, 2018; Räisänen and Laamanen, 2014; Zhan and Walker, 2018; Zhan et al., 2017). Nevertheless, although the craft industry has had its ups and downs, there are signals that craft production has a new beginning, especially connected to new ways of sharing and sustainability (e.g., Walker, Evans and Mullagh, 2019). Thus, mentoring support for craft start-ups and building strong collaboration networks within the cottage industry is needed (Farrer and Watt, 2015). Although recycling on its own is not enough to turn around the systems of material flows (Ceschin and Gaziulusoy, 2016), sustainable cities and communities could be effective recycling centres open tor givers and takers of materials, efficient recycling for upcycling, the circular economy and social collaboration (cf. König, 2013). Circularity and social responsibilities can also be promoted more effectively through already existing practices (Ellen MacArthur Foundation, 2013).

Ehrenfeld (2014) calls for cultural change from having to being, meaning to reduce consumption and owning things for short-term hedonistic satisfaction. Instead, crafting can preserve eudaimonic well-being and personal agency through reflections on quality and value, and through embodied interaction with the material world (Pöllänen and Weissmann-Hanski, 2020). Meaningful making by hand may offer an alternative to the emotional void being filled with shopping as addictive behaviour (Maraz, Griffiths and Demetrovics, 2016). Understanding how things are made could work as a mechanism for valuing and handling things we possess on a sustainable basis and turn into responsible consumption and production as steps for climate action to take place (Räisänen and Laamanen, 2014).

3.   PERSPECTIVES ON SUSTAINABLE CRAFT EDUCATION IN FINLAND

Because education in general has moved towards educating twenty-first-century competencies that address themes of ways of thinking and working, with tools for working and living in the world (Binkley et al., 2012), crafts as a means with participatory and empowering elements may help realize the SDGs (UN, 2015). Co-crafting your 'ecological handprint' (Biemer et al., 2013) can be concretized through the elements of the system of sustainable craft (see Figure 8.1) at different levels of education and in leisure activities (Pöllänen, 2015). Leal Filho et al. (2015) remind us that we need to prepare individuals for the unknown, fear of which can produce negative feelings and can trigger fight-or-flight stress reactions (Huotilainen et al. 2018), thus turning into a flow (Kouhia, 2016; Pöllänen, 2015). Thus, the idea is to focus on increasing co-crafting actions with a positive impact and empower students as future citizens for meaningful participation as change agents instead of focusing only on actions that decrease the negative impact (Kuthe et al., 2019).

3.1   Early Childhood Education and Elementary School

In Finnish early childhood education and elementary school, education could benefit from three main principles: material encounters, rehearsing skills and holistic craft process (Yliverronen and Seitamaa-Hakkarainen, 2016). Material to be recycled can be upcycled to children's creative rethink and redesign-based learning to reduce and reuse items. Thereby, the children take on social responsibility as the first basis of recycling and the circular economy. However, the most important task in early childhood is to rehearse skills and to become acquainted with a variety of materials and tools in work that also require concentration, patience and accountability. This will shape the neural connections through the senses and brain (Huotilainen, 2019) and support the child's diverse development. Holistic craft process will stimulate the learner's cognitive, sensorimotor, emotional and social resources and make the pupils' learning meaningful and enjoyable through problem solving (Pöllänen, 2020).

3.2   Upper Elementary School

In Finland, in upper elementary school, the easiest way is to include product lifecycle education in small tasks, information seeking, videos, portfolio learning with participatory learning methods and holistic craft process-based education. Four main themes in sustainable craft education may be material knowledge, ethical and ecological choices, human development, and frugality (cf. Marjanen and Metsärinne, 2019). These can be communicated to pupils through lifecycle and levels of participation (Räisänen and Laamanen, 2014). Open and holistic hands-on learning tasks can be constructed on the principle of tuning, sustainable consumption or user-centred design, selecting appropriate materials and techniques to create a workable solution for a design challenge (FNBE, 2014; Pöllänen, 2020).

Ethical and ecological questions could be introduced into material knowledge – that is, recognizing a material, getting a sense of materials, and gaining knowledge of appropriate materials and product features (Fry, 2009). Thus, discussions on maintaining products, quality, textile standards and eco-labels or ethical consuming from a social perspective help deepen consumer responsibility (Räisänen and Laamanen, 2014). According to Ihatsu (2002), the knowledge of different materials and techniques and the manufacturing process acquired through authentic experience creates a sense of commitment and responsibility as transferable skills. Holistic craft processes with material considerations implies being bodily, emotionally and cognitively active in developing the requisite skills for creativity and innovation, but also strengthening the psychomotor skills that are not only emphasized in studio craft but also in many different kinds of specialist labour (Bughin et al., 2018).

3.3   Secondary School, Vocational School and Higher Education

In Finnish secondary school, vocational school and in higher education, the framework of sustainable craft (Figure 8.1) may be used as the basis for education as well for students' designing tasks (Väänänen et al., 2017). The illustrated system can be dismantled into its elements and then viewed individually, so that the whole picture is reassembled again. It can be used as a base for visual culture analysis and designing sustainable fashion (Aakko, 2016), but also as an assistant for evaluation of one's design and crafting process (Väänänen, 2020). Beginning from hands-on learning tasks and connecting concept mapping and development (Novak, 2010) may deepen understanding and reflection, and, thereby, diversify students' conceptions (Kröger, 2016). Reflection through a variety of design assignments where students themselves acquire information helps in understanding the principles of ethical design and production (Räisänen and Laamanen, 2014). The more familiar students are with the subject, the deeper and more abstract the reflection (Bayliss and Dillon, 2010; Väänänen et al., 2018). It is catalysed by the socio-technological developments that make co-creating easier and more sustainable, in both the physical and the digital world. Co-creating in networked communities helps interaction within a larger socio-technological system for the generation of a pool of knowledge and ideas within a collective intelligence (Härkki et al., 2018).

4. CONCLUSIONS

In the Finnish context, craft education as single compulsory subject for all students in basic education, is an excellent setting for beginning support for the SDGs (UN, 2015) among young people – to provide them with resources and competencies to empower them as future citizens for meaningful participation as change agents (see Binkley et al., 2010; Kuthe et al., 2019; Räisänen and Laamanen, 2014). Consequently, this chapter has reviewed these goals as themes through craft as products, practice, lifestyle, cultural presentation and as historically connected to humans with the use of hands, bodies, minds, tools, methods, technologies, in sync in local environments, sharing knowledge and traditions.

Because craft is something inherently human (Kojonkoski-Rännäli, 1995), the human action and practices in the circular lifecycle can be understood something quite natural to human beings (Dissanayake, 1995; Dillon, 2018), providing inclusive pedagogy that combines hands-on activities with understanding of the social and cultural nature of human activity against fast fulfilment of needs and overconsumption (Dissanayake et al., 2017; Markkula, 2011). The holistic craft process, including ideation, design, manufacturing and reflection and evaluation (Pöllänen, 2020), means that craft education can be perceived as larger whole, rather than just making products at different levels of education. Therefore, sustainable craft as a system of practice, products and immaterial craft can be approached through these elements individually or holistically, meaning that all the aspects and elements are carefully considered in the making process (Väänänen et al., 2018). Finally, craft is about values and attitudes, the system of production and ethical consumption, and moreover, learning critical thinking (Räisänen and Laamanen, 2014).

As a multi-material learning environment (FNBE, 2014; Pöllänen, 2020), crafts allow creative, innovative and practical combination and experimenting with materials and techniques to ground the learning experiences for new ways of thinking and doing in a sustainable way (cf. Binkley et al., 2012). For instance, the expression of the 'ecological handprint' (Biemer et al., 2013) begins from materials, knowledge, skills and learning to understand the meaning of design, but can ultimately turn into holistic understanding of crafting as a lifestyle and a viable alternative for a sustainable future (Väänänen, 2020). Through their own designs and production as well as reflections on ethical design, fashion, advertising, and the entire lifecycle of the product, students are able to see the impact of their own choices (Räisänen and Laamanen, 2014; Väänänen, 2020). Materials and textiles are concrete ways to open up a holistic understanding of things, including economic systems, production, humanity, corporeality and aesthetics. As a counterweight, crafts can also transform eco-anxiety into actions that support awareness and sustainable behaviour with positive examples, instead of focusing on the problems (Norton, 2015).

Traditionally self-crafted products have been a part of the conscious home economy. Today, there are trends and cultural recognition that value tradition while bringing a contemporary sensibility to designing, making and repairing by hand with specialized skills and knowledge (Walker et al., 2019). For example, new domesticity with traditions and leisure-based crafting or downshifting a stressful career articulates anti-consumerism, environmentalism and sustainable consumption, and reinterpreting the past in the context of contemporary needs and politics (Kouhia, 2016; Pöllänen, 2015). In traditional-based crafts, specialized skills and knowledge are linked with creativity and accumulation of meanings of the diverse local cultures that can still be identified (Zhan and Walker, 2018; Zhan et al., 2017). As Nugraha (2018) and Kokko (2018) remind us that to keep traditions alive they need to be transformed to satisfy the needs of contemporary societies and kept in the curriculum.

The growing craft-related maker movement also exemplifies how crafting can serve as stress-reducing, meaning-making and increasing well-being (Pöllänen, 2015), providing a sense of belonging to people's lives and contributing to a new active participatory and responsible culture and society (Kouhia, 2016). Although there are strong connections between craft and sustainability, there are, in practice, several problems and contradictions to be overcome, however (Walker et al., 2019; Zhan et al., 2017). As Nugraha (2018) has stressed, this begins with understanding the disadvantages of the consumption-based lifestyle. It can be concluded that sustainable craft as hands-on learning about manufacturing, materials, as well as traditions and technologies, has a special opportunity to strive for the SDGs (UN, 2019b) and redefine aspects of design, manufacturing and consumption.

While the context and impetus for this chapter derives from the Finnish educational system, in which craft enjoys its own distinct subject area, we hope that the findings may be applied to product design and art education in general, when craft materials and processes are part of art programmes. More widely, we hope that this review will give theoretical and practical perspectives for educators and policy makers to see the benefit of the integration of sustainable development in education.

REFERENCES

Aakko, M. (2016). Fashion in-between: artisanal design and production of fashion. Doctoral dissertation. Aalto University.

Bayliss, P. and Dillon, P. (2010). Cosmologies and lifestyles: a cultural ecological framework and its implications for education systems. *Anthropological Journal of European Cultures*, 19(2), 7–21.

Biemer, J., Dixon, W. and Blackburn, N. (2013). Our environmental handprint: the good we do. Paper presented at the 1st IEEE Conference on Technologies for Sustainability (SusTech), Portland, USA.

Binkley, M., Erstad, O. and Herman, J. et al. (2012). Defining twenty-first century skills. In P. Griffin, B. McCaw and E. Care (eds), *Assessment and Teaching of 21st Century Skills* (pp. 17–66). Dordrecht: Springer.

Bughin, J., Hazan, E. and Lund, S. et al. (2018). Skill shift: automation and the future of workforce. McKinsey Global Institute Discussion Paper.

Ceschin, F. and Gaziulusoy, I. (2016). Evolution of design for sustainability: from product design to design for system innovations and transitions. *Design Studies*, 47, 118–63.

Dillon, P. (2018). Making and its cultural ecological foundations. In S. Walker, M. Evans and T. Cassidy et al. (eds), *Design Roots: Culturally Significant Designs, Products and Practices* (pp. 102–17). London: Bloomsbury.

Dissanayake, D.G., Perera, S. and Wanniarachchi, T. (2017). Sustainable and ethical manufacturing: a case study from handloom industry. *Textiles and Clothing Sustainability*, 3(2), 1–10.

Dissanayake, E. (1995). *Homo Aestheticus: Where Art Comes From and Why*. Seattle, WA: University of Washington Press.

Ehrenfeld, J.R. (2014). The real challenge of sustainability. In K. Fletcher and M. Tham (eds), *Routledge Handbook of Sustainability and Fashion* (pp. 57–63). Abingdon, UK and New York: Routledge.

Ellen MacArthur Foundation. (2013). *Towards the Circular Economy: Opportunities for the Consumer Goods Sector*. Accessed 13 August 2018 at https://www.ellenmacarthurfoundation.org/assets/downloads/publica tions/TCE_Report-2013.pdf.

Farrer, J.M. and Watt, C.A. (2015). The true value of materials: BRIDGE (Building Research and Innovation Deals for the Green Economy). *Textiles and Clothing Sustainability*, 1(10), 1–14.

Finnish National Board of Education (FNBE). (2014). *Perusopetuksen opetussuunnitelman perusteet* [National Core Curriculum for Basic Education]. The Finnish National Board of Education. Accessed 9 February 2021 at https://www.oph.fi/sites/default/files/documents/perusopetuksen_opetussuunnitelman_perusteet_2014.docx.

Fletcher, K. (2008). *Sustainable Fashion and Textiles*. London: Earthscan.

Fry, T. (2009). *Design Futuring: Sustainability, Ethics and New Practice*. Oxford: Berg.

Härkki, T., Seitamaa-Hakkarainen, P. and Hakkarainen, K. (2018). Hands on design: comparing the use of sketching and gesturing in collaborative designing. *Journal of Design Research*, 16(1), 24–46.

Harrod, T. (2013). 'Visionary rather than practical': craft, art and material efficiency. *Philosophical Transactions of the Royal Society A*, 371(1986), 1–12.

Huotilainen, M. (2019). *Näin aivot oppivat* [This Is How Brains Learn]. Helsinki: PS-Kustannus.

Huotilainen, M., Rankanen, M. and Groth, C. et al. (2018). Why our brains love arts and crafts: implications of creative practices on psychophysical well-being. *FORMakademisk*, 11(2), 1–18.

Ihatsu, A.-M. (2002). *Kasvatustieteellisiä julkaisuja Volume 73: Making Sense of Contemporary American Craft*. Joensuu: University of Eastern Finland.

Kojonkoski-Rännäli, S. (1995). Ajatus käsissämme: käsityön käsitteen merkityssisällön analyysi [The thought in our hands: an analysis of the meaning of the concept handicraft]. University of Turku.

Kokko, S. (2018). The role of higher education in sustaining culturally significant crafts in Estonia. In S. Walker, M. Evans and T. Cassidy et al. (eds), *Design Roots: Culturally Significant Designs, Products, and Practices* (pp. 252–63). London: Bloomsbury.

Kokko, S., Eronen, L. and Sormunen, K. (2015). Crafting maths: exploring mathematics learning through crafts. *Design and Technology Education: An International Journal*, 20(2), 22–31.

Kokko, S., Kouhia, A. and Kangas, K. (2020). Finnish craft education in turbulence: conflicting debates on the current National Core Curriculum. *Techne Series A*, 27(1), 1–19.

Kokko, S. and Räisänen, R. (2019). Craft education in sustaining and developing craft traditions: reflections from Finnish craft teacher education. *Techne Series A*, 26(1), 27–43.

Komiteamietintö. (1952). *Kansakoulun opetussuunnitelmakomitean mietintö II* [Elementary School Curriculum Committee Report II]. Helsinki: Valtioneuvoston kirjapaino.

König, A. (2013). A stitch in time: changing cultural constructions of craft and mending. *Culture Unbound*, 5, 569–85.

Kouhia, A. (2016). Unraveling the meanings of textile hobby crafts. Doctoral thesis. Faculty of Behavioural Sciences, Department of Teacher Education, Craft Science, University of Helsinki.

Kröger, T. (2016). Diverse orientations in craft education: student teachers' conceptions and perceptions. *Techne Series A*, 23(1), 1–14.

Kuthe, A., Körfgen, A., Stotter, J. and Keller, L. (2019). Strengthening their climate change literacy: a case study addressing the weakness in young people's climate change awareness. *Applied Environmental Education and Communication*, 18(3), 1–14.

Lappalainen, E.-M. (2014). Effective multicultural learning in iterative cycles: language learning breaking gender barriers in doing crafts. *Techne Series A*, 21(1), 1–16.

Le, T.H., Tran, V.T. and Le, Q.V. et al. (2016). An integrated ecosystem incorporating renewable energy leading to pollution reduction for sustainable development of craft villages in rural area: a case study at sedge mats village in Mekong Delta, Vietnam. *Energy, Sustainability and Society*, 2(21), 1–12.

Leal Filho, W., Manolas, E. and Pace, P. (2015). The future we want. *International Journal of Sustainability in Higher Education*, 16(1), 112–29.

Lepistö, J. and Lindfors, E. (2015). From gender-segregated subjects to multi-material craft: student teachers' views on the future of craft subject. *FORMakademisk*, 8(3), 1–20.

Luckman, S. (2015). Women's micro-entrepreneurial homeworking. *Australian Feminist Studies*, 30(84), 146–60.

Maidment, J., Tudor, R., Campbell, A. and Whittaker, K. (2019). Women's place-making through craft in post-earthquake Christchurch. *Aotearoa New Zealand Social Work*, 31(1), 17–30.

Maraz, A., Griffiths, M.D. and Demetrovics, Z. (2016). The prevalence of compulsive buying: a meta-analysis. *Addiction*, 111(3), 408–19.

Marjanen, P. and Metsärinne, M. (2019). The development of craft education in Finnish schools. *Nordic Journal of Educational History*, 6(1), 49–70.

Markkula, A. (2011). Consumers as ecological citizens in clothing markets. Doctoral dissertation. Aalto University.

Norton, B.G. (2015). *Sustainable Values, Sustainable Change: A Guide to Environmental Decision Making.* Chicago, IL: University of Chicago Press.

Novak, J.D. (2010). *Learning, Creating, and Using Knowledge: Concept Maps as Facilitative Tools in Schools and Corporations.* New York: Taylor & Francis.

Nugraha, A. (2018). Transforming tradition in Indonesia: a method for maintaining tradition in a craft and design context. In S. Walker, M. Evans and T. Cassidy et al. (eds), *Design Roots: Culturally Significant Designs, Products and Practices* (pp. 236–58). London: Bloomsbury.

Nussbaum, M. (2011). *Creating Capabilities: The Human Development Approach.* Cambridge, MA: Harvard University Press.

Pöllänen, S. (2009). Craft as context in therapeutic change. *The Indian Journal of Occupational Therapy*, XLI(2), 43–7.

Pöllänen, S. (2015). Elements of crafts that enhance well-being: textile craft makers' descriptions of their leisure activity. *Journal of Leisure Research*, 47(1), 58–78.

Pöllänen, S. (2020). Perspectives on multi-material crafts in basic education. *International Journal of Art and Design Education*, 39(1), 255–70.

Pöllänen, S.H. and Pöllänen, K.M. (2019). Beyond programming and crafts: towards computational thinking in basic education. *Design and Technology Education: An International Journal*, 24(1), 13–32.

Pöllänen, S. and Voutilainen, L. (2017). Crafting well-being: meanings and intentions of stay-at-home mothers' craft-based leisure activity. *Leisure Sciences*, 40(6), 617–33.

Pöllänen, S. and Weissmann-Hanski, M.K. (2020). Hand-made well-being: textile crafts as a source of eudaimonic well-being. *Journal of Leisure Research*, 51(3), 348–65.

Räisänen, R. and Laamanen, T.K. (2014). Tieto, kritiikki, toiminta, vastuu – pohdintaa kestävän kehityksen ja eettisen kuluttamisen näkökulmista käsityössä [Knowledge, critique, action, responsibility – discussions about sustainability and ethical consumption in textile craft]. In S. Karppinen, A. Kouhia and E. Syrjäläinen (eds), *Kättä pidempää: Otteita käsityön tutkimuksesta ja käsitteellistämisestä* (pp. 48–61). Helsinki: University of Helsinki.

Salonen, A.O. (2019). Transformative responses to sustainability. In W. Leal Filho (ed.), *Encyclopedia of Sustainability in Higher Education* (pp. 1–8). Cham, Switzerland: Springer.

Thomas, A. (2006). Design, poverty, and sustainable development. *Design Issues*, 22(4), 54–65.

United Nations (UN). (2015). *Transforming Our World: The 2030 Agenda for Sustainable Development.* New York: United Nations.

United Nations (UN). (2019a). *The Future Is Now – Science for Achieving Sustainable Development.* Accessed 12 November 2019 at https://sustainabledevelopment.un.org/content/documents/24797GSDR_report_2019.pdf.

United Nations (UN). (2019b). *The Sustainable Development Goals Report.* Accessed 4 November 2019 at https://unstats.un.org/sdgs/report/2019/The-Sustainable-Development-Goals-Report-2019.pdf.

United Nations Educational, Scientific and Cultural Organization (UNESCO). (2003). Convention for the Safeguarding of the Intangible Cultural Heritage. Accessed 9 February 2021 at https://ich.unesco.org/en/convention.

Väänänen, N. (2020). Sustainable craft: dismantled and reassembled. *Dissertations in Education, Humanities, and Theology No. 149.* Joensuu: University of Eastern Finland.

Väänänen, N. and Pöllänen, S. (2020). Conceptualizing sustainable craft: concept analysis of literature. *The Design Journal*, 23(2), 263–85.

Väänänen, N., Pöllänen, S., Kaipainen, M. and Vartiainen, L. (2017). Sustainable craft in practice – from practice to theory. *Craft Research*, 8(2), 257–84.

Väänänen, N., Vartiainen, L. and Kaipainen, M. et al. (2018). Understanding Finnish student craft teachers' conceptions of sustainability. *International Journal of Sustainability in Higher Education*, 19(5), 963–86.

Walker, S., Evans, M. and Mullagh, L. (2019). Traditional maker practices and sustainable futures: the implications of expertise. *The Design Journal*, 22(S1), 835–48.

World Commission on Environment and Development (WCED) (1987). *Our Common Future.* Oxford: Oxford University Press.

Yliverronen, V. and Seitamaa-Hakkarainen, P. (2016). Learning craft skills: exploring preschoolers' craft-making process. *Techne Series A*, 23(2), 1–15.

Zhan, X. and Walker, S. (2018). Value direction: moving crafts toward sustainability in the Yangtze River Delta, China. *Sustainability*, 10(1252), 1–20.

Zhan, X., Walker, S., Hernandez-Pardo, R. and Evans, M. (2017). Craft and sustainability: potential for design intervention in crafts in the Yangtze River Delta, China. *The Design Journal*, 20(S1), S2919–S2934.

9. Infusing education for sustainable development (ESD) into curricula: teacher educators' experiences within the School of Education at The University of the West Indies, Jamaica

Carmel Roofe, Therese Ferguson, Carol Hordatt Gentles, Sharon Bramwell-Lalor, Loraine D. Cook, Aldrin E. Sweeney, Canute Thompson and Everton Cummings

1. INTRODUCTION

As a Small Island Developing State (SIDS), Jamaica like its other island and mainland nation counterparts in the Caribbean faces various economic, social, environmental and governance development issues. Although sustainable development (SD) (i.e., development that embraces all four of the aforementioned dimensions) is critical for the island given its inherent socio-economic and environmental vulnerabilities, it is also challenged by various issues including environmental degradation, crime and violence, and poverty. Whilst education for sustainable development (ESD) is undoubtedly important for the global community, it becomes especially critical for SIDS such as Jamaica.

Section 36 of *Agenda 21*, one of the earliest global reports on SD, outlines that 'Education is critical for promoting sustainable development and improving the capacity of the people to address environment and development issues' (UNCED, 1992, Section 36.3). *Agenda 21* speaks to both formal and non-formal education at all levels, and specifically highlights the need for pre- and in-service teacher training programmes (ibid., Section 36.5d). ESD as part of curriculum reorientation efforts in teacher education is therefore critical in educating for a sustainable world. More recently, the Global Action Programme (GAP) on ESD highlights under Priority Action Area 3 the need to build capacities of educators and trainers in the effective delivery of ESD, stating that 'Educators and trainers are powerful agents of change for delivering the educational response to sustainable development' (UNESCO, 2014, p.20). Further, it calls for the integration of ESD into pre- and in-service teacher training. Such integration will need to occur in the curricula of teacher training programmes; however, simply integrating ESD into curricula alone will not suffice. It requires purposeful and intentional actions from those who work in teacher education.

Integrating ESD in curricula is essentially about integrating ESD in teaching and learning. Such integration may occur using different approaches, one of which is through infusion. Hungerford, Volk and Ramsey (1989) define curriculum infusion as the 'integration of the content and skills into existing courses in a manner as to focus on that content (and/or skills) without jeopardizing the integrity of the courses themselves' (p. 57). This therefore allows teacher educators to address issues from a multidisciplinary perspective without adding another course to their programme.

Given the importance of both curriculum development and teacher training and development, it is important to engage with processes and practices of ESD infusion in teacher education institutions (TEIs) as a long-term, systemic means of engendering the change needed. Teacher educators specifically, and academic staff in general, are cited as crucial in bringing about these long-term transformative changes (Barth and Rieckmann, 2012). Yet, there are fewer studies that focus on academic staff as drivers of change and on means and mechanisms to institutionalise this long-term change (ibid.). Cebrián, Grace and Humphris (2015) also argue that there is a gap with respect to research studies that focus on 'staff understandings, attitudes and challenges faced when trying to embed the principles of ESD in real practice' (p. 80). Indeed, some of the challenges with respect to curriculum orientation towards sustainability in higher education include factors such as lack of knowledge and competencies for ESD integration and the lack of collaboration and interdisciplinary practice among educators (Cebrián, 2017; Cebrián et al., 2015).

With this in mind, the ESD Working Group (comprising the teacher educators from various specialisations authoring this chapter) within the School of Education (SOE) at The University of the West Indies (UWI) Mona Campus in Jamaica decided to address these gaps in the literature alongside some of the challenges cited, by undertaking a Collaborative Action Research (CAR) project to infuse ESD into their courses. The rationale for this approach was based on the premise that as a Working Group promoting ESD in teacher education, members were limited in their understanding about the specific ESD practices and strategies employed by teacher educators in the courses they teach in the programmes in the SOE. Additionally, not much was known about the most suitable strategies for integrating ESD in the SOE context. Furthermore, the decision to undertake this research was also grounded in the view of Bertling and Rearden (2018) that to foster a deep commitment to sustainability actions, education should be rooted in the embodied locales of a place. The ESD Working Group sought to explore practices and strategies for ESD infusion in the curricula of their different specialisations. The intent of the ESD Working Group is that these practices and strategies could thereafter be shared with the wider SOE for further ESD infusion, as well as the wider UWI. The project was guided by the following research questions:

1. How do a group of teacher educators infuse ESD into the university courses they deliver?
2. What collaborative processes are employed by teacher educators in infusing ESD?
3. What strategies and practices can be utilised to infuse ESD into university-level courses?
4. In what ways has the process of ESD infusion enhanced students' awareness of and commitment to ESD?

The chapter begins with an overview of ESD and the role of teachers and teacher education in supporting ESD and ESD pedagogy. This is followed by details of the CAR methodological approach utilised, and discussion of the findings, focusing on the first three research questions specifically. The chapter ends with lessons learnt from the process and recommendations with respect to ESD infusion in teacher education curricula.

2.   LITERATURE REVIEW

2.1   Education for Sustainable Development

The 1992 United Nations Conference on Environment and Development (UNCED), also known as the Rio Summit, marked a pivotal moment for the global community with respect to SD. *Agenda 21*, one of the seminal documents emerging from the Summit, offered the world community a global plan of action for SD. Education was one of the key components underscored in this blueprint for action, with Section 36 of the document devoted to education, emphasising that 'education is critical to the achievement of sustainable development and identified core strategies to improve learning opportunities in this area' (Tilbury, 2010, p. 101). As Chin et al. (2019) point out, education can result in 'informed engagement, empowerment of stakeholders and cultivation of their creativity and enthusiasm' and result in more lasting change than mechanisms such as policy and incentives.

ESD has gained momentum since, noticeably through global forums such as the 2002 World Summit on Sustainable Development in Johannesburg, South Africa and the 2012 United Nations Conference on Sustainable Development in Rio de Janeiro, Brazil, as well as through initiatives such as the Decade of Education for Sustainable Development (DESD) (2005–14), the GAP on ESD and the Sustainable Development Goals (SDGs), with explicit mention in Target 4.7 under SDG 4.

Whilst there are various perspectives on what ESD is (Kopnina and Meijers, 2014; Leal Filho et al., 2019), ESD:

> is commonly understood as education that encourages changes in knowledge, skills, values, and attitudes to enable a more sustainable and just society for all. ESD aims to empower and equip current and future generations to meet their needs using a balanced and integrated approach to the economic, social and environmental dimensions of sustainable development. (Leicht, Heiss and Byun, 2018, p. 7)

Articulated another way, 'ESD aims at developing competencies that empower individuals to reflect on their own actions, taking into account their current and future social, cultural, economic and environmental impacts, from a local and global perspective' (UNESCO, 2017a, p. 7). Pearson and Degotardi (2009) posit that 'ESD is unique in that, unlike other educational models designed to address environmental and/or global development issues, it takes an holistic approach, incorporating aspects of both environmental and global education' (p. 98). They further posit that ESD goes beyond environmental education through its promotion of social and cultural factors alongside environmental ones. It is seen as key for supporting the integration of education into SD priorities. To accomplish this, ESD must be infused into education (Leicht et al., 2018). This work is critical at all stages of learning, and in formal and non-formal education.

2.2   The Role of Teacher Education in ESD

The core work of ESD is focused on developing key competencies within individuals, including systems thinking, visioning, collaboration, critical thinking and problem solving (see Rieckmann, 2018 for a comprehensive list of key competencies). The task of helping individuals to develop these competencies has been recognised as the responsibility of educators who are seen as 'powerful change agents who can deliver the educational response needed to achieve the SDGs. Their knowledge and competencies are essential for restructuring educational processes and educational institutions towards sustainability' (UNESCO, 2017a, p. 51). Teachers should not only have these competencies themselves; they must also be able to utilise creative pedagogies to develop these same competencies in their students (Rieckmann, 2020).

The preparation of educators to acquire and apply these key competencies is identified by UNESCO as the work of teacher education; academics, of course, echo this as well (e.g., Brandt et al., 2019; Hordatt Gentles, 2018; Rieckmann, 2020). TEIs are seen as ideal spaces in which to build awareness, develop capacity, experiment, innovate, implement and document good ESD practices. This is so because it is TEIs that provide programmes for initial or in-service training and certifying teachers. Many, particularly those housed in tertiary institutions, also offer programmes for in-service education and development of teachers and teacher educators at the graduate level. It is these programmes that provide opportunities for professional capacity building by teaching prospective, new and experienced educators about ESD. TEIs also provide spaces and resources for research on ESD theory and practice (McKeown and Hopkins, 2014).

During the DESD, much work was done across the globe to reorient programmes in TEIs to incorporate ESD. This was achieved primarily through small-scale initiatives, including establishing ESD teacher networks; development, documentation and sharing of best practices; and lobbying for the development and implementation of education policies that provide political and economic support for ESD. The value of this work has been acknowledged in UNESCO's Visby Report (International Centre of Education for Sustainable Development [SWEDESD], 2017) on recommendations for advancing Agenda 2030 and the United Nations SDGs with an urgent call for continued and scaled-up ESD initiatives by TEIs. This is expressed explicitly in the GAP: Priority Action Area 3, which sets out the aim to 'increase the capacities of educators and trainers to more effectively deliver ESD' (UNESCO, 2017b, p. 9). This should involve helping them to 'acquire the necessary knowledge, skills, attitudes and values . . . and develop the requisite motivation and commitment to facilitate ESD' (UNESCO, n.d.).

2.3   Developing ESD Pedagogy

There has been research focused on various aspects of ESD in higher education. Examples include an action research project on academic staff members' views in relation to ESD and the factors influencing their engagement with ESD at a university in the United Kingdom (Cebrián, 2017; Cebrián et al., 2015); an assessment of the infusion of sustainability into curricula at two universities in Jordan (Biasutti, De Baz and Alshawa, 2016); and the development of a programme in the Ukraine to promote ESD through teacher training (Kostyuchenko and Smolennikov, 2018). Studies such as these are important with respect to the embedding of ESD in higher education curricula.

While the stated aims of using teacher education to promote ESD are clear, the literature suggests there are challenges to enacting these aims because knowledge of specific ESD pedagogy is still limited. Critics argue that these aims are often lofty and ambiguous (Stevenson, 2007), pointing out that the success of ESD has been hampered by a lack of clear guidelines. They suggest that while curricula have evolved to support ESD, the development of appropriate new pedagogies to deliver these has been lacking, with negative implications for effective evaluation of ESD work and its social and cultural outcomes (Eilam and Trop, 2010). This should be a concern for TEIs whose mandate is to produce teachers who have both knowledge of content in addition to knowledge of how to deliver the content. With respect to ESD there is the additional responsibility of teaching in ways that will lead students to acquire and enact behaviours that promote sustainability (Goldman, Yavetz and Peer, 2006; Marcinkowski, 2004). This absence of specific guidelines for ESD pedagogy suggests that the generation of ESD pedagogy and its dissemination should be a key activity for faculty. Given the importance of teacher collaboration (Berry, Daughtrey and Wieder, 2009; Burton, 2015; Ronfeldt et al., 2015), the members of the Working Group decided to utilise this as a focal point for the research undertaking.

3.   METHODOLOGY

In conducting the study, a CAR design was utilised to not only sensitise and enhance teachers in training to ESD principles but also to develop a commitment to ESD among teacher educators. Coghlan and Brydon-Miller (2014) note that one of the aims of CAR is to achieve change for a group of people through working in partnerships with each other. A CAR project thus draws on the principles of research to improve practice of the individual group members and offer useful opportunities for professional development (PD) of those involved (Garces and Granada, 2016). In this sense, CAR enabled the teacher educators to conduct research as a team and to reflect on their practice. Furthermore, the rationale for the use of CAR is based in Burns's (1999) view that 'collaborative action research processes strengthen the opportunities for the results of research on practice to be fed back into educational systems in a more substantial and critical way' (p. 13).

The teacher educators were therefore interested in exploring how ESD could practically be infused into different courses, since the principles of ESD transcend disciplines. This infusion of ESD principles in selected courses involved a series of meetings and email exchanges in planning, designing, implementing and documenting the ESD infusion. A qualitative pre- and post-test in the form of a concept map was used to ascertain students' level of ESD awareness. At the same time, the teacher educators recorded ESD infusion reflections.

3.1   Participants

Of the six teacher educators who participated in the infusion aspect of the study, five are females and one is a male, and each taught a different course. One hundred and forty students at the undergraduate and graduate levels also participated in the study.

3.2   Data Collection Procedures

Concept map
A concept map was designed as the pre-test and post-test instrument used for ascertaining students' ESD awareness. It comprised two sections. The first section required

demographic details such as course name, student ID number, programme of study and their subject specialisation(s) as prospective teachers. Section two comprised four open-ended questions presented in the form of a concept map that required students to explain their understanding of the following concepts:

- SD;
- ESD;
- teachers promoting ESD;
- ESD actions required of the individual teacher.

Drawing on Novak and Cañas (2008), the instrument comprised four circles. Each circle contained one of the four terms with lines provided for participants to write their understanding of the term. This is consistent with the view that concept maps are useful 'graphical tools for organizing and representing knowledge' (Novak and Cañas, 2008, p. 1).

Reflection

The teacher educators carrying out the research were provided with the following four questions to guide their reflections:

1. In what ways has the collaborative process enhanced or inhibited my capacity to infuse ESD?
2. How did I feel about infusing ESD into the course?
3. What were my students' reactions/responses to the infusion of ESD into the course?
4. What new learning have I derived from this process?

The infusion of ESD principles

Prior to the implementation of the infusion, each teacher educator was asked to identify the course for infusion and submit infusion plans to the research group. Following the sharing and discussion of the plans, the plans were enacted and each teacher educator journaled the process and outcomes. Appendix Table 9A.1 provides the listing of courses and the ESD principles that were infused in each course. Additionally, the teacher educators were provided with the ESD Sourcebook (UNESCO, 2012) to aid in identification of possible ESD skills, issues, perspectives and/or values for infusion. Other support materials provided included:

- *A Rounder Sense of Purpose: Educational Competencies for Sustainable Development.*[1] This document provides guidelines on how the teacher educator can help learners develop competencies for SD by thinking holistically about the world, envisioning change, and for achieving transformation.
- Video recording providing an overview of ESD. The video was developed and produced by the current and past leaders of the ESD Working Group.
- A journal article on the reorientation of teacher education to address sustainability (Hordatt Gentles, 2018).

Meetings

The team of teacher educators met at least seven times over the duration of the project. The first meeting entailed a discussion of the idea of the collaborative project (November 2018). Thereafter, two meetings were held to conceptualise the research, clarify understanding of the aim of the project and what is meant by infusion, and design action plans for the intervention (December 2018 and January 2019). Additionally, updates on the infusion of ESD were received at regular meetings of the ESD Working Group (March 2019 and September 2019). Ideas for clarification were shared and discussed via emails.

3.3   Data Analysis

The analysis and findings shared in this chapter are based on the data from the action plans and reflections. Data analysis was undertaken collaboratively during two work sessions. Data from the action plans were analysed using direct interpretation of instances (Moustakas, 1990) while thematic analysis was undertaken for the data from the reflections. The data analysis for the reflections entailed individual transcription and group coding to develop categories and derive themes. The themes that emerged were agreed, validated and used to present findings. This collective analysis helped to add rigour and consistency to the qualitative analysis process (Creswell, 2016).

3.4   Ethical Considerations

The research proposal was submitted for review and approval from the SOE Director and the UWI Ethics Committee, respectively. Each teacher educator sensitised his or her students to the CAR project at the beginning of the semester. During the sensitisation session, students were asked to indicate their willingness to participate in the study by signing Informed Consent Forms. Only students who signed the Informed Consent Form were asked to complete the pre- and post-test.

4.   FINDINGS

4.1   How Do a Group of Teacher Educators Infuse ESD into the University Courses They Deliver?

All of the teacher educators were from a variety of disciplines and infused ESD using different approaches and activities. Based on the data received from the infusion plans, all had a shared understanding of what was expected for the infusion. Therefore, a variety of ESD-related skills, issues, perspectives, knowledge, and values were infused in the courses. Three of the six courses identified the specific ESD content that was infused while three courses did not specify this (see Appendix Table 9A.1).

Regarding the infusion of ESD skills, the skill *work co-cooperatively with other people in taking action* was common among three courses – namely, Environmental Education, History of Science and Science Teaching, and Principles of Curriculum Development and Implementation (see Table 9A.1). The approach of specifying the ESD content and skill to be infused aligns with Leicht et al.'s (2018) view of using ESD as an approach to change values, skills, knowledge and attitudes and Biasutti et al.'s (2016) view that ESD infusion should be deliberate.

ESD infusion in the respective courses mainly occurred in the teaching of content and the completion of activities in specified components of each course (Table 9.1). For each course, sensitisation and consent for participating in the ESD infusion occurred during weeks 1–2 while the specific infusion activities occurred at specific junctures of the course (Table 9.1). The infusion activities were carried out through mini-lectures; video and PowerPoint presentations; class discussion of ESD-related articles; completion of projects to include ESD-related principles; and the use of resource persons from agencies external to the university to aid the delivery of content. The data suggest that except for the Teacher Leadership course, ESD-specific content was infused in two or more class sessions for each course. For the courses Environmental Education, Fundamentals of Data Analysis, and History of Science and Science Teaching, infusion of ESD principles continued from the point of sensitisation until the end of the course. Additionally, three courses (Environmental Education, Fundamentals of Data Analysis, and Principles of Curriculum Development and Implementation) included ESD concepts as a component of an assessment. This would have allowed for deep rather than surface-level learning (Stimpson, 2006). Surface learning involves the learner having minimum interaction with the learning tasks by memorisation, applying procedures mechanically with the intent to gain a grade. Deep learning, on the other hand, involves 'an intention to understand and impose meaning' (Smith and Colby, 2007, p. 206).

4.2   What Collaborative Processes Are Employed by Teacher Educators in Infusing ESD?

In infusing ESD, the CAR process involved collaborative planning, implementation, data analysis and dissemination. Reflection was an integral aspect throughout the process. With respect to macro-level planning, all the participating teacher educators engaged in meetings to conceptualise the wider action research process, including the research purpose, questions and methodology. At the micro level, each teacher educator planned his or her own implementation – what course would be utilised, what ESD components would be infused, and how the infusion would occur. Reflection was ongoing throughout, serving as part of the data set but also serving as an intellectual and emotional exercise to record feelings, outcomes, surprises and other aspects of the process.

Implementation was also collaborative. Colleagues created one resource – a video – to utilise in class sessions as a common introduction to the concepts of SD and ESD. Colleagues also served as support persons for one another by visiting others' classes as guest lecturers. This was particularly useful for those colleagues who were new to the field and so benefited from the intervention of more seasoned peers.

Data analysis was also a collaborative undertaking with two half-day sessions devoted to qualitative analysis of individuals' reflections. The teacher educators worked in groups to code and cluster codes to produce larger-scale categories, and create assertions surrounding each reflective question.

Finally, the teacher educators disseminated – and continue to disseminate – the research findings in a collaborative manner. One medium was through presentation of preliminary findings at a graduate students' research seminar series in December 2019 to model

Table 9.1   How ESD infusion occurred in each course

Courses	Infusion Activities
Changing Cultures, Changing Schools	Sensitisation to research activity and pre-test (Week 1)
	Viewing of *Pricey Bargains* video; PowerPoint presentation and discussion on SD; listening to song 'Mother Earth's Cry'; paired activity identifying and discussing sustainability issues (Week 11)
	Mini lecture with PowerPoint and discussion on the concept of ESD; video presentation and discussion of a case of a school looking at sustainability (Week 12)
Environmental Education	Sensitisation to research activity and pre-test (Week 1)
	Video presentation on overview of ESD and discussion (Week 3)
	Weekly in-class discussions focusing on changing consumption patterns, climate change, solid and hazardous wastes
	Guest presenters from the Climate Change Division of the Ministry of Economic Growth and Job Creation in Jamaica, and the United Nations Development Programme (Weeks 6 and 7)
	Completion of action project as course assessment to include ESD focus
Fundamentals of Data Analysis	Sensitisation to research activity (Week 1)
	Mini guest lecture focusing on ESD-related concepts by ESD Working Group member (Week 5)
	Reading of at least three journal articles on ESD and summary of the literature on ESD (Weeks 2–13)
	Design of mini project collecting teachers' views on ESD included as part of course assessment (Weeks 3–13)
	Two-page reflection on ESD infusion
History of Science and Science Teaching	Sensitisation to research activity and pre-test (Week 1)
	PowerPoint presentation and discussion on what is sustainability; educational challenges for sustainability; implications of ESD for scientific literacy (Week 3)
	Ongoing discussion of ESD-related concepts as they emerged throughout the course
Principles of Curriculum Development and Implementation	Sensitisation to research activity and pre-test (Week 2)
	Video presentation on overview of ESD followed by class discussion (Week 5)
	PowerPoint presentation and discussion on ESD; peer teaching based on analysis of article by the International Bureau of Education-United Nations Educational, Scientific and Cultural Organization (IBE-UNESCO, 2015)
	Repositioning and reconceptualising the curriculum for the effective realisation of SDG 4, for holistic development and sustainable ways of living; and one chapter from the text *SDG4 – Quality Education: Inclusivity, Equity and Lifelong Learning For All* (Ferguson et al., 2019, pp. 49–69) (Week 8)
	Designing of units to include ESD principles as part of course assessment (Weeks 7–12)
Teacher Leadership	Sensitisation to research activity and pre-test (Week 1)
	Video presentation on overview of ESD and discussion, two YouTube videos about the Millennium Development Goals, Education for All and the SDGs that explained the significance of concern and action for sustainability through education; PowerPoint presentation and discussion on ESD as an option for advocacy (Week 6)

the CAR process whilst simultaneously introducing the concept of ESD. This chapter represents a more formalised presentation of the process and the findings.

A community of learners was formed through the sharing of resources, modelling of practices and collegiality in drawing on each other's expertise. The following comments are reflective of views shared:

> Colleagues keep referring to me as an 'expert' and I do not feel that way at all. However, seeing everyone's commitment, seeing people read more and research to understand sustainable development and ESD has been inspiring and encouraging, and has made me stop doubting that this work is important. I felt teary-eyed when a colleague emailed their PowerPoint presentation to share what they had put together for their students. It was so much work! It demonstrated so much research! And it drew on some of the influential thinkers in sustainability such as Sterling and Orr. This has bolstered my own personal passion and strengthened me to forge ahead with the infusion and with this collaborative undertaking. (Participant 5)

> Because of my minimal knowledge about ESD, the collaborative process enhanced my capacity to infuse ESD. Therefore, the infusion allowed access to colleagues who have more knowledge than me about ESD. Drawing on this resource, a colleague was invited to do a 15-minute presentation on ESD to students . . . Also, two colleagues were integral in the development of the assignment for the students' final project for the course using an issue in ESD. (Participant 3)

4.3   What Strategies and Practices Can be Utilised to Infuse ESD into University-level Courses?

The study found at least four strategies and practices that can be utilised to infuse ESD into university-level courses (Figure 9.1).

The first is that of seeking to be self-critical about one's experience and expertise, and being open to new ideas. Participant 1 highlights the utility of this approach:

> Although I felt I had no major challenges about infusing ESD into my EE course, I just wondered in a tentative way whether I had any 'new' way/s of infusing ESD in a course that I had been teaching since 2015 in which ESD is already one of the themes . . . I had quickly realised that the field had moved on since then and I had only heard of ESD since joining as a Faculty member in the SOE . . . I have had to read more about ESD in order to improve my understanding so that I can make it as explicit as possible in my course. Improved reading has also helped me to be more aware of the ESD themes in order to make linkages for the students more easily in class discussions.

Kumar (2008) highlights the importance of self-criticism as a foundation of an educational enterprise that is committed to revolution versus reproduction. According to Kumar (2008), education is intended to result in social change and thus there is a fundamental need for the education system to ensure that its processes do not merely reproduce the existing social order. The same principle applies to the educator whose ability to effect social change rests in large measure in his or her openness to new ideas. Cheng et al. (2015) reinforce the position of Kumar (2008) in explaining the importance of self-critical reflection for university students to become successful learners. The field of ESD represents a new frontier in education and one in which every educator needs to be adept. The process of infusing ESD in university courses is a tool for achieving the goal of social change, and if the university is to be successful in achieving this goal, then one critical starting point is a disposition of self-criticism.

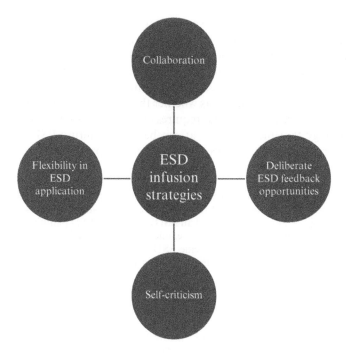

Figure 9.1   Strategies to infuse ESD into university-level courses

The second strategy emerging from the data is that of being deliberate about creating ongoing opportunities for students' feedback about the process of ESD inclusion as well as the content of what is being taught. The reflections and experiences of Participant 1 were instructive:

> I am always curious to find out what my students are thinking about this . . . course that I teach. At first it is difficult to gauge their true feelings . . . I got a mixture of responses from the first few classes that I had. There was mostly enthusiasm, however, one female student commented . . . that she did not understand what was happening and she even felt bored. I felt disappointed at first but right after she made that comment another . . . student summarised very enthusiastically what he was learning which was in line with what the focus of the course was.

The reflections of Participant 2 highlight the critical importance of actively engaging students:

> As I shared the ideas with the students, they were keen on being involved but wanted to know what extra would be required of them. I found myself spending more time reassuring them that this was all going to be integrated into the course and was not added extra work.

Andersson et al. (2013), struggled with this issue and shared the findings of their work using the 'values–beliefs–norms' framework. The study was conducted to determine whether participating in a teacher education course on SD can generate pro-SD beliefs and norms among future teachers. The study found that there is a probability that student-teachers who have a strong interest in environmental issues alongside a conviction that they should influence future students to commit to SD are more influenced by a teacher ESD course designed to provide the tools needed to teach about SD. The findings of the study by Andersson et al. (2013) suggest that the ideal targets for advancing the SD agenda should be those who are either already passionate about the cause or have an interest in becoming passionate. One of the concerns that seem to emanate from the reflections of the participants in the current study was whether the attempt at infusion was going to be merely a theoretical exercise or one that requires commitment on their part.

The third strategy that the study found can be used to infuse ESD is that of being flexible in the application of the process. Participant 2 captured the importance of this in the following:

> I found that I did not stick slavishly to the weekly schedule I planned for the infusion but integrated ESD at points when the content allowed and when the students asked certain questions that I thought would be best answered with an ESD concept . . . ESD planning requires carefully thought out strategies and a systematic yet flexible approach to deliberately infuse ESD. From this process I realise that even when we decide ESD will be infused in a particular topic we have to be open to those ideas being infused in other areas as the need allows.

The fourth strategy for effective infusion is collaborating with colleagues. The value of this approach is emphasised in the words of Participant 3, who wrote:

> Because of my minimal knowledge about ESD, the collaborative process enhanced my capacity to infuse ESD. Therefore, the infusion allowed access to colleagues who have more knowledge than me about ESD. Drawing on this resource, a colleague was invited to do a 15-minute presentation on ESD.

There have been multiple attestations concerning the importance of teacher collaboration in the literature (Berry et al., 2009; Burton, 2015; Ronfeldt et al., 2015), and this is borne out by the reflections of the teacher educators in this study.

5.   LESSONS LEARNT

5.1   Faculty Collaboration

Through this study, the ESD Working Group members have learned that collaboration provided an opportunity for the construction of 'collective knowledge' and expertise among faculty members (Burns, 2015). This collective knowledge served as a means of enhancing personal knowledge of ESD, and how it may be infused into classroom teaching and course outlines. Collaboration was also viewed as an opportunity to create and share resources. Collaboration therefore was seen to be an enabler, rather than an inhibitor, because it created an opportunity to develop a working relationship with others who were pursuing the same pedagogical goals and objectives. This was viewed as empowering and a benefit to professional growth.

Collaboration, as an effective means of expanding collective educational knowledge, was a significant lesson learnt, as it could allow for participants to express and share knowledge (Lantoff and Thorne, 2006 in Burns, 2015) and reflect (Burns, 1999, 2015; Garces and Granada, 2016) on ways of incorporating ESD in their teaching. Acquisition of knowledge and ideas as to how to infuse ESD in practice, through collaboration, could also potentially be disseminated widely and consistently amongst stakeholders, courses, disciplines and, possibly, faculties.

Another lesson learnt was that collaboration complements and can augment the process of action research. On its own, action research is a valid means of facilitating teacher and professional development (Gall and Acheson, 2011). When carried out collaboratively, action research becomes a socially constructive process by which reflection, higher-order thinking and problem solving are utilised to create knowledge (Woo et al., 2011 in Burns, 2015) and find solutions to common problems (Garces and Granada, 2016). These benefits and positive outcomes present CAR as an effective strategy for enhancing professional development (ibid.).

Given the possibilities that collaboration between faculty presents for the creation of collective knowledge and strategies that are designed to improve pedagogical practices and scaffolding, it may be beneficial for educational institutions to encourage and increase opportunities for academic staff to work together. This may be achieved through creative timetabling, team/co-teaching, and CAR. Facilitating collaboration may also provide an opportunity for the development of relevant and effective PD, such as PD models that are embraced, designed and directed by colleagues who share the same school-based, lived experiences (Burns, 2015). Professional development of this nature would have to be collegial and collaborative and may require the leeway for staff to form action research, lesson study or critical friends grouping (Gall and Acheson, 2011). Furthermore, though the teacher educators worked collaboratively, to a large extent they infused different ESD principles. This suggests that working together does not mean sameness of ESD infusion. Additionally, ESD infusion can occur in curricula when faculty possess a pedagogical disposition that allows them to be self-critical, flexible, deliberate and collaborative.

5.2 Faculty Development and Learning

The formation of a CAR group was viewed as a good opportunity for staff to share knowledge about ESD and how to incorporate it into their teaching. However, in spite of this benefit, some members of the group expressed that they still did not have sufficient understanding of ESD and how best to include it in their teaching. Some expressed that they felt inadequate, limited and unprepared to effectively infuse ESD in the courses they were teaching. From what was expressed, it would appear that during the process different interpretations and understanding of infusion of ESD could have occurred; therefore, contributing to the ambivalence of ESD and how to include it in classroom teaching.

The lesson that appears to be emerging from these sentiments is that collaboration, in spite of all its benefits, may not necessarily be the best or the only procedure to enable teachers understanding, acceptance and implementation of new and different ways of teaching. This should not be surprising given what educators know about how individuals learn differently, and that learning is a dynamic and continuous process that does not necessarily begin or end at a specific time. If educators do not expect the students in their classrooms to learn in the same ways and at the same pace, then why should this be expected within a multifarious group of university lecturers?

It may be prudent to offer other approaches and strategies for learning new concepts, and methodologies that support and supplement the collaborative approach. This may mean implementing strategies such as peer mentoring/coaching, videos of instruction or modelling as further PD strategies designed to facilitate a clearer understanding and infusion of ESD in teaching. Time should also be considered a key factor in terms of when a faculty member feels confident and comfortable enough to infuse the new methodology into their teaching. It may be in the best interest of the institution to expect that not all will infuse ESD in their programmes at the same time, at the same level and in the same ways. To accommodate this, individualised PD plans may be just as useful as group PD plans.

5.3 Faculty Commitment

An important lesson from this study was that effective collaboration occurred as a result of commitment to achieving a common goal. Commitment was an enabler – in other words, the common interest in the task of ESD infusion created the appropriate environment to foster professional commitment. Work environments can sometimes be complex, with faculty members having various tasks to complete and various roles to play. In this environment, it is often difficult to make commitments to complete tasks other than those related to job responsibilities. Faculty commitment in this study was fuelled by collegiality within the community of learning. Collegiality created a psychological bond and a strong sense of accountability that resulted in positive attitudes, behaviours (Choi and Tang, 2011) and determination to complete the requirements of ESD infusion.

There was a sense that each teacher educator felt highly responsible for maintaining his or her role in the collaborative process of infusing ESD into the courses. This commitment appeared to be influenced by a 'professional obligation' to learn more about ESD. Learning is dynamic – it is a life-long process. In this study, the teacher educators learned by 'doing'. They learned more about ESD and ESD infusion – the related concepts, skills and pedagogies – by remaining committed to the learning process. The teacher educators also displayed commitment to serving as positive and productive contributors to the group process. This obligatory commitment seemed to fuel a determination to persevere despite feelings of inadequacy, in order not to disappoint colleagues. It is not clear, however, whether the commitment demonstrated occurred because the teacher educators wanted to participate in the project or because as members of the Working Group they felt they had to participate.

It is recommended that in order to be successful members of collaboration teams, the work environment should encourage and support collegiality. This could be assisted by assembling members with similar goals, positive attitudes and reliable work ethics. New faculty should be socialised by senior faculty into a work culture requiring academic commitment and collegial responsibility. Senior faculty members should model professional obligations and be dependable in their responsibilities.

6.   CONCLUSION

A multidisciplinary group of teacher educators within an ESD Working Group carried out a CAR project that was designed to explore how to infuse ESD into the teaching of university courses. The hope is that the findings from this research eventually may be shared with other SOE staff members, as well as across faculties and departments within UWI's academic community to inspire ESD actions.

In conjunction with the research questions, the teacher educators reflected on the collaborative process and the strategies and practices as a means to facilitate the infusion of ESD in teaching and student learning. Each teacher educator was generally supportive of the process in that each shared time, resources, ideas and skills in order to ensure the success of the project. The inter-/multidisciplinary approach to ESD infusion brought various knowledge, ideas, content, skills and pedagogies to produce a unique infusion model that generated new ideas, content and pedagogies.

The findings from the project revealed that collaboration strengthened capacity and commitment to infuse ESD. This occurred largely due to the formation of a collegial community of learners where ESD was modelled, and resources and practices were shared. There were four key strategies and practices that were found useful for infusing ESD into university-level courses: self-critique and openness to new ideas; creating consistent opportunities for students' feedback; flexible application of the process; and collaboration with colleagues. It is also worth noting that the successful infusion of ESD required creativity and student-centred approaches to teaching.

Three notable/noteworthy lessons resulted from this CAR project. The first lesson related to collaboration as an effective means of expanding collective educational knowledge. For this reason, it may be worthwhile to encourage and increase opportunities for academic staff to work together. This may be achieved through creative timetabling, team/co-teaching, and CAR. Second, in spite of its benefits, collaboration was viewed as only one way of enabling teacher educators to infuse ESD in their teaching. Therefore, other approaches and strategies that complement collaboration should be utilised when appropriate. This could happen through the implementation of strategies such as peer mentoring/coaching, videos of instruction or modelling. The process created within each member of the Working Group a sense of responsibility, a 'professional obligation' to learn more about ESD and to infuse the pedagogy into their teaching and learning. For this reason, educational environments should encourage and support collegiality by selecting members with similar goals, positive attitudes and reliable work ethics. Additionally, as teacher educators seek to improve the level of ESD awareness and action, institutions should provide systems and structures that support open dialogue of efforts to infuse ESD at the individual and institutional levels. This will help to build community and foster the socially constructive processes needed to facilitate a multidisciplinary and cohesive approach to ESD infusion. Such efforts, however, must be underpinned by collegiality and commitment to do what it takes to actively infuse ESD in teaching. Only then can the appropriate strategies and practices for the context be discerned, and institutions can begin to work more cohesively to address the infusion of ESD in curricula.

NOTE

1.   Accessed 6 January 2020 at https://www.aroundersenseofpurpose.eu/uk/home.

REFERENCES

Andersson, K., Jagers, S.C., Lindskog, A. and Martinsson, J. (2013). Learning for the future? Effects of education for sustainable development (ESD) on teacher education students. *Sustainability*, 5(12), 5135–52.

Barth, M. and Rieckmann, M. (2012). Academic staff development as a catalyst for curriculum change towards education for sustainable development: an output perspective. *Journal of Cleaner Production*, 26, 28–36.

Berry, B., Daughtrey, A. and Wieder, A. (2009). Collaboration: closing the effective teaching gap. Centre for Teaching Quality. Accessed 5 January 2020 at https://files.eric.ed.gov/fulltext/ED509717.pdf.

Bertling, J. and Rearden, K. (2018). Professional development on a sustainable shoestring: propagating place-based art education in fertile soil. *Discourse and Communication for Sustainable Education*, 9(2), 5–20.

Biasutti, M., De Baz, T. and Alshawa, H. (2016). Assessing the infusion of sustainability principles into university curricula. *Journal of Teacher Education for Sustainability*, 18(2), 21–40.

Brandt, J., Burgener, L., Barth, M. and Redman, A. (2019). Becoming a competent teacher in education for sustainable development: learning outcomes and processes in teacher education. *International Journal of Sustainability in Higher Education*, 20(4), 630–53.

Burns, A. (1999). *Collaborative Action Research for English Language Teachers*. Cambridge, UK: Cambridge University Press.

Burns, A. (2015). Renewing classroom practices through collaborative action research. In K. Dikilitaş, R. Smith and W. Trotman (eds), *Teacher Researchers in Action* (pp. 2–3, 9–18). Faversham, UK: IATEFL.

Burton, T. (2015). Exploring the impact of teacher collaboration on teacher learning and development. [Doctoral dissertation]. Accessed 5 January 2020 at http://scholarcommons.sc.edu/etd/3107.

Cebrián, G. (2017). A collaborative action research project towards embedding ESD within the higher education curriculum. *International Journal of Sustainability in Higher Education*, 18(6), 857–76.

Cebrián, G., Grace, M. and Humphris, D. (2015). Academic staff engagement in education for sustainable development. *Journal of Cleaner Production*, 106, 79–86.

Cheng, M., Barnes, G. and Edwards, C. et al. (2015). *Transition Skills And Strategies: Critical Self-reflection*. Accessed 5 January 2020 at https://www.enhancementthemes.ac.uk/docs/ethemes/student-transitions/critical-self-reflection.pdf.

Chin, C.K., Munip, H. and Miyadera, R. et al. (2019). Promoting education for sustainable development in teacher education integrating blended learning and digital tools: an evaluation with exemplary cases. *EURASIA Journal of Mathematics, Science and Technology Education*, 15(1), Article em1653.

Choi, P. and Tang, S. (2011). Satisfied and dissatisfied commitment: teachers in three generations. *Australian Journal of Teacher Education*, 36(7), 45–75.

Coghlan, D. and Brydon-Miller, M. (2014). Collaborative action research. In D. Coghlan and M. Brydon-Miller (eds), *The SAGE Encyclopedia of Action Research*. London: SAGE Publications.

Creswell, J. (2016). *Thirty Essential Skills for the Qualitative Researcher*. Thousand Oaks, CA: SAGE Publications.

Eilam, E. and Trop, T. (2010). ESD pedagogy: a guide for the perplexed. *The Journal of Environmental Education*, 41(1), 43–64.

Ferguson, T., Iliško, D., Roofe, C. and Hill, S. (2019). *Quality Education: Inclusivity, Equity and Lifelong Learning For All*. Bingley, UK: Emerald.

Gall, M.D. and Acheson, K.A. (2011). *Clinical Supervision and Teacher Development: Preservice and Inservice Applications* (6th edition). Hoboken, NJ: John Wiley & Sons.

Garces, A. and Granada, L. (2016). The role of collaborative action research in teachers' professional development. *Profile*, 18(1), 39–54.

Goldman, D., Yavetz, B. and Peer, S. (2006). Environmental literacy in teacher training in Israel: environmental behaviour of new students. *Journal of Environmental Education*, 38(1), 3–22.

Hordatt Gentles, C. (2018). Reorienting Jamaican teacher education to address sustainability: challenges, implications and possibilities. *Caribbean Quarterly*, 64(1), 149–66.

Hungerford, H.R., Volk, T.L. and Ramsey, J.M. (1989). *A Prototype Environmental Education Curriculum for the Middle School: A Discussion Guide for UNESCO Training Seminars on Environmental Education*. UNESCO–UNEP International Environment Education Programme Series 29.

International Bureau of Education-United Nations Educational, Scientific and Cultural Organization (IBE-UNESCO). (2015). Repositioning curriculum in education quality and development-relevance. Accessed 15 February 2020 at http://www.ibe.unesco.org/en/blogs/repositioning-curriculum-education-quality-development-relevance-join-conversation.

International Centre of Education for Sustainable Development (SWEDESD). (2017). *Visby Recommendations for Enhancing ESD in Teacher Education*. SWEDESD. Accessed 15 January 2020 at https://www.swedesd.uu.se/digitalAssets/611/c_611672-l_3-k_btgvisby2016.pdf.

Kopnina, H. and Meijers, F. (2014). Education for sustainable development (ESD): exploring theoretical and practical challenges. *International Journal of Sustainability in Higher Education*, 15(2), 188–207.

Kostyuchenko, N. and Smolennikov, D. (2018). Education for sustainable development through teacher training. *Studia Periegetica*, 3(23), 11–20.

Kumar, A. (2008). The place of critical self-awareness in social education for revolution. Paper presented to the Rouge Forum Conference, Education: Reform or Revolution, University of British Colombia, 13–16 March.

Leal Filho, W., Shiel, C. and Paço, A. et al. (2019). Sustainable Development Goals and sustainability teaching at universities: falling behind or getting ahead of the pack? *Journal of Cleaner Production*, 232, 285–94.

Leicht, A., Heiss, J. and Byun, W.J. (2018). Introduction. In A. Leicht, J. Heiss and W.J. Byun (eds), *Issues and Trends in Education for Sustainable Development* (pp. 7–16). Paris: UNESCO.

Marcinkowski, T. (2004). Using a logic model to review and analyze an environmental education program. [Monograph]. Washington, DC: North American Association for Environmental Education.

McKeown, R. and Hopkins, C. (2014). Teacher education and education for sustainable development: ending the DESD and beginning the GAP. [Monograph]. Toronto: York University.

Moustakas, C. (1990). *Heuristic Research: Design, Methodology and Applications*. Newbury Park, CA: SAGE Publications.

Novak, J.D. and Cañas, A.J. (2008). *The Theory Underlying Concept Maps and How to Construct and Use Them*. Technical Report IHMC Cmap Tools 2006-01 Rev 01-2008. Florida Institute for Human and Machine Cognition. Accessed 27 February 2019 at http://cmap.ihmc.us/Publications/ResearchPapers/TheoryUnderlyingConceptMaps.pdf.

Pearson, E. and Degotardi, S. (2009). Education for sustainable development in early childhood education: a global solution to local concerns? *International Journal of Early Childhood*, 41(2), 97–111.

Rieckmann, M. (2018). Learning to transform the world: key competencies in education for sustainable development. In A. Leicht, J. Heiss and W.J. Byun (eds), *Issues and Trends in Education for Sustainable Development* (pp. 39–59). Paris: UNESCO.

Rieckmann, M. (2020). Education for sustainable development in teacher education: an international perspective. In S. Lahiri (ed.), *Environmental Education*. Delhi: Studera Press.

Ronfeldt, M., Farmer, S., McQueen, K. and Grissom, J. (2015). Teacher collaboration in instructional teams and student achievement. *American Educational Research Journal*, 52(3), 475–514.

Smith, T.W. and Colby, S.A. (2007). Teaching for deep learning. *The Clearing House: A Journal of Educational Strategies, Issues and Ideas*, 80(5), 205–10.

Stevenson, R. (2007). Schooling and environmental/sustainability education: from discourses of policy and practice to discourses of professional learning. *The Journal of Environmental Education*, 13(2), 265–85.

Stimpson, P. (2006). Orientation and approaches to environmental and geographical education for sustainability. In Z.C.-K. Lee and M. Williams (eds), *Environmental and Geographical Education for Sustainability: Cultural Contexts* (pp. 66–75). New York: Nova Science Publishers Inc.

Tilbury, D. (2010). Are we learning to change? Mapping global progress in education for sustainable development in the lead up to 'Rio Plus 20'. *Global Environmental Research*, 14, 101–7.

United Nations Conference on Environment and Development (UNCED). (1992). *Agenda 21: Programme of Action for Sustainable Development*. New York: United Nations. Accessed 23 December 2019 at https://sustainabledevelopment.un.org/content/documents/Agenda21.pdf.

United Nations Educational, Scientific and Cultural Organization (UNESCO). (n.d.). Building capacities of educators and trainers. Accessed 15 January 2020 at http://en.unesco.org/gap/priority-action-areas/building-capacities.

United Nations Educational, Scientific and Cultural Organization (UNESCO). (2012). *Education for Sustainable Development Sourcebook*. Paris: UNESCO.

United Nations Educational, Scientific and Cultural Organization (UNESCO). (2014). *UNESCO Roadmap for Implementing the Global Action Programme on Education for Sustainable Development*. Paris: UNESCO.

United Nations Educational, Scientific and Cultural Organization (UNESCO). (2017a). *Education for Sustainable Development Goals: Learning Objectives*. Paris: UNESCO.

United Nations Educational, Scientific and Cultural Organization (UNESCO). (2017b), Education for sustainable development: partners in action; halfway through the Global Action Programme on Education for Sustainable Development. Accessed 9 February 2021 at https://unesdoc.unesco.org/ark:/48223/pf0000259719.

APPENDIX

Table 9A.1   Courses and ESD principles infused

Courses and Level	ESD Principles
Changing Cultures, Changing Schools (postgraduate)	General sensitisation
Environmental Education (postgraduate)	*Skills:*
	The ability to move from knowledge and awareness to taking action for the environment
	Work cooperatively with other people in taking action
	Using the arts
	Whole-systems approach
	Values:
	Environmental values education strategies
	Issues related to the local community:
	Changing consumption patterns, climate change, solid and hazardous wastes
Fundamentals of Data Analysis (postgraduate)	General sensitisation
History of Science and Science Teaching (undergraduate)	*Knowledge:*
	The implications of the distribution of resources in determining the nature of societies and the rate and character of economic development
	The role of science and technology in the development of societies and the impact of these technologies on the environment
	The interconnectedness of present world political, economic, environmental and social issues
	Skills:
	Apply definitions of fundamental concepts, such as environment, community, development and technology, to local, national and global experiences
	Develop hypotheses based on balanced information, critical analysis and careful synthesis and test them against new information and personal experience and beliefs
	Develop cooperative strategies for appropriate action to change present relationships between ecological preservation and economic development
	Values:
	An appreciation of the challenges faced by the human community in defining the processes needed for sustainability and in implementing the changes needed
	A sense of balance in deciding among conflicting priorities. Personal acceptance of a sustainable lifestyle and a commitment to participation in change
	A realistic appreciation of the urgency of the challenges facing the global community and the complexities that demand long-term planning for building a sustainable future

Table 9A.1   (continued)

Courses and Level	ESD Principles
Principles of Curriculum Development and Implementation (postgraduate)	*Skills:* The ability to use multiple perspectives to understand another person's viewpoint The ability to analyse values underlying differing positions The ability to work co-cooperatively with other people *Perspectives:* There must be a balance and integration of environment, society and economy Systems thinking or a whole-systems approach should be used in problem solving rather than looking at problems in isolation Differing views should be considered before reaching a decision or judgment *Values:* Build democratic societies that are just, participatory, sustainable and peaceful Treat all living beings with respect and consideration Promote a culture of tolerance, non-violence and peace
Teacher Leadership (postgraduate)	General sensitisation

10. Teaching leadership skills to sustainability professionals
R. Bruce Hull, David P. Robertson and Michael Mortimer

1.   INTRODUCTION

Sustainability challenges are wicked and thus not easily resolved by scientific or technical solutions; that is, sustainability challenges are complex, uncertain, conflicted, dynamic, and social. Thus, they require a special set of competencies variously called soft skills, people skills, influence, collaboration, innovation, transdisciplinarity, and more – a bundle of skills and practices we call *leadership*. To meet this need, prominent professional societies (e.g., National Association for EHS&S Management, International Society of Sustainability Professionals), as well as numerous universities, now offer programs to teach leadership competencies to sustainability professionals (Brundiers and Wiek, 2017; Gallagher, 2012; MacDonald and Shriberg, 2016; Shriberg and MacDonald, 2013). The aim of this chapter is to explain why sustainability professionals need leadership skills, define this skill set, and describe an approach for teaching it to working sustainability professionals. Specifically, with respect to this book, these leadership skills will be needed to meet the 2030 Agenda for Sustainable Development and achieve the Sustainable Development Goals.

2.   LEADERSHIP

Leadership is a celebrated topic discussed in countless journals, self-help books, and professional development programs and is taught extensively in business, public administration, and military curricula (Northouse, 2015). The core concepts – the ontology – of traditional leadership theories include a leader, followers, and the things leaders get followers to do. Hence, traditional leadership theories emphasize attributes and actions of leaders (e.g., leaders are authentic, charismatic, honest, empathetic, visionary, servants) and how they motivate followers (e.g., through transformative motivation or transactional exchange) (Bennis, 2007; Northouse, 2015; Shriberg, 2012). This approach was recently applied to explore efforts by leaders of institutions of higher education to promote their institution's commitment to sustainability (Leal Filho et al., 2020). This focus on leaders and their characteristics has been popular and effective but, as discussed in the next section, it is less appropriate for professionals facing wicked sustainable development challenges.

The wicked challenges of sustainable development require a different theory and ontology of leadership, one where the responsibility is shared by all actors and where the basic elements of leadership are direction, alignment, and commitment (Drath et al., 2008; Hull, Robertson and Mortimer, 2020) (Table 10.1). Direction results when stakeholders

Table 10.1   Basic elements of leadership

Direction	Alignment	Commitment
Direction exists when stakeholders agree on the gap between aspirations and reality, what they are aiming to accomplish, what success looks like, and how they will achieve it. In wicked situations, when conditions are changing and clouded by uncertainty, such clarity requires a process of continuously creating and refining direction. It may involve orchestrating conflict and exposing internal contradictions that mobilize people to clarify what matters most and what can be traded off. Would-be collaborators without direction are uncertain about what they should accomplish together and may feel pulled in different directions by competing goals	Stakeholders must coordinate their efforts to do the work needed to produce the desired outcomes. Diverse stakeholders bring different resources to bear: they have different expertise, pull different levers to create change, and exercise different types of influence. Some tasks are glamorous and thus generate too many volunteers. Other tasks are less popular because they are expensive, risky, boring, or thankless. Stakeholders with weak alignment work in isolation, do not see how their tasks fit into the larger set of tasks to be done, risk working at cross-purposes, and leave some tasks undone	Stakeholders must willingly sacrifice some self-interests and be willing to invest their resources to achieve shared goals. Stakeholders with strong commitment feel responsible for the success and well-being of the collective effort and know that other stakeholders feel the same. They trust one another, will stick with the effort through difficult times, and allow other stakeholders to make demands on their time and energy. If commitment does not exist, then people make promises but do not follow through, or worse, drag their feet and sabotage progress

Source: Based on Drath et al. (2008); Hull et al. (2020).

agree on goals and strategies to achieve these goals. Alignment results when stakeholders coordinate resources to implement the strategies to achieve those goals. Commitment results when stakeholders willingly work toward those goals, even at some sacrifice of self-interest. When all three outcomes – direction, alignment, *and* commitment – are present, then group action occurs and can be sustained. This ontology shifts attention from attributes of leaders to the practices of stakeholders that promote direction, alignment, and commitment. Responsibility for leadership is shared and everyone can and should lead from where they are. Importantly, everyone can learn, apply, and improve upon practices that make direction, alignment, and commitment occur; that is, leadership can be taught and learned.

Leadership guru Ronald Heifetz (1994) offers us a thought experiment to illustrate the critical difference between shared versus leader–follower theories of leadership: imagine the different responsibilities and outcomes that occur when stakeholders assume that leadership means they will follow a leader's vision versus assuming that leadership means influencing one another to face shared challenges. In the leader–follower ontology, the vision of the desired future condition comes from the leader and if something goes wrong with that vision or the process leading to it, fault lies with the leader. In the shared leadership model, goals emerge from the stakeholders who must hold themselves accountable for the future they create and the process for creating it.

All three outcomes – direction, alignment, *and* commitment – must be present for leadership to occur. You are probably familiar with frustrating situations when one or more of these conditions did not exist. For example, when stakeholders have direction but no alignment, they agree on a mission statement but, perhaps because they are competitors for funding, will not share resources or not do the mundane and unnoticed tasks. Conversely, if stakeholders have commitment without direction or alignment, people head off in all directions at once, often working at cross-purposes as well as risking burnout and damaging the reputation of the group. Most perversely, a group can have direction and alignment but no commitment, so feet get dragged and time, money, and goodwill get wasted; or, worse, the effort gets sabotaged.

Nothing in this conception of leadership diminishes the critical roles played by people in recognized leadership positions, at the top of the hierarchy, elected or promoted to corner offices, with authority over people and budgets in their organizations and networks. They have an enormous impact and can facilitate or delay achieving direction, alignment, and commitment. In some situations, direction, alignment, and/or commitment can't be achieved without them. But, still, for reasons reviewed in this chapter, these few individuals can't do it alone. They must focus their energies on facilitating direction, alignment, and commitment among stakeholders. Navigating the wicked challenges of sustainable development requires both strong leadership from above as well as shared leadership from below, the middle, outside in, and inside out.

3. WICKED LEADERSHIP

Wicked problems require a special type of leadership. Many readers will be familiar with Rittel and Webber's (1973) classic work describing the attributes of wicked problems. Heifitz (1994), Norton (2015), and Grint (2005) extend that classic work to suggest leadership challenges associated with attributes of wicked problems (Table 10.2). Wicked problems, to paraphrase former UN Secretary-General Kofi Annan, are 'problems without passports'. Their impacts cross geographic and political boundaries and their solution must as well. Also, because wicked problems are unique, no one has experience solving them and thus stakeholders' understandings of a problem will change as they learn more about it and while they simultaneously try to solve it. Many wicked problems are tragic in that someone or something will lose: win–win solutions don't exist (i.e., people are trading off prosperity, identity, health, history, and biodiversity). And solutions are hotly contested because no objective, external criterion exists by which to determine the best or optimal solution. The dynamism and uncertainty of wicked problems confound understanding, prediction, and control. Science, expertise, and technology may be of limited a priori use. Because many wicked problems are unsolvable, failure is inevitable and continuous effort and learning are required.

If these illustrative attributes of wicked problems aren't challenging enough, the second half of Table 10.2 explores attributes of what Levin and colleagues (2012) call superwicked problems. Climate change is a good example of a super-wicked problem. Everyone

Table 10.2   Attributes of wicked problems

Problem Definition	*Scales* Across Which Actions and Impacts *Connect*	*Diversity* of Stakeholders Who Must *Collaborate*	*Uncertainty* to Which Stakeholders Must *Adapt*
Iterative: engaging the problem changes stakeholder understanding, which changes the problem definition	No one with authority over everyone who must be engaged	Contested: no win–win (someone loses)	High uncertainty
			Unknown unknowns
	Key actors don't know or interact with one another	Very diverse expertise needed	Unpredictable, unclear cause–effect
Each situation is unique	Open systems with unclear boundaries	Transdisciplinary	Interventions cause ripples that create new problems
No optimal, calculated, objectively best outcome		Requires working well beyond existing institutions and arrangements	Dynamism requires continuous learning
	Multi-scalar risks: local, regional, national, global		Relentless: can't be solved, only improved or delayed
Slow, unseen impacts don't mobilize concern		Those who define the problem also cause it and thus must change to solve it	
	Tragedy of commons (individual rational actions don't lead to rational aggregate outcome)		Requires continuous attention and learning
Worsened by waiting		Extensively cross-sector	
Will cause enormous harm and suffering if ignored		International, cross-cultural	Requires sensemaking rather than problem solving
	Long time horizon	Can't consult some stakeholders such as future generations	
Interconnectedness with other problems necessitates designing to fail without bringing down the whole	Risks increase with scale to create global tipping points		

on Earth is both responsible and impacted. These impacts and responsibilities are perceived differently and distributed unevenly. Further, delay is not a good option because unknown tipping points might produce irreversible changes with potentially catastrophic consequences. Confoundingly, super-wicked problems are not isolated: deep interdependencies with factors that ignore geographic, political, and other boundaries can cause unanticipated changes to ripple through global systems, further changing conditions and people and further causing unanticipated changes to ripple back through global systems.

The direction-alignment-commitment theory of leadership is extremely robust. Direction, alignment, and commitment are properties of leadership that generalize to most cultures, contexts, and situations. Pretty much anywhere or anytime that leadership occurs, even for wicked problems, stakeholders have achieved direction, alignment, and commitment. However, and this is important, the *practices* that produce direction, alignment, and commitment vary by situation.

To have real influence and relevance, sustainability professionals need a large toolbox of leadership practices that work in wicked situations. Table 10.3 illustrates how leadership practices that help stakeholders *connect across scale, collaborate across diversity,* and

Table 10.3   Cross-walking leadership theory and practice

Leadership for Wicked Challenges of Sustainable Development		Leadership Theory		
		Direction	Alignment	Commitment
Illustrative Leadership Practices	Connect	A shared story that describes the gap between current and desired conditions.	Learning networks that help actors find one another, devise, and share strategies.	Transparent reporting that motivates responsibility via shame and fame.
	Collaborate	Reframe to focus on shared values and interests rather than facts and positions.	Build trust with process that is participatory, correctable, and accountable.	Promote identity in new, shared goals and community.
	Adapt	Double-loop learning that questions and refines goals.	Tolerance for stakeholder failure as novel solutions and partnerships get tested.	Continuous feedback that explains and rewards course corrections.

adapt to uncertainty can promote direction, alignment, and commitment in the wicked situations. Additional connective, collaborative, and adaptive leadership practices are listed and illustrated in the next section and explained in detail in Hull et al. (2020).

1. *Connecting actors distributed across scale.* Many of the most pressing sustainability challenges and opportunities, such as climate change and supply chain risks, are distributed across vast, complicated, tele-connected, and sometimes global systems. No 'leader' has authority over or even awareness of all the stakeholders who must be engaged because stakeholders reside in different organizations and nations. Most actors will neither meet nor interact. Some actors will not even realize they are connected to the problem. Nonetheless, connection and coordination must occur to generate and maintain direction, alignment, and commitment across these different scales of political, economic, and ecological units, crossing boundaries of space, time, culture, and politics as solutions emerge, falter, and/or scale (Geels, 2015).
2. *Collaborating across differences.* Sustainability challenges require collaboration among people that have different assumptions, values, cultures, disciplines, and organizational obligations. Stakeholders often do not agree on what the situation is or what to do about it, and they may resist or ignore those who attempt to define it for them. Stakeholders must do this difficult work themselves; it can't be done for them by a 'leader'. They must voluntarily explain, defend, and develop shared interests and positions if direction, alignment, and commitment are to be sustained (Heifetz, 1994; Norton, 2015).
3. *Adapting to uncertainty.* Sustainability challenges require being adaptable to continual change and high uncertainty. The rate of technological, social, and environmental

change has never been greater (Steffen et al., 2015). Moreover, stakeholders are unpredictable. They change as they encounter and learn about new conditions and new opportunities (Norton, 2015). Their changed values and new goals trigger feedback loops that create new, unique system dynamics that require new interventions and course corrections that in turn require continuous re-engagement, learning, and compromise. Causation will be unknowable and control impossible in these dynamic and emergent conditions, making less effective rational problem-solving leadership styles that rely on mobilizing stakeholders to analyze, predict, and control situations. Instead, we need leadership approaches that put the burden on stakeholders for learning-by-doing, which requires transparency, communication, failing, and adapting (Dreier, Nabarro and Nelson, 2019).

4.　METHOD FOR TEACHING LEADERSHIP

MacDonald and Shriberg (2016) and Shriberg and MacDonald (2013) survey higher education programs in North America that teach leadership to environmental professionals. Many approaches exist. This section describes an approach delivered over ten years to working sustainability professionals pursuing a graduate degree (Figure 10.1). It combines wicked leadership practices with the traditional scientific and technical content professionals need. Evaluations of this pedagogy suggest it does deliver the listed leadership competencies (Hull, Robertson and Mortimer, 2018).

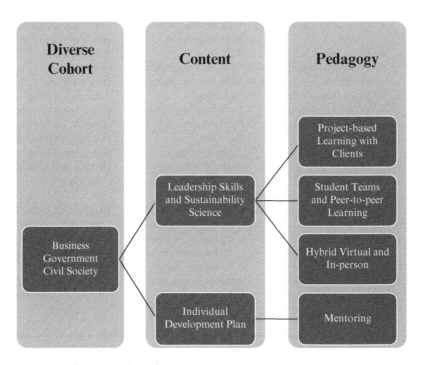

Figure 10.1　Key elements of graduate program

A cohort is assembled of 20–35 mid-career professionals (age range is 25–65; the average age is ~40) who have diverse academic, disciplinary, and professional backgrounds. Regardless of background, students must have significant professional work experience and be currently employed so they can use and bring job experiences to the classroom. Approximately equal representation from each of three sectors – business, government, and civil society – creates opportunity for significant peer-to-peer learning. The approximately one-year program meets face-to-face one weekend a month, near Washington, DC, where students can engage with peers, faculty, guest experts, and project clients. In the intervals between meetings, the hybrid curriculum includes asynchronous online learning units and synchronous virtual teamwork on projects.

The multidisciplinary program begins with a 'boot camp' to bring everyone up to the same level of understanding of sustainable development concepts, communication skills, systems thinking, and leadership tools commonly found in other graduate programs (MacDonald and Shriberg, 2016). The program then takes a deep dive into leadership practices relevant to the different levels of social interaction where sustainability professionals work: individual, team, organization, network, and societal scales (Table 10.4 contains more detail). The program also paces students through a series of learning modules

Table 10.4   Illustrative wicked leadership competencies

Outcome Type	Connect/Coordinate	Collaborate	Adapt
Awareness (of self and others)	Influence without authority style Control and inclusion traits Reflection	Personality, values Cross-cultural awareness Transdisciplinary Interdisciplinary Reflection	Learning style Conflict styles Tolerance for uncertainty and need for closure Reflection
Tools (strategies, best practices, approaches)	*Collective impact* Community of practice Scaling up innovation Systems mapping Social marketing Storytelling Impact words and writing	*Cross-sector partnering* Boundary-spanning leadership Ladder of inference Fist-to-Five Yes-And Team principles Project management Conflict facilitation Negotiation	*Sensemaking* Improvisation After action review Receive and give feedback Adaptive management Holding environments Social innovation Double- and triple-loop learning
Networks (examples, connections, and information shared among peers)	Examples of exemplary professionals who discuss their careers and influence working in distributed networks Access relevant global knowledge networks Peer network	Examples of exemplary professionals who discuss their history and success due to collaboration Access relevant global knowledge networks Peer network	Examples of exemplary professionals who discuss their ability to work with uncertain and dynamic situations Access relevant global knowledge networks Peer network

Note: Items in italic are discussed in more detail below. Other items are explained in Ernst and Chrobot-Mason (2010); Fisher and Shapiro (2005); Hull et al. (2020); and Runde and Flanagan (2010).

about the science and technology of sustainable development challenges in the US (e.g., water, climate, energy, food and agriculture, urbanization, supply chains). Instructors and guest experts represent a mix of government, business, and civil society perspectives. Students work as 'consultancy' teams on real projects and interact with clients. The program then transitions to global issues and cultural competencies. It concludes with international travel and project work allowing students to interact with peers from other countries and cultures. Throughout the program, students also focus on expanding their professional networks, refining their career plans, and advancing an independent study project designed to complement their professional development goals.

The program uses monthly learning modules that, although differing in content, all have the same four elements: (1) reading and prep-work done remotely; (2) synchronous meetings with peers, faculty, experts, clients that also provides time to do teamwork, practice leadership, and interact socially; (3) virtual teamwork and study time to complete project analysis, priority setting, and to prepare deliverables; and (4) individual reflections about lessons learned that can generalize to other situations to careers. We use pedagogies that are problem based and require shared inquiry (Barrett and Moore, 2010; Kolb, 2014), create opportunity to be reflective about lessons being learned (Bolton, 2010), and provide multiple touches on key topics so students can work through the learning cycle (Kolb, 2014). Thus, our program shares the common attributes that MacDonald and Shriberg (2016) found in their survey of programs: network building, project-based learning, and systems thinking. Importantly, the experiential nature of our program provides students a safe space to try out and practice leadership tools, roles, and styles.

Table 10.4 lists connective, collaborative, and adaptive leadership competencies taught in the program (the list is illustrative as the year-long program covers additional topics). These leadership competencies and practices facilitate direction, alignment, and commitment in wicked situations.

The rows in Table 10.4 distinguish among three types of leadership competencies: awareness, tools, and network. Leadership begins with *awareness* of self and others. To influence others, one needs to first know one's own traits, tendencies, biases, values, and assumptions before being able to recognize, understand, and manage those attributes in others. Students take and interpret multiple diagnostics designed to facilitate this self-awareness. *Tools* are frameworks, best practices, and strategies that people use to facilitate leadership outcomes. They are 'tools' in the sense that they fit different situations, produce different outcomes, and are stored in a metaphorical toolbox to be brought out and applied as need arises. *Networks* further enhance a person's leadership competencies because they provide access to role models, mentors, peers, opportunities, support, feedback, and just-in-time useful information.

One leadership competency from each column (noted in italic in Table 10.4) is elaborated in the text below. Limitations of space prevent full descriptions of all table entries.

1.   *Connect and coordinate action using collective impact.* The collective impact method is a set of best practices that help coordinate people distributed across space and time, working in different organizations, who may never meet one another. Successful efforts at generating collective impact tend to share five conditions: common agenda, shared measurement, mutually reinforcing activities, continuous communication, and backbone support (Kania and Kramer, 2011). Practicing collective impact is difficult

to replicate within the limitations of academic semesters, especially when students have full-time jobs and are geographically separated. So, ongoing efforts are studied using problem-based learning. For example, students form consulting teams to advise a nearby city that is using a multi-stakeholder collaborative effort to reduce local carbon emissions. The student teams review how actors, organizations, and public and private programs coordinate their efforts, including green building programs, transit-oriented development, renewable and low-carbon fuels, district energy, and 'green games' to motivate business and household conservation (Hull and Dooley, 2019). Key stakeholders are invited to class and describe their processes, successes, and struggles. Students use the collective impact tool to analyze and suggest improvements to the processes.

2. *Collaborate using cross-sector partnering.* Challenges such as climate change are not only beyond the scope of individual organizations, they are beyond the scope of any single sector (i.e., business, government, or civil society). Solutions, therefore, require, among other things, cross-sector, inter-organizational partnering. Partnering best practices include doing due diligence on partners' strengths and risks, establishing mutually beneficial shared goals, creating a learning culture, and designing governance structures that are transparent and hold actors accountable (Tennyson, 2003). Students use problem-based learning to learn these practices. They study an ongoing innovative cross-sector partnership addressing a sustainability challenge and use partnering best practices to study and critique the partnership's efforts. Stakeholders from each sector (business, government, and civil society) come into the classroom to discuss their roles, motivations, and partnering tips and challenges. Students prepare a report for these 'clients', summarizing observations, recommendations, and lessons learned.

3. *Adapt to uncertainty using sensemaking.* Rational problem analysis and reductionism do not work well when confronted with the immense complexity, uncertainty, and dynamism of major sustainability challenges (Bennis, 2007). Sensemaking is an alternative and more appropriate approach for these highly uncertain, contentious, wicked challenges (Snowden and Boone, 2007). It avoids analysis paralysis of rational planning by emphasizing actions that help make sense of and bring order to a situation rather than expecting to eliminate uncertainty, impose control, and solve the problem. Students use a sensemaking tool to map stakeholders' concerns and influence, the strategies they use to affect change, the system properties and feedback loops where leverage can be exercised, and the outcomes used to guide and evaluate success. For example, over a several-month effort they make sense of a project and situation new to them (most projects are based in rapidly developing countries such as India and China). They begin with desk research using reports by stakeholder organizations, and follow with email and phone interviews, as well as a site visit to ground truth and dig deeper.

5.   CONCLUSION

Sustainability professionals and technical education programs often emphasize science and technology. This chapter argues that leadership skills will also be needed to meet the 2030 Agenda for Sustainable Development. In particular, the direction-alignment-commitment theory of shared leadership is appropriate for the wicked problems typical of sustainable development. Sustainability professionals will be more influential and relevant if they have a toolbox of leadership practices designed to address the connective, collaborative, and adaptive aspects of wicked systems. Importantly, professionals can learn these competencies – leadership is not an innate quality of leaders, but rather something that can be learned. Higher education programs can teach these leadership skills and practices.

Over a decade of experience with the program described here and the hundreds of students graduating from it have taught the authors some powerful lessons. Career success and professional impact, as well as the hope and promise of sustainable development, are clearly enhanced by leadership skills and practices that mobilize people to solve wicked problems. Yet many aspiring professionals look to higher education primarily for technical, scientific expertise rather than leadership competencies. Likewise, many academic faculty and programs focus primarily if not exclusively on technical and scientific skills. A challenge to empowering sustainability professionals is finding the right balance between teaching leadership and teaching science and technology. There needs to be more research and debate about that balance. There also needs to be a concerted effort to match leadership skills to specific sustainable development challenges. Differing approaches to leadership are needed for different situations. There exists a large body of literature and practice about leadership and a growing body of literature and practice about the science and technology of sustainable development goals. Efforts such as those cited here are working to expand the overlap between these areas of knowledge and practice with the intent of helping achieve the SDGs. Trial and error will need to be tolerated as programs evolve to meet the needs of working professionals and as the leadership toolbox expands and refines.

REFERENCES

Barrett, T. and S. Moore (2010), *New Approaches to Problem-Based Learning: Revitalizing Your Practice in Higher Education*, Abingdon: Routledge.

Bennis, W. (2007), 'The challenges of leadership in the modern world: introduction to the special issue', *American Psychologist*, **62**, 2–5.

Bolton, G. (2010), *Reflective Practice: Writing and Professional Development*, Los Angeles, CA: SAGE.

Brundiers, K. and A. Wiek (2017), 'Beyond interpersonal competence: teaching and learning professional skills in sustainability', *Education Sciences*, **7** (1), Article 39.

Drath, W.H., C.D. McCauley and C.J. Palus et al. (2008), 'Direction, alignment, commitment: toward a more integrative ontology of leadership', *The Leadership Quarterly*, **19** (6), 635–53.

Dreier, L., D. Nabarro and J. Nelson (2019), *Systems Leadership for Sustainable Development: Strategies for Achieving Systemic Change*, Cambridge, MA: Corporate Sustainability Initiative, Harvard Kennedy School.

Ernst, C. and D. Chrobot-Mason (2010), *Boundary Spanning Leadership: Six Practices for Solving Problems, Driving Innovation, and Transforming Organizations*, New York: McGraw Hill Professional.

Fisher, R. and D. Shapiro (2005), *Beyond Reason: Using Emotions as You Negotiate*. New York: Penguin.

Gallagher, D.R. (ed.) (2012), *Environmental Leadership: A Reference Handbook*, Los Angeles, CA: SAGE.

Geels, F.W. (2011), 'The multi-level perspective on sustainability transitions: responses to seven criticisms', *Environmental Innovation and Societal Transitions*, **1** (1), 24–40.

Grint, K. (2005), 'Problems, problems, problems: the social construction of "leadership"', *Human Relations*, **58** (11), 1467–94.

Heifetz, R.A. (1994), *Leadership Without Easy Answers*, Cambridge, MA: Harvard University Press.

Hull, R.B. and R. Dooley (2019), 'Collective impact for climate mitigation', *The Solutions Journal*, **10** (3), 39–42.

Hull, R.B., D. Robertson and M. Mortimer (2018), 'Wicked leadership competencies for sustainability professionals: definition, pedagogy, and assessment', *Sustainability: The Journal of Record*, **11** (4), 171–7.

Hull, R.B., D. Robertson and M. Mortimer (2020), *Leadership for Sustainability: Strategies for Tackling Wicked Problems*, Washington, DC: Island Press.

Kania, J. and M. Kramer (2011), 'Collective impact', *Stanford Social Innovation Review*, **9** (1), 36–41.

Kolb, D.A. (2014), *Experiential Learning: Experience as the Source of Learning and Development*, New York: Pearson FT Press.

Leal Filho, W., J.H.P.P. Eustachio and A.C.F. Caldana et al. (2020), 'Sustainability leadership in higher education institutions: an overview of challenges', *Sustainability*, **12** (9), Article 3761.

Levin, K., B. Cashore, S. Bernstein and G. Auld (2012), 'Overcoming the tragedy of super wicked problems: constraining our future selves to ameliorate global climate change', *Policy Sciences*, **45**, 123–52.

MacDonald, L. and M. Shriberg (2016), 'Sustainability leadership programs in higher education: alumni outcomes and impacts', *Journal of Environmental Studies and Sciences*, **6** (2), 360–70.

Northouse, P.G. (2015), *Leadership: Theory and Practice*, Los Angeles, CA: SAGE.

Norton, B. (2015), *Sustainable Values, Sustainable Change: A Guide to Environmental Decision Making*, Chicago, IL: University Chicago Press.

Rittel, H.W. and M.M. Webber (1973), 'Dilemmas in a general theory of planning', *Policy Sciences*, **4** (2), 155–69.

Runde, C.E. and T.A. Flanagan (2010), *Developing Your Conflict Competence: A Hands-on Guide for Leaders, Managers, Facilitators, and Teams*, San Francisco, CA: John Wiley & Sons.

Shriberg, M. (2012), 'Sustainability leadership as 21st-century leadership', in D.R. Gallagher (ed.), *Environmental Leadership: A Reference Handbook*, Los Angeles, CA: SAGE, pp. 469–80.

Shriberg, M. and L. MacDonald (2013), 'Sustainability leadership programs: emerging goals, methods and best practices', *Journal of Sustainability Education*, **5**, 1–21.

Snowden, D.J. and M.E. Boone (2007), 'A leader's framework for decision making', *Harvard Business Review*, **11**, 69–76.

Steffen, W., W. Broadgate and L. Deutsch et al. (2015), 'The trajectory of the Anthropocene: the great acceleration', *The Anthropocene Review*, **2** (1), 81–98.

Tennyson, R. (2003), *The Partnering Toolbook*, London: International Business Leadership Forum.

11. Sustainability goals, mental health and violence: convergent dialogues in research and higher education

Sonia Regina da Cal Seixas and João Luiz de Moraes Hoeffel

1. INTRODUCTION

Brief History and Objectives

Our research and teaching work have been guided by a preceding theme, which can be synthesised as the relationship between environmental changes, quality of life and subjectivity. In those analyses, we consider the model of economic development and its relationship to the adequate use, or not, of natural resources, which through accelerated urbanisation promotes changes in land use patterns, new social and political dynamics, and which impose negative consequences on society and the individual, including increased poverty and violence. However, here we focus on the objective to be achieved – a sustainable development model that provides better living conditions for the population, creating real possibilities to tackle the challenges for adaptation and mitigation to a new scenario.

The development model that was established on the planet after World War II until the end of the 1980s was constituted by a logic of economic development at all costs, destruction of natural resources and industrialisation. However, the hypothesis of our study is that this model has driven urban expansion and concentration, population growth, environmental degradation, especially of water resources and atmospheric pollution, and impairment of physical and mental health, violence and social conflict.

It was only after the 1990s that, timidly, society began to glimpse the real meaning of this exclusive pursuit of economic development and its models. The first milestone of this understanding was the United Nations Conference on Environment and Development (the Rio de Janeiro Earth Summit in Brazil), where the debate on the development model, as well as the search for a guarantee for future generations of the right to development, materialised.

Until the first decade of the 2000s, the debate was intense, mainly led by the United Nations and expressed in several global documents that prioritised a sustainable development model focused on human beings and protecting the environment. In this sense, we can highlight the Rio Declaration on the Environment and the adoption of Agenda 21 as our major indicator of global intentions on the theme – to promote, on a planetary scale, a new standard of development for the twenty-first century.

Once again, Brazil hosted a conference in 2012, known as Rio+20, which aimed to evaluate the efforts made in previous years, to recognize gaps and new challenges, summarised in the green economy, eradication of poverty, and consolidation of the institutional framework for sustainable development. In its final document *The Future We Want* (United Nations, 2012), the formulation of useful goals is aimed at global action focused on sustainable development. This document guided the efforts of the international community towards a worldwide consultation process for the construction of a set of universal sustainable development goals beyond 2015, known as the Millennium Development Goals (MDGs). There is a set of eight general objectives: eradicate extreme poverty and hunger; achieve universal primary education; promote gender equality and empower women; reduce child mortality; improve maternal health; combat HIV/AIDS, malaria and other diseases; ensure environmental sustainability; and establish a global partnership for development.

At the same time, systematic advances in science have taken place, culminating in the Intergovernmental Panel on Climate Change (IPCC) reports on climate change (1990, 1992, 1995, 2001, 2007, 2013, 2014, 2018).[1] However, starting in the year 2010, there was an acceleration in the implementation of the MDGs and the preparation of recommendations on the next steps after 2015 to discuss a new development agenda. The results were synthesised and presented in the first report dedicated to the future agenda: *A Life of Dignity for All*,[2] which shows that a new post-2015 era requires a new vision and a responsive structure. Sustainable development – driven by the integration of economic growth, social justice and environmental sustainability – becomes a guiding principle and a standard operating procedure.

The construction of a post-2015 agenda became a priority and a joint collaboration of the Open Working Group for the Development Sustainable Development Goals (GTA-ODS), which includes specialised contributors from civil society, the scientific community and the United Nations. In August 2014, the GTA-ODS compiled inputs received, finalised the text and submitted the proposal for the 17 Sustainable Development Goals (SDGs, or ODS in Portuguese) and 169 goals associated with the UN General Assembly's consideration in 2015. The document adopted at the General Assembly UN in 2015, *Transforming Our World: The 2030 Agenda for Sustainable Development* (United Nations, 2015) is a guide to the actions of the international community in the coming years. It is also a plan of action for all people and the planet. The phrase that best defines the Agenda is 'people, planet, prosperity, peace and partnerships'. Its 17 objectives are: eradicate poverty; to end hunger; healthy life; quality education; gender equality; water and sanitation; renewable energy; decent work and economic growth; innovation and infrastructures; reduce inequalities; cities and communities; production and consumption; combat climate change; oceans, seas and marine resources; terrestrial ecosystems and biodiversity; peace and justice; and partnerships for development (Jowell, Zhou and Barry, 2017; Kraas et al., 2014).

Combining the MDGs and those resulting from Rio+20, Agenda 2030 and the SDGs inaugurate a new phase for the development of the planet, seeking to fully integrate all components of sustainable development and engaging all countries in the construction of a desired and socially planned future. However, in the face of a project of this magnitude it is worth highlighting that some fundamental points can be synthesized through the premise of 'mind the gaps' (Phelps and Silva, 2018), which are that the countries of the world have profound differences in the social and political characteristics, in social vulnerability, and the quality of social and economic policies. Also, there are substantial environmental risks, and a series of extreme events that are already under way, under pressure from climate change. So, our studies have been based on seeking to overcome these gaps, considering that this will only be possible through (1) the role of science, with investments in research and the search for diagnoses and solutions; (2) social participation; and (3) construction of effective social policies.

With regard to combatting climate change, a good example is the National Plan for Adaptation to Climate Change (PNA) (Ordinance No. 150, May 2016), an instrument prepared by the Brazilian federal government in collaboration with civil society, the private sector and state governments, with the objective of promoting the reduction of national vulnerability to climate change, and managing risk associated with climate change. The adaptation strategy involves identifying the country's exposure to current and future impacts based on climate projections, identifying and analysing vulnerability to these potential impacts, and defining actions and guidelines that promote the adaptation of 11 specific sectors – namely, agriculture, water resources, food and nutrition security, biodiversity, cities, disaster risk management, industry and mining, infrastructure, vulnerable peoples and populations, health, and coastal areas (Brasil, 2016; Mpandeli et al., 2018; Salmoral and Yana, 2018; Ziegler, 2018). It is worth remembering that the planning and implementation of this plan occurred in the period from 2009 to 2016 (under the Lula and Dilma Rousseff governments in Brazil) and the first monitoring report was presented to society in 2017, in a very different political context from the time of its implementation.

Thus, the contribution of the authors of this chapter is centred on the fundamental aspect that the 17 objectives of the 2030 Agenda for Sustainable Development are much more than technical issues for a development model compatible with quality of social life and natural resources preservation. In reality, it is a communication to individuals and institutions on how we can build a more just and fulfilling society for all. They are interrelated in their premises and have been addressed by the research theme of this study, which involves socio-environmental changes and implications of violence and the mental health of the population of specific regions in São Paulo state, Brazil, especially on the north seacoast and the Campinas-São Sebastião road axis.

These are diverse conservation areas, created for the management of water resources and conservation of Atlantic Forest areas. However, currently, they undergo intense processes of urbanisation and industrialisation with profound socio-environmental effects. For more than two decades, the authors have analysed these themes in their research. In this chapter, we present how the objectives of Agenda 2030 aim to improve both socio-environmental quality and the quality of life of the population of these study areas, especially with regard to improvement of mental health and reduction in violence.

2. ENVIRONMENTAL CHANGES, MENTAL HEALTH AND VIOLENCE: CONTRIBUTIONS TO THE SUSTAINABLE DEVELOPMENT GOALS (SDGs)

In 2015, the United Nations General Assembly with all member states of the United Nations adopted the 2030 Agenda for Sustainable Development (Kjaerulf et al., 2016). This Agenda, called *Transforming Our World: The 2030 Agenda for Sustainable Development*, contains 17 Sustainable Development Goals (SDGs), and 169 sub-targets (United Nations, 2015). Kjaerulf et al. (2016, p. 863) emphasise that 'history has shown that setting visionary goals can help unite leaders and decision-makers with researchers and practitioners worldwide towards an overarching, common cause'.

The 17 SDGs are integrated and blend, in a balanced way, the three dimensions of sustainable development: economic, social and environmental. They work like a list of tasks to be fulfilled by governments, civil society and the private sector in a cooperative project for a sustainable world by 2030, aiming to stimulate actions in areas of crucial importance for humanity, represented by five keywords: people, planet, prosperity, peace and partnerships. Despite the integrative context of all SDGs, five of them will be fundamental to our analysis, namely: SDG 3: good health and well-being; SDG 5: gender equality; SDG 11: sustainable cities and communities; SDG 13: combatting climate change; and SDG 16: peace and justice.

Contextualising Our Theme: Mental Health and Violence in the Context of the Chosen SDGs

Mental health and the impact of violence are complex problems (Hannigan and Coffey, 2011) because of their magnitude in the contemporary world, the way they challenge and promote theoretical and methodological dilemmas, and in how they can be addressed and analysed. In addition, there is another point of great importance, which concerns the interdisciplinary character of the subject, and which is the most striking feature of the research we have done in the last decades. Recognising the complexity of the theme, we also highlight the need for multiple approaches. In our research, we have systematically devoted ourselves to analysing these connections, either through full reviews of the scientific literature or through case studies in the state of São Paulo (Seixas, Hoeffel et al., 2012; Seixas, Hoeffel, Botterill et al., 2014; Seixas, Renk et al., 2012; Seixas et al., 2016).

The study of mental health is very important to individuals and to the community because it is a critical determinant of physical health (*The Lancet*, 2016), and as such is grounded in a project to include mental health indicators in the next SDGs by 2030 (Mental Health Foundation, 2016; Thornicroft and Votruba, 2016). This fact has encouraged researchers to include the theme within the dimension of sustainability and public policy. Thornicroft and Votruba (2016) emphasize that this is a historic opportunity and should be centred on a global effort to reduce the impact of mental illness, regarding the role that such diseases represent for society within the global burden of disease, premature mortality, stigma, and human rights violations. Moreover, in most of the world's countries, most people with mental disorders are not treated properly, and about 3000 people die daily from suicide (ibid.).

Violence, for its part, has become a widespread problem faced by society, and it also has a substantial negative impact on health due to the resulting occurrence of physical and mental disorders. The issue of urban violence in both the national and international literature presents a wealth of analysis, allowing broad discussion and recognition of a significant concern (Adorno, 2002; Bellis et al., 2012; Brender and Muggah, 2012; Caddick and Porter, 2011; Diniz, Nahas and Moscovitch, 2013; Netto and Jelvez, 2007; Rosa et al., 2012; Silva, Valadares and Sousa, 2013; Souza and Lima, 2007; Zaluar, 2010; Zaluar and Barcellos, 2013).

Reichenheim et al. (2011) point out that violence and injuries have been significant causes of morbidity and mortality in Brazil since the 1980s. In 2007, they accounted for 12.5 per cent of all deaths, especially in young men (83.5 per cent). The pattern of violence in Brazil differs from other parts of the world, as most of the deaths in the country are due to murder or traffic accidents, as opposed to most of the member countries of the World Health Organization (WHO), where 51 per cent of deaths from external causes are suicides and 11 per cent are due to civil war and conflict.

In Brazil, in 2007, there were 47 707 homicides and 38 419 traffic-related injuries and deaths, which together contribute 67 per cent of the total of 131 032 deaths from external causes. However, Brazil and other countries in Latin America there are similar figures in relation to domestic violence, which is an aspect that needs attention from society and from government because is a critical problem and has severe and permanent consequences for individuals, families and society (Guerrero et al., 2011; Reichenheim et al., 2011).

Reichenheim et al. also point out that insecurity is a feeling that is part of the way of life of Brazilians. According to the authors, this sentiment results from a combination of high crime rates, especially interpersonal violence, which cannot rely on an adequate police system as it is often ineffective and corrupt, and impunity in general. Other aspects such as the use of alcohol and illicit drugs, along with a large number of weapons in circulation, form the background for violence. Finally, insufficient and inadequate long-standing responses from public security and justice systems have helped to increase feelings of impunity and insecurity (ibid.).

The intersection of violence with mental health can be analysed through its direct impacts, from analyses of post-traumatic stress in victims of violence (Cervantes, Schuelter-Trevisol and Jornada, 2013; Gomes, 2012; Miller, 2012; Stevens et al., 2013), or from analyses that prioritize violent, antisocial or risky behaviours, presence of childhood maltreatment, and the association of violence and mental co-morbidities (mainly schizophrenia and bipolar disorder) or abuse of psychoactive substances or alcohol (Fazel et al., 2009, 2010; Lim et al., 2012; Murray, Farrington and Eisner, 2009; Murray et al., 2010; Pera and Dailliet, 2005; Richard-Devanto, Olie and Gourevitch, 2008; Sands et al., 2012; Siever, 2008; Soyka, 2000; Swartz et al., 1998; Volavka and Swanson, 2010; Woodwart et al., 2000).

The importance of studying violence is present in the SDGs as defined for the 2030 Agenda, and aims to offer a real opportunity to achieve commitments on violence prevention, especially against women and children. As García-Moreno and Amin (2016) point out, this is the first time that a global development agenda has addressed all forms of violence against women and girls, as well as violence against children in general, and that it is an important objective and its reduction as a target for 2030 is fundamental to achieving sustainability.

Brief Scenario: Bom Jesus dos Perdões: Mental Health and Violence

Several municipalities in the state of São Paulo have faced significant environmental changes, allied to the lack of priority for the sustainability of natural resources, in favour of a model of economic development supported by megaprojects in areas of environmental conservation that foster social and technological risks (Seixas, Hoeffel et al., 2012; Seixas, Hoeffel and Barrett, 2018; Seixas, Hoeffel and Botterill et al., 2014; Seixas, Hoeffel and Renk et al., 2014; Seixas, Renk et al., 2012). The question that has guided these researchers is: 'How do environmental changes negatively impact the quality of life of the population, especially considering the data on mental health and violence?'

The region of our studies – São Paulo State North Coast and Bragantina Region

(Figure 11.1) – has a strong tourist vocation and a vast expansion of development projects along the D. Pedro I–Tamoios exporter road axis. With this, it suffers strong population pressure, generating intense impacts on the region's natural resources, resulting from the construction of condominiums, hotels, inns and other types of structures that negatively alter the landscape and culture of these places (Seixas, Hoeffel et al., 2012; Seixas, Renk et al., 2012).

The natural areas required for tourism development are often privatised, thus opening doors to widespread real estate speculation, which, through the creation of new spaces, relegates the original environments to second place, forcing local populations to often change their homes and to change the professional activities that they developed traditionally. People can be expelled physically through pressure to sell their land and go elsewhere, often outside the local economy, or see their cultural habits become secondary, thus being induced to adopt new values brought in by tourists or by new residents (Hoeffel et al., 2010; Mendonça, 2006; Seixas, Hoeffel et al., 2012; Seixas, Renk et al., 2012; Suarez et al., 2009; Suarez et al., 2010).

To better understand the scope of our analysis, this chapter presents a brief overview of the problems related to the mental health situation and violence that occurs in the population of one of the municipalities analysed – Bom Jesus dos Perdões. It is worth mentioning that the research that consolidates the empirical basis of this chapter represents a long trajectory of authors' research in this region (e.g., Seixas et al., 2016; Seixas, Hoeffel et al., 2014). A set of ten municipalities along the D. Pedro I–Tamoios exporter road axis was analysed on several aspects directly related to the SDGs of Agenda 2030. The municipality of Bom Jesus dos Perdões was used as a case study due to its historically atypical performance under several of the indicators such as SDG 3: good health and well-being; SDG 5: gender equality; SDG 11: sustainable cities and communities; SDG 16: peace and justice; and SDG 13: combatting climate change, already mentioned above.

We sought to select some indicators that have an intimate relationship between mental health and violence. For mental health, there are rates of two morbidities specially chosen and systematized from Chapter V of the *International Statistical Classification of Diseases and Related Health Problems 10th Revision* (ICD-10) 'Mental and Behavioural Disorders', since they are the most sensitive to social and environmental issues in the area of mental health for the period 1998 to 2016. These morbidities are mental and behavioural disorders due to abusive use of alcohol (Figure 11.2) and other psychoactive substances (Figure 11.3). With regard to violence, we decided to analyse the data on domestic violence, sexual violence and other violence against children and adolescents from 2009 to 2016 (Figure 11.4). These selected periods correspond to the period available in the DATASUS system (System of Epidemiological Surveillance [SINAN], System of Ambulatory Care [SIASUS], and Violence and Accident Surveillance System [VIVA]), of the Brazilian Ministry of Health (Ministério da Saúde). The occurrence rates of the selected indicators were calculated for each 100 000 inhabitants, according to the recommendations of the World Health Organization (WHO), due to the international standardization.

Mental Health

In all countries of the world, the use and abuse of alcohol and psychoactive substances has become a severe public health problem that can result in detrimental effects for

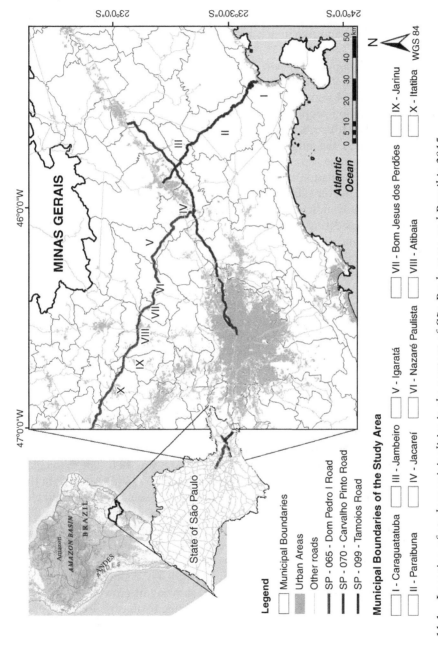

Figure 11.1   Location of study municipalities in the context of São Paulo state and Brazil in 2015

the family and social environment of the user, as well as high rates of morbidity and mortality, mainly when associated with psychiatric complications (Fernandes et al., 2017; Scheffer, Pasa and Almeida, 2010). Both of these groups of researchers point out that these disorders may be remarkably related to violent and criminal behaviours such as traffic accidents and family violence, especially for individuals with a history of aggression and medical and psychiatric complications (Fernandes et al., 2017; Scheffer et al., 2010, p. 533).

According to the *World Drug Report 2006* of the United Nations Office on Drugs and Crime (UNODC, 2006), it was estimated that in that year, 5 per cent of the world's population between 15 and 64 years of age has used illicit drugs at least once, accounting for approximately 200 million people. Among the licit substances, alcohol is the world's most consumed, followed by tobacco. These rates are growing significantly. In 2016, according to Lucchese et al. (2017), the ratio between the number of cases of illness and the number of inhabitants linked to the use and abuse of alcohol and illicit drugs corresponds to 5.4 per cent of the world population, approximately 243 million people, in the same age group (15–64). Of these, one in every 200 people in the world's adult population is a regular user of drugs or has drug use/addiction disorders, that is, approximately 27 million people.

In our study and considering the bases of the SDGs of Agenda 2030 we opted to analyse two categories of mental disorders: mental and behavioural disorders due to abusive use of alcohol, and mental and behavioural disorders due to abusive use of psychoactive substances, directly supported by SDG 3: good health and well-being, systematised from ICD-10 and compiled from the Brazilian Ministry of Health's SINAN/DATASUS for hospitalisation cases, presenting them as rates per 100 000 inhabitants according to the international standard (Figures 11.2 and 11.3, respectively). Over the years of research, it has been observed that among the ten municipalities chosen along the D. Pedro I–Tamoios exporter road axis, the Bom Jesus dos Perdões municipality has historically presented atypical behaviour when compared to the others. To illustrate this observation, in the figures we try to show these patterns, using the municipalities of Atibaia and Nazaré Paulista and the average of the state of São Paulo for the period 1998 to 2016, as references.

Observing Figure 11.2 – Mental and behavioural disorders due to abusive use of alcohol – what can be highlighted is that the average of the state of São Paulo for the analysed period presented a marked decline in rates per 100 000, since in the initial year it was 84.05 (1998) and in the last analysed year (2016) it was 18.6. The municipality of Nazaré Paulista begins the period with 24.80, peaks in 2001 at 40.79, and, from then on, maintains a dramatic decrease to 5.54 (2016). In Atibaia, some differentiated elements were observed: in 1998, its rate was 59.73, in 2001 there was a significant peak of 120.96, and from then on, a steady decrease until arriving in the last analysed year (2016) at a rate of 18.57. The municipality of Bom Jesus, on the other hand, presents four critical aspects – namely: a sharp peak in 2001 (132.14) from a rate in 1998 of 53.18; a substantial drop in 2004 to 67.97; a significant increase in 2007 (98.45); ending the analysed period (2016) with a higher rate than the others, of 62.11, showing its growth.

In Figure 11.3 – Mental and behavioural disorders due to abusive use of psychoactive substances – it was observed that the municipality studied again shows atypical behaviour compared to the average of the state and the two other districts analysed. In 2010, it presented a very significant evolutionary peak of 91.33 per 100 000, compared in the same year to Atibaia (26.07), Nazaré Paulista (18.28) and the state average (31.44). In the

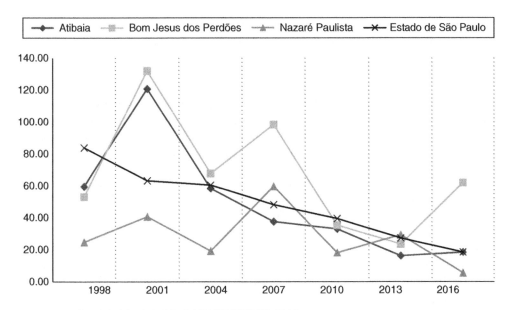

Source: Brasil, Ministério da Saúde, DATASUS/SINAN (2018).

Figure 11.2   Mental and behavioural disorders due to abusive use of alcohol

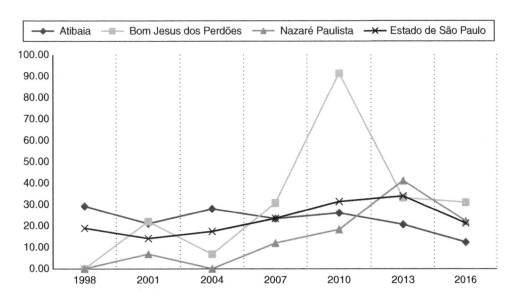

Source: Brasil, Ministério da Saúde, DATASUS/SINAN (2018).

Figure 11.3   Mental and behavioural disorders due to abusive use of psychoactive substances

last year considered (2016), the same municipality is also above all others, 31.05, against Atibaia (12.4), Nazaré Paulista (22.17) and the state average (21.24).

Violence

In 2005, the Secretariat of Surveillance of the Brazilian Ministry recognised violence as a severe public health problem (Brasil, 2005). The report emphasizes that the recognition of violence as a public health problem does not exclude the fact that it is also 'the result of a complex interaction of several factors, which may be individual, social, economic, cultural, among others' (Brasil, 2005, p. 6). The authors emphasized that the approach to violence must be interdisciplinary, based on theoretical and methodological advances in science, and on overcoming social inequalities, seeking to articulate public safety, health and social development, as well as confronting it by the various actors and sectors of society and the state, and supported by a broad debate with society.

In order to analyse violence in the context of the SDGs, it was decided to use the rates for 100 000 inhabitants of Bom Jesus dos Perdões Municipality between 2009 and 2016 for domestic violence, violence and other violence against children and adolescents. This category is directly related to the goals of Agenda 2030 (SDG 5: gender equality) and associated with the two groups of mental health analysed previously, and allowed us to understand the dynamics of the region of the study adequately.

Data for this analysis was collected from the Violence and Accident Surveillance System (VIVA), created by the Brazilian Ministry of Health in 2006. Given the complexity and magnitude of the violence in the national territory, it is worth emphasising essential aspects. In the period from 2006 to 2008, surveillance was implemented in referral centres (referral centres for violence, sexually transmissible disease/AIDS, specialised outpatient clinics, maternity hospitals, among others). As of 2009, VIVA became part of the Notification Aggravation Information System, integrating the Compulsory Notification List into Sentinel Units. In 2011, the notification of domestic violence, sexual violence and other violence for all health services was universalised, including it in the list of diseases and diseases of compulsory information that are registered in SINAN, and in 2014 it was mandated that cases of sexual violence and attempted suicide should be reported immediately (within 24 hours) to the municipal health departments. The Ministerial Ordinance in force that deals with the compulsory notification of interpersonal and self-inflicted violence in public and private health services was consolidated in 2017.

In Figure 11.4, Bom Jesus dos Perdões data are systematised, following the same comparison criteria, with the municipalities of Atibaia and Nazaré Paulista and the average of the state of São Paulo. What is striking is the primacy of Bom Jesus dos Perdões in the most significant number of cases, especially in the years 2012, 2013 and 2014.

3. CONTRIBUTIONS TO THE OBJECTIVES OF AGENDA 2030 AND EXPERIENCES IN RESEARCH AND HIGHER EDUCATION

The rates presented above should be analysed together with the historical context and other aspects of the reality studied. In this sense, the data shown on mental disorders and

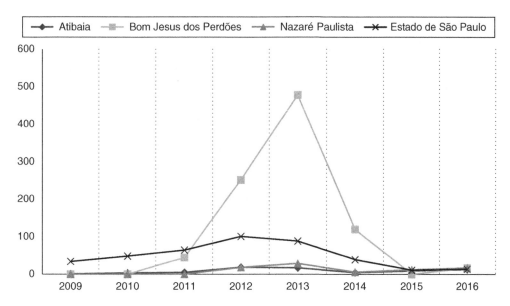

Source: Brasil, Ministério da Saúde, VIVA (2018).

Figure 11.4 Domestic violence, sexual violence and other violence against children and adolescents

violence serve to clarify that their impacts on the community may be impeding the full achievement of the SDGs for the region of the D. Pedro I–Tamoios exporter road axis.

In our view, all 17 SDGs are fundamental to achieving sustainability and a good quality of life. However, here we will highlight five of them: SDG 3: good health and well-being; SDG 5: gender equality; SDG 11: sustainable cities and communities; SDG 13: combatting climate change; and SDG 16: peace and justice. This choice is because the region of our study has undergone significant changes – environmental, economic and demographic – and has tended to worsen due to the shift in the profiles of the state and federal governments from January 2019, which are quite conservative, to say the least, especially about environmental issues.

As we have already described in more detail in other work (Seixas et al., 2019), Bom Jesus dos Perdões is a municipality in the state of São Paulo with an intense religious tradition and natural attractions that give it recognition in both the tourist and religious circuits (Prefeitura Bom Jesus dos Perdões, 2018). It covers an area of 109 km², with an estimated population of 24 023 inhabitants in 2017 and a population density of 181.87 inhabitants/km² in 2010 (IBGE, 2018), with significant urban and especially industrial growth occurring alongside D. Pedro I highway (SP-65) (ibid.).

According to Hoeffel et al. (2010), this municipality is peculiar in its exclusion, not justified, from a vital conservation unit, the Cantareira System Environmental Protected Area (Cantareira System EPA). This EPA was created in 1998 with the objective of maintaining and improving water quality mainly in the municipalities around Cantareira System reservoirs, which supply the São Paulo Metropolitan Region (São Paulo, 2000) and regulate the flow of water to the Metropolitan Region of Campinas.

Bom Jesus dos Perdões is located in an industrial area alongside the D. Pedro I highway that passes through the municipal area, and has caused urban and industrial expansion and several environmental problems. These municipalities also present an ecological richness and biodiversity that must be preserved, a fact that reinforces the need for sustainable measures and its inclusion in the Cantareira System EPA (Seixas et al., 2018).

Given this scenario, our contribution to achieving sustainable development in the region goes beyond the analysis of the rates presented, and contributes to understanding the dynamics that choreograph these rates, with a view to achieving health and human well-being and the construction of policies to solving these issues. In this way, the SDGs with the greatest synergy with our theme are those of SDG 3: To ensure a healthy life and promote well-being for all, in all ages; SDG 5: Achieve gender equality and empower all women and girls; SDG 11: Make cities and human settlements inclusive, secure, resilient and sustainable; and SDG 16: Promote peaceful and inclusive societies for sustainable development, provide access to justice for all, and build effective, accountable and inclusive institutions at all levels (PNUD, 2015).

The goals and targets set out in Table 11.1 represent in our view an ambitious proposal to change a complex set of environmental, social and economic problems in a region that

Table 11.1   Summary of the chosen goals and targets for the analysis

Goal	Target	Statement
3	3.4	By 2030, to reduce premature mortality from non-communicable diseases (NCDs) by one-third through prevention and treatment, and to promote mental health and well-being
	3.5	Strengthen the prevention and treatment of substance abuse, including narcotic drug abuse and harmful use of alcohol
5	5.1	To end all forms of discrimination against all women and girls everywhere
	5.2	Eliminate all forms of violence against all women and girls in public and private spheres, including trafficking and sexual and other types of exploitation
	5.2.c	Adopt and strengthen sound policies and applicable legislation for the promotion of gender equality and the empowerment of all women and girls at all levels
11	11.3	By 2030, to increase inclusive and sustainable urbanization and the capacity for participatory, integrated and sustainable management of human settlements in all countries
	11.6	By 2030, reduce the per capita negative environmental impact of cities, including paying special attention to air quality, municipal and other waste management
	11.6.a	Support positive economic, social and environmental relations between urban, peri-urban and rural areas, strengthening national and regional development planning
16	16.1	Significantly reduce all forms of violence and related death rates, everywhere
	16.6	Develop effective, accountable and transparent institutions at all levels
	16.6.b	Promote and enforce non-discriminatory laws and policies for sustainable development

Source: Based on PNUD (2015).

ends up converging in a complex context of mental disorders and violence, mainly against women and girls. The choice of these categories is related to the synergy they have, and that when contemplated by a research agenda and interaction with local governance will contribute to improving the quality of life of the population of the region and at the same time to sustainable development.

It is worth emphasizing, once again, that Agenda 2030 objectives, and especially those focused on this work and highlighted in Table 11.1 above, have a scope that goes beyond essentially technical aspects, but point to a development model that seeks to bring together in a single proposal the maintenance of quality of life and conservation of natural resources.

4. FINAL CONSIDERATIONS

As highlighted in this chapter, the 17 SDGs of Agenda 2030 bring together the three dimensions of sustainable development – namely, economic, social and environmental. These dimensions and objectives are integral to the presentation of this chapter, which involves in the current analysis questions about sustainability, mental health and violence in a region of relevant importance for the state of São Paulo and Brazil, but which in its ongoing process of expansion and economic development has presented socio-environmental severe issues.

It is hoped that these analyses on the SDGs of Agenda 2030, on the study area of this work, the D. Pedro I–Tamoios exporter road axis, may determine, through the results of research and teaching activities in higher education institutions, reflections, proposals for action and the implementation of projects that allow changes and improvements in relation to regional sustainability and quality of life, as well as opportunities to reach effective commitments that focus on the prevention of violence against women and children and a positive change with regard to mental health data.

ACKNOWLEDGMENTS

We thank FAPESP (2016/18585-3) for its support for the project 'Complex Problems in the Context of Environmental Change: Contributions to Mental Health Analysis', which supports this chapter. And to CNPq/Brazil for the Research Productivity grant to the first author.

NOTES

1. See https://archive.ipcc.ch/. Accessed 22 February 2021.
2. Accessed 1 March 2021 at https://www.un.org/millenniumgoals/pdf/A%20Life%20of%20Dignity%20for %20All.pdf.

REFERENCES

Adorno, S. (2002). Exclusão sócio econômica e violência urbana. *Sociologias*, 4(8), 84–135.

Bellis, M.A., Hughes, K., Perkins, C. and Bennett, A. (2012). *Protecting People, Promoting Health: A Public Health Approach to Violence Prevention for England*. Liverpool: North West Public Health Observatory, Liverpool John Moores University.

Brasil, Ministério de Minas e Energia/Empresa de Pesquisa Energética (2016). *O compromisso do Brasil no combate às mudanças climáticas: produção e uso de energia*. Accessed 17 October 2018 at http://www.epe.gov.br/sites-pt/publicacoes-dados-abertos/publicacoes/PublicacoesArquivos/publicacao-308/NT%20COP21%20iNDC.pdf.

Brasil, Ministério da Saúde, Secretaria de Vigilância em Saúde (2005). *Impacto da violência na saúde dos brasileiros*. Brasília: Ministério da Saúde.

Brender, N. and Muggah, R. (2012). Researching the urban dilemma: urbanization, poverty and violence: summary. International Development Research Centre. Accessed 9 February 2021 at https://idl-bnc-idrc.dspacedirect.org/handle/10625/53539.

Caddick, A. and Porter, L.E. (2011). Exploring a model of professionalism in multiple perpetrator violent gun crime in the UK. *Criminology & Criminal Justice*, 12(1), 61–82.

Cervantes, G.V., Schuelter-Trevisol, F. and Jornada, L.K. (2013). Transtorno de estresse pós-traumático em vítimas de violência. *Revista Brasileira de Clínica Médica*, 11(2), 145–9.

Diniz, A.M.A., Nahas, M.I.P and Moscovitch, S.K. (2013). Análise espacial da violência urbana em Belo Horizonte: uma proposição metodológica a partir de informações e indicadores georreferenciados. *Anais dos Encontros Nacionais da ANPUR/10*. Accessed 4 July 2018 at www.anpur.org.br.

Fazel, S., Langström, N. and Hjern, A. et al. (2009). Schizophrenia, substance abuse, and violent crime. *Journal of the American Medical Association*, 301(19), 2016–23.

Fazel, S., Lichtenstein, P. and Grann, M. et al. (2010). Bipolar disorder and violent crime: new evidence from population-based longitudinal studies and systematic review. *Archives of General Psychiatry*, 67(9), 931–8.

Fernandes, M.A., Pinto, K.L.C. and Teixeira Neto, J.A. et al. (2017). Transtornos mentais e comportamentais por uso de substâncias psicoativas em hospital psiquiátrico. *SMAD: Revista Eletrônica Saúde Mental Álcool e Drogas*, 13(2), 64–70.

García-Moreno, C. and Amin, A. (2016). The Sustainable Development Goals, violence and women's and children's health. *Bulletin of the World Health Organization*, 94, 396–7.

Gomes, R.M. (2012). Mulheres vítimas de violência doméstica e transtorno de estresse pós-traumático: um enfoque cognitivo comportamental. *Revista de Psicologia da IMED*, 4(2), 672–80.

Guerrero, R., Lozano R., and Espinosa R. et al. (2011). Violencia e saúde: o desafio de um problema social nas Americas. In L.A.C. Galvão, J. Finkelman and S. Henao (eds), *Determinantes ambientais e sociais da saúde*. Washington, DC: OPAS, FIOCRUZ, pp. 497–512.

Hannigan, B. and Coffey, M. (2011). Where the wicked problems are: the case of mental health. *Health Policy*, 101(3) 220–27.

Hoeffel, J.L.M, Fadini, A.A.B. and Seixas, S.R.C. (2010). Caracterização geral das Áreas de Proteção Ambiental do Sistema Cantareira (SP) e Fernão Dias (MG). In J.L.M. Hoeffel, A.A.B. Fadini and S.R.C. Seixas (eds), *Sustentabilidade, qualidade de vida e identidade local. Olhares soobre as APA's Cantareira, SP e Fernão Dias, MG*. São Carlos/São Paulo: RIMA/FAPESP, pp. 5–12.

IBGE (2018). Território e população. Accessed 27 October 2018 at https://www.ibge.gov.br/cidades-e-estados/sp/bom-jesus-dos-perdoes.html.

Jowell, A., Zhou, B. and Barry, M (2017). The impact of megacities on health: preparing for a resilient future. *The Lancet: Planetary Health*, 1(5), E176–E178.

Kjaerulf, F., Lee, B. and Cohen, L. et al. (2016). The 2030 Agenda for Sustainable Development: a golden opportunity for global violence prevention. *International Journal of Public Health*, 61, 863–4.

Kraas, F., Aggarwal, S., Coy, M. and Mertins, G. (eds) (2014). *Megacities: Our Global Urban Future*. Dordrecht: Springer.

Lim, S.S., Vos, T. and Flaxman, A.D. et al. (2012). A comparative risk assessment of burden of disease and injury attributable to 67 risk factors and risk factor clusters in 21 regions, 1990–2010: a systematic analysis for the Global Burden of Disease Study 2010. *Lancet*, 380, 2224–60.

Lucchese, R., Silva, P.C.D. and Denardi, T.C. et al. (2017). Common mental disorder among alcohol and drug abusers: a cross-sectional study. *Texto & Contexto – Enfermagem*, 26(1), http://doi.org/10.1590/0104-07072017004480015.

Mendonça, R. (2006). Turismo ou meio ambiente: uma falsa oposição? In A. Lemos (ed.), *Turismo: impactos sócio-ambientais*. São Paulo: Hucitec, pp. 19–25.

Mental Health Foundation (2016). *Better Mental Health for All: A Public Health Approach to Mental Health Improvement*. London: Mental Health Foundation.

Miller, L. (2012). Posttraumatic stress disorder and criminal violence: basic concepts and clinical-forensic applications. *Aggression and Violent Behavior*, 17, 354–64.

Mpandeli, S., Naidoo, D. and Mabhaudhi, T. et al. (2018). Climate change adaptation through the water–energy–food nexus in Southern Africa. *International Journal of Environmental Research and Public Health*, 15(1), Article 2306.

Murray, J., Farrington, D.P. and Eisner, M.P. (2009). Drawing conclusions about causes from systematic reviews of risk factors: the Cambridge Quality Checklists. *Journal of Experimental Criminology*, 5(1), 1–23.

Murray, J., Irving, B. and Farrington, D.P. et al. (2010). Very early predictors of conduct problems and crime: results from a national cohort study. *Journal of Child Psychology and Psychiatry*, 51(11), 1198–207.

Netto, V. and Jelvez, A. (2007). O espaço urbano como dimensão ativa na incidência do crime. Accessed 1 March 2021 at https://docplayer.com.br/7163204-O-espaco-urbano-como-dimensao-ativa-na-incidencia-do-crime.html.

Pera, S.B. and Dailliet, A. (2005). Homicide by mentally ill: clinical and criminological analysis. *Encephale*, 31(5), 539–49.

Phelps, N.A. and Silva, C. (2018). Mind the gaps! A research agenda for urban interstices. *Urban Studies*, 55(6), 1203–22.

Prefeitura Bom Jesus dos Perdões. Cidade. Accessed 3 August 2018 at https://bjperdoes.sp.gov.br/cidade.

Programa das Nações Unidas para o Desenvolvimento (PNUD) [UNDP] (2015). *Acompanhando a agenda 2030 para o desenvolvimento sustentável: subsídios iniciais do Sistema das Nações Unidas no Brasil sobre a identificação de indicadores nacionais referentes aos objetivos de desenvolvimento sustentável*. Brasília: PNUD.

Reichenheim, M.E., Souza, E.R. and Moraes, C.L et al. (2011). Violence and injuries in Brazil: the effect, progress made, and challenges ahead. *The Lancet*, 377(9781), 1962–75.

Richard-Devantoy, S., Olie, J.P. and Gourevitch, R. (2008). Risk of homicide and major mental disorders: a critical review. *Encephale*, 35(6), 521–30.

Rosa, E.M., Souza, L., Oliveira, D.M. and Coelho, B.I. (2012). Violência urbana, insegurança e medo: da necessidade de estratégias coletivas. *Psicologia: Ciência e Profissão*, 32(4), 826–39.

Salmoral, G. and Yana, X. (2018). Food–energy–water nexus: a life cycle analysis on virtual water and embodied energy in food consumption in the Tamar catchment, UK. *Resources, Conservation & Recycling*, 133, 320–30.

Sands, N., Elsom, S., Gerdtz, M. and Khaw, D. (2012). Mental health-related risk factors for violence: using the evidence to guide mental health triage decision making. *Journal of Psychiatric and Mental Health Nursing*, 19(8), 690–701.

São Paulo, Secretaria de Estado do Meio Ambiente (SMA) (2000). *Atlas das unidades de conservação 568 ambiental do Estado de São Paulo*. São Paulo: SMA.

Scheffer, M., Pasa, G.G. and Almeida, R.M.M. (2010), Dependência de álcool, cocaína e crack e transtornos psiquiátricos. *Psicologia: Teoria e Pesquisa*, 26(3), 533–41.

Seixas, S.R.C., Hoeffel, J.L.M. and Barrett, P. (2018). Water resources in the context of global environmental change: some perspectives for sustainability. In W. Leal Filho (ed.), *Handbook of Sustainability Science and Research*. Cham, Switzerland: Springer, pp. 87–102.

Seixas, S.R.C., Hoeffel, J.L.M. and Botterill, D. et al. (2014). Violence, tourism, crime and the subjective: opening new lines of research. In H. Andrews (ed.), *Tourism and Violence*, Farnham, UK: Ashgate, pp. 145–63.

Seixas, S.R.C., Hoeffel, J.L.M. and Renk, M. et al. (2016). Weather variability and climate change impacts on the mental health of a seaside community. *Journal of Scientific Research & Reports*, 11(3), 1–17.

Seixas, S.R.C., Hoeffel, J.LM., Renk, M. and Silva, B.N. (2012). Quality of life and socio-environmental degradation in the Cantareira System Environmental Protected Area, EPA SP/Brazil. *Urban Studies Research*, Article 918931.

Seixas, S.R.C., Hoeffel, J.L.M. and Renk, M. et al. (2014). Percepção de pescadores e maricultores sobre mudanças ambientais globais, no litoral Norte Paulista, São Paulo, Brasil. *Revista da Gestão Costeira Integrada*, 14, 51–64.

Seixas, S.R.C., Renk, M. and Hoeffel, J.L.M. et al. (2012). Global environmental changes and impacts on fishing activities in the northern coast of São Paulo, Brazil. In W.G. Holt (ed.), *Urban Areas and Global Climate Change: Volume 12*. Bingley, UK: Emerald Group Publishing Limited, pp. 299–317.

Seixas, S.R.C., Renk, M., Hoeffel, J.L.M. and Asmus, G.F. (2019). Social projects and the internalization of sustainability and social responsibility: concepts for the improvement of quality of life. In W. Leal Filho (ed.), *Social Responsibility and Sustainability*. Dordrecht: Springer, pp. 93–108.

Siever, L.J. (2008). Neurobiology of aggression and violence. *American Journal of Psychiatry*, 165(4), 429–42.

Silva, J.G., Valadares, F.C. and Souza, E.R. (2013). O desafio de compreender a consequência fatal da violência em dois municípios brasileiros. *Interface, Comunicação, Saúde e Educação*, 17(46), 535–47.

Souza, E.R. and Lima, M.L.C. (2007). Panorama da violência urbana no Brasil e suas capitais. *Ciência & Saúde Coletiva*, 11, 1211–22.

Soyka, M. (2000). Substance misuse, psychiatric disorder and violent and disturbed behavior. *British Journal of Psychiatry*, 176, 345–50.

Stevens, N.R., Gerhart, J. and Goldsmith, R.E. et al. (2013). Emotion regulation difficulties, low social support, and interpersonal violence mediate the link between childhood abuse and posttraumatic stress symptoms. *Behavior Therapy*, 44, 152–61.

Suarez, C.F.S., Barbosa, S.R.C.S. and Hoeffel, J.L.M. et al. (2010). Reflexões sobre turismo sustentável e qualidade de vida em unidades de conservação. In J.L.M. Hoeffel, A.A.B. Fadini and S.R.C. Seixas (eds), *Sustentabilidade, qualidade de vida e identidade local. Olhares sobre as APA's Cantareira, SP e Fernão Dias, MG*. São Carlos/São Paulo: RIMA/FAPESP pp. 135–48.

Suarez, C.F.S., Silva, G.D. and Barbosa, S.R.C. et al. (2009). Turismo, urbanização e sustentabilidade na APA do Sistema Cantareira – um estudo de caso em Vargem/SP – Brasil. *OLAM*, 1, 113–20.

Swartz, M.S., Swanson, J.W. and Hiday, V.A. et al. (1998). Violence and severe mental illness: the effects of substance abuse and nonadherence to medication. *American Journal of Psychiatry*, 155, 2.

The Lancet (2016). Editorial: What can public health do for mental health? *The Lancet*, 387(10038), 2576.

Thornicroft, G. and Votruba, N. (2016). Does the United Nations care about mental health? *The Lancet: Psychiatry*, 3(7), 599–600.

United Nations (2012). *The Future We Want: Outcome Document of the United Nations Conference on Sustainable Development, Rio de Janeiro, Brazil, 20–22 June, 2012*. New York: United Nations.

United Nations (2015). *Transforming Our World: The 2030 Agenda for Sustainable Development*. New York: United Nations.

United Nations Office on Drugs and Crime (UNODC) (2006). *World Drug Report 2006*. Accessed 12 February 2021 at https://www.unodc.org/unodc/en/data-and-analysis/WDR-2006.html.

Volavka J. and Swanson, J. (2010). Violent behavior in mental illness: the role of substance abuse. *Journal of the American Medical Association*, 304(5), 563–4.

Woodward, M., Nursten, J., Williams, P. and Badger, D. (2000). Mental disorder and homicide: a review of epidemiological research. *Epidemiologia e Psichiatria Sociale*, 9(3), 171–89.

Zaluar, A. (2010). A abordagem ecológica e os paradoxos da cidade. *Revista de Antropologia*, 53(2), 611–44.

Zaluar, A. and Barcellos, C. (2013). Mortes prematuras e conflito armado pelo domínio das favelas no Rio de Janeiro. *Revista Brasileira de Ciências Sociais*, 28(81), 17–31.

Ziegler, M.F. (2018). Desafios globais envolvem acesso à água, alimento e energia. Agencia FAPESP. Accessed 23 October 2018 at https://agencia.fapesp.br/desafios-globais-envolvem-acesso-a-agua-alimento-e-energia/29007/.

12. The Sustainable Development Goals in the context of university extension projects: the Brazilian case of the Federal University of Rio de Janeiro (UFRJ)

Luan Santos, Victória Fernandes da Silva,
Isabella Arlochi de Oliveira and Bruno Neves Amado

1. INTRODUCTION

Emerging in the 1980s, the term sustainable development arose from the relationship between preserving the planet and meeting human needs (International Union for Conservation of Nature [IUCN], 1980). The Brundtland Report (WCED, 1987) explains the same term simply as the development that 'meets the needs of the present without compromising the ability of future generations to meet their own needs'. Although heavily criticized, this definition is enduring because it is flexible and open to interpretation (Prugh and Assadourian, 2003).

More recently, in September 2015, world leaders gathered at the United Nations headquarters in New York and drew up the 2030 Agenda for Sustainable Development (Santos and Santos, 2017). This agenda is a collective plan and it comprises 17 Sustainable Development Goals (SDGs), that would assist the development of a more just, sustainable and safe planet (United Nations Development Programme [UNDP], 2015). These goals embrace topics like eradicating poverty, zero hunger, good health and well-being, gender quality, clean water and sanitation, climate action, life below water and on land, sustainable cities and communities, and quality education (Santos and Santos, 2017; UNDP, 2015).

Given this context and considering the nature of their activities and their mission, universities have an important responsibility in transforming societies and contributing to the development of a more sustainable society (Barth and Rieckmann, 2012) and to the achievement of the SDGs. Higher education institutions (HEIs) can implement sustainability concepts and translate them into practices in different domains, such as education and curricula, research design, institutional framework and community outreach (Lozano, Ceulemans, Alonso-Almeida et al., 2015; United Nations Educational, Scientific and Cultural Organization [UNESCO], 2012), generating positive spillovers (externalities) in several economic sectors.

Indeed, diverse efforts are being made by universities worldwide to make sustainable development part of their institutional frameworks by proposing new teaching and pedagogical approaches and curricula, besides encouraging campus sustainability life experiences (Lozano et al., 2013; Ramos et al., 2015). The international literature highlights the high potential that HEIs have in order to make rapid progress in implementing sustainable development into their operations (e.g., Cantalapiedra, Bosch and López, 2006; Ferrer-Balas, Buckland and de Mingo, 2009; Lozano and Lozano, 2014; Verhulst and Lambrechts, 2015; Wu and Shen, 2016), curricula (e.g., Aktas et al., 2015; Alonso-Almeida et al., 2015; Azeiteiro et al., 2015; Dlouhá and Burandt, 2015; Lozano, Ceulemans and Scarff Seatter, 2015; Rose, Ryan and Desha, 2015; Verhulst and Lambrechts, 2015; von Blottnitz, Case and Fraser, 2015; Watson et al., 2013), and research (e.g., Cantalapiedra et al., 2006; Ferrer-Balas et al., 2009; Lozano and Lozano, 2014).

However, although there have been successful developments in the field of HEI for sustainable development over the past 15 years or so, there are numerous challenges that must be overcome (Leal Filho, Manolas and Pace, 2015). According to Lozano et al. (2013), there is still the need for HEIs to improve the integration of sustainable development into curricula and research, and most importantly, to include it holistically into extension projects, reducing the difficulties of translating sustainability from theory to practice. These points highlight the importance of deepening the analysis of university extension projects.

According to Araújo (2004), the role of HEIs in sustainability discussions goes beyond the research and teaching/learning seen in classrooms. It advances towards extracurricular projects involving the surrounding community, seeking effective solutions to the local population, which reinforces the importance of fostering academic projects (extension, junior enterprises, competition teams, among others) aligned to the theme of sustainable development in universities. After all, with these activities, students put all learned theory into practice, produce scientific and technological knowledge, and impact not only their personal and professional lives, but also all those of academia and civil society in the region.

In this context, this chapter analyzes the Federal University of Rio de Janeiro (UFRJ), Macaé campus, as a case study for developing sustainable extension projects, especially in the context of the SDGs and the 2030 Agenda. The UFRJ is considered the second-best university in Brazil and the best in the Rio de Janeiro state (UFRJ-Macaé, 2016), the Macaé campus currently being responsible for several extension projects. Such projects represent a great ripening potential in environmental and social issues and in the internalization of the SDGs, so the present chapter aims to conduct a survey of the ongoing projects in the engineering courses at UFRJ-Macaé in terms of sustainable development and SDG practices. Nor can we forget that the main activity developed in the Macaé region is the oil and gas market, responsible for significant environmental, climatic and social impacts, so the analysis of projects in this region is even more relevant. From the results, it was possible to propose some actions that could better align the assessed projects with the 2030 Agenda, inspiring new attitudes both within the university environment and beyond that sphere.

The chapter is structured into four further sections. Section 2 deals with the theoretical framework, discussing the university extension projects and their relation with sustainable projects at UFRJ-Macaé. Section 3 covers the methodology used in the work and Section 4 refers to the analysis of the results and the discussion of some proposals for improvements that could be adopted by projects evaluated. Finally, Section 5 presents the main conclusions of the research.

2.   (SUSTAINABLE) UNIVERSITY EXTENSION PROJECTS AND THE SDGs

2.1   Theoretical Framework

The extension project is the proposal of proximity between the university and the community, developing research and teaching in a dialogical exchange directed to the community, thus meeting their demands and reducing social inequalities (Jezine, 2004). Thus, the academic function of the extension project is based on the theory–practice relationship, representing an alternative path to the development of a more complete academic education, allowing an exchange of knowledge between the agents involved. Through this action, socialization and construction of new knowledge take place.

Particularly in Brazil, after the Brazilian University Reform in 1968, the concept of a university extension project became linked to learning and research, to such an extent that these interrelated components became indissoluble, also guaranteed and reinforced by the Federal Brazilian Constitution of 1988 (Brazil, 1988). As provided in Article 207 of the Brazilian Constitution, extension projects, together with teaching and research, must be governed by the principle of inseparability, thus collaborating in a democratic project of society (Serrano, 2010).

According to Martins (2012), within the scope of Brazilian public universities, the teaching–research–extension triad is one of its greatest virtues and expression of social commitment. The relationship between these three spheres, when well articulated, leads to significant changes in the teaching and learning processes, substantiating, didactically and pedagogically, the professional and citizen training.

The role of education institutions, therefore, must be based on teaching, research and extension activities, which fully constitute these institutions, and which complement each other. As a continuity of teaching, extension activities must correspond to educational, cultural and scientific processes, making the results of academic activities available and aiming at cooperation and integration between teaching institutions and the society in which they operate.

Considering this perspective, HEIs should be able to catalyze and/or accelerate a societal transition towards sustainability (Stephens et al., 2008). Therefore, it is necessary to develop activities aimed at environmental awareness, one of which is environmental education, seen as capable of providing a change in habits and conduct of actions in relation to the positive environment, considering all its complexity (Pedrini, 2000). Environmental awareness, therefore, came to be seen as a powerful tool in the search for sustainable development, and strategies with a focus on education have become of fundamental relevance in view of the worsening of environmental problems.

A very significant movement towards sustainability at universities in Latin America was the creation of the International Organization of Universities for Sustainable Development and the Environment (OIUDSMA) in 1996 by Latin American universities. Its main purpose is the incorporation of the concept of environmental responsibility in the professional activity of engineers, architects and other graduates as a key role in the evolution of society towards sustainability. According to Tilbury and Wortman (2004), all careers have to be trained in their respective fields of thought in relation to environmental and sustainable criteria and values, so that, in the future, they can approach their professional activities from the point of view of sustainability.

Progress has been noticeable specifically regarding the development of sustainable education (Disterheft et al., 2015a, 2015b, 2016), and barriers to the implementation of sustainability practices are being addressed by HEIs (e.g., Aleixo, Azeiteiro and Leal Filho, 2016, 2017a, 2017b, 2018; Ávila et al., 2017). Verhulst and Lambrechts (2015) provided extensive information and discussion about these barriers, and more recently, Aleixo et al. (2017b, 2018) have provided an overview of these barriers.

However, the United Nations SDGs are an opportunity for overcoming these barriers to achieving sustainability implementation in HEIs (Leal Filho et al., 2017). The SDGs were approved in 2015 after a global consultation process that began in 2013 from the document *The Future We Want* (United Nations, 2012) established at the United Nations Conference on Sustainable Development (Rio+20). This process was very broad and involved institutions, organizations, private companies, academia, media and civil society, therefore allowing a variety of experiences and perspectives. In total, there are 17 goals and 169 targets divided into five major areas: people, planet, peace, prosperity and partnerships, in which the main focus is based on the three pillars of sustainable development: social, environmental and economic (Santos and Santos, 2017; UNDP, 2015).

Therefore, the opportunities offered by the SDGs to strengthen sustainable development at universities and the relevance of this topic and its international dimension require HEIs' preparation to play this relevant role actively. Moreover, the SDGs offer universities a unique opportunity to reflect on the ways they operate and may encourage them to make further efforts to become more sustainable, not only in respect of their operations but also in the field of teaching, research and extension (Leal Filho et al., 2018).

Sibbel's (2009) claim that it is important to consider the practicality of developing programs of study that can actually prepare graduates with the necessary knowledge and values, a capacity for critical thinking and the motivation to deal with the multitude of diverse problems associated with non-sustainable states is now more pertinent than ever. It directly addresses the university extension projects. In the context of SDGs, HEIs must be able to create knowledge and effectively transfer it to the community (Leal Filho et al., 2018; Stough et al., 2017) and, at the same time, prepare students for their role in society (Disterheft et al., 2013).

2.2   Extension Projects at UFRJ-Macaé: A Case Study

UFRJ is a national reference in the academic world, being the first federal university created in Brazil. Founded in 1920, UFRJ looks to provide quality education and build a just, modern and competitive society. Its tradition and quality are reflected in the classification as the best Brazil's federal university in the QS World University Rankings 2015 (UFRJ-Macaé, 2016) and in the University Ranking of Folha de São Paulo (RUF) in 2017 (ibid.).

Its geographical location is mainly concentrated in the city of Rio de Janeiro, but UFRJ also has operations in ten different cities in the Rio de Janeiro state, including in the city of Macaé. In this city, UFRJ has been present since the 1980s with the work of the Center for Ecology and Socio-Environmental Development of Macaé (NUPEM). Physically, the university is laid out in Macaé in three 'poles', namely Polo Universitário, Polo Barreto and Polo Ajuda, and it has about 2357 students enrolled on 11 undergraduate courses and

Table 12.1 Description of researched projects

Project	Objective	Area of Expertise
Catena Consultoria (Junior Enterprise)	Encourage the entrepreneurial spirit, develop technical, academic, personal and professional skills of its members, through the elaboration of industrial, civil and mechanical engineering projects for companies and entities in general	Entrepreneurship
Programa de Educação Tutorial Engenharias Macaé (Macaé Engineering Tutorial Education Program)	Develop activities in different areas such as the open-source electronic platform Arduino, composites, Excel, computational fluid dynamics (CFD) and teaching physics concepts. It aims to bring knowledge to students from inside and outside the university through lectures, courses, workshops, and academic research	Education
Mentes à Obra (Minds to Work)	Primarily engaged in carrying out reforms in philanthropic non-profit institutions	Civil engineering
Centro Interativo de Divulgação Científica (Interactive Center of Science Communication)	Consists of a teaching and scientific dissemination laboratory in the area of exact sciences	Science
Petrus	Develop a complete project and build a prototype of a formula-style race car to participate in a national competition	Mechanical and industrial engineering
Ali Babaja	Build an off-road vehicle to participate in several regional and national competitions (Baja SAE). Students are responsible for developing an entire project, from the theoretical to the assembly part respecting the competitions rules	Mechanical and industrial engineering
1/14 Bees	Build a small-scale radio-controlled airplane to represent UFRJ-Macaé in the SAE Aero Design competition	Aero design
Equipe Fernando Amorim (Team Fernando Amorim)	Promote sustainability, research and scientific study by developing a solar-powered boat to participate in national competitions	Renewable energy/ mechanical engineering
Liga de Investimentos de Macaé (Macaé Investment League)	Analyze and provide training to students on financial markets and investment issues through study groups, courses, lectures, competitions and other events	Finance
Associação Atlética Acadêmica Engenharia UFRJ Macaé (Academic Athletic Association Engineering UFRJ-Macaé)	Promote physical activities for university students and prepare them for regional sport competitions between universities in Rio de Janeiro	Sports

Table 12.1   (continued)

Project	Objective	Area of Expertise
Centro de Referência em Inovação para Operações Sustentáveis (Innovation Reference Center for Sustainable Operations)	Develop the entrepreneurial skills of UFRJ-Macaé and transform its region of influence into an ecosystem of entrepreneurship and innovation	Entrepreneurship
Aprenda a Programar Jogando (Learn to Program by Playing)	Present programming and computing concepts, showing children and young people that it is possible to develop the technology they use in everyday life	Computational programming
Inovar e Aprender (Innovation and Learning)	Develop technological literacy of students from municipal schools through educational robotics kits, guiding participants to solve real problems on a smaller scale	Innovation

Source: Own elaboration based on the interview answers.

three postgraduate courses, and over 248 teachers circulate on campus (UFRJ-Macaé, 2016). Although UFRJ-Macaé has only had a campus for ten years in Macaé, its development in the locality has been notorious, due to the excellence of professors, researchers, technicians and an increasingly engaged and participative student body.

The survey was applied to 13 projects of the engineering courses of UFRJ-Macaé and the information presented in this section was collected both from answers to questionnaires and interviews with the project members. The questionnaire is available in the Appendix at the end of the chapter.

3.   METHODS

This section presents the study method used, its rationale and the procedures for gathering information.

3.1   Research Method

The study adopted data collection as a research model, guided by the need to determine the behavior of a population, whereby from the application of the methodology it would be possible to achieve objective results without the influence of external factors (Gil, 2008). Thus, the population selected was from the Macaé campus of the UFRJ, considering all engineering extension projects from the industrial, mechanical and civil engineering courses, regardless of their involvement with SDGs.

3.2 Instrument and Data Collection

This study considered data collection from focal members of the projects analyzed using a form from Google Forms tool. It was sent electronically to these members (a total of 13 students), on 25 February 2018, in order to verify the knowledge these projects had on sustainable development and their commitment to practices focused on the SDGs and the 2030 Agenda.

In the collection instrument, physical evidence was requested to justify the presence or absence of actions on the various issues that permeate the concept of sustainable development and the 2030 Agenda. The following points were discussed: integration of sustainable practices into the design of the team's strategies; design of social, economic and environmental outcomes generated; which activities are considered important to improve the environmental performance of the project; identification of the advantages and obstacles in implementing sustainable policies; recognition of actions taken with waste and natural resources; investment in technologies to reduce their impacts; training in environmental education of their members to continuously improve the processes. In addition, project members were asked more specifically whether they know what the SDGs are and which of the 17 goals they are committed to, as well as what actions the groups take to achieve those goals.

3.3 Processing and Analysis of Data

Data evaluation was carried out using the Excel tool to verify and compare the projects, in order to analyze the scope of campus impacts. It is emphasized that the research did not show imperfect data, since the respondents were unable to send the questionnaire if any question was not answered.

4. RESULTS AND IMPROVEMENT PROPOSALS

From the 13 academic projects selected from the engineering courses at UFRJ-Macaé, all respondents answered the questionnaire proposed, so we had 100 percent of the engineering extension projects included in this research.

Based on the results of the questionnaires, cross-referencing of the data allows a better understanding of the current projects' landscape regarding sustainable development and the SDGs, their main socio-environmental actions and opportunities for improvement in this area. The data showed that more than half of the projects (54 percent) often considered socio-environmental issues in their planning and definition of strategies, and 31 percent said they always take these issues into account (Figure 12.1).

As expected, most projects consider environmental and social issues as an opportunity for improvement and innovation (Figure 12.2), and only one project did not consider them strategic. This answer may indicate the need to review the processes performed by this project, noting points to be optimized.

To improve the environmental performance of academic projects, the factors that have been considered most relevant are: reducing the amount of raw materials used; reducing energy consumption; and reuse of materials. The result, shown in Figure 12.3,

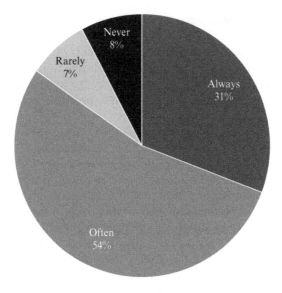

Source: Own elaboration based on the questionnaire results.

Figure 12.1   Frequency of consideration of environmental and social issues in the formulation of strategies

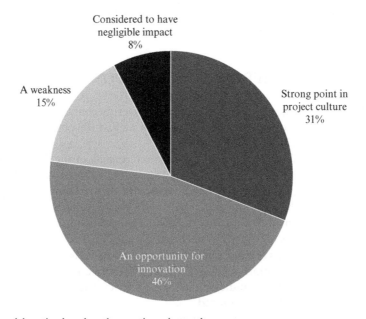

Source: Own elaboration based on the questionnaire results.

Figure 12.2   Vision of the environmental issue in projects

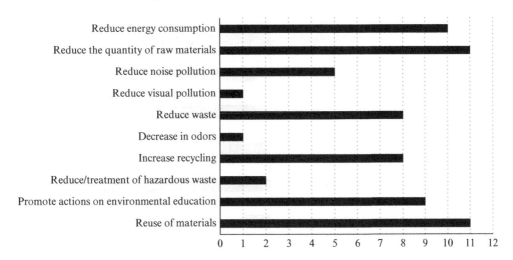

Source: Own elaboration based on the questionnaire results.

Figure 12.3 Most important activities to improve the environmental performance of the project

demonstrates the concern about the reduction, reuse and recycling of raw materials used in the processes carried out by the projects and the energy savings, from those who carry out more practical activities to those with a more theoretical orientation. These points are directly related to SDGs like SDG 9 (industry, innovation and infrastructure) and SDG 12 (responsible consumption and production), so we can consider that both SDGs – very much related to the engineering area – are the focus of the extension projects analyzed, suggesting a lack of integrative vision with other areas and subjects.

According to the answers, the main advantages in implementing sustainable policies in the university projects are: development and encouragement of environmental solutions; reduction and control of costs; public statement of commitment to environmental management; and concern for a more sustainable, safe and fair planet. Thus, it is evident that many projects are interested in the social and environmental context while aiming at the possibility of reducing costs, even if investment is necessary and the return happens in the long term.

As shown in Figure 12.4, it is noted that the biggest obstacle to the implementation of sustainable policies are the habits already established in the projects (cultural perspective), lack of knowledge and high costs. Thus, a paradigm shift is important for members in order to change their mindset, to begin to study improvement points and to make modifications in their structures in favor of attitudes that promote positive impacts on the environment. This point is directly related to SDG 4 (quality education).

More than half of respondents (54 percent) stated that their projects carry out continuous social impact activities. This shows the extent that actions taken by students can have on society. An example was the donation campaign held in December 2017 for the Casa do Idoso, a philanthropic entity in Macaé that gathered together all the projects studied in this survey and succeeded in joining the academic body, contributing to the development of the institution (SDG 17 – partnerships for the goals). In the same way, from

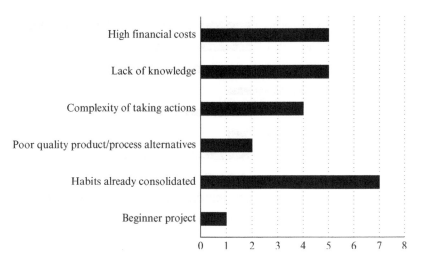

Source: Own elaboration based on the questionnaire results.

Figure 12.4   Main obstacles to the implementation of sustainable policies

the inclusion of environmental education in the university agenda and the consequent diffusion of this knowledge, it would be possible to establish specific actions and projects for the sustainable development of the community.

Regarding the waste generated by the activities carried out, 69 percent of them claimed to have negative externalities: papers, newspapers, plastics, scrap metal, wood, paints and resins. In addition, most projects do not have indicators to estimate the amount of waste produced weekly by their tasks. As for waste disposal, 56 percent have actions to find an adequate destination and 78 percent do not have programs to minimize them, which is clearly a matter to be analyzed. Those who have such programs, reuse the material to the maximum or donate what is still useful.

Concerning the consumption of natural resources, only 23 percent of respondents said they could estimate this amount and that they take steps to increase the efficiency of processes in order to minimize their impacts. In addition, 89 percent of the responses were negative regarding the amount of waste generated weekly by project activities. These facts corroborate the fact that 77 percent of the groups do not define the responsibility for environmental management, putting it in second place in their team guidelines and do not invest in technology to make a better use of resources, although 69 percent of the teams have development and training policies aiming at the continuous improvement of their members.

Finally, 77 percent of the projects declared that they did not know the SDGs, a result that creates opportunities of improvements that can be implemented from the environmental education perspective. According to the survey, teams that have knowledge about them are mainly responsible for SDGs 4, 8, 9, 12 and 17 – quality education; decent work and economic growth; industry, innovation and technology; responsible consumption; and production and partnerships for the goals – highlighting the perception of the need to integrate education with the use of technology to achieve sustainable development.

Among the perspectives for implementing improvements for the year 2019, the teams highlighted the sustainable use of energy invested in their products (goods or services) and investment in simple ways to reduce and reuse inputs such as paper and material used in experiments and projects. In addition, basic attitudes can be encouraged by the groups, given their visibility in the academic environment, collaborating for socio-environmental education. For example, recycled paper can be used for printing, as well as promoting the implementation of checklists in laboratories and rooms occupied by groups in order to verify sustainable practices and thus reduce energy consumption. This checklist could be useful to make sure that the lights and air conditioners in a certain environment were properly turned off at the end of the day or when the location was empty. These are simple measures, but they have a positive impact on the environment and stimulate a cultural change that is more aligned with the SDGs.

5. CONCLUSIONS

This chapter focuses on extension projects and university communities for two reasons. First, universities, being generators of cutting-edge research, can be expected to be leaders in new and innovative sustainable practices. Second, the demographic diversity within the university community (i.e., staff and students) is in itself a microcosmic society. Consequently, it is potentially a good test bed for the purpose of this research in developing a conceptual framework for community engagement.

The World Engineers' Convention (WEC, 2008), through the Brasilia Declaration, highlights the importance of engineering as a profession that leads to technological innovation and plays a fundamental role in social, economic and sustainable development. This type of professional is critical for achieving the SDGs and they are required in both developed and developing countries to invent, design and implement technologies and systems related to essential themes, such as water and energy, capable of improving the population's quality of life. However, engineering institutions around the world recognize that there is global shortage of engineers with the requisite skills to address the challenges of sustainable development (World Federation of Engineering Organizations [WFEO], 2018, 2019).

In this sense, research and extension activities, in interaction with teaching, the university and society, make it possible to operationalize the relationship between theory and practice, the democratization of academic knowledge and the return of that knowledge to the university, tested and reworked. Thus, the university must recommend an inseparability between teaching, research and extension activities, a fundamental factor for changing habits, conduct of actions and knowledge of society. It is understood, therefore, that extension activities, developed with a sustainability bias, are an important way to promote environmental awareness.

In this way, some Brazilian universities are encouraging environmental and sustainable practices to improve this scenario. The UFRJ developed some initiatives with this focus, such as the sewage treatment plant on the UFRJ campus for wastewater treatment with an advanced technology. There is also a project to implement a solar-powered air conditioning system. In this case, the university's parking lot roof was used to deploy panels using light and the heat from the sun to generate energy (Maio, 2017). In addition to the projects developed, it is equally important to add to the curriculum guidelines for engineering, mandatory subjects about sustainability from the first semesters of the course, arousing the interest of the students and motivating them to develop final projects focused on this area. To this end, it is necessary that supervising teachers have experience in the theme, which can be achieved through initiatives such as the Rhodes University Environmental Education & Sustainability Unit, in which professionals are encouraged to carry out activities with a focus on environmental management and related matters (UNESCO, 2015).

This particular research dealt with engineering extension projects at UFRJ-Macaé and allowed us to observe the level of knowledge shown by their members about the concept and practices of sustainable development and the SDGs. Results showed a huge range of possibilities and opportunities, so the groups, acting within an extension project and using the infrastructure provided by the university, can make greater impacts on the society in which they operate, promoting innovation and entrepreneurship in the region.

For these reasons, we would conclude that the integration of engineering expertise and environmental education can promote a more just society and one focused on sustainable development, considering the SDGs in the context of 2030 Agenda. In addition, process of the knowledge limited to the academic environment is demystified and diffused through simple practices implemented for continuous improvement and alignment to the SDGs as a strong agent of change in production systems and forms of consumption.

The study also raised some points that should be better explored in future research, especially with regard to concrete actions and improvements, as a way of reinforcing these projects with the 2030 Agenda. It must not be forgotten that these projects deal directly with the society of Macaé and its surroundings, so the proper knowledge and alignment of the projects with the 2030 Agenda will also support the dissemination of the objectives and goals of the SDGs in this region. This impact can also be reinforced with the participation of other extension projects, not only linked to engineering courses, as well as involving other universities that operate in the analyzed region.

REFERENCES

Aktas, C.B., Whelan, R. and Stoffer, H. et al. 2015. Developing a university-wide course on sustainability: a critical evaluation of planning and implementation. *Journal of Cleaner Production*, 106, 216–21.

Aleixo, A.M., Azeiteiro, U.M. and Leal, S. 2016. Toward sustainability through higher education: sustainable development incorporation into Portuguese higher education institutions. In J.P. Davim and W. Leal Filho (eds), *Challenges in Higher Education for Sustainability*. Cham, Switzerland: Springer, pp. 159–87.

Aleixo, A.M., Azeiteiro, U.M. and Leal, S. 2017a. UN decade of education for sustainable development: perceptions of higher education institution's stakeholders. In W. Leal Filho, U.M. Azeiteiro, F. Alves and P. Molthan-Hill (eds), *Handbook of Theory and Practice of Sustainable Development in Higher Education*. Cham, Switzerland: Springer, pp. 417–28.

Aleixo, A.M., Azeiteiro, U.M. and Leal, S. 2017b. Conceptualizations of sustainability in Portuguese higher education: roles, barriers and challenges toward sustainability. *Journal of Cleaner Production*, 172, 1664–73.

Aleixo, A.M., Azeiteiro, U.M. and Leal S. 2018. The implementation of sustainability practices in Portuguese higher education institutions. *Journal of Sustainability in Higher Education*, 19(1), 146–78.

Alonso-Almeida, M.D.M., Marimon, F., Casani, F. and Rodriguez-Pomeda, J. 2015. Diffusion of sustainability reporting in universities: current situation and future perspectives. *Journal of Cleaner Production*, 106, 144–54.

Araújo, M.I.O. 2004. A universidade e a formação de professores para a educação ambiental. *Revista Brasileira de Educação Ambiental*, No. 0, 71–8. Accessed 11 December 2019 at https://d3nehc6yl9qzo4.cloudfront.net/downloads/revbea_n_zero.pdf.

Ávila, L.V., Leal Filho, W. and Brandli, L. et al. 2017. Barriers to innovation and sustainability at universities around the world. *Journal of Cleaner Production*, 164, 1268–78.

Azeiteiro, U.M., Bacelar-Nicolau, P., Caetano, F.J.P. and Caeiro, S. 2015. Education for sustainable development through e-learning in higher education: experiences from Portugal. *Journal of Cleaner Production*, 106, 308–19.

Barth, M. and Rieckmann, M. 2012. Academic staff development as a catalyst for curriculum change towards education for sustainable development: an output perspective. *Journal of Cleaner Production*, 26, 28–36.

Brazil. 1988. *Constituição Federal*. Accessed 8 January 2020 at http://www.planalto.gov.br/ccivil_03/constitui cao/constituicao.htm.

Cantalapiedra, I.R., Bosch, M. and López, F. 2006. Involvement of final architecture diploma projects in the analysis of the UPC buildings energy performance as a way of teaching practical sustainability. *Journal of Cleaner Production*, 14, 958–62.

Disterheft, A., Azeiteiro, U.M., Leal Filho, W. and Caeiro, S. 2015a. Sustainable universities – a study of critical success factors for participatory approaches. *Journal of Cleaner Production*, 106, 11–21.

Disterheft, A., Azeiteiro, U.M., Leal Filho, W. and Caeiro, S. 2015b. Participatory processes in sustainable universities – what to assess? *International Journal of Sustainability in Higher Education*, 16(5), 748–71.

Disterheft, A., Caeiro, S., Azeiteiro, U.M. and Leal Filho, W. 2013. Sustainability science and education for sustainable development in universities – a way for transition. In S. Caeiro, W. Leal Filho, C.J.C. Jabbour and U.M. Azeiteiro (eds), *Sustainability Assessment Tools in Higher Education Institutions –Mapping Trends and Good Practices Around the World*, Cham, Switzerland: Springer, pp. 3–28.

Disterheft, A., Caeiro, S.S., Leal Filho, W. and Azeiteiro, U.M. 2016. The INDICARE-model – measuring and caring about participation in higher education's sustainability assessment. *Ecological Indicators*, 63, 172–86.

Dlouhá, J. and Burandt, S. 2015. Design and evaluation of learning processes in an international sustainability oriented study programme: in search of a new educational quality and assessment method. *Journal of Cleaner Production*, 106, 247–58.

Ferrer-Balas, D., Buckland, H. and de Mingo, M. 2009. Explorations on the university's role in society for sustainable development through a systems transition approach: case-study of the technical University of Catalonia (UPC). *Journal of Cleaner Production*, 17, 1075–85.

Gil, A.C. 2008. *Methods and Techniques of Social Research*, São Paulo: Atlas SA.

International Union for Conservation of Nature (IUCN). 1980. *The World Conservation Strategy: Living Resource Conservation for Sustainable Development*. Gland, Switzerland: UNEP-UNDP-WWF.

Jezine, E. 2004. As práticas curriculares e a extensão universitária. Paper presented at the Anais do 2° Congresso Brasileiro de Extensão Universitária, Belo Horizonte. Accessed 16 April 2020 at www.ufmg.br/congrext/ Gestao/Gestao12.pdf.

Leal Filho, W., Azeiteiro, U.M. and Alves, F. et al. 2018. Reinvigorating the sustainable development research agenda: the role of the Sustainable Development Goals. *International Journal of Sustainable Development & World Ecology*, 25(2), 131–42.

Leal Filho, W., Manolas, E. and Pace, P. 2015. The future we want: key issues on sustainable development in higher education after Rio and the UN Decade of Education for Sustainable Development. *International Journal of Sustainability in Higher Education*, 16, 112–29.

Lozano, R., Ceulemans, K. and Alonso-Almeida, M. et al. 2015. A review of commitment and implementation of sustainable development in higher education: results from a worldwide survey. *Journal of Cleaner Production*, 108(Part A), 1–18.

Lozano, R., Ceulemans, K. and Scarff Seatter, C. 2015. Teaching organisational change management for sustainability: designing and delivering a course at the University of Leeds to better prepare future sustainability change agents. *Journal of Cleaner Production*, 106, 205–15.

Lozano, F.J. and Lozano, R. 2014. Developing the curriculum for a new bachelor's degree in engineering for sustainable development. *Journal of Cleaner Production*, 64, 136–46.

Lozano, R., Lukman, R. and Lozano, F.J. et al. 2013. Declarations for sustainability in higher education: becoming better leaders, through addressing the university system. *Journal of Cleaner Production*, 48, 10–19.

Maio, G. 2017. Práticas de gestão sustentável na Universidade Federal de Rondônia. Final Project Accounting Science, Federal University of Rondonia, Porto Velho.

Martins, L.M. 2012. *Ensino–pesquisa–extensão como fundamento metodológico da construção do conhecimento na universidade*. São Paulo: Editora da Unesp.

Pedrini, A. 2000. *Educação ambiental: reflexões e práticas contemporâneas* (3rd edition). Petrópolis: Vozes.

Prugh, T. and Assadourian, E. 2003. What is sustainability, anyway? *World Watch*, 16(5), 10–21.

Ramos, T.B., Caeiro, S. and van Hoof, B. et al. 2015. Experiences from the implementation of sustainable development in higher education institutions: environmental management for sustainable universities. *Journal of Cleaner Production*, 106, 3–10.

Rose, G., Ryan, K. and Desha, C. 2015. Implementing a holistic process for embedding sustainability: a case study in first year engineering, Monash University, Australia. *Journal of Cleaner Production*, 106, 229–38.

Santos, L. and Santos, T. 2017. Os ODS e seus indicadores: novas classes gramaticais, uma mesma morfologia. *Pontes*, 13(2), 13–17.

Serrano, R.M.S.M. 2010. Conceitos de extensão universitária: um diálogo com Paulo Freire. João Pessoa: UFPB/PRAC. Accessed 8 January 2020 at http://www.prac.ufpb.br/copac/extelar/atividades/discussao/artigos/conceitos_de_extensao_universitaria.pdf.

Sibbel, A. 2009. Pathways towards sustainability through higher education. *International Journal of Sustainability in Higher Education*, 10, 68–82.

Stephens, J.C., Hernandez, M.E. and Román, M. et al. 2008. Higher education as a change agent for sustainability in different cultures and contexts. *International Journal of Sustainability in Higher Education*, 9, 317–38.

Stough, K., Ceulemans, W., Lambrechts, V. and Cappuyns, V. 2017. Assessing sustainability in higher education curricula: a critical reflection on validity issues. *Journal of Cleaner Production*, 172, 4456–66.

Tilbury, D. and Wortman, D. 2004. *Engaging People in Sustainability*. Gland, Switzerland: IUCN Commission on Education and Communication.

UFRJ-Macaé. 2016. Presentation. Accessed 18 January 2019 at http://www.macae.ufrj.br/index.php/2016-02-15-16-00-04/2016-02-22-14-38-42.

United Nations. 2012. *The Future We Want: Outcome Document of the United Nations Conference on Sustainable Development, Rio de Janeiro, Brazil, 20–22 June, 2012*. New York: United Nations.

United Nations. 2015. *Transforming Our World: The 2020 Agenda for Sustainable Development*. New York: United Nations.

United Nations Educational, Scientific and Cultural Organization (UNESCO). 2012. *Shaping the Education of Tomorrow: 2012 Full Length Report on the UN Decade of Education for Sustainable Development*. Paris: UNESCO. Accessed 6 November 2019 at http://unesdoc.unesco.org/images/0021/002164/216472e.pdf.

United Nations Educational, Scientific and Cultural Organization (UNESCO). 2015. Guidelines and recommendations for reorienting teacher education to address sustainability. *Education for Sustainable Development in Action, Technical Paper No. 2*. Accessed 3 April 2020 at https://unesdoc.unesco.org/ark:/48223/pf0000143370.

Verhulst, E. and Lambrechts, W. 2015. Fostering the incorporation of sustainable development in higher education: lessons learned from a change management perspective. *Journal of Cleaner Production*, 106, 189–204.

von Blottnitz, H., Case, J.M. and Fraser, D.M. 2015. Sustainable development at the core of undergraduate engineering curriculum reform: a new introductory course in chemical engineering. *Journal of Cleaner Production*, 106, 300–307.

Watson, M.K., Lozano, R., Noyes, C. and Rodgers, M. 2013. Assessing curricula contribution to sustainability more holistically: experiences from the integration of curricula assessment and students' perceptions at the Georgia Institute of Technology. *Journal of Cleaner Production*, 61, 106–16.

World Commission on Environment and Development (WCED). 1987. *Report of the World Commission on Environment and Development: Our Common Future* [The Brundtland Report]. Accessed 7 April 2020 at https://sustainabledevelopment.un.org/content/documents/5987our-common-future.pdf.

World Engineers' Convention (WEC). 2008. The Brasilia Declaration: Engineering and Innovation for Development with Social Responsibility: World Engineers' Conference Brasilia, 5 December 2006. Accessed 7 May 2020 at https://www.wec2019.org.au/world-engineers-convention-2008-brasilia/.

World Federation of Engineering Organizations (WFEO). 2018. *Paris Declaration: Advancing the United Nations Sustainable Development Goals through Engineering*. Accessed 7 May 2020 at http://www.wfeo.org/wp-content/uploads/declarations/WFEO-UNESCO-Paris_Declaration.pdf.

World Federation of Engineering Organizations (WFEO). 2019. *Declaration: Global Engineering Education Standards and Capacity Building for Sustainable Development*. Accessed 7 May 2020 at http://www.wfeo.org/wp-content/uploads/declarations/UNESCO_IEA_WFEO_Declaration_Global_Engg_Education.pdf.

Wu, Y.-C.J. and Shen, J.-P. 2016. Higher education for sustainable development: a systematic review. *International Journal of Sustainability in Higher Education*, 17, 633–51.

APPENDIX: SUSTAINABLE DEVELOPMENT QUESTIONNAIRE

1. What's the project's name?
2. What's the main activity of the project?
3. When was the project created?
4. In the project, are environmental and social concerns considered in the definition of strategies?
    a. Never
    b. Rarely
    c. Often
    d. Always
5. Environmental issues in the project are:
    a. A weakness
    b. Considered of negligible impact
    c. A strength present in the project's culture
    d. An opportunity for innovation
6. Among the mentioned activities below, choose the five most important for improving the environmental performance of the project:
    a. Reducing energy consumption
    b. Reducing the amount of raw materials used
    c. Reducing noise pollution
    d. Reducing visual pollution
    e. Reducing waste
    f. Reducing odors
    g. Increasing recycling
    h. Reducing/treating hazardous waste
    i. Promoting actions on environmental education
    j. Reuse of materials
7. For you, what are the main advantages to implementing sustainable policies? Choose three:
    a. Reducing/controlling costs
    b. Public demonstration of the commitment to environmental management
    c. Continuous improvement of environmental performance
    d. Concern for the future of the planet
    e. Maintaining good public relations with all stakeholders
    f. Improvement of image, notoriety and acceptance in the real and potential market
    g. Developing and encouraging environmental solutions
8. What are the main obstacles to implementing sustainable policies? Choose two:
    a. High financial costs
    b. Lack of knowledge
    c. Complexity in taking actions (i.e., treatment of toxic wastes)
    d. Poor quality product/process alternatives
    e. Consolidated habits
    f. Beginner projects
9. Does the project have any continuous activities of social impact? If so, which ones?

10.   Are there any wastes generated by the project activities? If so, which ones?
11.   Are there any actions for proper disposal of this waste? If so, which ones?
12.   Are there any programs to minimize this waste? If so, which ones?
13.   Is it possible to estimate the amount of residue that the project generates (solids, effluents, air emissions and vibrations)? If so, how is it estimated?
14.   Is it possible to estimate the consumption of natural resources (water, electricity, fuels, coal and mineral resources)? If so, how is it estimated?
15.   Is responsibility for environmental management defined and documented?
      a.   Yes
      b.   No
16.   Does the project provide detailed information on environmental damage resulting from the use and disposal of your products to the people involved?
      a.   Yes
      b.   No
17.   Is the project aware of the origin of the inputs, raw materials and products used in the operations and is it guaranteed that, in these origins, human rights and the environment are respected?
      a.   Yes
      b.   No
18.   Does the project invest in technology to reduce environmental/social impact?
      a.   Yes
      b.   No
19.   Does the project perform selective collection of the waste it generates?
      a.   Yes
      b.   No
20.   Does the project have development and training policies, aiming for the continuous improvement of all its staff?
      a.   Yes
      b.   No
21.   Does the project know what the Sustainable Development Goals (SDGs) are?
      a.   Yes
      b.   No
22.   What are the SDGs for which the project is responsible?
      a.   No poverty
      b.   Zero hunger
      c.   Good health and well-being
      d.   Quality education
      e.   Gender equality
      f.   Clean water and sanitation
      g.   Affordable and clean energy
      h.   Decent work and economic growth
      i.   Industry, innovation and infrastructure
      j.   Reduced inequalities
      k.   Sustainable cities and communities
      l.   Responsible consumption and production
      m.   Climate action

n. Life below water
o. Life on land
p. Peace, justice and strong institutions
q. Partnerships for the goals
23. What are the actions developed to achieve these goals?
24. Does the project have any prospect of implementing sustainable actions over the course of this year? If so, which ones?

13. Teachers' training as a way of increasing sustainable traditional livelihoods in the coastal region of Paraty, Brazil

Marina Alves Novaes e Cruz, Ana Claudia Campuzano Martinez, Cecilia Maria Marafelli, Katherine Cilae Benedict, Maria Inês Rocha de Sá, Leonardo Esteves de Freitas and Edmundo Gallo

1. INTRODUCTION

Climate change is a consequence, mainly, of a hegemonic model of development, production and consumption. While the profits generated by this model are appropriated by a small part of humanity, the deleterious effects of these changes affect, in particular, the most vulnerable part of the world's population, which is often exposed to climate-related risks (Bowen and Friel, 2012; Magrin et al., 2014).

Education is an important tool in addressing climate change related to the unequal model of development adopted in the world. The central role of education is widely recognized among researchers and public managers at various scales, locally as well as globally. The UNESCO Climate Change Initiative advocates investing in education so that societies are able to understand, mitigate and adapt to climate change (United Nations Educational, Scientific and Cultural Organization [UNESCO], n.d.).

In spite of this relevance, it is only since the second half of the last decade that we can observe investments being made in an education focused on the discussion of climate change; even today, this theme is not relevant in most educational processes (International Alliance of Leading Education Institutes [IALEI], 2009; Silva, Costa and Borba, 2016).

It is essential to discuss this issue from a strategic standpoint that does not address climate change solely from scientific logic or from individual behavior, which tend to reduce the causes of climate change to issues such as carbon emissions, effluent recycling and waste and transport. This approach needs to focus on the discussion of structural issues, such as the development of critical thinking and democratic participation (IALEI, 2009). This same perspective is observed at the national level, since much of the education work that deals with climate change in Brazil addresses scientific and behavioral issues, leaving aside the unequal development model (Jacobi et al., 2011). Due to this reality, the panel of Brazilian educators – gathered to discuss the relations between climate change and education – focused on the elaboration of human resources from a perspective that highlights the hegemonic development model (ibid.).

However, it is still common in basic education that the discussion of climate change is focused on this strictly scientific and behavioralist perspective, which 'fails to acknowledge and value the enormous potential of issues that fall more within the scope of citizenship and ethics from a critical perspective' (Jacobi et al., 2011, p. 140). Therefore, teacher training from a critical perspective about the relationship between climate change and development is essential to the search for sustainable development models that are effective for mitigating and adapting society to climate change.

2.   TRADITIONAL COMMUNITIES AT PARATY/RIO DE JANEIRO, ANGRA DOS REIS/RIO DE JANEIRO AND UBATUBA/SÃO PAULO

The main characteristics of traditional communities are the occupation of a specific territory by several generations; the key role played by family units and kinship relations in the exercise of economic, social and cultural activities; and the relevance of myths and rituals associated with hunting, fishing, extractive activity and farming – that is, knowledge and activities related to the environment, which presuppose a close connection with the cycles of nature and predominance of an essentially oral culture. These livelihoods value sustainable means of production and consumption, generating few impacts on the environment and thus causing only a small impact on climate change, since they do not produce large amounts of effluents such as sewage and garbage, do not require large amounts of energy for production and do not lead to the destruction of forests (Cappucci, 2016; Cortines et al., 2017; Stevens et al., 2016).

Adaptation of these populations to climate change depends on the promotion of sustainable production and consumption practices based on cooperation and solidarity. These aspects are valued in the ways of production and consumption of different traditional communities such as the *caiçara* (fishing communities), *quilombola*[1] and indigenous peoples that live in the Bocaina region, encompassing the municipalities of Angra dos Reis, Paraty and Ubatuba in the states of Rio de Janeiro and São Paulo, Brazil (Freitas et al., 2016).

Adaptation to climate change and the future of sustainable development in this region involves strategies that ensure the reproduction of the traditional way of life, bringing to the forefront educational processes that take those traditions into account. The present chapter intends to discuss the need to construct differentiated pedagogical practices for traditional communities as a way to strengthen their ways of life and, consequently, the processes of adaptation to climate change.

2.1   Land Disputes and Pressures on Traditional Communities

The greatest pressure on the maintenance of the way of living of these traditional communities is related to land issues: protected areas and real estate capital dispute the communities' territory (Freitas et al., 2016). This process is materialized, on a local scale, in a recurrent situation in Brazil, a country of continental dimensions that has a history of conflicts related to the possession of land and permanence of the rural workers and traditional peoples in their territories. The country's land structure has been the subject of countless debates and confrontations throughout history and, over the last 50 years, social movements have been strengthening and seeking to guarantee people in the countryside the right to own and work the land as well as decent living conditions.

The inequality of Brazil's land structure can be observed in areas of environmental preservation and great tourist appeal, such as the Bocaina region. Hundreds of families of small *caiçara* communities in this area are often pressured to leave their lands due to real estate speculation carried out by groups with strong economic and political power (Diegues, 2016; Freitas et al., 2016; Toledo, 2001).

The existence of territories differentiating urban spaces from rural ones is an effective characteristic of traditional communities. For Gomes da Silva, 'territory is a locus appropriate to the physical and cultural reproduction of the members of a certain traditional community' (Gomes da Silva, 2016, p. 43). Educational processes that make it possible to understand that the way of life of these communities is sustainable are essential for society and traditional communities to value these ways of life, strengthening the struggle for permanence in their territories.

This model of education, however, is counter-hegemonic. Only in recent years has it found any space in Brazil's educational policies. The *caiçara* communities were declared traditional peoples by Decree No. 6.040/2007, which establishes the National Policy for the Sustainable Development of Traditional Peoples and Communities. The recognition that communities that live in the 'countryside', a term used here as a counterpoint to the urban space, are entitled to an education different from that offered to those who live in urban agglomerations, is new and innovative, and gained strength from the institution, in 2002, of the *Operational Guidelines for Basic Education in Inland Schools*, drawn up by the National Education Council. This recognition goes beyond the notion of geographical space and understands cultural needs, social rights and the integral formation of these individuals (Cadernos Secad, 2007).

The rights of traditional peoples, although legally guaranteed, are commonly disregarded. Factors such as lack of representation in privileged decision-making spaces, absence or lack of access to public policies, and disinformation in general, greatly contribute to this situation. One of the most serious threats to traditional communities in the Bocaina region is the fact that they live in an extremely valued region of great natural beauty, a constant target of illegal occupation, disorderly and predatory tourism and real estate speculation.

Protected by the law, but neglected by the government, traditional communities have been, year after year, sidelined from their cultural and natural heritage and, consequently, from their identity. Expelled from their lands, they increase the number of citizens in precarious conditions in urban centers, with little or no access to decent housing, employment, healthcare, leisure and education (Cortines et al., 2017; Freitas et al., 2016). This direct threat to traditional communities poses an indirect threat to society as a whole, since the expulsion of these communities from their territories, followed by the construction of condominiums, hotels and other activities, directly related to mass tourism and high luxury, tends to strengthen the pattern of non-sustainable production and consumption, generating lasting impacts on climate change.

Allying itself with different programs and institutions that seek to resist this situation, the NEPEDif[2] has been working, since 2015, with *caiçara* communities in the construction of a 'differentiated education' project that, combined with the struggle for representation, permanence in the territory and the recognition of the identity of these communities, seeks to value their way of life.

The objective of the program is to guarantee the provision of public education that takes into account the particular dimension of *caiçara* culture, seeking to strengthen it and raise awareness of its importance in the process of resistance and struggle for its rights and territory. It is this permanence, with the sustainable use of the land, that can reduce the continuous and unbridled growth of deforestation of important areas, reducing the environmental impact that aggravates the climatic changes, as demonstrated by the relationship between deforestation and global warming (Scott et al., 2018).

2.2 From the Threat to Defense of the Territory

There are dozens of *caiçara* communities in the Bocaina region (Figure 13.1), many of which are accessed only by sea or trails. Among these are the Ponta Negra, Ponta da Joatinga, Araújo Island, Saco do Mamanguá, Sono Beach, Ponta Grossa, Pouso da Cajaíba and Calhaus Beach communities. These communities have been dealing for a long time with problems related to their children's education. As a rule, these communities rely on multi-age[3] schools for students aged six to ten years on average, which cover the first stage of Elementary School. In some cases, children in some of these locations need to travel to attend school on nearby beaches.

Regarding the second stage of Elementary and Secondary Education, there is simply no provision for regular education. For this reason, young people of school age need to study in the urban nucleus of Paraty. It is noteworthy that this gap left by the public administration was, on several occasions, filled by the offer of supplementary and/or vocational education offered by private groups, from a perspective that does not value the traditional knowledge and ways of life of these communities.

What then is implied by the non-provision of regular education to *caiçara* communities? The answer is simple: moving to the city of Paraty or dropping out of school. In both cases, the effects are perverse – families or young people who leave their territory to live in precarious conditions on the outskirts of the city, or young people without access to formal education, leaving the territory unprotected, either due to the decrease in the number of residents, or the impossibility of those who remain to articulate and fight for their defense and preservation. Therefore, we have a weakening of the livelihoods of these communities and territories linked to these ways of life, increasing the environmental impact on them and reducing the possibilities of strengthening sustainable livelihoods.

The territory in which these communities live comprises several islands, beaches, mountains and areas *in natura*, some protected by the public administration in protected areas, while others are exploited by real estate speculation, predatory tourism and large enterprises. However, the traditional communities that live in these territories are a hindrance to the realization of projects destined to benefit, for the most part, people of very high purchasing power. Vulnerable in their traditions and impacted by the difficulties of subsistence, *caiçara* communities are increasingly subject to abandoning their territories, opening space for these areas to be taken by large real estate ventures, with little concern for their preservation.

How, then, can *caiçara* communities protect themselves, defend and demand their rights? 'Defending their territory is the basic determinant of the sustainability of these communities'[4] and this defense involves the valuing of traditional manners and

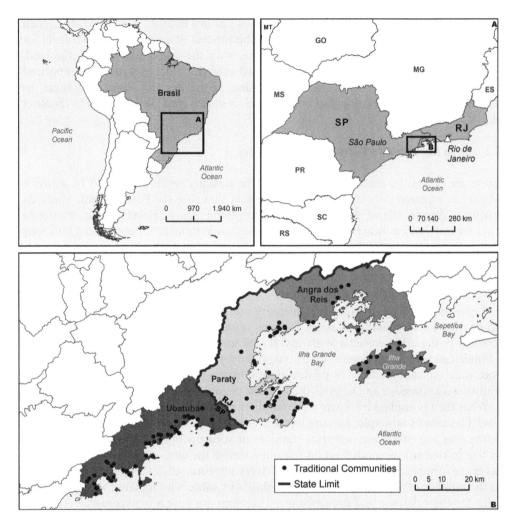

Figure 13.1   Territory of OTSS[5]/NEPEDif

customs, the community's articulation to preserve these characteristics, the knowledge of their rights and the search for the necessary mechanisms of resistance. In this sense, to strengthen the existence – and survival – of traditional communities of coastal regions is also to intervene in sustainability, as Cortines et al. (2017) argues: 'Maintaining livelihoods and traditional practices positively influences sustainability, creating conditions for the implementation of sustainable development goals in their territory and for the prevention and adaptation to climate change' (Cortines et al., 2017, p. 454). The school and a differentiated education play a fundamental role in the preservation of these people's way of life.

3.   DIFFERENTIATED SCHOOL EDUCATION

Differentiated education means a school education that recognizes and values the traditions, struggles and knowledge of traditional communities, valuing a knowledge based on a way of life that is less aggressive to the environment, focused on patterns of production and sustainable consumption. However, there is a tendency to counteract the traditional mode of ethnic-cultural, usually stereotyped and timeless way of life, with the so-called civilized, modern and urban way, without establishing a dialogue between the representations of environment and development that allows a sustainable subsistence economy attuned to technological advances, combining the old and the new society, maintaining a cultural identity that preserves the right to the territory. A differentiated school education becomes an emancipatory practice in the quest for social and environmental justice. A differentiated education, therefore, becomes a means of strengthening and enhancing a sustainable and climate-adjusted way of life, without disregarding that this way of life, even if inserted in a modern society, can and should maintain its essential characteristics.

To achieve this, it is necessary to challenge paradigms of common sense and to deconstruct concepts such as the existence of a universal knowledge produced by a hegemonic mercantile society that must be taught to all. This conception of education that attends to the dominant groups disregards the interests and needs of those living in other spaces, implicitly implying the idea that the rural people should be educated according to that model for a future life in the city. As a result, the public educational system in Brazil is marked by huge discrepancies in supply and results, especially in terms of attending the needs of the populations living on the edge of urban space.

The deconstruction of the myth of universal school education must be accompanied by the desire for a contextualized education that respects the ways of living, producing and thinking of the different ethnic groups in the countryside, and which is configured as a means of accessing citizenship. In the complex network of emancipatory knowledge, cultural and environmental preservation, the challenge of constructing a differentiated school education is under way.

For traditional communities, school education is understood as a strategy of struggle and resistance aiming at the protection of natural resources and traditional territories. Therefore, it is also a climate change adaptation strategy, since the promotion of an emancipatory education capable of protecting nature and enhancing sustainable production and consumption patterns is one of the main strategies to promote this adaptation.

The concept that thus emerges, of a 'countryside education', refers to populations characterized by a way of life in which a traditional culture permeates social and work relations. But which are these populations? Farmers, indigenous populations, extractivists, fishermen, *caiçaras*, *quilombola*, rubber tappers. And, according to Souza and Loureiro:

> An education that contributes to the transformation of the oppressive and expropriating reality of *caiçaras* must be committed to reaffirm the political and cultural identities of these peoples and their ways of relating to nature, as well as producing knowledge that helps to understand the structures of social inequality and environmental destruction . . . To guarantee the permanence of these groups in the traditional territories and to preserve the ways of life and their traditional practices is to combat deterritorialization, dispossession, expropriation and alienation. (Souza and Loureiro, 2017, p. 504)

The historical human/nature dichotomy, accentuated since the Industrial Revolution and the mercantile way of relating to natural resources, poses an increasingly greater impact on climate change. The sea, besides being a source of food and medicine, a climatic balancer and oxygen supplier, is the basis of the *caiçara* way of life. Without the sea, there is no longer a *caiçara* population, which combines small-scale, subsistence farming with small-scale (or artisanal) fishing.

In this way, we can conclude that the impacts of global warming affect the *caiçara* way of life, threatening its survival as a traditional population. On the other hand, these traditional communities maintain management techniques that can contribute to the preservation of ecosystems, since a relevant aspect in the definition of 'traditional cultures' is the existence of natural resource management systems, based on knowledge acquired by inherited tradition, of myths and symbologies, which are characterized by the respect for natural cycles and their exploitation within the capacity of recovery of the species of animals and the plants used. *Caiçara* cultures can favor the maintenance and sustainable use of natural ecosystems, understood as the resources that people rely on to survive, if these techniques are recognized as legitimate and important knowledge. This recognition and appreciation of traditional knowledge is one of the central objectives of a differentiated school education, enabling the debate over climate change inside traditional communities.

The struggle for regular and good-quality schools, and the offering of a differentiated education, has been supported, mainly, by these three institutions that have been working together with *caiçara* communities: NEPEDif, OTSS and IEAR.[6]

In one of NEPEDif's first field activities it was possible to elaborate, in collaboration with Pouso da Cajaíba *caiçara* residents, the following concept for a '*caiçara* differentiated education': 'Education that respects and values the culture and the knowledge of the territory. Critical education, connected with local and global reality, aiming at a better quality of life in a sustainable way' (Cruz at al., 2017, p. 95). Clearly, this is a concept of differentiated education that values a climate-adjusted way of life and dialogues with a school education that discusses the importance of sustainability in the context of global climate change. It was from this perspective and from the local school teachers' demands for the construction of a specific political pedagogical plan that the planning of the program of continuous formation began with the teachers who worked at Paraty's *caiçara* schools.

NEPEDif, OTSS and IEAR have been working since the beginning of 2017, developing this program and fostering the exchange of knowledge and experiences among their members and *caiçara* teachers, aiming to jointly bring about a curricular reorientation that allows the implementation of a true school education; in other words, an education in which these communities' reality is not only present but also guides the school life of their children, emphasizing aspects of culture, ways of life and difficulties faced by these populations.

It is important to emphasize that, if education alone cannot be the promoter of the many necessary changes, it is one of the instances that can make these changes possible, through school practices that prioritize the formation of subjects, aware of their role and which are active in their society. Thus, believing in the recovery of traditional knowledge and in strengthening fundamental aspects of community life, and also through formal, contextualized and qualified education, it is hoped that the next *caiçara* generations will grow up with a greater awareness of the richness and importance of their culture, and their commitment to the territory and environment in general.

4.   TRAINING *CAIÇARA* TEACHERS AS RESISTANCE

NEPEDif's strategy and purpose for strengthening *caiçara* communities, valuing their wisdom and knowledge, is the ongoing training of public school teachers who work in *caiçara* communities. To support the training of teachers capable of enhancing traditional culture and the sustainable way of life that these communities lead is one of the structuring strategies to implement educational processes capable of discussing climate change (Jacobi et al., 2011).

The Continuing Education Program at Education *Caiçara* School for the Coastal Schools of the First Stage of Elementary Education in Paraty/RJ, prepared by IEAR includes approximately 30 teachers, including coordinators, from the 15 municipal schools that work in the communities of the coastal region: Grajaú, Araújo Island, Laranjeiras, Paraty-Mirim, Sono Beach, Ponta Grossa, Ponta da Joatinga, Pouso da Cajaíba, Ponta Negra, Calhaus Beach, Trindade, Saco do Mamanguá, São Gonçalo, São Roque and Tarituba.

The training takes place through monthly meetings with the participation of members of NEPEDif, OTSS and IEAR and has a duration of four years, divided into three stages (Figure 13.2) (Cruz et al., 2018). The first stage, held throughout the first half of 2018, is called *awareness* and aims to bring together everyone involved and to discuss the proposed four-year plan.

Begun in the second half of 2018, the second stage or *theoretical deepening*, refers to the questioning of themes such as differentiated education, field education, national and regional curriculum guidelines on differentiated and field education, the concept of what is to be a *caiçara*, the difference between 'conventional curriculum' and '*caiçara* curriculum'. At this stage, the relevance of the *caiçara* way of life was addressed in a context in which production and consumption are unsustainable. This fact made it possible to value the *caiçara* way of life from a critical vision that approached sustainability and the

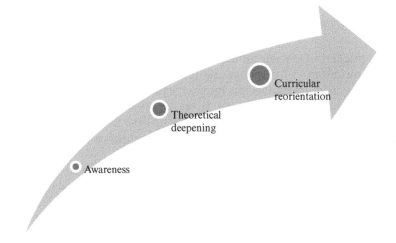

Source: Cruz et al. (2018).

Figure 13.2   Methodological stages of formation

climatic changes from a holistic perspective and not only from a scientific and behavioral perspective (IALEI, 2009; Jacobi et al., 2011).

Finally, during the third and last stage, from 2019 to 2021, called *curricular reorientation*, the methodological steps will be based on the proposal of the Curriculum Matrix of the Municipal Department of Education of São Paulo[7] which is briefly described below.

The first step, begun in 2019, consists of a study of reality through socio-cultural diagnoses of schools and communities. This study, based on social representation[8] methodology, treats information collected through the planning instrument called Strengths, Weaknesses, Opportunities and Threats (SWOT analysis)[9] and surveys allow the data to be grouped by semantic field for the construction of the thematic network.

The second step, also begun in 2019, encompasses the study of the curriculum itself, with the study and discussion of the epistemology of each area of knowledge (mathematics, Portuguese language, science, history, geography, arts, and physical education), the pedagogical tendencies underlying them, and their integrating concepts.

The third step in 2020, is the elaboration of an interdisciplinary curriculum, organized by generative themes – identified from the thematic network built previously – and that opposes the education offered by the regular school, in which the school curriculum is organized with reference to a 'universal' knowledge.

The last step, in 2020 and 2021, is the construction of a planning matrix in which the interdisciplinary and contextualized projects are effectively the daily reality of *caiçara* school education.

Both the methodological steps and the objectives of this training program corroborate Gallo et al.'s (2015) statement, according to whom the populations living in the coastal regions of Brazil – such as, in this case, the traditional *caiçara* communities of Paraty – are recognized as being vulnerable to the socio-environmental impact of climatic changes related to extreme events, such as floods, landslides, desertification, rising sea levels and rising temperatures.

5.   CONCLUSIONS

Residents and teachers of *caiçara* communities face several difficulties in their daily life, such as the precariousness of communication – electricity arrived in many places only between 2015 and 2016, telephone and Internet signals are unstable – and the distance between these communities and mainland. However, other challenges are also associated with teachers' routines, such as the accumulation of functions, tasks overload and the difficulties in crossing the sea, which depends not only on sea conditions but also on the availability of boats sent by the education department.

Because of all these difficulties, the number of residents is decreasing, especially young people who face both the pressure of living as *caiçaras* and the idealized image of an easy city life, thus abandoning their traditional territories. They often live in precarious conditions in urban centers, leaving a situation of sustainable social reproduction and adapted to the climatic changes in their traditional territories to a situation of poverty and social and environmental unsustainability (Cortines et al., 2017; Freitas et al., 2016).

The lack of schooling is one of the reasons that lead many to go away. Without a differentiated education, which reinforces and values the importance of their knowledge, related to their practices and ways of life, and makes them fight for their recognition within the system, facing situations of subordination, *caiçara* people tend to disappear. It is of fundamental importance to build an education system on which the transformation of this reality can be based, in which the traditional peoples can decide about the processes of organization and environmental management of their territories – an education that favors the appropriation of the fundamental knowledge so that they continue resisting and defending their rights.

Although the objectives pursued by this program of teacher training do not totally overcome these difficulties, they aim above all to contribute to the rescue and valorization of *caiçara* identity, fundamental for the maintenance of this culture, symbolically and concretely, through its resistance and permanence in the territory. We believe, based on our understanding of differentiated education and the characteristics of traditional communities, that the importance and centrality of a school project located in the territory that meets the demands and specificities of these communities are clear.

NEPEDif was, at the end of 2018, finishing the theoretical deepening stage and planning the beginning of the curricular reorientation stage. The next steps will strengthen issues related to sustainable livelihoods and their relation to climate change, always focusing on the valorization of these ways of life as a form of continuance in the territory and insertion into society.

The teachers' training program discussed in this chapter does not provide the desired objectives in itself, because the work is still limited to the *caiçara* communities of the municipality of Paraty, not the entire scope of the OTSS, which includes the municipalities of Angra dos Reis and Ubatuba as well, and neither the *quilombola* nor the indigenous communities. It is clear that this limitation will not be overcome solely by the action of NEPEDif, OTSS or IEAR. A possible way to overcome this challenge would be to turn the work developed so far into a training model incorporated by the three municipalities, broadening its scope.

NOTES

1. Communities of people of African origin who were originally maroons, that is, escaped slaves.
2. Center for Studies and Research on Differentiated Education (in free translation) formed by educators from the Pedro II College, a 180-year-old public institution of basic education.
3. Multi-age schools are schools that have, in the same classroom and with a single teacher, students attending different levels of teaching.
4. OTSS (2018), 'Defesa do território'. Accessed October 2018 at https://www.otss.org.br/defesa-do-territorio.
5. The Observatory of Sustainable and Healthy Territories of Bocaina, the result of the partnership between the Oswaldo Cruz Foundation and the Forum of Traditional Communities of Angra dos Reis, Paraty and Ubatuba, constitutes a techno-political space for the development of territorialized solutions based on the ecology of knowledge, articulated at different scales – regional, state, national and global.
6. The Institute of Education of Angra dos Reis, linked to the Fluminense Federal University, through the research group Educational Spaces and Cultural Diversities, coordinated by Professor Domingos Barros Nobre, works to implement curriculum restructuring in schools of traditional communities.
7. Curriculum matrix elaborated under the management of Mayor Luiza Erundina, whose Secretary of Education was Paulo Freire (1989 to 1993).
8. 'Social representation is a contemporary theory that seeks to understand how the individual or the community interprets social phenomena. It is fragmented, partial, has to do with visions of the world, with ideologies, with common sense, with ideas that are conveyed, with knowledge. Social representations circulate, communicate as a given theme is seen, and reflect the socio-historical and cultural context in which

the subject is inserted. They can be modified, become more elaborate, more contextualized' (Azevedo, 1999, p. 70).
9.   SWOT is an instrument that assists in the strategic planning of a particular institution or social group. Its purpose is to detect strengths and weaknesses in order to outline more specific goals.

REFERENCES

Azevedo, G.C. (1999). Uso de jornais e revistas na perspectiva da representação social de meio ambiente em sala de aula. In M. Reigota (ed.), *Verde cotidiano – o meio ambiente em discussão*. Rio de Janeiro: DP&A, pp. 67–82.

Bowen, K.J. and Friel, S. (2012). Climate change adaptation: where does global health fit in the agenda? *Globalization and Health*, 8(1), 10–17.

Cadernos Secad 2 (2007), *Educação do campo: diferenças mudando paradigmas*. Brasilia, DF: Secad. Accessed October 2016 at http://portal.mec.gov.br/secad/arquivos/pdf/educacaocampo.pdf.

Cappucci, M. (2016). Aspectos fundiários das comunidades caiçaras. In P.S. Neto (ed.), *Direito das comunidades caiçaras*. São Paulo: Café com Lei, pp. 105–31.

Cortines, A.C., Possidonio, R.D. and Bahia, N.C.F. et al. (2017). Social cartography and the defense of the traditional Caiçara Territory of Trindade (Paraty, RJ, Brazil). In W. Leal Filho and L.E. Freitas (eds), *Climate Change Adaptation in Latin America: Managing Vulnerability, Fostering and Resilience* (1st edition). New York: Scientific Publishing Services, pp. 445–56.

Cruz, M.A.N., Lino, F.A.M., Marafelli, C. and Sá, M.I.R. de (2018). Desafios da educação diferenciada: uma proposta de formação de professores de comunidades caiçaras. Paper presented at the Encontro Nacional de Didática e Prática de Ensino, 2018, Salvador. *Anais do ENDIPE*, Volume 19.

Cruz, M.A.N., Lino, F.A.M. and Teixeira, J. et al. (2017). A comunidade tradicional do Pouso da Cajaíba e o tradicional Colégio Pedro II. In R. Lima, A. Vianna, F.I. Ferreira and F.R. Mattos (eds), *A comunidade tradicional do Pouso da Cajaíba e o tradicional Colégio Pedro II* (1st edition). Rio de Janeiro: Colégio Pedro II, pp. 90–100.

Diegues, A.C. (2016). Prefácio. In P.S. Neto (ed.), *Direito das comunidades tradicionais caiçaras*. São Paulo: Café com Lei, pp. 11–19.

Freitas, L.E., Cruz, J.C.H.O., Cortines, A.C. and Gallo, E. (2016). Observatory of Sustainable and Healthy Territories (OTSS) GIS: geo-information for the sustainability of traditional communities in Southeastern Brazil. In W. Leal Filho, U.M. Azeiteiro and F. Alves (eds), *Climate Change and Health: Improving Resilience and Reducing Risks* (1st edition). Cham, Switzerland: Springer, pp. 353–67.

Gallo E., A.F. Setti and T. Ruprecht et al. (2015). Territorial solutions, governance and climate change: ecological sanitation at Praia do Sono, Paraty, Rio de Janeiro, Brazil. In W. Leal Filho, W.M. Azeiteiro and F. Alves (eds), *Climate Change and Health: Improving Resilience and Risks*. Cham, Switzerland: Springer, pp. 515–22.

Gomes da Silva, P.T. (2009). Conceito de comunidade tradicional. In P.S. Neto (ed.), *Direito das comunidades caiçaras*. São Paulo: Café com Lei, pp. 39–47.

International Alliance of Leading Education Institutes (IALEI) (2009). *Climate Change and Sustainable Development: The Response from Education*. Copenhagen: IALEI.

Jacobi, P.R., Guerra, A.F., Sulaiman, S.N. and Nepucemo, T. (2011). Mudanças climáticas globais: a resposta da educação. *Revista Brasileira de Educação*, 16(46), 35–148.

Magrin, G., Marengo, J. and Boulanger, J.P. et al. (2014). Central and South America. In V.R. Barros, C.B. Field and D.J. Dokken et al. (eds), *Climate Change 2014: Impacts, Adaptation and Vulnerability: Part B: Regional Aspects. Working Group II Contribution to the Fifth Assessment Report of the Intergovernmental Panel on Climate Change*. Cambridge, UK: Cambridge University Press, pp. 1499–566.

Scott, C.E.S., Monks, A. and Spracklen, D.V.S. et al. (2018). Impact on short-lived climate forcers increases projected warming due to deforestation. *Nature Communications*, 9, Article 157.

Silva, C.M.L.F., Costa, F.A. and Borba, G.L. (2016). A educação em mudanças climáticas: uma abordagem interdisciplinar. *Holos*, 4, 176–88.

Souza, V.M. de and Loureiro, C.F.B. (2017). Educação diferenciada e povos tradicionais caiçaras: resistência e luta diante da expansão do capital sobre os territórios tradicionais. In M.M.D. de Oliveira, M. Mendes, C.M. Hansel and S. Damiani (eds), *Cidadania, meio ambiente e sustentabilidade*. Caxias do Sul, RS: Educs, pp. 483–509.

Stevens, C., Winterbottom, R., Springer, J. and Reytar, K. (2016). *Securing Rights, Combating Climate Change: How Strengthening Community Forest Rights Mitigates Climate Change*. World Resources Institute. Accessed December 2018 at https://files.wri.org/s3fs-public/securingrights-full-report-english.pdf.

Toledo, V.M. (2001). Povos comunidades tradicionais e a biodiversidade. Translated by A. Diegues. In S. Levin (ed.), *Encyclopedia of Biodiversity*. Cambridge, MA: Academic Press.
United Nations Educational, Scientific and Cultural Organization (UNESCO). (n.d.). Climate change education and awareness. Accessed 12 February 2021 at https://en.unesco.org/themes/addressing-climate-change/climate-change-education-and-awareness.

14. Field notes: teaching sustainable business to environmental scientists
Diana Watts

1. INTRODUCTION

The call is clear – the search for multidisciplinary solutions to complex problems, new knowledge construction and an urgency to integrate scientific evidence in social system solutions (Cornell et al., 2013; O'Brien et al., 2013; Wallace and Clark, 2018). The question is also recognizable – namely, are we prepared to design sustainability curricula to prepare future professionals and citizens? Can we identify cognitive models, methodologies and competencies to support education, advocacy and action (Krasny, 2020)? Given the significance of economics and business organizations for environmental futures, my own focus has been to consider curricular development and educational practices from the perspective of markets and the growing emergence of sustainable business (Chandler, 2019; Raworth, 2017). As a social scientist, the question of interest has been to rethink future market systems that (might) extend beyond the role of profit maximization and neoliberal trade policies. Could sustainable business become a positive co-collaborator in creating emergent environmental solutions? This discussion will address teaching practices intended for graduate-level environmental science students, typically on the cusp of defining their professional pathway. The focus is to encourage students to re-examine sustainable business as a more dynamic interplay across business, government and civil society. Given the immediate and urgent role for science and science professionals noted by Sachs (2015), this also suggests a possible future contributing role to market adaptation (Olson and Rejeski, 2018; Wallace and Clark, 2018).

2. METHODOLOGY: COURSE OVERVIEW

The term sustainable business will be used to refer to the broad categories of actions comprising both corporate and entrepreneurial activities that address environmental and social externalities through a range of policies including internal governance and external compliance (Chandler, 2019; Fogel, 2016). The course curriculum and projects described here have been designed specifically for graduate students in an environmental sciences and policy program. From the outset, the overall course design prepares students to undertake individual exploratory reading to provide context for several directed projects. The syllabus and lectures have been developed with specific modules providing foundational concepts in economics, business and political sociology. These are intended to provide scaffolding. Overall, the lectures and readings are less about conveying specific content and more about preparing students to become comfortable with wrestling with competing ideas. This idea wrestling proved to be an important element throughout the course.

The overall course design has been based on three primary learning outcomes:

1. To engage students with cognitive models based on socio-ecological system adaptation that include multi-level actors with multiple, competing agendas (Folke, 2006).
2. To prepare students to consider multidisciplinary solutions. Students are invited to build on their own disciplinary base (natural science) while developing fluency in social science concepts and models (Stein, 2007).
3. To intentionally develop an inquiry-based approach premised on accepting emergent rather than established boundaries (Jahn, Bergmann and Keil, 2012). This open-ended framing is of particular interest when considering the emergent roles of business, government and civil society.

It should be noted that the course has never been intended to develop a 'pro' business bias but instead to encourage a greater appreciation for the complexity of the social, environmental and economic relationships. The course 'Sustainable Business' consists of five modules:

Module 1 – Setting the Framework: Economic Growth Models and the Ecosystem
Module 2 – Evolution of Corporate Social Responsibility from Philanthropy to Strategy
Module 3 – Regulatory Regimes in Practice: Do These Work?
Module 4 – Is there a Business Case for Sustainable Business?
Module 5 – Sustainable Futures

While the general readings and lectures provide a guideline, the crux of the learning process is focused on a series of assigned course projects. These projects have been designed to challenge students' existing premises around markets, economics and the emerging contours of sustainable business. Two specific examples will be discussed. The intention here is to offer preliminary insights into this larger issue of bringing scientific literacy together with a more nuanced understanding of the emerging role of markets and business in contributing to future sustainability solutions. The chapter will first discuss the conceptual basis for the courses and then provide a discussion of two class projects. The final section will conclude with the larger issue of preparing environmental science students to engage as co-collaborators not only in rethinking the role of markets but that of complex system adaptation (Krasny, 2020).

3.   CHALLENGING KEY ASSUMPTIONS

Sustainable business is not a neutral term for many environmental science students. This necessitates unpacking the cognitive model of the roles and relationships across business, government and society. Students typically begin the semester with a shared perspective that corporations are primarily enablers of the extractive take/make/waste economy (Dauvergne and Lister, 2013). Profit maximization is considered to be the key economic driver, and neoliberal economic policies are assumed to frame an unending growth

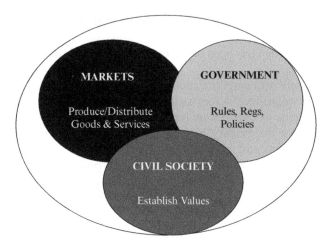

Source: Based on Steiner and Steiner (2012).

Figure 14.1   Business/government/society as stable institutions

curve in gross domestic product (GDP) (Alier, 2009; Raworth, 2017). Natural capital or environmental impacts are absent or marginalized. Perhaps most importantly for future policy makers, the primary role of governance is to create laws and regulations as well as improved accountability through voluntary reporting and monitoring systems (Sieuw, 2015). Civil society plays an advocacy role through non-profits (NPOs), social movements, and related civic organizations. In this institutional model, business, government and society are distinctive, with each serving a particular stable set of roles and functions (Figure 14.1). Policy regulation in turn is based on an assumption of potentially altering outcomes through a change in norms and behaviors based on policies of rule setting, monitoring, and adjudication. This is an oversimplification but highlights the essential premises.

There is an alternative to this perspective. In multilateral policy discussions, business is also described as making a *contribution* to climate change mitigation/adaptation (Intergovernmental Panel on Climate Change [IPCC], 2018). Business and industry working with governments and civil society are identified as key stakeholders in creating positive future-oriented policies (Laszlo and Zhexembayeva, 2011). Corporations are called upon to innovate alternative technological solutions through a general reliance on market signals (Chandler, 2019; Eastin, Grundmann and Prakash, 2011). This creates a contrast between companies viewed to be largely the focus of regulatory policies needing to be constrained from creating negative externalities, and an emerging role as social innovators, essential to developing new business processes. In this second perspective, governance is less about compliance mechanisms, although these still remain viable. The focus becomes complex interactions across business, civil society and governance systems. These may involve multiple actors and competing agendas (Olsson, Folke and Hahn, 2004). Regulation continues but may be one of many approaches to supporting sustainable business (Loconto and Fouilleux, 2014).

To fully appreciate this second perspective, the course also addresses another central issue – profit maximization. If students consider business organizations as the 'villain', then it becomes difficult to unfreeze this mental image in order to examine these more differentiated relationships. The course does not challenge the environmental damage of large corporations but does support thinking about more complex business relationships. Strategic business logic may include more than 'only' goals of profit, including social values (Chandler, 2019). Attention to these nascent strategic corporate social responsibility (CSR) initiatives is still worthwhile considering even if only viewed as representative 'bright spots' of adaptive behaviors (Ellis, 2010; Olson and Rejeski, 2018).

The aim of these courses is not to convince students to choose one or the other as prescription. Rather, the intention is to enable students to straddle these two prevailing perspectives. Both are empirically valid and require understanding of corporate supply chains and the cross-cutting of national, geographic and socio-cultural boundaries. For example, there is still much to be learned about reporting frameworks, certification and regulation in terms of social as well as economic consequences (Barkemeyer, Preuss and Lee, 2015; Gutierrez et al., 2016). Companies that demonstrate business strategy based on environmental stewardship models are still emergent (Chandler, 2019). But combining a more fluid understanding of institutional stakeholders presents a dynamic understanding that allows for shifting relationships across business, government and civil society. This more complex perspective is important for environmental education in that it presents an image of polycentric governance that includes business as an inclusive actor within the governance system (Krasny, 2020; Loconto and Fouilleux, 2014; Meadows, 1996).

4. DISCUSSION OF CLASS PROJECTS

With this background, we will now turn to a description of two projects. For our purposes here, a class project will refer to a specific set of structured activities that include instructions, readings and individual feedback from peer and faculty. Although these projects were used for student assessment (grading) the emphasis, largely through student–faculty feedback, was to build a more complex understanding of sustainability and proposed solutions specifically integrating environmental, economic and social outcomes. The following observations are based on the author's role as course designer and instructor working with approximately 60 students during four semesters between 2017 and 2020.

Project A: Changemaker Chats

The Changemaker Chats provide an opportunity for environmental science students to engage directly with business practitioners. Crossing this boundary between their science background and entrepreneurial or corporate settings may not be in the normal purview of many science students, either through absence of awareness that opportunities exist or lack of a proclivity to enter the business sphere. Students are invited in a pre-course survey to describe their own definition of sustainability and the role of sustainable business. This offers the instructor an initial insight into the self-reported starting point in terms of a student's perspective on business. The chat sessions are held at mid-point in the course and provide a second opportunity to assess the student's perspective.

The format for the chat sessions is a small group video interview between students and a business professional. There is some leeway in terms of identifying the changemaker, but priority is given to individuals with an environmental science background who are employed within the business sector on projects related to sustainability. Large corporations as well as start-ups are included in the contact list that the faculty member provides. Students identify the interview questions and facilitate the individual calls. The final step is a discussion board where the conversation is focused on comparing/contrasting the chat session experiences and student observations. For example, one student observed after speaking with an entrepreneur:

> [This start-up] takes food waste from restaurants and lets grubs grow on the food waste (this sounds gross, I know!), and then sells the grubs as animal feed . . . I love this concept because it's simultaneously addressing food waste and healthy animal feed. In prior sustainable food courses, I've learned that animal feed can often consist of questionable ingredients, so [it] is hitting two birds with one stone by minimizing waste going into the landfill and generating healthy feed for animals. (Communication with author)

This statement shows an insight into extending a natural waste system (use of grubs) and a new business opportunity (composting and sales of healthy animal feed). While recognizing this comment for what it is – an insight that has landed within the student's radar – it appears to have created a small 'aha' moment where business presents a solution.

The Changemaker Chats most closely align with the learning outcome focused on multidisciplinary solutions intended to encourage the crossing of (social/disciplinary/professional) barriers. These discussions are designed to bring together young practitioners, often with similar environmental science backgrounds, who have launched or are in the process of launching their own careers in the green economy. This provides a deliberate focus on professionals who are in the business setting but continue to wrestle with the ambiguity and novelty of applied science in the marketplace. A pertinent follow-up to the chat sessions would be to evaluate if these interactions lead students to a wider appreciation of this interplay between economic opportunities and science expertise.

Project B: Mapping the Value Chain

This mapping project is repeated twice – at the mid-point and the conclusion of the course. The instructions and source material are designed to be intentionally iterative and provide scaffolding across the semester. The primary aim is to focus students' attention on the complexity of multi-actor systems where social/economic/political and science-based relationships may compete and conflict.

The projects involve three defined (sub)assignments with the focus on a specific food commodity in relation to the value chain that supports it. Specifically, the project tasks students to describe a global value chain for a specific food commodity or sector (Figure 14.2). The mid-semester project is devoted to fish stock/fisheries, while the final project permits students to identify their own food commodity. Note that the focus of this analysis is less on conventional strategic issues of control or efficiencies across operations of value-adding activities (Chandler, 2019); instead, the research is to identify and construct the interactions of multiple stakeholders across the value chain (Dicken, 2015; Lang and Heasman, 2015). The value chain template designed for this course is heavily indebted to the work of Lang and Heasman, who argue that, as well as corporations, it is the actions

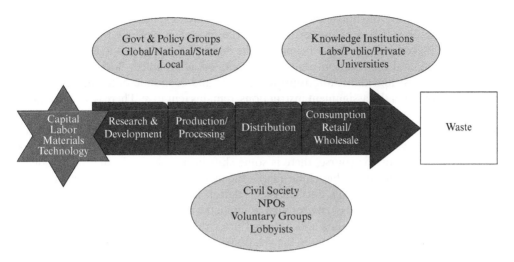

Source: Based on Dicken (2015) and Lang and Heasman (2015).

Figure 14.2 Food production/distribution value chain

and interactions of consumers and policy makers that comprise the current food system as we know it. This value chain framework directs students' attention to identify and parse these relationships.

The initial step of this project is to research key actors and activities relevant to the food production/distribution value chain. Students are provided with a graphic organizer that helps to track and develop this rudimentary map of primary relationships across economic/social/political/environmental actors. Based on this mapping exercise, the second step is to develop a policy memo. The memo is directed to describe tension points across social/economic and ecological relationships. For example, one student noted that increased certification outcomes may hold a negative impact for fisher communities (communication with author). Students are also instructed to write policy recommendations as well as identify areas for future research. The final step is peer review of narrated PowerPoint presentations to compare and contrast projects. This last step is of particular significance in allowing students to recognize the array of possible outcomes across food sectors as well as offer their own insights.

This assignment can be particularly challenging given that science students must research and explicitly address the economic/ecological interface through the lens of multi-actor perspectives without directly privileging one over the other. Economic considerations, social implications, as well as environmental consequences are identified and logged onto the map. In most cases the environmental aspects are most thoroughly reported. The intended outcome of the final paper is modest. Policy recommendations are developed. However, assessment of the recommendations is less about the actual quality of the proposals. Instead, it is about insight into the complexity and overlap of these various key actor positions and their identified points of tension.

In reviewing student papers, the primary difference between the mid-semester and final assignment is the development of the students' appreciation for the complexity of these relationships. During the mid-semester assignment, which explicitly links the preservation/depletion of a fish stock to certification, the project is typically framed in terms consistent with compliance. Overwhelmingly, the result of the project is to assess whether the monitoring and certification processes functioned as intended. Social implications tend to be modest and the relationship to markets and economic outcomes, although explicitly required in the assignment instructions, remains tentative. There is an awareness that fish are shipped and marketed throughout the world, but these tend to be stated in generic terms. Not surprisingly, central to many of the student policy recommendations is a call for improved monitoring and reporting.

Towards the end of the course, there is some shift in perspective in the final student projects. Constructing the value chain map, students begin to demonstrate a growing awareness of the overlapping and messier relationships across key actors/agendas. Connections between business, environmental impacts and social outcomes are reflected in their policy recommendations and narrated presentations. For example, one student reporting on avocado growers notes the relationship among the (local) role of gangs, changing tastes of upscale consumers largely in the US and Europe and depletion of domestic agricultural land. These outcomes are discussed in terms of the influence of consumers (civic society) driving the price/supply of avocados (markets), leading to the rise of gangs (absence of government) and the depletion of agricultural land (environment). It would be overstating it to claim that the second perspective of a multi-actor system has been reached, but there is at least growing *awareness* of embedded social, economic and environmental agendas that may co-create the food sector (Lang and Heasman, 2015). The student project description may appear to be a rather tentative breakthrough but suggests there is growing insight that the system is socially constructed from interactions across multiple actions and agendas.

It should also be noted that while this mapping activity is relatively easy to describe, it is one where students do push back. Encouraging environmental science students to explore relevant actors and agendas with this open framing of the value chain may frustrate students who are trained to think in more exact natural science models. This requires the challenge of multidisciplinary thinking where students utilize their scientific knowledge but at the same time are encouraged to gain fluency in a second discipline, in this case business and economics (Jahn et al., 2012). This is not equally attractive or possible for all students. The rewards come when (some) students are able to appreciate the complexity of the empirical referents they are describing even if they cannot yet carry out a completely satisfying analysis. Success is defined in terms of appreciating new issues and questions rather than clear analysis at the conclusion of the project. In a few cases, the mapping project is rejected, with students opting out. They claim that the source material is not available or that the instructions are not clear. Even with active faculty support it has been accepted that not all students will be successful in adopting this multidisciplinary framing that challenges core assumptions.

5.   ANALYSIS: WHAT HAVE WE LEARNED?

In keeping with offering field notes, these comments will be suggestive rather than evaluative. Our question at the outset concerned environmental education, particularly for science students with an emphasis on directing attention to markets and business as inclusive actors. It is argued that this focus is valid given the role (innovation/production/allocation) that industry is anticipated to play in terms of mitigation/adaptation policies. To re-emphasize, we are not interested in a prescriptive approach to examine market/private sector behaviors; rather, the question is a conceptual one.

The argument made here is that models do matter! More specifically, the question raised is whether the functionally based linear models do justice to current empirical referents. Is there sufficient appreciation for emerging developments such as social businesses, circular economy supply chains, B Corps, hybrid organizations and sustainability professionals as a new type of manager (Fogel, 2016; Hawkin, 2017; Holt and Littlewood, 2015)? Are entrepreneurs, corporations, and local business communities viewed as potential stakeholders in sustainable solutions or as on ongoing part of the problem? This relationship between cognition and action is significant (Krasny, 2020). If governance is viewed primarily as compliance-based reporting, monitoring and regulation of market behavior, then potential future actions remain similarly circumscribed.

Environmental education will continue to challenge educators to develop an ambitious learning/teaching agenda. Krasny (2020) argues that attributes of socio-ecological adaptation may provide a potential framework (2020). This discussion has focused on two specific aspects: polycentric governance or multi-actor relationships and complex adaptation. These provide the basis for the course projects. This can be seen in the constructed dialogue of the student–practitioner video conferences where interaction with sustainability practitioners is used to challenge initial premises. The mapping projects, similarly, encourage students to craft their own version of an issue (problem) as well as the policy solution (recommendations). But, designing curricular activities to promote imagining new futures is not easy. The projects described here have been run multiple times during the past four years. Each semester it appears from the student evaluations that the 'needle has moved' for some if not all of the students. Using words such as 'exposed me to' or 'pushed me to think about' suggests that student outcomes result more in raising new, tentative questions rather than leading to outright reformulations. Students observed:

> This course exposed me to the existence of various interesting sustainable business models and pushed me to think about the complex relationships across value chains and among business, government and civil society in new ways.

> I've realized that businesses must be included in the decision-making process and their needs must be addressed in order to make lasting environmental changes. It is the culmination of the actions of civil society, governments, and businesses that drive us toward a more sustainable future. (Communications with author)

Currently, we are working on the development of pre-/post-course evaluations that may offer a more analytic assessment of this cognitive shifting. One suggestion has been to engage students in concept mapping exercises to help evaluate individual changes. Assessing learning at the conclusion of the semester has its own inherent pitfalls, however, in that much of the actual progress may occur only *after* leaving the program. This process of formulation, reformulation and integration based on multidisciplinary thinking is a journey. The breakthrough may only occur when students are confronted with their own subsequent professional experiences that promote this more differentiated approach (communication with author). This experience is difficult to replicate in a course, but it can help lay the groundwork.

6.   CONCLUSION: CRITICAL ROLE OF SCIENTISTS IN CREATING SUSTAINABLE FUTURES

This discussion focuses on integrative class projects intended to provide illustrations of the type of activities that could encourage students to question existing formulations of business/government/society into more fluid relationships of polycentric governance, adaptive learning and systems thinking. Could this change in cognitive models lead to a wider range of possible future actions as well? Could environmental scientists and their science literacy engage in a wider spectrum of participation with a more diverse set of actors? If sustainability education 'is a future-oriented activity', then curricular design, if not to be reflective of the past, must directly engage students in redefining ecosystem futures that go beyond current thinking (Iliško, Skrinda and Micule, 2014; Krasny, 2020). This discussion has focused specifically on market actors/activities and suggested that in order to be prepared to contribute to sustainable business initiatives, students require a richer working vocabulary and grounded set of models. But this is only one slice! In order for environmental science students to contribute and participate in the larger issue of system adaptation then a more complicated range of stakeholders, actions and outcomes may need to be imagined (Folke et al., 2010). The closing observation from educating environmental science students with more complex cognitive models of social and economic realities is that it remains a work in progress. As noted at the outset, only through a broader framing of environmental education will students be prepared to co-collaborate and use their vital scientific literacy to address future issues of ecosystem stewardship (Cornell et al., 2013; Olson and Rejeski, 2018).

REFERENCES

Alier, J.M. (2009). Socially sustainable economic de-growth. *Development and Change*, 40(6), 1099–119.

Barkemeyer, R., Preuss, L. and Lee, L. (2015). On the effectiveness of private transnational governance regimes – evaluating corporate sustainability reporting according to the Global Reporting Initiative. *Journal of World Business*, 50(2), 312–25.

Chandler, D. (2019). *Strategic Corporate Social Responsibility: Sustainable Value Creation* (5th ed.). New York: SAGE Publications.

Cornell, S., Berkhout, F. and Tuinstra, W. et al. (2013). Opening up knowledge systems for better responses to global environmental change. *Environmental Science and Policy*, 28, 60–70.

Dauvergne, P. and Lister, J. (2013). *Eco-Business: A Big Brand Takeover of Sustainability.* Cambridge, MA: MIT Press.

Dicken, P. (2015). *Global Shift: Mapping the Changing Contours of the World Economy.* New York: Guilford Press.

Eastin, J., Grundmann, R. and Prakash, A. (2011). The two limits debates: 'limits to growth' and climate change. *Futures*, 43(1), 16–26.

Ellis, T. (2010). *The New Pioneers: Sustainable Business Success Through Social Innovation and Social Entrepreneurship.* Chichester: John Wiley & Sons, Ltd.

Fogel, D. (2016). *Strategic Sustainability: A Natural Environmental Lens on Organizations and Management.* New York: Routledge.

Folke, C. (2006). Resilience: the emergence of a perspective for social-ecological systems analyses. *Global Environmental Change*, 16(3), 253–67.

Folke, C., Carpenter, S. and Walker, B. et al. (2010). Resilience thinking. *Ecology and Society*, 15(4), Article 20.

Gutierrez, N.L., Defeo, O. and Bush, S.R. et al. (2016). The current situation and prospects of fisheries certification and ecolabelling. *Fisheries Research*, 182, 1–6.

Hawken, P. (2017). *Drawdown: The Most Comprehensive Plan Ever Proposed to Reverse Global Warming*. New York: Penguin Books.

Holt, D. and Littlewood, D. (2015). Identifying, mapping, and monitoring the impact of hybrid firms. *California Management Review*, 57(3), 107–25.

Iliško, D., Skrinda, A. and Micule, I. (2014). Envisioning the future: bachelor's and master's degree students' perspectives. *Journal of Teacher Education for Sustainability*, 16(2), 88–102.

Intergovernmental Panel on Climate Change (IPCC). (2018). Summary for policymakers. In IPCC, *Global warming of 1.5°C: an IPCC Special Report on the impacts of global warming of 1.5°C above pre-industrial levels and related global greenhouse gas emission pathways, in the context of strengthening the global response to the threat of climate change, sustainable development, and efforts to eradicate poverty*. Geneva: IPCC.

Jahn, T., Bergmann, M. and Keil, F. (2012). Transdisciplinarity: between mainstreaming and marginalization. *Ecological Economics*, 79, 1–10.

Krasny, M. (2020). *Advancing Environmental Education Practice*. Ithaca, NY: Cornell University Press.

Lang, T. and Heasman, M. (2015). *Food Wars: The Global Battle for Minds, Mouths and Markets*. New York: Routledge.

Laszlo, C. and Zhexembayeva. N. (2011). *Embedded Sustainability: The Next Big Competitive Advantage*. Stanford, CA: Stanford Business Books.

Loconto, A. and Fouilleux, E. (2014). Politics of private regulation: ISEAL and the shaping of transnational sustainability governance. *Regulation and Governance*, 8(2), 166–85.

Meadows, D. (1996). Envisioning a sustainable world. In R. Constanza, O. Segura and J. Martinez-Alier et al. (eds), *Getting Down to Earth: Practical Applications of Ecological Economics*, Cambridge, UK: Cambridge University Press, pp. 117–26.

O'Brien, K., Reams, J. and Caspari, A. et al. (2013). You say you want a revolution? Transforming education and capacity building in response to global change. *Environmental Science and Policy*, 28, 48–59.

Olson, R.L. and Rejeski, D. (2018). Slow threats and environmental policy. *Environmental Law Reporter*, 48(2), Article 10116.

Olsson, P., Folke, C. and Hahn, T. (2004). Social-ecological transformation for ecosystem management: the development of adaptive co-management of a wetland landscape in Southern Sweden. *Ecology and Society*, 9(4), 2.

Raworth, K. (2017). *Doughnut Economics: Seven Ways to Think Like a 21st Century Economist*. White River Junction, VT: Chelsea Green Publishing.

Sachs, J. (2015). *The Age of Sustainable Development*. New York: Columbia University Press.

Siew, R.Y.J. (2015). A review of corporate sustainability reporting tools (SRTs). *Journal of Environmental Management*, 164, 180–95.

Stein, Z. (2007). Modeling the demands of interdisciplinarity: toward a framework for evaluating interdisciplinary endeavors. *Integral Review*, No. 4, 91–107.

Steiner, J. and Steiner, G. (2012). *Business, Government and Society: A Managerial Perspective*. New York: McGraw-Hill Publishers.

Wallace, R. and Clark, S. (2018). Environmental studies and sciences in a time of chaos: problems, contexts, and recommendations. *Journal of Environmental Studies and Sciences*, 8(1), 110–13.

PART II

INNOVATION AND NEW TECHNOLOGIES

15. Innovations in curriculum and pedagogy in education for sustainable development
Hock Lye Koh and Su Yean Teh

1. INTRODUCTION

The progress of sustainability has been characterized as sluggish, uneven and negligible (Leal Filho, Manolas and Pace, 2015), three decades after the launch of the *Brundtland Report* (World Commission on Environment and Development [WCED], 1987). The 1987 *Brundtland Report*, while being non-specific and ambiguous in many ways, carries an undeniable implication that sustainable development must deal with complex and uncertain planetary systems and issues. The complexity of the uncertain interconnected systems confronting the current and future generations, are viewed and interpreted within diverse societies beset with vastly different values, beliefs and cultures.

1.1 Sustainability: A Contested Concept

It is therefore inevitable that vagueness in the definition of sustainability has rendered sustainability a contested concept, with multiple interpretations and different ways of implementation. What are broadly agreed upon are the desired outcomes of a sustainable future, but the actions by which specific outcomes are to be achieved are often contested (Carew and Mitchell, 2008). Given the phobia of climate change, some advocated decarbonization as the ideal path to a sustainable future, with limited success anticipated. Others opted for innovative engineering and social solutions as mitigation and adaptation measures (Boyle, 1999). Putting forward a strong case in favour of community consultations in major decision processes involving sustainability constitutes yet another action plan (Clift, 1998). This call for community engagement is relevant and is consistent with the Maslow's (1987) hierarchy of human needs (MHHN), in which the emotional need for self-esteem and community-esteem is ranked the second highest tier of human needs. While confusing to some, this contested concept of sustainability is healthy, as ambiguity in the *Brundtland Report* encourages deep reflections, promotes wide-ranging social innovations, enables fruitful cultural–economic dialogues and empowers active community engagement in reaching a common goal.

It is generally accepted that sustainability may be divided into three subordinate concepts: environmental, social and economic sustainability. However, there are two competing representations of this subordination, which have deep implications for education for sustainable development (ESD) and the United Nations Sustainable Development Goals (SDGs). One representation conceptualizes the three sub-systems as concentric and nested circles, in which the environmental system represents the most important and hence the outermost and the largest circle. The second smaller social system is nested within the larger environmental system, with the third and smallest economic system being nested within the social system (Mitchell, 2000). This representation suggests that the economic system is subordinate to both the social and environmental systems, with vast implications to ESD. In contrast, Clift (1995) and many others interpreted the active interaction among the three systems as an intersecting Venn diagram. The small core zone of triple intersection represents concurrent environmental, social and economic sustainability. The smallness of this triple intersection presents difficult issues confronting sustainability. These two contrasting representations may have vast implications for the design of curriculum and pedagogy of sustainability education. This contest of subordination leads to a search for best practices in curriculum and pedagogy designs founded on core values of educational institutions and its relationship with society and the environment.

1.2 Education–Society–Environment Nexus

The intimate connections among education, society and the environment were articulated by John Dewey, a founding voice in pragmatism, in student-centred experiential learning and in functional psychology (McDonald, 2004). One interpretation of the intimate relationship among the triplets consisting of education, society and environment would lead to a representation of three concentric and nested circles, in which the environment is the most important outermost circle and educational institutions, albeit very important, are the smallest innermost circle nested within the society and the environment (Figure 15.1). The immediate implication of this nested arrangement of the triplets is that education must serve or service both society and the environment. This nested triplet (education–society–environment) philosophy has been endemic in many civilizations, including those in the East and Far East, for millennia. Similarly, the supreme importance of education grounded in student-centred, skill-based pedagogy as advocated by Dewey has been commonly acknowledged and widely practised for millennia in the East. The search for continuing educational reform in confronting a fast-changing socio-economic environment is crucial in seeking a socio-intellectual framework that would be capable

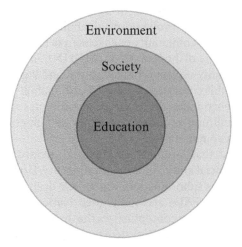

Figure 15.1   Connections in which education must serve society and the environment

of flexible adaptation to the diversity of changes experienced in real life. This continuous educational reform takes place within a socio-moral context that is subject to a constant state of flux. In such a dynamic world that is constantly evolving, knowledge is acquired by solving real-world place-based problems in context. As the product of an adaptive process of social engagement, genuine knowledge and creativity are the offspring of *doing*, as exemplified by the intricate silk and tea culture in the East. Adaptation is an ongoing negotiation between existing core social values and constantly changing circumstances. The pragmatic focus on adaptive problem-solving based upon student-centred learning, as advocated by Dewey and widely practised over the millennia in the East, has a profound impact on the evolving concepts of contemporary sustainability (Tarrant and Thiele, 2016), and on the core competences essential to ESD (Koh and Teh, 2019).

1.3   Integrated Water Resource Management: Water and Food Security

Water and food security have always been the essential key to sustainability of all civilizations, ancient and modern. It is therefore not surprising that SDG 2 (no hunger) and SDG 6 (clean water and sanitation) are two important goals critical to sustainability. For coastal communities living in low-elevation coastal zones such as Pantai Acheh of Penang Island, Malaysia, salinization of groundwater caused by sea level rise (SLR) could pose a daunting challenge to water supply and crop cultivation, thereby undermining local water security (SDG 6) and food security (SDG 2) (Kh'ng, Teh and Koh, 2021). Hence, integrated water resource management (IWRM) has evolved to become an important area of core competences essential to ESD and critical to the long-term sustainability of low-elevation coastal zones such as Pantai Acheh.

2.   LITERATURE REVIEW

The silo mentality of individual discipline has historically ensured academic rigour within the discipline. It has also ensured that curriculum and learning outcomes met the needs of the respective professional organizations and the wider community they served. However, silo mentality hinders problem-driven and solution-oriented fields, such as sustainability, that inherently rely on the integration of knowledge and action across multiple disciplines to solve complex, real-world problems (Wiek et al., 2011). Take, for example, mainstream economics as represented in Econ101 classrooms that presumes a model of competitive markets in which firms seek to maximize their profits. In these competitive markets, rational and self-interested individuals fulfil their insatiable demands, consume goods and services and seek to optimize their utility (Marglin, 2008). Hence, leading Econ101 textbooks devote a mere 3.2 per cent of their total printed area to externalities, public goods and other sustainability-related topics (Green, 2012). Broad consensus indicates that Econ101 courses are highly standardized across North American universities because the course textbooks are typically selected from a handful of leading mainstream economists (Colander, 2000). Econ101 curriculum and pedagogy have faced considerable criticism for their failure in creating awareness regarding the three pillars of sustainability consisting of the environment–society–economy nexus and for their inability to deliver socially optimal sustainability learning outcomes. Improved prospects for sustainability, therefore, require new economic goals and models, and mandate innovative Econ101 textbooks, curriculum and pedagogy that devote appropriate attention to sustainability learning outcomes.

Modern universities have the capacity and mandate to develop problem-driven and solution-oriented curricula that are highly effective in developing integrated and use-inspired knowledge that is sustainability oriented. Universities should devise curricula and pedagogy to deliver sustainability learning outcomes (SLOs) to serve the society and the environment, as implied in Figure 15.1. Delivery of sustainability-related curriculum to undergraduate students can be problematic due to this silo mentality of curriculum in each traditional discipline. Few entry-level courses focusing on sustainability, which are broad enough for all disciplines, are available to students. In promoting and supporting sustainability curriculum development, it is essential to develop a university-wide programme to connect different disciplines working and teaching in sustainability areas.

Facing a steep learning curve, sustainability in higher education (SHE) is a long arduous journey, best exemplified in the cases of the University of Vermont and the University of British Columbia. It is hoped that this brief literature review will provide good insights into how to develop innovative curriculum and pedagogy for promoting SHE.

2.1   University of Vermont

At the University of Vermont (UVM), SHE is defined as 'the pursuit of ecological, social and economic vitality with the understanding that the needs of the present must be met without compromising the ability of future generations to meet their own needs'. The UVM spent the 2014–15 academic year developing a convincing narrative that sustainability is an interdisciplinary concept that allows for each respective discipline to introduce and reinforce ecological, social and economic sustainability topics in a discipline-specific manner (Hill and Wang, 2018). Since 2015, the UVM has adopted a model in which SLO is a university-wide requirement and in which sustainability is embedded throughout the university curriculum and pedagogy. However, most higher education institutions (HEIs), such as the Universiti Sains Malaysia (USM), are not yet ready to embark on this ambitious goal. Instead, a 'second-best' alternative model is adopted in which SLO elements can be embedded into stand-alone courses. The UVM has long been an outstanding leader in the teaching and research of environment and natural resources (ENR)-related issues and programmes. These ENR programmes have played a leading national role in adopting an interdisciplinary approach in educating the next generation of ENR and sustainability practitioners (ibid.). The faculty within the disciplines are encouraged to teach sustainability under a disciplinary-specific framework. This practical approach to SHE appears to be attractive as it is implementable for many (HEIs).

2.2   University of British Columbia

In 1997, the University of British Columbia (UBC) adopted a sustainable development policy that encouraged sustainable practices in all aspects of its actions and that mandated all students be educated about sustainability (Moore et al., 2005). In 2009, UBC prepared a 'Sustainability Academic Strategy (SAS)' that aimed to provide a vision and implementable goals for enhancing sustainability across the university. A key product of SAS was an entry-level, interdisciplinary sustainability course (SUST 101), available to all students across the university, regardless of faculty or year level. With about 50 000 degree-seeking students enrolled in many diverse programmes across 14 faculties, UBC recognized that innovative pedagogies, such as experiential learning and team teaching, were not as cost-effective as a standard lecture course. However, based upon the experience in delivering SUST 101 on a pilot basis and subsequent analysis, UBC recognized that the course can be self-supporting financially, if delivered efficiently. The lesson learned is that the curriculum developers should strive for interdisciplinarity content, broad-based student enrolment, use of innovative pedagogies that promote sustainability behaviour and dialogue both in teaching and content development.

3. EDUCATION FOR SUSTAINABLE DEVELOPMENT

The aim of education is not just knowledge per se but knowledge that leads to fruitful action (Short, 2010, p. 7). Aiming for fruitful actions, ESD plays two important roles in achieving the SDGs. First, ESD bridges the gaps and disconnect among the three sustainability pillars consisting of the social, environmental and economic dimensions (Figure 15.2, top part). Second, ESD trains future professionals and citizens to manage and adapt to complex sustainability challenges. Towards achieving the SDGs and the sustainability learning outcomes, HEIs need to collaborate with societies and communities to strengthen three ESD learning pathways: (1) knowledge and skill-based learning; (b) real-world learning; and (3) place-based learning (Figure 15.2, middle part). The integration of these three ESD pathways would create research collaborations richly rooted in nature–human interactions. Communities and societies would provide the 'pathway' for this adaptive real-world learning to take 'place', by providing the space for place-based learning. Transferable across locations, experiences and disciplines, this place-based inquisitive learning can cultivate life-long competences essential to active community engagement (Gruenewald, 2003; Koh and Teh, 2020a) in the context of real-world problem-solving. Traditional discipline-specific knowledge and skills as well as general awareness of environmental issues are certainly important. But to confront the complexity of the interconnected ecological, social and economic challenges associated with sustainability would demand more than stand-alone siloed knowledge, skills and awareness. Thus, transdisciplinary learning, research and inquiry involving critical system thinking, integrated knowledge generation and community-centred collective action are essential elements in ESD and sustainability. While Dewey formulated the concepts of education and its intimate relationship with society and the environment, Abraham Maslow articulated a hierarchy of human needs (Figure 15.2, bottom part) to guide and prioritize learning outcomes, a scheme that has been implicitly recognized for millennia in the East.

3.1 MHHN: Maslow's Five-tier Hierarchy of Human Needs

The MHHN is a motivational theory in psychology comprising a five-tier model of human needs, often depicted as hierarchical levels within a pyramid (Figure 15.2, bottom part). From the bottom of the pyramid upwards, the five tiers of needs are: (1) fundamental physiological needs for food, water and thermal requirement; (2) personal needs for

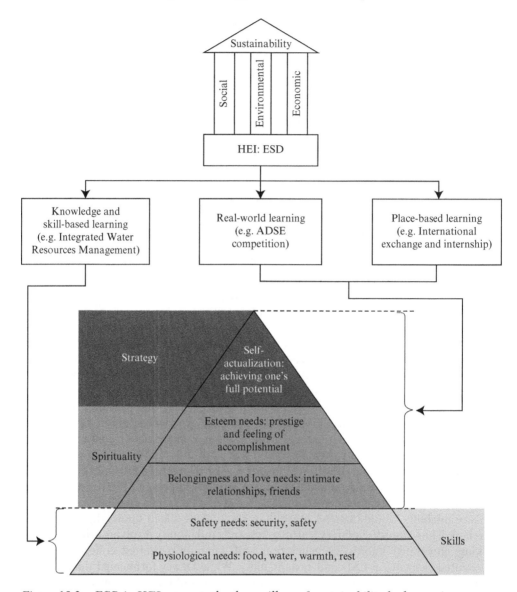

Figure 15.2   ESD in HEI supports the three pillars of sustainability by leveraging on Maslow's hierarchy of human needs

safety from physical harm, fear or threat; (3) psychological need for love and belonging in community; (4) emotional need for the self and community esteem; and (5) need for self-actualization and fulfilment of personal potential (Maslow, 1987). Deep understanding and appreciation of this MHHN is useful in the search for sustainability concepts and best practices essential to ESD. Given the spiritual and psychological need for love and belonging in community, well-planned educational transformation should promote the humanization of HEIs while developing a sustainable strategy for transformation and deep learning to attain self-fulfilment and the SDGs. To achieve the higher tiers of the MHHN, educators help students achieve self-realization and fulfilment of personal potentials, and help transform their goals and perspectives for a better self, a better community and a better society. In the framework of ESD, education helps students acquire the skills to reconfigure their worldview in the context of sustainability and empowers them with the strategy to examine the complexity of sustainability challenges from multiple perspectives, through engagement with multiple stakeholders, and through embracing spiritual, ecological and socio-economic aspirations (Koh and Teh, 2019).

3.2   Three Core Competences for Sustainability

The curriculum and pedagogy for ESD must effectively leverage on these five tiers in the MHHN (Figure 15.2, bottom part) to develop three core sustainability competences consisting of skills, spirituality and strategy: (1) *skills* to ensure food, water and personal security; (2) *spirituality* for community esteem; and (3) *strategy* for self-actualization beneficial to community. Leveraging on the strength of ESD and the MHHN, pragmatic and versatile educators can facilitate transdisciplinary critical system thinking beyond the confine of siloed mono-disciplinary approaches and effectively conduct deep inquiry, leading to profound discovery (Hensley, 2018). In this way, students will be able to connect and align their self-fulfilment with the fulfilment of the SDGs. ESD develops capability in a student in critical system thinking, in communication and in collaboration. ESD strategizes a student to be an informed and critical analyst, to be a steward and an agent of change of the global environment, by cultivating the skills, spirituality and strategy that enable adaptive learning and innovation for the good of human–nature relationships.

3.3   Four Goals of the Decade of Education for Sustainable Development

The UN Decade of Education for Sustainable Development (DESD) highlighted the importance of developing four capacities in students: (1) an integrative capacity that allows for a holistic perspective; (2) a critical capacity that questions taken-for-granted patterns; (3) a transformative capacity that moves from simple awareness to transformative change; and (4) a contextual capacity that embeds the values of pluralism in learning (Wals, 2012). The MHHN provides the mechanism for motivating and empowering students to achieve these four essential goals of DESD. The pragmatic focus on adaptive problem-solving as advocated by Dewey and practised over the millennia in the East by *doing* has a phenomenal impact on the achievement of the three core competences consisting of skills, spirituality and strategy critical to the SDGs by solving global problems with local solutions (Koh and Teh, 2019). By doing, learning and engaging in local solutions for solving global problems, such as those encountered in IWRM, students will be empowered to: (1) develop the three sustainability core competences; (2) fulfil the four essential goals of DESD; and (3) satisfy their quest for the five Maslow human needs.

3.4   Paradigm Shift in Curriculum and Pedagogy

Various studies have shown that knowledge about the environment, its associated ecosystems and the ecosystem services provided are positively correlated with desirable personal and social attitudes toward conservation (Bradley, Waliczek and Zajicek, 1999). This is hardly surprising as the knowledge of ecosystem services provided by nature can induce a positive response in individuals and societies to protect that provision of services out of self-interest. This positive response is possible only if the link between the natural ecosystem and its services provided to society can be positively imprinted and firmly established in those who are equipped with the competences to reflect deeply on the linkage. But many others may lack that capacity of deep reflection, as modern technical education does not automatically equip them with that capacity. Many studies, however, indicated that knowledge alone might not be readily translated to intended attitudes for change; and that intended attitudes might not lead to desirable behaviour to act in an environmentally responsible manner. As may be seen from Figure 15.2 (bottom part), knowledge acquisition (skill) merely fulfils the lowest tier in the MHHN for reason of job and food security. Attitude change entails a higher and more demanding tier in the MHHN for self-esteem and community esteem (spirituality). Behavioural motivations require an even higher tier in the MHHN for self-actualization and fulfilment of personal potentials (strategy). The gap between cognitive goals (skills, knowledge) and affective goals (love, community esteem, self-actualization) can be wide in an education system that focuses primarily on the attainment of cognitive achievement of knowledge and skills to fulfil economic demand of human resources. ESD must effectively address this apparent disconnect among knowledge, attitude and behaviour for SDGs to be achieved. This will require a transformational and innovative paradigm shift in curriculum and pedagogy for ESD to narrow the gaps among the five tiers of the MHHN and to bridge the disconnect among the three pillars of sustainability.

4.   INNOVATIONS IN CURRICULUM AND PEDAGOGY

Innovation in curriculum and pedagogy of ESD (CPESD) should aim at engaging students' awareness and knowledge of how and why a diversity of values, viewpoints and actions might assist them in developing flexible, creative solutions, given the contested nature of sustainability. This CPESD must address the basic concepts embodied in the MHHN and adopt the pragmatic approach of Dewey for adaptive student-centred learning by problem-solving.

4.1   National Oceanic and Atmospheric Administration-funded MWEE

The evaluation conducted by the Meaningful Watershed Education Experiences (MWEE) programme funded by the United States National Oceanic and Atmospheric Administration (NOAA) showed that students' intention to be environmentally responsible was positively influenced by three core activities: (1) outdoor learning; (2) hands-on learning experiences; and (3) inclusion of topics and localities that students viewed as important to their life (Zint, Kraemer and Kolenic, 2014). This important finding of NOAA is consistent with the adaptive problem-solving approach of Dewey, as the three NOAA learning activities focusing on outdoor and hands-on experiences are intimately linked to adaptive problem-solving activities at the local levels to enhance place-based learning experiences. Unfortunately, many existing universities' curriculum and pedagogy in many courses across diverse disciplines do not appear to engage adaptive problem-solving activities as embraced by Dewey and MWEE. For example, many departments of mathematical sciences continue to teach classical mathematics subjects such as calculus, algebra and statistics in the 'old' ways, without engaging students and teaching staff in the three core activities listed in the MWEE programme. In the following sub-sections, we outline several CPESD concepts, initiatives and discoveries essential to ESD.

4.2 Holling Adaptive Co-management Concepts

With deep understanding and acceptance of the inherent instability of natural systems, and systems impacted by humans, Holling (1973) shifted the focus of ecosystem study from the maintenance of equilibrium within ecosystems, which is difficult to achieve, to the management of change and the associated dynamic human–nature relationships. Through the concept of collaborative strategies, Holling laid the foundation of the theory and practice of adaptive co-management (Holling and Gunderson, 2002). Adaptive co-management promotes the iterative interactions of multiple stakeholders (for example, citizen conservationists, resource consumers, resource managers, industry representatives and government officials) to generate local-scale strategies for sustaining human–nature relationships. Ecosystem management has the dual purpose of conservation and the production of knowledge through structured feedback of implemented procedures. Through the repetitions of the stakeholder-involvement process of evaluation and deliberation, local knowledge and expertise is generated. Adaptive co-management has become a foremost example of innovations in curriculum and pedagogy critical to sustainability science.

4.3 Shaping Knowledge, Attitudes and Behaviours

Influenced by many factors within their learning environment, students will go through significant changes in their knowledge, attitudes and behaviours regarding sustainability – some positive and some negative. Knowledge alone, sitting at the lowest bottom tier in the MHHN, is not likely to change attitudes and behaviours that sit at the higher upper tiers of the MHHN unless and until further actions are taken. For example, it is difficult to overcome scepticism about decarbonization, about sustainability or about climate change (CC), if social networks consistently reinforce this scepticism. At the upper tier 3 or 4 of the MHHN, the human need for community esteem and community well-being overwhelms the lowest tier 1 need for knowledge (for job security). In communicating real-world sustainability challenges, there is a need for an integrated programme that highlights legitimacy and credibility of sustainability (involving tier 3, the need for belonging in a community) in order to motivate individuals and communities to change their attitude and behaviour (involving tier 4, the need for self- and community esteem) for a better future by taking appropriate actions (involving tier 5, the need for self-actualization and fulfilment of personal potential). The MHHN helps to understand the barriers to and potential enablers of positive behaviour change and the effective communication channels that will make sustainability issues personally relevant, without contradicting or compromising community acceptance. There is a need to examine how and why the perceptions, attitudes and behaviour of students would change with new sustainability awareness and knowledge acquired. The understanding of these processes permits recommendations for future curriculum and pedagogy designs for ESD. Community-based education aimed at influencing positive attitudes and desirable behaviour, made possible by reference to the MHHN, needs to be developed as an ongoing programme to complement efforts at the HEIs. An active engagement with nature and the environment, the larger 'community' hosting society (Figure 15.1), is desirable for creating positive emotions and for sustaining an intrinsic motivation for actions that favour sustainable development, both as an individual and as a community.

4.4   Place-based Real-world Learning

Place-based, real-world learning cultivates the ability to investigate deeply into the life of a real community, explore its connections to national, regional and global influences and assess its impacts on other systems (Sobel, 2004), making it critical for sustainability teaching and learning (Gruenewald and Smith, 2008). Knowledge and skill-based learning, place-based learning and real-world learning are three crucial sustainability learning pathways that support ESD and sustain the three pillars of sustainability (Figure 15.2). Solutions for many challenges facing the real world reside in the understandings held by stewards of place who have devoted themselves to a long-term investment in the well-being of a place and the living things that inhabit it. The *place* concept is transferable across experiences, across technical skills and across the features of real-world problems. Once a student learns how to discover the meanings, functions and ecosystem values of a place, he or she will have the life-long skills for active place-based community and environmental engagement for real-world problem-solving (Gruenewald, 2003). Going beyond the conventional classroom settings, ESD delivers quality education (SDG 4) that creates the opportunity for students to solve place-based, real-world problems by applying their knowledge and skills acquired from lectures and elsewhere. Such active engagement of students in a diverse place-based and real-world setting would require them to seek knowledge and skills outside their traditional disciplines, and to accelerate their understanding and appreciation of multi-faceted goals of SDGs through partnerships and collaboration.

5.   PEDAGOGY OF LIVING EXAMPLES

The development of a sustainable campus environment driven by innovation in sustainability curriculum and pedagogy would involve significant financial resources. It would require a thorough understanding of the cultural, social and ecological imperatives and perspectives within the campus. A campus has multiple levels of governance system, in which the students, academics and administration have their respective hierarchy, not necessarily in harmony with each other. Research has suggested that optimal results could be delivered by a top-down approach, in which campus administration and management are actively involved in the environmental stewardship and sustainability programmes of the campus (Lukman and Glavic, 2007). The direction and governance of campus sustainability programmes and practices could be formulated by multi-sector iterative consultations among top management, academics and students. However, due to various constraints in many universities, this top-down initiative is not commonly adopted. Individual educators and students are left to explore their creative pathways to sustainability, often in isolation and in an ad hoc manner. In the long run, this blossoming of individual contributions might lead to fruitful collective outcomes in the pursuit of sustainability. Various small-group endeavours towards environmental stewardship and sustainability goals in and out of campus will be presented in the following three sub-sections to encourage further deliberations on innovations and best practices regarding sustainability curriculum and pedagogy. The connectivity among the three learning pathways of ESD in supporting the three pillars of sustainability is illustrated in Figure 15.2. Knowledge and skill-based learning, real-world learning and place-based learning have been identified as the three pathways that can produce promising sustainability learning outcomes.

5.1 Knowledge and Skill-based Learning

Knowledge and skill-based learning, as embodied in IWRM, is crucial in enhancing water security (SDG 6) and food security (SDG 2). Under the threats of groundwater salinization due to SLR, IWRM is critical to the long-term sustainability of low-elevation coastal zones such as Pantai Acheh of Penang. It has become an important expertise domain essential to ESD worldwide. Appropriate IWRM strategy along coastal and estuarine zones promotes vibrant mangroves and wetland ecosystems, as well as viable coral communities. The valuable ecosystem services provided by mangroves, wetlands and corals directly support the aspirations of SDG 8 (meaningful employment), SDG 14 (life below water) and SDG 15 (life on land).

Water is a critical component of the biosphere. It links land, water bodies, estuaries, ocean and atmosphere to form a complex system, whose intimate interrelationships are just beginning to emerge under CC initiatives. Failures in the water sector will have severe consequences to many SDGs (Koh and Teh, 2020b). Proper IWRM supports socio-economic development (SDG 8) as well as maintains sustainable cities (SDG 11). IWRM literacy entails the competence to (1) understand the entire water cycle; (2) assess the impacts of human activities on the water cycle; (3) evaluate the viability of associated resources and ecosystems; and (4) develop the strategy to make environmentally responsible decisions and actions based upon sound knowledge and desirable attitudes. IWRM may, thereby, be defined as the process that promotes the coordinated development and management of water, land, and related natural–human resources, in order to maximize the economic and social welfare in an equitable manner without compromising the sustainability of vital ecosystems (Snellen and Schrevel, 2004) and without compromising the well-being of the future generations. IWRM in ESD must seek to develop the three core sustainability competences (skills, spirituality, strategy) relevant to IWRM. ESD in IWRM empowers the following three competences within the broad water sector: (1) the transmission of technical skills and knowledge needed for understanding the intimate relationships among the water components; (2) the cultivation of spiritual and socio-cultural coherence through the transformation of attitudes and behaviour that leads to a sustainable water environment; and (3) the strategic capability to negotiate and implement IWRM programmes. Hence, IWRM seeks to promote the conservation of water resources and aquatic ecosystems by low-carbon, low-input and sustainable means (Koh, Tan and Teh, 2018). This can be accomplished by (1) enhancing technical skills and knowledge of IWRM-related problems and their solutions; (2) inducing desirable spiritual, social, attitudinal and behavioural changes towards the goals of IWRM; and (3) empowering the strategic capacity to efficiently deliver the goals of IWRM.

While most students recognize water as an important natural resource, they might not have the competence to fully assess the impacts of anthropogenic activities on water resources and associated aquatic or marine ecosystems. Hence, IWRM education must develop the competence to recognize and conceptualize the connections within this complex aquatic system. The interconnections within the complex IWRM systems would often require quantitative analysis and mathematical modelling involving multiple components across diverse disciplines. This transdisciplinary feature of IWRM provides a golden opportunity for students and educators majoring in quantitative sciences such as mathematical sciences to engage with other disciplines and with multi-stakeholders, as well as with other SDGs. These engagements empower the students and educators to develop higher-order skills essential to integrated system thinking beneficial to their career and communities.

This integrated system thinking in IWRM involves the abilities to (1) distinguish individual elements of the aquatic system and the intimate relation among the elements; (2) understand the behaviour of the entire aquatic system by analysing the complexity in the interdependencies of its elements and interconnected relations; and (3) develop qualitative and quantitative solutions and strategies for sustainable management of the aquatic environment (Covitt, Gunckel and Anderson, 2009). For example, numerical simulations have been used to evaluate the combined effects of environmental and chemical stressors on a model *Daphnia* population, within the context of an IWRM programme (Koh, Hallam and Lee, 1997). Similarly, model simulations were used to identify the best discharge options for urban sewage disposal into the coastal zones in Penang that would maintain a balance among the environment, the society and the economy (Koh, Lim and Lee, 1997) for optimal IWRM. Climate change and population growth will exert increasing pressure on the balance between demand and supply of water to society, particularly in highly urbanized areas in emerging economies with limited resources. Two IWRM approaches are generally used to address this mismatch between water demand and supply. The first approach is based upon science, technology, engineering and mathematics (STEM) to increase water supply, while the second relies on behavioural innovation to reduce water consumption (Clark and Finley, 2008). The STEM-based development of new water resources will be constrained by CC, sea level rise and population growth, particularly in low-lying coastal cities such as Miami and Guangzhou (Teh et al., 2019). Back-to-nature soft engineering such as the 'sponge systems' should be considered as a solution in this water mismatch, particularly in urbanized future cities (Koh and Teh, 2020b). Concerted and innovative efforts must be devoted to changing consumer behaviour to reduce water consumption demand. ESD in IWRM needs to innovate to address this water mismatch and seek long-term sustainable solutions to the water crisis looming over the horizon, by paying attention to water education and conservation.

School-based water education and conservation programmes play an important role in understanding the water cycle and in inducing desirable changes in water conservation behaviour for a sustainable future. Water-security programmes and research have generally focused on technology for increasing water supply rather than on behavioural innovations for reducing water consumption. This unsustainable approach to water demand–supply imbalance will not work in the long run, given the constraints on water supply and the unconstrained demand for water. Hence, IWRM must address this chronic water crisis, as a large proportion of the world population is currently subject to water stress and is exposed to increasingly threatened water security (Vörösmarty et al., 2010). The prospects for water security in the future looks even more menacing for low-lying coastal regions subject to threats of CC, sea level rise and population growth.

5.2   Real-world Learning

Innovations in curriculum and pedagogy for ESD must encompass informal education and student-oriented self-learning. Active engagement of students in real-world problems and solutions related to SDG is the key to sustainability. Students working on sustainability-focused projects need to seek knowledge outside their traditional disciplines and beyond their classrooms, and to collaborate with others in accelerating their understanding and appreciation of SDGs. Community engagement and informal education beyond the traditional classroom provide the platform for students and educators to enhance their awareness and development of problem-solving skills in the broader spectrum of sustainability. For this purpose, students and educators are encouraged to take an active part in sustainability-focused projects and competitions, and be involved in community outreach and awareness events. Recognizing the importance of informal education and community engagement, the Association of Southeast Asian Nations (ASEAN) Foundation and German multinational software corporation SAP sponsor the annual ASEAN Data Science Explorers (ADSE) competition, with the goal to engage in SDG real-world projects focusing on promoting regional sustainability. Launched in 2017, the ADSE annual competition enlists regional universities to promote positive social impact of SDGs in the ASEAN region. ADSE provides a platform for students across ASEAN nations to engage with each other on real-world problem-solving through collaboration on issues intimate to SDGs. By focusing on student-centred self-learning, ADSE empowers young people with the skills and a spiritual sense of ownership to play a strategic role in solving various SDG issues endemic in ASEAN nations.

ADSE contributes to the strategy of realizing the ASEAN Socio-Cultural Community Blueprint 2025 vision of creating an ASEAN community that is inclusive, sustainable, resilient and dynamic, the key to SDGs. Enablement sessions are held at key HEI partners including USM to familiarize educators and trainers with data analytic skills using the SAP Analytics Cloud (SAC) software. The trained educators are then required to train students and are encouraged to mentor the students to take part in the ADSE competitions. In a team of two members, the participating teams must be full-time tertiary students who are nationals of ASEAN member countries. They must be above the age of 16 and are currently pursuing their diploma or undergraduate studies in one of the tertiary institutions in ASEAN nations. The competitions equipped students with ICT skills and other sustainability competences by encouraging them to provide sustainable solutions and strategy for solving challenging social and economic issues in ASEAN.

For the 2019 ADSE competition, six UN SDGs were chosen as thematic foci. The six SDGs are: SDG 3: good health and well-being; SDG 4: quality education; SDG 5: gender equality; SDG 8: decent work and economic growth; SDG 9: industry, innovation and infrastructure; and SDG 11: sustainable cities and communities. Each participating team must first choose one of the six thematic SDGs, compile relevant sources of data and research information for ASEAN nations and develop sustainable solutions for their chosen thematic SDG. A total of 192 teams participated in the ADSE Malaysia 2019, out of which ten best teams were chosen to present their SDG research in the national finals. At the regional finals, each ASEAN member state will be represented by the winning team of the national finals. Two USM teams, one of which is mentored by the second author, made it to the national finals consisting of ten teams. With the entry entitled 'Protect Women from Violence', which is central to SDG 5, the team of two second-year USM undergraduates leveraged on SAP data analytics to find sustainable solutions to the prevalence of violence against women in ASEAN. This valuable experience working on real-world place-based problem solution is a key component in ESD.

5.3   Place-based Learning

Flexible arrangement among universities for promoting academic and cultural exchange is critical to place-based, real-world learning and research that cut across disciplines and that transcend regional differences in beliefs and cultures. Internships and other exchange arrangements have made it possible for students and educators to visit local and foreign universities for short durations to learn and conduct collaborative research on diverse fields in sustainability science. The authors have recently hosted visitations of interns and exchange scholars from Cambridge, Peking and Princeton Universities as well as from elsewhere to work on research on sustainability. The authors have been repeatedly invited to visit the International Centre of Theoretical Physics in Italy, the University of Miami, the University of Tennessee and several Chinese universities to collaborate on place-based research related to IWRM and sustainability science. Research on climate change impact on coastal vegetation and water security within the context of the Greater Everglades Ecological Restoration programme (GEER) have been an ongoing international collaboration for over three decades. These flexible international exchanges are fruitful in promoting research outcomes such as refereed high-impact journal publications (Kh'ng et al., 2021; Koh, Hallam and Lee, 1997; Teh et al., 2019). These international exchanges promote mutual understanding on cultural diversity and enhance the appreciation of the ecological values of biodiversity. For example, biodiversity in coral communities contributes to the resilience of a complex adaptive ecosystem to absorb disturbances and bounce back quickly (Bellwood et al., 2004), with its resilience being enhanced by complementarian attributes inherent in biodiversity. Coral resilience is enhanced by adapting to live within constantly changing ecosystems instead of incessantly trying to confront the changes. Similarly, human communities enhance their resilience to cope with disruptive events, such as the COVID-19 pandemic, by adapting, by reorganizing, by renewing or by flipping into an alternative path (Holling and Gunderson, 2002). Resilience to catastrophic disasters such as COVID-19 is a hallmark of sustainability (Koh and Teh, 2020c).

6.   DISCUSSION

In order to achieve sustainability learning outcomes, changes in curriculum and pedagogy in HEIs must be made to encompass three ESD learning pathways: (1) knowledge and skill-based learning; (2) real-world learning; and (3) place-based learning. IWRM embodies knowledge and skill-based learning that fulfils the basics of ESD. The acquired ESD knowledge and skills alone does not necessarily translate to desirable sustainable action or attitude. To link knowledge and action for sustainable development, students must be exposed to real-world learning and place-based learning that go beyond classroom and across technical skills, as exemplified in Section 5. A key challenge for ESD is the development of new curriculum and pedagogy that facilitate an integrated and place-based real-world learning of the hazards confronting humanity and the options for dealing with them. Global problems such as IWRM (water insecurity, water quality degradation), climate change, biodiversity loss, unsustainable energy consumption and disease emergence (COVID-19) are complex, involving many dimensions such as cultural, social and political issues. The complexity of the interconnectivity between many components cannot be solved within the confines of a single STEM discipline (Teh and Koh, 2020). Hence, educators need to change the types of problems they work on and the way they address these problems in the integration of traditional disciplines in STEM education.

Traditional STEM curriculum and pedagogies provide a foundation that is vital for the understanding of scientific content in each discipline. However, innovation in STEM education is essential to (1) incorporate new advances in pedagogy; (2) keep faculty current with the latest advances in STEM disciplines (Colbeck, O'Meara and Austin, 2008); and (3) engage a wide variety of students in STEM hands-on transdisciplinary learning. Thus, traditional STEM education must innovate to include an awareness of a new class of problems, such as IWRM and climate change impacts, with sustainability as a unifying theme. This will require higher-order competences such as enhanced teamwork and communication skills, to empower students and educators to concentrate on connections between disciplines and to develop the ability to solve problems that span multiple content areas.

Technology-enhanced e-learning and teaching can be an effective tool to improve and enrich students learning experiences (Koh and Teh, 2014). In conjunction with digital online educational resources, these ICT-enabled technologies have empowered off-campus teaching institutions to offer cost-efficient learning experiences, leading to blended learning becoming a key higher education (HE) scenario. In off-campus HE systems, pedagogical designs using ICTs have the potential to achieve significant carbon reductions in comparison with classic on-campus teaching (Caird et al., 2015). When dealing with global problems such as CC impacts, food insecurity, water shortages and energy crisis, it is essential for HEIs to efficiently produce knowledge useful for society with social-cultural input from the community. As the human–nature disconnect is the root cause of current environmental degradation and ecological crisis, the reconnection between universities and societies and the integration between humans and nature could accelerate sustainable development.

7.   CONCLUSIONS

ESD plays an important role in equipping future professionals and citizens with the appropriate sustainability attitudes, attributes and skills to manage and adapt to complex and uncertain sustainability challenges in their careers (Leal Filho et al., 2015). This chapter suggests that for ESD to bridge the gaps and disconnect among the three sustainability pillars (social, environmental and economic), its curriculum and pedagogy must effectively develop three core sustainability competences consisting of skills, spirituality and strategy: (1) skills to ensure food, water and personal security; (2) spirituality for community esteem; and (3) strategy for self-actualization beneficial to community. For this purpose, HEIs need to collaborate with societies and communities to strengthen three ESD learning pathways: (1) knowledge and skill-based learning; (2) real-world learning; and (3) place-based learning. While traditional discipline-specific knowledge and skills are certainly important, knowledge and skills acquired by solving real-world, place-based problems are essential to confront the complexity of the interconnected ecological, social and economic challenges associated with sustainability. Place-based, real-world learning cultivates the ability to investigate deeply into the life of a real community, explore its connections to national, regional and global influences and assess its impacts on other systems.

The following concluding remarks summarize the contributions of this chapter in clarifying concepts and practices that are pertinent to issues of curriculum and pedagogy appropriate for addressing the complexity and uncertainty of sustainability challenges. This chapter attempts to demonstrate that interdisciplinary systems thinking around sustainability should be a central part of ESD across all disciplines. This chapter demonstrates how problem-solving curriculum and pedagogy can be integrated into campus sustainability efforts through knowledge and skill-based learning focusing on IWRM, through placed-based learning and through real-world learning.

HEIs must recognize the importance of curriculum and pedagogy reform for sustainability goals in higher education. While faculty may possess expertise in their disciplinary speciality, they are often not well versed in the knowledge and concepts that underlie sustainability. Many faculties excel in the classroom and have excellent teaching skills. Few, however, have explored effective curriculum and pedagogy design methodologies tailored to sustainability. Faculty must, therefore, be encouraged into new ways of thinking and teaching by promoting faculty awareness, commitment and knowledge of environmental stewardship initiatives. HEIs must develop the ability of faculty to incorporate good sustainability pedagogical practices into courses and to redesign courses that clearly connect with sustainability. Integrating sustainability concepts into disciplinary content throughout the entire course would shift the learning outcome of the course from acknowledge acquisition to sustainability goals. This integration would highlight how the learning outcomes relate to and have impact on sustainability ideas, attitude, behaviours and actions. For this to happen, faculty should reinvent their courses around sustainability themes, behaviours and actions to create innovative courses that foster active place-based, real-world learning oriented to problem-solving that has lasting impact on society. To enable HEIs to make a meaningful and lasting contribution to sustainable development, curriculum framework and pedagogy practices need to be transformed. Systems thinking should engage the larger community by working on concrete living examples of how they are used in real practice.

There are two shortcomings regarding ESD that need to be addressed. First, in theory, values, ethics and human–nature interdependence must be strengthened in ESD to connect the environment, society and economics dimensions. In reality, however, ESD is mostly not practised within the classrooms. And when ESD is practised, teaching methods remain the same as when it is not practised. This indicates that ESD is not currently engaged with curriculum and pedagogical innovation for sustainability, as noted by Christie et al. (2013). Second, in theory, a competence-based curriculum and pedagogy that cultivate skills, spirituality and strategy toward sustainability outcomes is better suited to the complexity of acting in sustainable ways in the workplace and beyond, as illustrated in Figure 15.2. However, in reality, curriculum and pedagogy adopted in many universities do not appear to endorse this competence-based approach.

Driven by a desire to work towards sustainability goals, sustainability competences are underpinned by a combination of sustainability-focused discipline-specific knowledge and skills. However, it is essential to cultivate transdisciplinary higher-order skills such as holistic system thinking, critical reflective analysis for decision making, effective social communication and coherent teamwork. This chapter attempts to draw attention to the realization that this set of transdisciplinary higher-order skills is crucial for effective decision making and timely actions for sustainability. HEIs need to reorientate their curriculum and pedagogy that would enhance this higher-order skill set. Finally, many practical, theoretical and philosophical questions relevant to sustainability remain unexplored and unresolved in addressing deep issues on ESD, the complexity of which is beyond the scope of this chapter.

REFERENCES

Bellwood, D.R., Hughes, T.P., Folke, C. and Nystrom, M. (2004). Confronting the coral reef crisis. *Nature*, 429(6994), 827–33.

Boyle, C. (1999). Education, sustainability and cleaner production. *Journal of Cleaner Production*, 7, 3–7.

Bradley, J.C., Waliczek, T.M. and Zajicek, J.M. (1999). Relationship between environmental knowledge and environmental attitude of high school students. *The Journal of Environmental Education*, 30(3), 17–21.

Caird, S., Lane, A. and Swithenby, E. et al. (2015). Design of higher education teaching models and carbon impacts. *International Journal of Sustainability in Higher Education*, 16(1), 96–111.

Carew, A.L. and Mitchell, C.A. (2008). Teaching sustainability as a contested concept: capitalizing on variation in engineering educators' conceptions of environmental, social and economic sustainability. *Journal of Cleaner Production*, 16(1), 105–15.

Christie, B.A., Miller, K.K., Cooke, R. and White, J.G. (2013). Environmental sustainability in higher education: how do academics teach? *Environmental Education Research*, 19(3), 385–414.

Clark, W.A. and Finley, J.C. (2008). Household water conservation challenges in Blagoevgrad, Bulgaria: a descriptive study. *Water International*, 33(2), 175–88.

Clift, R. (1995). The challenge for manufacturing. In J. McQuaid (ed.), *Engineering for Sustainable Development*. London: The Royal Academy of Engineering.

Clift, R. (1998). Engineering for the environment: the new model engineer and her role. *Transactions of the Institution for Chemical Engineering*, 76(B), 151–60.

Colander, D. (2000). Telling better stories in introductory macro. *The American Economic Review*, 90(2), 76–80.

Colbeck, C., O'Meara, K. and Austin, A. (2008). *Educating Integrated Professionals: Theory and Practice on Preparation for the Professoriate*. San Francisco, CA: Jossey-Bass.

Covitt, B., Gunckel, K.L. and Anderson, C.W. (2009). Students' developing understanding of water in environmental systems. *The Journal of Environmental Education*, 40(3), 37–51.

Green, T.L. (2012). Introductory economics textbooks: what do they teach about sustainability? *International Journal of Pluralism and Economics Education*, 4(3), 189–223.

Gruenewald, D.A. (2003). The best of both worlds: a critical pedagogy of place. *Educational Researcher*, 32(4), 3–12.

Gruenewald, D.A. and Smith, G.A. (2008). Introduction: making room for the local. In D.A. Gruenewald and G.A. Smith (eds), *Place-based Education in the Global Age: Local Diversity* (pp. xiii–xxiii). New York: Lawrence Erlbaum Associates.

Hensley, N. (2018). Transforming higher education through trickster-style teaching. *Journal of Cleaner Production*, 194, 607–12.

Hill, L.M. and Wang, D. (2018). Integrating sustainability learning outcomes into a university curriculum: a case study of institutional dynamics. *International Journal of Sustainability in Higher Education*, 19(4), 699–720.

Holling, C.S. (1973). Resilience and stability of ecological systems. *Annual Review of Ecology and Systematics*, 4(1), 1–23.

Holling, C.S. and Gunderson, L.H. (2002). Resilience and adaptive cycles. In L.H. Gunderson and C.S. Holling (eds), *Panarchy: Understanding Transformations in Human and Natural Systems* (pp. 25–62). Washington, DC: Island Press.

Kh'ng, X.Y., Teh, S.Y. and Koh, H.L. (2021). Sea level rise undermines SDG2 and SDG6 in Pantai Acheh, Penang, Malaysia. *Journal of Coastal Conservation*, 25(1), https://doi.org/10.1007/2-021-00797-5.

Koh, H.L. and Teh, S.Y. (2014). e-Learning for college physics: bridging knowledge gap in science. *International Journal of Humanities and Arts Computing*, 8(Supp.), S167–S178.

Koh, H.L. and Teh, S.Y. (2019). Skills, spirituality and strategy: three core competences in education for sustainability. Paper presented at the 2nd International Conference on Sustainable Development Goals, 30–31 July 2019, Penang, Malaysia.

Koh, H.L. and Teh, S.Y. (2020a). University and community engagement: toward transformational sustainability-focused problem solving. In W. Leal Filho, U. Tortato and F. Frankenberger (eds), *Universities and Sustainable Communities: Meeting the Goals of the Agenda 2030* (pp. 791–804). Cham, Switzerland: Springer Nature.

Koh, H.L. and Teh, S.Y. (2020b). Sustainable and resilient cities: a discourse on the water nexus. In W. Leal Filho, A. Azul and L. Brandli et al. (eds), *Sustainable Cities and Communities: Encyclopedia of the UN Sustainable Development Goals*. Cham, Switzerland: Springer Nature.

Koh, H.L. and Teh, S.Y. (2020c). Covid-19 simulation in Malaysia for assessing effectiveness of MCO: implications on social economic resilience. Keynote speech at the 10th ICEII2020 and the 7th ICCOE2020, Nanyang Technological University, Singapore, 22–24 April.

Koh, H.L., Hallam, T.G. and Lee, H.L. (1997). Combined effects of environmental and chemical stressors on a model *Daphnia* population. *Ecological Modelling*, 103(1), 19–32.

Koh, H.L., Lim, P.E. and Lee, H.L. (1997). Impact modeling of sewage discharge from Georgetown of Penang, Malaysia on coastal water quality. *Environmental Monitoring and Assessment*, 44, 199–209.

Koh, H.L., Tan, W.K. and Teh, S.Y. (2018). Regime shift analysis and numerical simulation for effective ecosystem management. *International Journal of Environmental Science and Development*, 9(8), 192–9.

Leal Filho, W., Manolas, E. and Pace, P. (2015). The future we want: key issues on sustainable development in higher education after Rio and the UN Decade of for Sustainable Development. *International Journal of Sustainability in Higher Education*, 16(1), 112–29.

Lukman, R. and Glavic, P. (2007). What are the key elements of a sustainable university? *Clean Technologies and Environmental Policy*, 9(2), 103–14.

Marglin, S.A. (2008). *The Dismal Science: How Thinking Like an Economist Undermines Community*. Cambridge, MA: Harvard University Press.

Maslow, A.H. (1987). *Motivation and Personality*. New York: Longman.

McDonald, H.P. (2004). *John Dewey and Environmental Philosophy: SUNY Series in Environmental Philosophy and Ethics*. Albany, NY: State University of New York Press.

Mitchell, C. (2000). Integrating sustainability in chemical engineering practice and education: concentricity and its consequences. *Transactions of the Institution for Chemical Engineering*, 78(B), 237–42.

Moore, J., Pagani, F. and Quayle, M. et al. (2005). Recreating the university from within: collaborative reflections on the University of British Columbia's engagement with sustainability. *International Journal of Sustainability in Higher Education*, 6(1), 65–80.

Short, P.C. (2010). Responsible environmental action: its role and status in environmental education and environmental quality. *The Journal of Environmental Education*, 41(1), 7–21.

Snellen, W.B. and Schrevel, A. (2004). IWRM: for sustainable use of water 50 years of international experience with the concept of integrated water. Background paper for the FAO/Netherland Conference on Water for Food and Ecosystems. Wageningen: Ministry of Agriculture, Nature and Food Quality.

Sobel, D. (2004). *Beyond Ecophobia: Reclaiming the Heart in Nature Education*. Great Barrington, MA: The Orion Society and the Myrin Institute.

Tarrant, S.P. and Thiele, L.P. (2016). Practice makes pedagogy – John Dewey and skills-based sustainability education. *International Journal of Sustainability in Higher Education*, 17(1), 54–67.

Teh, S.Y. and Koh, H.L. (2020). Education on sustainable development: the STEM approach in Universiti Sains Malaysia. In W. Leal Filho, A. Lange Silvia and R.W. Pretorius et al. (eds), *Universities as Living Labs for Sustainable Development: Supporting the Implementation of the Sustainable Development Goals* (pp. 567–87). Cham, Switzerland: Springer Nature.

Teh, S.Y., Koh, H.L. and DeAngelis, D.L. et al. (2019). Modeling $\delta^{18}O$ as an early indicator of regime shift arising from salinity stress in coastal vegetation. *Hydrogeology Journal*, 27(4), 1257–76.

Vörösmarty, C.J., McIntyre, P.B. and Gessner, M.O. et al. (2010). Global threats to human water security and river biodiversity. *Nature*, 467, 555–61.

Wals, A.-E.-J. (2012). *Shaping the Education of Tomorrow: 2012 Full-Length Report on the UN Decade of Education for Sustainable Development*. Paris: UNESCO.

Wiek, A., Withycombe, L., Redman, C.L. and Mills, S.B. (2011). Moving forward on competencies in sustainability. *Environment: Science and Policy for Sustainable Development*, 53(2), 3–13.

World Commission on Environment and Development (WCED). (1987). *Our Common Future* [The Brundtland Report]. Oxford: Oxford University Press.

Zint, M., Kraemer, A. and Kolenic, G. (2014). Evaluating meaningful watershed educational experiences: an exploration into the effects on participating students' environmental stewardship characteristics and the relationships between these predictors of environmentally responsible behavior. *Studies in Educational Evaluation*, 41, 4–17.

16. Digital storytelling as OER-enabled pedagogy: sustainable teaching in a digital world
Daniel Otto

1. INTRODUCTION

The latest Fridays for Future protests against climate change have re-emphasised the importance of education for sustainable development (ESD). Sustainable development (SD) is a crucial concept that students should be familiarised with during their educational career. Therefore, formal education can operate on two different levels. On the one hand, ESD can be the content of courses and other educational measures that are not only offered inside, but also outside formal curricula (Otto et al., 2019). On the other hand, students can become aware of SD as the result of a self-reflective process triggered by their own educational practices. This chapter intends to reconcile both objectives by discussing digital storytelling (DS) in light of the concept of open educational resources (OER)-enabled pedagogy. DS can be regarded as a pedagogical approach to educate students about SD topics in an innovative and motivating way and instruct them on the use of digital technology. OER-enabled pedagogy is an analytical lens that pinpoints pedagogical opportunities to strengthen the students' role in and beyond educational practices.

Starting from a broader perspective, DS has gained prominence as an approach for teaching and learning in the digital age (Bilen, Hoştut and Büyükcengiz, 2019; Challinor, Marín and Tur, 2017; Otto, 2017; Robin and McNeil, 2019). DS combines the art of telling stories with a mixture of digital media – for instance, texts, pictures, audio and video material (Robin, 2016). The objective is to produce (alone or in groups) a relatively short video (two to five minutes), which is then shared and discussed with the course members or uploaded onto the Internet to receive a wider audience. The final products of a DS process are personal narratives created with digital tools and shared with others to present and distribute information, ideas and opinions on a broad range of topics. In this perspective, DS renders a compelling teaching practice to acquire twenty-first-century skills such as global, digital, technology and information literacy (Niemi and Multisilta, 2016; Robin, 2008).

The idea of OER has recently gained prominence through the release of the United Nations Educational, Scientific and Cultural Organization (UNESCO) recommendation concerning OER (UNESCO, 2019). The recommendation highlights the intended contribution of OER to the United Nations 2030 Agenda for Sustainable Development, primarily Sustainable Development Goal (SDG) 4 (quality education) by offering open access to various forms of education and learning. However, the basic idea of OER was already established in 2002 by the UNESCO's Forum on the Impact of Open Courseware for Higher Education in Developing Countries. The primary objective of OER is to allow people to retain, reuse and revise, remix, and redistribute teaching and learning materials (the 5Rs). In this manner, OER broaden access to education, reduce costs of materials and improve the overall quality of teaching and learning (Green, 2017). The subsequent concept of OER-enabled pedagogy intends to strengthen students' role in educational processes by empowering them in practices only made possible through the 5R permissions of OER (Wiley and Hilton, 2018). Therefore, OER-enabled pedagogy provides criteria to evaluate whether teaching and learning practices constitute this form of pedagogy. However, the authors call for further studies that examine questions about the additional benefits of the criteria associated with OER-enabled pedagogy. This brings up questions of whether DS could benefit from taking on board OER-enabled pedagogy or whether it already fulfils its criteria.

A glance at the literature indicates that, hitherto, DS and OER-enabled pedagogy have not yet been combined. Nonetheless, it could be hypothesised that DS is more powerful as well as sustainable when it is carried out in combination with OER-enabled pedagogy. While OER by itself can be a facilitator for DS in terms of finding and using appropriate material, OER-enabled pedagogy strengthens the students' role and value in and beyond the DS process. It ensures that students are recognised as the creators of their stories and that their products are made publicly available (social media platforms, OER repositories). Thereby, their stories can be further used and carry value beyond the creator's own learning.

Surprisingly, the different perspectives and concepts have rarely been linked to each other explicitly. While DS advocates the importance of copyright issues in the compilation of materials, there is often no explicit reference to Creative Commons (CC) licences and OER repositories to search and collect materials. Moreover, the created videos themselves are not provided with CC licences to permit further use. Vice versa, proponents of OER-enabled pedagogy have so far not recognised DS as an appropriate teaching approach that fulfils their pedagogical requirements.

In a nutshell, this chapter merges both perspectives to investigate whether both can mutually benefit from each other. Therefore, this chapter is structured as follows. Section 2 describes DS on a conceptual basis and outlines steps for the implementation of DS in teaching in general. Correspondingly, empirical examples of DS are outlined. Section 3 presents OER as a way to use and provide openly licensed material for teaching and learning scenarios. OER-enabled pedagogy serves as an approach to develop scenarios based on OER. Section 4 amalgamates both perspectives by presenting a case study that used DS in an international university teaching project about climate change. The analytical lens of OER-enabled pedagogy renders recommendations to enhance the students' role and the value of their artefacts during and beyond the teaching project. Section 5 provides a conclusion and outlook.

2. DIGITAL STORYTELLING FOR TEACHING IN THE DIGITAL AGE

As mentioned in the introduction, DS combines the ancient tradition of telling stories with the use of digital tools and artefacts to compose and share stories. Although digital stories are the outcomes of this process, it is essential to state that the value of DS lies rather in the educational process than in the final product. Assessments of digital stories should, therefore, focus on the manner in which they have been composed and conveyed rather than, for instance, how they are technically implemented. Hence, the story is at the centre of the DS process.

Because educational practitioners widely use DS, it has similarities and overlaps with other concepts and methodologies such as interactive stories, narrative computer games, and so forth (Robin and McNeil, 2019). A coherent definition is puzzling, and individual perceptions and classifications of DS may differ. Nevertheless, there are certain elementary characteristics as well as specific values and concepts inherent in DS. Against this background, at least three types of stories can be classified that constitute DS (Robin and McNeil, 2012):

- personal narratives – stories that enclose crucial events in personal life;
- historical documentaries – comprising dramatic and emotional events that help the viewer to understand the past;
- stories that inform or educate viewers on a particular concept or practice.

While the first type of stories are primarily found in the health sector (medical or nursing schools), the second are frequently used in teaching history or social sciences. Although the suitability of the different types of stories varies based on learning and teaching objectives, the third type of stories are used more broadly in education to convey complex concepts or relationships to make them more compelling and understandable for the audience. These characteristics render it an appropriate instrument for addressing complex environmental issues (e.g., climate change or air pollution) and making them comprehensible for the viewer.

From a pedagogical standpoint, carrying out DS in teaching is found to strengthen the following competencies (Becker and Otto, 2016; Otto, 2017):

- *research competence*: development and implementation of an idea based on scientific concepts and results; learn to identify and evaluate relevant material;
- *problem-solving competence*: ability to organise decision-making processes autonomously; cope with various hurdles during this process;
- *interpersonal competence*: ability to successfully work in groups; assign and fulfil different roles in the process;
- *technological competence*: ability to use a range of digital techniques and tools such as recording devices and video editing software.

With regard to the latter competence, DS contributes to teaching students twenty-first-century literacy skills (Robin, 2008). Students are empowered in the effective use of technology by actively participating, communicating and collaborating during the DS process.

For the implementation of DS, various concepts are outlined in the literature on how to structure the process. Although these concepts vary concerning their abstraction and elaborateness, they revolve around some essential steps that need to be integrated:

1. Develop first idea/sketch.
2. Conduct research.
3. Write script and develop storyboard from it.

4. Collect and create material.
5. Assemble material and create a digital story.
6. Present to receive feedback and reflect.

A bandwidth of different concepts exists that take on board these different core steps adequately. With her eight-step approach to DS, Morra (2013) presents a rather pragmatic but very instructive and intuitive concept (Figure 16.1).

In addition, on her website, Morra (2019) offers more detailed guidance on how to implement each of the eight steps and DS in general.

A more advanced concept to steer the DS process is introduced by Robin and McNeil (2012) who draw on the ADDIE instructional design model. The ADDIE model is one of the most popular models to design courses or training and comprises five phases of

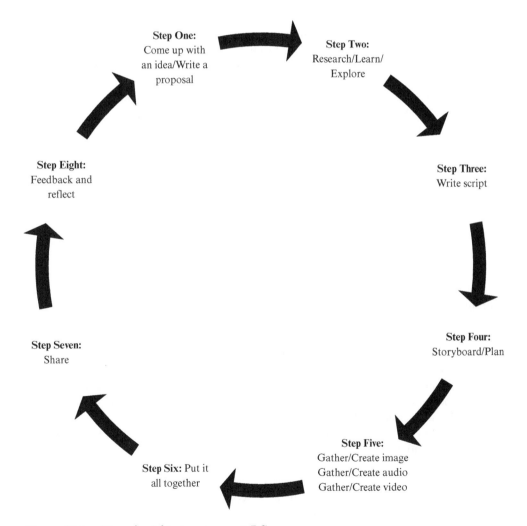

Figure 16.1   Morra's eight steps to great DS

Figure 16.2   ADDIE model for DS process

analysis, design, development, implementation and evaluation (Branch, 2009). It offers the advantage of detailed instructions for teachers for the planning process. The authors systematically operationalise the ADDIE model to assist in organising and structuring the DS process. For each of the five steps, they present essential aspects to consider regarding the teachers' own role and the role and tasks of the students (Figure 16.2).

In a nutshell, while the concept of Morra is more than appropriate for rather short-term offerings such as workshops or training, the ADDIE model of Robin and McNeil is appropriate for teachers who require detailed instruction or want to incorporate DS in regular courses or for curriculum integration.

A crucial aspect of the DS process in educational contexts is the overall assessment of the student-created digital stories (Boase, 2008; Jenkins and Lonsdale, 2007). As already mentioned, because the focus is preferably on the DS process, a formative assessment is to be given preference over a summative assessment. This form of assessment can occur during the decisive intermediate steps displayed in the different DS concepts (Jenkins and Lonsdale, 2007; Ohler, 2009). Of particular importance is the step from a first idea/script to the design of a storyboard. Therefore, this step appears to be suitable for teacher intervention. Teachers should provide constructive feedback and steer the further process.

From a pedagogical perspective, it is also preferable to involve students in the feedback or even assessment process. Depending on the target group, students' feedback can be integrated at various points. However, at least an open discussion and feedback round at the end of the DS process ought to be mandatory when the students present their digital story to each other. Peer assessment is another method for students to comment on each other's work and has been proven to increase students' competences and collaboration (Boud, Cohen and Sampson, 1999; Whitelock, 2009). It can also trigger self-reflection on their own DS idea/concept. The latter aspect is why it is vital to implement peer assessment early in the DS process so that students have the time to reflect, react and revise based on the recommendation of others. The first script or the storyboard is an occasion where peer assessment can be included.

For recording and editing the digital stories, recent technical developments have made it possible to record advanced and high-quality videos with standard mobile devices (Robin and McNeil, 2019). For editing and putting together materials, standard video software – for example, by Microsoft (MovieMaker) and Apple (iMovie) – already provides all necessary functions. Microphones and a tripod can be helpful equipment upgrades that significantly improve the quality of the recordings. Additional apps and software for DS can be found on several websites that provide examples for software to create the storyboard (e.g., Google Slides, Storyboard That, Storybird) to do online video editing (e.g., WeVideo).[1]

Several studies have demonstrated the positive effects of DS on academic achievement across educational sectors (Yuksel, Robin and McNeil, 2010). For instance, a school study encompassing three countries reveals that the implementation of DS can enhance student engagement and motivation and contribute to twenty-first-century skills, especially when working in groups (Niemi and Multisilta, 2016). However, empirical studies mostly focus on the school sector, where DS is frequently used (Smeda, Dakich and Sharda, 2014). Studies for higher education are rare (Kocaman-Karoglu, 2016; Yuksel et al., 2010). Nonetheless, recent studies reinforce the effects observed in schools for higher education, where it also contributes to increased motivation of students (Aktaş and Yurt, 2017). However, SD topics that use DS are yet seldom (Otto, 2018).

In terms of OER and DS, Tur, Marín and Challinor (2017) provide a stimulating DS study. At two universities, DS was used to support the development of reflection and digital skills in professional education. Students, either individually or in groups, produced artefacts that reflected on different aspects of their courses. The authors analysed the artefacts for recurring themes, levels of reflection and digital competence, particularly the use of OER. They suggest that DS can be a highly engaging way of introducing both reflective and open educational practices.

3.   OER-ENABLED PEDAGOGY TO ENHANCE SUSTAINABILITY IN TEACHING

The term OER was coined by the UNESCO's 2002 Forum on the Impact of Open Courseware for Higher Education in Developing Countries (UNESCO, 2002). Notwithstanding that no canonical definitions exist, the latest definition provided by UNESCO defines OER as: 'Learning, teaching and research materials in any format and medium that reside in the public domain or are under copyright that have been released under an open license, that permit no-cost access, reuse, re-purpose, adaptation and redistribution by others' (UNESCO, 2019, pp. 3f.). OER cover a variety of materials, ranging from the abstract to full course units. Examples of OER are lectures, quizzes, pictures, graphics, or pedagogical materials. The CC licences have been established as the standard to licence OER and thereby signal to others how to use the materials further.[2]

Especially during the last decade, OER and the general striving towards open education (OE) has gained momentum (Bozkurt, Koseoglu and Singh, 2019). Not least, this is visible in the recent release of the UNESCO recommendation concerning OER at the 40th General Conference (UNESCO, 2019). OER is a powerful concept that is firmly embedded in education (Cronin and MacLaren, 2018; Koseoglu and Bozkurt, 2018) and the underlying idea is perceived as a precondition for OE (OPAL, 2011).

In addition to the release of the UNESCO recommendation, OER intend to support the implementation of the 2030 Agenda for SD, especially SDG 4 (quality education). The recommendation states the importance of 'nurturing the creation of sustainability models for OER: supporting and encouraging the creation of sustainability models for OER at national, regional and institutional levels, and the planning and pilot testing of new sustainable forms of education and learning' (UNESCO, 2019, p. 4). The latter aspect of sustainable forms of education and learning is one of the core ideas of OER. This is codified in the aim to facilitate access to educational material and empower people to use the 5Rs – retain, reuse and revise, remix and redistribute teaching and learning materials – as well as to develop collaborative and innovative learning scenarios based on them (Green, 2017). Thereby, the concept of OER ascribes to broadening access to education, reducing the costs of materials and to improving the overall quality of teaching and learning. The last two decades have reinforced this for all fields of education (Clements, Pawlowski and Manouselis, 2015; Otto, 2019).

Regarding the technical infrastructure for OER, several repositories exist where material can be found, mostly located in Europe or North America (Santos-Hermosa, Ferran-Ferrer and Abadal, 2017; Zancanaro, Todesco and Ramos, 2015). These repositories make OER widely available and permit users to find and use them. However, how to best design these repositories, technically and conceptually, has been a subject of discussion (Butcher, 2011; Kerres and Heinen, 2015).

Notwithstanding the recognised benefits of OER and the emerging number of OER repositories, various analyses have revealed that the actual adoption of OER in education, and especially OER practices are low (Otto, 2019). As a consequence, several studies have been conducted to identify barriers and obstacles for the adoption of OER (Belikov and Bodily, 2016; de Hart, Chetty and Archer, 2015; Luo et al., 2019; Perryman and Seal, 2016). One central problem, often overlooked, is that OER are primarily content based and not an educational model per se. Efforts to solve this shortage of OER are visible in the following discussions that have, among others, introduced the nexus of OER-enabled pedagogy (Wiley and Hilton, 2018). While open pedagogy has a long history in education, the term OER-enabled pedagogy proposes teaching and learning practices that are only possible in the light of the 5R permissions of OER. The underlining idea is to establish a pedagogy that empowers students to occupy a more active role in the teaching and learning process and to be the creator rather than the recipient of the content. One possibility to integrate OER-enabled pedagogy in teaching and learning is to enable students to improve or create course content throughout their learning process.

To evaluate whether a teaching practice constitutes OER-enabled pedagogy, the authors provide criteria for evaluation (ibid.). Therefore, they draw on the concepts of Wiley and Hilton's (2018) renewable assignment and classify different types of assignment.

Table 16.1 shows a matrix to examine whether a preferred teaching or learning approach can be considered as OER-enabled pedagogy. In order to assist teachers in verifying teaching approaches as being a renewable assignment, the authors suggest four questions that must be answered to decide whether OER form an essential part of the teaching practice:

1. Are students asked to create new artefacts (e.g., paper, videos, songs) or revise/remix existing OER?
2. Does the new artefact have value beyond supporting the learning of its author?
3. Are students asked to share their new artefacts or revised/remixed OER publicly?
4. Are students asked to license their new artefacts or revised/remixed OER openly?

Table 16.1   Criteria distinguishing different kinds of assignments

	Student Creates an Artefact	The Artefact Has Value Beyond Supporting Its Creator's Learning	The Artefact Is Made Public	The Artefact Is Openly Licensed
Disposable assignments	X			
Authentic assignments	X	X		
Constructionist assignments	X	X	X	
Renewable assignments	X	X	X	X

Source: Wiley and Hilton (2018).

By answering these four questions, teachers are able to determine a plan and/or revise/improve their teaching approach.

To sum up, this chapter has demonstrated the importance of OER and OER-enabled pedagogy for teaching and learning in the digital age. OER facilitate access to teaching and learning material and enhance the overall quality of education. Because OER are facing limitations in being primarily content, OER-enabled pedagogy has emerged to increase OER practices that are only made possible by the 5R permissions. However, hitherto, few examples examine whether OER-enabled pedagogy brings additional benefits to the sustainability of teaching scenarios.

4.   DIGITAL STORYTELLING AS OER-ENABLED PEDAGOGY

With regard to aforementioned lack of research on OER-enabled pedagogy, this section contributes a case study that used DS in a teaching project of two universities in Tunisia and Germany. The teaching project has already been completed, and the results have been analysed and published (see Otto, 2017, 2018). Although the evaluation of the students' and teachers' experiences with DS were positive, there was no use neither of OER-enabled pedagogy nor of OER. This makes the teaching project a compelling case study to analyse whether OER-enabled pedagogy renders additional benefits for the teaching project in terms of pedagogy and sustainability. In the following, the case study is presented, and the main results are outlined. Afterwards, OER-enabled pedagogy is applied to the case study to investigate its potential benefit.

The teaching project used DS in the context of climate change (Otto, 2017, 2018). Against the boundary conditions of the project – an interdisciplinary group of students and specific learning objectives – DS turned out to be the most suitable teaching approach.

The idea for the teaching project was born out of the Arab Spring celebrated in 2010 in countries of the Maghreb region. Tunisia has taken a unique role in the Arab Spring, as it is the (only) democratic success story. Education plays a central role in a transition process towards the establishment of democratic culture, as it is a prerequisite for civic engagement. Environmental education and the associated concept of SD are core elements for the sustainable use of resources. Against this background, the teaching project aimed to educate students on the topic of climate change, a core aspect of SD.

The university course was based on the concept of the lived experience of climate change (LECH) (Abbott and Wilson, 2015). Beyond the scientific facts about climate change, the concept captures lay rationalities of climate change and the local and indigenous knowledge associated with it. Thereby, the concept intends to bridge the gap between political and lay rationalities to support improved decision making by incorporating these lived experiences in the political spin. Lived experiences are understood as being embedded in cultural imprints comprising specific individual and collective belief systems. Self-conceptions of people and their activities are always enabled as well as constrained by structural forces that construct their lived experience (ibid.). These structural forces can be 'broader contextual influences' like cultural, socio-economic and power relation or 'proximate influences' like livelihoods, the capacity to adapt, and engagement with others (ibid.).

As learning outcomes after the course, the students should be able to:

● demonstrate knowledge and understanding of climate change as an interdisciplinary problem;
● deal critically with the concept of lived experiences;
● be able to compare and contrast lived experiences in the Global North and Global South;
● engage and interact with each other to share expertise and experiences;
● critically scrutinise the scientific and political discourse about climate change.

The implementation of the project was facing some central hurdles:

● an interdisciplinary group of students;
● different cultural backgrounds;
● different learning cultures;
● different levels of knowledge about climate change.

To address these challenges and accomplish the desired learning outcomes, DS was chosen as the teaching approach. It was expected that implementing DS would bring significant pedagogical benefits for the students. The increased interaction throughout the DS process enhances students' collaboration and engagement. Creating stories in groups increases creative thinking and the development of new ideas. DS allows the students to connect the topics of climate change with their livelihood and present their personal ideas and stories to the audience. By using digital technology, for instance, multi-media software and computer technologies to create and present their stories, DS contribute to digital literacy. With regard to the topics of climate change, DS reveals the students individual and collective experiences with climate change and allows them to reflect on these experiences from an intercultural perspective.

The course design was based on the Morra's (2013) DS concept mentioned in Section 2. Therefore, the course was divided into four phases:

1. Preparation phase (content delivery).
2. Group work phase (collaboration in small groups).
3. Sharing and discussion phase (sharing and presenting the digital stories).
4. Reflection phase (reflecting one's own and group work).

During the preparation phase, the LECH concept was conveyed to the students. The second group work phase consisted of planning and implementing the digital story. For this purpose, the students formed groups of four or five learners with the task of collecting and editing a digital story on a chosen topic of climate change. The chosen topics had to be investigated from different disciplinary and national perspectives, and the stories had to comprise different types of knowledge (from experts, laypeople, scientists, etc.). In order to be able to evaluate the learning process in the form of a formative assessment, the script was submitted to the teachers to give constructive feedback and recommend improvements. The final sharing and discussion phase was a joint presentation meeting, including a dialogue about each of the digital stories. Afterwards, in the reflection phase, students reflected on their course experiences in a written individual reflection report. The underlying concept of written debriefing draws on the assumption that a renewed examination of events and experiences leads to a more in-depth recollection and thus to a better processing of experiences. Moreover, it allows teachers to gain deeper insights into the learning experiences of their students. At the same time, the reports served as a part of formative evaluation.

Experiences and the evaluation of the course (for details see Otto, 2017, 2018) reveal that using DS fulfilled the expectation of enhancing student motivation and student engagement in an intercultural exchange about climate change. It also broadened students' experience in terms of their cultural and disciplinary perspective.

From a pedagogical perspective, students were able to develop or increase competences in all four areas stated in Section 2:

- *Research competence.* Students identified a climate change-related topic (e.g., wheat cultivation, tourism) and researched it to develop their story in which different lived experiences occurred (from experts, laypeople and politicians).
- *Problem-solving competence.* Students were able to transform a complex problem in the field of climate change into a short digital story. They managed and organised their group working and overcame different obstacles at various stages of the process.
- *Interpersonal competence.* Students were able to work and collaborate in different interdisciplinary and intercultural groups on a joint climate change topic.
- *Technological competence.* Students compiled their digital story by using self-recorded material and applied digital tools and software to create and edit it.

While the project disclosed positive outcomes in terms of motivation and competence development, applying the framework of OER-enabled pedagogy suggests opportunities for improvement.

In summary, the case study highlighted the overall benefits of DS and stated its positive impact on the students' learning achievements. It also showed that DS was a suitable approach for the given teaching context. In a second step, OER-enabled pedagogy was

Table 16.2   Project reassessment applying OER-enabled pedagogy

OER-enabled Pedagogy (Renewable Assignment)	DS Teaching Project	Suggested Improvement
1. Are students asked to create new artefacts (e.g., paper, videos, and songs) or revise/remix existing OER?	Students were asked to create an artefact (digital story) and to record/ collect appropriate material	Students can be instructed to recognise OER as their material
2. Does the new artefact have value beyond supporting the learning of its author?	Students were invited to upload and share their digital stories via YouTube to reach a wider audience	The digital stories could be uploaded in OER repositories to increase discoverability and sustainable use through others
3. Are students asked to share their new artefacts or revised/remixed OER publicly?	Students used self-recorded material. Stories were shared with other participants	Students can be invited to use OER repositories (of their institution if existing) to share and to discuss outcomes publicly
4. Are students asked to license their new artefacts or revised/ remixed OER openly?	Students were not asked to license their material	Students can be tutored to use CC licences for their material and thus enable others to reuse, revise or remix their material or digital stories

used to examine whether applying the concept to the case study renders additional benefits. Table 16.2 illustrates that the additional benefits of OER-enabled pedagogy mainly occur regarding students' recognition in and beyond the teaching project and the sustainability of the created artefacts. Recognition refers to the fact that the digital story can be reused, revised or remixed by others. Students thus receive credit for their digital story, which can increase their motivation and the overall quality of their products. Sustainability is enhanced when students make their digital story publicly available, preferably by publishing in OER repositories. In this manner, the digital story or parts of it can be further used or serve as instructional material for others.

5.   CONCLUSION AND OUTLOOK

This chapter scrutinised the benefits and prospects of reconciling DS and OER-enabled pedagogy to serve as a combined pedagogical approach for teaching in a digital world. First, the idea and benefits of DS were presented. It became evident that DS constitutes a promising pedagogical approach to impart twenty-first-century skills to students and to strengthen their research, problem-solving, interpersonal and technology competences. Several studies suggest that DS can also increase students' motivation, a pivotal aspect to trigger student engagement. It is not only regarding SD that the type of stories that inform or educate viewers on a particular concept or practice appear to be promising. Nevertheless, for the case of SD, there are only limited examples in higher education that empirically verify this assumption.

In the next step, OER and the related concept of OER-enabled pedagogy were introduced. OER is understood as openly licensed material that allows users to use 5Rs. OER-enabled pedagogy builds on this concept and enables practitioners to develop teaching scenarios that allow students autonomy, interdependence, responsibility and participation.

When both perspectives are considered, the question arises whether the adoption of OER-enabled pedagogy for DS creates added value. To investigate this question, a case study was analysed that encompassed the implementation of DS in an international and interdisciplinary university teaching project about climate change.

The case study demonstrated that reassessing the teaching project through the lens of OER-enabled pedagogy discloses benefits regarding the students' role in the DS process and the value as well as the sustainability of their products. Although the students in the DS teaching project created artefacts, their recognition and visibility can be increased by using OER. Moreover, using open CC licences and uploading the artefacts into OER repositories enables further use by others beyond the course duration and gives students the chance to be credited for their work. This can also be understood as a way to enhance the sustainability of DS beyond the course duration.

For further research, two ways seem promising. First, to expand the range of empirical studies in higher education that use DS as a teaching method to convey SD topics to students. Second, OER-enabled pedagogy and the related criteria can be applied to existing studies as a lens to identify suitable teaching approaches or to identify cases where the application of the concept can improve the sustainability of the artefacts and improve the students' role in the teaching process.

ACKNOWLEDGEMENT

The chapter was written by the author as part of the project OERinfo II funded by the Federal Ministry of Education and Research (BMBF) in Germany under grant number: 01PO18015C. The content of the publication lies within the responsibility of the author.

NOTES

1. See, for example, http://digitalstorytelling.coe.uh.edu/; https://samanthamorra.com/2014/04/12/5-fantastic-apps-for-digital-storytelling-on-ipads/; https://elearningindustry.com/18-free-digital-storytelling-tools-for-teachers-and-students;https://www.educatorstechnology.com/2018/04/9-great-digital-storytelling-tools-for.html. Accessed 10 January 2020.
2. See https://creativecommons.org/. Accessed 2 February 2020.

REFERENCES

Abbott, D. and Wilson, G. (2015). *The Lived Experience of Climate Change: Knowledge, Science and Public Action.* Cham, Switzerland: Springer International Publishing.

Aktaş, E. and Yurt, S.U. (2017). Effects of digital story on academic achievement, learning motivation and retention among university students. *International Journal of Higher Education*, 6(1), 180–96.

Becker, S. and Otto, D. (2016). Lernkulturen im (Klima-)Wandel. Digital Storytelling zur Kompetenzvermittlung in interkulturellen Lehr-Lernsettings. In O. Dörner, C. Iller, Henning Pätzold and S. Robak (eds), *Differente Lernkulturen – Regional, National, Transnational* (pp. 101–14). Leverkusen-Opladen: Verlag Barbara Budrich.

Belikov, O.M. and Bodily, R. (2016). Incentives and barriers to OER adoption: a qualitative analysis of faculty perceptions. *Open Praxis*, 8(3), 235–46.

Bilen, K., Hoştut, M. and Büyükcengiz, M. (2019). The effect of digital storytelling method in science education on academic achievement, attitudes, and motivations of secondary school students. *Pedagogical Research*, 4(3), Article em0034.

Boase, K. (2008). Digital storytelling for reflection and engagement: a study of the uses and potential of digital storytelling. Centre for Active Learning & Department of Education, University of Gloucestershire. Accessed 10 January 2020 at https://gjamissen.files.wordpress.com/2013/05/boase_assessment.pdf.

Boud, D., Cohen, R. and Sampson, J. (1999). Peer learning and assessment. *Assessment and Evaluation in Higher Education*, 24(4), 413–26.

Bozkurt, A., Koseoglu, S. and Singh, L. (2019). An analysis of peer reviewed publications on openness in education in half a century: trends and patterns in the open hemisphere. *Australasian Journal of Educational Technology*, 35(4), 68–97.

Branch, R.M. (2009). Instructional design: the ADDIE approach. In R.M. Branch, *Instructional Design: The ADDIE Approach*. Boston, MA: Springer Science.

Butcher, N. (2011). *A Basic Guide to Open Educational Resources (OER)*. Prepared for the Commonwealth of Learning & UNESCO. Edited by A. Kanwar and S. Uvalić-Trumbić. Accessed 19 February 2021 at https://unesdoc.unesco.org/ark:/48223/pf0000215804?posInSet=10&queryId=b84da8c2-5070-4bb2-9093-3a8fc37b42ff.

Challinor, J., Marín, V.I. and Tur, G. (2017). The development of the reflective practitioner through digital storytelling. *International Journal of Technology Enhanced Learning*, 9(2–3), 186–203.

Clements, K., Pawlowski, J. and Manouselis, N. (2015). Open educational resources repositories literature review – towards a comprehensive quality approaches framework. *Computers in Human Behavior*, 51, 1098–106.

Cronin, C. and MacLaren, I. (2018). Conceptualising OEP: a review of theoretical and empirical literature in open educational practices. *Open Praxis*, 10(2), 127–43.

de Hart, K., Chetty, Y. and Archer, E. (2015). Uptake of OER by staff in distance education in South Africa. *The International Review of Research in Open and Distributed Learning*, 16(2), 1–15.

Green, A.G. (2017). What is open pedagogy? *Green Geographer*. Accessed 16 February 2021 at https://greengeographer.com/what-is-open-pedagogy/.

Jenkins, M. and Lonsdale, J. (2007). Evaluating the effectiveness of digital storytelling for student reflection. In *ICT: Providing Choices for Learners and Learning: Proceedings Ascilite Singapore 2007* (pp. 440–44). Accessed 16 February 2021 at https://www.ascilite.org/conferences/singapore07/procs/jenkins.pdf.

Kerres, M. and Heinen, R. (2015). Open informational ecosystems: the missing link for sharing educational resources. *International Review of Research in Open and Distance Learning*, 16(1), 24–39.

Kocaman-Karoglu, A. (2016). Personal voices in higher education: a digital storytelling experience for pre-service teachers. *Education and Information Technologies*, 21(5), 1153–68.

Koseoglu, S. and Bozkurt, A. (2018). An exploratory literature review on open educational practices. *Distance Education*, 39(4), 441–61.

Luo, T., Hostetler, K., Freeman, C. and Stefaniak, J. (2019). The power of open: benefits, barriers, and strategies for integration of open educational resources. *Open Learning*, 35(1), 1–19.

Morra, S. (2013). 8 steps to great digital storytelling. *Samanthamorra.com*. Accessed 15 March 2020 at https://samanthamorra.com/2013/06/05/edudemic-article-on-digital-storytelling/.

Morra, S. (2019). Transform learning. *Samanthamorra.com*. Accessed 15 March 2020 at https://samanthamorra.com/digital-storytelling/.

Niemi, H. and Multisilta, J. (2016). Digital storytelling promoting twenty-first century skills and student engagement. *Technology, Pedagogy and Education*, 25(4), 451–68.

Ohler, J. (2009). Digital and traditional storytelling part IV – assessing digital stories, new media narrative. *Jasonohler.com*. Accessed 10 January 2020 at http://www.jasonohler.com/storytelling/assessmentWIX.cfm.

OPAL (2011). *Beyond OER: Shifting Focus to Open Educational Practices. OPAL Report 2011*. Accessed 19 February 2021 at https://nbn-resolving.org/urn:nbn:de:hbz:464-20110208-115314-6.

Otto, D. (2017). Lived experience of climate change – a digital storytelling approach. *International Journal of Global Warming*, 12(3/4), 331–46.

Otto, D. (2018). Using virtual mobility and digital storytelling in blended learning: analysing students' experiences. *Turkish Online Journal of Distance Education*, 19(4), 90–103.

Otto, D. (2019). Adoption and diffusion of open educational resources (OER) in education. *The International Review of Research in Open and Distributed Learning*, 20(5), 122–40.

Otto, D., Caeiro, S. and Nicolau, P. et al. (2019). Can MOOCs empower people to critically think about climate change? A learning outcome based comparison of two MOOCs. *Journal of Cleaner Production*, 222, 12–21.

Perryman, L.-A. and Seal, T. (2016). Open educational practices and attitudes to openness across India:

reporting the findings of the Open Education Research Hub Pan-India Survey. *Journal of Interactive Media in Education*, 2016(1), 1–17.

Robin, B.R. (2008). Digital storytelling: a powerful technology tool for the 21st century classroom. *Theory into Practice*, 47(3), 220–28.

Robin, B.R. (2016). The power of digital storytelling to support teaching and learning. *Digital Education Review*, 30(3), 17–29.

Robin, B.R. and McNeil, S. (2012). What educators should know about teaching digital storytelling. *Digital Education Review*, 22, 37–51.

Robin, B.R. and McNeil, S.G. (2019). Digital storytelling. In R. Hobbs and P. Mihailidis (eds), *The International Encyclopedia of Media Literacy*. New York: John Wiley & Sons.

Santos-Hermosa, G., Ferran-Ferrer, N. and Abadal, E. (2017). Repositories of open educational resources: an assessment of reuse and educational aspects. *International Review of Research in Open and Distance Learning*, 18(5), 84–120.

Smeda, N., Dakich, E. and Sharda, N. (2014). The effectiveness of digital storytelling in the classrooms: a comprehensive study. *Smart Learning Environments*, 1(1), Article 6.

Tur, G., Marín, V.I. and Challinor, J. (2017). The development of the reflective practitioner through digital storytelling. *International Journal of Technology Enhanced Learning*, 9(2/3), 186–203.

United Nations Educational, Scientific and Cultural Organization (UNESCO). (2002). *Forum on the Impact of Open Courseware for Higher Education in Developing Countries Final Report*. Paris: UNESCO.

United Nations Educational, Scientific and Cultural Organization (UNESCO). (2019). Draft recommendation on open educational resources. General Conference, 40th Session, Paris, 2019. Accessed 1 May 2020 at https://unesdoc.unesco.org/ark:/48223/pf0000370936.

Whitelock, D. (2009). Editorial: e-assessment: developing new dialogues for the digital age. *British Journal of Educational Technology*, 40(2), 199–202.

Wiley, D. and Hilton, J. (2018). Defining OER-enabled pedagogy. *International Review of Research in Open and Distance Learning*, 19(4), 133–47.

Yuksel, P., Robin, B.B.R. and McNeil, S. (2010). Educational uses of digital storytelling around the world. *Elements*, 1, 1264–71.

Zancanaro, A., Todesco, J.L. and Ramos, F. (2015). A bibliometric mapping of open educational resources. *International Review of Research in Open and Distance Learning*, 16(1), 1–23.

17. Addressing the SDGs through an integrated model of collaborative education

Wendy Stubbs, Susie S. Y. Ho, Jessica K. Abbonizio,
Stathi Paxinos and Joannette J. (Annette) Bos

1. INTRODUCTION

Complex problems like climate change, rising inequality and entrenched poverty are interconnected sustainability issues and hence call for multidimensional collaborative approaches. Such 'wicked' problems, or grand societal challenges (Waddock and McIntosh, 2011), and efforts to address the United Nations Sustainable Development Goals (SDGs), need integrated solutions. Higher education is criticised for its traditional monodisciplinary courses (Boden, Borrego and Newswander, 2011; Noy et al., 2017). These do not adequately prepare students to develop innovative solutions to address the Goals. While many tertiary courses provide some degree of breadth, most nonetheless take a distinct disciplinary focus. For example, often sustainability courses are taught from a business, engineering, environmental science, or social science viewpoint. As such, sustainability courses do not deliver a balanced curriculum, with content and perspectives from across different domains. This is problematic, as sustainability practitioners need to explicitly value, include and interweave knowledge, skills and perspectives from different disciplines, industries and cultures.

It is well-recognised that understanding and managing environmental and social issues require a particular set of skills, capabilities and insights (Roome, 2005). Students need to acquire knowledge, learn and apply new skills and shift attitudes and behaviours (Rands, 2009; Stubbs, 2013; Stubbs and Cocklin, 2008). This requires a strategic and well-formulated course for sustainability. It is clear that a piecemeal, monodisciplinary approach inhibits 'transformative change' (Sipos, Battisti and Grim, 2008), 'deep learning' (Warburton, 2003) or a 'paradigm shift' (Down, 2006), which are considered essential for teaching sustainability (Stubbs and Schapper, 2011).

This chapter describes how Monash University (Australia) educators from different disciplines and faculties (Faculty of Arts, Faculty of Business and Economics, Monash Sustainable Development Institute and Faculty of Science) co-designed an integrated sustainability course, the Master of Environment and Sustainability (MES), to prepare students to address the complex issues underlying the SDGs. The MES is a two-year course with four parts: (1) interdisciplinary environment and sustainability core studies; (2) specialisation preparatory studies; (3) specialist studies; and (4) interdisciplinary advanced practice. Building on the core subjects (Part 1), students can choose from five specialisations (Parts 2 and 3). They are provided the opportunity to work in real-world contexts, combining theory and practice to learn how to respond to local and international, corporate, government and social environmental concerns (Part 4).

This chapter is structured as follows. Section 2 presents a brief literature review that provides the context for the design and development of the MES. Section 3 discusses the research approach, while Section 4 presents the Research Skills Development framework (Willison and O'Regan, 2007) and SDG framework (United Nations, 2018a), which were used to build a sound skills curriculum to enable graduates to support solutions for the SDGs. Section 5 describes the design and delivery of the MES course. The chapter concludes with personal reflections on, and key learnings from, academics' and students' experiences (Sections 6 and 7). The insights gained and lessons learnt from designing the MES course will be useful to other universities attempting to create courses that address the SDGs.

2.   LITERATURE REVIEW

Sustainability, which may be defined as 'development that meets the needs of the present without compromising the ability of future generations to meet their own needs' (World Commission on Environment Development [WCED], 1987), is inherently interdisciplinary. Specifically, sustainable development is concerned with enhancing the quality of life for future generations while avoiding harm to the environment and the economy (McCormick et al., 2015). Sustainability issues, such as climate change, are typically underpinned by three interconnected pillars: the environment, economy and society (Aktas, 2015). Sustainability, therefore, requires us to critically examine the social, economic and ecological consequences of contemporary paradigms and practices and engage with diverse stakeholders. Indeed, UNESCO (1978) states that 'interdisciplinarity may be regarded as the necessary educational approach for reflecting and conveying the fundamental unity and complexity of life' (p. 8).

Globally, higher education is increasingly interdisciplinary (Irani, 2018). The number of undergraduate and postgraduate offerings have grown substantially over the past 25 years (Brandenburg and Kelly, 2019). University strategies, funding agencies and organisations such as the United Nations support this trend (e.g., American Association for the Advancement of Science, 2011; Annan-Diab and Molinari, 2017; Australian Research Council, 2018; Sustainable Development Solutions Network [SDSN] Australia/ Pacific, 2017; Wals, 2009). This is in recognition of the fact that traditional monodisciplinary models of education are criticised for not developing the broader understanding necessary to approach complex problems (Boden et al., 2011; Cooper et al., 2001; Noy et al., 2017; Wineburg and Grossman, 2000). Ultimately, a boundary-crossing skill-set is needed beyond that developed by narrow monodisciplinary tertiary education (Burns, 2013).

To investigate solutions to global sustainability challenges, graduates require integrated knowledge and boundary-spanning skills associated with understanding the perspectives and constraints of different sectors, disciplines and communities (Millar, 2016; United Nations, 2017; Wilson, Ho and Brookes, 2018). Specifically, graduates may be working in diverse multidisciplinary teams and across societal sectors. Such diverse teamwork requires an appreciation of others' roles and worldviews as well as identifying creative multi-win solutions (Walker, Cross and Barnett, 2019). Indeed, employers in sustainability value the T-shaped professional, defined as individuals with an area of expertise as well as a broader knowledge base and interpersonal skills to engage with other professions (Alkaher and

Goldman, 2018; Hansen and von Oetinger, 2001). Interdisciplinary education, therefore, often presents students with integrative conceptual and teamwork tasks that build their interpersonal, critical and reflective thinking skills (Eastwood, 2010; Howlett, Ferreira and Blomfield, 2016). These transferable skills equip sustainability graduates for interdisciplinary professions of the future that require knowledge brokering and innovation (e.g., Dinmore, 1997; Ernst and Young LLP and Federation of Indian Chambers of Commerce and Industry, 2018).

2.1   Challenges to Effective Interdisciplinary Education

While interdisciplinary education is well recognised as beneficial to students and society, there are known challenges to building an effective interdisciplinary curriculum. A major hurdle is building a cohesive yet diverse and multifaceted curriculum. Designing and delivering interdisciplinary degrees is challenging because it requires extensive collaboration amongst a range of discipline experts, and even industry and government partners, with different pedagogical perspectives and worldviews. A key challenge in developing a sustainability curriculum is: How can educators effectively co-design a harmonised curriculum across multiple domains that both supports a diverse cohort and all areas of sustainability? How do educators draw together many different domain specialists and forms of knowledge into a harmonious whole with a strong skills curriculum and overarching vision? Doing so requires deep collaboration across educators, meaning that interdisciplinary instruction is more time and resource intensive than monodisciplinary approaches (Boyer and Bishop, 2004; Jones, 2010; Moslemi et al., 2009; Sims and Falkenberg, 2013). Specifically, effective design and co-delivery of materials often requires educators to negotiate the difficulties and discomfort of operating outside their core discipline (Dyment and Hill, 2015).

Additionally, educators must design a curriculum that recognises the challenges of interdisciplinary learning from the student perspective (e.g., Brewer, 1999; Coops et al., 2015; de Greef et al., 2017). Students can find the absence of disciplinary boundaries confusing because there is no contained knowledge base to master; rather, one can feel overwhelmed with the range of disciplines to understand and integrate. Students often report they lack the skills to integrate new and unfamiliar domains of knowledge (Falcus, Cameron and Halsall, 2019). The integration method is not always taught explicitly (ibid.). Students can also face language barriers related to disciplinary jargon, particularly in assessment (Klaassen, 2018). A dominant challenge is ensuring that assessment is appropriately clarified, and skills development is mapped to support a range of students (Coops et al., 2015). Any language barrier is particularly challenging when approaching assessment, also due to many students' lack of familiarity with assessment types used outside their home discipline (Klaassen, 2018). Interdisciplinary assessment tasks typically involve the integration of a range of disciplines, but each single assessment will usually favour the style and language of one particular discipline – for example, critical analysis in the social sciences and technical formats in science, technology, engineering and mathematics (STEM). Educators must ensure that assessment is appropriately clarified in language that does not assume tacit knowledge of a particular discipline's pedagogy, assessment types or jargon. Appropriate skills development must also be mapped (Coops et al., 2015). While students will be on different learning trajectories, depending upon their particular background and home discipline, a core skills curriculum must be integrated that supports and challenges all learners and builds competencies for the SDGs.

Perhaps the most important challenge for educators and students is that an interdisciplinary curriculum can be perceived as disjointed at the subject or course level unless it is underpinned by a model under which different content, assessment, skills, experts/staff (Lindvig, Lyall and Meagher, 2017), perspectives, pedagogies, languages and learning cultures (Tripp and Shortlidge, 2019) can be harmonised or integrated. Essentially, this is contingent on the strength of the collaborative partnership formed among educators and the establishment of a shared language and approach to the curriculum development (Bardecki and Millward, 2020; Tinnell et al., 2019).

3.   RESEARCH APPROACH

This chapter uses a case study approach (Yin, 1994) to describe how Monash University educators designed a new postgraduate sustainability course, the MES, to address the SDGs. The Research Skills Development (RSD) conceptual framework guided the MES curriculum and assessment design, and is used to guide the discussion of the MES in Section 5. The MES case study is supplemented by feedback from a small sample of educators and students (Section 6). These comments provide personal reflections on staff and students' experiences with the MES in its first two years of operation. It is not a representative sample of the student cohort but provides some preliminary insights that can inform the development of a larger survey of MES students and alumni to enhance the MES.

The MES was launched in 2017 and the first cohort of students completed the course in November 2019. In December 2019, a small qualitative research project sought feedback from educators who coordinate specialisations and/or teach subjects in the MES, and students who had just completed the MES. Each participant was asked a series of open questions about their experiences with the MES course; reflections on their key learnings/teachings; the interdisciplinary nature of the course; the SDGs; and, where the course could be strengthened. The interviews were transcribed for analysis to draw out key themes. Two of the authors independently analysed the interviews and agreed on the key themes. Table 17.1 summarises the participants.

4.   FRAMEWORK

The key challenge in developing the MES was, how can we effectively co-design a harmonised curriculum across multiple disciplines of sustainability, and deliver assessment and scaffolded skills development appropriate for a vastly diverse student cohort? We integrated two frameworks to form our model for collaboration: Research Skills Development and the United Nations SDGs.

Table 17.1   Participant summary

Code	Staff/ Student	Specialisations; Disciplines	Cultural Background
ED1	Staff	Coordinator Leadership for Sustainable Development; MSDI	Dutch
ED2	Staff	Leadership for Sustainable Development; MSDI	Australian
ED3	Staff	Coordinator Environmental Security; Faculty of Science	Australian, Malaysian
ED4	Staff	Coordinator Corporate Environmental and Sustainability Management, Environment and Governance, International Development and Environment; Faculty of Arts	Australian
ST1	Student	Environmental Security	Australian
ST2	Student	Corporate Environmental and Sustainability Management	Australian
ST3	Student	Corporate Environmental and Sustainability Management and Leadership for Sustainable Development	Indian, UAE
ST4	Student	Environmental Security	Australian
ST5	Student	Leadership for Sustainable Development	Australian
ST6	Student	Corporate Environmental and Sustainability Management	Vietnamese
ST7	Student	Leadership for Sustainable Development	Australian

Note: MSDI = Monash Sustainable Development Institute.

4.1   The Research Skills Development (RSD) Framework

The RSD framework has two axes: facets of research skills are listed against different levels of autonomy or independence required by students. It is a well-known, robust and flexible framework primarily for scaffolding the development of research skills across year levels. It can create a ladder of learning that bridges content (Paterson, Rachfall and Reid, 2013; Willison and Buisman-Pijlman, 2016; Yoshida, 2015). The RSD framework (Willison, 2018; Willison and O'Regan, 2007) has been used in various educational contexts and was adopted as a strategic educational priority for Monash University. It has been particularly successful for building collaborative partnerships between disciplines and academics (Torres and McCann, 2014). While it has a specific focus upon skills development, it has a wide range of applications and flexibility, and provides a common language for curriculum design that transcends discipline and country.

The RSD framework was deemed appropriate for addressing the objective for five main reasons (Table 17.2). Overall, the educators felt confident in applying the tool to the challenge because of the documented rigour and success of the RSD framework (Pretorius, Bailey and Miley, 2013; Taib and Holden, 2013; Willison, 2012, 2014; Yoshida, 2015).

Table 17.2   The five rationales and contexts for applying the RSD framework to the design and development of the MES

Rationale	Summary of Studies and Applications
Previous use as a collaborative model for complex education teams and projects	The scholarly literature shows the framework has been successfully applied as a collaborative model It builds educational partnerships and thus the capacity for integrated curriculum (Paterson et al., 2013; Willison, 2014) For example, in their meta-analysis of a range of studies, the Australian Office for Teaching and Learning (Willison, 2014) concluded that the RSD framework creates a collaborative environment (instead of competitive) It is valuable for underpinning collaboration because of its flexibility and relevance to any discipline and subject matter
Creates a common language for diverse education teams	The framework's terminology has previously been used as a common language among educators This increases team confidence in 'learning and assessment in course-level context in a variety of disciplines' (Willison, 2014, p. 16) The RSD provides accessible terminology that transcends disciplines, while still providing sufficient flexibility for different disciplines to develop pedagogy within their learning context
Scaffolding of skills development at the course level	The framework was an appropriate foundation for thematic harmonisation and scaffolding of skills across the MES In building a course that is coherent for students, one must evaluate how the different skills and knowledge being developed in each distinct disciplinary course map out and contribute to course-level skills development (Loveys et al., 2014; Pretorius et al., 2013; Willison, Sabir and Thomas, 2017)
Frame for clearly articulating assessment tasks	Academics have used the RSD framework to reframe their assessment tasks and marking rubrics (Willison, 2012) The tool increases the clarity of assessment purpose and coherence of learning objectives (Willison, 2012), which is particularly important when students are working across different disciplines and may not have tacit knowledge of a discipline It allows educators to design assessment of content and skills intentionally and appropriately in a targeted, explicit manner (Willison et al., 2017) Students and academics have reported that they recognise and acknowledge the development of their own or their students' research skills, respectively, as a result of using the framework (Willison and Buisman-Pijlman, 2016) Pretorius et al. (2013) state that in working with nursing and midwifery studies, 'The RSD framework proved a valuable tool in the redesign of a second year Midwifery assignment by providing an explicit guide to build and assess student skills' (p. 383) The demonstrated benefit to students is the clarity of expectations in learning (Jonsson, 2014; Pretorius et al., 2013; Willison, 2012) Educators report they can more comprehensively embed essential research skills and sustainability-specific skills into the curriculum (Willison, Le Lievre and Lee, 2010) Studies of undergraduate cohorts have demonstrated the effectiveness of applying the RSD framework (Paterson et al., 2013; Willison and O'Reagan, 2007)

Source: Adapted from Castillo and Ho (forthcoming).

4.2   The United Nations Sustainable Development Goals

The SDGs provide a globally recognised framework for approaching sustainability issues and education (United Nations, 2018a). The Goals inherently recognise and communicate the interconnected and boundary-spanning nature of contemporary global issues. These Goals recognise the complex social, environmental, economic and political dimensions of issues and create a framework for advanced and interdisciplinary learning (United Nations, 2015). Due to the interconnections between the Goals, and the breadth across the 17 SDGs, they are also relevant to all domain areas and flexible enough to use in any educational context – for example, for interdisciplinary and industry-aligned parts of the curriculum.

The SDGs set out a network of 17 objectives, 169 specific targets and 232 unique indicators that cross traditional policy agendas and disciplinary boundaries, including physical and social sciences (ibid.). To illustrate, SDG 13 (Climate Action) includes targets for national policy, climate change education and adaptation across governments, private sectors and civil society to ensure water, food and energy security into the future (Le Blanc, 2015; United Nations, 2017). Goals regarding public health logically interact with SDG 13 – for example, SDG 6 (Clean Water and Sanitation) focuses on optimising water efficiency and aquatic ecosystem management as well as ensuring access to clean and affordable water and hygiene education in vulnerable communities (Le Blanc, 2015; United Nations, 2018b). Such multifaceted Goals and targets necessitate that graduates are at least to some extent literate across economic development, human rights, international collaboration, cultural diversity and environmental management.

The educators utilised the framework to contextualise and map curriculum, to promote a multifaceted approach, and as a framework for presenting content to students within a broader view of sustainability. This tool was used to ensure a comprehensive coverage of issues across the two-year MES course, with a broad coverage of SDGs in the interdisciplinary core and capstone subjects and more focused coverage of particular Goals within specialisations.

5.   COLLABORATIVE MODEL OF EDUCATION: CASE STUDY OF THE MASTER OF ENVIRONMENT AND SUSTAINABILITY

5.1   The Case: A New Interdisciplinary Degree

In 2016, the Faculties of Science and Arts, the Monash Sustainable Development Institute, and the Monash Business School were tasked with co-developing the MES. All faculty stakeholders would contribute different expertise and perspectives to the issue of sustainability and in doing so, contribute to the SDGs. The faculties wished to form a partnership in alignment with SDG 17 (Partnerships for the Goals) that emphasises interdisciplinary collaboration (Stafford-Smith et al., 2017) to help break down traditional departmental silos.

The different faculty academics faced a challenge not only in terms of the level of collaboration required for integrating disciplines but also in providing teaching and learning for students from all backgrounds. Students were drawn from 35 different nations, from

Botswana to France, and a plethora of disciplinary backgrounds (e.g., fashion, marketing, communications, biomedical studies, engineering). Due to the diversity of students' educational and cultural backgrounds, it was expected that each student would experience a different learning trajectory within the course. Scaffolding would need to be built for various learning trajectories. The educators also needed a conceptual map to unify and contextualise the different concepts within the domains.

5.2   The Collaborative Design and Delivery

The educators ran a series of workshops to introduce all faculty teaching into the MES to the RSD and SDG frameworks to gain academic buy-in as well as foundational understanding of the frameworks. In terms of the SDG framework, the workshops involved discussing cross-dimensional disciplinary aspects of the various Goals and mapping units to multiple SDGs at the course level. These alignments were then applied to the vision and core learning outcomes of individual subjects. The skills curriculum for developing change agents was also assessed and mapped to individual subjects. Special emphasis was placed on focusing upon different complementary skills in individual subjects, to create a breadth of skills development, whilst reinforcing core competencies, such as reflection, at increasing levels of sophistication from year one to two. The topic and skills mapping unearthed broad coverage of Goals within interdisciplinary subjects, with particular suites of Goals and skills emphasised for the relevant specialisations (see Table 17.3 for a summary of the course structure, the specialisations and learning outcomes for the whole course and each of the specialisations). For example, the environmental security subjects focused upon Life On Land and Life Below Water, and evidence-based practice for decision making. The course was mapped to the 17 SDGs pre-delivery, and then annually as the course evolved from 2017 to 2019. Further skills mapping is required to track progress.

The SDG language and framework was employed across the 22 main (core) subjects. Subjects in particular specialisations focus upon different but complementary elements of the Goals in introductory weeks. For example, students focused upon the development of the indicators for Goals, and assessing the evidence base underpinning these, in environmental security subjects. Complementarily, students focus upon critically assessing multiple stakeholder perspectives on the issues addressed by the SDGs in the environmental governance and corporate specialisations. These different elements and skills are integrated in practice components of the more advanced capstone units in the final year, strengthening and integrating prior learning.

Monash University Library experts introduced the RSD to academics via two workshops during course ideation. Using the RSD and SDG frameworks in workshops, across and within specialisations, the academics began to unpack their assessment tasks. The tasks were then interrogated with the guidance and expertise of library teams also participating in the workshop alongside their academic colleagues. The range of tasks, skills and competencies that students were being asked to demonstrate in these assignments were identified and mapped in alignment with the facets of research and student autonomy in the RSD framework. Utilising and sharing their particular disciplinary lenses, educators from disparate disciplines explained to each other what could be unclear for non-cognate students. At this point, cross-disciplinary collaborations were initiated, as well as a strong rapport. This fostered multidisciplinary learning by educators.

Table 17.3   Structure and learning outcomes of the MES

Component	Learning Outcomes	Core Subjects
Whole course	1. Evaluate, analyse and integrate knowledge of global change and sustainability and the interdependence of society, the economy and the environment 2. Evaluate, analyse and integrate approaches to environment and sustainability within their specialisations, including environmental security, international development, leadership, policy and governance or business management 3. Apply expert, specialised cognitive, research, technical and communication skills to analyse and design solutions to environment and sustainability problems 4. Reflect and participate constructively in ethical decision making consistent with sustainability principles	*Interdisciplinary foundation* Global challenges and sustainability Perspectives on sustainability *Interdisciplinary capstones* Interdisciplinary consultancy Sustainability project (group) Sustainability project (group) Sustainability internship Sustainability research thesis

Specialisation	Learning Outcomes	Core Specialisation Subjects
Corporate environmental and sustainability management	1. Demonstrate advanced and integrated knowledge of global environmental, social and economic issues facing business and the key sustainability management theories, concepts and principles 2. Apply expert skills and specialised knowledge of the key sustainability management theories, concepts and principles to critically evaluate the global environmental, social and economic issues facing business	Corporate sustainability management Sustainability measurement Corporate sustainability regulation
Environment and governance	1. Demonstrate advanced and integrated knowledge of key environmental challenges and environmental policy and management approaches to address these challenges 2. Apply expert skills and specialised knowledge to critically evaluate environmental policy and management approaches and the design and implementation of fit for purpose policy and management approaches	Environmental analysis Environmental governance and citizenship Field studies in environmental governance

Table 17.3   (continued)

Specialisation	Learning Outcomes	Core Specialisation Subjects
Environmental security	1. Demonstrate advanced and integrated knowledge of the biological, chemical, and physical basis of global environmental change, its impacts on the natural environment and its implications for society 2. Apply expert skills and specialised knowledge to analyse and interpret the science required for policy and environmental management within the field of environmental security	Securing biodiversity and ecosystems Climate change, energy and human security Water security and environmental pollution
International development and environment	1. Demonstrate advanced and integrated knowledge of the theory and practice of international development, and frameworks for understanding the environmental impacts of development 2. Apply expert skills and specialised knowledge to analyse the causes of poverty, disadvantage and environmental change, and plan and implement international development projects and programmes	Deconstructing development Political ecology: critical explanations of socio-environmental problems
Leadership for sustainable development	1. Demonstrate advanced and integrated knowledge tools, mechanisms and skills required to influence and lead change processes to enhance positive environmental, economic and social outcomes for sustainability 2. Apply expert skills and specialised knowledge of critical drivers of individual behaviour affecting sustainability practice to analyse and to design solutions to target these drivers	Processes to influence change Understanding human behaviour to influence change Leading change for sustainable development

Source: *Monash Handbook*: S6002 – Master of Environment and Sustainability, accessed 17 February 2021 at https://handbook.monash.edu/2020/courses/S6002.

Essentially, through using the RSD and SDG frameworks, educators developed a common language to discuss and articulate assessment within the course and a shared framing and understanding to contextualise course content and assessment. The model was effective because it allowed a consistent approach but enough room for flexibility, so that academics could apply the model within their particular context and section of the course.

5.3   The Transformational Outcomes in Support of SDG 17: Partnership for the Goals

The SDG and RSD framework worked as a robust, effective model to ensure constructive alignment of framing, learning objectives, content and assessment within the MES. The workshops were successful in terms of promoting awareness amongst academic staff of the expertise, both scholarly and practice-based, across the education community of more than 50 educators. This facilitated the cross-pollination and harmonisation of ideas and learnings, but also cross-referencing of materials and skills across different units in the degree. The workshops enabled the successful application of the RSD in particular. For example, educators were empowered to map key skills across the core entry-level subjects through to final capstone and research subjects. The RSD and SDG model facilitated the peer review by academics of their subjects, leading to revision of assessments to ensure they were scaffolded at the appropriate level, built upon one another and encompassed a range of academic skills for advancing the Goals. The rubric workshop also led to educators creating RSD-informed rubrics that ensured constructive alignment and resulted in the creation of clear, explicit assessment rubrics suitable for diverse learners. Overall, academics improved their own practice in curriculum assessment design and students received an SDG aligned, harmonised and contextualised learning experience and progressive skills curriculum through their course.

An essential element to building and maintaining rapport is the ongoing communication and professional development. The course and domain coordinators have been instrumental in providing networking and communication opportunities in the form of hosting education days for the course academics and the library team; end-of-term social get-togethers; and online team drives to share resources for continued pedagogical discussions. Educators also participate in United Nations Climate Change Conferences and other external industry, government, and UN events. This has created a community of practice that has extended out now to industry, intergovernmental committees, and government in the spirit of Goal 17 Partnerships for the Goals. The cohesive and comprehensive nature of the course, and its transformation capacity, has been recognised by an Australian Banksia Foundation Sustainability Award in 2019. The course provides strong employability outcomes for graduates across corporate, not-for-profit, research, governance and intergovernmental organisations worldwide, and a strong transformational education experience, as reflected in the next section.

6.   REFLECTIONS FROM EDUCATORS AND STUDENTS

6.1   Course Structure and Delivery

Scholars have noted the challenges of building a cohesive yet diverse curriculum that integrates different disciplinary approaches and knowledge domains. This requires deep collaboration (Boyer and Bishop, 2004; Jones, 2010; Moslemi et al., 2009). The educators worked closely to design the MES course, focusing on specialisations that supported students' career paths. The MES stands apart from other courses because of the collaboration of educators from different disciplines at all stages of the course's development. The ongoing collaboration ensures the course is 'truly co-owned':

I think what's unique, is that we all sat down as educators to design this and see how we could actually integrate it more closely and I haven't had that experience before. It's normally, the course director creates a master's course and they say, 'Oh, can you teach this course, can you teach that course?'. There's very little where the educators come together and say, 'How can we actually integrate this (and) what are the key things we want to get across? (ED4)

Students highlighted the integration of disciplines within the course design and structure, which encouraged interactive and collaborative learning. The course provides 'exposure to different worldviews' from leaders in their fields, which enables students to 'learn how we can make a difference following their footsteps'.

The MES's range and choice of specialisations allows students to 'specialise in a field of sustainability rather than being a generalist'. However, the students felt that it was important to be exposed to a spread of subjects as sustainability 'covers such a broad aspect of life'. In addition, the course provides a variety of industry guest speakers and different pathways – industry project, internship, group research project and research thesis – which provides greater opportunities to build industry connections. While 'flexibility of the course was a big bonus', students found that it could be more of a challenge to design their course if they don't have a clear direction. In these cases, strong guidance from the course coordinators is required to help students align their subject choices with their aspirations and career ambitions.

Highlighted subject areas that could be added, or expanded, to enhance the MES, include health, gender equality, education and poverty issues; increased focus on the social pillar of sustainability; an indigenous course; green infrastructures and technologies; big data analytics; artificial intelligence and sustainable development; sustainable agriculture and food systems; and more case studies from the Southeast Asia and Pacific regions.

The sustainability field is evolving very quickly, and educators emphasised the need to keep the MES up to date by constantly exploring new specialisations to prepare students for careers of the future. Industry advisory boards are important to ensure the course is providing students with the necessary knowledge and skills. However, one educator suggested that 'something that's edgier or more radical' could be injected into the course by looking at activist and non-conventional approaches to prepare students to be change makers. This could take the form of students experimenting with creating and running some of their own events.

6.2 Diversity

As Tripp and Shortlidge (2019) point out, it is important to recognise and integrate different disciplinary backgrounds, levels and learning cultures. A strength of the course is its student diversity in cultures and disciplinary backgrounds. As one student noted, people wanted to contribute in class and they brought so much life and professional experience with them. Students valued the diversity of opinions, but also support, from fellow students. The discussions enabled students to learn about themselves – who they were as a person and how they impact others on the planet:

You never knew what idea from which part of the world or which discipline came out to be the best idea in a group discussion. And that was absolutely really, really nice to have that engagement with so many new perspectives and very refreshing ones to say the least. (ST3)

However, another student warned about the danger of 'group think' and noted that in a few situations, conservative views were ridiculed among the cohort rather than 'properly dissected and discussed'. This can exclude people who 'need to be brought into this space'. It is therefore important to engage with a good range of perspectives, including those that are critical of sustainability.

For the educators, highlights include the transformations in students as they discover how they can make a contribution or find a new career path; giving students a structure and a platform to transition into a sustainability leadership role; the collaboration, creativity and critical thinking shown by the students along with their passion to drive the sustainability agenda:

> I feel like sometimes, on a good day, at its best, the course is helping people find meaning and finding a way to contribute to the global crisis that can sometimes otherwise feel very overwhelming . . . seeing students go onto strategic leadership roles and to have a positive impact in society is incredible. (ED3)

6.3   Skills Development

A lack of skills to integrate disciplinary knowledge domains is a challenge for students (Falcus et al., 2019). Students' learning is enhanced though collaborating with people from different disciplines and cultures. Discussing different perspectives provides a broad foundation that helps students respect different worldviews. The skills that students developed included how to research; bridging the research and action gap; using reflective and systems thinking; effective communication with people with different perspectives on sustainability; and being open-minded, willing to change personal perspectives and take personal responsibility. One student noted that the focus on skills development and the flexible structure of the course aligns with the idea of the T-shaped sustainability professional (Alkaher and Goldman, 2018; Hansen and von Oetinger, 2001). This prepared students to work in the sustainability sector, as suggested by previous feedback from an ex-student:

> The strong academic foundation I built during the Master of Environment and Sustainability enables me to be a more effective and informed communicator. It helps me take into account the complex elements at play in environmental communication. This ability is something that the MES was integral in helping me to perfect. (Climate Change Communications Manager)

A key learning for one of the educators was that 'collaboration takes lots of time and lots of talking':

> I try to convey that sustainability and the world is a contest of ideas and worldviews and that there are many different ways of understanding what sustainability is and that this a very personal thing . . . sustainability is not about the status quo. It's about encouraging the students to think about how things could be different and then try and attempt to take action, implement change and use strategies and tactics to influence those. (ED2)

Educators pointed to providing more scaffolding to help students transition into the sustainability field; supporting students to deal with the emotional cost of being a sustainability practitioner; and the systematic review of the skills students are learning and how they can be improved.

6.4 Interdisciplinarity

Educators must design a curriculum that recognises the challenges of interdisciplinary learning from the student perspective (e.g., Brewer, 1999; Coops et al., 2015; de Greef et al., 2017). Students found that the educators' different disciplinary backgrounds and the course design helped them 'get inside the heads of different decision makers in science, and governance, and corporate spheres' and learn 'how to speak their language (and) how to speak to their values'.

However, one area of weakness was the electives that were managed by staff who do not teach core subjects in the MES. The subjects managed by the MES staff were regarded as stronger because they built on each other. Other challenges of an interdisciplinary approach include raising awareness about the significance of interdisciplinarity; melding teaching philosophies and approaches between educators in the core subjects; and managing administrative differences between faculties (e.g., submission of late assessments and special consideration policies). There is still work to be done to address these issues.

6.5 SDGs

Some students had not been exposed to the SDGs before starting the MES, while others had little or a basic understanding. After completing the course, the students felt that they were 'fully aware of the SDGs and their importance and what they are set up to achieve'. They found the SDG framework to be a powerful framework to examine 'real-world problems' and learn about solving complex sustainability problems:

> The Master of Environment and Sustainability is a truly unique course that lays the foundation for future innovators and change makers to work toward achieving the SDGs. Key to this is its multidisciplinary approach, which provides a holistic understanding of the skills and expertise required to cross traditional boundaries. (ST2)

However, students did find the SDGs challenging. One felt 'a bit down when thinking about how much had to be achieved by 2030'. Another lamented that hardly anyone uses the SDGs in the 'real world' outside of international bodies like the Intergovernmental Panel for Climate Change (IPCC) and UN and questioned how to engage people and businesses with them.

The educators stressed the importance of discussing the SDGs both critically (e.g., critiquing the highly negotiated agenda with necessary trade-offs and compromises) and positively, and integrating them into the assessments to expose students to a 'diversity of ways of thinking and problem solving'. The SDGs provides a conceptual framework under which the different disciplines and sectors 'can come together and be cohesive'.

One area that needs to be reviewed is the focus on the SDGs by different subjects in the MES. The two foundation core subjects explicitly draw upon the SDGs by delving into the challenges underlying the 17 Goals, how the Goals interrelate and integrative solutions to address the SDGs. While the educators committed to integrating the SDGs into their subjects, the students pointed out that in reality, a number of the specialisation subjects did not explicitly refer to the SDGs. However, the students do not believe every subject needs to explicitly 'revolve around' the SDGs because 'there are so many other ways to change the world' and address global sustainability issues. This is useful feedback for educators in revising the MES curriculum to ensure students understand how each subject addresses issues encapsulated by the SDGs.

6.6   Recommendations

Figure 17.1 and Table 17.4 provide key recommendations for others embarking on interdisciplinary course design, based on the educators' personal learnings and the reflections from students and staff captured in this chapter. The framework in Figure 17.1 is underpinned by collaborative co-design and co-teaching. This forms the basis for all other elements of the course design and delivery.

7.   CONCLUSION

Waddock (2007) argued that the world needs leaders and managers who are capable of integrating complexity, who understand the long-term consequences of their decisions, and who will make decisions that benefit people, societies and the natural environment. The Master of Environment and Sustainability is Monash University's first serious attempt

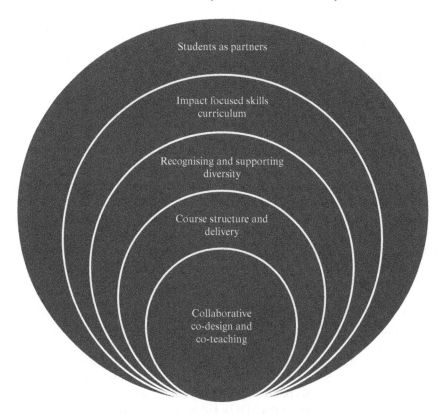

Figure 17.1   A recommended framework for collaborative interdisciplinary course design to support future sustainability leaders

Table 17.4   Summary of recommendations

Recommendation	Key Points
1. Collaborative co-design and co-teaching	Course design and delivery are underpinned by ongoing collaboration amongst educators
	Supported by an interdisciplinary governance structure and ongoing education design activities and training
	Identify and address educators' disciplinary and cultural boundaries
2. Integrate collaborative interdisciplinary learning and co-teaching approaches into course structure and delivery	Comprehensive coverage of all SDGs through curriculum mapping
	Exposure to a broad diversity of perspectives
	Interdisciplinary foundation and advanced practice subjects complemented by multidisciplinary specialisations
	Enable T-shaped professionals through interdisciplinary and specialist knowledge and skills
3. Recognise and support diversity within the learning environment and assessment design	Identify assumed and tacit domain knowledge and student training needs
	Use accessible language
	Interweave students' intercultural and professional experience within the curriculum to enable social learning and leverage diversity
4. Integrate impact-focused skills development into curriculum	Map and integrate skills development to the SDGs and RSD
	Support scaffolding from first year to advanced capstones
	Provide opportunities to practise interdisciplinary and career skills
5. Promote students as partners in learning	Feature student experiences: disciplinary, intercultural and professional
	Seek feedback and adapt rapidly
	Seek input from employers and alumni
	Promote students as an interdisciplinary community of sustainability practitioners
	Promote interdisciplinary teamwork, scaffolded to increase in complexity from foundational through to advanced capstone subjects
	Encourage diversity in teams and cohorts

at creating a truly interdisciplinary course, reflecting the university's commitment to the SDGs and recognising that solving sustainability issues is inherently interdisciplinary and collaborative. The RSD and SDG frameworks guided the design and development of the MES to ensure that outcomes were delivered that prepared students to deal with the complex issues underlying the SDGs. While there is still work to be done, reflections from students from the first cohort to complete the MES suggest that this approach helps to prepare students to be effective communicators, collaborators, critical thinkers, problem solvers and change makers in the sustainability sector.

This chapter provides guidance to faculty on one approach to creating interdisciplinary curricula using the RSD framework and may provide a catalyst for sharing learning experiences in designing courses to address the SDGs. The key lessons from using the RSD and SDGs frameworks to develop the Master of Sustainability may help other educators design interdisciplinary sustainability courses. First, deep collaboration can help to build a cohesive yet diverse curriculum that appropriately integrates different disciplinary approaches and knowledge domains. Second, interdisciplinarity can be achieved by exposing educators and students to multiple disciplines and developing the knowledge, skills and opportunities to both integrate disciplines and specialisations. Third, diverse cohorts can be supported by recognising and accommodating different learning trajectories within the learning environment and assessment design. Fourth, enable students to develop effective skills continuously and progressively for integrating domain concepts, to prepare them for sustainability careers. Finally, recognise the rapidly shifting sustainability field and diverse student needs.

However, this case study offers only a glimpse of the range of interdisciplinary approaches to designing curriculum to prepare students to address global sustainability challenges. The research was limited by a small sample of educators' and students' experiences and insights in the new course, and hence further research is required to assess the student outcomes of the MES. The reflections in Section 6 could inform the design of a survey of students and alumni to gather data to assess the impact of the MES, such as placements. More broadly, future research could investigate other transformative curricula that address the SDGs.

REFERENCES

Aktas, C.B. (2015). Reflections on interdisciplinary sustainability research with undergraduate students. *International Journal of Sustainability in Higher Education*, 16(3), 354–66.
Alkaher, I. and Goldman, D. (2018). Characterizing the motives and environmental literacy of undergraduate and graduate students who elect environmental programs – a comparison between teaching-oriented and other students. *Environmental Education Research*, 24(7), 969–99.
American Association for the Advancement of Science. (2011). *Vision and Change in Undergraduate Biology Education: A Call to Action*. Accessed 30 May 2019 at http://visionandchange.org/finalreport.
Annan-Diab, F. and Molinari, C. (2017). Interdisciplinarity: practical approach to advancing education for sustainability and for the Sustainable Development Goals. *The International Journal of Management Education*, 15(2), 73–83.
Australian Research Council (2018). ARC statement of support for interdisciplinary research. Accessed 30 June 2019 at https://www.arc.gov.au/policies-strategies/policy/arc-statement-support-interdisciplinary-research.
Bardecki, M. and Millward, A. (2020). Interdisciplinary cooperation and collaboration in undergraduate sustainability-based programs: a Canadian example of environment and urban sustainability (EUS). In W. Leal Filho, R.W. Pretorius and U. Azeiteiro et al. (eds), *Universities as Living Labs for Sustainable Development* (pp. 399–416). Cham, Switzerland: Springer.
Boden, D., Borrego, M. and Newswander, L.K. (2011). Student socialization in interdisciplinary doctoral education. *Higher Education*, 62(6), 741–55.
Boyer, S.J. and Bishop, P.A. (2004). Young adolescent voices: students' perceptions of interdisciplinary teaming. *RMLE Online*, 28(1), 1–19.
Brandenburg, C. and Kelly, M. (2019). Integration as the new (general education). *Journal of Interdisciplinary Studies in Education*, 8(1), 21–9.
Brewer, G.D. (1999). The challenges of interdisciplinarity. *Policy Sciences*, 32(4), 327–37.
Burns, H. (2013). Meaningful sustainability learning: a study of sustainability pedagogy in two university courses. *International Journal of Teaching and Learning in Higher Education*, 25(2), 166–75.
Castillo, T. and Ho, S. (forthcoming). Mastering environment and sustainability: how the RSD brought harmony to an interdisciplinary program. In L. Torres, F. Salisbury and B. Yazbeck et al. (eds), *Connecting the Library to the Curriculum: Effective Approaches that Enhance Skills for Learning*. Cham, Switzerland: Springer.

Cooper, H., Carlisle, C., Gibbs, T. and Watkins, C. (2001). Developing an evidence base for interdisciplinary learning: a systematic review. *Journal of Advanced Nursing*, 35(2), 228–37.

Coops, N.C., Marcus, J. and Construt, I. et al. (2015). How an entry-level, interdisciplinary sustainability course revealed the benefits and challenges of a university-wide initiative for sustainability education. *International Journal of Sustainability in Higher Education*, 16(5), 729–47.

Coulibaly, A.W. (2019). Overview of the international framework on education for sustainable development, UNESCO. Accessed 31 January 2020 at https://unfccc.int/documents/197160.

de Greef, L., Post, G., Vink, C. and Wenting, L. (2017). *Designing Interdisciplinary Education: A Practical Handbook for University Teachers.* Amsterdam: Amsterdam University Press.

Dinmore, I. (1997). Interdisciplinarity and integrative learning: an imperative for adult education. *Education*, 117(3), 452–68.

Down, L. (2006). Addressing the challenges of mainstreaming education for sustainable development in higher education. *International Journal of Sustainability in Higher Education*, 7(4), 390–99.

Dyment, J.E. and Hill, A. (2015). You mean I have to teach sustainability too? Initial teacher education students' perspectives on the sustainability cross-curriculum priority. *Australian Journal of Teacher Education*, 40(3), 1–16.

Eastwood, J. (2010). The effects of an interdisciplinary undergraduate human biology program on socioscientific reasoning, content learning, and understanding of inquiry. PhD Thesis, Indiana University.

Ernst and Young LLP and Federation of Indian Chambers of Commerce and Industry (2018). *University of the Future: Bringing Education 4.0 to Life October 2018.* New Delhi: Ernst & Young LLP and FICCI.

Falcus, S., Cameron, C. and Halsall, J.P. (2019). Interdisciplinarity in higher education: the challenges of adaptability. In M. Snowden and J.P. Halsall (eds), *Mentorship, Leadership, and Research: Their Place Within the Social Science Curriculum* (pp. 29–145). Cham, Switzerland: Springer.

Hansen, M.T. and von Oetinger, B. (2001). Introducing T-shaped managers: knowledge management's next generation. *Harvard Business Review*, March, 107–16.

Howlett, C., Ferreira, J. and Blomfield, J. (2016). Teaching sustainable development in higher education: building critical, reflective thinkers through an interdisciplinary approach. *International Journal of Sustainability in Higher Education*, 17(3), 305–21.

Irani, Z. (2018, 24 January). The university of the future will be interdisciplinary. *The Guardian.* Accessed 30 January 2019 at https://www.theguardian.com/higher-education-network/2018/jan/24/the-university-of-the-future-will-be-interdisciplinary.

Jones, C. (2010). Interdisciplinary approach – advantages, disadvantages, and the future benefits of interdisciplinary studies. *Essai*, 7(1), Article 26.

Jonsson, A. (2014). Rubrics as a way of providing transparency in assessment. *Assessment and Evaluation in Higher Education*, 39(7), 840–52.

Klaassen, R.G. (2018). Interdisciplinary education: a case study. *Journal European Journal of Engineering Education*, 43(6), 842–59.

Le Blanc, D. (2015). Towards integration at last? The Sustainable Development Goals as a network of targets. *Sustainable Development*, 23(3), 176–87.

Lindvig, K., Lyall, C. and Meagher, L.R. (2017). Creating interdisciplinary education within monodisciplinary structures: the art of managing interstitiality. *Studies in Higher Education*, 44(2), 347–60.

Loveys, B.R., Kaiser, B.N. and McDonald, G. et al. (2014). The development of student research skills in second year plant biology. *International Journal of Innovation in Science and Mathematics Education*, 22(3), 15–25.

McCormick, M., Bielefeldt, A.R., Swan, C.W. and Paterson, K.G. (2015). Assessing students' motivation to engage in sustainable engineering. *International Journal of Sustainability in Higher Education*, 16(2), 136–54.

Millar, V. (2016). Interdisciplinary curriculum reform in the changing university. *Teaching in Higher Education*, 21(4), 471–83.

Moslemi, J.M., Capps, K.A. and Johnson, M.S. et al. (2009). Training tomorrow's environmental problem solvers: an integrative approach to graduate education. *BioScience*, 59(6), 514–21.

Noy, S., Patrick, R., Capetola, T. and McBurnie, J. (2017). Inspiration from the classroom: a mixed method case study of interdisciplinary sustainability learning in higher education. *Australian Journal of Environmental Education*, 33(2), 97–118.

Paterson, G., Rachfall, T. and Reid, C. (2013). Building a culture of research: using undergraduate research to advance the TR profession, build research capacity and foster collaborative relationships. *Therapeutic Recreation Journal*, 47(4), 259–75.

Pretorius, L., Bailey, C. and Miley, M. (2013). Constructive alignment and the Research Skills Development framework: using theory to practically align graduate attributes, learning experiences, and assessment tasks in undergraduate midwifery. *International Journal of Teaching and Learning in Higher Education*, 25(3), 378–87.

Rands, G. (2009). A principle–attribute matrix for environmentally sustainable management education and its application: the case for change-oriented service-projects. *Journal of Management Education*, 33(3), 296–323.

Roome, N. (2005). Teaching sustainability in a global MBA: insights from the OneMBA. *Business Strategy and the Environment*, 14(3), 160–71.

Sims, L. and Falkenberg, T. (2013). Developing competencies for education for sustainable development: a case study of Canadian faculties of education. *International Journal of Higher Education*, 2(4), 1–14.

Sipos, Y., Battisti, B. and Grimm, K. (2008). Achieving transformative sustainability learning: engaging head, hands and heart. *International Journal of Sustainability in Higher Education*, 9(1), 68–86.

Stafford-Smith, M., Griggs, D. and Gaffney, O. et al. (2017). Integration: the key to implementing the Sustainable Development Goals. *Sustainability Science*, 12(6), 911–19.

Stubbs, W. 2013. Addressing the business–sustainability nexus in postgraduate education. *International Journal of Sustainability in Higher Education*, 14(1), 25–41.

Stubbs, W. and Cocklin, C. (2008). Teaching sustainability to business students: shifting mindsets. *International Journal of Sustainability in Higher Education*, 9(3), 206–21.

Stubbs, W. and Schapper, J. (2011). Two approaches to curriculum development for educating for sustainability and CSR. *International Journal of Sustainability in Higher Education*, 12(3), 259–68.

Sustainable Development Solutions Network (SDSN) Australia/Pacific (2017). *Getting Started with the SDGs in Universities: A Guide for Universities, Higher Education Institutions, and the Academic Sector*. Melbourne: SDSN Australia/Pacific.

Taib, A. and Holden, J. (2013). 'Third generation' conversations – partnership approach to embedding research and learning skills development in the first year. A practice report. *The International Journal of the First Year in Higher Education*, 4(2), 131–6.

Tinnell, T.L., Tretter, T.R., Thornburg, W. and Ralston, P.S. (2019). Successful interdisciplinary collaboration: supporting science teachers with a systematic, ongoing, intentional collaboration between university engineering and science teacher education faculty. *Journal of Science Teacher Education*, 30(6), 621–38.

Torres, L. and McCann, L. (2014). Transforming the libraries impact in curriculum: reconceptualising the library's impact to student's research skills development. Paper presented at the National Alia Conference, 15–19 September, Melbourne. Accessed 19 August 2019 at https://read.alia.org.au/content/transforming-librarys-impact-curriculum-reconceptualising-librarys-contribution-students.

Tripp, B. and Shortlidge, E.E. (2019). A framework to guide undergraduate education in interdisciplinary science. *CBE – Life Sciences Education*, 18(2), Article es3.

United Nations. (2015). *Transforming Our World: The 2030 Agenda for Sustainable Development*. Accessed 30 January 2020 at https://www.un.org/en/development/desa/population/migration/generalassembly/docs/globalcompact/A_RES_70_1_E.pdf.

United Nations. (2017). *UNDP Strategic Plan, 2018–2021*. Accessed 30 January 2020 at https://undocs.org/DP/2017/38.

United Nations. (2018a). The 17 Goals. Accessed 30 January 2020 at https://sustainabledevelopment.un.org/sdgs.

United Nations. (2018b). Water supply sanitation and hygiene (wash). Accessed 30 January 2020 at https://sustainabledevelopment.un.org/partnership/?p=26313.

United Nations Educational, Scientific and Cultural Organization (UNESCO). (1978). *Intergovernmental Conference on Environmental Education Organized by UNESCO in Co-operation with UNEP, Tbilisi, USSR, 14–26 October 1977: Final Report*. Paris: UNESCO.

Waddock, S. (2007). Leadership integrity in a fractured knowledge world. *Academy of Management Learning and Education*, 6(4), 543–57.

Waddock, S. and McIntosh, M. (2011). Business unusual: corporate responsibility in a 2.0 world. *Business and Society Review*, 116(3), 303–30.

Walker, L.E., Cross, M. and Barnett, T. (2019). Students' experiences and perceptions of interprofessional education during rural placement: a mixed methods study. *Nurse Education Today*, 75, 28–34.

Wals, A.E. (2009). *Review of Contexts and Structures for Education for Sustainable Development*. Paris: UNESCO.

Warburton, K. (2003). Deep learning and education for sustainability. *International Journal of Sustainability in Higher Education*, 4(1), 44–56.

Willison, J. (2012). When academics integrate research skill development in the curriculum. *Higher Education Research and Development*, 31(6), 905–19.

Willison, J.(2014). *Outcomes and Uptake of Explicit Research Skill Development Across Degree Programs*. Sydney: Office of Learning and Teaching. Accessed 17 February 2021 at http://hdl.voced.edu.au/10707/325831.

Willison, J. (2018). Research skill development spanning higher education: critiques, curricula and connections. *Journal of University Teaching & Learning Practice*, 15(4), Article 1.

Willison, J. and Buisman-Pijlman, F. (2016). PhD prepared: research skill development across the undergraduate years. *International Journal for Researcher Development*, 7(1), 63–83.

Willison, J., Le Lievre, K. and Lee, I. (2010). *Making Research Skill Development Explicit in Coursework: Final Report*. Australian Learning & Teaching Council. Accessed 17 February 2021 at https://ltr.edu.au/resources/CG7-497%20Adelaide%20Willison%20Final%20Report%202010.pdf.

Willison, J. and O'Regan, K. (2007). Commonly known, commonly not known, totally unknown: a framework for students becoming researchers. *Higher Education Research and Development*, 26(4), 393–409.

Willison, J., Sabir, F. and Thomas, J. (2017). Shifting dimensions of autonomy in students' research and employment. *Higher Education Research and Development*, 36(2), 430–43.

Wilson, L., Ho, S. and Brookes, R.H. (2018). Student perceptions of teamwork within assessment tasks in undergraduate science degrees. *Assessment and Evaluation in Higher Education*, 43(5), 786–99.

Wineburg, S. and Grossman, P. (eds) (2000). *Interdisciplinary Curriculum: Challenges to Implementation.* New York: Teachers College Press.

World Commission on Environment Development (WCED) (1987). *Our Common Future*. New York: Oxford University Press.

Yin, R.K. (1994). *Case Study Research: Design and Methods*. Thousand Oaks, CA: SAGE.

Yoshida, A. (2015). Facilitating learning and research engagement in 4th year undergraduate students: the outcomes of student self-assessment survey. *Qualitative and Quantitative Methods in Libraries*, 4, 871–81.

18. Measuring transformative learning for sustainability in higher education: application of an augmented Learning Activities Survey
Elizabeth Sidiropoulos

1. INTRODUCTION

Society is facing global socio-economic and environmental challenges that require a determined transition towards greater sustainability. However, sustainability issues are complex and often identified as 'wicked problems' (Rittel and Webber, 1973), which are characterised as being unique, difficult to define, socially complex and lacking knowable solutions or outcomes. Therefore, prescribed solutions or linear pathways to sustainability may not be known. Education is of critical importance to assist societal transitions toward sustainability and achieve the United Nations (UN) Sustainable Development Goals (SDGs) (UNESCO, 2016). Education is nominated as a specific goal in SDG 4.7 and contributes to every other major goal. UNESCO (2016) identified that learners can transform themselves and their societies by developing knowledge, skills, attitudes and competencies to address such complexity and uncertainty and learn their way forward (Wals and Benavot, 2017). This calls for a shift in teaching, particularly in higher education (HE), from transmission of knowledge to transformation of learning where students can deepen their sustainability perspectives and shift their mindsets through active participation, critical thinking and reflexivity (Sterling, 2011).

Evaluating whether transformative learning occurs in sustainability education (SE) is not a simple task due to the wide range of possible learning outcomes, such as changes in worldview, self, epistemology, ontology, behaviour and capacity (Hoggan, 2016). There is no standard test to assess transformative learning in SE in HE and this represents a gap in the literature and practice of SE. Previous empirical studies have adopted diverse theoretical approaches and metrics to assess learning outcomes (see El-Deghaidy, 2012; Miller, 2016; Quinn and Sinclair, 2016; Zoller, 2015). The Learning Activities Survey (LAS; King, 2009), developed for an HE setting, has been used to measure transformative learning in various adult learning contexts (see Schwartz, 2013). The LAS has rarely been applied to SE in HE and may be an effective tool for this purpose. This chapter addresses the gap and reports on a study that applied transformative learning theory and an augmented LAS instrument to evaluate SE in a HE context.

Transformative Learning Theory

Transformative learning (TL) refers to shifts in the way a person 'experiences, conceptualises and interacts with the world' (Pallant, 2016, p.71). Transformative learning (TL) theory was launched in 1978 when Mezirow published his theory of perspective transformation (PT) and has since evolved to become prominent in the field of adult learning (Taylor, 2017). According to Mezirow (2000), each person interprets the world based on their perceptions of experience, which create *frames of reference* that influence their thinking, beliefs and actions. Frames of reference consist of *meaning perspectives* or habits of mind (worldview, mindset) that manifest directly into *meaning schemes* or points of view. Mezirow's theory of PT is a ten-step process (see Appendix Table 18A.1) triggered by a *disorienting dilemma*, which challenges a person's existing frame of reference. By critically reflecting on one's underlying values and assumptions and through constructive dialogue with self or others, a person revises their problematic frame of reference and decides to act on their reflective insight. The type of transformation experienced is, in turn, influenced by the type of learning and reflection. Mezirow (2009) distinguished between instrumental learning (a task-oriented approach to validate truth claims), communicative learning (a dialogic approach to assessing another's frame of reference), and emancipatory or self-reflective learning (to assess one's own frame of reference). Mezirow also distinguished between reflection on the content or process in problem solving and reflection on the premises or presuppositions in problem posing. Transformative learning can be experienced as a straightforward transformation of a person's meaning scheme (point of view) or as a profound transformation of a meaning perspective (habit of mind). Further, PT may be cumulative with incremental changes in meaning schemes occurring over time, leading to a transformed perspective, or can occur as an epochal event with a sudden, major reorientation in perspective.

Mezirow's theory has drawn criticism for its emphasis on individual transformation as a rational and cognitive process. Diverse theoretical perspectives and outcomes were brought to TL theory by scholars including Cranton (1994, 1996), Boyd and Myers (1988), O'Sullivan (1999) and Gunnlaugson (2007), who examine different facets of transformation in terms of process, outcomes and context (Cranton and Kasl, 2012). These contributions yield a broader interpretation of TL and address 'the role of spirituality, positionality, emancipatory learning, and neurobiology' (Taylor, 2017, p. 19). Mezirow responded by including perspectives such as emotions (Dirkx, 2001; Merriam, 2004) and the social and cultural learning context (Dirkx, 2006; Dirkx, Mezirow and Cranton, 2006; Mezirow, 2000; Taylor, 2000, 2007).

The term TL is often used interchangeably with Mezirow's theory of PT and as a broad holistic term encompassing diverse views of profound change at the personal, social or cultural level (Hoggan, 2016). Accordingly, various research methods are adopted to investigate TL, although most studies rely on qualitative methods (Cheney, 2010; Taylor and Snyder, 2012). The few quantitative studies in TL used numerical scores to measure changes in cognitive, affective or behavioural aspects of TL. Cheney (2010) found only three out of 51 studies adopted mixed methods, of which two used the LAS. Since 2010, quantitative researchers have increasingly adopted the LAS to assess PT/TL in HE contexts. Two such studies investigated TL outcomes from undergraduate business education (Brock, 2010) and from study-abroad programmes (Stone et al., 2017).

Transformative Learning in Sustainability Education

In this chapter, sustainability education (SE) is used to encompass the spectrum of interpretations on holistic sustainability including education for sustainable development

(ESD). Holistic sustainability, as the interlinked dimensions of environment, society and economy (Pace, 2010), is a complex epistemology (Taylor and Snyder, 2012) that can present multiple challenges to students' frames of reference and potentially disrupt their conceptual, affective and relational experience of the world. It is often approached from an interdisciplinary perspective with a TL intent (Noy et al., 2017; Ryan and Cotton, 2013) designed to empower learners and develop their competencies as change agents to help achieve the UN SDGs (Miller, 2016; UNESCO, 2016). Key sustainability competencies for graduates are expounded by many scholars and include systems thinking, anticipatory, normative, strategic and interpersonal competencies (Wiek, Withycombe and Redman, 2011).

The fields of TL and SE are conceptually congruent and share several elements. These include a constructivist paradigm of learning, changes in cognitive, conative and affective components (Mezirow, 2009; Sipos, Battisti and Grimm, 2008), an emphasis on epistemic learning and change in worldview (Mezirow, 1994; Sterling, 2011), and outcomes in instrumental and communicative learning as well as individual/social actions (Leal Filho et al., 2018; Ryan and Cotton, 2013). Finally, both TL and SE have unpredictable outcomes that are influenced by a constellation of personal, situational and contextual factors.

While TL approaches are more popular in HE, there is limited research on analysing TL outcomes in SE contexts (Winter et al., 2015). The author reviewed 22 empirical TL studies in SE conducted during 2008–17 and found a variety of learning contexts, theoretical frameworks, research methods and learning outcomes (Singer-Brodowski, 2017; Zoller, 2015). The reviewed studies focused on individual subjects (e.g., Hales and Jennings, 2017; Kalsoom and Khanam, 2017; Karol and Mackintosh, 2011; Kokkarinen and Cotgrave, 2013), interdisciplinary units (e.g., Howlett, Ferreira and Blomfield, 2016; Noy et al., 2017) and across a whole institution (Winter et al., 2015). In these studies, rates of TL reported by students varied from none to all participants, with some studies reporting strong negative reactions and even 'resistance' to critical self-reflection (Kelly, 2010). Holistic sustainability was found to be a strong trigger, or 'disorienting dilemma' and firm links were evident between formal and informal learning. The reviewed studies relied predominantly on qualitative approaches, with quantitative studies limited to pre-test/post-test surveys or retrospective pre-test surveys to measure changes in knowledge or attitudes. Only one study by Feriver et al. (2016) used the LAS to investigate SE in an HE setting. Despite the growing call to implement and evaluate TL in HE, there is no standard assessment instrument to examine ESD outcomes and compare results across studies or to justify educational interventions that promote TL (Cheney, 2010).

Study Context and Purpose

The purpose of this study was to apply the LAS to investigate learning outcomes from dedicated SE units in HE. The study contributes to the field by reporting on the efficacy of an augmented LAS instrument to detect PT/TL outcomes from SE in HE. It represents a useful first step towards developing a context-specific instrument for this purpose and can inform SE practice. Specific objectives of the study were to apply an augmented LAS to determine (1) the incidence of PT/TL; (2) the contribution and importance of Mezirow's ten steps towards TL; (3) the influence of demographic, academic, study-related and situational factors on TL outcomes; (4) the type of learning outcomes; and (5) the development of competence, personal agency and advocacy for sustainability.

2.   METHOD

Participants

The research was conducted with undergraduate respondents at two universities in Australia, one in an urban location and another in a regional setting. At one university, the SE unit was compulsory for all students enrolled in business-related programmes and was delivered through a blended learning model with online content/resources for self-study complemented by weekly on-campus workshops during the semester. Assessment included both individual and group tasks. At the other university, the SE unit was compulsory for students in sustainability or environmental science majors and was also delivered in a blended model, with most students enrolled in a distance (off-campus) mode. Assessment was based entirely on individual tasks with no formal group work. Both SE units were available as elective options to students from other faculties. These SE units were chosen for this study as they drew on students from across diverse locations and disciplines and with different reasons for enrolment (i.e., compulsory and elective).

This chapter focuses on cohorts enrolled in these SE units in the first semester of 2017. An estimated 1008 students were enrolled, of which 301 provided useable responses to an online post-course survey. Respondents were mostly from Anglo-Saxon countries (40 per cent), with the second largest group from the North Asia region (24 per cent). The majority had lived in Australia for more than five years (40 per cent) although a significant portion had lived there for less than three years (32 per cent). The sample was evenly split between male and female, and the majority were aged from 18 to 25 years (63 per cent). Most respondents had completed one to three semesters (40 per cent) and nominated business-related programmes as their study major (63 per cent). The majority were enrolled in SE units as a compulsory subject (78 per cent).

Data Collection

This study was based on a concurrent mixed methods approach (Creswell, 2009) as it provided useful insights from the triangulation of quantitative and qualitative findings in the survey (Johnson and Onwuegbuzie, 2004), and aligned with the constructivist-interpretivist paradigm of the study (Crotty, 1998). The research was approved by the Human Ethics Committee at each university and authorised the investigator to contact, recruit and collect data from students in these SE units. All students were informed about the research study on their university learning management system and invited to participate in the survey. Students were informed their participation would be voluntary and anonymous and were given an informed consent form.

Survey Instrument

The LAS is a self-reporting assessment instrument used in adult education to determine the learning activities that contribute to PT. It was originally developed by King (1998) based on Mezirow's ten stages (precursor steps) of PT and informed by insights from Brookfield, Cranton and other scholars (King, 2009). The standard LAS instrument has four sections and consists of fixed-choice and open-ended responses. King (2009) validated the instrument through pilot studies and interviews that included member-checking, a critical review by an expert panel and by supplementary follow-up interviews. Internal consistency of the LAS was demonstrated through favourable pairwise correlations between items. Reliability was approached from a hermeneutical perspective, where several individual items are evaluated separately to determine whether an adult learner experienced PT in relation to their educational experience. Validity and reliability of the LAS have since been tested by many studies on TL in adults (e.g., Brock, 2010; Feriver et al., 2016; Glisczinski, 2007; Madsen and Cook, 2010). Strange and Gibson (2017) reported the internal consistency of the LAS using Cronbach's alpha ($\alpha = 0.80$), which compared favourably with King's test result ($\alpha = 0.86$) (King, 1998, cited in Strange and Gibson, 2017). In this study, the internal consistency of the LAS was established using Cronbach's alpha ($\alpha = 0.78$) and found to be consistent with values reported above.

While the LAS was designed by King (2009) as a pre-screening survey for a sequential exploratory study in a mixed-methods approach, it has since been utilised by researchers as a quantitative tool only (Brock, 2010; Madsen and Cook, 2010; Stone et al., 2017). Nevertheless, the LAS has been criticised by Taylor and Snyder (2012), who argue that it does not reflect broader theoretical psychological constructs of TL or empirical findings on how people experience TL. To address these concerns and reduce possible error and bias in self-reported measures of PT (Mayhew et al., 2016), the LAS was augmented in this study with supplementary questions (see the Appendix) informed by the literature on TL and SE (e.g., El-Deghaidy, 2012; Noy et al., 2017). The supplementary questions explored the incidence and type of TL, respondents learning experience during the semester and the influence of various background and contextual factors. This strengthened the mixed-methods approach (Creswell, 2009) and served to qualify, enrich and triangulate findings from the standard LAS. In summary, the LAS was regarded as a suitable tool for this study for several reasons: its simplicity, widespread use in TL research and reported validity and reliability; the emphasis on cognitive epistemological change regarding holistic sustainability; and the flexibility to add questions to further explore student *perceptions* of their TL outcomes.

In Section 1 of the LAS, Q1 provides a checklist of statements that correspond to Mezirow's ten phases of PT (Appendix Table 18A.1), with respondents able to select all statements that apply to them. In Q2, respondents indicate whether there has been a change in their values, beliefs, opinions or expectations and Q3 asks for a description of the perceived change. Section 2 provides a checklist for respondents to indicate the potential contribution of three categories of items during the semester/unit: (1) significant persons, that is, a challenge by the teacher and support by the teacher or other persons; (2) educational factors (learning activities) such as classroom discussions, critical thinking, personal reflection, and so on; and (3) significant life events such as marriage, birth/ adoption of a child, moving, and so on. Section 3 provides a checklist for the influence of the same three categories of items (i.e., significant persons, educational factors and significant life events) during their overall study programme, and includes a checklist of their typical reflection practices. Respondents could also specify other options and provide short-answer descriptions. Section 4 relates to demographic and educational information such as gender, age, degree programme and specialisation, number of terms completed, country of origin and years in Australia.

The determination of PT is a subjective assessment made by the researcher according to guidelines specified by King (2009) – namely, student responses to Q1 (indicated at least one precursor step), Q2 (reported a change in their perspectives), and Q3 (provided a description of the change). In this study, the determination of potential PT was also based on triangulation with responses to supplementary questions. Thus, the term PT was replaced by the term Overall PT/TL to encompass the wider range of potential learning outcomes from SE (Hoggan, 2016).

Data Analysis and Interpretation

Survey data was analysed using SPSS 22 and included two-tailed t-tests, analysis of variance (ANOVA), chi-square tests and Cronbach's alpha (Pallant, 2016). Significance was set at the 5 per cent level. Open responses to LAS and supplementary questions were coded and interpreted via Mezirow's (2000) learning domains (instrumental, communicative and transformative) and by key factors and influences in the augmented LAS (King, 2009).

3. FINDINGS AND DISCUSSION

Findings from the augmented LAS are reported here in terms of the five specific study objectives and discussed in the context of potential learning influences and outcomes from TL theory (Hoggan, 2016) and SE studies.

Incidence of TL

In this study, TL experiences were broadly interpreted as any change in respondents' worldviews, attitudes and behaviour, as well as the development of their skills for systems/complex thinking, teamwork/collaboration and their intended advocacy. An estimated 57 per cent of respondents experienced Overall PT/TL at varying levels towards sustainability. The rate is comparable to the study by Brock (2010) who found a rate of 48.8 per cent for undergraduate business students in a traditional classroom (US) and by Stone et al. (2017), who reported a rate of 59.0 per cent for students in overseas study programmes.

Importance of Precursor Steps

Individual precursor steps reported by respondents who experienced Overall PT/TL compared with those who did not experience Overall PT/TL are depicted diagrammatically in Figure 18.1. The relationship between the number of precursor steps and Overall PT/TL was examined with an independent samples t-test and a significant difference was found

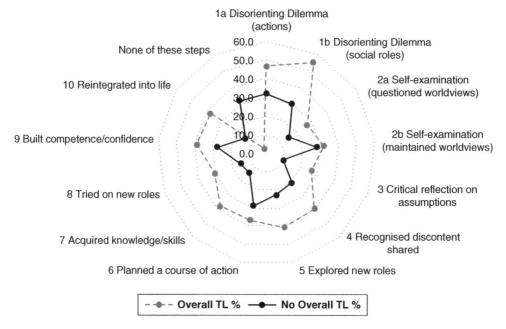

Figure 18.1   Precursor steps reported by Overall TL outcome

($t = -6.626, p < 0.001$) between groups. Those who experienced Overall PT/TL reported a mean of 4.49 precursor steps ($SD = 2.989$), while those who did not experience Overall PT/TL reported a mean of 2.50 steps ($SD = 1.955$). This finding supports the contention that experiencing more precursor steps enhances the potential for PT/TL in SE and may be useful in guiding curriculum design.

The relationship between individual precursor steps and Overall PT/TL is presented in Table 18.1. As expected, all steps were significant except item 2b of maintaining one's perspective. These findings provide empirical support for earlier studies (Brock, 2010; Stone et al., 2017) and highlight the importance of the disorienting dilemma, which is considered a key element in TL. Respondents' comments referred to a greater awareness of their own impact on sustainability, their own ignorance and the challenges and opportunities of fostering social change.

Both TL theory and previous research posit that critical reflection and self-reflection are important triggers for experiencing TL (Madsen and Cook, 2010). However, this study found a low rate of critical reflection and a low correlation with Overall PT/TL (refer to Step 3 in Table 18.1). Students may have misinterpreted the LAS statements on 'reflection' (see the Appendix) or not recognised the critical reflection inherent in learning complex conceptual frameworks such as 'systems thinking'. Indeed, the low rate of critical reflection in this study (only 26.3 per cent of respondents with Overall PT/TL) was similar to results for undergraduate business students (26.6 per cent) reported by Brock (2010). To foster more reflexive and deeper student learning, educators are encouraged to include learning and assessment activities that specifically embed critical and self-reflection and the sharing of learning experiences.

Table 18.1 Frequencies of reported precursor steps and association with Overall PT/TL

Phase/PT Precursor Step	Total Responses (n)	Share of Total Respondents (%) (n = 301)	Number (n) and Share (%) of Overall PT/TL Respondents[a] (n = 171)	Chi-square[b] (Yates Correction)	P[c]	Number (n) and share (%) of No Overall PT/TL Respondents[a] (n = 130)
1a: Disorienting dilemma (actions)	112	37.2	80 (46.8)	14.600	< 0.001**	32 (24.6)
1b: Disorienting dilemma (social roles)	124	41.2	94 (55.0)	29.709	< 0.001**	30 (23.1)
2a: Self-examination (questioned worldviews)	61	20.3	46 (26.9)	9.856	0.002**	15 (11.5)
2b: Self-examination (maintained worldviews)	82	27.2	54 (31.6)	3.267	0.071	28 (21.5)
3: Critical reflection on assumptions	55	18.3	45 (26.3)	15.928	< 0.001**	10 (7.7)
4: Recognised discontent shared	89	29.6	68 (39.8)	18.655	< 0.001**	21 (16.2)
5: Explored new roles	93	30.9	70 (40.9)	17.615	< 0.001**	23 (17.7)
6: Planned a course of action	92	30.6	63 (36.8)	6.682	0.010*	29 (22.3)
7: Acquired knowledge/skills	79	26.2	65 (38.0)	26.925	< 0.001**	14 (10.8)
8: Tried out new roles	67	22.3	52 (30.4)	14.128	< 0.001**	15 (11.5)
9: Built competence/confidence	93	30.9	66 (38.6)	10.174	< 0.001**	27 (20.8)
10: Reintegrated into life	78	25.9	64 (37.4)	25.966	< 0.001**	14 (10.8)
None of these steps	37	12.3	5 (2.9)			32 (24.6)

Notes:
a. Number and share of Overall PT/TL (or No Overall PT/TL) respondents who selected the precursor step.
b. Relationship between individual precursor steps and the experience of Overall PT/TL.
c. Significance levels: * $p < -0.05$, ** $p < -0.01$.

Influences on TL

The personal context or 'positionality' (Taylor, 2017) of students was expected to influence their 'readiness to change' (Griswold, 2007; Sidiropoulos, 2018; Taylor, 2000). However, Overall PT/TL was not influenced by any demographic or educational variable or by their reason for enrolling in the unit (compulsory or elective). One possible explanation is that holistic sustainability simply overwhelmed the general positionality of learners. That is, a student's personal context may not have influenced whether they experienced Overall PT/TL, but only the type of learning outcome. This could be investigated further in future studies through qualitative inquiries.

The only significant influence of positionality on Overall PT/TL was the perceived importance of sustainability to the learner's study programme [X^2 (4, $n = 301$) $= 32.55$, $p < 0.001$], their profession [X^2 (4, $n = 301$) $= 22.93$, $p < 0.001$)] and everyday lives [X^2 (4, $n = 301$) $= 32.81$, $p < 0.001$)]. As shown in Figure 18.2, the magnitude of perceived importance was asymmetric in its effect, particularly the importance of sustainability to their study programme and profession. Respondents who regarded sustainability as 'very important' were twice as likely to experience Overall PT/TL, while respondents who perceived sustainability as 'unimportant' were two to four times more likely not to experience Overall PT/TL. This finding confirms previous studies on the influence of motivation and resistance to TL (Glisczinski, 2007; Karol and Mackintosh, 2011) and supports the contention that 'transformations need strong motivation and cannot be expected to occur without this' (Illeris, 2014, p. 583). To enhance motivation in SE, educators could connect to the 'psychological or practical potentials in learners' existence and life world . . . (to) . . . justify the exertion required for transformation' (ibid., pp. 583–4). Educators are encouraged to highlight the importance of sustainability at the outset to motivate students and provide the 'fuel' for TL.

The influence of situational factors during the semester/unit on Overall PT/TL was explored through chi-squared and ANOVA tests. Overall PT/TL ($p < 0.001$) was influenced by personal support – specifically teacher support and support by others (friends and partners) – and by educational activities – specifically class/group projects, term papers/essays, class activities/exercises, assigned readings and online resources. These findings reinforced the importance of having a safe and supported space within which to voluntarily reflect on, discuss and traverse the discomfort of a disorienting dilemma (Lange, 2004; Pace, 2010). Educators are encouraged to provide support and tools to navigate their students through the challenge of holistic sustainability.

Learning Outcomes of SE

A range of learning outcomes was expected based on the TL and SE literature, with students challenged to 'reflect on the *content* of the problem, the *process* of problem solving, or the *premise* of the problem' (Mezirow, 1994, p. 224; original emphasis). The key learning outcomes are summarised and presented in Table 18.2.

As expected, reported learning outcomes extended beyond epistemic change and covered the cognitive, affective and conative domains. Outcomes spanned changes in worldview, self, epistemology, ontology, behaviour and capacity and aligned with many UN SDGs. Respondents often reported multiple learning outcomes that were coded as

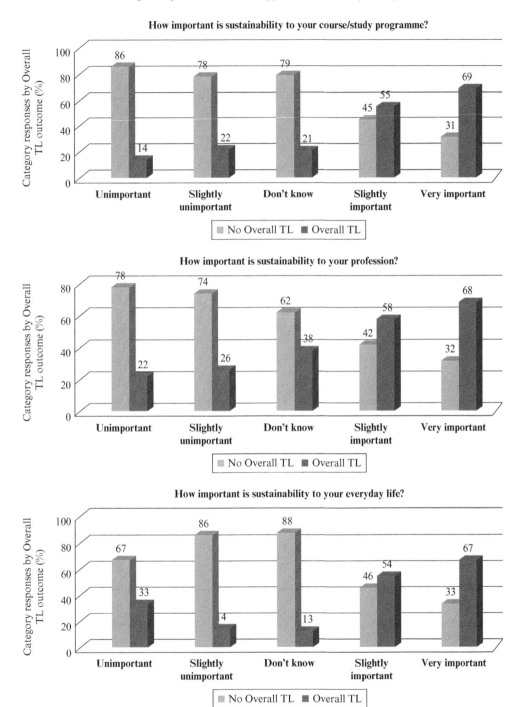

Figure 18.2   Overall TL outcome by measures of perceived importance of sustainability

Table 18.2   Types of reported educational outcomes in Overall PT/TL

Type of Transformative Learning Experience Reported[a]	Number of Responses ($n = 223$)	Share of Responses (%)	IL/CL[b]
Re-evaluating/planning to take OR have taken stronger actions for sustainability personally (3)	26	12	IL
Realised importance of sustainability issues and human impacts (8)	26	12	IL
More acutely aware of limited resources, inefficiency/waste and protecting the environment (9)	19	9	IL
The power of systems thinking to address problems (13)	19	9	IL
Developed stronger/deeper analytical skills, critical thinking (12)	16	7	IL
Appreciation of wicked problems (4) and iceberg model (5)	14	6	IL
See the positive effect and need for individual behaviour change (6)	14	6	IL
Broadened/widened perspectives (5)	13	6	IL
Recognised need (2)/difficulty (2)/capability (3) to act for wider social change	12	5	CL
Appreciate complexity/importance of three pillars of sustainability (5)	8	4	IL
Greater self-awareness (1) and independent views/thinking process	7	3	CL
Feel stimulated to take greater action to cause change	5	2	CL
Greater knowledge of business/economics (3)	5	2	IL
Worldview shifted with respect to social issues (1)	5	2	IL
'Woken up'/'opened eyes'/'mindstorm'/shifted values	4	2	CL
Concerned/cared more about sustainability	4	2	CL
Re-evaluated business and government role to create sustainability (1)	4	2	CL
Importance and value of teamwork/interpersonal relationships (1)	4	2	CL
Changed behaviour with family and friends (1)	3	1	CL
See new sustainable business opportunities	2	1	CL
Re-evaluated overall roles and expectations of people generally	1	0	CL
No answer	9	4	

Notes:
a. Numbers in brackets refer to responses to supplementary question on key skills/knowledge learnt during the SE unit.
b. IL denotes instrumental learning and CL represents communicative learning.

instrumental learning (IL), that is, knowledge, skills and cognitive understandings or communicative learning (CL), that is, insights into both one's own and others' values and interests.

The dominance of IL and CL outcomes in this study is consistent with TL theory and with previous studies in SE (El-Deghaidy, 2012; Howlett et al., 2016; Kokkarinen and

Cotgrave, 2013). Both IL and CL are important enablers that scaffold the development of sustainability competencies. Instrumental learning is an important contributor to TL, contributing directly to foundational knowledge and skills (Hales and Jennings, 2017; Noy et al., 2017), indirectly in combination with CL (Quinn and Sinclair, 2016) and over time (Singer-Brodowski, 2017; Winter et al., 2015; Zoller, 2015). Respondents reported IL as greater knowledge and awareness of environmental and sustainability issues as well as building cognitive skills. Findings in this study support the complementarity between IL and CL and reinforce the importance of IL as potential triggers of TL and as key elements of sustainability competencies. Accordingly, educators are encouraged to integrate holistic sustainability concepts into all core units of tertiary programmes in order to foster IL and incremental changes, instead of relying exclusively on interdisciplinary SE units for more substantive TL outcomes.

Communicative learning (CL) is given primacy in TL and SE where understanding one's own and others' values and motives is critical to collaboratively co-creating more sustainable outcomes (Wiek et al., 2011). In this study, CL was evidenced as greater autonomy and independence, a greater realisation of the importance and development of skills for teamwork/collaboration and an appreciation of the mechanisms, challenges and opportunities for social change. These findings highlight the importance of investigating diverse perspectives in holistic sustainability and demonstrate how SE contributes to the development of sustainability literacy and competence in students.

Transformative learning does not generally occur from a single experience (Taylor, 2017) but can build over long periods of time and emerge as a result of 'synergistic conditions'. In this study, respondents reported varying degrees of personal change from none to incremental change and even epochal transformation. Most respondents reported PT as gradual, with limited cases of epochal transformation. Findings in this study support the notion that TL builds over incremental learning experiences and often requires great effort.

Competency, Personal Agency and Advocacy for Sustainability

Significant relationships were found between Overall PT/TL and the development of self-reported competence, advocacy and agency for sustainability ($p < 0.001$). Respondents who experienced Overall PT/TL reported very high rates of individual learning (i.e., competence) to identify and address sustainability challenges (94 per cent) with progressive declines in their agency to advocate for the environment/sustainability (89 per cent) and for wider social change (65 per cent). Respondents indicated changes in their actual and planned personal behaviour and in their intended advocacy within their private sphere. Few students mentioned changes in behaviour or actions in their professional sphere with limited instances of advocacy/agency for wider societal change. These results are consistent with findings in previous SE studies of limited effects on wider system change (Kalsoom and Khanam, 2017; Lange, 2004; Miller, 2016; Quinn and Sinclair, 2016).

4.   CONCLUSION

The renewed emphasis on sustainability education (SE) and transformative learning (TL) by the United Nations (UNESCO, 2016) heightens the imperative to measure learning outcomes in HE. Yet, there is no standard quantitative measure to assess TL outcomes from such interventions. The Learning Activities Survey (LAS) is a simple instrument used to investigate TL for adults in a variety of contexts. This chapter reports on a study that applied an augmented LAS instrument to measure TL in SE units at two universities in Australia. The LAS was augmented with supplementary questions to explore key learning influences and outcomes in a SE context.

The study demonstrated TL theory as a relevant conceptual framework to guide pedagogy and assess outcomes in SE. Holistic sustainability was a confronting concept that triggered a wide range of learning outcomes in worldview, self, epistemology, ontology, behaviour and capacity. Instrumental and communicative learning outcomes were important contributors to students' TL experiences and supports the notion of cumulative learning over time from repeated SE exposure. To enhance the likelihood of TL for sustainability in HE, this chapter recommends both disciplinary and interdisciplinary approaches to SE in the curriculum. This study also demonstrated the effectiveness of an augmented LAS, which is proposed as a useful first step to assess SE in an HE context.

The standard LAS instrument has some limitations, with further research recommended to test, refine and calibrate the instrument in other SE settings. The use of self-reported data for measures of worldview, knowledge, attitudes and behaviour face limitations of reliability and validity (Gonyea, 2005). Statements intended to operationalise the TL constructs of 'reflection', 'action' and 'building confidence' could be misunderstood by students. To address this shortcoming, scholars could augment the LAS with triangulating questions (Creswell, 2009) and/or include complementary qualitative methods such as in-depth interviews and/or reflective journals to enable deeper explorations of how students experience TL. Another limitation is that the LAS is based on retrospection and a respondent's ability to accurately recall their previous knowledge, attitudes, abilities and behaviour, which are subject to error and bias (Mayhew et al., 2016). An alternative is to adopt a pre-post method, preferably with matched respondents. Results from the LAS would also be further strengthened by including comparable control groups. Finally, findings in this study are limited to SE units at two Australian universities and may not generalise to other HE settings in Australia or in other contexts.

Despite these limitations, it is considered that the augmented LAS could be applied across a wider range of settings to ascertain any generalisability of results and to compare predictors of TL and outcomes from SE in different contexts. Further research could investigate the relationship between students' 'positionality' and the type of learning outcome experienced during their studies. The research could investigate the influence of a range of facilitative conditions, the discipline of study and learner characteristics, including 'transformational readiness' (Griswold, 2007). Future studies could explore student perceptions of their agency to impact sustainability in their personal and professional lives and identify key influences on the emergence of wider agency. Finally, future research could investigate whether students' perceived competence for sustainability issues/challenges translates into professional skills/competencies.

Tertiary educators planning to incorporate SE could reference the TL model and

Mezirow's precursor steps to scaffold their students' TL and utilise an augmented LAS to track learning outcomes and identify the key factors that contribute to cognitive, affective and conative changes in student sustainability dispositions. Transformation is complex and deeply personal (Kelly, 2010) and while it cannot be predicted or guaranteed, sustainability educators can create 'synergistic conditions' for TL by connecting the pedagogic 'tools' with student 'fuels' of personal motivation and life experiences.

ACKNOWLEDGEMENTS

Sincere thanks are extended to research collaborators at participating universities and especially to students who participated in the study. Reviewer comments on earlier drafts of this chapter are greatly appreciated. This work was supported by funding from the Australian Government Research Training Program Scholarship.

REFERENCES

Boyd, R.D. and Myers, J.G. (1988). Transformative education. *International Journal of Lifelong Education*, 7(4), 261–84.

Brock, S.E. (2010). Measuring the importance of precursor steps to transformative learning. *Adult Education Quarterly*, 60(2), 122–42.

Cheney, R.S. (2010). Empirical measurement of perspective transformation, 1999–2009. Paper presented at the 29th Annual Midwest Research-to-Practice Conference in Adult, Continuing, Community and Extension Education, Michigan State University, 26–28 September.

Cranton, P. (1994). *Understanding and Promoting Transformative Learning: A Guide for Educators of Adults.* San Francisco, CA: Jossey-Bass.

Cranton, P. (1996). *Professional Development as Transformative Learning: New Perspectives for Teachers of Adults.* San Francisco, CA: Jossey-Bass Publishers.

Cranton, P. and Kasl, E. (2012). A response to Michael Newman's 'Calling transformative learning into question: some mutinous thoughts'. *Adult Education Quarterly*, 62(4), 393–8.

Creswell, J.W. (2009). *Research Design: Qualitative, Quantitative, and Mixed Methods Approaches* (3rd ed.). Thousand Oaks, CA: SAGE Publications.

Crotty, M. (1998). *The Foundations of Social Research: Meaning and Perspective in the Research Process.* London: SAGE Publications.

Dirkx, J.M. (2001). The power of feelings: emotion, imagination, and the construction of meaning in adult learning. *New Directions for Adult and Continuing Education*, 2001(89), 63–72.

Dirkx, J.M. (2006). Engaging emotions in adult learning: a Jungian perspective on emotion and transformative learning. *New Directions for Adult and Continuing Education*, 2006(109), 15–26.

Dirkx, J.M., Mezirow, J. and Cranton, P. (2006). Musings and reflections on the meaning, context, and process of transformative learning: a dialogue between John M. Dirkx and Jack Mezirow. *Journal of Transformative Education*, 4(2), 123–39.

El-Deghaidy, H. (2012). Education for sustainable development: experiences from action research with science teachers. *Discourse and Communication for Sustainable Education*, 3(1), 23–40.

Feriver, Ş., Teksöz, G., Olgan, R. and Reid, A. (2016). Training early childhood teachers for sustainability: towards a 'learning experience of a different kind'. *Environmental Education Research*, 22(5), 717–46.

Glisczinski, D.J. (2007). Transformative higher education: a meaningful degree of understanding. *Journal of Transformative Education*, 5(4), 317–28.

Gonyea, R.M. (2005). Self-reported data in institutional research: review and recommendations. *New Directions for Institutional Research*, 2005(127), 73–89.

Griswold, W. (2007). Transformative learning in a post-totalitarian context: professional development among school teachers in rural Siberia. Doctor of Philosophy dissertation, Kansas State University. Accessed 17 October 2017 at http://hdl.handle.net/2097/454.

Gunnlaugson, O. (2007). Shedding light on the underlying forms of transformative learning theory: introducing three distinct categories of consciousness. *Journal of Transformative Education*, 5(2), 134–51.

Hales, R. and Jennings, G. (2017). Transformation for sustainability: the role of complexity in tourism students' understanding of sustainable tourism. *Journal of Hospitality, Leisure, Sport & Tourism Education*, 21(Part B), 185–94.

Hoggan, C. (2016). A typology of transformation: reviewing the transformative learning literature. *Studies in the Education of Adults*, 48(1), 65–82.

Howlett, C., Ferreira, J.-A. and Blomfield, J. (2016). Teaching sustainable development in higher education: building critical, reflective thinkers through an interdisciplinary approach. *International Journal of Sustainability in Higher Education*, 17(3), 305–21.

Illeris, K. (2014). Transformative learning re-defined: as changes in elements of the identity. *International Journal of Lifelong Education*, 33(5), 573–86.

Johnson, R.B. and Onwuegbuzie, A.J. (2004). Mixed methods research: a research paradigm whose time has come. *Educational Researcher*, 33(7), 14–26.

Kalsoom, Q. and Khanam, A. (2017). Inquiry into sustainability issues by preservice teachers: a pedagogy to enhance sustainability consciousness. *Journal of Cleaner Production*, 164(Suppl. C), S1301–S1311.

Karol, E. and Mackintosh, L. (2011). Analysing the lack of student engagement in the sustainability agenda: a case study in teaching architecture. *International Journal of Learning*, 17(10), 219–36.

Kelly, P. (2010). Can we make the changes? Insights from the edge. *Journal of Futures Studies*, 15(1), 77–90.

King, K.P. (1998). Facilitating perspective transformation in adult education programs: a tool for educators. Paper presented at the Pennsylvania Adult and Continuing Education Research Conference, Chester, Pennsylvania, 21 March.

King, K.P. (2009). *The Handbook of the Evolving Research of Transformative Learning Based on the Learning Activities Survey*. Charlotte, NC: Information Age Publishing.

Kokkarinen, N. and Cotgrave, A.J. (2013). Sustainability literacy in action: student experiences. *Structural Survey*, 31(1), 56–66.

Lange, E.A. (2004). Transformative and restorative learning: a vital dialectic for sustainable societies. *Adult Education Quarterly*, 54(2), 121–39.

Leal Filho, W., Raath, S. and Lazzarini, B. et al. (2018). The role of transformation in learning and education for sustainability. *Journal of Cleaner Production*, 199, 286–95.

Madsen, S.R. and Cook, B.J. (2010). Transformative learning: UAE, women, and higher education. *Journal of Global Responsibility*, 1(1), 127–48.

Mayhew, M.J., Hoggan, C., Rockenbach, A.N. and Lo, M.A. (2016). The association between worldview climate dimensions and college students' perceptions of transformational learning. *Journal of Higher Education*, 87(5), 674–700.

Merriam, S. (2004). The changing landscape of adult learning theory. *Review of Adult Learning and Literacy: Connecting Research, Policy, and Practice*, 14(6), 199–220.

Mezirow, J. (1994). Understanding transformation theory. *Adult Education Quarterly*, 44(4), 222–32.

Mezirow, J. (2000). Learning to think like an adult: core concepts of transformation theory. In J. Mezirow and Associates (eds), *Learning as Transformation: Critical Perspectives on a Theory in Progress* (pp. 3–33). San Francisco, CA: Jossey-Bass.

Mezirow, J. (2009). An overview on transformative learning. In K. Illeris (ed.), *Contemporary Theories of Learning: Learning Theorists . . . In Their Own Words* (pp. 90–105). New York: Routledge.

Miller, H.K. (2016). Undergraduates in a sustainability semester: models of social change for sustainability. *The Journal of Environmental Education*, 47(1), 52–67.

Noy, S., Patrick, R., Capetola, T. and McBurnie, J. (2017). Inspiration from the classroom: a mixed method case study of interdisciplinary sustainability learning in higher education. *Australian Journal of Environmental Education*, 33(2), 97–118.

O'Sullivan, E. (1999). *Transformative Learning: Educational Vision for the 21st Century*. New York: Zed Books.

Pace, P. (2010). Education for sustainable development: current fad or renewed commitment to action? *Journal of Baltic Science Education*, 9(4), 315–23.

Pallant, J. (2016). *SPSS Survival Manual: A Step by Step Guide to Data Analysis Using IBM SPSS* (6th ed.). Maidenhead, UK: McGraw-Hill.

Quinn, L.J. and Sinclair, A.J. (2016). Undressing transformative learning: the roles of instrumental and communicative learning in the shift to clothing sustainability. *Adult Education Quarterly*, 66(3), 199–218.

Rittel, H.W.J. and Webber, M.M. (1973). Dilemmas in a general theory of planning. *Policy Sciences*, 4(2), 155–69.

Ryan, A. and Cotton, D. (2013). Times of change: shifting pedagogy and curricula for future sustainability. In S. Sterling, L. Maxey and H. Luna (eds), *The Sustainable University: Progress and Prospects* (pp. 151–67). London: Earthscan.

Schwartz, T. (2013). Examination of factors that promote transformative learning experiences of college-level adult learners of foreign languages. Dissertation, Auburn University. Accessed 2 December 2017 at http://etd.auburn.edu/handle/10415/3857.

Sidiropoulos, E. (2018). The personal context of student learning for sustainability: results of a multi-university research study. *Journal of Cleaner Production*, 181, 537–54.

Singer-Brodowski, M. (2017). Pedagogical content knowledge of sustainability: a missing piece in the puzzle of professional development of educators in higher education for sustainable development. *International Journal of Sustainability in Higher Education*, 18(6), 841–56.

Sipos, Y., Battisti, B. and Grimm, K. (2008). Achieving transformative sustainability learning: engaging head, hands and heart. *International Journal of Sustainability in Higher Education*, 9(1), 68–86.

Sterling, S. (2011). Transformative learning and sustainability: sketching the conceptual ground. *Learning and Teaching in Higher Education*, 5, 17–33.

Stone, G.A., Duerden, M.D. and Duffy, L.N. et al. (2017). Measurement of transformative learning in study abroad: an application of the learning activities survey. *Journal of Hospitality, Leisure, Sport and Tourism Education*, 21(Part A), 23–32.

Strange, H. and Gibson, H.J. (2017). An investigation of experiential and transformative learning in study abroad programs. *Frontiers: The Interdisciplinary Journal of Study Abroad*, 29(1), 85–100.

Taylor, E.W. (2000). Analyzing research on transformative learning theory. In J. Mezirow (ed.), *Learning as Transformation: Critical Perspectives on a Theory in Progress* (pp. 151–80). San Francisco, CA: Jossey-Bass.

Taylor, E.W. (2007). An update of transformative learning theory: a critical review of the empirical research (1999–2005). *International Journal of Lifelong Education*, 26(2), 173–91.

Taylor, E.W. (2017). Transformative learning theory. In A. Laros, T. Fuhr and E.W. Taylor (eds), *Transformative Learning Meets Bildung: An International Exchange* (pp. 17–29). Rotterdam: Sense Publishers.

Taylor, E.W. and Snyder, M.J. (2012). A critical review of research on transformative learning theory, 2006–2010. In E.W. Taylor, P. Cranton and Associates (eds), *The Handbook of Transformative Learning: Theory, Research, and Practice* (pp. 37–55). San Francisco, CA: Jossey-Bass.

UNESCO (2016). *UNESCO Global Action Programme on Education for Sustainable Development: Information Folder*. Paris, Accessed 29 March 2018 at https://unesdoc.unesco.org/ark:/48223/pf0000246270.

Wals, A.E.J. and Benavot, A. (2017). Can we meet the sustainability challenges? The role of education and lifelong learning. *European Journal of Education*, 52(4), 404–13.

Wiek, A., Withycombe, L. and Redman, C.L. (2011). Key competencies in sustainability: a reference framework for academic program development. *Sustainability Science*, 6(2), 203–18.

Winter, J., Cotton, D., Hopkinson, P.G. and Grant, V. (2015). The university as a site for transformation around sustainability. *International Journal of Innovation and Sustainable Development*, 9(3–4), 303–20.

Zoller, U. (2015). Research-based transformative science/STEM/STES/STESEP education for 'sustainability thinking': from teaching to 'know' to learning to 'think'. *Sustainability*, 7(4), 4474–91.

APPENDIX

Supplementary Questions in LAS

The LAS was augmented with supplementary questions related to respondents' main geographical region of residence, length of time in Australia and mode of study to reflect the characteristics of the population. Other questions explored prior learning for sustainability, conceptions of sustainability and sustainable development, perceived key skills required for graduates in their profession, and the importance of sustainability to their course, profession and personal lives. Questions also explored respondents' learning experiences during the subject/unit, important influences on their learning and types of learning outcomes, as follows:

- their tutor's role in perceived perspective change on sustainability;
- the most important sustainability skills/knowledge learnt in the subject/unit;

Table 18A.1   Correspondence between Mezirow's ten steps of PT and LAS item

Phase/Precursor Step to PT	LAS Item Wording in Q1
	Thinking back over the subject:
1a: Disorienting dilemma (actions)	I had an experience that caused me to question the way I normally act
1b: Disorienting dilemma (social roles)	I had an experience that caused me to question my ideas about social roles (e.g., how a graduate or professional should act)
2a: Self-examination (questioned worldviews)	As I questioned my ideas, I realised I no longer agreed with my previous beliefs or role expectations
2b: Self-examination (maintained worldviews)	As I questioned my ideas, I realised I still agreed with my beliefs or role expectations
3: Critical reflection on assumptions	As I questioned my ideas, I felt uncomfortable with traditional social expectations
4: Recognised discontent shared	I realised that other people also questioned their beliefs
5: Explored new roles	I thought about acting in a different way from my usual beliefs and roles
6: Planned a course of action	I tried to figure out a way to adopt these new ways of acting
7: Acquired knowledge/skills	I gathered the information I needed to adopt these new ways of acting
8: Tried out new roles	I tried out new roles so that I would become more comfortable or confident in them
9: Built competence/confidence	I began to think about the reactions and feedback from my new behaviour
10: Reintegrated into life	I took action and adopted these new ways of acting
	I do not identify with any of the statements above

Source: King (2009).

- the change in their attitudes and perceptions of sustainability/environment;
- the most important topic or activity during the subject and reason;
- their perceived capability to address sustainability challenges/issues, their intention to advocate more actively for the environment/sustainability and to become more involved in social change movements.

19. The need to build the concept of environment within the framework of the Sustainable Development Goals

Rocío Jiménez-Fontana, Esther García-González and Antonio Navarrete

1. INTRODUCTION

The Education Department of the University of Cádiz has been working for 11 years on the concept of environment with its students on the Andalusian Interuniversity Master's Degree in Environmental Education, as a prelude to their accessing the concept within the subject Environment and Environmental Education. This master's course has a multi-university character, with seven Andalusian universities participating. Classes are taught online simultaneously from all the universities through the Adobe Connect platform. The versatility of the system allows for continuous communication of the participants with their peers in the different universities, as well as the sharing of different types of information and documents.

The environmental educator must acquire a complex and systemic perspective on the environment to be able to recognize and identify opportunities to develop environmental education. And, due to the open and participatory nature of the United Nations Sustainable Development Goals (SDGs) and their considerable reception in different fields, their rise in importance represents an opportunity to be able to conduct environmental education. Given this situation, the question arises as to what extent research in the systemic and complex construction of the concept of environment might contribute to students' access to the SDGs, since these goals should guide actions towards a sustainable present and future (Shiel et al., 2016).

2. THEORETICAL FRAMEWORK

2.1 The Concept of Environment in the Twenty-first Century

Environment articulates and integrates high-level basic concepts – meta-concepts – which enable its understanding and allow its application to be extended to very diverse fields of knowledge. These are unity-diversity, interaction, system and change (García, 1988, 1995; García and García, 1992; Grupo Investigación en la Escuela, 1991). From this perspective, environment can also itself be considered a meta-concept. For those afore-mentioned authors, meta-concepts are bridge notions that facilitate connections between disciplines – integrating concepts that function as an axis when articulating and guiding the formulation and organization of knowledge. Environment is in turn a structuring concept, since it serves as a junction type of node, generates a network of connections and forms a paradigmatic core (Morin, 1991) that, when constructed, allows data to be treated from another conceptual perspective and new knowledge to be reorganized and elaborated. In the present research study, understanding environment from this complex and systemic perspective allows one to address the major problems of humanity and their possible solutions – basic issues for a prospective environmental educator – from the perspective of the logic of the SDGs.

Historically, the concept of environment has evolved at the same time as knowledge about environmental issues. It has gone from being understood as an inexhaustible provider of resources and capable of self-generation to be conceived of as a fragile system threatened by its interaction with humans. Thus, in many cases, one observes that there still exists a utilitarian naturalistic vision, as is reflected in several papers about conceptions related to environment (Álvarez-García, Sureda-Negre and Comas-Forgas, 2018; Quintero and Solarte, 2019; Sauvé, 2004a).

This naturalistic vision of environment is a clear reflection of the simplifying vision of previous times (Morin, 1991). The controversy arises from an epistemological and, therefore, philosophical and scientific point of view. Positivism and classical science have left an inheritance based on individualism, objectivity, rigour, an elitist access to certain knowledge as the only and absolute truth, a system of values, superficiality and a simplifying culture that has had serious implications for the way people develop as individuals, society and a species (Jiménez-Fontana et al., 2014), as well as conditioning knowledge of the world. One of the main objectives of classical science for several centuries was to eliminate the uncertain, indeterminate, imprecise and complex, and to be able, through knowledge and action, to control and dominate the world (Morin, 1984).

To this one must add that people are consumers of pre-formulated scientific ideas (Flores, 2008), which also include aspects such as opinions, beliefs, perceptions and conceptions. With regard to environment, this translates into a patching-things-up type of policy to try to mitigate the effects of environmental problems. It does not, however, facilitate any understanding of their causes, and thus hinders any modification of those causes (Flor, 2005). This philosophical–scientific paradigm is highly consistent with the structures of advanced capitalism (García, 1995). Reaching an understanding of environment that goes beyond the boundaries of what is understood as a natural ecosystem (a pond or a forest) requires the involvement of other dimensions. For instance, as noted by Novo (1997), it is crucial to understand that the city, the classroom and economic systems, among others, are also environmental systems that have a huge effect on global impacts (Quintero and Solarte, 2019). Sauvé (2004b) argues that the environment, being a culturally and contextually determined, socially constructed, reality, escapes from any precise, global and consensual definition.

For all these reasons, an environmental education limited to one or another of these representations would be incomplete, and would respond to just a reduced vision of the relationship with the world. Leff (2006) argues that environment is not ecology, but rather the field of relationships between nature and culture, of the material and the symbolic, of the complexity of being, and of thought.

2.2   Dialogue with Environmental Education

With what has been expressed so far in environmental education, one should work on the complementarity of order and disorder, of the logical and the contradictory, of certainties and uncertainties, when wishing to train people to provide alternatives to the problems generated by one's way of explaining how the world functions and of intervening in it (Flor, 2005). However, in the field of education, it is common to find that, in environmental education, ecology is still considered to be the centre of discourse, obviating all the cultural, political and economic aspects that configure the environment as an object of reflection (Quintero and Solarte, 2019).

Thus, the type of environmental education promoted by environmental educators constitutes a key indicator of their worldviews and of how they actually teach about the environment (Cottereau, 2001; González, 2003; Sauvé, 2004a, all cited in Calafell and Bonil, 2014). Therefore, there have been efforts made to characterize the worldviews on the environment that society, and environmental educators in particular, function under. Cardona (2012), cited in Quintero and Solarte (2019), argues that behind every environmental education practice there may be found the figure of an environmental educator, and, with this, a whole foundation based on the mobilization of previous knowledge, practices and conceptions that condition the construction of the corresponding pedagogical content knowledge.

2.3   The Trampoline of the Sustainable Development Goals

The United Nations Educational, Scientific and Cultural Organization (UNESCO) has been insisting on the need to formulate systems to train educators so that they can face the challenges in social and political contexts and the urgent needs that educational institutions must systematically address. An example is the Agenda 2030, which includes the SDGs (UNESCO, 2016). In this agenda, education is recognized as a means to achieve these objectives (Kioupi and Voulvoulis, 2019).

The SDGs adopted by the United Nations in 2015 contain the most ambitious global agenda approved by the international community to mobilize collective action for common goals, putting forward systemic responses to a global and interrelated vision of sustainable development. These goals are universal, transformative and inclusive, and describe the main developmental challenges for humanity. They focus on key systemic barriers to sustainable development, such as inequality, sustainable consumption patterns, weak institutional capacity and environmental degradation (UNESCO, 2017).

2.4   SDGs in the Field of Education

Environmental education is not just about teaching sustainable development and adding new content to courses and training. Formal and non-formal contexts should be conceived of as places of learning and experience for sustainable development (UNESCO, 2017). This includes re-thinking different spheres, including research (UNESCO, 2014a), and recognizing them as key elements for institutional-level approaches (UNESCO, 2014b) so as to create diverse and multidisciplinary learning contexts, and holistically and comprehensively illustrate the SDGs (UNESCO, 2017). In this sense, environmental education allows every individual to contribute to achieving the SDGs by equipping that individual with the knowledge and skills needed not only to understand what these goals are, but also to contribute as an informed citizen to achieving the necessary transformation (ibid.).

However, similarly to the conceptualizations associated with the environment, the worldviews associated with environmental education and sustainable development themselves do not escape from reductionism and the parcelization separating environmental from economic perspectives (Bond and Morrison-Saunders, 2011; Borg et al., 2014; Fien and Tilbury, 2002). Moreover, the social aspects or the relationships between ecological and social problems (Sachs, 2012) are almost never taken into account (Albareda-Tiana, Vidal-Raméntol and Fernández-Morilla, 2018). As noted above, this occurs through a perpetuation of the reductionism existing in the base structure, the environment. In this way, it is to be expected that the SDGs will also be understood as separate entities, breaking the systemic spirit they possess and hindering their holistic application, which is key to facing humanity's socio-environmental problems.

In Spain, SDGs have been the subject of analysis of their presence in the teaching practices of the International University of Catalonia (ibid.). They have also been used as learning content in tune with active teaching methods, and thus to analyse the evolution of prospective teachers in their sustainability competencies and the decrease in their carbon footprint at the end of a didactic experience (Albareda-Tiana et al., 2019). However, there has yet to be any in-depth study of such students' knowledge about SDGs (Zamora-Polo et al., 2019).

In this sense, the present study focuses on determining which SDGs are to be found in the conceptions that a group of students who are prospective educators have about the environment. Knowledge of these conceptions is needed to design and implement training activities for environmental educators, since it constitutes an opportunity to address their models of environmental education and stimulate processes of change (Calafell and Bonil, 2014).

3.   METHODS

3.1   Context: The Didactic Sequence

The study was implemented in the framework of the subject Environment and Environmental Education in the Andalusian Interuniversity Master's Degree in Environmental Education. The instructional strategy aimed at stimulating the students' conceptions as future environmental educators has a duration of 12 presential hours and 36 non-presential hours. It is based on a constructivist-type participatory-collaborative process. The conceptions of those involved, the contrasts and reflections made in group sessions, the debates, consultation, collation and analysis of information, as well as inquiry and search for new sources, are the elements of the process with which this concept is constructed.

The didactic sequence comprises five activities. In the first, the students are asked:

Activity 1
To begin the process we ask you to individually take a sheet of paper and make a list of the words, concepts, actions, ideas . . . that come into your head upon hearing the word 'ENVIRONMENT'.

> ATTENTION: Not paragraphs, not definitions, a list of simple terms!
> This is an individual task!

The intention is for the students to explain their conceptions related to environment and to become aware of them.

Once this is done, they are asked to form contrast groups and do the second activity:

Activity 2
Now form small groups of 3, 4, or 5 people (not more than 4 or 5, not less than 3).
Without changing anything in each person's own list, you have to contrast the lists of the group members.

Exchange the information, see similarities in the meanings, concepts and ideas, as well as the disagreements. Discuss what you agree or disagree with.

Then
Make a new list of terms, now as a group, putting in first place those that a greater number of members agree on, 4 or 5, then 3 or 2, and finally 1 (after each term, indicate the number).

Express what concepts, words, ideas, relationships, groupings . . . have come up during the discussion that did not appear in the individual lists (list 2).

Express what discrepancies, issues, conflicts, or doubts have appeared during the 'discussion' process (list 3).

> ATTENTION: This is not a mechanical process. The intention is for the reflection and exchange of ideas as a way to go deeper into the theme we are dealing with.
> Later you will be given the format for sharing the information.

This activity seeks that on the one hand, upon detecting coincidences, they feel reinforced and secure in their contributions and trust the process, and that on the other, when they detect differences, they progress by discovering new terms and start the debate about which terms are part of the environment and which are not. They are also asked to list new terms (list 2), and also to express the discrepancies or doubts that arise (list 3).

Following this, all the groups present their three lists to the rest of the groups of their own university as well as those of the other universities. In this comparison among all the universities, they have to take notes and reflect both on the new terms in relation to their own individual and small group lists, and on the doubts and discrepancies the other groups have. In this way, the scope of the concept of environment is gone into in greater depth, and the difficulty of covering it is visualized, all in terms of their personal conceptions as well as those they have taken in during the process.

Once this is done, each small group is asked to draw up a three-column table in which the first column lists the new terms to be added to those already existing; the second, the new doubts or discrepancies that arose after the whole class large group pooling; and the third, those terms they reject.

Before analysing the results provided by this activity, they are asked to do the third activity:

Activity 3
We are going to leave the classroom, and go to the centre, the street, and if it is possible to a rooftop patio of a building, a terrace, or any high point that will allow one to view most of the surrounding landscape, environment.

We have to sharpen our sight and other senses to detect what is part of the environment during the outing, try not to miss anything. During the outing, one of you (chosen to be group secretary) will have to make a comprehensive list of all the terms mentioned by their fellow group members. They have to be written down in the same order as they are mentioned.

The intention with this activity is to make a more physical contact with the nearby environment in a group experience in which all the senses will be deployed as a resource for gathering new information.

With the results obtained from this, the fourth activity is put to them:

Activity 4. Contrast in groups the information gathered in the Activities 1 and 2 with that gathered during the outing, Activity 3.
1. When looking at, hearing, feeling, perceiving, our surroundings, what appeared that was not there before?
2. Has anything disappeared?
3. What was different?
4. In what we are doing, does anything catch your attention or is there anything that seems significant to you?

The last activity is done in the large group at each of the universities:

Activity 5. Back in class at each university, draft a poster-type size pictogram on paper.
Draw elements you identify as part of the environment. Let's all draw! Look at what the others are drawing to avoid repetitions! Don't take up too much space.
   Everyone should explain why they have drawn something if their classmates ask.
   As we continue with the process, join the elements that are present with arrows.
   ➤ ATTENTION: This is not a symbolic drawing representing the environment but a summa- tion of elements and relationships.

The intention with this activity is to capture a group pictorial image at each university in which, in addition to the constituent elements of the environment, there also appear the relationships established between them.

The photographs of the pictograms from the different universities are subsequently analysed in class, and the process of theoretical formalization of the concept of environ- ment begins. The spatiotemporal component is addressed first so as to discern the evolu- tion and change of certain complex relationships between diverse elements that function as a changing system, that is, the environment as a meta-concept.

3.2 Research Problem

The question orienting this research is focused on determining which SDGs are present in the conception of environment that a group of prospective environmental educator students who are doing the Andalusian Interuniversity Master's Degree in Environmental Education have after completing the subject Environment and Environmental Education. In the study, ten of the 11 academic years were selected: those from 2010–11 to 2019–20. A total of 458 students participated in the experi- ence. They came from various disciplines – biology, engineering, geology, education, sociology, geography, environmental sciences, marine sciences, and so on – given that the characteristics of the master's degree accommodate many areas of knowledge in line with the transdisciplinary nature of environment. To approach this problem, the following questions are gone into in depth:

1. What terms do the students of the master's programme associate with the concept of environment at the beginning and at the end of the process?
2. What is the difference between the SDGs present at the beginning of the subject and those present at the end?
3. How does the presence of the areas of natural, social and economic sustainable development, as well as their combinations (natural/social, natural/economic, and economic/social), vary from the beginning to the end of the process according to the SDGs identified?

The responses to these questions may, in a secondary plane, provide information about the validity for its purpose of the didactic sequence implemented in the subject Environment and Environmental Education.

The nature of the problem formulated oriented the research towards a qualitative approach. This allows phenomena to be studied in their natural context, in this case an educational process, with the intention of making sense of them from the analysis of the data (Denzin and Lincoln, 2005).

3.3   Instruments for the Collection and Analysis of Information

To obtain the information, the terms used in the different student lists were subjected to a content analysis procedure. Specifically, the sources of information were Activities 2 and 5 described in the didactic sequence section, which correspond to the initial and final moment of the said sequence. The intention was to analyse the concepts reflected in the documents (López-Noguero, 2002; Piñuel, 2002) and those deriving from iconic communication (Porta and Silva, 2003).

The information was classified, according to meaning, into the 17 SDGs (Figure 19.1) and the description that UNESCO makes of each. Prior to this classification, the data were cleansed, excluding terms that were not strictly related to the SDGs as well as those that were only contributed by a single member of the group in Activity 2 since it was a group activity.

1 NO POVERTY	2 ZERO HUNGER	3 GOOD HEALTH AND WELL-BEING	4 QUALITY EDUCATION	5 GENDER EQUALITY
6 CLEAN WATER AND SANITATION	7 AFFORDABLE AND CLEAN ENERGY	8 DECENT WORK AND ECONOMIC GROWTH	9 INDUSTRY, INNOVATION AND INFRASTRUCTURE	10 REDUCED INEQUALITIES
11 SUSTAINABLE CITIES AND COMMUNITIES	12 RESPONSIBLE CONSUMPTION AND PRODUCTION	13 CLIMATE ACTION	14 LIFE BELOW WATER	15 LIFE ON LAND
16 PEACE, JUSTICE AND STRONG INSTITUTION	17 PARTNERSHIPS FOR THE GOALS	SUSTAINABLE DEVELOPMENT GOALS		

Figure 19.1   SDGs

Table 19.1 *Relationship between the priority areas of sustainable development and the SDGs*

Natural	Social	Economic
SDG 6: Clean water and sanitation	SDG 2: Zero hunger	SDG 1: No poverty
SDG 13: Climate action	SDG 3: Good health and well-being	SDG 8: Decent work and economic growth
SDG 14: Life below water	SDG 4: Quality education	SDG 9: Industry innovation and infrastructure
SDG 15: Life on land	SDG 5: Gender equality	SDG 10: Reduced inequalities
	SDG 7: Affordable and clean energy	SDG 12: Responsible consumption and production
	SDG 11: Sustainable cities and communities	
	SDG 16: Peace, justice and strong institutions	
	SDG 17: Partnerships for the Goals	

Source: Adapted from Albareda-Tiana et al. (2018).

The cleansing process left two lists of terms, concepts, or ideas. One – the initial case – corresponded to Activity 2, and the other – the final case – to Activity 5. The nature of the information from the two activities was different. For Activity 2, it was a list of terms from which only information irrelevant for the research had been removed. For Activity 5, the symbols that appeared in the different pictograms were assigned terms that had been agreed on by consensus in the research team. Once the two lists had been prepared, a maximum of two SDGs were assigned to each of the terms since these are not necessarily exclusive to a single SDG, but can refer to more than one. An example in this regard is the word 'nature', which can refer to both SDG 14 'life below water' and SDG 15 'life on land'. As the result of this process, the list corresponding to Activity 2 comprised 1837 terms, of which 183 were different, and that corresponding to Activity 5 comprised 1537 terms, of which 393 were different.

In order to know how the scope of the concept of sustainable development varied according to the SDGs identified, an adaptation was applied of the relationship proposed in Albareda-Tiana et al. (2018) between the priority areas of sustainable development and the SDGs (Table 19.1).

The data were processed using the NVivo12 software package. This allowed one to determine the frequencies of the different SDGs identified in the analysis and create the corresponding word clouds.

4. RESULTS

The results will be organized in accordance with the three research questions listed in the preceding section.

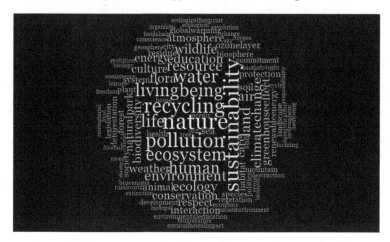

Figure 19.2   Initial words

4.1   Research Questions

Q1: What terms do the students of the master's programme associate with the concept of environment at the beginning and at the end of the process?
As noted above in the Methods section, the initial list of terms comprised a total of 183 different items. The different frequencies with which these were referred to are represented in Figure 19.2 by means of a word cloud in which how often the word is repeated is reflected in its size. Among the more frequent are *nature, sustainability, pollution, recycling, living being, ecosystem* and *water*. Less representative are *environmental education, global warming, ecological footprint* and *responsibility*. The presence of *human* is worth highlighting.

Similarly, Figure 19.3 shows the word cloud corresponding to the final list. In total, there are now 393 words, more than double the number of the initial cloud, which denotes that there has been an enrichment in the conceptualization of environment. Those that stand out are *cloud, sun, tree, mountain* and *rain*. New words appear that have less naturalistic connotations. Examples of this are *wind turbine, solar panel, telecommunications, factory, city, nuclear power station, emissions, car* and *money*. Also noteworthy, as in the initial case, is the presence of *human*, now with somewhat larger letters. This will be discussed in greater detail below. It gives clues to the opening of horizons towards dimensions of a more social and economic nature in the process of constructing the concept of environment.

Q2: What is the difference between the SDGs present at the beginning of the subject and those present at the end?
The differences that exist address two issues – the diversity and the frequency of the SDGs (Figure 19.4). With regard to diversity, all the SDGs are present at both times except for SDG 5 at the beginning. This gives clues to the presence of all the areas of sustainable development in the students' conceptions about environment. With regard to the frequency of the SDGs, it can be observed that the most significant at the beginning

Figure 19.3   Final words

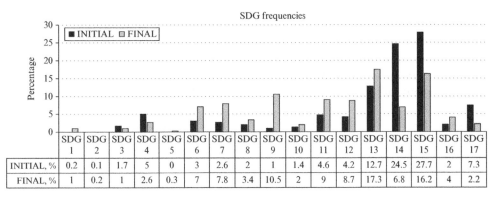

	SDG 1	SDG 2	SDG 3	SDG 4	SDG 5	SDG 6	SDG 7	SDG 8	SDG 9	SDG 10	SDG 11	SDG 12	SDG 13	SDG 14	SDG 15	SDG 16	SDG 17
INITIAL, %	0.2	0.1	1.7	5	0	3	2.6	2	1	1.4	4.6	4.2	12.7	24.5	27.7	2	7.3
FINAL, %	1	0.2	1	2.6	0.3	7	7.8	3.4	10.5	2	9	8.7	17.3	6.8	16.2	4	2.2

Figure 19.4   Initial and final SDG frequencies

of the process are SDG 14 (24.5 per cent) and SDG 15 (27.7 per cent), both linked to the natural area of sustainable development (Table 19.1). This leads one to think that the natural component is more present in the students' initial conceptions of environment. Indeed, as is shown in Figure 19.2, the most repeated terms for these SDGs are *nature, life, ecosystem, living being, tree, river, mountain*.

It is notable that the presence of both these SDGs has declined at the end of the process. For SDG 14 there is a decrease of 17.7 per cent, and for SDG 15 a decrease of 11.5 per cent. This means that the natural area lost weight at the end of the process in favour of the social and economic areas, and therefore that the students' conceptions to some extent evolved towards a more holistic view.

The third highest value at the beginning of the process corresponds to SDG 13. Some of the most representative terms that characterize this SDG are: *climate change, cloud, greenhouse, climate, emissions, air*. However, it has a greater presence at the end of the process where it represents 17.3 per cent versus the initial 12.3 per cent. Indeed, it is the most representative SDG at the end of the process. While it is true that this SDG is related to the natural area (Table 19.1), the actions necessary to fight climate change are not strictly natural as they were in the case of SDGs 14 and 15, which refer directly to life in ecosystems. Climate change is indirectly or directly attributed to human action (United Nations, 1992).

Focusing on the end of the process, in addition to the above, the frequency differences for SDG 9 (10.5 per cent compared to the initial 1 per cent) and for SDG 12 (8.7 per cent versus the initial 4.2 per cent) also stand out. Both SDGs are classified in the economic area of sustainable development. Some examples of the most repeated terms for these SDGs are *industry, power lines* and *telecommunications* for SDG 9, and *recycling, pollution* and *orchard* for SDG 12.

With regard to the SDGs classified in the social area, it is noteworthy that SDG 11 has doubled at the end of the process (9 per cent). Some terms corresponding to this SDG are *car, society* and *city*. The case is similar for SDG 7, affordable and clean energy, which has increased threefold over the initial value (7.8 per cent as against 2.6 per cent), and is characterized by terms such as *renewable energy* and *nuclear power plant*. However, SDG 17 has an insignificant presence at the end of the process as it is only 2 per cent of the total, while at the beginning it was 7.3 per cent. Classified in this SDG are terms such as *sustainability* and *awareness*.

Q3: How does the presence of the areas of natural, social and economic sustainable development, as well as their combinations (natural/social, natural/economic and economic/social) vary from the beginning to the end of the process according to the SDGs identified?

To answer this question, the classification presented in Table 19.1 was used. The possible combinations of SDGs were taken into account in calculating the representativeness, so that each combination resulted in a single datum, that is, a total of six possibilities were obtained: natural, social, economic, natural/social, natural/economic and economic/social.

Figure 19.5 shows how the representativeness of the different sustainable development areas, both classic and combined (which shall henceforth be denoted as hybrids), varied from the beginning to the end of the process. With regard to the hybrid areas, it is significant that two SDGs of different areas can be assigned to a same given term, as this indicates that the process that was developed, the conceptualization of environment, helps to overcome the parcelized vision of sustainable development by revealing the relationships between different areas. This is a necessary step to being able to progress towards a complex vision of sustainable development (Jabareen, 2008).

It is clear in the figure that the natural area is the most representative. The terms assigned to the two SDGs in this area constitute the majority. This reflects the strong natural tendency of the students' conceptions at both the initial and the final moments, coherent with the findings of other studies (Summers, Childs and Corney, 2005), although there was a relative decline at the end of the process. This is the case even though, in the classification used (Table 19.1), there are more SDGs in the social (8) and economic (5) areas than in the natural one (4). The natural area is followed in representativeness by the social area, which decreases at the end of the process. Together,

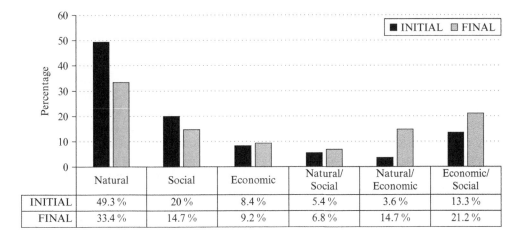

	Natural	Social	Economic	Natural/ Social	Natural/ Economic	Economic/ Social
INITIAL	49.3 %	20 %	8.4 %	5.4 %	3.6 %	13.3 %
FINAL	33.4 %	14.7 %	9.2 %	6.8 %	14.7 %	21.2 %

Figure 19.5   Initial and final classic and hybrid areas of sustainable development

the classic natural and social areas account for almost three-quarters at the beginning, and decrease to half of the total at the end. The economic area, however, does not undergo any variation.

With respect to the hybrid areas, the natural/social area undergoes practically no change, but the natural/economic area increases four-fold from an initial 3.6 per cent to a final 14.7 per cent, and the economic/social area goes from 13.3 per cent to 21.2 per cent. These increases reflect the relationships between areas, a fundamental characteristic of a systemic understanding of environment. In sum, combined with the other two areas, the economic area gains ground by the end of the process.

Looking more deeply into the results obtained for the hybrid areas with the greatest differences, and taking into account that these correspond to SDGs assigned to each area of sustainable development, one can see that, at the beginning of the process, the areas most closely related are the economic and social. This is illustrated by terms such as *public transport*, which is an economic investment made available to all of society, *health*, which is a right that not all people have access to, and *food*, which, with responsible production and consumption, should help overcome famine. These terms are included in SDG 2, SDG 3, SDG 8, SDG 9, SDG 10, SDG 11, SDG 12 and SDG 16 At the end of the process, further SDGs appear – SDG 4, SDG 5 and SDG 7 – through such terms as *equality*, which alludes to gender, race and human beings in general, or *monuments* because of their consideration as infrastructure of a cultural nature.

The case of the natural/economic hybrid stands out because it undergoes the greatest increase. Some examples of its terms are *dumping into the sea*, as this has a direct impact on the natural environment and generally comes from an industrial economic activity, and *chicken* or *egg* as both are directly related to the food industry. The SDGs involved in this case are SDG 6, SDG 9, SDG 10 and SDG 12, SDG 13 and SDG 15. At the end, other SDGs are added – SDG 8, SDG 10 and SDG 14. There are terms such as *fishing vessel*, which corresponds to an economic activity whose resource is life below water, or *factory*, which corresponds to an economic activity that generates jobs but has serious consequences for climate change.

4.2   Other Results of Interest

As set out in the Methods section, an analysis was made of the two lists of terms extracted from the students' productions. From these lists, those terms without any strict relationship to the SDGs were removed. In both lists, *human* appeared as an element that the students identified as being part of environment. While this is not classifiable in any particular SDG, it is a key agent for the definition of SDGs, and therefore transversal to them. It is a structural element in the construction of the concept of environment that cannot be understood without the presence and interactions of humans in the areas that comprise it (Novo, 1985). At the beginning of the process, it has a representativeness of 41.38 per cent, which increases to 58.38 per cent at the end. In this sense, one might ask not so much about the quantification of its presence, but rather about the nature of that presence. In the pictogram of the final activity, there is evidence that the human is seen as an integral part of the environment since the term appears in the central positions of the chart and is related to the rest of the elements, when, in the more simplistic conceptions, humans are understood to be an external agent, outside of the concept of environment itself. The next step in utilitarian worldviews is usually to include this element as a consumer of resources, and therefore their administrator, but this does not mean that it is considered a part of environment. In more evolved, systemic and complex worldviews it begins to be integrated as simply another element. It would be interesting therefore to inquire into the specific characteristics for the inclusion of humans in the concept of environment. In any case, this finding is a clear indication that evolution of the concept of environment is taking place.

5.   DISCUSSION

An interpretation of the results presented above is that SDGs are always present in the conceptions that the master's course students have of the environment, although with nuances that can be broken down along the following lines.

First, there are more than twice as many terms associated with the concept of environment at the end (393) than at the beginning (183) of the course, indicative of an increase in diversity. The students' concept of environment at the end of the process thus has a much richer, more diverse, and more detailed meaning.

Second, the difference in the SDGs detected at the beginning and the end of the process is almost exclusively in their frequencies since, except for SDG 5, which only appears at the end, they are all present at both times. With regard to their representativeness, the most abundant at the beginning are SDGs 14 and 15, followed by SDG 13. The first two decline in abundance at the end, giving way to allusions to SDG 6, SDG 7, SDG 8, SDG 9, SDG 10, SDG 11, SDG 12, SDG 13 and SDG 16. It can therefore be affirmed that the fact of bringing out the complexity of the notion of the environment that future environmental educators are dealing with works as an integrating concept that articulates and guides the formulation and organization of knowledge, a structuring concept that generates a web of interconnections (Morin, 1991). At the same time, the didactic sequence fostering recognition of this complexity leads to greater diversity in the allusions to SDGs.

Third, the objective of the study was to see how these SDGs related to both the classic (natural, social and economic) and hybrid (natural/social, natural/economic and economic/social) areas of sustainable development, since reductionist visions tend to separate environmental and economic perspectives (Bond and Morrison-Saunders, 2011; Borg et al., 2014; Fien and Tilbury, 2002), and usually do not take social aspects or the relationship between ecological and social problems into account (Albareda-Tiana et al., 2018; Sachs, 2012). The results showed that allusions to the natural and social areas decreased at the end, while those to the economic area practically did not vary. This decrease was reflected in an increase in the relationships between dimensions, supporting the premise that the perceptions of these prospective environmental educators are increasing in complexity, as is reflected in the increase in economic/social and natural/economic relationships. In addition, within these hybrid areas, there was also an increase in the diversity of the SDGs, with those present at the beginning being maintained, but new ones being added. In this sense, recognition of the complexity of the concept of environment enhances the students' relational vision, supporting the idea that environment articulates and integrates high-level basic concepts such as the fact of interactions. These make it easier to understand the concept of environment, and allow its application to be extended to very diverse spheres of knowledge by functioning as bridge-notions that facilitate connections between disciplines (García, 1988, 1995; García and García, 1992; Grupo Investigación en la Escuela, 1991). This aspect translates into greater diversification and less parcelization of SDGs, one of the limitations recognized in the literature (Gómez-Gil, 2017).

Fourth, although the representativeness of the human being does not show any significant increase from the beginning to the end of the process, the nature of this element's presence merits analysis since one would infer from the literature that its inclusion is gradual, from simple and more utilitarian worldviews to complex worldviews of the environment in which the human being is integrated as just another element. This aspect could be related to the fact that the least accessible SDGs were SDG 1, SDG 2 and SDG 5, with the core of the problem in all three being humans themselves. However, if this element is not accepted as being an integral part of the environment, neither will it be seen as being a direct recipient of environmental problems. This aspect also advocates for the study's starting premise, in which greater realization of the complexity of the notion of environment allows better access to understanding SDGs.

Fifth, all of the above leads one to think that the didactic process followed contributes to an enrichment in the prospective environmental educators' conceptions of environment, and therefore to their understanding of SDGs.

And sixth, the fact that the results show an imbalance in the distribution between the classic and the hybrid areas might suggest that the evolution in the concept of environment, although clear, does not reach the established expectations. It is necessary to bear in mind, however, that these results have been treated as a single entity due to the nature of the study. In order to determine more reliably the evolution generated in the students, an analysis would have to include the groups as specific case studies. An even finer analysis would include a final individual activity in which terms associated with environment were again requested, and a subject-to-subject contrast was made of the resulting data. This would also reveal all the diversity of terms that characterize each of the SDGs. This and other aspects remain as open lines for future research. As proposed by UNESCO (2014a), it is essential to raise the profile of research of this type, associated with places of learning and experience for sustainable development (UNESCO, 2017), so that environmental education can allow all citizens to contribute to achieving the SDGs.

6.   CONCLUSIONS

A series of conclusions can be drawn from this research. The SDGs most referred to at the beginning (SDG 14 and SDG 15) are of a strictly natural nature, as has already been reported in the literature and noted from experience. In this line, as a general rule, the least accessible SDGs for the students are SDG 1, SDG 2 and SDG 5, to the point that this last one does not appear even once in the initial allusions during any of the 11 courses involving more than 400 students analysed.

As was posited at the beginning of this communication, bringing out the complexity of the concept of environment, as was done with the didactic proposal implemented, helps the students to access the SDGs better and more often. With environment having a much richer and more comprehensive meaning by the end of the process, the terms they connect with it are doubled in number and their diversity is greatly increased. The allusions to SDGs not only increase overall, but those to SDGs 14 and 15, of a strictly naturalistic nature, decrease, to the benefit of an increase in the diversity of other SDGs.

In addition, it is seen that bringing out the complexity of the environment concept helps to add complexity and depth to the vision of the students (future educators), an aspect that is evident in the increased multiplicity of the number of relationships established between areas of sustainable development, enhancing the diversity and reducing the fragmentation. In other words, the SDGs are less atomized, a nuance of vital importance for the successful achievement of the Agenda 2030 goals. All this underlines the need to inquire into the conceptions of future environmental educators, and how these conceptions are organized and interact with each other. If one accepts that the practices of environmental education are founded on the concepts that the environmental educators use, one deduces how important it is to get them to evolve towards positions more in line with a systemic perspective, crucial for understanding sustainability and working with the SDGs.

REFERENCES

Albareda-Tiana, S., García-González, E., Jiménez-Fontana, R. and Solís-Espallargas, C. (2019). Implementing pedagogical approaches for ESD in initial teacher training at Spanish universities. *Sustainability*, 11(18), Article 4927.

Albareda-Tiana, S., Vidal-Raméntol, S. and Fernández-Morilla, M. (2018). Implementing the Sustainable Development Goals at university level. *International Journal of Sustainability in Higher Education*, 19(3), 473–97.

Álvarez-García, O., Sureda-Negre, J. and Comas-Forgas, R. (2018). Assessing environmental competencies of primary education pre-service teachers in Spain. *International Journal of Sustainability in Higher Education*, 19(1), 15–31.

Bond, A. and Morrison-Saunders, A. (2011). Re-evaluating sustainability assessment: aligning the vision and the practice. *Environmental Impact Assessment Review*, 31(1), 1–7.

Borg, C., Gericke, N., Höglund, H.O. and Bergman, E. (2014). Subject- and experience-bound differences in teachers' conceptual understanding of sustainable development. *Environmental Education Research*, 20(4), 526–51.

Calafell, G. and Bonil, J. (2014). Identificación y caracterización de las concepciones de medio ambiente de un grupo de profesionales de la educación ambiental. *Enseñanza de las Ciencias*, 32(3), 205–25.

Denzin, N.K. and Lincoln, Y.S. (2005). *The SAGE Handbook of Qualitative Research*. London: SAGE.

Fien, J. and Tilbury, D. (2002). The global challenge of sustainability. In D. Tilbury, R.B. Stevenson, J. Fien and D. Schreuder (eds), *Education and Sustainability: Responding to the Global Challenge*. Gland, Switzerland: IUCN.

Flor, J.I. (2005). *Claves par la educación ambiental*. Santander: Centro de Estudios Montañeses.

Flores, R.C. (2008). Representaciones sociales del medio ambiente. *Perfiles Educativos*, 30(120), 33–62.

García, J.E. (1988). Fundamentos para la construcción de un modelo sistémico del aula. In R. Porlán, J.E. García and P. Cañal (eds), *Constructivismo y enseñanza de las ciencias*. Sevilla: Diada.

García, J.E. (1995). La transición desde un pensamiento simple hacia un pensamiento complejo en la construcción de un pensamiento escolar. *Investigación en la Escuela*, 27, 7–20.

García, J.E. and García F. (1992). Investigando nuestro mundo. *Cuadernos de Pedagogía*, 209, 10–12.

Gómez-Gil, C. (2017). Objetivos de Desarrollo Sostenible (ODS): una revisión crítica. *Papeles de Relaciones Ecosociales y Cambio Global*, 140, 107–18.

Grupo Investigación en la Escuela (1991). *Proyecto curricular IRES (Investigación y renovación escolar). Introducción y cuatro volúmenes*. Sevilla: Diada.

Jabareen, Y. (2008). A new conceptual framework for sustainable development. *Environment, Development and Sustainability*, 10(2), 179–92.

Jiménez-Fontana, R., Azcárate, P., García-González, E. and Navarrete, A. (2014). Sostenibilidad curricular en las aulas universitárias: el papel de los valores en la estructura del sistema de evaluación. Communication presented at the 26 Encuentros de Didáctica de las Ciencias Experimentales, Universidad de Huelva.

Kioupi, V. and Voulvoulis, N. (2019). Education for sustainable development: a systemic framework for connecting the SDGs to educational outcomes. *Sustainability*, 11, Article 6104.

Leff, E. (2006). Complejidad, racionalidad ambiental y diálogo de saberes. Article published in *Carpeta informativa del CENEAM 2000–2006*.

López-Noguero, F. (2002). El análisis de contenido como método de investigación. *XXI. Revista de Educación*, 4(4), 167–80.

Morin, E. (1984). *Ciencia con conciencia*. Barcelona: Anthropos.

Morin, E. (1991). *El método IV: las ideas, su hábitat, su vida, sus costumbres, su organización*. Madrid: Cátedra.

Novo, M. (1985). *Educación ambiental*. Madrid: Anaya.

Novo, M. (1997). *La educación ambiental: bases éticas, conceptuales y metodológicas*. Madrid: Universitas.

Piñuel, J.L. (2002). Epistemología, metodología y técnicas de análisis del contenido. *Estudios de Sociolingüística*, 3(1), 1–42.

Porta, L. and Silva, M. (2003). La investigación cualitativa: el análisis de contenido en la investigación educativa. *Anuario Digital de Investigación Educativa*, 14, 1–8.

Quintero, M. and Solarte, M.C. (2019). Las concepciones de ambiente inciden en el modelo de enseñanza de la educación ambiental. *Entramado*, 15(2), 130–47.

Sachs, J.D. (2012). From Millennium Development Goals to Sustainable Development Goals. *The Lancet*, 379, 2206–11.

Sauvé, L. (2004a). Uma cartografia das corrientes em educaçao ambiental. In M. Sato and I. Carvalho (eds), *Educação ambiental – pesquisa e desafios* (pp. 17–46). Porto Alegre: Artmed.

Sauvé, L. (2004b). Perspectivas curriculares para la formación de formadores en educación ambiental: reflexiones sobre educación ambiental. Article published in *Carpeta informativa del CENEAM 2000–2006*.

Shiel, C., Leal Filho, W., do Paço, A. and Brandli, L. (2016). Evaluating the engagement of universities in capacity building for sustainable development in local communities. *Evaluation and Program Planning*, 54, 123–34.

Summers, M., Childs, A. and Corney, G. (2005). Education for sustainable development in initial teacher training: issues for interdisciplinary collaboration. *Environmental Education Research*, 11(5), 623–47.

United Nations (1992). *United Nations Framework Convention on Climate Change*. Accessed 18 February 2021 at https://unfccc.int/resource/docs/convkp/conveng.pdf.

United Nations Educational, Scientific and Cultural Organization (UNESCO) (2014a). *Informe de Seguimiento de la EPT en el Mundo 2013/4. Enseñanza y aprendizaje: lograr la calidad para todos*. Paris: UNESCO.

United Nations Educational, Scientific and Cultural Organization (UNESCO) (2014b). *Declaración final de la Reunión Mundial sobre la EPT de 2014: el Acuerdo de Mascate*. Paris: UNESCO.

United Nations Educational, Scientific and Cultural Organization (UNESCO) (2016). *Education 2030: Incheon Declaration and Framework for Action for the Implementation of Sustainable Development Goal 4*. Paris: UNESCO.

United Nations Educational, Scientific and Cultural Organization (UNESCO) (2017). *Educación para los Objetivos de Desarrollo Sostenible. Objetivos de aprendizaje*. Paris: UNESCO.

Zamora-Polo, F., Sánchez-Martín, J., Corrales-Serrano, M. and Espejo-Antúnez, L. (2019). What do university students know about Sustainable Development Goals? A realistic approach to the reception of this UN program amongst the youth population. *Sustainability*, 11, Article 3533.

20. Interdisciplinary training for the transformation of teaching in the context of sustainability

Osvaldo Luiz Gonçalves Quelhas, Sergio Luiz Braga França, Marcelo Jasmim Meiriño, Gilson Brito Alves Lima, Luís Perez Zotes and Nicholas Van-Erven Ludolf

1. INTRODUCTION

Humankind has been going through a sustainability crisis that can be related to 'production and consumption patterns that are incompatible with the capacity of the biosphere to provide minimal biophysical conditions to support the human welfare of the present and future generations' (Comissão Econômica para a América Latina e o Caribe/Friedrich Ebert Stiftung [CEPAL/FES], 2019, p. 3). Such crisis brings along new challenges and opportunities for the sustainable development of organizations and society.

In this regard, continuing education is crucial to promote more sustainable lifestyles within the current context, and education for sustainable development (ESD) can prepare individuals to deal with problems that threaten sustainability (economic, social and environmental issues). ESD also aims to change attitudes and behaviors and foster the necessary competencies to shape a sustainable future beyond the knowledge and understanding of social and environmental issues (Segalàs Coral, Drijvers and Tijseen, 2018; United Nations Educational, Scientific and Cultural Organization [UNESCO], 2007).

According to Mintz and Tal (2013), sustainable development (SD) is one of the biggest challenges to be confronted by humankind in the twenty-first century. In this context, ESD, together with other actions, becomes an important agent for the promotion of a culture that, in addition to economic outcomes, take account of environmental and social outcomes to the same extent. ESD in higher education has a recent origin – most initiatives started after the Rio Earth Summit in 1992 and Agenda 21. Moreover, the role of education in the context of sustainability was only officially recognized by the United Nations (UN) through the declaration of the Decade of Education for Sustainable Development (DESD) (2005–14). Research studies and evaluations emerged after DESD, showing that higher education is seeking to transform teaching and research, so that higher education institutions (HEIs) can increasingly become agents in the promotion of sustainable living, although there is still a long way to go for these institutions in this regard (Dahlin and Leifler, 2018; Rose, Ryan and Desha, 2015; Segalàs et al., 2018).

Bringing the discussion into the context of Latin America and the Caribbean, a study conducted by CEPAL pointed out several challenges to be overcome by SD in the region. The study revealed an industrial standard: specialization in products with low technological complexity due to difficulties in the incorporation of technical progress, and the development of capacities that enable the access to dynamic markets with more added value, aggravating the external vulnerability of those countries in relation to developed countries (CEPAL/FES, 2019).

In the specific case of Brazil, the study shows high levels of structural heterogeneity of the production system. We can also observe deep production unevenness within specific economic sectors, among distinct sectors and different regions in Brazil. This unevenness is far above the average of those in developed countries, creating a core that generates inequalities that are spread and reproduced in society. This situation is represented by social and regional inequalities that might deepen because of some aspects of the sustainability crisis: global warming, for example, will increase the temperature in the Brazilian semi-arid regions and beyond, and might even increase the external vulnerability of Brazilian agriculture exports. In Brazil, this factor leads to the concentration of workforce in sectors with low productivity, remuneration and formality, in addition to few perspectives of social mobility.

According to CEPAL/FES (2019), without actions to confront this crisis, developing countries will deal with more serious structural problems, including poverty, migration, food security, loss of competitiveness and external vulnerability. In this sense, Mello et al. (2019) highlight some of the major challenges for Brazil in this context: improving the capacity of its workforce with focus on skill development; strengthening the link between education and employability; providing greater flexibility and mobility in labor markets; and an economic growth model that can create jobs. These authors also point out that, without updating workers' skills, the social disparity may rise to a level twice as high in the next decade. Increasing the skills of workers will require coordination between educators, governments and employers with a focus on the individuals with the lowest skills.

This case study discusses the Postgraduate Program in Management Systems (PPSIG), which is connected with the School of Engineering of Fluminense Federal University (UFF). It can be understood as a study in the research, teaching and extension areas, addressing projects for education, professionalization, training and innovation linked with the development of competencies, skills and attitudes for sustainability in businesses and society.

The main goal of PPSIG is meeting the current and future demands of national, regional and local SD through the training of professionals with systematic and diversified vision, capable of acting in the socio-environmental and economic transformation of institutions and society in an innovative way. Research projects and institutional exchange programs are proposed in order to achieve these results, in terms of economic, social, environmental and scientific impacts.

For this purpose, PPSIG is an articulation between the Doctorate in Sustainable Management Systems (DSM) and the Master's in Management Systems (MMS) to align academic, research and extension efforts that intend to combine areas of knowledge (hard and earth sciences, biological sciences, engineering, health sciences, agricultural sciences, management, humanities, linguistics, Portuguese and arts) and their applications with a focus on the qualification of researchers and on the needs of society.

Concerning the skills to be developed by those who participate in the PPSIG, the program considers that some skills deserve to be highlighted, such as systemic thinking, problem-solving abilities, working in interdisciplinary groups, critical thinking, contextualization and vision of the future. Researching sustainability skills, Quelhas et al. (2019)

found that these competencies are among the most important to stimulate the sustainable performance of organizations.

Three strategic guidelines stand out in the PPSIG:

1. Building competencies, promoting technological innovation and scientific development for the solution of problems with high social, economic and environmental impacts. Associated goals: integration with governments, private and third-sector institutions to promote applied research to solve problems with high social, economic and environmental impacts through the MMS and DSM. Promotion of the growth of employment, competitiveness and R&D.
2. Enhancing inter-institutional cooperation mechanisms with interdisciplinary postgraduate programs. Associated goals: development and enhancement of the technical-scientific events at the National Congress on Management Excellence (CNEG)/Innovation in Corporate Social Responsibility (INOVARSE) event aiming at the exchange of experiences to reduce social inequality, to improve work conditions and efficiency in the use of natural resources.
3. Internationalization of the PPSIG. Associated goals: integration through actions and permanent pragmatic mechanisms with the World Sustainable Development Research and Transfer Centre (WSD-RTC) and the international scientific event, the World Symposium on Sustainability Science and Research. These partnerships are relevant because their goal is to increase the incentives given to professors to further improve their actions at several levels, such as the elaboration of international cooperation projects, exchange of students and special visiting researchers, joint publications with renowned international researchers, and participation on the editorial board of international journals, among others, especially in the area of sustainable management systems.

The PPSIG strategic guidelines are continuously enhanced at the Annual Governance Meeting, with the participation of professors, students and former students, as well as representatives of public and private institutions from the third sector and society. From these annual meetings, practices, goals and broad themes of the program are updated, aiming to meet the current and future demands of society, in the context of SD. In this sense, Saboya et al. (2017) and Oliveira et al. (2019) highlight the importance of strategic planning to support decision making.

Much of the research carried out at PPSIG is applied research focused on the business environment and other areas. This model enables a partnership between academia and other sectors of society, strengthening the interdisciplinary character of the program.

There was a real inversion in the way potential research problems are constructed and favored: from an endogenous way, internally generated by research groups based on literature gaps, to an exogenous way, constructing empirical knowledge from real demands, which will inform or feed the creation of interdisciplinary theories.

Adopting a systematic approach, a holistic and interdisciplinary view means considering all aspects, as well as the intention among them and the attempt to foresee conflicts or problems by taking into account the environmental, social, economic and technical dimensions without subordinating any of them (Björnberg, Skogh and Strömberg, 2015; Guerra, 2016; Thürer et al., 2017).

The PPSIG is an integrative, comprehensive and dynamic proposal, aligned with socially relevant demands, without losing sight of the universalist perspective that characterizes science. The program understands that qualification, learning and research must advance together, without restricting the application of the results obtained from research projects in a specific sector, but shifting its critical and analytical potential to the demands and challenges of the state of Rio de Janeiro and other regions of the country.

The goals established by the PPSIG are linked with the UN Sustainable Development Goals (SDGs) and Agenda 2030. In this sense, the scope of the program is aligned with the following SDGs:

- SDG 4: Ensure inclusive and equitable quality education and promote lifelong learning opportunities for all.
- SDG 6: Ensure the availability and sustainable management of water and sanitation for all.
- SDG 8: Promote sustained, inclusive and sustainable economic growth, full and productive employment and decent work for all.
- SDG 9: Build resilient infrastructure, promote inclusive and sustainable industrialization and foster innovation.
- SDG 11: Make cities and human settlements inclusive, safe, resilient and sustainable.
- SDG 12: Ensure sustainable consumption and production patterns.
- SDG 13: Take urgent measures to combat climate change and its impacts.

2.   METHODOLOGY

In 1993, the Laboratory of Technology, Business Management and Environment (LATEC) was created. The laboratory is part of the School of Engineering at UFF. During its first years, it was composed of academics and market professionals with the most varied academic backgrounds. Nowadays, the LATEC/UFF is a national reference center that offers opportunities for management qualifications with a systematic approach aimed at fostering SD. Therefore, although the PPSIG conception had existed for 19 years in 2019, its multidisciplinary groundings were established more than 25 years ago when the LATEC was created.

Concerning its strategy, this study can be classified as bibliographic research, through which the concepts and discussions associated with the promotion of SD by graduate programs were raised. These concepts were necessary to analyze the results of the actions developed by PPSIG regarding sustainability, and, for the data survey, the authors of this chapter used scientific documents published in databases such as Scopus, Elsevier, Web of Knowledge, Emerald Insight and Scielo: 23 documents were selected for addressing the topic.

On the other hand, this research can also be characterized as a case study. According to Gil (2010), this type of approach is developed from all types of studies that have important information about the object of interest. In this sense, in addition to the bibliographic research, we searched PPSIG management reports of the last five years and information available on the website about the DMS and MMS (open information). A case study, according to Yin (2003), is a more directed and comprehensive research on a specific topic – here, the actions related to teaching and structuring of skills in the management of sustainable organizations. In this sense, we focused on PPSIG actions that could contribute to the formation of graduates capable of working in organizations in the context of sustainability, as well as the performance of the program in scientific and technological development. In the latter case, a survey was carried out in PPSIG's thesis and dissertation database, identifying those that contribute to the development of sustainability, whether in the social, environmental or economic dimension. This identification was carried out by reading the titles and abstracts of the dissertations and theses, and, when necessary, the conclusion.

Considering its nature, this study can be classified as applied (exploratory) research, since it describes and analyzes results without proposing new theories. Gil (2010) argues that in exploratory research, the idea is to deepen the topic of interest with interviews, bibliographic survey, and analyzing examples that help understanding, among other actions.

3.   IMPLEMENTATION PROCESS OF THE PPSIG

This section presents the main PPSIG programs and actions, and their relation to the promotion of sustainability.

3.1   Master's in Management Systems (MMS)

The efforts for the development of this interdisciplinary program (PPSIG) dates from the first semester of 1999, when UFF professors developed a plan for a master's program for the engineering area. The plan provided the integration of researchers who acted in the management area, and, from diverse theoretical, methodological and professional perspectives, they elaborated a project for the development of the MMS. As a result of the master's program, a project for the interaction of the various areas of knowledge interested in developing interdisciplinary research in management systems was elaborated. At that time, the Professional Master's Program in Management Systems was created (Resolution #36/99 CUV, from 31 March 1999), accredited by CAPES[1] with an initial grade 3 (Approval Letter CAA/CTC/49, on 20 June 2000).

Since its origins, the MMS already had multidisciplinary characteristics, placing researchers with different educational trajectories side by side, and adopting as its mission the technological and scientific development in the organization and strategy concentration area. Its evolution resulted in an interdisciplinary path, producing knowledge and qualifying people in lines of research in total quality management systems, environmental management systems, workplace safety management systems and social responsibility and sustainability management systems. The natural outcome was the later creation of the Interdisciplinary Doctorate in Sustainable Management Systems (DSM).

3.2   Doctorate in Sustainable Management Systems (DSM)

In 2012, due to the strategic planning of the MMS, its interdisciplinary character became more evident, not only because of the professors and researchers of the program, but also because of the students interested in comprehending and dealing with the interdisciplinary challenges experienced in the world of business and sustainable production. Obtaining grade 4, at the end of the 2010–12 period (CAPES MEC Ordinance 1077, of 31 August 2012, DOU 13 September 2012), motivated the staff of researchers of the master's program to begin the discussion about the creation of a doctoral course in the interdisciplinary area of CAPES.

In 2013, the graduate program had its doctorate course approved by the UFF (CUV Decision No. 036/2013) and the respective recognition by CAPES (Approval Letter No. 264-28/2013/CTC/CAAIII/CGAA/DAVCAPES of 17 December 2013), starting its academic activities in the second semester of 2014, with the opening of its First Public Selection Notice.[2] The program retained grade 4 in its first evaluation (2014–17 period), being the original grade granted during its approval process.

In this aspect, the DSM is the result of the evolution of the competencies and academic extension and research strategies of the professors involved in the MMS, working in an interdepartmental way with professors with distinct backgrounds (exact sciences, applied social sciences, social and earth sciences, chemical, civil, production and mechanical engineering areas) from various educational units of the university.

The faculty of the doctoral program is characterized by its goal to extend the borders of knowledge, develop technologies and promote sustainable innovation with experience, competence and productivity. Its multidisciplinary background, as well as its professional performance in diversified research, are coherent with the proposal of the doctoral program and aligned with the idea of contributing to the extension of knowledge and deepen the collaboration in productive sustainable processes.

The doctoral program has attracted candidates from various higher educational institutions of Rio de Janeiro and other states. The initial qualification area presented a distribution within a set of areas that encompassed engineering (about 50 percent), applied social sciences, hard and earth sciences, humanities, linguistics, Portuguese and arts, and multidisciplinary (about 50 percent). The selection process has an eliminatory stage (assessment of documents and foreign language content test) and then a classificatory stage (assessment of thesis proposal and assessment of the candidate's curriculum).

The doctoral thesis proposals are distributed among three lines of research of the DSM: management of sustainable organizations, technologies applied to sustainable organizations, and decision-making support in sustainable organizations, which currently represent 50 percent, 21.43 percent and 28.57 percent of the proposals, respectively.

The qualification process for the first class occurred in the 2013–16 period. Regarding international partnerships, the program invited and encouraged the participation of prominent professors from international institutions in the qualification and thesis defense boards, highlighting the participation of Professor Walter dos Santos Leal Filho, PhD from the Hamburg University of Applied Sciences, and Professor Clara Maria Rodrigues da Cruz Silva Santos, DSc from the University of Coimbra.

At the end of the second semester of 2017, with the expected scheduled period for the students' activities, and after fulfilling the regulatory requirement of the PPSIG (passing a qualification test and publishing articles in journals with Qualis[3] grades B1–A1, with SCOPUS and/or JCR index), the thesis defense process of the first class started.

With collegiate deliberation, the selection process for the fourth class started in January 2017 with the offer of ten places. About 40 candidates applied for them, and ten were approved and enrolled in the Student Module of the Sucupira Platform.[4]

Keeping the same philosophy of the previous years, the basis of the program consists in developing methodologies linked with its lines of research, which can be applied to different productive sectors. The search for diversity and multiple composition of the four classes – represented by the profile of the candidates from several areas (hard sciences, humanities, social and applied sciences and technological sciences) – is a factor that reaffirms the focus of the collegiate on the interdisciplinary character of the program.

By complying with its first strategic guideline, building competencies, the PPSIG has succeed in promoting its integration with government, private and third-sector institutions in order to foster applied research projects aimed at the solution of problems with high social, economic and environmental impacts through the MMS and DSM. Thus, cooperation partnerships were established with the National Nuclear Energy Commission (CNEN), D. Pedro II School, Federal Center for Technological Education Celso Suckow da Fonseca (CEFET-RJ), PETROBRAS, the Industry Federation of the State of Rio de Janeiro (FIRJAN), Federation of Industries of the State of Espírito Santo, Industrial Federation of the State of Minas Gerais, National Industrial Training Service (SENAI RJ), Industry Social Service (SESI RJ), Banco do Brasil, Brazilian Navy, Peugeot Citroen, the Court of Appeals of the State of Rio de Janeiro and other industrial production and service companies from Rio de Janeiro and other Brazilian states.

In this sense, the PPSIG has been acting as a reference center in Brazil for research, teaching and extension with effective impact on the improvement of the environmental, social and economic performance of organizations. The integration work with the organizations generated a replicable model for other institutions interested in aligning their organizational management and training programs with the principles of SD.

Table 20.1 presents the main aspects that contributed to the training of graduates who may face issues related to sustainability in organizations, and to the production of research projects that stimulate improvements in the economic, social and environmental dimensions at the local and regional level. The table also provides references found in the literature that reinforce the importance of each aspect for the quality of teaching and the promotion of sustainability.

3.3   National Congress on Management Excellence (CNEG)

Regarding the second PPSIG strategic guideline – enhancing inter-institutional cooperation mechanisms with interdisciplinary postgraduate programs – CNEG and INOVARSE were created by the group of professors that developed the PPSIG and became a huge event, evolving from a regional into an international event. The 14th CNEG/INOVARSE in 2018, the was held in Rio de Janeiro, at the headquarters of FIRJAN, with the theme: Industry 4.0, Lean and Organizational Sustainability. This event had the participation of 28 lecturers and authors of 360 approved articles representing various Brazilian states and foreign countries, among them: Portugal, Argentina, Uruguay, Chile, Angola and Canada. The International Opening Lecture by Professor Elaine Mosconi, PhD from Université de Sherbrooke (Canada), stood out.

The CNEG/INOVARSE became the main Latin American event engaging universities, governments and companies in the reflection on SD and innovation, by offering students from PPSIG and other national and international institutions opportunities to publish articles.

Table 20.1   Aspects and actions of PPSIG for the promotion of sustainability

Aspects	Actions	References
Integration with government, private and third-sector institutions	1. Annual Governance Meeting with the participation of professors, students, graduates and representatives of public and private institutions from the third sector and society 2. Professional master's degree 3. Applied research in partnership with institutions from multiple sectors 4. Promotion of scientific events (congresses, symposia etc.)	Pereira et al. (2016); Rübenich, Dorion and Eberle (2019)
Search for integration with other educational institutions	1. Promotion of scientific events 2. Development of research in participation with other institutions	Fioreze and McCowan (2018)
Search for internationalization	1. Development of international cooperation projects 2. International exchange students 3. Joint publications with renowned international researchers 4. Participation in international scientific events 5. Partnerships with international education institutions 6. Participation in the editorial board of renowned international journals 7. Participation of prominent professors of international institutions in the qualification and thesis councils	Signorini (2018)
Curriculum that promotes sustainability and innovation	1. MMS has three lines of research: environmental management systems and occupational safety, social responsibility and sustainability management systems, organizational management systems. The program has disciplines related to the three dimensions of sustainability. The disciplines stimulate debates and problem solving in interdisciplinary groups 2. DSM has three lines of research: decision support in sustainable organizations, management of sustainable organizations, applied technologies for sustainable organization. The program has disciplines related to the three dimensions of sustainability. The disciplines stimulate debates and problem solving in interdisciplinary groups	Dahlina and Leifler (2018)
Promotion of interdisciplinarity	1. Construction of research problems from sources exogenous to the university, generating empirical knowledge from the real demands of organizations, society and the environment 2. Adoption of systematic vision and holistic view in research	Freitas Júnior, Barros and Barbirato et al. (2015)

Table 20.1   (continued)

Aspects	Actions	References
	3. Faculty and students with different educational and professional trajectories	
	4. Stimulus to applied and interdisciplinary research	
	5. Doctoral candidates have advisors and co-advisors, both from different areas of knowledge	
	6. Search for an interdisciplinary student body via the following selection process elimination stage (document evaluation and test on specific content and foreign language) and later in a qualifying stage (evaluation of the dissertation proposal and evaluation of the candidate's curriculum), seeking to combine quality with diversity	

3.4   Internationalization

The third PPSIG strategic guideline is internationalization. In this sense, the PPSIG aims at integrating, through actions and research mechanisms, techno-scientific production and organization of programs with the Inter-University Sustainable Development Research Program (IUSDRP) and with WSD-RTC. Of the achievements resulting from this integration a good example is the World Symposium on Sustainability Science scientific event in Manchester, United Kingdom, in April 2017, which produced the *Handbook of Sustainability Science and Research* (Leal Filho, 2017).

In 2019, the second symposium with the theme 'Implementing the UN Sustainable Development Goals' took place. This event had the participation of professors and students from the PPSIG in the scientific committee and in the presentation of the selected articles. The symposium was organized along with the University of Hamburg/School of Applied Sciences (Germany), PPSIG, Pontifical Catholic University of Paraná (PUC-PR) and in cooperation with various UN organizations, agencies, government offices and authorities, universities, companies, non-governmental organizations and other organizations from all over the world.

With regard to the mechanisms to promote international cooperation, the PPSIG has been developing innovative research studies for the program through the exchange of professors for postdoctoral programs, visits and collaborations, as well as hosting renowned visiting professors who, associated with the regional effort, develop competencies for applied research in management systems. Now there are several international exchange programs with foreign universities – for instance, the exchange program attended by the DSM students Jean Carlos Machado Alves and Fabio Ribeiro de Oliveira, who participate in teaching and research activities at the University of Coimbra (Portugal) and at the University of Nova Lisboa (Portugal), respectively.

4.   RESULTS AND DISCUSSIONS

The analysis of the experience of developing and implementing the PPSIG reveals interesting aspects of the qualification of master's degrees and doctorates in the scientific, extension and teaching areas. The sensitivity of professors and coordinators when identifying the difficulties of the students and choosing the research themes represents a differential that improves the PPSIG's performance.

The program coordination provides adequate support for the solution of problems associated with regional, national and international sustainability. This paradigm transformed the quality of the teaching process, research and interaction with society according to the guidelines and specific directions for each research project. The systematic follow-up by the professors was important to minimize dropout rates and strengthen the positive results related to the doctoral process. Moreover, after the conclusion of dissertations and theses, there is a natural support for the inclusion of former students in the academic environment or in the professional field in private, public or third-sector organizations.

The follow-up of PPSIG former students highlights behaviors, skills and attitudes that contribute to different perspectives for the solution of social, economic and environmental problems. As an example, research carried out at PPSIG by Santos, Méxas and Meiriño (2017) demonstrated that it is possible to establish a set of sustainability indicators for the hospitality industry, respecting its diversity. The authors proposed a set of sustainability indicators for the sector based on a broad methodological framework. The study allowed a clear prioritization of environmental aspects to the detriment of others. In another research developed at PPSIG, Moraes et al. (2019) carried out a techno-economic feasibility analysis to convert ethanol into hydrogen gas (H_2) to be used as fuel for automobiles. The result showed the techno-economic feasibility of producing hydrogen for power generation using an ethanol processor.

Encouraging researchers to solve sustainable issues, with relevant results for regional development is one of the main goals of the program, by preparing students to apply and improve techno-scientific knowledge in methodologies, practices and tools that can contribute to collective, organizational or regional knowledge, and more specifically, to the advancement of knowledge management systems (KMS). In this regard, PPSIG former students are ethical professionals with critical thinking skills, a contextualized and interdisciplinary theoretical foundation, and other attributes such as:

1.   Acting in the field of applied sciences and technologies, developing studies and research projects.
2.   Creativity and leadership to apply the scientific method guided by sustainability principles, and acting in the job market by focusing on investigation and implementation of new technologies.
3.   Developing innovating ideas and strategic actions capable of broadening and enhancing his or her acting area from the sustainability perspective.
4.   Broadening their humanist, entrepreneurial and innovative qualifications, enabling them to solve problems in society and contributing to the technological, scientific and social development in the country.

5. Acting in multi-professional and inter-professional teams in the different fields of science and technology, being able to model, analyze and solve problems in the area, by applying ethical and scientific principles.
6. Acting in multidisciplinary teams (supervising, planning, coordinating or executing actions at a higher complexity level) in interdisciplinary partnerships with other academic programs, as well as with public, private, environmental organizations and regulatory agencies.

The result of the qualifying process of former students provided benefits in terms of integrating knowledge and development of systematic competences, highly valued by the job market and by academia in the knowledge society.

In the 2013–16 period, PPSIG produced doctors who are now part of the permanent faculty at public universities throughout the country, such as the Federal University of Ouro Preto (UFOP), Federal Rural University of Rio de Janeiro (UFFRJ), CEFET-RJ and the UFF. In addition, more than 80 percent of the doctors attending the program act in research groups that are recognized by the university. Several former PPSIG students are in the productive sector occupying top management positions, or acting as professors and coordinators in *sensu lato* and *sensu stricto* undergraduate courses or graduate courses in private HEIs. Among them are:

● Alberto Almeida dos Santos: public official at CNEN, where he occupies the position of Acting Chief of the Logistics and Infrastructure Service at the CNEN headquarters.
● Alexandre Elias Ribeiro Denizot: Professor of Work Safety at the CEFET-RJ in December 2018.
● Jean Carlos Machado Alves: Exclusive Dedication Professor at UFOP.
● Marcelo Arese: Substitute Professor of the Production Engineering course at UFF, Petrópolis Campus, in 2018.
● Rodrigo dos Santos Amado: Exclusive Dedication Professor of the Bachelor's Degree in Hotel Management and Graduate Course in Tourism at the UFF. He is also a Professor of the Professional Master's Course of the Postgraduate Program in Strategic Management at UFRRJ.
● Rodrigo Goyannes Gusmão Caiado: accepted for a postdoctoral internship in the Postgraduate Program in Production Engineering (Master's and Doctorate), Department of Industrial Engineering at PUC-RJ, in July 2018, to develop a project with the title 'Research and Development of the VSM 4.0 Dynamic Model for the Optimization of Supply Chain Management in Manufacture'.

The articulation between qualified research and the solutions to organizational problems is at the core of the PPSIG. This proximity can be observed in the research topics demanded by the most diverse productive sectors. The applicability of the PPSIG research studies can also be seen in the letters sent by the researched organizations available on the MMS website, where, in many cases, the researchers compose the workforce.

The PPSIG has made efforts to develop competencies, abilities and capacities for organizational sustainability and improvement of life in society. After years of learning and experience, some principles have been established to accomplish its goals:

- Work with the institutional and individual partners from other national and international institutions who act in the production of knowledge for the solution of problems that afflict society; emphasis on the measurement of the scientific, economic and social results for society, generated by the intellectual production for the qualification of doctors and masters.
- Permanent planning and self-assessment as fundamental elements for constant improvement and the establishment of continuing education in the program.
- Emphasis on integration/articulation with the several sectors of society: industrial, governmental, economic and financial.
- Appreciation of the faculty through the acknowledgment of its accomplishments, demonstrated in the awards event in the first semester of each year, by granting a commemorative plaque to the professors who published studies in international journals which broaden impact on science development.
- Appreciation of the culture of passion for the scientific production work, for teaching and for the inclusion of sustainability in the professional and academic activity of each component of the PPSIG, in synergy with individual values.

The PPSIG presents results that bring positive impacts to the dimensions of economic, social and environmental sustainability. As already presented in the text, one of the main PPSIG goals is to establish partnerships with governments, private and third-sector institutions to promote applied research aimed to solve problems with high social, economic and environmental impacts through the MMS and DSM.

In the last five years and seven months (January 2014–July 2019), at the time of writing, the PPSIG has produced 448 term papers, 14 doctoral theses and 474 master's dissertations. The results of 488 term papers were analyzed for their compliance with the indicators of each SD dimension (economic, social, and environmental). Of these, 385 of the theses and dissertations complied with the respective indicators, meaning 79 percent of compliance with the topic. These 385 who defended theses and dissertations represent the following percentage of the SD dimensions: 65 percent economic, 26 percent social and 9 percent environmental (Figure 20.1).

The following figures present the relation between the theses and dissertations developed by the PPSIG and sustainability dimensions. Figure 20.2 shows the result for the economic dimension:

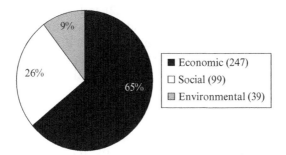

Figure 20.1   Quantity of PPSIG theses and dissertations × sustainable development dimensions

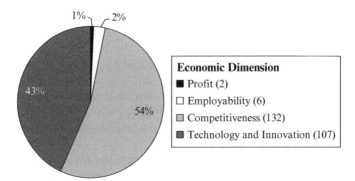

Figure 20.2   Quantity of PPSIG theses and dissertations × economic dimension indicators

In this sense, according to what is presented by the figure, the theses and dissertations complied with the following indicators:

- increase in the gross domestic product, added value and/or gross income: two PPSIG studies;
- creation of new work positions: growth of the employment rate and/or creation of new professional careers: six PPSIG studies;
- increase in competitiveness, understood as cost reduction; increase in productivity; improvement of the quality of products and/or services; increase in market share (national or global) and/or conquering of new markets: 132 PPSIG studies;
- building technological and innovative capacities: increase of R&D; hiring of experts in technological development; partnerships between science, technology and innovation institutions with companies; new and/or better implemented products or productive processes or increase in the number of registered patents: 107 PPSIG studies.

These indicators are related to SDG 8 and SDG 9 as they are linked to economic growth, innovation, and skills promotion, among others. According to Frey (2017), the global development agenda clearly includes goals related to economic growth (Goal 8.1), business creation (Goal 8.3), productivity (Goal 8.2), technological innovation (Goal 8.2) and consumption (Goal 8.4), while SDG 9 addresses issues such as promoting resilient infrastructure, inclusive and sustainable industrialization and innovation (Kynčlová, Upadhyaya and Nice, 2020). Figure 20.3 explains these results for the social dimension.

For this dimension, the PPSIG studies complied with the following indicators:

- better access to the formal job market, education, health and/or social protection: six PPSIG studies;
- reduction of income differences; gender, race, ethnicity, generation, social-origin inequalities; and/or other structural gaps: 14 PPSIG studies;
- improvement of work, health conditions and/or the relationship with consumers: 79 PPSIG studies.

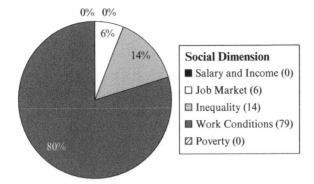

Figure 20.3   Quantity of PPSIG theses and dissertations × the social dimension indicators

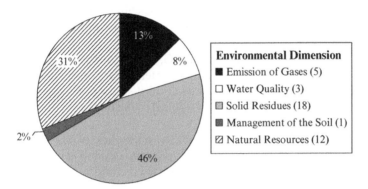

Figure 20.4   Quantity of PPSIG theses and dissertations × the environmental dimension indicators

These indicators are related to SDG 4 and SDG 8 as the data presented in the figure are related to the access to education and the labor market, quality of work, as well as to the reduction of inequalities. SDG 4 focuses on ensuring inclusive, equitable and quality education. Research in this area, as well as the training and qualification of teachers, can contribute to the achievement of this goal (Sunthonkanokpong and Murphy, 2019). In addition, quality and inclusive education can provide better access to quality work and reduce inequalities. One of the objectives of SDG 8 is also to improve quality of life and safety at work – 79 studies were developed in this area by PPSIG, and many of these are applied in the work environment of organizations.

Last, Figure 20.4 addresses the environmental dimension.

The PPSIG developed research studies that observe the following indicators in the environmental dimension:

- reduction of the emission of greenhouse gases and/or other atmospheric pollutants: five PPSIG studies;
- improvement of water availability and/or water quality: three PPSIG studies;
- reduction and management of solid residues; circular economy: 18 PPSIG studies;

- better management of the soil: 1 PPSIG study;
- better use of natural resources (energy, silviculture, minerals, materials, etc.): 12 PPSIG studies.

These indicators are related to SDG 6, SDG 11, SDG 12 and SDG 13 as they concern the preservation of water quality, sustainable management of solid waste, reduction of gas emissions, and better use of natural resources, among others. We can also highlight the partnership of PPSIG with private organizations from the third sector and the government to carry out research focused on teaching quality. Kavvada et al. (2020) emphasize the importance of these interactions to promote the achievement of these goals.

5. FINAL CONSIDERATIONS

In general, the main problems associated with the teaching of organizational sustainability are related to identifying the real needs of organizations and society, and the analysis of the adding value according to the actions developed.

When analyzing the results obtained by PPSIG, we can say that they are well structured and may be a solution to real problems faced by contemporary organizations. The research studies arose from the needs of public, private or third-sector organizations. Thus, we can conclude that the teaching of sustainability applied to the operation of organizations can produce significant and recognized results.

This study addressed the PPSIG actions for the promotion of SD. Besides promoting sustainable development education (SDE), the program develop applied research studies in partnership with institutions from the most varied sectors, in order to develop professionalization, training and innovation linked with the creation of sustainable competencies and capacities.

For this purpose, several PPSIG actions were analyzed to verify their results and benefits to institutions and society in the context of sustainability in its social, economic and environmental dimensions. The study shows that the PPSIG results can improve the economic, social and environmental indicators of companies and society, being a catalyst for socio-environmental and economic demands, and contributing to the development of projects, social actions, internationalization, inter-institutional integration and development of solutions for complex problems of society.

In this regard, the PPSIG goals and results establish a set of investments capable of promoting a virtuous cycle of economic growth, creation of employment, development of productive chains, decrease of environmental impacts, and recovery of the productive capacity of the natural capital.

NOTES

1. Coordenadoria de Aperfeiçoamento de Pessoal de Nível Superior, a government agency linked to the Brazilian Ministry of Education.
2. The selection process that allows students access to the doctorate. It is an impersonal procedure where equal opportunities are ensured for everyone interested in participating in the program, allowing the identification and selection of the most suitable students according to objective criteria.

3. A Brazilian official system with the purpose of classifying scientific production. It is maintained by CAPES.
4. An online application built to collect and analyze data from the Postgraduate National System.

REFERENCES

Björnberg, K.E., I.-B. Skogh and E. Strömberg (2015), 'Integrating social sustainability in engineering education at the KTH Royal Institute of Technology', *International Journal of Sustainability in Higher Education*, 16(5), 639–49.

Comissão Econômica para a América Latina e o Caribe/Friedrich Ebert Stiftung (CEPAL/FES) (2019), 'O Big Push Ambiental no Brasil: investimentos coordenados para um estilo de desenvolvimento sustentável', *Perspectivas*, No. 20/2019.

Dahlin, J. and O. Leifler (2018), 'Attitudes towards curriculum integration of sustainable development among program directors in engineering education', in *EESD 2018 Proceedings, Rowan University, June 3–6*, pp. 198–205.

Fioreze, C. and T. McCowan (2018), 'Community universities in the South of Brazil: prospects and challenges of a model of non-state public higher education', *Comparative Education*, 54(3), 370–89.

Freitas Júnior, O.D.G., P.A.M. Barros and J.C.C. Barbirato et al. (2015), 'Reestruturando o modelo de universidade pública brasileira para atender aos novos desafios gerenciais', paper presented at XV Colóquio Internacional de Gestão Universitária – CIGU, October 2017, pp. 1–15.

Frey, D.F. (2017), 'Economic growth, full employment and decent work: the means and ends in SDG 8', *The International Journal of Human Rights*, 21(8), 1164–84.

Gil, A. (2010), *How to Develop Research Projects*, São Paulo: Atlas.

Guerra, A. (2017), 'Integration of sustainability in engineering education: why is PBL an answer?', *International Journal of Sustainability in Higher Education*, 18(3), 436–54.

Kavvada, A., G. Metternicht and F. Kerblat et al. (2020), 'Towards delivering on the sustainable development goals using earth observations', *Remote Sensing of Environment*, 247, Article 111930.

Kynčlová, P., S. Upadhyaya and T. Nice (2020), 'Composite index as a measure on achieving Sustainable Development Goal 9', *Applied Energy*, 265, Article 114755.

Leal Filho, W. (ed.) (2017), *Handbook of Sustainability Science and Research*, Cham, Switzerland: Springer.

Mello, S.L.M., N.V.-E. Ludolf and O.L.G. Quelhas et al. (2019), 'Innovation in the digital era: new labor market and educational changes', *Ensaio: Avaliação e Políticas Públicas em Educação*, 28(106), 66–87.

Mintz, K. and T. Tal (2013), 'Sustainability in higher education courses: multiple learning outcomes', *Journal of Cleaner Production*, 41, 113–23.

Moraes, T.S., H.N.C. da Silva and L.P. Zotes et al. (2019), 'A techno-economic evaluation of the hydrogen production for energy generation using an ethanol fuel processor', *International Journal of Hydrogen Energy*, 44, 21205–19.

Oliveira, M. Méxas, M. Meiriño and G. Drumond (2019), 'Critical success factors associated with the implementation of enterprise risk management', *Journal of Risk Research*, 22(8), 1004–19.

Pereira, G.M.C., F.N. Castro, L.N.M. Lanza and D.C.F. Lanza (2016), 'Panorama de oportunidades para os egressos do ensino superior no Brasil: o papel da inovação na criação de novos mercados de trabalho', *Ensaio*, 24(90), 179–98.

Quelhas, O.L.G., G.B.A. Lima and N.V.-E. Ludolf et al. (2019), 'Engineering education and the development of competencies for sustainability', *International Journal of Sustainability in Higher Education*, 20(4), 614–29.

Rose, G., K. Ryan and C. Desha (2015), 'Implementing a holistic process for embedding sustainability: a case study in first-year engineering, Monash University, Australia', *Journal of Cleaner Production*, 106, 229–38.

Rübenich, N.V., E.C.J. Dorion and L. Eberle (2019), 'Organizational learning and benchmarking in university technology courses: a Brazilian experience', *Benchmarking: An International Journal*, 26(2), 530–47.

Saboya, G.L., O.L.Q. Quelhas and R.G.G. Caiado et al. (2017), 'Monte Carlo simulation for planning and decisions making in transmission project of electricity', *IEEE Latin America Transactions*, 15(3), 431–8.

Santos, R.A., M.P. Méxas and M.J. Meiriño (2017), 'Sustainability and hotel business: criteria for holistic, integrated and participative development', *Journal of Cleaner Production*, 142(Part 1), 217–14.

Segalàs Coral, J., R. Drijvers and J. Tijseen (2018), '16 years of EESD: a review of the evolution of the EESD conference and its future challenges', in *EESD 2018 Proceedings, Rowan University, June 3–6*, pp. 12–19.

Signorini, I. (2018), 'Legitimation of local scientific policies due to the internationalization requirements of the university', *Cadernos CEDES*, 38(105), Article 205221.

Sunthonkanokpong, W. and E. Murphy (2019), 'Quality, equity, inclusion and lifelong learning in pre-service teacher education', *Journal of Teacher Education for Sustainability*, 21(2), 91–104.

Thürer, M., I. Tomaşević and M. Stevenson et al. (2017), 'A systematic review of the literature on integrating sustainability into engineering curricula', *Journal of Cleaner Production*, 181, 608–17.
United Nations Educational, Scientific and Cultural Organization (UNESCO) (2017), *Education for Sustainable Development: Learning Objectives*', accessed 24 May 2018 at http://unesdoc.unesco.org/images/0024/002474/247444e.pdf.
Yin, R.K. (2003), *Case Study Research: Design and Methods*, Thousand Oaks, CA: SAGE.

21. Extra-curricular activities as a way of teaching sustainability
Gert-Olof Boström, Katarina Winka and Katarzyna Wolanik Boström

1. INTRODUCTION

This chapter takes its point of departure in the complexity of education for sustainable development (ESD) as pointed out by Leal Filho and Pace (2016) and Longhurst (2014). This inherent complexity demands different approaches to teaching and in this chapter the value of extra-curricular activities (ECAs) will be elaborated upon. Two examples of ECAs that have been conducted at Umeå School of Business, Economics and Statistics in Sweden will be presented, discussed and analyzed. The chapter brings together a series of linked concepts, namely ESD, ECAs and experiential learning theory (ELT).

1.1 The Classroom Is Not Enough When Teaching Sustainability

The United Nations Educational, Scientific and Cultural Organization (UNESCO, 2017) has suggested that the following key competences are needed to achieve the UN Sustainability Development Goals (SDGs): systems thinking competency, anticipatory competency, normative competency, strategic competency, collaboration competency, critical thinking competency, self-awareness competency and integrated problem-solving competency. These competences might appear well known and rather basic in the eyes of a university teacher, but everyone addressing them in their courses in relation to sustainability can acknowledge the challenge of supporting the development of these competences in students. A closer look reveals their complexity and hence the demand for a substantial effort from the teacher to effectively communicate and relate these competencies to the reality of the students.

ESD is an approach to teaching that is recommended when designing courses and curricula to align with the SDGs and develop the key competences (de Haan, 2010; Leicht, Heiss and Byun, 2018). It focuses on *what* to teach (SDG learning outcomes and content) as well as *how* (pedagogical strategies and design of learning environments). ESD also encourages a widening of learners' perspectives to enable deeper learning and understanding (Leal Filho and Pace, 2016). The ESD approach recommends that the key competencies should be integrated throughout the curriculum, but there is also an additional option: ECAs can play a vital role in contributing to the students' development of these competencies.

ECAs are, by definition, not part of the curriculum but take place in the educational environment outside of normal classroom time (Bartkus et al., 2012). These activities can be directly or indirectly linked to the curricula, or be completely unrelated. Some are organized by the students and others by the educational institution. Another term for

ECAs is 'informal learning', as opposed to the formal learning setting of the curriculum. ECAs can be a way to bring in glimpses of the students' potential future working life into the setting of the university.

Even though ECAs take place outside regular courses, this does not mean that they are less relevant for student learning. Both formal as well as informal learning settings at universities are relevant for the advancement of competencies for sustainable development (Barth et al., 2007). From the perspective of the institution, or teacher, it is possible to regard ECAs as an arena where contents or competencies that do not easily or logically fit within the curriculum can be included. These activities also open up for external voices and discussions not regularly present at the university. This characteristic means that ECAs can serve the purpose of providing examples and role models for actions and behaviors that are used in society outside the university.

Until now, ESD discourse has focused on methods, techniques and activities mainly taking place in the classroom and within the course curriculum. The key competencies required for addressing sustainability are under debate (Eizaguirre, García-Feijoo and Laka, 2019, p. 2) and there may be other competencies that might serve the purpose better. The focus in this chapter is not, however, on what the competences specifically are; instead, the question is: what role can ECAs play in order to stimulate student learning of complex competencies? The nature of these competencies is that they are generic and complicated and consequently demanding and difficult to both teach and learn. The ability to apply different problem-solving frameworks to complex sustainability problems and develop viable, inclusive and equitable solutions that promote sustainable development is demanding. To reach this objective, there is a need for carefully designed ECAs, as activities in the classroom are not enough. The students need to be exposed to additional situations in which the complexity of the UN SDGs can be experienced (see also Teslenko, 2019; Tortora, 2019).

What happens outside the classroom, for example in ECAs, is, however, not isolated from what happens inside the classroom. Together they represent different activities promoting learning and they can be regarded as prerequisites for each other. The experiences and perspectives that the students gain from ECAs are brought into the classroom, and what the students learn in the classroom is brought into the ECA. By means of this transfer of knowledge, a significant leap in the students' learning may take place. Teaching and learning are closely related, and by approaching the same SDGs in two different environments there is potential for interplay between the classroom setting and the ECA.

Addressing the SDGs and the core competencies outside the classroom has several benefits that may play a significant role in the student learning process. One aspect is the possibility for people from outside the university to participate in these activities, which will expose the student to authentic stories and arguments that are not just created in the academic world. Depending on the setting, these contributions might have more or less significance but, in general, input from practitioners in the discipline is likely to have a positive effect on the students' motivation and learning. These voices coming from outside the university represent examples from the students' future work setting. Following this line of argument, another aspect appears – credibility. People coming from industry tend to be considered to have high credibility among students with regard to describing what is happening outside the university.

Another benefit is that the core competencies and their relationship to the SDGs can be addressed from different angles. The core competencies were identified as a way to communicate what is needed for the purpose of approaching the UN goals. However, these goals have a dynamic nature and therefore demand a dynamic approach. ECAs are a means to update the status of these goals by inviting people from outside the university to share their perception of the goals and the competencies needed to approach and achieve them. ECAs also have an inverted power by welcoming professionals from outside the university into academia to learn from current research and scholarly practice. Perhaps the most important impact from the ECA is in the cross-fertilized learning environment that is created when both these groups meet in discourse.

What the students bring into the classroom in the form of experiences, attitudes and prior knowledge influences their learning (Ambrose et al., 2010; Kolb, 1984) – so does their motivation and approach to learning (Marton and Säljö, 1997; Trigwell, Prosser and Waterhouse, 1999). Experiential learning theory (ELT) posits that learning is a result of reflection and the processing of experiences. It highlights the value of different teaching modes to offer students various ways to gather experiences and it also positions learning as an experience that stretches beyond the classroom. ECAs are excellent opportunities to gain experiences, motivation and knowledge that can have a positive impact on student learning. The learning achieved by participating in ECAs depends on the characteristic of the activity, whether or not it has an academic focus. Students engaging in ECAs have been found to achieve higher interpersonal competency skills and improved success in attaining leadership roles (Rubin, Bommer and Baldwin, 2002).

This chapter brings together a series of linked concepts, namely: ESD, ECA and ELT. The empirical focus will be on two different but complementary cases of ECAs. The nature of these cases will be outlined in detail, as well as how they evolved and were implemented. Their relationship to student learning will be discussed and implications for future actions outlined. The aim is to highlight the potential of expanding the idea of a 'learning environment' to include the surrounding academic milieu to promote experience of, engagement in and reflection on sustainability issues.

1.2   The Environment – Umeå School of Business, Economics and Statistics

Umeå School of Business, Economics and Statistics (USBE) at Umeå University was founded in 1989. Umeå University, founded in 1965, is located in the northern part of Sweden but only one-third of the students at USBE come from the region. Thus, the recruitment area of students is the whole of Sweden as well as internationally. There are about 3000 students enrolled on one or another of the 12 programs or 165 courses at USBE and in 2018 there were 172 exchange students.

USBE has a strong sustainability profile. The school mission states that: 'Through interplay with the surrounding society, we provide education and research that contributes to the understanding, ability, and responsibility of individuals in relation to societal challenges and the importance of sustainable development' (USBE, 2020). The sustainability profile at USBE is strengthened by its Association to Advance Collegiate Schools of Business (AACSB) accreditation and being an advanced signatory of the Principles for Responsible Management Education (PRME), and being certified according to the environmental management standard ISO 14001 and the specific policy for sustainable development. Moreover, the school has an organization that signals the importance accorded sustainability, namely: a dean that actively promotes sustainability; a sustainability council (including a student representative);[1] an administrative manager who also serves as sustainability coordinator at USBE; a head of teaching and learning clearly devoted to sustainability; and a career center coordinator in charge of alumni work with a great interest in sustainability. Description of these environmental settings provides a necessary understanding for the two cases that will be described as ECAs offered at USBE. These cases are: first, a series of independent guest lectures and the Sustainability Day; and second, the campaign #17goals17weeks.

To appreciate the impact of the ECAs, it is fruitful to understand the range and nature of the educational programs that USBE offers. The professional degree programs are, in terms of students, the largest, and prepare students directly for business life or the public sector. By completing one of these programs, the student can apply directly for a position in the business sector as well as in the public sector or start their own business (cf. Leal Filho and Pace, 2016). This circumstance is essential to bear in mind when reading about the cases, since the people invited who come from outside the university represent the students' future labor market. Thus, there is a mutual interest and benefit, as the people coming into the university have an interest in understanding what is going on in higher education and frequently wish to identify talented students, while the students and staff at USBE want to hear what is going on outside the university.

2.   DATA COLLECTION AND ANALYSIS

The main empirical basis of this qualitative study is two narrative interviews: one with a career center coordinator in charge of the alumni work; and one with the administrative manager who also serves as sustainability coordinator at USBE. Additional material consists of an internal *Final report #17goals17weeks*, a printed program on 'Theme days on sustainability issues in business administration', USBE's sustainability policy, USBE's strategy for 2019–25 and other relevant documents indicated in and supported by the interviewees (including students' feedback and comments on the activities). Media material including USBE's self-presentation on the website and in social media (including promotion of the guest lectures and #17goals17week campaign on Facebook) were also included. The main author, Gert-Olof Boström, is a lecturer at the USBE, but has not been active in the cases presented. The interviews were carried out by the co-authors. The interviews were transcribed verbatim and subjected to an exploratory approach of applied thematical analysis (Guest, MacQueen and Namey, 2012).

2.1   Theoretical Framework

In the constructivist paradigm attributed to Dewey (1938) and Piaget (1954), learning is perceived as the process of creating knowledge and acquiring skills through the processing of experiences. We construct knowledge of the world based on what we experience, and we specifically learn from experiences that challenge our prior knowledge and beliefs. Conflict, differences and disagreement are drivers for the learning process. This view of how learning works has had a fundamental impact on modern-day teaching practices in higher education. The one-way communication model based on lectures has been challenged by student-active methods where students are encouraged to engage in the subject and develop their critical thinking through discussions with peers and experts (Biggs and Tang, 2011; Dorestani, 2005).

Experience is at the core of the learning process according to ELT (Kolb, 1984). According to this theory, self-study, being taught and being exposed to various situations are all considered experiences that can lead to learning. Learning is defined as 'the process whereby knowledge is created through the transformation of experience. Knowledge results from the combination of grasping and transforming experience' (ibid., p. 41). From this perspective, providing students with opportunities for meaningful experiences is the main purpose of higher education. This also means that the design of learning environments where these experiences can happen is of great importance (Kolb and Kolb, 2005).

The learning environment, where teaching and learning occurs, has received increased attention in the last two decades (Choi, Van Merriënboer and Paas, 2014; Entwistle and Peterson, 2004). A learning environment can refer to an educational approach, a cultural context, or a physical setting in which teaching and learning occur. Often, the term 'learning environment' addresses the physical classroom or an online environment (Oblinger, 2005; Thomas, Pavlechko and Cassady, 2019). However, learning does not only happen in the classroom. Biggs and Tang (2011, p. 74) emphasize that 'we need to stop assuming that learning is only taking place when it is located inside a teacher-directed classroom'. There is a great potential in regarding the surrounding environment as a resource and complement to the classroom and curricular activities (Brooks, 2011; see also Teslenko, 2019).

ECAs are 'academic or non-academic activities that are conducted under the auspices of the school but occur outside of normal classroom time and are not part of the curriculum' (Bartkus et al., 2012, p. 698). Non-academic ECAs may comprise sports, music, drama, dance and student journals, while academic ECAs will vary depending on who the organizer is and where they take place. For ECAs to contribute to student engagement and learning there are some prerequisites that need to be fulfilled (Barth et al., 2007). The existence of various and manifold contexts is significant. In formal settings, multifaceted contexts have to be created; informal learning offers these per se. For this to be successful, however, universities need to create spaces for informal learning and appreciate and support informal learning processes. Interdisciplinarity is important to promote reflective processes, developing competency in interdisciplinary collaboration and developing motivational dispositions. The learners' individual responsibility is also of great significance, as this maximizes the number of possibilities for learning and acquiring competencies. Learners can be supported by making spaces for informal learning processes available to them.

Teaching complex competencies to students is a challenge and this is a well-known situation when teaching about, and for, sustainability. Hence, new approaches to teaching have been proposed under the term ESD (Leicht et al., 2018). The key characteristics of ESD are: (1) focus on the learner; (2) action-oriented learning; and (3) transformative learning (Rieckmann, 2018; Wiek, Withycombe and Redman, 2011).

ESD is recognized as a key enabler of sustainable development, since it relates to all 17 goals of the UN 2030 Agenda. It is specifically part of Goal 4, Target 4.7: 'ensure that all learners acquire the knowledge and skills needed to promote sustainable development, including, among others, through education for sustainable development and sustainable lifestyles'. Education for sustainable development targets formulation of learning outcomes, selection of learning content, choice of pedagogy and design of learning environments. The aim is to empower learners to take informed decisions and responsible actions for environmental integrity, economic viability and a just society, for present and future generations, while respecting cultural diversity (Leicht et al., 2018).

Discourse about teaching sustainability initially focused on methods, techniques and activities mainly taking place in the classroom and within the students' curriculum. However, since learning not only happens in the classroom, an institution-wide approach might yield greater effects. Rieckmann (2018, p. 46) recommends that 'Schools and universities, for instance, should see themselves as experiential places of learning for sustainable development, and should therefore orient all their processes towards principles of sustainability'. By offering students ECAs, the learning experience can reach beyond individual courses and programs and become an integral part of lifelong learning. This is about broadening perspectives, which is an integral part of teaching sustainability.

3.   THE TWO CASES OF ECAs

In this section, two cases of ECAs will be described: first, a series of independent guest lectures including the Sustainability Day at USBE; and second, the campaign #17goals17weeks. For each of these two activities the background and organization will be outlined. The focus of the presentation is on the implementation of the ECAs and how the stage was set for these kind of activities.

3.1   A Series of Independent Guest Lectures and the Sustainability Day

USBE has a tradition of inviting external guest lecturers to speak at the school. These guest lecturers are closely linked to the alumni of USBE, but other guests are also invited to give presentations, especially at the Sustainability Day. These include, for example, CEOs or sustainability managers of large and well-known companies. The choice of guest lecturer invited depends on the aim (i.e., topic) of the lecture. There is approximately one guest lecture a month, and all of them have a sustainability approach in terms of the SDGs. The particular approach is portrayed either by the topic chosen or encouraged by questions from the chairperson or the audience at the end of the lecture.

The career center coordinator, who studied on the degree program at USBE, manages work with alumnae at USBE and is in charge of setting the topic, identifying and inviting appropriate guest lecturers and chairing the session. The title of the lecture is developed in dialogue with the guest lecturer but the topic is identified before potential guests are approached. It is of interest to note that arranging these guest lectures is part of the study coordinator's regular work tasks in addition to monitoring current sustainability discourse and developments. The career center coordinator also holds a permanent chair on the sustainability council at USBE, which is the highest formal forum for both discussions about the SDGs and the planning of sustainability-related activities at the business school. The quality of work is also enhanced by the study coordinator's personal interest in questions related to sustainability.

The ECAs described here are in the form of independent guest lectures with no specific relation to any particular course, although some topics have a direct relevance and strong linkage to certain courses. Even though these guest lectures are arranged by USBE, they are not done on behalf of any ongoing course or program, meaning that they are extra-curricular. A significant compass for these lectures is sustainability, either as a direct part of the topic or made visible in other ways.

Once a year, a Sustainability Day is arranged at USBE. In this initiative, the invited speakers are required to talk about sustainability work in their respective organizations. The Sustainability Day is arranged as a half day since the students prefer this to a full day. The invited speakers are carefully identified in order to give the Sustainability Day a contemporary content, focusing on particularly interesting processes happening in the field. Both the Sustainability Day as well as the independent guest lectures are open to the public:

> It started partly as a student initiative, the first Sustainability Day as a 'theme day', when I, together with two students, formed the first program . . . But I also try to put sustainability into every guest lecture, no matter if it is the theme or not. (The study coordinator)

A common feature of all guest lectures, including presentations at the Sustainability Day, is that time for questions is provided at the end of the lecture. This part of the guest lecture, and actually all the other parts, is managed by the career center coordinator who is also the host for external people coming to the USBE. This time for questions is crucial in terms of connecting the guest lecture to its intended idea, and if necessary provides an opportunity to adjust the presentation to match the intentions. It is also a time for interaction with people from the audience, which comprises both students, academic staff and external visitors. Moreover, it is also a possibility to make sure that sustainability is elaborated in the presentation. The career center coordinator explained:

> I remember that when IKEA was here, then the questions put by a person from the external public were quite critical; they maybe had more courage than the students. When the presenters are people in high positions from big companies, the students tend to be a bit restrained. I have tried to make time for a panel or for questions at the end of these theme days, just to make sure that their presentation is not unchallenged, but you can look at it from different angles. I guess it is a way to nuance the discussion.

3.2 #17goals17weeks

In the autumn term of 2018, USBE ran a campaign called #17goals17weeks. The main purpose of this campaign was to present the breadth and the depth of USBE's sustain-ability work as efficiently as possible for internal and external stakeholders related to the 17 SDGs. Internal stakeholders are, for example, employees and students at the business school while external stakeholders can comprise people from industry. A further purpose of the campaign was to respond to the call from the UN regarding the dissemination of knowledge about the SDG.

The administrative manager, who also serves as sustainability coordinator at USBE, was in charge of the #17goals17weeks campaign. Inspired by a TED talk, it was in fact this manager who came up with the idea of the campaign to improve communication of the ongoing activities of the business school's sustainability work. As indicated by the name, the timeframe of the campaign was 17 weeks, which is equivalent to the number of the UN's SDGs. Every week, a specific goal was highlighted in relation to different activities going on at USBE, either in research, teaching and/or cooperation with society. Different communication channels were used for presentation, such as Facebook, LinkedIn and Instagram.

The design of the campaign was quite simple: each week, one of the SDGs was briefly presented, followed by a longer presentation of the activities at USBE that related to this particular goal. There was an ambition to balance the activities presented so that all three departments at USBE were highlighted in a similar number of presentations. Another balance was to present activities related to the three overall missions of Swedish universities: research, teaching and cooperation with society. The sustainability coordinator said in the interview:

> Well, we have learned that we do a hell of a lot of things at the USBE! We had . . . what was it? 41 different entries! 14 on research, nine on education, 12 on cooperation with society and some others. There could also be both research and education in the same entry.

One of the main audiences for the #17goals#17weeks were the internal stakeholders, including the employees at USBE. Specifically for this group, an additional channel for communicating the campaign was 'the social wall', which is the name for the strategically located screens at the business school. One screen is located in the lounge outside the dean's office and five others are located in corridors and in coffee rooms in the three departments. In addition, there are two screens placed in the student restaurant/coffee bar located just outside the premises of USBE. The latter screens are mainly directed to students and therefore they usually have a somewhat different content. However, all screens were used for communicating the #17goals17weeks campaign. The goal for the week and the activities related to that goal were presented throughout this period. All these screens were also used to advertise the independent guest lectures and the Sustainability Day.

4.   DISCUSSION

The two cases presented here are of a different nature and serve slightly different purposes. A common intention was to highlight the importance of sustainability and the SDGs and to provide opportunities for both students and academic staff to gain broader experience of the complexities of sustainable development. The independent guest lectures and the Sustainability Day were directed towards the public present when the activity took place, whereas the #17goals17weeks campaign used electronic channels that enabled an asynchronous and prolonged communication. As far as feedback possibilities are concerned, the campaign was based on one-way communication, while the guest lectures and the Sustainability Day encouraged, at least to some extent, two-way communication. An implication of this communication difference was the possibility to adapt the guest lectures and the Sustainability Day to the interests and questions from the audience present. On the other hand, the benefits of the #17goals17weeks campaign was the repeated possibility to become acquainted with the research, education and collaboration on sustainability that has been carried out at USBE. It also facilitated the integration of research examples into curricula and classes. Together, these activities represent a deliberate strategy to create spaces for informal learning and support for informal learning processes.

The time allowed for questions during the guest lectures and at the Sustainability Day deserves special attention. These opportunities for dialogue are valuable for many reasons. They enable the chairperson to guide the speaker further into SDG-related issues – for instance, how sustainability is currently discussed and practiced in different work-life settings. The knowledge and practice disseminated are highly relevant and up to date, and often demonstrate state-of-the-art practices. The question time also represents a shift in roles in the auditorium. The audience is invited to speak and the speaker becomes a listener and a participant in the dialogue. This transformation offers the participating students the possibility of experiencing different behaviors and responsibilities and also to observe how these roles are enacted by other people in the audience. The career-center coordinator has described how the students commonly ask rather respectful questions, but people coming from companies or other organizations can have much more challenging (and thought-provoking) questions and comments. This group also represents an important source of knowledge and experience. As research has found, interdisciplinarity can promote reflection processes (Barth et al., 2007). Observing and engaging in these discussions with peers and experts can thus help students develop competency in interdisciplinary collaboration and develop their critical thinking skills. Naturally, it is also of interest how the guest lecturer responds to the questions.

We know that student learning is influenced by their motivation and attitudes as well as prior experiences and knowledge (Ambrose et al., 2010; Marton and Säljö, 1997). From a student perspective, these ECAs provide an opportunity to see the value of the curricular content, as well as broadening their knowledge in areas that are not in the formal curriculum. Listening to people coming from an organization/company is a way to bring the students' future into the university (cf. Tortora, 2019). Meeting a potential employer increases their motivation and offers hands-on evidence of the importance and value of the SDG key competencies. A guest lecture might provide an opportunity to ask questions of personal interest and to exchange contact information.

Another argument for expanding the traditional learning environment to include ECAs is to approach the complexity of teaching sustainability issues in a more holistic way. Providing students with opportunities for meaningful experiences is the main purpose of higher education and the complexity of sustainability is hard to frame within a syllabus course. This can be due to a lack of knowledge on the part of the teacher, lack of updated course material, or that the time-frame of the course is too limited. The main value of these ECAs is to demonstrate how sustainability is discussed and practiced in society and how different organizations and companies tackle these issues. The activities represent purposefully designed experiential places where informal learning can take place. This highlights the close relationship between ECAs and the formal curriculum. Students can bring the knowledge and perspectives they have met in the ECA into the regular course setting to enrich their learning.

It is important to have a strategy with regard to who to invite to the guest lectures and to the Sustainability Day. At USBE, this strategy is based on policy, decided by the sustainability council and made operational by the study coordinator. The strategy here roughly means that there is a logic to the topics presented and that there is a match between the person invited and the topic. According to the study coordinator, it is important to be sensitive to the different corporate brands that the guest lecturers represent. A more well-known corporate brand means by definition that more students will attend the event. Another aspect of the strategy is to invite alumni, as these people serve as especially interesting and credible role models for students regarding future possible jobs. The ECAs presented here might also be considered a way for the organizer, in this case USBE, to demonstrate current activities within the organization for a broader audience. It is easy to underestimate the public's interest in what is going on at the university. Most of the participants have a university degree or are pursuing one, and they are interested in finding out what is currently happening at the university. This interest is even stronger when former students, alumni, come back as guests. In turn, these guests are curious to find out what has changed and what the current trends at the university are. As a consequence, the ECAs are arenas that promote lifelong learning and encourage transdisciplinary dialogue.

5. CONCLUSIONS

In this chapter, we have outlined the potential in regarding the surrounding environment as a resource and complement to the classroom and curricular activities. Extra-curricular activities can enable deeper learning and widen student perspectives of sustainable development (Leal Filho and Pace, 2016; Leicht et al., 2018). According to ELT, it is important to use different teaching modes in order to offer students various ways to gather experiences. Further, research has shown that learning does not only happen in the classroom, which makes ECAs an interesting complement (Biggs and Tang, 2011). The activities we have described provided experiences not possible to embrace within regular course syllabi and have the potential to benefit both students and teachers. The university, and in particular the USBE, has created spaces and activities to support informal learning processes (Barth et al., 2007). We have shown how a transdisciplinary context, where university and society meet in order to visualize the complexity of sustainability, can encourage dialogue and lifelong learning. A challenging dimension of sustainability is its dynamics, as development is continuous and therefore not always possible to frame in traditional university teaching. Therefore, we advocate closer collaboration and interaction between members of society, industry and the university.

A group that does not receive much attention when discussing ESD are the teachers. This group of people are key to integrating the SDGs into the curriculum and also need knowledge, interest and motivation for their own professional development. The ECAs presented here may be considered important not only for student learning, but also for the professionalization of university teachers. First, guest lectures and the Sustainability Day provided opportunities to stay updated and collect authentic examples and cases to be used in teaching. Second, the campaign #17goals17weeks highlighted good examples of ESD that might serve as role models and provide ideas on how to make linkages to the SDG. The dual focus of the campaign – research and teaching – also gave legitimacy and value to teaching sustainability.

Students engaging in ECAs have been found to achieve higher interpersonal competency skills and improved success in attaining leadership roles (Rubin et al., 2002). What has been less researched is the link between academic ECAs and how they contribute to reaching the educational objectives in an ongoing program. The two cases illustrated here are examples of how an organization can broaden the experience base for students and through this set the stage for enhanced interest and engagement in sustainable development.

We regard the ECAs described as a melting pot, as expressed by Moore (2005) – that is, a situation where transformative and transdisciplinary learning can take place when guest lecturers, researchers and students meet in a contemporary discourse about sustainability. There is a need for complex learning environments in order to support learning about SDGs and learning for sustainability. In this chapter, two examples of how to offer students experiences from outside the curriculum in order to enrich their knowledge and views on sustainability have been presented. Activities outside the classroom are necessary to achieve successful and multidimensional ESD.

NOTE

1. This student comes from the student association HHUS, which is a volunteer association for all students at USBE.

REFERENCES

Ambrose, S.A., Bridges, M.W. and DiPietro, M. et al. (2010), *How Learning Works: Seven Research-Based Principles for Smart Teaching*, San Francisco, CA: Jossey-Bass.

Barth, M., Godemann, J., Rieckmann, M. and U. Stoltenberg (2007), 'Developing key competencies for sustainable development in higher education', *International Journal of Sustainability in Higher Education*, 8(4), 416–30.

Bartkus, K.R., Nemelka, B., Nemelka, M. and P. Gardner (2012), 'Clarifying the meaning of extracurricular activity: a literature review of definitions', *American Journal of Business Education*, 5(6), 693–703.

Biggs, J. and C. Tang (2011), *Teaching for Quality Learning at University*, Maidenhead, UK: Open University Press.

Brooks, C.D. (2011), 'Space matters: the impact of informal learning environments on student learning', *British Journal of Educational Technology*, 42, 719–26.

Choi, H.H., Van Merriënboer, J.J. and F. Paas (2014), 'Effects of the physical environment on cognitive load and learning: towards a new model of cognitive load', *Educational Psychology Review*, 26(2), 225–44.

de Haan, G. (2010), 'The development of ESD-related competencies in supportive institutional framework', *International Review of Education*, 56(2), 315–28.

Dewey, J. (1938), *Experience and Education*, New York: Macmillan Co.

Dorestani, A. (2005), 'Is interactive/active learning superior to traditional lecturing in economics courses?', *Humanomics*, 21(1), 1–20.

Eizaguirre, A., García-Feijoo, M. and J.P. Laka (2019), 'Defining sustainability core competencies in business and management studies based on multinational stakeholders' perceptions', *Sustainability*, 11(8), Article 2303.

Entwistle, N.J. and E.R. Peterson (2004), 'Conceptions of learning and knowledge in higher education: relationships with study behaviour and influences of learning environments', *International Journal of Educational Research*, 41(6), 407–28.

Guest, G., MacQueen, K.M. and E.E. Namey (2012), *Applied Thematical Analysis*, Thousand Oaks, CA: SAGE.

Kolb, D.A. (1984), *Experiential Learning: Experience as the Source of Learning and Development*, Upper Saddle River, NJ: Prentice-Hall.

Kolb, A. and D. Kolb (2005), 'Learning styles and learning spaces: enhancing experiential learning in higher education', *Academy of Management Learning and Education*, 4(2), 193–212.

Leal Filho, W. and P. Pace (2016), 'Teaching education for sustainable development: implications on learning programmes at higher education', in W. Leal Filho and P. Pace (eds), *Teaching Education for Sustainable Development at University Level*, Cham, Switzerland: Springer, pp. 1–6.

Leicht, A., Heiss, J. and Byun, W.J. (eds) (2018), *Issues and trends in Education for Sustainable Development*, Paris: UNESCO.

Longhurst, J. (2014), *Education for Sustainable Development: Guidance for UK Higher Education Providers*, Gloucester, UK: The Quality Assurance Agency for Higher Education.

Marton, F. and R. Säljö (1997), 'Approaches to learning', in F. Marton, D. Hounsell and N.J. Entwistle (eds), *The Experience of Learning*, Edinburgh: Scottish Academic Press, pp. 39–58.

Moore, J. (2005), 'Is higher education ready for transformative learning? A question explored in the study of sustainability', *Journal of Transformative Education*, 3(1), 76–91.

Oblinger, D. (2005), 'Leading the transition from classrooms to learning spaces', *Educause Quarterly*, 1, 7–12.

Piaget, J. (1954), *The Construction of Reality in the Child*, New York: Basic Books.

Rieckmann, M. (2018), 'Learning to transform the world: key competencies in education for sustainable development', in A. Leicht, J. Heiss and W.J. Byun (eds), *Issues and Trends in Education for Sustainable Development*, Paris: UNESCO, pp. 39–59.

Rubin, R.S., Bommer, W.H. and T.T. Baldwin (2002), 'Using extracurricular activity as an indicator of interpersonal skill: prudent evaluation or recruiting malpractice?', *Human Resource Management*, 41, 441–54.

Teslenko, T. (2019), 'Engaging students and campus community in sustainability activities in a major Canadian university', in W. Leal Filho and U. Bardi (eds), *Sustainability at University Campuses: Learning, Skills Building and Best Practices*, Cham, Switzerland: Springer.

Thomas, C., Pavlechko, G. and J. Cassady (2019), 'An examination of the mediating role of learning space design on the relation between instructor effectiveness and student engagement', *Learning Environments Research*, 22(1), 117–31.

Tortora, M. (2019), 'Promoting sustainability and CSR initiatives to engage business and economics students at university: a study on students' perceptions about extracurricular national events hosted at the local university', in W. Leal Filho and U. Bardi (eds), *Sustainability at University Campuses: Learning, Skills Building and Best Practices*, Cham, Switzerland: Springer, pp. 477–96.

Trigwell, K., Prosser, M. and F. Waterhouse (1999), 'Relations between teachers' approaches to teaching and students' approaches to learning', *Higher Education*, 37, 57–70.

United Nations Educational, Scientific and Cultural Organization (UNESCO) (2017), *Education for Sustainable Development Goals: Learning Objectives*, UNESCO: Paris.

USBE (2020), 'Vision, mission and values', accessed 12 May 2020 at https://www.umu.se/en/usbe/about-us/vision-mission-and-values/.

Wiek, A., Withycombe, L. and C.L. Redman (2011), 'Key competencies in sustainability: a reference framework for academic program development', *Sustainability Science*, 6(2), 203–18.

22. Fostering empathy towards effective sustainability teaching: from the Food Sustainability Index educational toolkit to a new pedagogical model*

Sonia Massari, Francesca Allievi and Francesca Recanati

1. INTRODUCTION

Nowadays, transitioning towards a more sustainable society becomes everyone's duty. In education, and specifically higher education, the discussion on how curricula should evolve and contribute to this societal quest is thriving. However, the concept of sustainability itself is complex and hence risks remaining abstract; furthermore, students may face difficulties in grasping its interconnected nature, even when referring to the UN Sustainable Development Goals (SDGs) (UN, 2015).

When it comes to food sustainability, the connection between the food system and the desired sustainable societal transition is even harder to grasp. Three food paradoxes can be identified (Barilla Center for Food & Nutrition Foundation [BCFN], 2016): (1) worldwide, 821 million people suffer from a shortage of food, while 2.1 billion people are obese or overweight; (2) despite the need to feed a growing global population, 40 percent of the world's cereal resources are used to feed livestock and produce fuel; (3) one-third of the world's food production is wasted, causing economic losses and environmental impacts, and exacerbating the existing nutritional challenges. Besides the multifaceted challenge, the perspectives and priorities of the various stakeholders of the food system fail to be fully represented and understood. This may hinder sustainable development, which requires integrated approaches and actions in recognition that everything and everyone is interconnected (Ukaga, Maser and Reichenbach, 2010).

We argue that understanding and, consequently, acting towards sustainability will always be difficult unless it is perceived as a *value* for human beings. While providing students with knowledge on the connections among societal, environmental, and economic issues remains important, innovative approaches are needed for education to become a catalyst for sustainability. These approaches should be based on mechanisms of altruism: acting together to save the planet can only be done by enabling students to first see and then understand the other (Steffen et al., 2015). Focusing on food sustainability is relevant because food connects, in one way or another, all SDGs (Stockholm Resilience Centre, 2016).

The present work focuses on the activation of empathy in higher education, not only to enable a more comprehensive understanding of sustainability and the SDGs but, even more, to stimulate agency skills in students and enable them to develop creative solutions for a more sustainable society. Two classroom experiments based on the BCFN's Food Sustainability Index (FSI) are presented and analyzed, and the derived pedagogical model to foster empathy and make sustainability teaching more effective is introduced.

2. HUMAN LIMITS AND SUSTAINABILITY PRINCIPLES: THE ROLE OF EMPATHY

During an interview[1] the Italian astronaut Luca Parmitano underlined that '[l]ife on this planet will continue beyond the damages we are creating . . . it will continue to exist but it is possible that in the future humans will not be part of this system. If we want to preserve humankind, this is the moment to act'. As the end of the Earth is an event very far into the future, discussion about sustainability, especially with youth, should start from the opposite point of view: how long will humanity be able to survive on Earth? How are our daily choices affecting the planetary boundaries (Steffen et al., 2015)? How can humankind be educated about such boundaries and their implications for human activities?

Thousands of years of evolution have made the human brain increasingly powerful, but the most important skill that humankind has developed, and which has allowed cooperation with others, is empathy or the sharing of emotions (ibid.). More than any other species, humans have developed the ability to share each other's feelings, up to the point that it is possible to understand, or even anticipate, the thoughts and behaviors of others. As shown in various studies (Section 2.1), empathic mechanisms can also generate attitudes and behaviors targeted at environmental conservation and sustainability.

2.1 Empathy and Empathic Mechanisms

Even if the sense of altruism seems basic and simple, it is a complex function that aroused the interest of neuroscientists and psychologists. Among the latter, Tomasello investigated the drivers of rapid human evolution and progress (Tomasello, 2009) and discovered the crucial role of the *created* culture, a culture understood as an element capable of developing what he calls the 'ratchet effect'. For example, some monkeys can use tools (e.g., a stick to extract ants), but each monkey must learn the function of objects by itself. Humans are instead able to maintain knowledge transgenerationally, in short, thanks to active teaching. Moreover, a mechanism of transmission of knowledge selects only the most useful innovations in order to have tools that become increasingly functional. This is the *ratchet effect* –the ability to build a culture that evolves and is maintained over time. For this to happen, a collaborative type of interaction is needed, which would be impossible without empathic abilities.

Recently, interest in empathy has been relaunched thanks to the discovery of the mirror-neuron systems (Rizzolatti and Graighero, 2004) and the consequent growth of experiments in neuroscience and psychology. Empathy is now quickly projecting itself into other research fields, underlining the need for widespread empathy in the contemporary world. Proposals aimed at reactivating empathy are flourishing: in addition to cognitive sciences, recent contributions invest empathy with the quality of near salvation for the fate of a humanity entangled in global ecological and financial crisis. For instance, Rifkin (2009) and De Waal (2010) link the evolutionary perspective with that of contemporary financial, legal and political life, refuting aggressiveness and selfishness as basic components of human nature. In particular, Rifkin's proposal is centered on the egoism/altruism antithesis being replaced by a participatory, associative reading of human nature, where the empathic capacity is the psychological device that renews participatory bonds every time humans forget that energy is needed for communication. Therefore, the dark side of human development is no longer constituted by the logic of selfishness or competition, but by the historical, cultural, physiological, or pathological variation of the empathic component of human nature. Empathy is thus biologically innate but tends to be forgotten mainly due to the economic-driven growth perspective and standardized training received by many humans, despite being one of the skills that the World Economic Forum (2019) considers fundamental. Additionally, a positive link between empathy and environmental protection has emerged: the correlation of empathic engagement and sustainable practices could be exploited to engage citizens in environmental conservation practices and to optimize related policy and economic tools (Ericson, Kjønstad and Barstad, 2014).

Training students to adopt empathic behaviors when addressing environmental protection appears therefore to be a crucial objective for higher education to teach and so reinforce sustainability. The decrease in empathy found in college students in the last decades (Konrath, O'Brien and Hsing, 2011) further underlines the importance of fostering empathy through education.

3.   TEACHING SUSTAINABILITY IN HIGHER EDUCATION: THE MISMATCH BETWEEN INCREASING INTEREST AND ACTUAL LIMITATIONS

Sustainability, and especially food sustainability, is gaining popularity in higher education. With sustainable agriculture projects increasing in universities across the United States (LaCharite, 2016), and nearly 750 members in the Association for the Advancement of Sustainability in Higher Education (AASHE), the potential role of academia in shaping citizens who have (food) sustainability as a core value is evident. Additionally, the outcomes of sustainable agriculture projects in formal higher education include a deeper sense of community and enhanced critical thinking, two fundamental characteristics for the integration of sustainability in all aspects of society (ibid.). It has also been highlighted how those campuses most committed to sustainability may implement change in the surrounding community (Cortese, 2003).

However, difficulties remain in developing sustainability curricula. For example, in the context of food sustainability, education on sustainable agriculture techniques, as well as the understanding and application of sustainable diets into the courses and practices of universities and campuses, are still lagging behind. As shown in Allievi and Massari (2021), some types of non-formal education on sustainable food systems often fail to guide students towards more sustainable food choices, which could otherwise have a long-term impact on how they approach sustainability in general.

Other barriers are linked to the institutional and administrative structure, the overall lack of training, information, and leadership for sustainability goals, and the curriculum overload (Kioupi and Voulvoulis, 2019). In addition to these, the lack of pressure from society contributes to the low priority given to such transformation (ibid.). All these points diminish the allocation of budget and personnel dedicated to sustainability (ibid.).

It becomes clear that to achieve SDGs, courses and pedagogical aims need to be redesigned to include interdisciplinary collaboration, with sustainability being integrated into the mission, vision, and action plans of the institution (Blanco-Portela et al., 2017). In this context, the role of empathy also becomes fundamental.

3.1   The Role of Empathy for Sustainability Teaching

The authors argue that students can relearn empathy as they get back in touch with this skill through facilitated exercises and workshops. Empathy, in its affective and cognitive meaning, increases the chances that an individual will take action over another's suffering (Owoimaha-Church, 2017). Such an attitude would also be beneficial for the achievement of the SDGs: despite these 17 goals offering a rather anthropocentric point of view of the nature–human relationship, if an eco-centric perspective was accounted for, it would allow the empathic recognition of nature's inherent value and would ease the paradigm change necessary to tackle sustainability (Koiupi and Voulvoulis, 2019). In this context, previous studies have shown how empathy has a positive effect on the understanding of environmental knowledge and sustainability (Brown et al., 2019; Guergachi et al., 2010; Jensen, 2016; Owoimaha-Church, 2017), enabling feeling and caring, and enhancing the awareness of the needs of all life forms, both at the local and global scale.

A deeper understanding is needed of how teaching methods can effectively foster this process (Brown et al., 2019; Jensen, 2016) in order to narrow the knowledge–action gap that often characterizes sustainability and sustainable consumption learning (Barth et al., 2012; Kollmuss and Agyeman, 2002). Deep learning involves much more than information: Jensen (2016) underlined how practices of sustainability teaching were more effective when being innovative, and when including empathy to imagine other perspectives. This also raises the complexity of sustainability understanding, which needs to include new relationships between the self and the other, and the transition to sustainability becoming a value. This calls for a more transformative educational policy, in which educators can develop solutions to place empathy not only in the curriculum but also in the daily practices and environments of education. Previous research points out that this is possible through activities such as role playing, imagination, and personal stories (Owoimaha-Church, 2017).

It becomes clear that empathy has the power to promote sustainability, as individuals create empathic relations with sustainability issues, by forming identities that include elements beyond their locality. This is how the connection between empathy and sustainability can advance the understanding of human–environment relations, and in turn contribute to policies and international relations where, for example, harm to the environment is accounted for (Brown et al., 2019). By promoting and supporting empathy at the micro level of the interactions that take place among the individuals of a community, the community as a whole will also see its overall sustainability improved (Guergachi et al., 2010). With this in mind, it is possible to assume that enhancing empathy in students through experience will increase sustainability in the educational context as well as in the surrounding community, accounting for both environmental and social factors. Learning, thinking, and doing need to be aligned to facilitate the necessary cultural change in educational organizations (Kioupi and Voulvoulis, 2019).

4.   SOLVING THE CHALLENGES OF TEACHING FOOD SUSTAINABILITY: THE CASE OF THE FSI EDU TOOLKIT

The Food Sustainability Index (FSI) measures the sustainability of national food systems across three categories: food loss and waste, sustainable agriculture, and nutritional challenges. In its third edition in 2018, 67 countries have been ranked according to their final score scaled from 0 to 100, where 100 equals the most sustainable. This latter is obtained from the weighted sum of 89 qualitative and quantitative metrics (BCFN and Economist Intelligence Unit, 2018).

The FSI Edu is an educational module and toolkit for higher education based on the FSI and aiming at teaching food sustainability and its link to the SDGs. It has been tested in different universities around the world, reaching nearly 500 students so far (as of end of 2020).

It comprises five steps: a kick-off knowledge-assessment questionnaire, a theoretical lesson, two workshops, and a final knowledge-assessment questionnaire. The expected learning outcomes for students are to understand (1) the global challenges related to food sustainability and the role of food within the SDGs; (2) the complexity of the global food system; and (3) the need for multistakeholder dialogue to tackle food sustainability challenges.

4.1   Methodology: Application of the FSI to Foster Empathy in Food Sustainability Teaching

Two experiments using the FSI Edu have been carried out, each selecting one of the two workshops available in the module. In the first workshop called 'Being a Country', students were asked to use the FSI data to assess the situation of one specific country. This exercise aims at allowing students to grasp the complex and multifaceted nature of food sustainability. Additionally, it allows students to better understand the variety of dimensions and data to be taken into account when attempting to develop indicators and composite indexes for the assessment of the complexity of food sustainability. The second workshop called 'Being a Food System Agent' focuses on the different points of view of the food system's stakeholders (or agents) through the weighting process of the FSI. In practice, it is a role-playing game where students are divided into groups representing the different agents – that is, farmers, policy makers, food industry, or nutritionists. Both the workshops help the students to understand sustainability by being in 'others' shoes', thus activating the empathic mechanism. In the second phase of the experiments, students were asked to apply the newly acquired knowledge in their creative process. This phase aimed at detecting the actual impact of the FSI Edu, not only as a means to deliver valuable information on food sustainability but even more to engage the students in becoming active agents in the food system, thus contributing positively to a more sustainable society (Allievi, Dentoni and Antonelli, 2018).

The experiments presented involved three classrooms, during the Fall–Spring 2019–20 term: one in Roma Tre University, Italy, which also did a virtual exchange with one in JAMK University of Applied Sciences, Finland, and one in ISIA Design School, Italy.

The class from Roma Tre University had 20 students from different countries, mainly with an academic background in economics and business and attending the course on

'Sustainability Design Thinking'. The class from ISIA Design School had 26 students from the Master's Degree in Systems Design, all from Italy, mainly with an academic background in industrial design and communication and attending the course on 'Sociology of Change'. The class from JAMK University of Applied Sciences had 21 students from the Bachelor's Degree in Tourism and Hospitality Management attending the course on 'Food and Consumer', mostly coming from Finland.

The experiments also involved two lecturers (who are also two of the authors), one from JAMK University of Applied Sciences and the other teaching in both ISIA Design School and Roma Tre University.

4.2   First Experiment

In the first experiment, the students from Roma Tre University attended a two-hour co-teaching class with both lecturers online. After the introduction of the FSI, the first lecturer facilitated the 'Being a Country' workshop. In small groups, starting from the final score and rank of the selected country, they explored strengths and weaknesses in each of the three aforementioned areas, using the data available in the Excel workbook containing the FSI database. This first part lasted for 30 minutes and was followed by another half an hour, during which each group presented and discussed its findings to and with the rest of the classroom. In particular, the second lecturer moderated the discussion, promoted students' curiosity through live comments, and answered their questions. Reflections on sustainability issues were expressed by the lecturer and students commented cooperatively and interactively.

After this session, students implemented the knowledge acquired in their teamwork design thinking (DT) exercises. Throughout this course, each group learned the DT techniques needed to formulate ideas that are innovative in terms of sustainability and strategic to collaborate and cooperate. Divergent phases of design, like openness to different solutions, were alternated with convergent ones, such as the selection of best solutions. The outcome was a project in which all the DT phases (empathy, problem definition, ideation, prototyping, implementation, testing) were implemented.

Eighty percent of the team project was about learning ethnographic research methods and working in the field and 20 percent concerned the final ideation phase. When all the concepts were finalized, another co-taught online class was organized: this time, students from Roma Tre University presented the progress of their projects to the class at JAMK University of Applied Sciences and received their feedback. Again, by using DT, the two class groups were able to carry out a virtual exchange, with the lecturers in the two classrooms facilitating the discussion. The students then continued developing their projects for one week before giving a final presentation, in which they were also asked to highlight how their learning from the FSI Edu was useful for the development of their creative process and to give feedback to the tool in terms of its usefulness to understand sustainability.

4.3   Second Experiment

The second experiment was implemented with students from ISIA Design School. For this experiment, the second lecturer was not online but closely interacting with the students in the classroom. The workshop 'Being a Food System Agent' was proposed. Each group representing one agent in the food system had first to work separately for 30 minutes, identifying its vision, goal, and priorities, and translating them into the weighting system of the FSI Excel workbook (i.e., by changing the relative weights of the indicators, and weight being proportional to the relevance of the indicators). Second, each group presented their weights and the reasoning process behind the choice to the rest of the class. Finally, the whole classroom participated in an open discussion, during which the differences and common points of the agents' perspectives were presented.

The activities in the classroom were facilitated by the two lecturers, one online and one present in the classroom. After this session, the students had one week to prepare a 30-second creative video on the role of food in fighting climate change and achieving sustainability in Europe.

5. RESULTS OF THE EXPERIMENTS

This section illustrates the results of the two FSI Edu workshops used in the experiments.

5.1 'Being a Country' Workshop

Teaching DT methods proved to be the strongest asset of the course connected with the first experiment. DT is a transferable methodology of problem solving, a framework that can be used by any sustainability sector and actors (private company, public institutions, etc.) to solve complex problems. DT is an innovative approach, as it places users at its core, prioritizing their perspectives and preferences, and using soft skills such as empathy, creativity, and communication (Massari, 2017). This type of thinking was not easy to integrate into a formal educational environment such as business schools, where training is still provided traditionally. However, the final result was undoubtedly successful.

The keywords of the course were empathy, critical thinking, open-mindedness, and collaboration. The course's transdisciplinary nature is seen not only by the co-existence of information coming from different fields but also by how students worked in teams and in the field. It is important to highlight that the students who took part in this experiment have different backgrounds and nationalities. This was a real advantage, as both the empathy phase and the ideation phase were analyzed from an intercultural point of view. Furthermore, the opportunity to interact with the classroom in JAMK provided added value to the group, creating transcurricular discussions between different institutes and educational scenarios. Also, students had a background in business and marketing, but no knowledge of food studies, sustainability, or food sustainability.

Students' comments regarding the FSI Edu are summarized in Table 22.1.

Out of five groups, only two mentioned FSI Edu in their final presentations. One group focused on inequalities of food services on the campus and developed a solution that also accounts for invisible disabilities, such as mental health disorders. FSI supported their understanding of dietary patterns in Europe, but it is unclear how such data are connected to their creative process. Another group pointed out the difficulties in using FSI to enrich their project, which dealt with a range of plastic-free products for students and tourists.

Table 22.1   Strengths and weaknesses of the FSI as an educational tool

Strengths	Weaknesses
It is one of the most interesting tools with which to understand the differences among countries, to have a *wide* perspective on food sustainability issues	FSI is interesting for understanding country-level differences, but questions regarding the causes remain open
The need of business students for this sort of tool is irrefutable; having an analytical tool such as the FSI and related data is in line with students' academic needs. The tool proved to be innovative and, despite having been defined as similar to other educational tools, they appreciated the possibility for interaction	Two hours is too short to fully understand the tool and its uses; longer time during the class to deepen the analysis would have been beneficial
FSI data can be helpful for all students interested in food sustainability and who are approaching this topic. This tool can also be used in high schools to prepare younger students to deal with issues such as globalization when starting higher education. FSI Edu thus has the potential to be used as an *orientation tool*	The FSI enabled students to see the existing differences and inequalities, and students would like to act for a change, but also say that they do not have enough information to do that
FSI is also extremely important in offering support in debunking fake news and enabling students to become more aware readers. The variety of indicators has been valued positively as a way to start using system thinking, instead of approaching these issues separately	
It is key to be able to access reliable data to understand the critical points and then move to action; only those who know the facts can change the status of things and can improve their *problem-solving skills*	
Students identified other fields of study where this tool could be useful and impactful on a pedagogical level: political sciences and engineering. This could also contribute to putting in the foundations for new green jobs	

Despite the class as a whole giving positive feedback on the FSI, most students did not report using this tool for further analysis and self-learning on sustainability. Also, it seems that the workshop 'Being a Country' did not contribute to their creative process. This further confirms that sustainability is not easy to address in those classes where students are not majoring in the topic, and it is therefore necessary to captivate them from the start using innovative teaching styles.

The use of DT in this course was very innovative, not only because it provided the students with analysis and research tools to find alternative and creative solutions for emerging food sustainable systems, but also because it offered the participants reflection and interaction tools that could help them in their future professional career and throughout their life.

However, it seems that the data and analysis offered through the FSI Edu did not find their place as an instrument for research, thus enriching the first part of DT, called 'inspiration phase', even if the students considered it useful to improve their critical approach.

5.2 'Being a Food System Agent' Workshop

One of the most important current challenges in teaching students in design studies is the design of more sustainable solutions. In the past ten years, design pedagogy and project-based learning have evolved to prepare young designers for the complexities they face as citizens in a global community. However, the most widespread teacher-centered design pedagogy is not conducive to the development of 'sustainability designers and leaders', who instead need a variety of skills that are key in tackling the challenges outlined above, such as divergent thinking, creative problem solving, empathy, and self-reflection.

The present research also aimed at exploring how sustainability pedagogy can be transformed to equip an emerging generation of designers to meet these future challenges. The workshop 'Being a Food System Agent' was thus also useful to investigate the use of alternative and design-led approaches as methods for experiential learning, testing whether the combination of these methods encourages self-reflective practices as a key first step towards becoming leaders of sustainable futures (Angheloiu, Chaudhuri and Sheldrick, 2017). The students participating in this experiment had a background in industrial design and communication, but no knowledge of food studies and sustainability.

The most interesting points emerging from the discussion following the 'Being a Food System Agent' workshop were as follows:

- Transferring the abstract concept of SDGs into a more practical context is challenging.
- Some concepts, such as the difference between policy and politics, were completely new and fostered curiosity and discussion.
- In comparison with the first experiment, students made a lot of connections between what they learned through FSI and their real lives (e.g., the need for a special diet, and impact on the local economic, environmental, and social sustainability).
- In comparison with the first experiment, students had more difficulties in understanding the indicators and the methodology but had a more positive response to maps and interactive instruments.
- Students produced creative solutions to cooperate and work together: through the workshop, they understand both the differences in agents' (or stakeholders') priorities and what it means to create a balance in a system and ecosystem.

Among the main outcomes was a shift in mindset that is key to unlocking behaviors and attitudes that can enable designers gear themselves towards sustainable lifestyles. However, it is necessary to test whether these insights and reflections have a lasting effect on mindset. Additionally, out of 21 videos, more than half referred to sustainability as something personal, describing, through subjective content, personal history, and everyday practices, how to implement sustainability principles in practice.

When looking at the messages shared through the videos, the informational statements (dealing with macro scenarios) based on general and abstract data were fewer than those including guidelines for everyday life (micro scenarios), also including personal reflections. The topics addressed in the videos were water, health, natural resources, local versus global, packaging and plastic-free items, waste, climate change, ecology, SDGs, everyday grocery shopping, circular economy, activism, children.

Often, future scenarios seem intangible, especially when involving long timelines. A creative project-based approach enabled students to develop propositional artifacts, which facilitated a reflective conversation about what it might *feel* like to be alive in the respective scenarios. DT methods, such as video ideation and concept creation, enabled the students to move in a propositional space and sparked intense debate among students about what would and what would not be feasible in their respective scenarios, as well as what would be preferable and deemed to improve the quality of life in the future. The results suggest the potential for more experiential learning to enable students to test their dominant assumptions around the role and applications of creative solutions in achieving and maintaining sustainable societies over the next decades.

6.   THE EOE MODEL: AN EMPATHY-BASED MODEL

The human component in innovation was an important focus of research for both workshops. Thanks to the mix of formal and experiential education, both workshops provided a concrete foundation for the students' future working life: besides the solid knowledge on sustainability and the complexity of food systems, students learned fundamental soft skills, which are increasingly desired in workplaces. In particular, the complexity of sustainable systems demands creative problem solvers with aptitudes for empathy, non-linear thought, and risk taking.

As emerged from the results of the two experiments, DT as a methodology of learning and teaching is an exploratory process involving visualizing, experimenting, creating, and gathering feedback. This ensemble creates added value for both business and design schools. More conventional pedagogical approaches tend to be more common in higher education, with analytical tools targeted at improving critical thinking in students. On the other hand, in design schools, the focus on enriching creative skills gives less attention to the critical ones. A balance between these two types of skills and pedagogical approaches is needed.

The combination of analytical and critical tools, such as the FSI, with creative teaching models, for example based on experiential learning and DT, can lead to an effective learning path (Massari, 2017). However, critical and creative thinking are not enough to generate new behaviors in students and transform knowledge and skills into aware and sustainable actions.

The US National Education Association (NEA, 2012) identified four Cs as essential twenty-first-century skills that students should learn: collaboration, communication, critical thinking, and creativity. Collaboration (teamwork) and communication (debate and sharing) are at the basis of all the experiential teaching methods. Critical thinking and creativity are the necessary skills to activate all the processes of awareness and conscious learning and they are paramount in food and sustainability studies. Two more Cs can be added: choice and change. These are fundamental in students' agency, enabling their ability and will to positively influence their own lives in the world around them (Massari, 2020).

The workshop 'Being a Food System Agent' stimulated the analysis and research on the activation of cooperative mechanisms and students' awareness: more than half the class in the second experiment succeeded in translating the knowledge into practical actions, thus supporting the agency skills in students. From this analysis, the authors developed a more comprehensive understanding of the role of empathy in sustainability education and identified three different levels of empathy that need to be experienced for agency skills to be activated.

A mindset shift is required to realize sustainable actions: humans need empathy towards other humans and towards other life forms, as those at risk in the near future are not the Earth and its resources, but humankind itself. However, recognizing ourselves as part of a human system is not enough; various levels of empathy need to be put in place. First, the individual needs to use empathy to recognize oneself in the system. Second, empathy is necessary to recognize the point of view of others. Last, empathy needs to be activated to recognize what each individual can do with the other(s) to cooperate to change the status of things thanks to co-constructive and collaborative empathic processes.

The authors propose a new pedagogical model to teach sustainability in higher education. This innovative model, called EOE, is based on the three aforementioned empathy steps needed to move from the acquisition of knowledge to cooperation and active co-construction of meaning. The EOE model is defined according to the following parts (Figure 22.1):

E = empathy with one's self (ego-centric empathy)
O = altruistic empathy (other-centric empathy)
E = co-constructive empathy (eco-centric empathy)

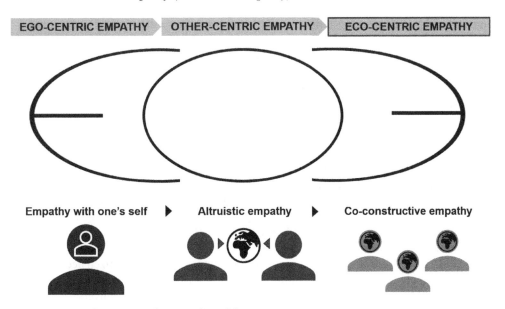

Figure 22.1   The EOE pedagogical model

This model can be implemented with analytical tools such as the FSI Edu and lead to interesting results, as shown in the second experiment. Additionally, the presence of DT learning processes may enhance the development of a better appreciation for the diversity of learning orientations exhibited by project team members. Finally, empathy and effective interaction with team members are also components of interpersonal and emotional intelligence competences. The presence of interdisciplinary student teams in design-thinking projects has the potential to provide a practice field for cross-functional interactions in work situations. Therefore, the integration of EOE and DT can help to develop the opportunity for students to become 'authors' of their experiences, rather than simply passive 'readers'. Students learn to become proactive and empathic problem solvers.

7.   DISCUSSION AND CONCLUSIONS

This chapter opened up, even more, the question of the role of empathy in sustainability teaching, with a particular focus on food sustainability. The workshops, in particular 'Being a Food System Agent', showed how students can be engaged in issues related to the food system by considering the different stakeholders. By guiding students to see food beyond its final consumption, and including the transdisciplinary sectors that it connects, they could better grasp and define sustainability. Furthermore, DT methods highlighted the concept of the interconnectedness of people, and people with nature: this should be one of the core concepts in education, as it has a fundamental role in developing competences and research methodologies that support sustainability with transdisciplinary approaches. This chapter shows how the boundary between quantitative analysis and qualitative creativity can be overcome, by introducing agency-centered reflection tools. In particular, in the 'Being a Country' workshop, the advantage is the possibility for a deep understanding of the food system's complexity in a specific context, as well as its suitability for students of, for example, engineering, who could make the most use of the ample data of the FSI database. On the other hand, this workshop, even when combined with an international virtual exchange, did not influence positively either the application of the FSI data into the following creative process, or the fostering of empathic mechanisms.

The strength of the workshop 'Being a Food System Agent', is that it can be considered a valid ally in enhancing processes of cooperation and co-creation. By seeing food sustainability through the eyes of a specific agent group, students experienced three levels of empathy, according to the EOE model described above. This was reflected in the results of the following creative process and video assignment. Nevertheless, this workshop limits the reflection on the context of one specific country and keeps the focus on the various agents that act within it. The EOE model contributes to the current research on the competences for sustainability and global citizenship, supporting the concept of sustainable development identified specifically in the Earth Charter (Earth Charter International, 2017).

The EOE model can be key to fostering the competencies that each citizen needs to support sustainability: a lifelong curriculum, adaptable to local needs and cultural contexts, could be developed in this sense; through the EOE model, clusters of universal soft skills (or emotional competences), based on eco-centric empathy and global co-construction of sustainability knowledge through empathy, could be identified. While the qualitative data gathered concern only two experiments, they support the thesis that when empathic mechanisms are enabled, the results in terms of sustainability understanding are better, and can activate more creative processes in the students. This leads to the merger of inspiration and action. More experiments are needed to test and validate the EOE model in a variety of settings. This is partly continuing through the testing of FSI Edu but the research will be further expanded.

The first International Day of Education – launched by the UN in January 2020[2] – coincides with the start of the UN Decade of Action[3] that highlights the crucial role of people's action for faster progress in addressing the current societal challenges and calls for youth and academia to push for the required transformation. In light of the increasing effects of climate change and the latest 'warning to humanity' (Ripple et al., 2017), this Decade of Action cannot fail to carry out the needed transformations towards a more sustainable world, including that of the educational system. It is time for educators to question what is being done wrong and what needs to be improved. Empathy is a prerequisite that would lead the way towards seeing the other and working together towards the SDGs.

ACKNOWLEDGMENTS

The authors would like to thank the Barilla Center for Food and Nutrition (BCFN) Foundation and the Economist Intelligence Unit for their efforts in developing the FSI. Special thanks to the BCFN Foundation also for the support in granting the development and dissemination of the FSI Edu toolkit, as well as its application in classrooms worldwide. Additionally, they wish to thank JAMK University of Applied Sciences, ISIA Design School and Roma Tre University for their support in implementing international and innovative teaching methods in the classrooms. Finally, they wish to thank all the students who took part in the experiments and gave their valuable feedback.

NOTES

* Sonia Massari carried out both of the experiments described in this chapter, developed the theoretical and pedagogical model, and wrote most of the theoretical background; she also edited and revised the whole chapter. Francesca Allievi carried out both of the experiments described in this chapter, developed the FSI Edu toolkit, and wrote some of the theoretical background; she also edited and revised the whole chapter. Francesca Recanati developed the FSI Edu toolkit, and edited and revised the whole chapter.
1. The interview was held on 8 February 2020 at the European Space Agency's European Astronaut Centre. See European Space Agency (2020), 'Luca speaks with European media' [video], accessed 11 May 2020 at https://www.esa.int/ESA_Multimedia/Videos/2020/02/Luca_speaks_with_European_media.
2. See UNESCO (2019), 'International Day of Education', accessed 10 May 2020 at https://en.unesco.org/commemorations/educationday.
3. See United Nations (n.d.), 'Decade of Action', accessed 11 May 2020 at https://www.un.org/sustainable development/decade-of-action.

REFERENCES

Allievi, F., Dentoni, D. and Antonelli, M. (2018). The role of youth in increasing awareness of food security and sustainability. In P. Ferranti, E.M. Berry and J.R. Anderson (eds), *Encyclopedia of Food Security and Sustainability Volume 3: Sustainable Food Systems and Agriculture.* Oxford: Elsevier, pp. 39–44.

Allievi, F. and Massari, S. (2021). Promoting sustainable food availability and behaviour on campus: current perceptions and potential food guidance. Accepted for publication in the special issue of *Canadian Food Studies.*

Angheloiu, C., Chaudhuri, G. and Sheldrick, L. (2017). Future tense: alternative futures as a design method for sustainability transitions. *The Design Journal,* 20, 3213–25.

Barilla Center for Food & Nutrition Foundation (BCFN) (2016). *Eating Planet.* Milan: Edizioni Ambiente.

Barilla Center for Food & Nutrition Foundation (BCFN) and Economist Intelligence Unit (2018). *Fixing Food 2018: Best Practices Towards the Sustainable Development Goals.* Accessed 5 May 2020 at https://foodsustain ability.eiu.com/whitepaper-2018/ and http://foodsustainability.eiu.com/resources/.

Barth, M., Fischer, D. and Michelsen, G. et al. (2012). Tackling the knowledge–action gap in sustainable consumption: insights from a participatory school programme. *Journal of Education for Sustainable Development,* 6(2), 301–12.

Blanco-Portela, N., Benayas, J., Pertierra, L.R. and Lozano, R. (2017). Towards the integration of sustainability in higher education institutions: a review of drivers of and barriers to organisational change and their comparison against those found of companies. *Journal of Cleaner Production,* 166, 563–78.

Brown, K., Adger, W.N. and Devine-Wright, P. et al. (2019). Empathy, place and identity interactions for sustainability. *Global Environmental Change,* 56, 11–17.

Cortese, A. (2003). The critical role of higher education in creating a sustainable future. *Planning for Higher Education,* 31(3), 15–22.

De Waal, F. (2010). *The Age of Empathy: Nature's Lessons for a Kinder Society.* New York: Broadway Books.

Earth Charter International (2019). *2018 Annual Report.* Accessed 11 May 2020 at https://earthcharter.org/library/2018-annual-report/.

Ericson, T., Kjønstad, B.G. and Barstad, A. (2014). Mindfulness and sustainability. *Ecological Economics,* 104, 73–9.

Guergachi, A., Ngenyama, O., Magness, V. and Hakim, J. (2010). Empathy: a unifying approach to address the dilemma of environment versus economy. Paper presented at the International Environmental Modelling and Software Society (iEMSs) 2010 International Congress on Environmental Modelling and Software Modelling for Environment's Sake, Fifth Biennial Meeting, Ottawa, Canada.

Jensen, S. (2016). Empathy and imagination in education for sustainability. *Canadian Journal of Environmental Education,* 21, 89–105.

Kioupi, V. and Voulvoulis, N. (2019). Education for sustainable development: a systemic framework for connecting the SDGs to educational outcomes. *Sustainability,* 11(21), Article 6104.

Kollmuss, A. and Agyeman, J. (2002). Mind the gap: why do people act environmentally and what are the barriers to pro-environmental behavior? *Environmental Education Research,* 8(3), 239–60.

Konrath, S., O'Brien, E. and Hsing, C. (2011). Changes in dispositional empathy in American college students over time: a meta-analysis. *Personality and Social Psychology Review,* 15, 180–98.

LaCharite, K. (2016). Re-visioning agriculture in higher education: the role of campus agriculture initiatives in sustainability education. *Agriculture and Human Values,* 33, 521–35.

Massari, S. (2017). Food design and food studies: discussing creative and critical thinking in food system education and research. *International Journal of Food Design,* 2(1), 117–33.

Massari, S. (2020). Food design methods to inspire the new decade. Agency-centered design. Towards 2030. In R. Bonacho, M.J. Pires and E.C. Carona de Soursa Lamy (eds), *Experiencing Food: Designing Sustainable and Social Practices: Proceedings of the 2nd International Conference on Food Design and Food Studies (EFOOD 2019), 28–30 November 2019, Lisbon, Portugal.* London: CRC Press.

National Education Association (NEA) (2012). *Preparing 21st Century Students for a Global Society: An Educator's Guide to the 'Four Cs'.* Washington, DC: NEA.

Owoimaha-Church, E. (2017). Develop & sustain empathy, reach our goals by 2030. Accessed 5 May 2020 at http://www.teachsdgs.org/blog/develop-sustain-empathy-reach-our-goals-by-2030.

Rifkin, J. (2009). *The Empathic Civilization: The Race to Global Consciousness in a World in Crisis.* New York: JP Tarcher/Penguin Putnam.

Ripple, W., Wolf, C. and Newsome, T. et al. (2017). World scientists' warning to humanity: a second notice. *BioScience,* 67(12), 1026–8.

Rizzolatti, G. and Graighero, L. (2004). The mirror-neuron system. *Annual Reviews of Neuroscience,* 27, 169–92.

Steffen, W., Richardson, K. and Rockström, J. et al. (2015). Planetary boundaries: guiding human development on a changing planet. *Science,* 347(6223), Article 1259855.

Stockholm Resilience Centre (2016). How food connects all the SDGs. Accessed 11 May 2020 at http://www.stockholmresilience.org/research/research-news/2016-06-14-how-food-connects-all-the-sdgs.html.

Tomasello, M. (2009). *The Cultural Origins of Human Cognition*. Cambridge, MA: Harvard University Press.

Ukaga, O., Maser, C. and Reichenbach, M. (2010). *Sustainable Development: Principles, Frameworks, and Case Studies*. Boca Raton, FL: CRC Press.

United Nations (2015). *Transforming Our World: The 2030 Agenda for Sustainable Development*. New York: United Nations.

World Economic Forum (2019). Can we create an empathic alternative to the capitalist system? Accessed 11 May 2020 at https://www.weforum.org/agenda/2019/08/empathy-can-create-a-new-economic-system/.

23. Making economics relevant: incorporating sustainability
Madhavi Venkatesan

1. INTRODUCTION

Globally, economies are measured in relative terms with respect to a single economic indicator – gross domestic product (GDP). This indicator, which was created to measure output, has become a synonym for standard of living, in direct opposition to the caution related to the same put forward by its creator, Simon Kuznets (1934). Further, quantification of economics in the decades that followed its deployment has successfully facilitated the perception of economics as a science and distanced the discipline from its moral philosophical roots. Instead of the behavioral discipline of economics providing evaluation and policy based on an explicit normative framework of seeking to attain societally optimal outcomes related to ecosystem symbiosis and quality of life attainment, inclusive of resource conservation and mental and physical optimality, economics has been molded by mathematics to project an objective observational stance. The latter, however, is an implicit normative judgment that has promoted business as usual without conscience-based responsibility. Failures in the market are labeled as 'externalities' and the teaching of economics has endogenized marketing and profit making by legitimizing that individuals are insatiable and driven by greed. That these assumptions, which are referenced as theory, are social norms borne into existence through social construction, is not addressed.

With 70 years of this standardized teaching, the economy has been molded by theory and its behavior is consistent with insatiability, with high resource use, excess production and consumption, as well as a lack of acknowledgement of non-market costs, such as the responsibility for waste. Arguably, this reality provides an opportunity for the discipline to acknowledge its relevance with respect to issues affecting global environmental health, as indeed it is the production-driven model along with an exclusion of moral responsibility that has created the social and environmental justice issues of the present and has been a direct contributor to climate change.

Even though it is a behavioral science, economics has been taught as though it is an optimization discipline, and that incentives like utility and profit maximization are immutable drivers of human behavior. Students are typically presented with a single perspective that reinforces the economic framework in operation. However, the teaching also bounds the rationality of the student to the extent that there is no critical assessment of the prevailing economic system, no discussion of moral responsibility of fundamental purpose other than accumulation. As early as 1938 Beach stated (p. 515):

> It has been the policy of many teachers of economics that beginners in economic theory should be taught only one theoretical explanation of each phenomenon. These teachers feel that the acquaintance of the student with other explanations can be postponed until the student has

become more familiar with economics in general and therefore has a better sense of judgment. The existence of other theoretical explanations can be mentioned, and this, it is thought, should be sufficient to keep the student aware of the fact that there are other sides to the story.

The effectiveness of this policy might be questioned. Even if the existence of other theories is mentioned, the significance of this existence is very seldom appreciated. Elementary students look for definite answers to their problems, and, lacking the power of discernment, will accept the one theoretical explanation as sufficient. If the students do not continue in this subject, this one explanation will always be the explanation. If the students continue, they will tend to have a bias in respect to this one explanation.

Therefore, for those phenomena for which no one theoretical explanation is entirely satisfactory, instead of offering one theory, which may indeed be the best, would it not be better to develop the power of discernment of the student by suggesting more than one theory? Two explanations should be enough, and if they could be introduced by emphasizing certain contrasting features, the additional time need not be great, and the original explanation may be made clearer. Perhaps the most important job of the teacher in social sciences is to develop the students' power of discernment. The students must learn that one idea does not contain the whole truth; and when this is learned, the students' progress will be more rapid.

In the present period, researchers have noted that the teaching of economics has not deviated much over the past 50 years, highlighting that the profession of the teaching of economics has lagged with respect to alignment of content with contemporary issues (Allgood, Walstad and Siegfried, 2015; Bowles and Carlin, 2020). This is a lost opportunity and a problem. The exclusion of application and limited tangibility in the classroom teaching of economics has limited recognition of the significance of economic literacy. Given that introductory economics is typically a requirement at most institutions, non-tangible and commoditized teaching does not allow the profession the opportunity to be relevant:

> More broadly, a few courses in undergraduate economics, and perhaps only an introductory course, are often the only interaction that the college graduates of tomorrow will have with the economics profession. Because they are the only opportunities that academic economists will have to educate the citizens and voters of tomorrow, they deserve our best efforts. (Becker, 2000, p. 117)

This chapter highlights aspects of the teaching of economics that can be incorporated in classroom instruction to promote a stronger understanding of how the economic system – consumption, investment and enfranchisement of the individual economic agent – can promote sustainable economic outcomes. As a starting point, the chapter begins with a discussion of the relationship between culture and environment. The basic question that is addressed is, is the environment a resource for use or an entity to steward and why? The role of culture as it relates to the perception of the environment is evaluated by comparing the perspectives of indigenous and colonial peoples specific to North America. Inclusion of a discussion on culture enables the introduction of comparative systems and most importantly the cultural attribution to the environment is foundational to understanding how economic outcomes can either promote or limit environmental sustainability. Further, it fosters understanding that the economic system is a social construction aligned to the culture of its origin, enabling discussion of how an imposed economic framework and indicator such as GDP can facilitate cultural convergence. This discussion is followed by an overview of how information asymmetries and price can be approached to highlight the significance of externalities in fostering excess consumption. Fundamentally, this addresses how over a product's lifecycle costs exceed price, and consumption based on price leads to over-use of resources, environmental degradation and social justice issues. This chapter highlights the significance of the opportunity presently available to instructors of economics to be facilitators for the adoption of sustainability through addressing the role of conscious consumption and responsible participation in consumer, investor and government decision making. In the concluding discussion, the role of economic literacy in sustainability is addressed.

2. TEACHING ECONOMICS FOR SUSTAINABILITY: THE ROLE OF CULTURE

Economics evaluates human behavior relative to wants, needs, and resource allocation within a natural environment. By definition, the parameters of the discipline include other life forms and the physical resources needed to maintain both life and environmental regeneration. To the extent that a human culture incorporates non-human elements in decision making, an economic system arguably should include an understanding of the holistic interdependence of living and non-living elements of the planet.

Culture is a significant contributor to what is perceived as valuable and is the determining parameter in the designations that ultimately yield to resource allocation within a society (Mokyr, 2017). Given that culture is a learned behavior, culture can either promote or diminish any given society's understanding of the interconnectedness of human and planetary life, thereby determining the extent of the anthropocentric, or human-centered, perspective. The United Nations Educational, Scientific and Cultural Organization (UNESCO, 2017, n.p.) defined culture as a significant component to attaining global sustainability:

> Placing culture at the heart of development policy constitutes an essential investment in the world's future and a pre-condition to successful globalization processes that take into account the principles of cultural diversity. It is UNESCO's mission to remind all States of this major issue. As demonstrated by the failure of certain projects underway since the 1970s, development is not synonymous with economic growth alone. It is a means to achieve a more satisfactory intellectual, emotional, moral and spiritual existence. As such, development is inseparable from culture.

The inputs and outputs of economic systems are dependent on the value structures of a society; and to the extent that economics explains observable phenomena and proposes optimal outcomes, the discipline can be both responsible for the maintenance of an economic framework and also the catalyst for a change. Economic outcomes in essence mimic the values of the participants in an economic system.

Evaluating the historical cultural progression of human society can promote a stronger understanding of the economic relationship with resource allocation, both intra- and inter-society. Most importantly, it can provide insights with respect to how perceptions of the world are shaped through cultural frameworks at a given point in time. The pace at which cultural attributes evolve may also provide a deeper understanding of why institutional and social frameworks may be inconsistent with the manifestation of contemporary challenges. The next section provides a summary overview of the relationship between culture and environmental domination by assessing the perspective of indigenous people and European colonists in North America. The discussion provides alternative cultural perspectives of the environment and economic stability and thereby promotes an understanding of culture being a learned social construction not necessarily a manifestation of innate human traits.

The colonization of North America is credited with a variety of reasons, from religious freedom, to economic betterment, and even to adventure. However, evidence suggests that the market value of the natural environment was an overall and significant driver of the interest in settlement. Given that the land was inhabited by indigenous populations at the time of European colonization, and colonists' records describe the environment as resource rich, there is evidence that culture is influential in promoting either resource preservation or depletion. Arguably, the legacy of the colonists' orientation toward the environment as a market-value asset has shaped current environmental sensitivities and the perception of the environment as a resource. However, perhaps more important to understand is that the environment can be embedded within a culture not as a resource for human use but as an entity that human life is dependent upon and a human responsibility to steward.

Many of the first settlers were a 'downtrodden and oppressed people with few skills to make it in a pioneering society. Despite the difficulties they experienced, the shift across the Atlantic resulted in one enormous benefit: it removed the pilgrims from competition with other Europeans. In Europe, they were at the bottom of the heap, persecuted and reviled as fanatics' (Flannery, 2001, pp. 271–3). Religion, along with the difficulty of survival and settlement, proved to be the cohesive element of early colonists. The Puritans adopted a stringent legal code as a reaction to the unknown and fearful outlook in their New England settlement, 'for they believed America to be a stronghold of the devil. Everything about the place seemed God-forsaken, from the natives (who they took to be devil worshippers) to the untamed landscapes and wild creatures' (ibid., p. 275).

The cultural values depicted in the early colonists were the 'outcome of enormous social stress', the 'emphasis of self-denial and extreme conformity with an uncompromising faith seems typical of social movements that arise at such times. Societies founded on such principles are like glass . . . they thrive during times of adversity, but during more prosperous periods their stringent belief systems may be either discarded or greatly modified' (ibid., p. 276). From the perspective of their settlement, the original Puritan settlers pose an enigma, though they adapted to the available crops (specifically, corn) and fowl of New England, growing corn and raising turkeys, 'their ecology was not so different from that of villagers in the old country. Thus, at an ecological level, despite the shift in continents, the Puritans continued to live very British lives' (ibid.).

Colonial cultural values as both documented at the time of settlement and related to the environment differed from those of the indigenous peoples. Where the indigenous populations migrated with the seasons and adapted to the environment, colonial values specific to their defining of civilization promoted the augmentation of the environment to conform to human needs. Where Europeans sought 'endless accumulation of capital which John Locke saw as a natural consequence of the human love for wealth' (Cronon, 1983, p. 79), natives found wealth in the abundance of their environment. The land supported their way of life and therefore they were by necessity stewards of their environment. The change to the indigenous populations came over a short time interval, as colonial dominance predicated on an accumulation-based culture forced the native population into geographically limited settlements and fostered a dependence that had its roots in seemingly benign trading arrangements between the two groups.

2.1 The Market Value of Discovery

Colonial records of the New England of the seventeenth century were not descriptive narratives related to the beauty or even objective assessment of the landscape. Instead, surviving descriptions provide an insight into the market focus of colonial settlers. As noted by Cronon (1983, p. 21), 'As often as not, their descriptions of New England contained implicit comparisons with England. Explorers describing a new countryside with an eye to its mercantile possibilities all too easily fell into this way of looking at things, so that their descriptions often degenerated to nothing more than lists'.

The colonial attitudes and appetite for what was coined as the 'New World' equated to a 'discovery' from the perspective that the resources found were thought of as accessible for the colonists' taking; the land for their ownership; and the native people for whatever resource that they could offer, inclusive of elimination in the event they proved useless. Their view was legitimized by religion and a sense of moral superiority in spite of whether their actions in the New World were contrary to those espoused in either. Initially, justification of the right to inhabited land was provided through religion via interpretation of Genesis to give land to those who used their God-given attribute of dominion over plants and animals and who followed God's pronouncement to multiply; neither of these characteristics were found to be in use by the indigenous populations. A secular version of this was established through the characterizing of the natives as 'savages', thereby exempting the natives from the protections of civilized society.

As a result, though the English did at times rely on indigenous hospitality, food, advice, and assistance in exploring and weathering the seasonal changes, this did not limit their interest or ambition toward increasing their claim on native land. As the colonial population increased due to procreation and continued immigration, encroachment and religiously justified claim to indigenously occupied areas also increased. The Bible was used as a justification for colonial encroachment and claim to native lands. Specifically, Genesis 1:28, which in the King James version of the Bible promoted the view that man had dominion over all other life and that man should multiply, was interpreted to equate to a European right to native land given that indigenous peoples had not exercised either the right of dominion or procreation. These actions undermined initially peaceful relations.

2.2 The Role of Marketed Want

Trade initially promoted the interaction between the native populations and Europeans. As Jennings (1975, p. 102) states: 'Although trade was eagerly sought by natives, as by Europeans, its effects upon the two societies were conditioned diversely by preexisting traits of their cultures. In the long run, it helped to make Europeans dominant and natives dependent. It stimulated European industry and enriched European merchants while destroying native crafts and impoverishing the tribes. It opened to the Europeans vast new territories and provided the means for their acquisition, but it set the native populations against each other in a deadly competition for subordinate supremacy that ultimately resulted in the dispossession of them all'. Calloway (1997) reported that after contact with European traders and participating in trading activities, many indigenous peoples began to 'participate in the systematic slaughter of animal populations with which they had formerly cultivated a symbiotic and spiritual relationship and on which they had relied for much of their livelihood' (pp. 15–16).

The trading relationship augmented indigenous society permanently and became incongruous with native practices and spiritual behaviors specific to the environment. Simply stated, dependence on trade and addiction to commodities of trade, primarily alcohol, promoted and propelled the indigenous contribution to the environmental degradation of the environment. Natives 'sacrificed harmony, balance, and conservation on the altar of chaos, commodities, and accumulation. Formerly restrained by traditional ideas from overexploiting animals, they abandoned tradition in the face of consumer temptations' (Krech, 1999, p. 152).

'There was a fundamental disparity in the exchanges between European and native peoples. After the Europeans had been taught how to make and use canoes, moccasins, buckskin clothing and backwoods shelters, they could dispense with native guides' (Jennings, 1975, pp. 40–41). The purchase of native land created a permanent transfer of property, while the indigenous dependence on European goods fostered a long-term dependence, as Jennings (1975. p. 41) notes: 'bow makers found no apprentices where hunters and warriors knew the advantages of guns, and an artisan gap of a single genera-tion can wipe out a craft in an illiterate society . . . When European farms and herds began to flourish, the demand for Indian-produced food dropped off. Commercial hunting and the sale of lands perpetually depleted the stocks of the very commodities on which the native population depended'.

The native advantage from trade was short-lived: 'Over the long-term the commercial transformation of their society implied its decay. To the calamities of epidemic disease and alcoholism were added trade wars of the most destructive sort. Firearms acquired in trade enabled particular tribes to gain advantage and supremacy in competition with other tribes . . . with these (territorial) large-scale beaver wars the native peoples secured the last stage of their own demise' (Jennings, 1975, pp. 88–9).

In the current period, the role of culture in economics has been significantly limited by the perception that the present neoclassical economic system is the outcome of natural evolution. As noted by Zein-Elabdin (2009, p. 1156), 'The assumption that modern European achievements represent a natural or historical norm – as in Smith's (1976, p. 405) "natural course of things" – leads to disavowal of culture. As the cultural framework is taken for granted, the realm of economy, or what is perceived to be economic tendency, is disembodied from culture; in other words, the materiality of life, habits of provisioning or accumulation are seen as supracultural'. At the time of Smith's writing, Christian religion and its evolving protestant forms did implicitly embed a common moral perspective related to a focus on Christian defined virtue. Independent of the implicit morally based cultural norms, an economic system developed. Arguably, the concept of 'otherness' allowed for differentiation with respect to the implementa-tion of ethics in practice, which eventually required and legitimized regulation to substitute for morality. Further and related, the dominance of neoclassical economics and its quantitative value of efficiency allowed for a uniform assumption of rational self-interest. Not accounting for the role of culture in promoting a commonalty of societal values, the practice of economics eliminated the explicit evaluation of moral and ethical parameters in decision making. In so doing, neoclassical economics in teaching and practice promoted a new cultural orientation consistent with its assumptions (Hardin, 2009). However, the reliance of market value in determining optimal use of resources has created an environmental and human health conundrum, as only market values rather than qualitative impacts are used to determine optimal production and consumption. As McCloskey (1996, p. 188; original emphasis) notes, 'To the extent that cultural attributions incorporate individual moral responsibility and community ethics, the focus on self-interest alone may have promoted economic outcomes devoid of moral orientation. But I believe now that neglecting the culture – for example, neglecting ethics – will make the economic analysis wrong. By this I mean "wrong" *in terms that economists themselves would recognize as relevant.* I believe now that an economics that wants to get the economy right has to know about ethics. And an economy that wants to get its business right has to practice ethics'. What McCloskey reaffirms is the significance of Smith's impartial spectator, with an embedded assumption that the spectator is directed by innate conscience: 'We can never survey our own sentiments and motives, we can never form any judgment concerning them; unless we remove ourselves, as it were, from our own natural station, and endeavor to view them as at a certain distance from us' (Smith, 1869, p. 99).

3.   THE ROLE OF CONSUMPTION IN SUSTAINABILITY

Consumption is a driver of trade and is also related to the perception of human needs and wants relative to the environment. Our cultural orientation toward consumption implicitly surfaces the perception of the human relationship with the environment as either one of symbiosis or dominion. In the case of the former, stewardship would prevail, consistent with the behavior of the indigenous peoples prior to European settlement and in the latter full utilization of resources to maximize market return as noted in colonial actions would be observed. To a large extent the perceived relationship between human systems and environmental systems affected the level of resource use and environmental augmentation. Culture in the form of religion and spiritual beliefs can be asserted to have contributed to the perception of stewardship relative to human needs and wants.

Our present society builds on the systems established at settlement and it is evident that the perception of the environment as a resource dominates economic thought. It is embedded within our discussion of the production possibilities frontier (PPF) and our policy interest in ensuring that we seek to maximize production subject to resource constraints at any given point in time. In the case of production this conforms to policy – monetary and fiscal – that seeks to maintain or establish the economy at its peak in business cycle terms or at its potential relative to the GDP measure.

The underlying and guiding assumption of production and consumption decisions is premised on the belief that individuals in an economy have insatiable desires to consume. This assumption is reflected in the PPF when efficiency is defined as any production

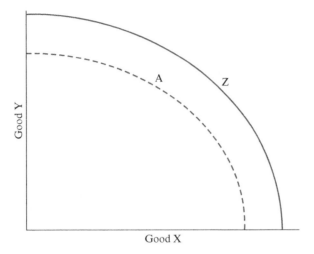

Figure 23.1   Production possibility frontier

combination found on the PPF line (Figure 23.1). On this line, the economy is maximizing production relative to resource constraints. Combinations of agricultural output along this can only be attained by allocating the resources in a way that maximizes production. To the extent that the allocation of resources at a given point in time considers intergenerational equity and threshold extraction rates consistent with the prevention of resource depletion, and enables repopulation for renewable resources, the trade-off decisions may or may not be consistent with sustainable resource utilization.

Further, to the extent that a society is taught or maintains the social norm of satiation of needs relative to that of wants, the efficient allocation of resources may not embody the maximum production related to the resources available from a long-term perspective. In Figure 23.1, the PPF line labeled Z represents a society for which insatiable wants have been embedded into the culture and the PPF represents the maximum production possible in an economy given resource availability at a given point in time. This society must rely on the identification of new resources and technology to enable future consumption or an outward shift of the PPF over time. On the other hand, the society depicted as operating on PPF A, while having the ability to attain PPF Z, would be inconsistent with full resource utilization. Society A, though representing a society that is guided by the cultural value of intergenerational equity and the satiation of needs relative to the balance of environmental and social sustainability, would be inefficient based on prevailing economic theory. The Z economy would consider A to represent an inefficient use of resources if some resources were left idle.

The PPF line labeled Z represents the maximum production possible in an economy given resource availability at a given point in time; Z also corresponds to a society for which insatiable wants have been embedded into the culture. This society will be dependent on the identification of new resources and technology to enable an increase in future production and related consumption. Increased resource access and technological advancement are reflected in an outward shift of the PPF over time.

3.1 Economic Growth and the Significance of Consumption

GDP is a measure of production capacity within a nation's domestic borders and what it essentially captures is the total value of goods and services sold at a specific point in time. In the United States, consumption expenditures account for more than 65 percent of GDP. Because prices change routinely, the value of GDP is found in its growth rate period to period and, in comparison, at a point in time to another country's GDP values. This comparative evaluation has become a proxy for the economic strength of a country. As an aggregate measure, it does not capture the changes in quality of life or standard of living or even income distribution. These are significant limitations that were noted by developers of the indicator. However, since the 1940s, in spite of its known limitations, GDP has been the international metric for economic progress. Given the significance of consumption in the calculation of GDP as well as the focus on GDP as an indication of economic strength, consumption is a significant driver of economic growth and as a result a focal point of monetary and fiscal policy.

Further, this linkage and the corresponding focus on GDP growth as a proxy for progress means that consumption decisions can have a significant ripple effect throughout

---

BOX 23.1   COMPONENTS OF GDP

By definition, GDP measures the market value of all (gross) final goods and services (product) produced within a country (domestic) at a specific point in time. From this perspective, GDP provides an aggregate value but no detail with respect to the distribution of goods and services, quality or standard of living of a country's inhabitants. However, given the relationship between employment, disposable income and consumption, there is an implied connection between employment growth and GDP. As a result, employment is a significant predictor for GDP growth and to the extent that increased GDP growth is a target metric for countries relative to their measurement of progress, employment growth and quality are also routinely evaluated.

GDP can be calculated by assessing total income generated in an economy or total expenditures made within an economy at a specific point in time. The components of the expenditure calculation of GDP include consumption (C), investment (I), government (G) and net exports ($X - M$), the formula for which is exports minus imports:

$$GDP = C + I + G + (X - M)$$

Consumption spending, C, is spending by households on goods and services, with the exception of new housing. Included in household expenditures are durable and non-durable goods as well as medical care and education. Investment spending, I, consists of the purchase of goods and services that will be used in the production of future goods and services. The expenditures include production facilities, inventory and new housing. Government spending, G, includes spending on goods and services by local and state and the national government, but it does not include transfer payments. Transfer payments do not reflect a direct purchase of a good or service; rather they reflect a reallocation of tax dollars. The expenditures of transfer recipients are already included in consumption spending, justifying their omission from G in the calculation of GDP. Net exports reflect the net amount of purchases by foreigners of domestically produced goods (X) relative to the amount of foreign goods purchased in the domestic market (M). Net exports provide the status of the balance of trade between countries and are influenced by and also as a result of relative demand between trading parties, influence foreign exchange rates. Foreign exchange rates reflect the demand of one currency relative to another.

a single economy as well as the finite global resource base. Consider, for example, the lifecycle of milk cartons. Polyethylene-lined, printed paper milk cartons have been created for the transport and preservation of milk from the production to the consumption stage. However, the components of the carton were not developed with waste disposal in mind; rather, increasing distribution and sales were the rationale for the carton. As a result, largely related to the focused basis of its creation, the milk carton serves a consumption purpose without consideration of the impact to the environment and potential future human and animal health due to its non-biodegradable or reusable composition. This illustration on a broader consumption scale provides a simplified perspective to evaluate the underlying values captured in consumption decisions. From this perspective, production for consumption may be expressed as a myopic activity focused on near-term satiation of a need or want to the exclusion of the evaluation of the impact or ripple effect of the satiation, excluding the moral and or stewardship responsibility to environmental and human health.

As another example, consider the price of a t-shirt produced in an emerging market. It will include the cost of the laborer who cut and sewed the shirt, but not the social cost resulting from his exploitive wage (given the price differential from his payment for labor and the return to the producer who will sell the product at a US boutique). The price does not include the carbon footprint related to the ultimate transportation of the t-shirt to the store, or the waste cost related to the landfilling of a shirt that cannot biodegrade because it is not made of natural fibers. In net, the cost of the consumption of the t-shirt is only partially borne by the purchaser; other societies and the environment subsidize the price. The outcome allows a developed society to have more than needed, to satisfy wants, while unknowingly or knowingly using more resources and creating environmental and social externalities. The process of 'efficiency' without the inclusion of morality results in an unsustainable outcome but one that is considered quantitatively optimal based on the prevailing quantitatively driven and market price-dependent economic model.

The limitation of the calculation of GDP to market value in conjunction with firm profit maximization and consumer insatiability, two endogenized tenets of neoclassical economics, has resulted in externalities to the environment and societies. Externalities are observable in environmental degradation, and depletion of environmental resources as well as in exploitation of labor markets.

3.2   Economic Growth and Climate Impacts

The most significant environmental impact attributed to economic growth has been the increased speed in climate change as a result of fossil fuel-based energy production and the growth in energy dependence in both direct consumer use and in the production of consumer goods. However, there is a distinction in the use of energy. Developed countries' use of energy is significantly higher than that of developing countries, with the United States being the cumulatively highest contributor to greenhouse gas emissions (Ge, Friedrich and Damassa, 2014).

Evidence suggests that profitability parameters on the part of businesses promote a circumvention of regulatory restrictions on the production and responsibility for externalities, leading to production shifting to developing countries where regulations may be limited and the focus on GDP growth may result in the trade-off between environmental

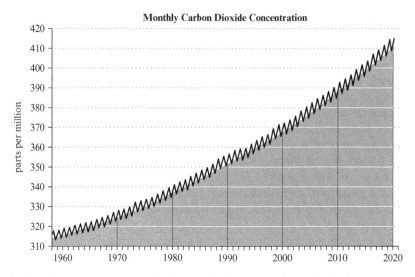

Source: Scripps CO$_2$ Program. Accessed 23 February 2021 at http://scrippsco2.ucsd.edu.

Figure 23.2   Atmospheric carbon dioxide concentration: 1960–2020

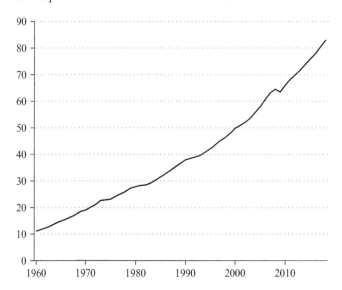

Sources: World Bank National Accounts data and OECD National Accounts data files.

Figure 23.3   Global GDP (constant 2010 US dollars, trillions)

and social protection to growth in production capacity, as depicted in the historical increase in CO$_2$ relative to production highlighted in Figures 23.2 and 23.3.

Economic growth has been achieved through the use of resources and the advancement of technology, where the latter has promoted more efficient use of resources. However, growth has not been without adverse consequences to the environment. Atmospheric greenhouse gas emissions are one of a number of externalized impacts related to the coupling of economic growth with environmental exploitation and degradation. Sustainable development challenges the present context of growth by relying on a decoupling of economic growth rates and environmental impacts. Decoupling is defined by the OECD as 'breaking the link between "environmental bads" and "economic goods" (Organisation for Economic Co-operation and Development [OECD], 2002, p. 1). Decoupling would yield a lower rate of increase in environmental degradation relative to economic growth (e.g., GDP):

> Decoupling may be either absolute or relative . . . Absolute decoupling is said to occur when the environmentally relevant variable is stable or decreasing while the economic driving force is growing. Decoupling is said to be relative when the growth rate of the environmentally relevant variable is positive, but less than the growth rate of the economic variable. (Ibid.)

There has been considerable discussion as to whether growth can continue with decoupling. Ecological modernization theory posits that while economic development requires inputs and generates waste, both of which contribute to various forms of environmental problems, the magnitude of economic development's impact on the environment is likely to decrease through time. As a result, decoupling is likely to occur first in developed countries. In contrast, the treadmill of production theory suggests that the national-level environmental impacts of economic development should remain stable or perhaps increase in magnitude through time, regardless of whether countries are relatively more developed or less developed. Jorgenson and Clark (2012) test both theories with respect to CO_2 emissions and developed/developing country status. Their findings corroborate that there is a decrease in emissions in developed countries due to technological progress and also that emissions are correlated with developing status. However, they suggest that exploitation of regulatory differences may be a stronger contributing factor to the variation in emissions. In other words, the measured emissions increase in developing countries may be the result of the movement of production to nations with lower regulation, lower production/economic growth, and cheaper more exploitable labor. Further, developing country emissions are related to the production of products that will be consumed in the developed countries.

Given the strength of the consumer expenditures in developed countries' GDP, sustainability transformation to sustainable development may be catalyzed through education – economic literacy – that promotes a shift in consumption value orientation to include a responsibility for the holistic impact of a given consumption choice – a moral framework. The result would potentially lead to internalization of externalized costs of production to ensure sustainable use of environmental resources as well as labor.

If consumers had the information to make a rational choice – to be the rational economic agents that the pricing model of economics assumes but that social frameworks and institutions do not universally foster or develop – consumers would be better empowered to exercise the power inherent in consumption decisions.

For example, there is no market price for air; it is free, and it is also required for life. But, in spite of it being essential for life, it is a costless component of the production process; waste has been released into the air for years. If there had been a cost for disposal, or even better a social value that prevented the release of airborne waste that was embedded in demand, the pollution that has collected in the atmosphere for the past 300 years would be significantly less to potentially non-existent. As simple as it may sound, consumers could have promoted the welfare of the atmosphere through their collective demand that air quality be preserved.

The moral values embedded and communicated within demand and supply determine the manner in which a need or want is attained. To the extent that there is no discussion of the values and behavioral factors assumed and reflected in demand and supply – arguably, implicit values – the values and the subsequent behaviors become endogenous to the economic system. Explicit awareness of present behavioral assumptions inclusive of the 'unlimited wants' of consumers, the profit maximization motivations of producers to meet investor returns, and the understated resource depletion resulting from externalized or understated costs offer the potential to modify active and embedded behavior.

Consumption choices are based on demand and supply of a good and are identified with satisfying a need or a want. The impact of consumption decisions can be significant when there is asymmetry of information; fundamentally, there is a relationship between economic and environmental outcomes and consumption choices. Purchases affect labor and environmental resource use. However, most purchase decisions are made through a market mechanism, where the consumer is not aware of the entire production process and waste is not a factor in the consumption decision. This limitation in information transparency often creates a disconnect between the social and environmental justice sensitivities of a consumer and the realities of their consumption choice in enabling and maintaining the values that they espouse.

3.3   Economic Literacy and Internalizing Externalities

In teaching economics, equilibrium, the point at which demand and supply are equal, is assumed to yield a market outcome where resources are efficiently allocated; neither demand nor supply can be made better without making the other worse off. The price at which the quantity demanded equals the quantity supplied is therefore expected to embody the cost associated with production, including return to the supplier and the benefit of consumption of the good or service. However, production and consumption are not limited to the transactional nature of exchange of the final good at the determined market price. In the process of production and consumption, there are costs that are not factored that impact the well-being of the economy at large and these are referenced as externalities. In essence, externalities arise when an individual or firm engages in activities that influence the well-being of others and where no compensation is provided in exchange for the imposition. The lack of inclusion of externalities in the cost assessment or consumption expense of a particular good, leads to the undervaluing of that good and potential for both over consumption and heightened waste. As depicted in Figure 23.4, along a product lifecycle, each step of the lifecycle may have costs that are not captured in price because firms have no incentive to include costs that they do not need to address. Their focus is profit maximization (investor returns) and individuals presently are assumed to be incentivized to maximize consumption subject to an income constraint – the lower the prices the more of their insatiable desire to consume can be fulfilled. Lifecycle assessment enables evaluation of a process from the stance of an impartial bystander and given the pre-existing moral responsibility of the observer, offers the opportunity to internalize externalities in production and consumption that are contributors to environmental and social justice, attributes of sustainability.

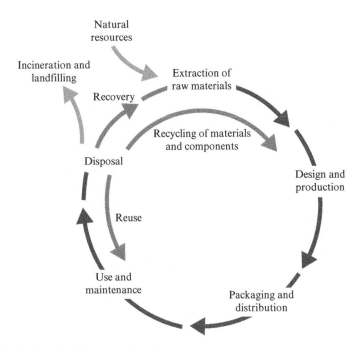

Figure 23.4 Lifecycle of a consumption product

3.4 Addressing Externalities and the Significance of Underpricing Resources

Typically, externalities are characterized as negative, signifying that the externality yields an adverse outcome. These externalities are referenced as being negative externalities. However, there is a potential that a positive outcome could be generated, leading to a positive externality. In the discussion of externalities, it is often assumed that market participants perceive the externalities generated by their actions as acceptable due to their focus on the immediate gratification of their needs. For the producer, this equates to externalizing the cost of the disposal of waste products into waterways and the air where no cost is directly borne to adversely impact profits, but arguably intertemporal costs can be assessed that may impact the enjoyment and longevity of multiple life forms and generations of human life. For the consumer, the externality can be evaluated in the indifference to waste creation at the point of the consumption decision or even the externalities associated with the production of the good or service being purchased. In the case of the former, the cost of the disposal of packaging material is typically marginal to zero, relatively negligible, but disposal creates a negative externality in the landfill, incinerator, or recycling plant that could have been avoided with a thoughtful exercise of demand.

At present, the type of internalizing of externalities that has occurred has been limited to quantifying the externality to an overt cost. However, to the extent that the costs may remain understated and the market mechanism is not cognizant and focused on the elimination of the externality-based cost but rather the minimization of overall costs, this process has yielded suboptimal outcomes. For example, assume that a firm produces ambient pollution as a result of the incineration of waste. If a governmental regulatory body institutes a fee or cost for pollution, effectively charging the firm for the ability to pollute the air, the producer is able to delegate responsibility for environmental stewardship to the price of pollution. Additionally, depending on the demand for the service offered, the producer may be able to not only transfer the costs now associated with polluting activity to the consumer, but may also be able to maintain the pollution level. Assuming that the good is a necessity, the consumer is *inelastic* to the change in price and maintains the needs quantity of the good. In this example, the negative externality related to internalizing the cost has not changed. Instead, only the responsibility of pollution has been transferred to a cost, revenue to the regulating body has been generated, and the consumer has suffered erosion in her overall disposable income and purchasing power. The impact of the latter outcome may be an unexpected contractionary phenomenon to GDP. Fundamentally, the consumer has continued to maintain demand arguably because the complete impact of the externality being created by their consumption is not understood.

Externalities are defined as a type of market failure based on the premise that optimal social outcomes result from individual economic agents acting in self-interest. However, if instead of being a market failure, externalities could be evaluated to assess and develop an optimizing strategy between individual interests and enhanced social outcomes, externalities could be internalized within the market model as a preference. Perhaps externalities only indicate a lack of holistic awareness on the part of the consumer and producer or a cultural bias toward immediate gratification. These characteristics can be potentially modified through education. Optimal and universally acceptable strategies could then be adopted to promote sustainability.

The success of this internalization strategy relies on the development of the educated rational economic agent as a consumer. If consumers are aware of the responsibility inherent in their consumption and are aware of the environmental and social impact of production processes, consumer demand can create the coalescing framework to augment preference to exhibit demand for sustainably produced products. The augmentation in demand does not allow for the opportunity of delegation of responsibility of pollution capacity to a cost or alternatively, the incorporation within a cost minimization framework. As a result, the change in preference and subsequent modification in demand promotes the development of market outcomes that are environmentally and socially optimal from the position of what is supplied.

4. CONCLUDING COMMENTS AND NEXT STEPS

The defining of sustainability is in close alignment with the objective of the discipline of economics. Economics, after all, is the study of human behavior in relation to a resource-constrained world. The ability of economics to add value to sustainability objectives requires the insertion of moral value parameters or normative thinking in conjunction with the positive or observational stance adopted by the discipline. The catalyst for the inclusion of moral values in the practice of economics rests with the ability to promote an understanding between prevailing economic assumptions of behavior and efficiency alongside the economic outcomes fostered. A comparison between moral values and the present social and environmental issues resulting from the present economic framework offers the opportunity to assess their inconsistency. Further, and related to classroom instruction, lifecycle assessments of consumer products can address the role of consumption, prices, and externalities relative to students' sensitivities to sustainability objectives: environmental and social justice, and economic equity. The educational process in this manner facilitates an understanding of the inconsistencies between the economic framework and sustainability, surfacing the role of consumer, investor and regulatory action and thereby establishing the holistic responsibility of a rational economic agent.

This chapter proffers that sustainability can be catalyzed through the instruction of economics within a normative framework that incorporates moral and ethical responsibility toward the present and future and where the rationale for sustainability is justified through the lens of the operation of the present economic system.

REFERENCES

Allgood, S., Walstad, W. and Siegfried, J. (2015). Research on teaching economics to undergraduates. *Journal of Economic Literature*, 53(2), 285–325.

Beach, E. (1938). Teaching economics. *The American Economic Review*, 28(3), 515.

Becker, W.E. (2000). Teaching economics in the 21st century. *The Journal of Economic Perspectives*, 14(1), 109–19.

Bentham, J. (1879). *An Introduction to the Principles of Morals and Legislation*. Oxford: Clarendon Press, p. 14.

Bowles, S. and Carlin, W. (2020). What students learn in Economics 101: time for a change. *Journal of Economic Literature*, 58(1), 176–214.

Calloway, C.C. (1997). *New Worlds For All: Indians, Europeans, and the Remaking of Early America*. Baltimore, MD: Johns Hopkins University Press.

Cronon, W. (1983). *Changes in the Land*. New York: Hill & Wang.

Flannery, T. (2001). *The Eternal Frontier: An Ecological History of North America and Its Peoples*. Melbourne: Text Publishing.

Ge, M., Friedrich, J. and Damassa, T. (2014). 6 graphs explain the world's top 10 emitters. Accessed 23 February 2021 at https://www.wri.org/blog/2014/11/6-graphs-explain-world-s-top-10-emitters.

Hardin, R. (2009). Culture. In R. Hardin, *How Do You Know? The Economics of Ordinary Knowledge* (pp. 161–84). Princeton, NJ: Princeton University Press.

Jennings, F. (1975). *The Invasion of America: Indians, Colonialism, and the Cant of Conquest*. Chapel Hill, NC: The University of North Carolina Press.

Jorgenson, A. and Clark, B. (2012). Are the economy and the environment decoupling? A comparative international study, 1960–2005. *American Journal of Sociology*, 118(1), 1–44.

Krech, S. (1999). *Myth and History: The Ecological Indian*. New York: W.W. Norton & Company, Inc.

Kuznets, S. (1934). *National Income, 1929–1932*. Cambridge, MA: NBER.

McCloskey, D. (1996). Missing ethics in economics. In A. Klamer (ed.), *The Value of Culture: On the Relationship between Economics and Arts* (pp. 187–202). Amsterdam: Amsterdam University Press.

Mokyr, J. (2017). Culture and economics. In J. Mokyr, *A Culture of Growth: The Origins of the Modern Economy* (pp. 3–15). Princeton, NJ: Princeton University Press.

Organisation for Economic Co-operation and Development (OECD). (2002). Indicators to measure decoupling of environmental pressure from economic growth. Accessed 21 February 2021 at https://www.oecd.org/environment/indicators-modelling-outlooks/1933638.pdf.

Smith, A. ([1779] 1976). *An Inquiry into the Nature and Causes of the Wealth of Nations*. Chicago, IL: University of Chicago Press.

Smith, A. (1869). *Essays On, I. Moral Sentiments: II. Astronomical Inquiries; III. Formation of Languages; IV. History of Ancient Physics; V. Ancient Logic and Metaphysics; VI. The Imitative Arts; VII. Music, Dancing, Poetry; VIII. The External Senses; IX. English and Italian Verses*. Edited by J. Black and J. Hutton. London: Alex Murray & Son.

United Nations Educational, Scientific and Cultural Organization (UNESCO). (2017). Culture and development. Accessed 23 February 2021 at http://www.unesco.org/new/en/culture/themes/culture-and-development/.

Zein-Elabdin, E. (2009). Economics, postcolonial theory and the problem of culture: institutional analysis and hybridity. *Cambridge Journal of Economics*, 33(6), 1153–67.

24. Towards sustainability as a frame of mind in higher education: thinking about sustainability rhizomatically

Dzintra Iliško

1. INTRODUCTION

Sustainability has been well embedded in the political and mission statements of many universities worldwide and has been integrated into green initiatives and coursework. The United Nations Educational, Scientific and Cultural Organization (UNESCO) has fostered understanding of sustainability at the political level via the Decade of Education for Sustainable Development (2005–14) and Global Action Programme (GAP) on Education for Sustainable Development (EDU) in schools, higher educational institutions, non-governmental organization (NGO) initiatives, municipalities, youth organizations and on an individual level.

There is a gradual shift taking place from a weak to strong understanding of sustainability. Educational models that are based on testing culture need to expand this narrow view on teaching and learning. Education for sustainability needs to empower students to act as agents of change. Much is needed to be done to make sustainability a vision of the whole university by building capacity of students to transcend subject boundaries and to build a more transdisciplinary view on sustainability issues. Universities need to rethink their role in educating leaders and agents of change who possess qualities such as wisdom, humility and respect for all forms of life (Martin and Jucker, 2005). Universities need to build students' capacity to challenge unethical actions and to think across subject borders by engaging with multiple stakeholders in co-creating a future vision and helping to face new challenges. This co-creation approach involves creating common space for diverse epistemologies, traditions, understandings and contexts where all parties involved can 'celebrate the messiness of knowledge', thus 'opening possibilities for being, thinking, and doing transdisciplinarity in higher education setting' (McClam and Flores, 2012, p. 241).

The discourse on the role of universities to respond to sustainability challenges in times of 'systemic global dysfunction' (Sisitka et al., 2015, p. 73) has widely been discussed. This requires reorienting education and research towards a transformation paradigm to enable the students to deal with unsustainable issues that require one's ability to accept complexity, ambiguity and uncertainty in order to engage in new forms of participation and living. Therefore, universities need to support openness to various ways of integrating sustainability, including the fourth less tangible pillar of sustainability – namely, culture. The Center of Sustainable Education at Daugavpils University, Latvia, plays a significant role in integrating sustainability issues and sustainability pedagogies in teaching in university's coursework in cooperation with the UNESCO chair at Daugavpils University who is the key player with respect to education for sustainable development in cooperation with non-governmental organizations (NGOs).

2. PHILOSOPHICAL FRAMEWORK: LEARNING TO THINK METAPHORICALLY

There are many models and definitions of sustainability that have been produced in academia since the term 'sustainability' was introduced for the first time in the eighteenth century in forest management and in *Our Common Future* in 1987 (the Brundtland Report) by the World Commission on Environment and Development (WCED). Since then, the three-dimensional model of sustainability (economic, social and environmental) was enriched by the fourth, culture dimension. There is an emerging need for the universities to conceptualize the new ways of thinking about sustainability by engaging students to envision a more sustainable future for local and a global community. The transition is taking place from being narrow and linear to becoming a more holistic and a long-term approach in understanding sustainability.

LeGrange (2009) and Deleuze and Guattari (1987) encourage one to rethink and reconceptualize sustainability in terms of rhizomatic thinking that view a sustainability in a more open, evolving and a dynamic framework. They refer to a colony of ants when explaining the phenomenon of deterritorialization, which, when being destroyed, are still able to become a part of or to form an animal rhizome and stay connected. This expands the meaning of sustainability education as constantly changing and evolving. The authors see the framework of sustainability as ever-evolving, dynamic and composed of heterogeneous elements that displace, join, circle and hold together in a synergetic way. This can be referred to as a rhizomic network of diverse stakeholders who bring in new possibilities for growth and for new understandings to emerge. Rhizomic networking allows ongoing, dynamic and open-ended design of a preferable and desired future. This also allows transdisciplinary knowledge to emerge as well as a more creative stance towards the sustainability issues. This partnership includes genuine reciprocity, mutual learning and relearning, building bridges between diverse areas of life where co-production of knowledge is taking place among diverse stakeholders in order to have a long-term perspective. Universities need to encourage building 'a multi-stakeholder platform by engaging with society in a mutual process of creation and transformation' (Trencher, Yarime and Kharrazi, 2014, pp. 44–5). Multiple stakeholders with different backgrounds and perspectives can contribute efficiently towards more informed and joint actions of sustainability transformations (Schneider at al., 2019).

This expands the reality of teaching within separate disciplines and challenges normalizing practices, thus encouraging transdisciplinary problem-solving opportunities for the students to engage actively in planning a sustainable future. This helped to build bridge between the academic community and society by providing students with the space for an encounter with uncertainty, ambiguity and complexity, and to reflect on diverse ways of doing and being in a responsible way. Tassone et al. (2018) argue about the need to engage students in an inquiry-based process by developing a sense of communities of practice by encouraging them to embrace new ways of doing things and learning from new experiences. This can be done by discussing and engaging with real-life issues as well as relate the issue of study to their real-life worlds and contexts (Savin-Baden, 2000).

3.   SUSTAINABILITY AS A FRAME OF MIND IN ACTION

Sustainability competencies that were developed as a part of the educational course 'Sustainability for Societal and Cultural Changes' at Daugavpils University is a part of the definition of quality education that was set as a priority in the framework of education for sustainable development (UNESCO, 2017) and formulated as a part of Sustainable Development Goal (SDG) 4. Students are seen as change agents who are able to deal with the challenges of a contemporary society. This requires a reorienting of higher educational practice from knowledge orientation to action orientation. This requires one to adapt current teaching practice to competency-based learning, enabling students to become change agents and transition managers or leaders for sustainable development (Rieckmann, 2012; Wiek et al., 2015; Wiek, Withycombe and Redman, 2011; Wilhelm, Foster and Zimmermann, 2019), as well as to equip them with the tools to deal with wicked and complex issues related to sustainable development. Similarly, Wiek and Key (2015) suggest action-oriented competence that involves implementing interventions, transitions and transformative governance towards sustainability. A number of international documents (Organisation for Economic Co-operation and Development [OECD], 2005; United Nations Economic Commission for Europe [UNECE], 2012) suggest a competency framework, part of which are action competencies – namely, one's ability to envision change, to explore alternative futures and engage in the present (UNECE, 2012) and one's ability to act autonomously by keeping a big picture in mind (OECD, 2005). All those suggested competency models enable individuals to shape their preferable and desired future and go beyond acquiring knowledge and develop one's ability to deal with complex problems and challenges. This requires transdisciplinarity perspectives and involvement of multiple stakeholders. The set of competencies to be developed at the university setting need to be based on individual teachers' values, epistemologies and theoretical perspective. When the teacher identifies their assumptions and theoretical models, they can further modify and align their didactic solutions of the educational objectives. This means reaching coherent alignment between the objective of developing 'change agents' with the underlying competency profile with a clear comprehension of epistemological boundaries and power issues (Wilhelm et al., 2019). Action-oriented competencies can best be developed in action-oriented learning environments employing participatory learning modes and constructivist learning.

4.   METHODOLOGY

For the purpose of this study the author chose the case study on integrating sustainability issues in one of the university courses for the master's level students. Case study was used as a methodological approach to investigate the efficiency of approaches and pedagogies oriented towards transforming students' meaning perspectives towards sustainability by engaging them in a transformative journey. The course offered for the students reflects different global sustainability issues, such as poverty, globalization, global education, inclusion, human rights and environmental challenges. The author has engaged the students in revealing their stories of how and when they have learned about sustainable ways of being in the world and how their experience has been reinforced and expanded by doing a coursework on sustainability for societal changes. The study involved the content analyses of students' essays on how their significant experience of life was supported and reinforced by learning about sustainability in the university setting. The careful coding of main and subcategories was carried out and the data gained as a result of study of essays was supported by the semi-structured interviews with five students who agreed on a voluntarily basis to comment on their transformative journeys during their studies.

5.   RESEARCH FINDINGS: CONCEPTUALIZATION OF SUSTAINABILITY AS DERIVED FROM THE STUDENTS' LIFE WORLDS

The university's course on 'Sustainability for Societal and Cultural Changes' is aimed at developing students' literacy – ability to engage in thinking, problem solving and decision making in regard to sustainability issues; therefore, the course involves an inquiry-based learning approach and experiential learning. The course involves not only knowledge about environment, culture, economic development, social justice and interdependency of all aspects of sustainability, but is also aimed at developing students' willingness and ability to engage in meaningful action for creating a sustainable future that includes stewardship, respect and a system thinking. The course is also aimed at developing students' system thinking on sustainability issues in their local communities and developing their anticipatory competence, ability to collectively assess, analyse and evaluate unsustainability of current issues and to envision the future of sustainability issues within a sustainability framework. The students are required to design and plan interventions and transformative strategies to improve the situation by undertaking individual actions (Lambrechts et al., 2013). Pedagogical approaches – for example, student-centred, action-oriented and transformative – that were used in the course were directed towards motivating learners to become active citizens who are able to participate in shaping sustainable futures in their communities. Chosen pedagogical approaches were directed towards challenging students' frames of reference and developing their innovative and creative ideas and choices in dealing with unsustainability in their neighbourhoods.

At the beginning of the course many students related sustainability to economic, political, social and cultural aspects. Key categories that derived from students' essays were as follows: sensitivity towards nature (as derived from the folk tradition, and as taught in the family); cultivating one's family land (eco-farming, care/love towards one's land, ownership); critical reflection on one's lifestyle (as taught in families, leading a sustainable lifestyle, childhood memories); transformative life journeys toward sustainability (revaluating one's consumption patterns, linking one's consumption patterns to global sustainability); envisioning a more sustainable lifestyle and community (connecting one's life to broader systems, recognizing structural and cultural aspects that embrace unsustainable practices and building alternative scenarios to overcome unsustainability in one's community).

Critical Reflection on One's Lifestyle

Sustainability pedagogies employed in this study course encouraged students to reflect on their experience in a group of other students. In the group with other students, they were invited to discuss unsustainability issues in order to build their capacity to deal with the complexity and uncertainty in a social world. The course was based on experiential learning in order to teach students how to apply their knowledge to real-life contexts. Reflection on unsustainability issues during the coursework has broadened students' knowledge about sustainability issues, but critical reflection helped them to reflect on existing values, norms and taken-for-granted assumptions. The author encouraged them to produce their own definition of the term, rather than by borrowing it from the assigned readings and to explore the term in relation to their experience and understanding, to choose an approach that allows them to find the differences among diverse views on sustainability. At the beginning of the course, they were asked to identify unsustainability locally and globally, but their main concerns reflected environmental issues. All interviewed students commented that, for them, the notion of sustainability was related only to environmental issues, and only at the end of the semester did they develop a more holistic vision of sustainability. Very few students talked about social sustainability and issues such as social justice and inequality of distribution of resources and poverty in their essays in reference to their understanding when undertaking the course on sustainability. Only a few talked about sustainability in a holistic and systemic way. One of the achievements as a result of undertaking the course was students' reference to the connection they could see among their lifestyles, consumption patterns and institutional conditions, as well as collective action towards sustainability. As one student remarked, 'Now I see more clearly how global issues are connected with my personal lifestyle as a consumer'.

Envisioning Ways to Live Sustainably

The Sustainable Development Strategy of Latvia outlines the sustainable development objectives of Latvia for 20 years and solutions for efficient and sustainable cultivation of land, culture, nature, and building a sustainable economy. After a critical reading of national and international legislation, several students concluded that the best changes are coming from the grassroots and individual levels: 'All changes begin with one's intention to do the best one can do for oneself, family, and the close neighbourhood'. For many students, the main source of inspiration for developing sustainable lifestyles was family upbringing, where students were taught sensitivity and care towards a non-human world and discussed their learnings at school. In addition, the lifestyle of many students is influenced by the reality of a consumerist society – namely, overconsumption. They admitted that much needs to be changed in their lifestyles in order to reduce their environmental impact. After numerous discussions on films and suggested reading materials, the students have revaluated their frames of reference towards a non-human world and adopted a more sustainable lifestyle. After watching the documentary film *Home* (2009), directed by French photographer, reporter and environmentalist Yann Arthus-Bertrand, and engaging in critical discussion, many students revaluated the harm humans did to the Earth during many centuries that led to the Anthropocene – a timeframe defined by the high level of pollution of land, air, and water and other waste products.

Building a Sustainable Lifestyle in One's Household: Intergenerational Learning

The best learning on sustainability issues were what the students gained from their families, particularly the way they have organized their households. Their parents taught them sensitivity towards nature, about the 'second life' of things, saving resources, gardening and growing their own vegetables. Almost all students had experiences of participation in cultivating the land, planting and gathering vegetables for their family needs. Almost all of them grew up in the situation of limited means where saving was both for economic reasons and a matter of values taught in the family related to saving natural resources and caring for one's land. The intergenerational learning and wisdom was deeply embedded in their lifestyles and attitude towards the Earth. As one of the students commented: 'Sustainability is deeply embedded in my family traditions and my lifestyle'. Another commented: 'We cultivate our land, we plant our crops and we take care of our land. This is what our grandparents have taught my parents and this is what parents taught me'. Most of the students reported being engaged in farming in their parents' households. One of the students commented: 'Here I have learned how to love and cultivate my land, how to stay connected with nature, to enjoy this beauty around me. By being a part of this I cannot be do harm to the Earth'.

Students' Transformative Life Journeys Toward Sustainability

This part of the course focused on involving students in envisioning a better future and building trajectories towards reaching their preferred and desired future. While visualizing the models of a preferable future, the students were engaged in building their capacity to cope with uncertainty, ambiguity, divergent norms, and values. The coursework aimed at engaging students in their transformative journeys by the use of participatory pedagogies that would hopefully lead to transformed habits of mind, which are an essential part of their transformative learning (Mezirow, 2000). Mezirow's theory offers theoretical foundations for one's transformative journey towards a sustainable lifestyle by connecting education for sustainability and transformative learning as one's ability 'to deal with complexity and uncertainty' (Leal Filho et al., 2018, p. 287; Ryan and Cotton, 2013). Transformation refers to questioning and redefining one's frames of mind, and assumptions that foster generating new meanings and new visions of the future. During one's journey, new understandings and meaning schemes emerge. Mezirow defines meaning schemes as sets of habitual expectations made up of theories, beliefs and stereotypes that need to be explored and revaluated. Meaning schemes are described as constructs, metaphors, and personal ideologies. Meaning perspectives contain criteria for making judgements and belief systems. This process of change of meaning schemes differs from the notion of growth as a rational and linear development. To put it metaphorically, for the transformation to take place in one's life, one needs to travel into a world of darkness, and then return, transformed with a radically new way of understanding of the world. As Mezirow comments, 'Nothing is different, yet all is transformed. Everything is seen differently. In this change of perspective, in the transformation of meaning, lies the meaning of transformation' (Mezirow, 1978, p. 100). The reality is still there, but the perspective and meaning have been profoundly transformed.

There are several 'Aha' moments in students' journeys that they have shared in their interviews as well. After watching the film *Home*, followed by the group discussions, one of the students commented that her perception of the world and things has changed immensely: 'I can define my life as a moment before watching the film, and life that is completely different after watching this film'. She has changed her meaning perspective towards a more sustainable one in terms of her consumption habits. Similar comments were made after watching the documentary film *Fashion Victims: Bangladesh 2013* on the unsustainability of fashion industry and overconsumption patterns. Several students made a commitment to buy less and to evaluate their actions critically. Students who participated in public actions on promoting sustainable ways of living and giving a second life to things, as well on how to participate in clean-up days, have also commented on how they rethought their current ways of being and doing: 'After watching this film, I re-evaluated my ways of consumption since I saw injustice in a fashion industry in the world and myself as a part of this industry. I do not want to support this chain of injustice by overconsuming things that are produced by exploitation of people in the third world countries'.

Some students reported transformative moments in their learning when they realized interconnectedness, an interdependency of things and the consequence of one's actions on local and global scales: 'Then people buy things; they do not think how much resources are being used in producing things, and almost never think about the social injustice and cheap labour. Before thinking about urgent ecological issues, I noticed only environmental aspects but did not see an overall picture or a sustainability worldview.' The intention of this study course was also to overcome disconnected thinking that was shaped by the contemporary educational approaches and structure by incorporating more of a holistic thinking. Therefore, the author introduced problem-based learning approaches by exploring complex real-life problems with planning the involvement of multiple stakeholders.

Envisioning a More Sustainable Lifestyle and Community

Students were encouraged to engage in planning, collectively analysing and evaluating complex and wicked societal issues, negotiating sustainability values underlying a specific case study, engaging with multiple stakeholders, planning the strategies for action, taking responsibility for initiatives, and envisioning change. Students developed a number of sustainability competencies for achieving desired transformations in the future. As one of the student's commented, 'By working in teams I have learned to work in interdisciplinary teams with my groupmates and to find alternative solutions to the issue of study and to plan interventions and transformative governance strategies towards sustainable solutions'. One commented on valuable learning in groups by gaining knowledge on diverse perspectives, engaging with the variety of contexts, and building a transdisciplinary design of an issue of study. While planning this inquiry type of learning, the author's epistemological orientation was compatible with constructivism's type of inquiry that forced her and her students to expand their knowledge to be aligned with this newly framed epistemological orientation. The author tried to provide students with multiple discourse opportunities that involved group discussions and critical writing. By engaging students in a real-world inquiry, they were asked to provide evidence, to recognize counterclaims and argue their claims.

6. CONCLUSIONS

Higher educational institutions worldwide have embedded sustainability in their mission statements, curriculum, research projects and coursework (Lozano et al., 2015; Shawe et al., 2019). But, as Leal Filho et al. (2019) argue, in developing a purpose, 'a complete rethinking and articulation of vision is needed to achieve SD [sustainable development] outcomes' (p. 679). Since sustainability efforts remain an individual issue, such as recycling, energy saving and sorting waste, this is necessary to develop a balanced and a holistic approach to sustainability efforts in a higher education institution. This holistic understanding needs to be negotiated by all stakeholders who build a commitment to this desired vision of a resilient, healthy and just community defined by planetary boundaries with efficient and transparent governance.

Universities need to be responsible not only for awarding degrees but also acting as agents of change and preparing students to apply knowledge in solving real-life problems. Young people are seen as future leaders who will work under the conditions of growing complexity and uncertainty of current day reality. They need to acquire competencies such as systems thinking, strategic competence and interpersonal competence (Rieckmann, 2012) that are necessary to deal with wicked issues and work towards the ideal of a sustainable future in their local communities.

Universities can play a huge role in shaping future society by addressing sustainability and fostering innovative research by involving the students in a co-creation of new knowledge within local communities and adopting local sustainability partnerships. Universities need to undertake this responsibility by building democratic, ecologically minded communities of learners. Students need to be engaged in solving complex issues that may require individuals' capacity to think critically and to take action. Being involved in the process of co-creation of knowledge with multiple stakeholders will help them to reveal the complexities of the world. Involvement of multiple stakeholders will open the space for transdisciplinarity in dealing with complex real-life issues and will help to overcome disciplinary barriers.

Employing experiential learning in the university setting will help students to apply gained knowledge. This will empower them to apply knowledge, skills and values for a sustainable way of life and to contribute to a sustainable development in their communities. Experiential learning will develop students' competencies to discover their own unsustainable patterns of life that can facilitate developing their action competency. For the efficient change to take place, desire and passion needs to come from an individual rather than being reinforced from above. The course was aimed at fostering change of lifestyle and frame of mind that involves physical, socio-emotional and spiritual dimensions by translating theoretical knowledge into students' worldviews. The analyses of students' narratives allows one to see a gradual process of change in one's mental thought models towards sustainability.

Experiential learning will develop students' capacity to participate as informed citizens who are able to identify unjust unsustainable practices and will exercise agency for building a more sustainable future. Students who were involved in a transformative journey towards more complex teaching epistemologies reported awareness of sustainability issues and intentions to make changes in their lifestyles. Case studies described in this chapter are an example of implementing a competency-based approach towards education for sustainable development that was oriented towards empowering future problem solvers and active citizens in shaping a sustainable future. Participative approaches towards learning fostered future agents of change by engaging students in developing more transformed knowledge, fostering collective action and enhancing competencies for reflective leadership.

REFERENCES

Deleuze, G. and Guattari, F. (1987), *A Thousand Plateaus: Capitalism and Schizophrenia*, Minneapolis, MN: University of Minnesota Press.
Fashion Victims: Bangladesh 2013 (2013), Documentary film, accessed 2 March 2021 at https://www.youtube.com/watch?v=6Dku_VWCsMY.
Home (2009), Documentary film, directed by Yann Arthus-Bertrand, produced by Luc Besson, accessed 2 March 2021 at https://www.youtube.com/watch?v=-GUeDISwZ3E&t=42s.
Lambrechts, W., Mulam, I. and Ceulemans, K. et al. (2013), 'The integration of competences for sustainable development in higher education: an analysis of bachelor programs of management', *Journal of Cleaner Production*, 48, 65–73.
Leal Filho, W., Raath, S. and Lazzarini, B. et al. (2018), 'The role of transformation on learning and education for sustainability', *Journal of Cleaner Production*, 199, 286–95.
Leal Filho, W., Skouloudis, A. and Brandli, L. et al. (2019), 'Sustainability and procurement in higher education institutions: barriers and drivers', *Journal of Clean Production*, 231, 1267–80.
LeGrange, L.L. (2009), 'Sustainability and higher education: from arborescent to rhizomatic thinking', *Educational Philosophy and Theory*, 43(7), 742–54.
Lozano, R., Ceulemans, K. and Alonso-Almeida, M. et al. (2015), 'A review of commitment and implementation of sustainable development in higher education: results from a worldwide survey', *Journal of Clear Production*, 108, 1–18.
Martin, S. and Jucker, R. (2005), 'Educating earth literate leaders', *Journal of Geography in Higher Education*, 29(1), 19–29.
McClam, S. and S. Flores (2012), 'Transdisciplinary teaching and research: what is possible in higher education?', *Teaching for Higher Education*, 17(3), 231–43.
Mezirow, J. (1978), 'Perspective transformation', *Adult Education Quarterly*, 28, 100–110.
Mezirow, J. (2000), *Learning as Transformation: Critical Perspectives on a Theory in Progress*, San Francisco, CA: Jossey-Bass.
Organisation for Economic Co-operation and Development (OECD) (2005), *The Definition and Selection of Key Competencies: Executive Summary*, Paris: OECD.
Rieckmann, M. (2012), 'Future-oriented higher education: which key competencies should be fostered through university teaching and learning?', *Futures*, 44(2), 127–35.
Ryan, A. and Cotton, D. (2013), 'Times of change: shifting pedagogy and curricula for future sustainability', in S. Sterling, L. Maxey and H. Luna (eds), *The Sustainable University: Progress and Prospects*, Abingdon: Routledge, pp. 151–67.
Savin-Baden, M. (2000), *Problem-based Learning in Higher Education: Untold Stories*, Buckingham, UK: Society for Research in Higher Education.
Schneider, F., Giger, M. and Harari, N. et al. (2019), 'Transdisciplinary co-production of knowledge and sustainability transformations: three generic mechanisms of impact generation', *Environmental Science and Policy*, 102, 26–35.
Shawe, R., Horan, W., Moles, R. and B. O'Regan (2019), 'Mapping of sustainability policies and initiatives in higher education institutes', *Environmental Science and Policy*, 99, 80–88.
Sisitka, H.L., Wals, A.E., Kronlid, D. and McGarry, D. (2015), 'Transformative, transgressive social learning: rethinking higher education pedagogy in times of systemic global dysfunction', *Current Opinion in Environmental Sustainability*, 16, 73–80.
Tassone, V.C., O'Mahony, C. and McKenna E. et al. (2018), '(Re-)designing higher education curricula in times of systemic dysfunction: a responsible research and innovation perspective', *Higher Education*, 76, 337–52.
Trencher, G., Yarime, M. and Kharrazi, A. (2013), 'Co-creating sustainability: cross sector university collaboration for driving sustainable urban transformations', *Journal of Clear Production*, 50, 40–55.
United Nations Economic Commission for Europe (UNECE) (2012), *Learning for the Future: Competencies in Education for Sustainable Development*, Geneva: UNECE.

United Nations Educational, Scientific and Cultural Organization (UNESCO) (2017), *Education for Sustainable Development Goals: Learning Objectives*, Paris: UNESCO.

Wiek, A. and Key, B. (2015), 'Learning while transforming – solution oriented learning for urban sustainability in Phoenix', *Current Opinion in Environmental Sustainability*, 16, 29–36.

Wiek, A., Bernstein, M.J. and Foley, R.W. et al. (2017), 'Operationalizing competencies in higher education for sustainable development', in M. Barth, G. Michelsen, M. Rieckmann and I. Tholas (eds), *Routledge Handbook of Higher Education for Sustainable Development*, Abingdon: Routledge, pp. 241–60.

Wiek, A., Withycombe, L. and Redman, C.L. (2011), 'Key competencies in sustainability: a reference framework for academic program development', *Sustainability Science*, 6, 203–18.

Wilhelm, S., Foster, R. and Zimmermann, A.B. (2019), 'Implementing competence orientation: towards constructively aligned education for sustainable development in university-level teaching-and-learning', *Sustainability*, 11, 1–22.

25. Implementing a green co-learning center to support sustainable campus development

Cahyono Agus, Nur Aini Iswati Hasanah, Aqmal Nur Jihad, Pita Asih Bekti Cahyanti, Muhammad Sulaiman and Suratman

1. INTRODUCTION

Indonesia has abundant natural resources, such as humid tropical forests, mineral mines, oil and gas, and soil fertility. Tropical ecosystems have high temperatures, rainfall, humidity, sunlight, and organic cycles throughout the year so that they have the highest biological productivity and biodiversity in the world (Agus, 2018, 2019; Agus et al., 2018; Agus, Anggari et al., 2019; Agus, Primananda, Faridah et al., 2019). Excessive exploitation of natural resources for economic reasons has resulted in severe environmental and global damage, and climate change is exacerbating the damage in tropical ecosystems and in Indonesia in particular (Agus, Primananda and Nufus, 2019; Agus et al., 2017; Cahyanti and Agus, 2017). Management of Indonesia's abundant natural resources still relies on the exploitation of resources-based development, and thus needs to become a more dignified and sustainable knowledge-based development (Agus et al., 2018; Agus, Ilfana et al., 2019; Agus, Primananda and Nufus, 2019).

The destruction of the human side of life in the world today has become a significant tragedy and occurs in all fields. Chris Hedges, a senior US journalist, reported that many doctors damage health, law enforcement has damaged the legal system, and higher education is damaging science (Agus et al., 2016). Agus et al. (2020) reported that government rogue elements have also destroyed freedom and power, a part of the press and social media have damaged public information, religious fanaticism has also damaged the morality of religion itself, while the bank mafia has damaged the nation's economy. Towards solving these ills, Nelson Mandela said that education is the most potent peaceful force and modifier for a better and more dignified world (ibid.).

Indonesia must change the paradigm from development that relies only on natural resources, to development based on scientific innovation. A new paradigm shift is necessary, from natural resource extraction based on the red economy of mass production towards empowering natural resources for sustainable development (Agus, 2018, 2019; Agus et al., 2020; Agus, Ilfana et al., 2019). Education is important, even crucial, in achieving welfare and social progress, and lies at the heart of sustainable development (Leicht, Heiss and Byun, 2018; van't Land and Herzog, 2017). Education can create leaders and communities who in turn can create future development solutions (United Nations Educational, Scientific and Cultural Organization [UNESCO], 2012).

UNESCO (2017) suggests that higher education can help overcome the problems of poverty; health and well-being; gender equality; government, employment, and economic growth; climate change; peace, justice, and lasting agreement. Thus, education for sustainable development (ESD) can nurture the human lives that change with time and generations. Indonesia is committed to successfully implementing the UN Sustainable Development Goals (SDGs) by achieving the 2030 Agenda. In this regard, Indonesia's Presidential Regulation No. 59/2017 concerning the implementation of SDGs has mandated the Ministry of National Development Planning of the Republic of Indonesia to provide the Roadmap of SDGs Indonesia (Bappenas, 2019).

A revolution is needed to realize the 2030 Agenda and associated SDGs through a performance-based program that is integrated, comprehensive, non-egocentric, and of real benefit. In addition to grand concepts, also needed are improvements in mindset, equalization of perceptions, program orientation not project orientation, empowerment of all resources, principles of needs and benefits – from upstream to downstream – performance indicators, monitoring and evaluation, follow-up and program sustainability. The leading critical indicator of success is not the completion of administrative and financial accountability and conformity with mere standard operating procedures; this program requires the full commitment and participation of all stakeholders in a synergistic, integrated, and comprehensive way. The main problem of coordination between government agencies, which are usually egocentric and more concerned with administration and project orientation, must be changed to systematic and integrated program orientation.

2. EDUCATION FOR SUSTAINABLE DEVELOPMENT

ESD was developed because education (formal, non-formal, and informal) is a powerful instrument that is effective for communicating, providing learning, raising awareness, and being able to mobilize communities and move the nation towards developing a more sustainable future life (UNESCO, 2012). ESD inculcates broad, deep, and futuristic insights and concepts about the global environment to seek cause-and-effect relationships and how to overcome them. However, it is not sustainable development education, but education to support sustainable development that gives awareness and the ability to all people (especially future generations) to contribute better to sustainable development in the present and the future.

ESD will increase the capacity of the community or nation to be able to build, develop, and implement planned activities that lead to sustainable development. Programs and activities can support sustainable economic growth by considering several ecosystems, including (1) development of the quality of human resources and technology; (2) preservation of the environment and diversity; (3) social justice; (4) cultural harmony and preservation; and (5) balance of production and consumption (UNESCO, 2012). ESD will increase awareness of individual responsibility, which in turn is expected to increase respect for the rights of others, nature, and diversity, and enable people to make choices/decisions that are responsible and to articulate all of that into real action. With ESD, we must make a real contribution to creating a better, safer and more comfortable life, both now and in the future for our children and grandchildren. This concept involves a comprehensive understanding of complexity and diversity and how to change all developments towards sustainability, implemented through wise planning and execution, and disseminated effectively and extensively.

Since the 1970s, environmental awareness has been emerging in the field of higher education. It is widely accepted that universities can play critical roles in promoting sustainability and many organizations and individuals have made efforts to promote the role of higher education in sustainable development (Zou et al., 2015). Education is a key agent for change towards sustainable development (United Nations Economic Commission for Europe [UNECE], 2009). In 2005, the UN's Decade of Education for Sustainable Development (2005–14) program established a series of goals and strategies to strengthen and focus global efforts in ESD (Zou et al., 2015). Based on UNECE (2009), ESD builds the capacity of individuals, communities, and society to make informed judgments and choices in favor of sustainable development. This promotion of sustainability at the university level has become a global trend.

A university is an educational institution that provides instruction and facilities for research in many branches of advanced learning (Zou et al., 2015). It is a center of universal knowledge (Van Weenen, 2000). It has a brand image of academic excellence, and it should place more emphasis on educational quality than on personal administrative support and professional advocacy services (Akareem and Hossain, 2016). Its primary role in sustainable development is to facilitate the fundamental moral and cultural changes necessary for creating a sustainable society (Zou et al., 2015). ESD is about the added value (quality) to existing education (UNECE, 2009).

3.   SDGs PROGRAM IN HIGHER EDUCATION

Policy strategies have been proposed towards Indonesia's implementation of SDG 4 on quality education, especially on higher education for the period 2020–30 (Bappenas, 2019): first, strengthening of autonomy in higher education; second, the development of higher education institutions as centers of excellence and development of science and technology; third, development of innovative study programs that suit development and industrial needs; fourth, strengthening the vocational competency certification system (Bappenas, 2019).

The involvement of higher education in assisting SDGs can be realized by (1) providing knowledge, innovations, and solutions for SDGs; (2) creating current and future implementers of the SDGs; (3) demonstrating how to support, adopt and implement SDGs in governance, operationalization, and culture; and (4) developing leadership cooperation between sectors to guide response to the SDGs. Meanwhile, the SDGs themselves will assist universities through (1) increasing the needs for SDGs related to education; (2) providing a comprehensive and global definition for responsible universities; (3) offering a framework for achieving goals; (4) creating new scheme funding; (5) and supporting collaboration with new internal and external partners (Bappenas, 2018). The SDGs program has not been well coordinated thus far and there is a need for integrated national development for all stakeholders involved. The programs of each ministry and institution are still egocentric; the implementation of each program is very dependent on the significant commitment of each leader. For this reason, Bappenas (the National Development Planning Agency) sector leaders need to be able to be more active in facilitating the coordination of the SDGs achievement program and building perfect synergism.

The Emancipated Learning (*Merdeka Belajar*) policy is expected to liberate educational institutions and encourage young people to innovate and promote creative thinking. This time, the focus is on the Liberated Campus (*Kampus Merdeka*), and there are several policy adjustments supported by changes in Ministerial Regulations, without having to change the Presidential Regulation and national law (Ministry of Education and Culture [MoEC], 2020). The four policies in the field of higher education include: (1) autonomy for state and private universities to open or establish new study programs; (2) automatic re-accreditation programs for all ranks, and voluntary ones for higher education institutions and study programs already ready to rise in rank; (3) freedom for a public university to become a Legal Entities University; and (4) granting the right to students to take courses outside the study program and make changes to the definition of Semester Credit Units (ibid.). This controversial policy must be guarded and anticipate the need for risk management that may arise, to be more productive and efficient. A good and effective policy can be implemented if the policy is grounded and functional. The Indonesian government will continue this program in 2021 to include: (i) smart Indonesian cards; (ii) school digitization; (iii) achievement and character strengthening; (iv) driving teachers; (v) a new curriculum; (vi) revitalization of vocational education; (vii) the Liberated Campus; and (viii) advancement of culture and language (ibid.). However, strong policies to create ecosystems and an atmosphere to encourage innovation and creativity in learning, methods of delivery, and exciting content creators during online learning during the COVID-19 pandemic were not appropriately handled. The edutainment of the *SariSwara* learning and education method, which Ki Hadjar Dewantara (KHD) develops, should be one of the right solutions to perfect it (Agus et al., 2020). Through the omnibus law scheme, fundamental legislation to educate the nation's life as the goal of the Republic of Indonesia seems to be urgent to change.

4. BLUE CAMPUS UGM

In order to maintain the earth's increasingly damaged environment, we will be very dependent on students who are problem solvers, critical thinkers, and, ultimately, change makers (Boca and Saraçlı, 2019), as well as being the key to success in achieving sustainable development goals (Pavlova, 2011). Environmental awareness plays an essential role in shaping individual attitudes, and environmental education is vital from preschool to higher education (Bozdogan, Sahinler and Korkmaz, 2016). Human consciousness also plays a vital role in maintaining the balance and preservation of nature (Nazarenko, 2018) so that a full understanding of the resolution of urgent environmental problems is needed for sustainable development (Parker, Prabawa-sear and Kustiningsih, 2018).

Parker et al. (2018) state that environmental values are not yet embedded in society, which leads to a lack of respect for natural resources and environmental services. Students tend to take notes with a low level of awareness about environmental problems in the community. Although tropical ecosystems have an impact on the global environment, the community has not been moved to contribute significantly to the improvement of the earth's environment, which is becoming increasingly damaged. The effort to improve the tropical environment, because it has the highest productivity in the world, can contribute greatly and significantly to the improvement of the global environment (Agus, 2018, 2019).

The green campus movement has been able to increase environmental awareness in the academic community through pro-environmental groups focusing campaigns on the love of nature, anti-waste, conservation of animal species, and preventing forest destruction (Nilan, 2017). Indonesia's young generation is aware of future natural conditions; however, the relationship between environmental awareness and the success of ESD is still unclear. It is expected that ESD can accommodate and maintain environmental awareness of students and, vice versa, awareness supports the success of ESD. Empowerment of land resources (land, water, minerals, air), biological resources (animals, plants, humans, and other living things), and environmental resources (interactions between creatures) must be synergistic and optimal. We need more hard work, smart work, actual work, cooperation within a harmonious and synergistic academic, business, community, government (ABCG) network. Of course, communication, coordination, consolidation, and full commitment that is all 'right' (the right people, time, ways, places, targets, forms), needs to continue to be pursued.

Our planet consists of blue oceans covering 72 percent, and blue skies more than 95 percent. The blue earth paradigm signifies that the green earth supports the blue sky and oceans and vice versa (Agus, 2018). Universitas Gadjah Mada (UGM) has long been known as a 'blue campus' because of the many writings and films about the subject. The sustainable blue campus paradigm needs to be revitalized. A campus with an ecosystem of education, research, and community service empowers all the potential elements of the universe on earth by strengthening the relationship between God, humans and nature so that economic, socio-cultural, religious, spiritual, human and environmental values can be achieved harmoniously, synergistically, and in balance. Breakthroughs, synergies, and significant innovations from the process of civilization, which are the result of re-exploration, re-identification, re-inventory, restoration, renaissance, and re-creation of cultures that were neglected due to modernization can make this possible. The use of information technology (IT) towards creating a cyber-campus is a revolution of increased quality and dignified environment and life. The unique culture of harmony in life, better attitudes and behavior are expected to be able to shape the characteristics of identity, self-esteem, self-confidence, and independence in order to create endurance, resistance, and developmental power.

Education should not only sharpen the intelligence of the brain but must also adopt the concept of *TriSakti* (Tri-Soul) to teach creativity, taste, and intention. This is a synergistic combination of thought processes, taste/feeling and motivation. The fourth industrial revolution (Industry 4.0) is developing rapidly with the support of advanced technology, artificial intelligence, Big Data, and mobile technology. Japan is even working towards Society 5.0 to overcome chronic social challenges. However, the revolution has as increased the ego of the self, the personal, and the group, as well as eliminating values of human, socio-cultural, environmental, family and togetherness. The teachings of KHD, who advocated education for all people regardless of sex, race, ethnicity, culture, religion, and social and economic status, have played a part in filling this emptiness by honing the brain, heart, and hands synergistically, not just for young people but for all generations (Agus et al., 2020). KHD's teachings are reflected in the Javanese concept of becoming *Jalma Kang Utama* (the ultimate human being). Education must sharpen the potential of students' talents and be a blessing to society and the universe (ibid.).

Destructive innovation has led to Education 4.0, which encourages millennial students to follow modern learning with the support of the latest smart IT, digital, and Big Data access. However, students tend to be solitary, egocentric, and lose their human values, social culture, togetherness, and kinship (ibid.). To that end, strengthening the characters of young people through atmospheric academic design and infrastructure in fulfilling the content of cultural, humanitarian, and corporate values must be introduced in a well-structured manner. Today, millennial co-working spaces and cafés are always crowded with millennial learners. Thus, Co-learning System 4.0 for the millennial student in an era of destructive innovation, with the support of sophisticated IT and significant data access, seems to be the most appropriate learning media (ibid.). The restoration of the millennial education system must be firmly rooted in the noble culture of the nation itself in order to prepare for the new civilization of a 'Golden Indonesia'. Also, we must dare to develop the concept of 'Out of the box, within the system' (ibid.).

5.   ESD-SDGs PROGRAM AT UGM

UGM was established during the struggle for independence of the Republic of Indonesia, and it took on the task of the *Tridharma* (the 'three teachings': education, research, and community service). In realizing a dignified and international standard campus and in the framework of UGM as the center of ESD, it is necessary to implement an environmentally friendly and disaster-mitigation campus program. The implementation of *Tridharma* needs to be supported by the management of an abiotic, biotic, socio-cultural, health, and security environment in order to realize the education of the future generations of a noble nation (Agus et al., 2020).

UGM launched its SDGs Centre in August 2019 to support the initiation and development of collaborative networking with other universities' SDGs Centres in the Java region in particular and throughout Indonesia in general. The establishment of the SDGs Centre at UGM becomes one of the remits of the Regional Centre of Expertise (RCE) Yogyakarta in supporting the implementation of the SDGs and achievements at UGM and the Special Region of Yogyakarta. The development of the UGM campus can inspire the realization of a campus area and its surroundings as green, blue, clean, healthy, resilient, and cultured. These campus programs are indicators for the application of the concept of ESD. The programs are aligned with the university's identity and in responding quickly to the issue of global warming and world climate change, energy, food, water, waste, health, and disasters. The management of the UGM blue campus environment is carried out comprehensively with co-management, co-participation, and self-regulation by involving the stakeholders. The pillars of the ecological, technological, and cultural approaches are integrated to realize an environmentally friendly campus of awareness and disaster response in the context of forming noble and dignified human beings (Agus et al., 2020).

UGM is a world-class research university characterized by the interests of the ordinary people and deeply rooted in Indonesian culture and society through the Indonesia–Managing Higher Education for Relevance and Efficiency (I–MHERE) project that is supported by World Bank. The aims of the project are, first, research-based teaching and learning; second, increasing international academic reputation and accreditation in education, research, and community service; third, increasing international cooperation networks; and fourth, strengthening the role of UGM in its participation in overcoming national problems through Indonesia's bottom-up and socio-cultural approach and promoting local excellence at the global level.

With UGM's vision as a research university and in line with the *Tridharma* paradigm of education, research, and community service development, the university policy is oriented towards strengthening ESD. The background of the policy is that life at present is becoming increasingly complex and, going forward, chaotic, due to (1) the population multiplying and exceeding natural world production capacity; and (2) a fast-developing complex communication and transportation system, that is, economic, trading, development, poverty, environment, weather globalization (Agus et al., 2020). The people live in an unbalanced environment, which means more exploitation than conservation, which, in turn, will mean unsustainable development and disaster in the future (Agus, 2018).

ESD has developed into a broad, profound, and revolutionary global environment concept and perception, which includes a cause–effect relationship and problem-solving capacity. It is not an education of sustainable development, but education for supporting sustainable development. These programs provide people – especially the next generation – with awareness and capability to contribute to sustainable development now and in the future. These programs have enriched the curriculum, learning process, and university development. Synergism with other programs has resulted in the better achievements in the ever-increasing performance indicators.

Nevertheless, the implementation of education, research, and community service programs separately and individually resulted in ego-sectoral and reduced learning impacts. Students still find it challenging to integrate into the whole learning process and its applications in the community. Therefore, the paradigm of three pillars of mandatory tasks has shifted at UGM, from education, research, and community service individually, to became more integrated into research-based community service and education. The results and impacts of the program are measured to ensure their sustainable improvement. The program has been and is being implemented through network collaboration between UGM and the regional government, industry, community, and professional associations. Student mobilization in the village community became a formal program known as Student Community Services (SCS) at UGM and has been practiced since the 1970s. The empowerment paradigm of the research-based Student Community Services – Community Empowerment Learning program (SCS-CEL) through a multidisciplinary approach has been applied since 2007. Every year there are around 7000 students deployed in the community for two months, which is equivalent to a three-semester credit unit for undergraduate students. This empowerment paradigm must follow the principles of win–win solutions, co-creation, co-finance, flexibility, and sustainability.

UGM, as a sustainable blue campus, has a noble aspiration to be a forum for building excellent human resources capable of being lifelong examples who can help to realize a great world civilization. Therefore, UGM aims to be a center of light in the darkness for life on earth and the universe through the development of intelligent science and technology. UGM is a channel through which to hone clairvoyant, noble cultural morals as a field of education, research, and community service to continuously create a universal life that is peaceful and happiness for future generations.

UGM is determined to become a source of the birth of world leaders who can build a new civilization through various sustainable blue campus programs, namely (1) as a pioneering campus for environmental conservation; (2) as an ESD development center for the SDGs program; (3) as a civilized campus of culture; (4) as a resilient and independent campus in times of disaster; (5) as a blue campus to maintain noble and wise values; (6) as a pro-climate campus; (7) as a campus that respects gender and young people; (8) as a campus as a center of sociopreneurship; and (9) as a cyber-campus. All of this is intended to realize the creation of a dignified, dynamic, innovative campus life that is rooted in national culture and is world class. Higher education must also develop *Tridharma* that is innovative, efficient, and become a guide for the development of countries in a sustainable world.

UGM continues to develop campus infrastructure and superstructures based on its values and national culture and on the inspiration of the sustainable blue campus, in addition to efforts to enhance national and global cooperation to advance knowledge for humanity and world peace. The UGM campus layout contains nuances of the sustainable blue campus, which starts from the line of imagination and consists of several zones as representative of a science, health, socio-humanities and agro-complex cluster.

6.   CO-LEARNING CENTERS

Collaboration is a philosophy of interaction and personal lifestyle so that everyone must be responsible for their actions, including learning and respecting the abilities and contributions of others. There is a division of authority and acceptance of responsibility among group members for group actions. Collaborative learning is an educational approach to teaching and learning that involves groups of students who work together to solve problems, complete tasks, or make products (Laal and Ghodsi, 2012). Collaborative learning is based on building consensus through collaboration between group members, which is very different from competition to be the best individual in the group.

The development of human knowledge and learning has developed rapidly, so the development of more effective educational systems and practices is also very much needed. This requires the integration of insights from various fields – from biology and neuroscience to psychology, sociology, developmental science, and learning – and connecting them with knowledge of the successful approaches that have emerged in education (Darling-Hammond et al., 2019). The basic knowledge provided by learning and development science, coupled with decades of insights gained through educational research, has provided a framework for supporting the welfare of young people throughout the world in their various contexts (ibid.). Darling-Hammond et al. (2020) demonstrate the way that schools can organize relationships that support development with coherent and integrated approaches that are both effective and supportive. This program includes home and school connections, instruction with scaffolding designed to support social, emotional, and academic skills development, habits, and mindset, and responses that are culturally and competently adjusted to the assets and needs of each young person

The co-learning center is one of the methods of organization that facilitates students to be actively involved in small group instruction, practical activities, discussions, and joint learning. Educators must design according to diverse student needs in general and particular education settings (King-Sears, 2007). The industrial revolution has dramatically influenced the development of the world (Caliskan, 2015). Globalization has influenced technology, the young generation, and the human lifestyle (Scholl and Gulwadi, 2015). The whole world has the same global and local challenges when facing new and increasingly complex life challenges. Higher education institutions must become vigilant in the development of the latest technological knowledge by developing holistic learning systems for millennial students (Agus et al., 2020). Millennial generation education requires a revolution in learning systems, including facilities, infrastructure, and learning superstructure.

To this end, libraries as co-learning centers have an essential role in enhancing the scientific base, fostering critical thinking and enhancing the educational experience (Freeman, 2005) in order to adapt to more complex millennial societies (Johnson, 2013). Learning resources and media need to adjust to keep pace with changes in student behavior and needs. In line with the latest technological changes, print collections have gradually become less important in research (Dempsey and Malpas, 2018), shifting to digital information or databases. The traditional paradigm of the function of libraries that are indoors and outdoors has shifted and developed into a place of learning that is friendly, safe and warm to provide social interactions, meetings, discussions and works (Head, 2016). The Library 4.0 model no longer distinguishes between digital space and real life, with features such as cloud storage, integrated accounts, creative space, high technology, Big Data, open-source, and discussion space, both formal and informal (Noh, 2015).

UGM has innovated to provide and support new ways of learning for millennial young people. Several café spaces and co-learning spaces have been built on campus to build collaborative media, cross-field discussions of science, and programs to create innovative start-ups. The design of study rooms make them simpler, more open-concept, modern, appropriate, and adaptive. Johnson (2013) emphasizes various design principles such as accessibility, inclusivity, visibility, connectivity, flexibility, and adaptability. Millennial students are more interested in an independent and attractive learning style that is supported by the high-speed Internet. The flexibility to access Big Data with more flexible time and place is suited to the young people of today. Universities and faculties that develop co-learning spaces are becoming more popular and targets for students to interact intensively and better academically. The implementation of independent learning in an independent campus means that millennial students not only get good grades, but today's soft skills are more structured and systemized.

7.   EDUCOPOLIS PARK

Millennial students have several options from which to choose what space they will use as a study room both on- and off-campus. UGM Educopolis Wisdom Park is a multidisciplinary ESD concept embodiment with educational, economic, environmental, cultural, social, edutainment, health, entrepreneurship, and universal characteristics. This area is built with high complexity involving various orientations or goals, which not only fulfills aesthetic functions but becomes a showroom for the application of ESD-style nature-based management.

The integrated concept of Educopolis refers to an environment that is conducive to

Table 25.1   Matrix of functions and spaces in Wisdom Park

	Open Space	Blue Space	Green Space
Flood control	Flood emergency area	Detention, retention, calculation of water discharge	Flood emergency area
Water utilization	–	Recharge area, conditioning, water purification	–
River environment	River border with multi-function	Microclimate	Green and biodiversity areas (400 trees, 38 native species

the learning process in the context of developing multidisciplinary collaboration and responding to ecological problems to achieve the university's vision. Lestan, Erzen and Golobic (2014) argue that universities must pay attention to the quality of good outdoor learning centers, influencing the effectiveness of learning and human health (Agus et al., 2020).

Wisdom Park, as a green space, provides several environmental, social, and human services with a multidisciplinary, multifunctional yet straightforward concept. Holt et al. (2019) revealed that students who actively interacted with green space had a good overall mood, a higher quality of life, and a lower perceived level of stress. Wisdom Park must be a system with a sustainable city or district landscape. Rakhshandehroo et al. (2017) mention the various benefits of urban green open spaces such as nature conservation of biodiversity; reduced air temperature, heat islands, and air pollution; improved air quality; and reduced noise and contaminants.

Wisdom Park will comprise several components to achieve certain functions, for example, as an educational park, open space, blue space, and green space. The university designed Wisdom Park with several functions in mind: the role and mechanism of water catchment, education, housing, worship, recreation areas, and sports (Table 25.1).

The educational garden has been designed to be complete, futuristic, and functional. It functions as a learning zone outside the classroom, regardless of the combined functions of the area directly adjacent to the campus and the related residential area. The combination of learning and the presence of the real world make it a perfect open space with holistic functions. Asamoah et al. (2017) highlighted several important factors for the utilization of green space co-learning, including Wi-Fi connectivity, proximity to lecture and living areas, aesthetic nature of the space, and quiet environment.

Cahyanti et al. (2019) proposed the concept of an integrated 'Shaft Garden' waste management park using the shaft as the point of view of multi-story buildings, a continuous channel connecting all the floors (Figure 25.1). The garden refers to an area containing the components of hard and soft materials that support each other and are intentionally constructed for humans for relaxation. This concept combines the integrated management of the agricultural and non-agricultural sectors by utilizing the advantages of landscape, temperature, intensity and length of sun exposure, humidity, microbial activity, organic matter cycle, growth, and high land productivity throughout the year in tropical ecosystems.

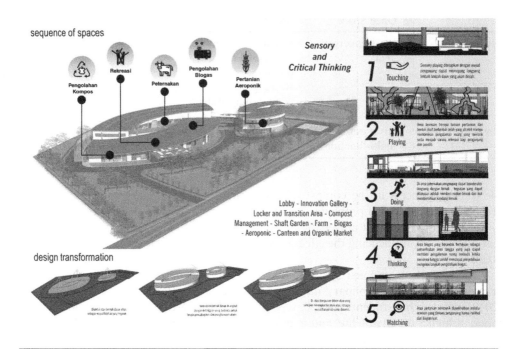

Source: Cahyanti et al. (2019).

Figure 25.1   Development of integrated 'Shaft Garden' waste management park, UGM

An academic and non-academic atmosphere to support the integrated education, research, and community service processes in universities in the current era must be developed following the style of millennial students. Education for the freedom of the soul needs to be facilitated with modern, fun, and appropriate infrastructure, curriculum, ecology, and academic atmosphere.

8.   CONCLUSIONS

The paradigm of three pillars of mandatory tasks has shifted at blue campus UGM, from education, research, and community service individually to became more integrated into research-based learning and community service. The empowerment paradigm implements the principles of win–win solutions, co-creation, co-finance, flexibility, and sustainability. The program must be implemented through a network of collaboration between the university, the regional government, industry, community, and professional associations. Co-learning System 4.0 for millennial students in the era of destructive innovation with sophisticated IT support and access to Big Data seems to be the most appropriate learning media. The development of student character through a program of togetherness, family, and humanity can enrich the development of human resources. The restoration of the millennial education system must be firmly rooted in the noble culture of the nation itself, in order to prepare for the new civilization of 'Golden Indonesia'.

REFERENCES

Agus, C. 2018. Development of blue revolution through integrated bio-cycles system on tropical natural resources management. In W. Leal Filho, D.-M. Pociovalisteanu, P. Borges de Brito and P.R. Borges de Lima (eds), *Towards a Sustainable Bioeconomy: Principles, Challenges and Perspectives*. Cham, Switzerland: Springer, pp. 155–72.

Agus, C. 2019. Integrated bio-cycle system for sustainable and productive tropical natural resource management in Indonesia. In H.B. Singh (ed.), *Bioeconomy for Sustainable Development*. Singapore: Springer, pp. 201–16.

Agus, C., Anggari, P.E. and Faridah, E. et al. 2019. Role of watering interval and organic pot on the growth of exotic fast-growing species on coal mining soil. *IOP Conference Series: Earth and Environmental Science*, 308, Article 012055.

Agus, C., Azmi, F.F. and Ilfana, Z.R. et al. 2018. The impact of forest fire on the biodiversity and soil characteristic of tropical peatland. In W. Leal Filho, A.L. Salvia and R. Pretorius et al. (eds), *Handbook of Climate Change and Biodiversity*. Cham, Switzerland: Springer, pp. 287–303.

Agus, C., Cahyanti, P.A.B. and Widodo, B. et al. 2020. Cultural-based education of Tamansiswa as a locomotive of Indonesian education system. In W. Leal Filho, A.L. Salvia and R. Pretorius et al. (eds), *Universities as Living Labs for Sustainable Development*. Cham, Switzerland: Springer, pp. 471–86.

Agus, C., Ilfana, Z.R. and Azmi, F.F. et al. 2019. The effect of tropical peat land-use changes on plant diversity and soil properties. *International Journal of Environmental Science and Technology*, 17, 1703–12.

Agus, C., Primananda, E. and Faridah, E. et al. 2019. Role of *arbuscular mycorrhizal fungi* and *Pongamia pinnata* for revegetation of tropical open-pit coal mining soils. *International Journal of Environmental Science and Technology*, 16, 3365–74.

Agus, C., Primananda, E. and Nufus, M. 2019. Integrated bio-cycle system for rehabilitation of open-pit coal mining areas in tropical ecosystems. In Leal Filho, W. (ed.), *International Business, Trade and Institutional Sustainability*. Cham, Switzerland: Springer, pp. 515–28.

Agus, C., Wulandari, D. and Primananda, E. et al. 2017. The role of soil amendment on tropical post tin mining area in Bangka Island Indonesia for dignified and sustainable environment and life. *IOP Conference Series: Earth and Environmental Science*, 83, Article 012030.

Akareem, H.S. and Hossain, S.S. 2016. Determinants of education quality: what makes students' perception different? *Open Review of Educational Research*, 3(1), 52–67.

Asamoah, Y., Mensah, I. and Adams, O. et al. 2017. Usage of green spaces at University of Cape Coast by non-African foreign students. *Journal of Global Initiatives*, 11(2), 49–67.

Bappenas. 2018. Challenges and strategy for the implementation of Sustainable Development Goals (SDGs). Public lecture. Padjadajaran University Bandung, 4 April 2018 [In Indonesian].

Bappenas. 2019. *Roadmap of SDGs Indonesia: A Highlight*. Jakarta: Ministry of National Development Planning/National Development Planning Agency RI.

Boca, G.D. and Saraçlı, S. 2019. Environmental education and student's perception, for sustainability. *Sustainability*, 11(6), Article 1553.

Bozdogan, E., Sahinler, S. and Korkmaz, E. 2016. Environmental awareness and attitudes in university students. An example from Hatay (Turkey). *Oxidation Communications*, 39(1), 661–72.

Cahyanti, P.A.B. and Agus, C. 2017. Development of landscape architecture through geo-eco-tourism in tropical karst area to avoid extractive cement industry for dignified and sustainable environment and life. *IOP Conference Series: Earth and Environmental Science*, 83, Article 012028.

Cahyanti, P.A.B., Widiastuti, K. and Agus, C. et al. 2019. Development of an edutainment Shaft Garden for integrated waste management in the UGM green campus. *IOP Conference Series: Earth and Environmental Science*, 398, Article 012001.

Caliskan, H.K. 2015. Technological change and economic growth. *Procedia – Social and Behavioral Sciences*, 195, 649–54.

Darling-Hammond, L., Flook, L. and Cook-Harvey, C. et al. (2020). Implications for educational practice of the science of learning and development. *Applied Developmental Science*, 24(2), 97–140.

Dempsey, L. and Malpas, C. 2018. Academic library futures in a diversified university system. In N. Gleason (ed.), *Higher Education in the Era of the Fourth Industrial Revolution*. Singapore: Palgrave Macmillan.

Freeman, G.T. 2005. The library as place: changes in learning patterns, collections, technology and use. In G.T. Freeman, *Library as Place: Rethink Roles, Rethink Space*. Washington, DC: Council on Library and Information Resources.

Head, A.J. 2016. Planning and designing academic library learning spaces: expert perspectives of architects, librarians, and library consultants. In A.J. Head, *A Project Information Literacy Research Project: The Practitioner Series*. Washington, DC: Project Information Literacy.

Holt, E.W., Lombard, Q.K. and Best, N. et al. 2019. Active and passive use of green space, health, and well-being amongst university students. *International Journal of Environmental Research and Public Health*, 16(424), 1–13.

Johnson, I.M. 2013. Development goals after 2015 – the role of information, books, and libraries. *Information Development*, 29(4), 294–96.

King-Sears, M.E. 2007. Designing and delivering learning center instruction. *Intervention in School and Clinic*, 42(3), 137–47.

Laal, M. and Ghodsi, S.M. 2012. Benefits of collaborative learning. *Procedia – Social and Behavioral Sciences*, 31, 486–90.

Leicht, A., Heiss, J. and Byun, W.J. 2018. *Issues and Trends in Education for Sustainable Development*. Paris: UNESCO.

Lestan, K.A., Erzen, I. and Golobic, M. 2014. The role of open space in urban neighborhoods for health-related lifestyle. *International Journal of Environmental Research and Public Health*, 11, 6547–70.

Ministry of Education and Culture (MoEC). 2020. *Merdeka Belajar: Kampus Merdeka*. Jakarta: MoEC [In Indonesian].

Nazarenko, A.V. 2018. Raising environmental awareness of future teachers. *International Journal of Instruction*, 11(3), 63–76.

Nilan, P. 2017. The ecological habitus of Indonesian student environmentalism. *Environmental Sociology*, 3(4), 370–80.

Noh, Y. 2015. Imagining Library 4.0: creating a model for future libraries. *The Journal of Academic Librarianship*, 41, 786–97.

Parker, L., Prabawa-sear, K. and Kustiningsih, W. 2018. How young people in Indonesia see themselves as environmentalists. *Indonesia and Malay World*, 46(136), 263–82.

Pavlova, M. 2011. Environmental education and/or education for sustainable development: what role for technology education? *Proceedings of PATT 25: CRIPT 8 Perspectives on Learning in Design and Technology Education Conference*, Queensland, Australia, pp. 333–9.

Rakhshandehroo, M., Yusof, M.J.M. and Arabi, R. et al. 2017. The environment benefits of urban open green spaces. *Alam Cipta*, 10(1), 10–16.

Scholl, K.G. and Gulwadi, G.B. 2015. Recognizing campus landscapes as learning spaces. *Journal of Learning Spaces*, 4, 53–60.

United Nations Economic Commission for Europe (UNECE). 2009. *Learning from Each Other: The UNECE Strategy for Education for Sustainable Development*. Geneva: UNECE.

United Nations Educational, Scientific and Cultural Organization (UNESCO). 2012. *Education for Sustainable Development*. Paris: UNESCO.

United Nations Educational, Scientific and Cultural Organization (UNESCO). 2017. *Education for Sustainable Development Goals, Learning Objectives*. Paris: UNESCO.

van't Land, H. and Herzog, F. 2017. *Higher Education Paving the Way to Sustainable Development: A Global Perspective*. Paris: International Association of Universities.

Van Weenen, H. 2000. Towards a vision of a sustainable university. *International Journal of Sustainability in Higher Education*, 1(1), 20–34.

Zou, Y., Zhao, W., Mason, R. and Li, M. 2015. Comparing sustainable universities between the United States and China: cases of Indiana University and Tsinghua University. *Sustainability*, 7, 11799–817.

26. An exploration of interdisciplinary settings as intellectual spaces for sustainability in higher education
Rudi W. Pretorius

1. INTRODUCTION AND AIM

1.1 Sustainability in Higher Education and the Interdisciplinary Turn

Academia has traditionally been organized according to disciplines, with many of them having a legacy of a century, and some even longer, in higher education (Rasmussen and Arler, 2010). The trend towards interdisciplinarity gained momentum with the realization that the sustainability challenges posed by twenty-first-century global environmental change cannot be confined by boundaries between disciplines. In most cases, inputs from various disciplines are required to gain a comprehensive understanding of the issues involved (Baerwald, 2010; Skole, 2004). Due to the complexities involved to deal effectively with these, students need to be empowered to engage with knowledge, skills and insights not confined to specific disciplines, and to be able to cross disciplinary boundaries (Yarime et al., 2012). This interdisciplinary intellectual space is dynamic, continuously changing and can be navigated through a diversity of approaches, with 'one-size-fits-all' solutions not relevant. In reality, this is easier said than done, since academia is still largely organized in terms of disciplinary structures and characterized by assessment and reward practices that reinforce disciplinary trajectories (Woelert and Millar, 2013).

1.2 Viewpoints on the Value of Disciplinary Versus Interdisciplinary Settings

Since the restructuring of knowledge towards greater acceptance of crossing the borders between disciplines gained momentum in the late twentieth century, domains with an integrative human–environment focus have most notably been affected (Turner et al., 2015). This provides a direct link with sustainability learning, as sustainability issues cut across a wide array of disciplines, involving the humanities, social and physical sciences, which implies interdisciplinarity, amongst other things (Yarime et al., 2012). It needs to be stated, however, that interdisciplinarity builds on the existence of disciplines (Rasmussen and Arler, 2010) and should not be regarded as the so-called 'death' of disciplines. For example, Jetzkowitz (2019) regards disciplines as representative of the state of scientific knowledge and methodological standards. More opportunities are required to explore the interface between disciplines to provide a space for sustainability learning. For this, a strong multidisciplinary foundation is required, implying a solid grounding in multiple disciplines. In this regard, Youngblood (2007) explains that interdisciplinarity can be thought of as a 'new form of problem-oriented critical thinking focusing on *process* rather than *domain*' (p. 2; original emphasis).

1.3   Aim, Methodology and Value of this Chapter

This chapter provides a critical reflection on the value of interdisciplinary intellectual spaces as required for sustainability learning versus the inherent contestation associated with these spaces. Since the challenges of interdisciplinarity (especially at undergraduate level) are easy to underestimate (Öberg, 2009), successful navigation of this space requires careful planning, implementation and assessment. These and related challenges are unpacked in this chapter with reference to geography's interdisciplinary linkages, which is based on the PhD research of the author (Pretorius, 2017), and which considered undergraduate geography at South African universities in relation to sustainability learning. The theoretical framework selected for this research is 'integral theory', which aligns well with the move towards interdisciplinarity and the interrelated nature of realities that humankind must deal with in the twenty-first century (Laszlo, 2008). As a discipline that bridges the humanities, social and physical sciences, geography has much experience in terms of the challenges associated with the interdisciplinary intellectual space. In conclusion, this experience is shared, which will be of value for not only other disciplines but for the facilitation of sustainability learning as well.

2.   THE NECESSITY OF INTERDISCIPLINARY APPROACHES FOR SUSTAINABILITY LEARNING

2.1   Realities Associated with Disciplinary Academic Structures

The ever-increasing focus on specialization during especially the past 100 years or so resulted in the division of academia into literally hundreds of individual disciplines/ fields of study, mostly functioning in an isolated, self-interested fashion (Bursztyn and Drummond, 2014). This structure gradually became entrenched, associated with an increasing number of specialized journals and establishment of corresponding institutional structures for accreditation, evaluation and funding. It has been observed, however, that it is exactly those processes that created disciplinary departments that amplify the disconnectedness between disciplines and real-world sustainability challenges (Lubchenco, 1998). The irony about this is that although the literature points towards agreement that disciplinary approaches are not effective to address complex sustainability issues, they also agree that interdisciplinary approaches need disciplines as counterpoint (Rasmussen and Arler, 2010; Turner et al., 2015). The strategy suggested is to deal with this tension as a necessary part of the process to advance interdisciplinary sustainability learning.

2.2   Structuring of Knowledge for Sustainability Learning

Appropriate structuring of knowledge is crucial for students to develop a complete understanding of sustainability issues, including their complexity and interconnectedness (Komiyama and Takeuchi, 2004). Course work from selected disciplines/fields of study should therefore first expose students to the required knowledge, concepts and methodologies to understand what sustainability entails. Second, courses that provide a holistic perspective and cover the linkages between the issues at stake should also be included (Yarime et al., 2012). This presupposes a comprehensive knowledge platform not only to facilitate review of the spectrum of sustainability issues, but also to systematically organize (disparate) disciplines/fields of study, thus supporting development of comprehensive solutions. To achieve this, alignment with an interdisciplinary and/or fully integrated curriculum model (Table 26.1) is required, towards which the humanities, physical and social sciences can contribute (Michelcic et al., 2003). Within this space, individual disciplines/fields of study can provide inputs consisting of sustainability criteria and indicators, while integration of these constitutes an important step towards learning to solve problems in the field of sustainability (Komiyama and Takeuchi, 2004).

Table 26.1 Positioning of interdisciplinarity within the spectrum of curriculum models

	Spectrum of Curriculum Models			
	Model based on traditional, subject-centered approach	Model based on exploration of connections between content areas	Model based on interdisciplinarity	Model based on full integration
Approach to content	Content taught as separate subjects with limited or no integration and connection	Focus still on subjects but with more emphasis on connections between subjects and on real life	Breaking down of rigid boundaries between subjects	All specifics associated with identifiable subjects disappear
Role of teacher	Teachers mostly convey and explain subject basics	Deliberate identification and reinforcement of common areas between subjects	Deliberate efforts to blend skills and concepts from different subjects to develop understanding of specific problems or themes	Teachers become facilitators of the learning process
Role of student	Students are receivers of what is taught	Students are more actively involved in doing	Scope for students to be more creative and contribute to decision making	Students are able to choose the topics they want to study with the assistance of their teachers
Impact/ effect	Provides knowledge on a specific subject	Facilitates application of knowledge in subject area	Builds problem-solving capacity	Leads to development of initiative and creative problem-solving capacity

Source: Based on and adapted from Kysilka (1998, p. 204, Fig. 1) and Annan-Diab and Molinari (2017, p. 76, Fig. 3).

2.3   Examples of Interdisciplinary Settings for Sustainability Learning in Higher Education

The recent increased prominence of interdisciplinary constructs in the human–environment domain has already been alluded to. Examples include human ecology (Bennett, 2017), environmental studies/science (Schackleton et al., 2011), earth system science (Lenton, 2016), sustainability science (Yarime et al., 2012) and environmental management (Bharagava, 2018). A commonality shared by these constructs lies in their aim to add to the understanding of the challenges associated with sustainability and environmental change. Despite their presence in the interdisciplinary space, their rooted-ness in their originating disciplines is still obvious. Although all of them have at some time been advanced by their followers as potential new disciplines, none of them have obtained this status yet (Rasmussen and Arler, 2010). The situation differs for geography and anthropology, both established disciplines, but known for their interdisciplinary character as each of them covers the humanities, physical and social sciences, with a focus on interrelationships between knowledge domains (Youngblood, 2007). The rest of this chapter considers one of these – namely, geography.

3.   THE CONTEXT OF GEOGRAPHY'S INTERDISCIPLINARY LINKAGES

3.1   The Interdisciplinary Nature of Geography Versus Geography's Own Intradisciplinarity

Although the quest for interdisciplinarity not only involves geography, the human–environment identity of this discipline (Skole, 2004, p. 742) resonates with the need to link natural and human systems. The literature of the past ten to 15 years provides several examples of geographers who support the interdisciplinary nature of geography and its perceived ability to integrate the humanities, physical and social sciences (Baerwald, 2010; Hedberg et al., 2017). However, while the call for interdisciplinarity implies the need for integration across the breadth of geography, geographers find it challenging to cross the methodological and epistemological divide between physical and human geography (Castree, 2015; Ziegler et al., 2013). The discipline therefore needs to develop an understanding of its own 'intradisciplinarity' to be able to make a contribution in the interdisciplinary space (Evans and Randalls, 2008). Recent trends in undergraduate geography curricula are in sync with calls on the discipline to move towards an integrative human–environment narrative. This can be seen as a turn in geography to holistic synthesis (Sui and DeLyser, 2012), wherein 'hybrid geographies' are well positioned to formalize the sought-after integration.

3.2   Positioning Geography within Interdisciplinary Collaborations and Shifting Institutional Realities

With reference to the range of topics covered, approaches and methods (Baerwald, 2010), the unbounded nature of geography provides geographers with ample opportunity for interdisciplinary efforts (Lave et al., 2014). The preparation of students at undergraduate level to participate in interdisciplinary work at later stages is not that easy and involves choices between the extent of coverage versus the depth to be achieved (Hedberg et al., 2017). Despite trends towards interdisciplinarity, contributions in the scholarly literature on how geography might respond in terms of supportive teaching and learning approaches, are to a large extent still lacking (ibid.). Suggestions include provision of room for interdisciplinary dialogue, a wider variety of course work and specifically courses in which aspects of human and physical geography are combined (Lave et al., 2014). A downside of the move towards interdisciplinarity is that geography increasingly seems to be losing its administrative autonomy (Gibson, 2007) and is being absorbed into multidisciplinary units (Holmes, 2002). Together with the questioning of the internal consistency of geography as a discipline and where exactly it fits in, geography may therefore become a victim of restructuring projects, which is what happened with some geography departments in Australia (ibid.) and in the United Kingdom (Chan, 2011).

3.3 Implications of Interdisciplinarity for Sustainability Learning in Geography

To increase the value of geography for sustainability learning, students need to be prepared for possible roles in interdisciplinary work. This is countered, however, by the reality of many geographers who tend to specialize in human or physical geography or further sub-specializations of geography, thus leading to the observation that undergraduate geography curricula seem to comprise a number of fragmented or weakly interacting parts, while a binding overall narrative is lacking (Castree, 2012). The growing need for geographers to participate in interdisciplinary contexts provides a golden opportunity for geography to align itself with a fully integrative narrative (Pretorius, 2019), instead of getting stuck in divisions and turf wars between sub-specializations (Skole, 2004). Inclusion of aspects of environmental science, environmental management and geographical information systems (GIS) as part of the academic offering by geography departments aligns with the move towards interdisciplinarity (Holmes, 2002). Although adding a vocational flavor to geography, the trade-off is that curricula may be viewed as demand led, thus resulting in debates on the balance between disciplinary orientation and vocational skills (Gibson, 2007).

4. GEOGRAPHY'S INTERDISCIPLINARITY AND SUSTAINABILITY LEARNING: THE CASE OF UNDERGRADUATE GEOGRAPHY IN SOUTH AFRICA

4.1 Contextual Setting

Assessment of the undergraduate curricula of 19 geography departments in South Africa (2014–15) with reference to divisions and approaches in geography (Pretorius, 2017) showcases the diverse nature of the curriculum being offered. Newer extensions of the geography curriculum to include environmental science, environmental management and GIS have become a feature of undergraduate geography at many South African universities. A newcomer is integrated/thematic geography, which is slowly but surely gaining a foothold. According to Pretorius (2017), sustainability does not feature prominently in the curricula of many geography departments in South Africa, although significant variations between departments exist. The rest of this section provides an assessment of linkages between interdisciplinarity and sustainability learning in the context of undergraduate South African geography.

4.2   Assessment Methodology

The assessment of linkages between interdisciplinarity and sustainability learning in geography as reported in this section follows the same protocol as used by Pretorius (2019) for assessment of linkages between the human–environment identity of geography and sustainability learning. Starting with exterior, third-person perspectives, the assumption was that assessment of the contribution of module content related to environmental science/management, GIS, cartography, remote sensing, meteorology and tourism would provide an indication of the move towards interdisciplinarity in geography. This included an assessment of linkages with sustainability learning.

For this purpose, the sustainability criteria as provided by the Sustainability Tracking, Assessment & Rating System (STARS) (AASHE, 2012) were used. The STARS curriculum section (Category 1, Education and Research – ER) makes a distinction between courses focused on sustainability and courses that relate to sustainability. Both these categories were used for this assessment. Data obtained from eight interviews with geography lecturers at South African universities were used for interior first-person perspectives. In addition, focus groups at four South African geography departments supplied data to obtain interior, second-person perspectives from (Pretorius, 2017). These three methodologies are associated with the All Quadrants (AQ) model of integral theory, with the following quadrants that have been selected (refer to Figure 26.1):

- lower right quadrant (objective observations; third-person perspectives);
- upper left quadrant (subjective observations; first-person perspectives);
- lower left quadrant (inter-subjective observations; second-person perspectives).

Esbjörn-Hargens (2006) explains that a coherent picture of the problem being researched can be obtained through triangulation and cross-correlation of the data collected through the various selected methodologies, while making observations from the inside and/or outside of the collective interior/exterior and/or individual interior/exterior. These observations are then considered and reflected on during the phase of data analysis. Using the AQ model this can be achieved by using first-, second- and third-person methodologies (one from each of the major groups – as indicated in Figure 26.1), which applies to the research reported on in this chapter.

4.3   Exterior, Third-person Perspectives

The results of the assessment of the combined contribution of environmental science/ management (Category E), GIS, cartography and remote sensing (Category G) and meteorology and tourism (Category O) to undergraduate geography in South Africa are depicted in Figure 26.2 and are based on the research by Pretorius (2017). Analysis of the stacked column presentation in this figure provides clear evidence of the substantial contribution of Categories E, G and O to undergraduate South African geography. This

Upper left (UL)			Upper Right (UR)
Methodology used: Individual interviews Interior view Individual; 'What I think or experience' Intentional Subjective, inward view of 'self' First-person perspective			*Methodology not used* Exterior view Individual; 'What she/he or it does' Behavioral Individual objectively viewed Third-person perspective
	I	**It**	
	We	**Its**	
Second-person perspective Inter-subjective dynamics Culture and world view of group Collective; 'What we think or should do' Interior view *Methodology used:* Focus groups			Third-person perspective Inter-objective dynamics Social and environmental systems Collective; 'What they do' Exterior view *Methodology used:* Curriculum assessment
Lower left (LL)			Lower Right (LR)

Source: Pretorius (2017); based on and adapted from Esbjörn-Hargens (2009, pp. 3–4, Figures 1 and 2).

Figure 26.1   Basics of the AQ model – the four quadrants of integral theory

contribution exceeded the 50 per cent level for seven departments and even exceeded the 70 per cent level for the University of Pretoria. The bulk of this contribution could be allocated to Categories E and G and was distributed more or less in equal proportions across these two categories. Category E varied from 5 per cent or less (e.g., at Rhodes University and North-West University – Mafikeng Campus) to almost 50 per cent (University of Zululand). Category G, on the other hand, varied from 5 per cent or less (e.g., Rhodes University, University of Zululand and University of Cape Town) to as high as 41 per cent (Nelson Mandela University). Based on this assessment it can be concluded that the move towards interdisciplinarity has a definite visibility and impact in undergraduate South African geography.

In terms of sustainability learning, the assessment by Pretorius (2017) showed a higher combined relative sustainability contribution for Categories E, G and O, compared to the full curriculum for 13 of the 19 departments (although the difference is not significant in some cases). This indicated the concentration, to some extent, of the sustainability contribution in modules associated with these three categories. The opposite applied to specifically the University of Venda, University of South Africa, North-West University (Mafikeng Campus), University of KwaZulu-Natal, Walter Sisulu University and Rhodes University. For these departments, the sustainability contribution occurred in significant proportions in various parts of the curriculum and was not necessarily concentrated in only Categories E, G and O.

Pretorius (2017) furthermore indicated that modules linked to Category E generally showed a relatively higher sustainability contribution, while modules associated with Category O (especially tourism) also seemed to perform quite well in this regard. However,

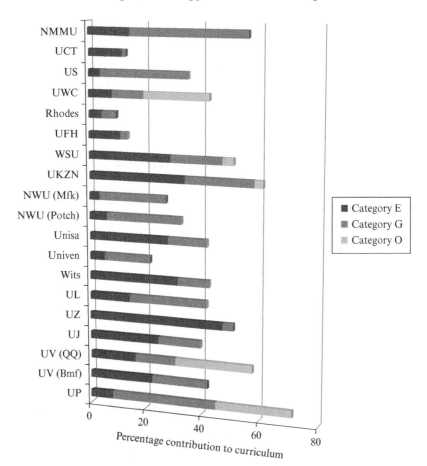

Note: Universities: UP – University of Pretoria; UV (Bmf/QQ) – University of the Free State (Bloemfontein/ QuaQua); UJ – University of Johannesburg; UZ – University of Zululand; UL – University of Limpopo; Wits – University of the Witwatersrand; Univen – University of Venda; Unisa – University of South Africa; NWU (Potch/Mfk) – North-West University (Potchefstroom/Mafikeng); UKZN – University of KwaZulu-Natal; WSU – Walter Sisulu University; UFH – University of Fort Hare; Rhodes – Rhodes University; UWC – University of the Western Cape; US – University of Stellenbosch; UCT – University of Cape Town; NMMU – Nelson Mandela Metropolitan University, subsequently renamed Nelson Mandela University.

Source: Pretorius (2017).

Figure 26.2   Stacked column presentation of the contribution of environmental science/ management (Category E), GIS, cartography and remote sensing (Category G) and meteorology and tourism (Category O) to undergraduate geography in South Africa, 2014–15

the sustainability contribution was hugely under-represented in modules associated with Category G, although exceptions can be mentioned – for example, University of Cape Town and University of Fort Hare. Noteworthy was that for the majority of departments, 50 per cent or more of the sustainability contribution for the modules linked to Categories

E, G and O was clustered at the advanced undergraduate level. This is a positive trend, indicating achievement of greater depth while engaging with the full complexity of sustainability, thus increasing the usefulness for sustainability learning.

4.4   Interior, First-person Perspectives

Based on the eight interviews conducted during 2016–17, an idea could be formed of the perspectives of South African geographers about interdisciplinarity and sustainability learning in the context of geography (Pretorius, 2017). This aligns with the upper left quadrant of the AQ model with the purpose of getting a view from the inside of individual, subjective perspectives.

The first topic dealt with in the interviews related to the issue of obtaining a balance in the curriculum between the integrity of the discipline and other needs and requirements, with reference to twenty-first-century sustainability challenges (Box 26.1 – Topic 1). The geographers who were interviewed clearly had definite ideas about the issue at hand, while revealing diverging opinions at the same time. Two of the interviewees (A4 and C2) referred to the challenges involved with geography's own intradisciplinarity, alluding to challenges experienced by the discipline to maintain a balance in terms of its varied composition. This, according to them, is impacting negatively on the discipline. Two interviewees (C1 and D1) referred to the issue of vocationalism, with the result that departments are obliged to offer modules required by industry, but which might not be aligned with the requirements of the discipline (they mentioned the example of GIS). Such involvement might not necessarily have negative implications for geography, with a balance indeed still possible, but this depends on how the process is managed (referred to by Interviewee D1 for environmental science/management).

The second topic dealt with in the interviews was about the realities of the inclusion of environmental and/or sustainability issues in undergraduate geography within an interdisciplinary context (Box 26.1 – Topic 2). The aim with this was to determine to what extent this presented an opportunity versus a threat to geography, as experienced in the selected departments. A trend that can be observed in the responses is that geographers appear to be concerned about the prospects and outcomes of interdisciplinary linkages. A concern referred to by Interviewee A4, was that the curriculum might begin to lean towards environmental science, which might be to the detriment of geography. Interviewee A5 was less negative but held the viewpoint that adjustments and/or reworking of the curriculum might be required. This implies a give-and-take situation that might not always have positive outcomes for geography. Interviewee E1 experienced this development as a threat to geography and its practitioners (although mentioning opportunities as well), while some positive feedback came from Interviewee D1, who mentioned that graduates with geography and environmental management as subjects should be well prepared for the job market.

4.5   Interior, Second-person Perspectives

To provide more depth and to expand on the inside views obtained through the interviews, focus groups were conducted at four targeted departments of geography in South Africa. This aligns with the lower left quadrant of the AQ model, with the purpose to obtain an

BOX 26.1   FIRST-PERSON PERSPECTIVES: GEOGRAPHY'S INTERDISCIPLINARY LINKAGES AND SUSTAINABILITY LEANING (PRETORIUS, 2017)

Topic 1: Striking a balance in the curriculum between the discipline's integrity and other needs and requirements

A4: '. . . there are aspects of Geography which are pure Physical Science and others which are Human Social Science . . . those divisions would always be there, but that's what makes Geography . . . A variety of aspects and the contestations between these various aspects, which is not a bad thing, provided . . . we keep all the aspects going in this attempt to strike a balance. If we move into a situation where some aspects are dying, then there is a problem.'

C1: '. . . the requirement to produce people for vocational kinds of training . . . can be done in ways which are unfortunate . . . which means that we direct a lot of the curriculum towards those things, you know. For example in GIS we've been with GIS people who've been pushing very strongly to get a certain kind of Plato accreditation and . . . they have to (do) that undergraduate here.'

C2: 'These are very important things. How do we ensure that the curriculum is balanced? Well, we have to actually go into a very deep and dark discussion of the value of Physical Sciences in Geography and the way in which it's valued . . . Physical Geography is not prepared to have that conversation. They are very arrogant and they are not prepared to engage with a conversation and I think they'll be the end of Geography.'

D1: '. . . but we are moving now towards Geography and Environmental Management . . . we believe that the two can co-exist. We can do good in Environmental Science as well as in Geography . . . We view Environmental Management as industry focused. We view it as a professional degree and as vocational source. Students have got to leave here with a set of skills, practical skills that they can do to do Environmental Management.'

Topic 2: Realities of addressing environmental/sustainability issues in the curriculum within an interdisciplinary context

A4: '. . . at one stage it was even thought in the department that we were leaning too much towards Environmental Science, towards . . . sustainability issues at the expense of purely Geographical issues and the argument . . . was that Environmental Science doesn't have a concrete theory the way Geography does and that if we lean too much towards that, we will begin to lose academic theorization which is essential for our departments because we are at an academic institution.'

E1: 'We develop the subject and then these other focus areas sort of come in . . . and become important actually. I think in South Africa that is happening. I think it's a threat to the established practitioners . . . but at the same time the introduction of all that is providing the opportunities. So . . . it's how we deal with it actually. My sense, in South Africa, is that there's an increasing threat to Geography as such. Whether this is happening elsewhere, I'm not sure sure.'

D1: '. . . there are also students who have done Geography and Environmental Management and I find those seem to be our strong studies when they go to Masters and PhD . . . I mean, Environmental Management teamed along with Geography makes a very good professional.'

A5: 'If I or somebody decide . . . I'm covering what you're covering is essentially the same thing, now the first question is . . . who should give it up? . . . Should they keep them and I should adjust mine? Whoever loses will have to fill it up with something else which means they will have to redesign their curriculum slightly and people I found aren't really into that.'

inside view of the collective interior by studying the various inter-subjectivities flowing from discussions. For the sake of comparison, the themes that were used were the same as for the individual interviews. Box 26.2 presents a snapshot of crucial aspects flowing from the focus group discussions.

Concerning the first topic – namely, the issue of maintaining a balance in the curriculum between the integrity of the discipline and other needs and requirements (Box 26.2 – Topic 1) – a number of rather skeptical comments were voiced during discussions with Group F. An example is Participant F1, who commented that the approach required when dealing with interdisciplinary themes triggers superficiality. This may be to the extent that themes are dealt with in such a general way that it becomes a meaningless exercise. Group B also exhibited skepticism but took a different angle: an example is Participant B3, who commented that delivering environmental managers seems to have become the ultimate goal in their department, but which is at the expense of opportunities for the other sub-disciplines of geography.

Concerning the second topic – namely, the realities associated with addressing environmental and/or sustainability issues in the geography curriculum in an interdisciplinary context (Box 26.2 – Topic 2), Group F continued to reveal skepticism. During the discussion participants took the opportunity to expand more on the perceived superficiality associated with interdisciplinary programs. An example is provided by the quote for Participant F1, who referred to sufficient scope in the 'horizontal' sense (i.e., in terms of coverage), but a lack of 'verticality' (i.e., in terms of depth). Participants in Group F also referred to the trend that departments associated with such collaborations often change their names – this might be to do with marketing of the resulting bigger units more effectively. Participant F2 viewed this as a 'survival strategy', while Participant F1 viewed it specifically from the marketing perspective. The views expressed by Group B were less skeptical. An example is Participant B3, who commented on the flexibility of geography to connect with a number of fields and disciplines. Accordingly, this is what makes geography attractive and provides geographers with an 'edge'.

5.   ANALYSIS OF RESULTS AND DISCUSSION OF KEY ISSUES

5.1   Geography's Interdisciplinarity as a Space for Sustainability Learning

Due to the complexity associated with issues in the sustainability domain, sustainability learning requires a holistic approach to acquaint students with how to go about with the integration of knowledge, skills and insights across boundaries of disciplines (Yarime et al., 2012). Geography is perceived to fit this requirement well, linked to its inherent interdisciplinary nature (Skole, 2004) and characteristics of a discipline that provides a bridge between the humanities, physical and social sciences (Youngblood, 2007). Due these qualities, for example, geography is suitable to fulfill the role of a core discipline in undergraduate interdisciplinary sustainability-related study programs, by providing structure to the learning experience (Pretorius and Fairhurst, 2015). The exploration of undergraduate curricula offered by South African departments of geography by Pretorius (2017) revealed a clear footprint of the move towards interdisciplinarity. This is specifically for modules linked to Category E, although also notable for Category O,

BOX 26.2   SECOND-PERSON PERSPECTIVES: GEOGRAPHY'S
INTERDISCIPLINARY LINKAGES AND SUSTAINABILITY
LEANING (PRETORIUS, 2017)

Topic 1: Striking a balance in the curriculum between the discipline's integrity and other needs and requirements

F1*: '... the more you integrate these things at undergraduate level, the more superficial you are making it. We see the value of it if you bring the different specialists together at a later stage, the one knows exactly how cities work, the other about climate, etc. and then you have the IT (read: GIS?) guy that assists in putting all these things together. To say that we now need to do all these things with our Geography students, expecting them to understand all this complexity, implies they will eventually know something about very little.'

B3*: 'I have questions about Environmental Management as an end-of-pipe aim in our department. This is in terms of our honors in which it still features prominently, serving as a building block for ... although we have moved away from it a bit ... I think we can still do more in our department to acknowledge other sub-disciplines in Geography and not only Environmental Management.'

J9*: 'I think Environmental Management did Geography a lot of good in terms of student numbers ... but what about the teachers, since now there are a lot of things there that are not mean for them ...'

H3: 'Yes, we have constantly debates about ... you know we're losing the classic part of Geography ...'

H3: 'The problem is that one starts to get people who have emphasis which is so far removed from traditional Geography that it can become a problem.'

Topic 2: Realities of addressing environmental/sustainability issues in the curriculum within an interdisciplinary context

F2*: 'This is the reason why many departments changed their names, to be able to claim EIA, Environmental Management ... It was a survival strategy.'

F1*: 'Actually a marketing strategy and the reason why we kept the name of our department as Geography ... the guys here are beyond it.'

F1*: 'Management is a science in its own right, so you actually need specialists in this regard ... but this is where the superficiality slips in ... with these interdisciplinary programs the students learn so much that eventually they know a little bit about many things, almost as a horizontal big picture.'

B3*: 'This is exactly what makes Geography such a fantastic field ... because you are involved with so many other (fields) ... and I think that is what gives geographers their edge, because you have that broader perspective on everything in society.'

J9*: 'The challenge with sustainability learning is to bring sustainability into all your modules without losing any of the knowledge in your own subject ... some of the subject knowledge that you wanted to convey as a geographer ...'

H3: '... that geographers will say, but we're already doing sustainability ...'

Note: * Translated from Afrikaans.

while not well presented very well in Category G. The research by Pretorius (2017) furthermore exposed that modules linked to Category E showed the highest sustainability contribution, followed by Categories O and G. This matches the feedback obtained with the interviews and focus groups that formed part of this research and dealt specifically with the virtues of the interdisciplinarity of the discipline and its perceived ability to work towards integration between the humanities and the sciences. However, given the methodological and epistemological divide between human and physical geography, the referred to integration is not that easy to achieve, but is a matter that needs to be addressed.

5.2 Geography's Interdisciplinarity as Space for Vocationally Oriented Sustainability Learning

In terms of the qualities of geography as an interdisciplinary as well as a bridging discipline, the links of geography with vocationally oriented fields of study such as environmental science/management, GIS and tourism provide several opportunities for sustainability learning. The disadvantage of this, as was frequently highlighted during the interviews and focus groups for this research, is a potential deterioration of the identity of undergraduate geography (i.e., Australia – Holmes, 2002), or the substitution of geography with environmental science/management (i.e., USA – Rasmussen and Arler, 2010). In addition, some scholars regard the focus on skills training and workplace requirements as potentially detrimental to the discipline (Fairhurst et al., 2003). However, a number of scholars (e.g., Arrowsmith et al., 2011; Whalley et al., 2011) hold the opinion that curricula can be designed in such a way that geography as a discipline is not impoverished, while it is possible to enhance employment opportunities for students at the same time. From this perspective, sustainability learning can fulfil a complementary role, due the strong linkages between the human–environment identity of geography and sustainability conceptualizations and constructs (Grindsted, 2013). The value of sustainability learning is that it is not focused on skills transfer per se, but on the integration of skills and knowledge linked to specific disciplines, in order to empower students to take an active part in the transformation to sustainability (Mochizuki and Fadeeva, 2010, p. 392).

5.3 Geography's Interdisciplinarity as Contested Space Versus Potential for Sustainability Learning

Different pathways towards interdisciplinarity are indeed possible and actively pursued by many scholars (Bursztyn and Drummond, 2014). However, contestation is unavoidable due to the deadlock resulting from the need for specialization, while simultaneously pressured to address complex issues that require more than can be offered by only specialization. This links with the debate on disciplinarity versus interdisciplinarity and the need for informed responses to complex, urgent sustainability issues (Oksen, Magid and de Neergaard, 2009). This can be illustrated with the example of the characteristics and functioning of the Earth's biogeochemical cycles, which may be adequately described from a disciplinary perspective but falls short in addressing aspects related to the role of human society (Bacon et al., 2011). It is therefore clear why interdisciplinarity is important for sustainability learning (Mochizuki and Fadeeva, 2010). Of concern is that although geography brings an integrative perspective to the interdisciplinary space, not all geographers necessarily appreciated this – an aspect that was highlighted during some of the interviews and focus groups for the research by Pretorius (2017). Simon and Graybill (2010) mention the example of the collaborators in an interdisciplinary project they investigated, who perceived geography as lacking a clear definition and being too general to produce solid scientific contributions. Similar objections may apply to sustainability learning due to its reliance on the contested concept of sustainability and also stigmatization due to generalization and lack of a clear definition (Missimer, Robèrt and Broman, 2017, pp. 32–3).

5.4 Integral View of the Move Towards Interdisciplinarity and Sustainability Learning in Undergraduate Geography

The stand-off in geography to deal with its own 'intradisciplinarity' versus participating in the interdisciplinary space acquires a new meaning if considered in the context of integral theory. Embracing an approach through which reality is not explored in a compartmentalized way but from the perspective of the integral spheres of the self (subjectivity), culture (inter-subjectivity) and nature (objectivity), may pave the way towards a comprehensive, integrative narrative for geography. This points the way for geography not to deal with twenty-first century sustainability issues through reductionism while either over-focusing on objectivity and/or over-valuing rationality, but rather through cooperation with related fields of study, but with clarity on its own position, role and potential contribution. As showed by Pretorius (2017), the variety of modules linked to Categories E, G and O (offered by South African departments of geography), together with their varied sustainability contributions, presents several challenges for the development of an integrative narrative for geography. This is because these modules are not tied to a specific identity of geography, but rather illustrate how geography can fit in with trends towards interdisciplinarity. In the context of teaching and learning, inclusion of these related study fields in geography are associated with challenges as merging interdisciplinarity and disciplinarity, balancing specialization and holism and countering claims and perceptions of generalization.

6.   CONCLUDING REMARKS

6.1   Lessons Learnt from Geography's Interdisciplinary Linkages with Sustainability

The skeptical perceptions of South African geographers towards further development of the interdisciplinary linkages between geography and sustainability have been highlighted in this chapter. This fits in with the picture that many scholars and most likely the majority of geographers have of the discipline of geography – namely as divided into a number of sub-disciplines, with sustainability as yet another addition. This, however, constitutes an important misconception that needs to be addressed, since interdisciplinarity refers to a process rather than a domain (Youngblood, 2007). What can be learnt from the experience with geography therefore alludes to the importance of not viewing sustainability as yet another domain (i.e., academic turf) that gradually develops its own territory and then aims towards increasing its dominance. The focus should rather be on the process (i.e., methodology) of developing solutions to problems and answers to important questions. This type of approach acknowledges the participation, existence and value of different disciplines (and sub-disciplines, as in geography) in the interdisciplinary space and avoids claiming and defending of academic turf.

6.2   Implications for Other Disciplines Involved with Sustainability Learning

Despite the need for collaboration and participation in the interdisciplinary space for sustainability learning to take place, the results presented in this chapter (Table 26.2) support the observations by Cook (2010) that such initiatives seem to have the best chance of success when practitioners are not in denial about their disciplinary backgrounds, but fully embrace them. Several tensions perceived by geographers about interdisciplinary linkages between geography and sustainability learning have been highlighted in this chapter, mostly referring to the difference between blending of multiple knowledge-generating processes into one perspective, versus acceptance of pluralistic knowledge processes and existence of multiple realities and perspectives (Turner et al., 2015).

These tensions are not unique to geographers but apply to all practitioners working in the interdisciplinary space. Tensions such as these cannot be prevented, but are an essential part of working, learning and researching in the interdisciplinary space. This space therefore facilitates opportunities for conversation, based on the disciplinary backgrounds of participants, but is not bounded by them.

Table 26.2   Mapping of key elements of interdisciplinarity as context for sustainability learning

Interdisciplinarity as Context for Sustainability Learning			
Complexity of issues Holistic approach required – students to be exposed to integration of knowledge, skills and insights across disciplinary boundaries	*Reasons for deadlock* Simultaneously requiring specialization while pressured to address complex issues requiring more than can be offered by only specialization	*Unavoidable tensions* Attempts to blend multiple knowledge-generating processes into one perspective, versus acceptance of existence of multiple perspectives	*Challenges* Perceptions of deterioration of the identity of undergraduate disciplines and generalization of issues
What to do Focus on the process (i.e., methodology) of developing solutions to problems and answers to questions	*What not to do* Viewing sustainability as yet another domain ('academic turf') that needs to be defended and expanded	*Implications* Interdisciplinary spaces facilitate opportunities for conversation based on the disciplinary backgrounds of participants but is not bounded by them	*Integral solutions* Exploration of reality from the perspective of the integral realms of subjectivity (the self), inter-subjectivity (culture) and objectivity (nature)

6.3 Limitations of this Research and Possible Further Research

As for all research, some limitations also apply to the research results as reported in this chapter. To be considered in this regard is the fact that the curriculum assessment, interviews and focus groups were conducted over a certain time period, and do not reflect the dynamics involved in the continuously changing academic environment. This work should therefore be supplemented by follow-up research on the same or on a related topic, which will be able to capture subsequent changes and developments, and which will facilitate comparisons over time. The mostly qualitative-based methodologies that were used in this research are associated with certain limitations as well, although these could largely be countered through the integral research design, which provides expression of the multidimensional nature of reality. This added the necessary rigor to the research since it allowed triangulation and cross-correlation between the methodologies and various perspectives that were used to investigate relationships between the move towards interdisciplinarity and the inclusion of sustainability in South African undergraduate geography.

REFERENCES

Annan-Diab, F. and Molinari, C. (2017). Interdisciplinarity: practical approach to advancing education for sustainability and for the Sustainable Development Goals. *The International Journal of Management Education*, 15(2), 73–83.

Arrowsmith, C., Bagoly-Simó, P. and Finchum, A. et al. (2011). Student employability and its implications for geography curricula and learning practices. *Journal of Geography in Higher Education*, 35(3), 365–77.

Association for the Advancement of Sustainability in Higher Education (AASHE). (2012). *STARS Version 1.2 Technical Manual*.

Bacon, C.M., Mulvaney, D. and Ball et al. (2011). The creation of an integrated sustainability curriculum and student praxis projects. *International Journal of Sustainability in Higher Education*, 12(2), 193–208.

Baerwald, T.J. (2010). Prospects for geography as an interdisciplinary discipline. *Annals of the Association of American Geographers*, 100(3), 493–501.

Bennett, J.W. (2017). *Human Ecology as Human Behavior: Essays in Environmental and Developmental Anthropology*. New York: Routledge.

Bharagava, R.N. (2019). *Recent Advances in Environmental Management*. Boca Raton, FL: CRC Press.

Bursztyn, M. and Drummond, J. (2014). Sustainability science and the university: pitfalls and bridges to interdisciplinarity. *Environmental Education Research*, 20(3), 313–32.

Castree, N. (2012). Progressing physical geography. *Progress in Physical Geography*, 36(3), 298–304.

Castree, N. (2015). Geography and global change science: relationships necessary, absent, and possible. *Geographical Research*, 53(1), 1–15.

Chan, W.F. (2011). Mourning geography: a punctum, Strathclyde and the death of a subject. *Scottish Geographical Journal*, 127(4), 255–66.

Cook, D.T. (2010). The promise of an unanswered question: multi-/cross-disciplinary struggles. *Children's Geographies*, 8(2), 221–2.

Esbjörn-Hargens, S. (2006). Integral research: a multi-method approach to investigating phenomena. *Constructivism in the Human Sciences*, 11(1/2), 88–116.

Esbjörn-Hargens, S. (2009). An overview of integral theory: an all-inclusive framework for the 21st century. *Integral Institute Resource Papers*, 1(1), 1–24.

Evans, J. and Randalls, S. (2008). Geography and paratactical interdisciplinarity: views from the ESRC-NERC-PhD studentship programme. *Geoforum*, 39(2), 581–92.

Fairhurst, U.J., Davies, R.J. and Fox, R.C. et al. (2003). Geography: the state of the discipline in South Africa: 2000–2001. *South African Geographical Journal*, 85(2), 81–9.

Gibson, C. (2007). Geography in higher education in Australia. *Journal of Geography in Higher Education*, 31(1), 97–119.

Grindsted, T.S. (2013). From the human–environment theme towards sustainability – Danish geography and education for sustainable development. *European Journal of Geography*, 4(3), 6–20.

Hedberg, R.C., Hesse, A. and Baldwin, D. et al. (2017). Preparing geographers for interdisciplinary research: graduate training at the interface of the natural and social sciences. *The Professional Geographer*, 69(1), 107–16.

Holmes, J.M. (2002). Geography's emerging cross-disciplinary links: process, causes, outcomes and challenges. *Australian Geographical Studies*, 40(1), 2–20.

Jetzkowitz, J. (2019). Interdisciplinarity from a social science perspective. Keynote lecture presented at the GESIS-Institutstag, 4 July 2019. Accessed 30 December 2019 at https://www.ssoar.info/ssoar/handle/document/63626.

Komiyama, H. and Takeuchi, K. (2006). Sustainability science: building a new discipline. *Sustainability Science*, 1(1), 1–6.

Kysilka, M.L. (1998). Understanding integrated curriculum. *The Curriculum Journal*, 9(2), 197–209.

Laszlo, E. (2008). *Quantum Shift in the Global Brain: How the New Scientific Reality Can Change Us and Our World*. Rochester, VT: Inner Traditions.

Lave, R., Wilson, M.W. and Barron et al. (2014). Intervention: critical physical geography. *The Canadian Geographer/Le Géographe Canadien*, 58(1), 1–10.

Lenton, T. (2016). *Earth System Science: A Very Short Introduction*. Oxford: Oxford University Press.

Lubchenco, J. (1998). Entering the century of the environment: a new social contract for science. *Science*, 279(5350), 491–7.

Michelcic, J.R., Crittenden, J.C. and Small, M.J. et al. (2003). Sustainability science and engineering: the emergence of a new metadiscipline. *Environment, Science and Technology*, 37, 5314–24.

Missimer, M., Robèrt, K.H. and Broman, G. (2017). A strategic approach to social sustainability – part 1: exploring the social system. *Journal of Cleaner Production*, 140, 32–41.

Mochizuki, Y. and Fadeeva, Z. (2010). Competences for sustainable development and sustainability: significance and challenges for ESD. *International Journal of Sustainability in Higher Education*, 11(4), 391–403.

Öberg, G. (2009). Facilitating interdisciplinary work: using quality assessment to create common ground. *Higher Education*, 57(4), 405–15.

Oksen, P., Magid, J. and de Neergaard, A. (2009). Thinking outside the box: interdisciplinary integration of teaching and research on an environment and development study programme. *Interdisciplinary Science Reviews*, 34(4), 309–26.

Pretorius, R.W. (2017). Repositioning geography in education for sustainability: the South African higher education context. Unpublished PhD thesis, University of South Africa, Pretoria.

Pretorius, R. (2019). Towards an integrated disciplinary narrative and an enhanced role for geography in education for sustainability: reflections on South African higher education. In W. Leal Filho and A. Consorte-McCrea (eds), *Sustainability and the Humanities*. Cham, Switzerland: Springer.

Pretorius, R.W. and Fairhurst, U.J. (2015). The role of geography in multi-inter-trans-disciplinary study programmes for environmental sustainability. In W. Leal Filho (ed.). *Transformative Approaches to Sustainable Development at Universities*. Cham, Switzerland: Springer.

Rasmussen, K. and Arler, F. (2010). Interdisciplinarity at the human–environment interface. *Geografisk Tidsskrift – Danish Journal of Geography*, 110(1), 37–45.

Shackleton, C.M., Scholes, B.J. and Vogel, C. (2011). The next decade of environmental science in South Africa: a horizon scan. *South African Geographical Journal*, 93(1), 1–14.

Simon, G.L. and Graybill, J.K. (2010). Geography in interdisciplinarity: towards a third conversation. *Geoforum*, 41(3), 356–63.

Skole, L. (2004). Geography as a great intellectual melting pot and the preeminent interdisciplinary environmental discipline. *Annals of the Association of American Geographers*, 94(4), 739–73.

Sui, D. and DeLyser, D. (2012). Crossing the qualitative–quantitative chasm I: hybrid geographies, the spatial turn, and volunteered geographic information (VGI). *Progress in Human Geography*, 36(1), 111–24.

Turner, V.K., Benessaiah, K., Warren, S. and Iwaniec, D. (2015). Essential tensions in interdisciplinary scholarship: navigating challenges in affect, epistemologies, and structure in environment–society research centers. *Higher Education*, 70(4), 649–65.

Whalley, W.B., Saunders, A. and Lewis, R.A. et al. (2011). Curriculum development: producing geographers for the 21st century. *Journal of Geography in Higher Education*, 35(3), 379–93.

Woelert, P. and Millar, V. (2013). The 'paradox of interdisciplinarity' in Australian research governance. *Higher Education*, 66(6), 755–67.

Yarime, M., Trencher, G. and Mino, T. et al. (2012). Establishing sustainability science in higher education institutions: towards an integration of academic development, institutionalization, and stakeholder collaborations. *Sustainability Science*, 7(1), 101–13.

Youngblood, D. (2007). Multidisciplinarity, interdisciplinarity, and bridging disciplines: a matter of process. *Journal of Research Practice*, 3(2), Article M18.

Ziegler, A.D., Gillen, J. and Newell, B. (2013). Comprehensive research in geography. *Area*, 45(2), 252–4.

27. Stepping toward a sense of place: a choreography of natural and social science
Michael-Anne Noble, Hilary Leighton and Ann Dale

1. INTRODUCTION

Through the development of critical knowledges and practices related to ecosystem structure and function, biodiversity and sustainability, we address prevailing dualisms between humans–nature, and subject–object through a curriculum designed to invite students to step into experiential outdoor spaces with time enough to develop an affective connection to place and a greater conscious awareness of belonging. Live cases and design examples from Royal Roads University faculty illuminate how natural and social science, when choreographed together for learning, are each critical to establishing a primary motive of 'relatedness' as it pertains to an indissoluble unity between people and place. Moving from nature as mere backdrop to co-implicating themselves in a continual process *of being in place*, students look *into* rather than merely *at* the environment and as such deepen their identification to place which can suggest a willingness to protect what has become in essence, part of their own sense of identity.

Sense of place research suggests a bonding of people to places (Low and Altman, 1992) through place attachment as determined by a strong emotional reaction or connection to a place and can be understood as related to one's identity in terms of cognitive connectivity or dependence on that place (Cleary et al., 2017). Place attachment, an affective, cognitive bond between people and their environment (Low and Altman, 1992; Masterson et al., 2017) can include both positive and negative responses (Clayton, 2003) and has been applied to solving sustainability issues, the study of social-ecological research (Masterson et al., 2017), natural resource management, pro-environmental and other social behaviours including resilience and transformation (Manzo and Devine-Wright, 2014; Masterson et al., 2017). Scannell and Gifford (2010) suggest that sense of place requires a triadic framework between the *person* (individual and cultural), the *place* (social and biophysical) and the *psychological process* (affective, cognitive and behavioural). Both knowledge and experience of a place can be important in terms of developing 'place identity' where meaningful, and sometimes spiritual, interactions may occur between people, physical environments, and other species.

Environmental educator David Orr (2004) offers that rootedness in place is critical for 'biophilia' to take effect (see Kellert and Wilson's, *The Biophilia Hypothesis*, 1993) – the innate tendency or urge humans have to connect and affiliate with the more-than-human world, or in literal terms, to *love the world*. This deep emotional connection, this being-in-the-world phenomenology of Heidegger ([1927] 1962) and Merleau-Ponty (1962) suggests a kind of inhabiting or *indwelling* with the world beyond mere attachment to place, steps toward a deeper affection where the distinction of the objective 'it' *out there*, finds confluence with the subjective 'me' *in here* in a subject-to-subject communion between self and world. Artificial boundaries with 'Other' become meaningless. Such nature-responsive epistemology is rarely conveyed and yet from a psychological perspective may in fact have more to do with human maturation than socialization and culture do.

Norwegian philosopher and deep ecologist, Arne Naess (1989), wrote that 'in the conception of the maturity of the self, nature is largely left out' (p. 174). He noticed that the places we inhabit and grow up in as children, the immediate natural spaces we call home, are mostly ignored in terms of our development and learning. And while society and human relationships are important, Naess (1988) professed that we are from the beginning, *in* and *of* nature, and that therefore developing a sense of *ecological identity* through sense of place (home), with its 'rich, constitutive relations' (p. 20) with all other living beings, is critical. He understood that when a very deep identification takes place – when we 'see ourselves in others' (ibid.) within the living world, that one's sense of self is no longer delimited by one's personal ego, rather 'one experiences oneself to be a genuine part of all life' (Naess, 1989, p. 174). A moral consideration for all life and our place in it holds critical implications for whether we place ourselves as part of nature or apart from nature. It also suggests a willingness to protect the places we know (and love) from harm, especially if we see them as part of our own identity.

The modernist view, however, has tended to devalue the interior dimensions of reality in favor of the exterior and material systems, and placed an emphasis on an exteriorization of knowledge, thus reducing nature to an objective science. This is typified by language such as 'organisms' rather than 'living beings'. While this concept may be valuable in some domains of inquiry and research, depending on the nature of the questions, such a reductionist approach can fail to illuminate the entire picture and to accurately provide for the interiority of natural phenomena, including that of the human being.

Therefore, in view of our proclivities toward a more blurred edge between the inside/out, the rational and the imaginary in teaching and learning, we argue for spaces that allow textual and rich descriptive, qualitative approaches using natural and human science methods that entail '(re)discovery of the subjective nature and storied quality of science' (Sandelowski, 1994, p. 47). This is in contrast to the dominant privileged and pure science approach that does not see a universe with inherent awareness of feeling and life in all things. This also tends to preclude any profound sense of understanding of the planet as a whole, interconnected, and integral system and the intrinsic part we play within that system.

In the School of Environment and Sustainability at Royal Roads University (RRU), British Columbia (where the authors are faculty) all programs are cohort-based with a strong emphasis on systems thinking, experiential learning, teamwork, and collaboration. Using a narrative description of curriculum design intended to integrate place considerations, demonstrating the critical necessity for the integration of natural and social sciences, we describe the living lab, a forest walk-shop, and a Sense of Place workshop.

2.   THE LIVING LAB

RRU is situated on the 565 acres of the Hatley Park National Historic Site, and includes examples of many distinct and significant ecosystems, such as the Garry Oak Ecosystem, Old Growth Coastal Douglas Fir Forest, numerous riparian areas, wetlands, a saltwater marsh and lagoon in addition to the manicured Japanese Garden, Italian Garden and Rose Garden. RRU is situated on the traditional and unceded territories of the Xwsepsum (Esquimalt) and Lekwungen (Songhees) families and their ancestors. It is also a migratory bird sanctuary. As a result of the convergence of all these aspects of the university lands, there are many special places for students to discover and connect with. Like other programs at RRU, the Bachelor of Science (BSc) program makes extensive use of the lands and gardens as both a living laboratory and as an inspiration for students to develop a strong sense of place to help anchor their studies and their sense of embeddedness in community.

Teaching with awareness of sense of place begins with meeting students where they are at, which is often a heavily laboratory-based education and the perception that science is meant to be objectively measured. It is not an uncommon experience for science students to have prior lab experiences that are designed for them to observe a specific result or effect, but which do not require the students to place the result in the context of the community and world.

One of the early experiences that we designed for the BSc students requires them to go to a creek on campus and collect water samples to test for phosphate as part of an undergraduate environmental chemistry course. However, the levels of phosphate in the creek are well below the detection limits of the assay. This exercise is useful in several ways: the students learn proper sampling techniques, how to collect field observations of the sampling site (which helps to establish a sense of place between the students and the creek), and how to perform a colorimetric assay to quantify phosphate. It teaches students that just because they test for something in an environmental sample, it does not mean that it is present. It also tends to lead to conversations like this:

> Student: My test result is wrong. There is no phosphate in my samples.
> Instructor: Hmm . . . Well, your positive control worked fine. What are some possible sources of phosphate in water?
> Student: Sewage, detergent, leaking septic systems . . .
> Instructor: So, given where your sample is from, would phosphate in the water be a good thing?
> Student (after a long moment to think): No?

By tying the lab results to a specific place on campus, this exercise is an example of a starting point for connecting science to its place in the world. In the above conversation, the real leap in understanding occurs not when the student can name possible sources of phosphate but rather when the student understands that a *lack* of phosphate is not only a desirable result for their samples but also the result that makes sense in the context of the creek from which the samples were drawn.

The BSc program, like the others described here, has a strong emphasis on teamwork, and the capstone course of the program involves a ten-month, team-based environmental consulting project for a sponsoring organization. These major projects are very open-ended problem-based learning experiences focusing on applied, real-world problems. One of the strengths of this type of learning is that the problems can be used to show students the complexity of the interconnections between ideas and disciplines in a way that rewards creativity and the ability to understand a situation from a variety of perspectives (Jonassen and Hung, 2008; Subramaniam, 2006). This is particularly true for fields like environmental science that by their interdisciplinary nature draw on a variety of knowledge, tools, concepts, and skills from both natural and social sciences increasing the student's ability to understand how those disciplines fit together. One of the major challenges initially for the science students is seeing the value of social science perspectives in contributing to solutions.

While all the problems have science components to them (such as measurement of metals in soils or establishing a baseline species inventory of an area), they also include a social science component, such as the use of surveys, interviews or focus groups to gather opinions of particular options or provide context for relationships and policy recommendations. One such major project, Hatley Park Educational Resource for Nature Kindergarten Program (Beckmann et al., 2014) is one example of the rewards and challenges posed by the integration of natural and social sciences and a product that demonstrates a choreography of the two. The overarching purpose of the project was to develop a guidebook to the flora, fauna and fungi of Hatley Park that incorporates kindergarten-level learning outcomes to support and enrich the quality of the Nature Kindergarten learning experience from a neighbouring school with access to the campus for its classes. Until this project was developed, the program had been using a variety of guidebooks written for an adult audience (ibid.). The BSc student team assigned to this project had no prior experience with educational communication or kindergarten-aged children. Some members of the team had experience with plant and animal identification, one had experience with photography, and one had some experience with computer photo editing. The team easily identified what the science part of the project would involve – going to the area of Hatley Park used by the kindergarten and identifying the plants, animals and fungi located there. The social science parts – how to best communicate the information, what children would find interesting, what Indigenous knowledge should be included, what language and science learning outcomes need to be included, and so on, were not as easily identifiable at the start of the project.

The team spent time on a literature review and as a result concluded that they would need to conduct interviews with various local experts, teachers and Elders to fill their knowledge gaps. The realization for these science students that interviews were 'real' research was the first awkward step in building the project. Their faculty advisor recommended a visit with a colleague with experience in constructing semi-structured interviews, which resulted in a transformative conversation about what might be possible beyond a collection of factoids and photos.

By working through the ethical review process, the team learned how to think through the qualitative research requirements of the project as well as how it would intersect with the 'sciencey bits'. The students learned how to respectfully ask questions and honour the experiences of place from a range of people that included teachers, Indigenous Elders and RRU grounds staff.

The next challenge was to actually spend time with the Nature Kindergarten class in the forest, something they were a bit nervous about. This step held an important revelation – that there was more to see during this than 'just kids playing'. With guidance from the teachers, the students learned to observe closely – to see what attracted the children's attention, how they made comparisons between different leaves, sticks, and so on, and what stories they told about their adventures.

As the team embraced the interaction between what they were learning about science and what they were learning about lived experience human science research, the project gained momentum. The guidebook they were designing started to include more pictures, stories, colours and age-appropriate vocabulary. They made comparisons for some pages to show how large things were, such as: 'Did you know a Western Red Cedar tree is as tall as five school buses end to end?' Or that 'a bald eagle has a wing-span larger than a person with their arms stretched out?' (Beckmann et al., 2014, p. 30).

Ultimately, the students produced and tested a field guide that was a practical, beautiful expression of both their learning and what the Nature Kindergarten program had been actively teaching hundreds of kids. When the integration of social and natural science becomes seemingly effortless, it provides the room for powerful, creative learning outcomes for the students and community alike such as this field guide. Although not all major projects have the same reach as this one, they are all influential for their sponsor organizations and provide similar opportunities to make room for new solutions that combine multiple disciplines and perspectives.

The major projects component creates an integrative space in the BSc program at RRU where students can learn to work using the interdisciplinary methods and vocabulary of the environmental field and prepare for futures in which they will be expected 'to share their knowledge and expertise in public forums and work effectively in their profession, but also to identify themselves as scholars and contributing members of the community of practice' (Dunlap, 2006, p. 39). They also provide the space and time to enable learning that is firmly anchored within the reality of life in the world, giving practical experience in being able to communicate complicated science concepts to diverse communities, and encouraging the students to be engaged in self-reflection and practical applications of their learning.

3.   A FOREST WALK-SHOP

At the Congress of Humanities and Social Science held at the University of British Columbia (UBC) in May 2019, a pre-conference 'walk-shop' designed to lead pre-service student-teachers out onto the coniferous campus through the arboretum and second-growth forest to the brink of the beach, was led by a small team of environmental educators (two from RRU).

We gathered early on the south end of the university grounds at the Reconciliation Pole (UBC, 2017) – an Indigenous totem carved between 2015–17 under the design and direction of Master Carver and Hereditary Haida Chief, 7idansuu (Edenshaw), James Hart, who used red and yellow cedar, oil paint, copper and abalone. We began by acknowledging those lands and the history of the peoples who had lived there for millennia, in gratitude and in awe of this magnificent 55-foot rendering. We lingered there to ask ourselves, 'Why does this matter?' – an invitation toward a deeper empathy for the ancestors of this place and a call to action in terms of how we were going to be together on these lands now, here, today. People began describing their connections to their homelands and favourite places, which naturally segued into a discussion on the importance of performing science education in connection to place.

We began by walking to the Orchard Commons, part of the campus arboretum and heard the story of the Giant Arbutus that can only grow in certain locations (iconic on the West Coast of Canada) and needs both a relationship with the soil and to be protected in order to thrive. We continued on in silence, focusing on sounds and sensations and the 'I wonder' questions that often naturally arise. Next, we stopped at an enormous Ponderosa Pine in front of the Student Commons Residence where a drawing exercise revealed that the numbers of ways we see and perceive something are as unique as we each are, meaning there is no right way to draw a tree! This opened up an opportunity for participants to share creative ways they have brought art into the science education curriculum and prompted the reading of a poem about this particular tree called, 'Pondering the Ponderosa Pine' by the late arts-based educator, Carl Leggo (2018) as homage to both man and tree:

> ever green, ever rooted, ever patient,
> ever willing to teach us if we are willing to learn
> teach us to remember we are guests
> on an ancient land with countless stories
> teach us to walk tenderly with one another,
> filled with memories and hopes for others, too . . . (n.p.)

Next, our walking journey took us to the foot of an old, healthy oak where we couldn't help but notice the biodiverse confluence of tree, birds, ferns and grasses, all flourishing together. We talked as educators about the necessity of getting to know a place over time before launching it into curriculum, allowing the place and the curriculum to percolate together, to inform each other for best results.

Just down the path at the First Nations Longhouse, our olfactory senses were piqued as we could smell fresh cedar before we saw the totem-pole-in-the-making. We were told this was in essence an education student's thesis being chipped away at, as the soft wood was revealing more to him about his mythic relations and stories yet to be told. According to a colleague in the crowd, the carver, although absent from his project at that moment, was keen to connect First Nations principles of teaching into the science curriculum – the type of learning that involves the well-being of all living things, is holistic and connects students with a sense of place, requires the exploration of identity, recognizes Indigenous knowledge and the power of story, and involves patience and time (see the First Nations Education Steering Committee [FNESC], n.d.).

We ended our walk soon after at a small second-growth forest where we were introduced to 'The Kicking Tree'. A poor old 'soul' that has been brutalized over time by frustrated students, where kicking it became a 'thing to go and do' to release tension and anger. Now, thankfully, this tree has a secure fence protecting it from further harm. It was a solemn moment as we stood in silence considering the affrontery of such unthinkable acts and felt the transference of shame that we humans can be capable of such a lack of awareness and care for another living being. Some were moved to share their feelings, including their tears.

While environmental education can be approached theoretically, we know it is primarily about relationships – with places, with other human communities, with our fellow creatures and with our own souls. The last exercise we offered, an adaptation of ecophilosopher, author, activist and teacher Joanna Macy's 'Council of All Beings' (Macy and Young Brown, 1998) is an experiential exercise that forms part of her lifework, The Work That Reconnects,[1] and as it turned out was a perfect antidote to the Kicking Tree experience. The instructions were simple and clear:

Wander. Let yourself be drawn in. Go feelingly. Find your place in nearby nature (or better yet, let it find you). Ask permission to sit. Listen for a clear 'yes' or 'no'. If you hear nothing, it's best to move on. Wait until you 'hear' a 'yes'. Be courteous and curious, spend some time getting to know this particular place and its inhabitants. You can start with the simple default question of, 'Who are you?' or 'Please tell me about yourself'. Repeat as necessary until there is nothing more (for the time being). Be silent. Keep listening. Later, write . . . (Leighton, 2020, p. 199)

More than merely taking in information and then interpreting the experience, this exercise requires a leap of curiosity as we ask students to spend some time looking *into* the life of another being through 'just listening' (Carbaugh, 1999). Intended to re-sensitize them to the ecopsychological terrain in which they live and move, students enter into the sensorial present and awaken to, 'the very voice of the trees, the waves and the forests' (Merleau-Ponty, 1962, p. vii) and with empathy and a kind of deep identification through wild 'teachings', get to know another being.

After suffusing themselves in nature, immersed in 'wild conversations' for a time, we all gathered in a final sharing circle, 'The Council of All Beings' (Macy and Young Brown, 1998). We asked the students to evoke their moral imaginations and make a conscious leap. Instead of speaking *about* their experiences, we encouraged them to speak *for* the more-than-human they encountered, and to use 'I' messages to do so (a concept quite foreign in natural science). For instance, rather than say, '*The* old pine is tall and *it* has far-reaching branches', the student teacher to go first tentatively offered, '*I* am very tall, with far-reaching branches and *I* have been here a long, long time'. Strangely (or not), she was a tall woman and as she spoke and spread her arms out, it was true, she had a wide embrace.

In line with Naess (1988, 1989), Macy (2007) urges that we seek a 'wider construct of identity' or what she calls the need for 'the greening of the self' (p. 148), which in some ways is an act of remembering more of our own true nature through nature connection. She argues that a more ecological consciousness with the worldview of 'self as inseparable from the web of relationships that sustain it' (p. 151) may hold profound implications for the fate of our planet because once we identify in this unified way, we shift from dominator to defender, from colonialist to community member, from the personal to planetary. Or one could imagine that Naess and Macy might say that if we realize we are the earth acting on its own behalf through human consciousness, we will behave in life-giving not life-threatening ways.

Each brave person who spoke in this council, who imagined the life of the Other, came to understand that they shared something of the traits of this particular more-than-human being (otherwise why would they have been attracted in the first place?) and in effect, could see themselves as more related than not. In this way, their human capacity for reflective awareness allowed them to see the importance of learning to include multiple perspectives in order to appreciate the aliveness in every aspect of the world, especially in those that are non-human. Moving from an 'I-It' subject-to-object encounter, participants moved to a subject-to-subject or 'I-Thou' (Buber, 1970) understanding:

An 'I–Thou' relationship calls up a kind of devotion to seeing beneath the shallow surface of things by asking us to look into rather than at; it urges a willingness to forgo our addiction to omnipotence in the presence of other life. As we start to see ourselves in each Other, we can see how much more alike we are than not. And as we gaze into the essence of Another, we see and are seen in a sensorial participation of interplay and intimacy. We are also in some ways looking into a mirror reflecting back to us something of ourselves at the same time. Side-by-side, we can regard the truth in Others and the true nature in ourselves at once. (Leighton, 2020, p. 200)

It soon became evident in our final discussion that participants saw the value and importance of the both/and[2] stance we had taken in our walk-shop. By embracing both critical and rational thinking with embodied and deeply imaginative ways of knowing the world (for the sake of their efficacy as environmental educators), this became an example of much needed reconciliation in action, a gestalt that brought us back to where we started at Hart's pole.

By showing up, paying attention, and listening closely, student-teachers began to (re)discover an intrinsic, interactive relationship with the living world and reclaim a sense of their place within that place. They were also keen to share the experience in turn with their own students. The walk-shop was (in the end) an invitation toward more conscious action through integrated knowledge with a strong emphasis on the educational value of the phenomenal dance between natural and human science as found at the confluence of lived experience (Van Manen, 1990).

4.   LESSONS LEARNED – SENSE OF PLACE WORKSHOP

The experience of designing the walk-shop and the feedback we received, combined with our desire to lay a greater groundwork between the social and natural sciences, led us to design a one-day Sense of Place workshop for the BSc students for the start of their program.

Beginning in the classroom with an introduction to the ideas of systems thinking, ecopsychology and sense of place, we used slides, discussion and drawing activities to help students understand their connection to special places in their earlier life. We provided campus guidebooks (developed by a previous cohort) and simple instructions to find a place that 'speaks' to you (e.g., you are attracted to) and spend about two hours getting to know that place and its inhabitants. Students took notes, took pictures, and took a buddy to share their experience with.

Later, we gathered under a tree in the Japanese Gardens to form a final sharing circle where students began by telling us something 'sciencey' about their interaction with the place they got to know. This was an easy first step for science students – everyone was willing to talk. From there, we asked that they speak about something special about that place from a more personal perspective. Again, everyone was fairly comfortable with their responses, which were descriptive and mostly enthusiastic. Finally, we asked them to tell us a story from the perspective (or voice) of the place or one of its inhabitants. This proved a bit more difficult and did require that we allow more space for silence and for students to drum up their courage as well as tap into their imaginations before sharing. However, nearly every student did in the end choose to share an alternate view in rich story-form and the momentum for sharing grew around the circle with each additional telling.

One learning objective of this day was to enlarge the students' capacity and awareness for the necessity to integrate multiple perspectives offered by social and natural sciences in order to address the larger more complex problems (such as climate pollution and loss of biodiversity) that we all face. As teachers, it is our obligation to help students develop both their own sense of agency and their sense of communion with the world, a dynamic tension that requires a dynamic and emerging curriculum in response to modern day challenges that extend beyond any one discipline, any one sector, or any one level of government to solve, and will require unprecedented collaboration.

5.   CONCLUSION

Many questions have been asked about why it has taken modern society so long to begin to respond to climate change pollution since the release of the first Intergovernmental Panel on Climate Change report in 1995 and successive reports to 2018 (IPCC, 2018). Indeed, there is evidence that in the decade 1979–89, the world's major powers came within several signatures of endorsing a binding, global framework to reduce carbon emissions – far closer than we've come since. Human societies have moved from an agricultural revolution to an industrial revolution in its history, and our failure to embrace the requisite energy revolution may well prove to be our downfall. Why, in the face of overwhelming scientific evidence, has this failure occurred?

There are, of course, many complicated factors. It is widely understood that as researchers we have failed to communicate the science in an accessible way to the public(s) and in so doing, have failed to convey the urgency of the problems. Another contributing factor is the traditional separation between the natural and social sciences. We are at a stage in our evolution where the big challenges facing modern society are ultimately not necessarily those of scientific or managed origin, but rather about people, their diverse cultures, interests, visions, priorities, behaviours and needs (Norgaard, 1994). The solitudes (between the natural and social sciences), the silos (between disciplines) and the stovepipes within (for example, between physical and human geographers) have actually contributed to our failures to communicate.

Overcoming the terrorism of either/or (Dale, 2012) requires a new kind of collaboration and integration through transdisciplinarity, which is more than a new discipline or super-discipline and actually a different way of seeing and experiencing the world, more systemic and more holistic (Max-Neef, 2005). Place-responsive curriculum (which denotes a relationship *with* place rather than nature as a backdrop or space to merely base our learning on) offers a way to bridge these artificial separations. A diverse and imaginative whole science pedagogy that equally values multiple modalities of learning and in this case includes experimentation, reflection, observation, drawing, analysis, walking, writing, sitting, imaginative and dialogic inquiry, suggests we are engaged in a study of the habits and rhythms, relationships and forms, currents and patterns of our earthly home, toward an ecology of learning. This can result in a co-created curriculum where learning communities acknowledge students as makers of real and meaningful connections for themselves based on what they have encountered, anchored in the living world. Making such spaces for sustainable education is only a starting point: when *both* social *and* natural sciences are obvious and equally valued, when they step together, refusing to be awkward dance partners, we bring a more wholesome and immersed perspective to learning, and what heuristically emerges is something more diverse and richer than could be achieved by any one of its singular parts.

By grounding learning in place-specific contexts and placing significance on a personal awareness of one's relationships *with* and *in* the world, emergent properties bring a spectrum of integrated space where day and night, particle and wave, sun and moon, masculine and feminine, physical and metaphysical, reason and emotion, logic and intuition, discipline and transdiscipline are no longer dichotomies, but complements that converge and merge toward something greater than the one without losing their unique and necessary identities (ibid.).

Each place is unique and diverse and while a place grounds the learning in real-life applications so critical to problem-based learning, each place also offers its particular wisdom, its own lessons for takeaway. This allows for lessons learned to be adaptive to new locations and new perspectives regardless of geography.

AUTHORS' NOTE

At the time of publication, Victoria, BC, home to RRU, and most of the world, was in lockdown in response to the COVID-19 pandemic. In our attempts to create a sense of continuance and calm for our students, we carried on by taking our face-to-face learning online and as such offered the Sense of Place workshop in a virtual space as orientation for incoming BSc students.

We first gathered in Collaborate™ (an online learning platform) to view the slide deck we use in class while encouraging questions throughout using a chatbox text option. Next, we sent the students outside into their own backyards or nearby nature (always at a safe distance from others) to experience getting to know another life form on their own. When they returned, they proceeded to report about the various physical attributes of the places they visited and then told something 'science-y' of that place, thus demonstrating a deepening of their understanding. Finally, each student was asked to speak from the perspective of that place – whether it was a muddy river, tree stump, lichen, rock or wildflower. It took a few students going first for the rest to get the hang of it and fall in. They spoke of moodiness and sometimes flooding (river), being home to other life while aging and disintegrating (stump), being part of a symbiosis and community of life barely detectable at times (lichen), strength and stability (rock) and getting ready to bloom into a new life (wildflower). Each offering left us breathless. Not only had students deeply and readily identified with another life, they morally imagined what it was like to *be* that life, and as they shared that perspective were revealing their knowledge of systems and symbiosis, of cycles of death, renewal and adaptation. Every student participated and each perspective shared was done in a sober, respectful and awe-inspiring way. Finally, each student's last words were some kind of (imagined) wisdom for us humans, which seemed a fitting way to end that class and this chapter.

NOTES

1. Joanna Macy's significant contribution has been The Work That Reconnects (TWTR) – found in *World as Lover, World as Self* (2007) and most prominently in *Coming Back to Life: Practices to Reconnect Our lives, Our World* (1998, with Molly Young-Brown). The website at https://workthatreconnects.org is the home of this work and a network space for practitioners of TWTR (of which co-author, Dr Hilary Leighton is a registered facilitator).

2. In contrast to more black-and-white Aristotelian thinking with options of 'either/or', 'both/and' thinking takes a holistic view that includes multiple perspectives and asks that we consider both options and then other possibilities as well beyond the binary in order to reach what Buddhism refers to as a 'third' or 'middle way' thinking that is neither one nor the other but 'both/and'.

REFERENCES

Beckmann, K., Antal, A., Xu, Z. and Anari, E. (2014). Hatley Park Educational Resource for Nature Kindergarten Program. Unpublished BSc Major Project Report, Royal Roads University, Victoria, BC.

Buber, M. (1970). *I and Thou* [Trans. W. Kaufmann]. New York: Charles Scribner's Sons.

Carbaugh, D. (1999). 'Just listen': 'listening' and landscape among the Blackfeet. *Western Journal of Communication*, 63(3), 250–70. https://doi.org/10.1080/10570319909374641.

Clayton, S. (2003). Environmental identity: a conceptual and an operational definition. In S. Clayton and S. Opotow (eds), *Identity and the Natural Environment* (pp. 43–66). Cambridge, MA: MIT Press.

Cleary, A., Fielding, K.S. and Bell, S.L. et al. (2017). Exploring potential mechanisms involved in the relationship between eudaimonic wellbeing and nature connection. *Landscape and Urban Planning*, 158, 119–28.

Dale, A. (2012). Synoikismos: overcoming the terrorism of the either/or. Wiley Lecture. Congress of the Humanities and Social Sciences, University of Waterloo and Wilfrid Laurier University.

Dunlap, J.C. (2006). The effect of a problem-centered, enculturating experience on doctoral students' self-efficacy. *Interdisciplinary Journal of Problem-Based Learning*, 1(2), 19–48.

First Nations Education Steering Committee (FNESC) (n.d.). 'Learning first peoples classroom resources'. Accessed November 2019 at http://www.fnesc.ca/learningfirstpeoples/.

Heidegger, M. ([1927] 1962). *Being and Time*. New York: Harper & Row.

IPCC (2018). Global warming of 1.5°C. An IPCC Special Report on the impacts of global warming of 1.5°C above pre-industrial levels and related global greenhouse gas emission pathways, in the context of strengthening the global response to the threat of climate change, sustainable development, and efforts to eradicate poverty. [V. Masson-Delmotte, P. Zhai, H. O. Pörtner, D. Roberts, J. Skea, P.R. Shukla, A. Pirani, W. Moufouma-Okia, C. Péan, R. Pidcock, S. Connors, J. B. R. Matthews, Y. Chen, X. Zhou, M. I. Gomis, E. Lonnoy, T. Maycock, M. Tignor, T. Waterfield (eds)].

Jonassen, D.H. and Hung, W. (2008). All problems are not equal: implications for problem-based learning. *Interdisciplinary Journal of Problem-Based Learning*, 2(2), 6–28.

Kellert, S.R and Wilson, E.O. (1993). *The Biophilia Hypothesis*. Washington, DC: Island Press.

Leggo, C. (2018, 13 February). Pondering the ponderosa pine [Poem]. *Medium.com*. Accessed November 2019 at https://medium.com/phoneme/pondering-the-ponderosa-pine-33537cc036b1.

Leighton, H. (2020). Mindscapes and landscapes: rendering (of) self through a 'body' of work. In E. Lyle (ed.), *Identity Landscapes: Contemplating Place and the Construction of Self* (pp. 197–209). Leiden: Brill/Sense Publishers.

Low, S.M. and Altman, I. (1992). *Human Behavior and Environment (Advances in Theory and Research), Vol. 12: Place Attachment*. Boston, MA: Springer.

Macy, J. (2007). *World as Lover, World as Self: Courage for Global Justice and Ecological Renewal*. Berkeley, CA: Parallax Press.

Macy, J. and Young Brown, M. (1998). *Coming Back to Life: Practices to Reconnect Our Lives, Our World*. Gabriola Island, BC: New Society Publishers.

Manzo, L.C. and Devine-Wright, P. (eds) (2014). *Place Attachment: Advances in Theory, Methods and Applications*. New York: Routledge.

Masterson, V.A., Stedman, R. and Enqvist, J. et al. (2017). The contribution of sense of place to social-ecological systems research: a review and research agenda. *Ecology and Society*, 22(1), Article 49.

Max-Neef, M. (2005). Foundations of transdisciplinarity. *Ecological Economics*, 53, 5–16.

Merleau-Ponty, M. (1962). *Phenomenology of Perception* [Trans. C. Smith]. London: Routledge.

Naess, A. (1988). Self-realization: an ecological approach to being in the world. In J. Seed, J. Macy, P. Fleming and A. Naess (eds), *Thinking like a Mountain: Toward a Council of All Beings*. Gabriola Island, BC: New Society Publishers.

Naess, A. (1989). *Ecology, Community and Lifestyle*. New York: Cambridge University Press.

Norgaard, R. (1994). *Development Betrayed: The End of Progress and a Coevolutionary Revisioning of the Future*. London: Routledge.

Orr, D.W. (2004). *Earth in Mind: On Education, Environment, and the Human Prospect*. Washington, DC: Island Press.

Sandelowski, M. (1994). The proof is in the pottery: toward a poetics for qualitative inquiry. In J.M. Morse (ed.),

Critical Issues in Qualitative Methods (pp. 46–63). Thousand Oaks, CA: SAGE Publications.

Scannell, L. and Gifford, R. (2017). Place attachment enhances psychological need satisfaction. *Environment and Behavior*, 49(4), 359–89.

Subramaniam, R.M. (2006). Problem-based learning: concept, theories, effectiveness and application to radiology teaching. *Journal of Medical Imaging and Radiation Oncology*, 50(4), 339–41.

UBC (2017, 7 April), 'Reconciliation Pole installed at UBC'. Accessed November 2019 at https://aboriginal.ubc.ca/2017/04/07/reconciliation-pole-installed-at-ubc/.

Van Manen, M. (1990). *Researching Lived Experience. Human Science for An Action Sensitive Pedagogy.* New York: SUNY Press.

28. Preserving sustainability: activating the ecological university through collective food practice
Monica Dantas, Sherif Goubran and Nadra Wagdy

1. INTRODUCTION

Raising awareness about sustainability and increasing the sustainability competencies of communities are critical determinants for achieving global change. The fundamental role of education, especially higher education institutions (HEIs), in the transition towards sustainable societies has been well recognized (Rowe, 2007; Sonetti, Lombardi and Chelleri, 2016; Washington-Ottombre and Bigalke, 2018). The post-2015 development agenda has specifically underlined the importance of high-quality education and lifelong learning in achieving the Sustainable Development Goals (SDGs) (Didham and Ofei-Manu, 2015). The SDGs call for transformative action (United Nations, 2015): they represent a call for action, for the development of complex and multidimensional approaches, and provide a clear sustainable development roadmap (Chineme, Herremans and Wills, 2019; Goubran, 2019).

Researchers and practitioners investigated how education can be best utilized to place societies on track to sustainable development (Frisk and Larson, 2011; Rowe, 2007). Frisk and Larson (2011) highlight that the main reason for this educational focus is rooted in the need for developing an understanding of the pillars of sustainability. Quoting ecologist Babia Dioum Senegalese and anthropologist Jane Goodall, Frisk and Larson (2011) indicate that care can only come from love, love comes from understanding, and understanding comes from what we are taught. Yet, many researchers are still pointing to the inadequacy of our educational system to transform knowledge into action (Chineme et al., 2019; Frisk and Larson, 2011).

Through this background, it is important to contextualize the role of different stakeholders within HEIs. Administrators, faculty and staff play an influential role in developing, establishing and maintaining a culture of sustainability on university campuses (Washington-Ottombre and Bigalke, 2018). However, and in many university and college campuses, students and alternative student movements have been at the forefront of the transition (Rosentrater and Burke, 2017; Sonetti et al., 2016).

This research uses autoethnography to reflect on the activities of one such student-led campus activity – 'Season Jars'. Home on Concordia University's Montreal campus, the project uses food preservation as a tool for delivering an experiential and multidisciplinary collective learning experience that combines science, history, and cultural knowledge with culinary techniques. The project aims to raise awareness on sustainability and food security as well as to create a sharing campus community around food transformation. The researchers will use observations and reflections collected from more than 50 workshops that took place between 2016 and 2019. Beyond simply describing the activities undertaken by the project in the last four years, the chapter aims to contextualize the project's approach to sustainability education within the multidisciplinary debates on the topic.

The chapter starts by providing an overview of the literature pertaining to sustainability education on university campuses, experiential learning theory and models, as well as the use of food as a medium for knowledge dissemination and development. The chapter then presents Season Jars within the context of Concordia students' sustainability and food movements. The chapter then confronts the available frameworks and models with the observations collected. The research specifically focuses on the food preservation workshops provided by Season Jars and investigates how the workshops' design and methodology contributed to bridging the knowledge-to-action gap reported in the literature. The chapter proposes that Season Jars' workshops were able to supply space (in the social sense) for sustainability solutions and knowledge to organically emerge while also transforming spaces (in the physical sense) on the university campus into sustainability hubs. However, the observations show that these transformations were accelerated and enabled through the innovative dynamic education approaches of the project.

2. BACKGROUND AND CONCEPTUAL UNDERPINNINGS

2.1 Sustainability, Higher Education, and Sustainable Development

In a recent study, Washington-Ottombre and Bigalke (2018) point to the fact that HEIs have played a significant role in promoting, and in some cases implementing, sustainable development on their campuses and in their local communities. The authors highlight that this has been primarily achieved through the launch, support and improvements of initiatives, declarations, and networks as well as voluntary assessments. Through their analysis of 454 innovations reported within the voluntary Sustainability Tracking Assessment & Rating System (STARS), Washington-Ottombre and Bigalke (2018) found that 'operations' was still the main mode of implementation for sustainability innovations on campuses by a large margin. While advances, improvements, and innovations in the operation of university campuses and educational facilities are important actions, Washington-Ottombre and Bigalke's findings echo some of the worries reported by literature regarding the shortcomings of the current approaches to sustainable development in HEIs. In a study focused on the sustainability perceptions, attitudes and habits of university students, Rosentrater and Burke (2017) found that most students learn or retrieve information about climate change through news media and the Internet (ranked first and second respectively). In the selected responses featured in their article, a number of students expressed concern that the university could do more to encourage sustainable practice (e.g., provide better access to sustainable services). However, the students interviewed perceived that, individually, they don't have the ability to create a 'strong impact' (ibid.). The findings highlight some key gaps in our approach to education that we need to address to empower students and communities to push towards transformative sustainable change.

Didham and Ofei-Manu (2015) point to the fact that education for sustainable development (ESD) should be viewed as a mode of implementation for providing the necessary capacity needed to achieve the ambitious SDGs. Such capacities could include (1) critical reflexivity; (2) cooperation and relationship building; and (3) holistic interpretation of knowledge, with the end goal to develop a sense of responsibility (ibid.). The authors emphasize that the broad and holistic ESD stems from what was previously known as environmental education, which was more focused on the environmental pillar (the planet) (ibid.). Interdisciplinarity has been advocated as the appropriate means for enabling the holistic approach to sustainability problems (Goubran, Emond and Cucuzzella, 2017). Washington-Ottombre and Bigalke (2018) identified this notion of cross-disciplinary education as an internal innovation factor on university campuses. Ingram (2012), Burns and Miller (2012), and Chineme et al. (2019) also underline the role interdisciplinarity plays in ESD and highlight that sustainability problems, which are often wicked in nature (Coyne, 2005; Rittel and Webber, 1973), can hardly be approached through one discipline or field.

While interdisciplinarity might enable students to appreciate the holistic nature of life (i.e., its natural, social, economic, and cultural dimensions) and help them overcome the fragmented image traditional disciplinary education paints (Burns and Miller, 2012), it does not necessarily help overcome the knowledge-to-action gap. Researchers have proposed examining the learning cycle to bridge this gap. The aim of such a bridge would be to overcome the current perception that individuals don't have the capacity to initiate transformation – and to transform learners into active agents of change that catalyze action towards sustainable development (Frisk and Larson, 2011; Washington-Ottombre and Bigalke, 2018).

2.2   The Experiential Learning Model and Its Relevance to Sustainability

The concept of experiential learning has been widely referenced and utilized since it was first developed by David Kolb (1984) and further elaborated in his recent work with his wife Alice (Kolb and Kolb, 2009). The basic premise of Kolb's model shifts the understanding of learning from a discrete activity to a progression. Kolb proposes that learning happens in a four-stage cycle that moves across concrete experiences (experiencing), reflective observation (observing), abstract conceptualization (thinking), and active experimentation (applying). In this context, experiential learning becomes the process of moving through these four modes (Kolb, 1984; Kolb and Kolb, 2009). In a chapter published in *The SAGE Handbook of Management Learning, Education and Development*, Alice and David Kolb (Kolb and Kolb, 2009) present six key propositions that are foundational to their theory: (1) learning is best understood as a process; (2) all learning is, in fact, re-learning; (3) the process requires resolving conflict between opposed modes of adaptation; (4) learning is a process of adaptation; (5) learning is a result of synergy between the individual and the environment; and (6) learning is a process of creating knowledge. They further clarify that learning happens across two intersecting axes: the 'transforming' (how we do things) and 'grasping' (how we think about things) dimensions (ibid.). Since its publication more than three decades ago, experiential learning theory (ELT) has been readily used to question the traditional didactic modes of teaching and learning. More importantly, the theory has been widely referenced in the context of sustainability education.

Maher and Burkhart (2017), in their study on how to engage nutrition undergraduate students with sustainability, use the experiential learning model. They point to the fact that 'experience, when coupled with reflection, will contribute to deeper learning than what may be seen with pure theoretical learning' (Maher and Burkhart, 2017, p. 1103). In their view, ELT can help in the implementation of adaption strategies and in using sustainability as a lens for students to understand their disciplinary knowledge (ibid.). Burns and Miller (2012), in their presentation of the Learning Gardens Laboratory (a living laboratory for sustainable food systems based on the hands-on application of organic gardening), place experiential learning at the foundation for their activities. They specifically point out the empowering nature of experiential and participatory learning models, their ability to create a sense of ownership, and their power to build the required capacity to approach complex sustainability issues (ibid.).

Frisk and Larson (2011) study the effective educational practices that can accelerate the behavioural changes required to achieve transformative action. They study the literature related to behavioural research, sustainability competencies, and education pedagogy. They conclude that four key domains of knowledge are known to predict behaviours: (1) declarative (understanding how the system works – supported by theories such as information deficit model); (2) procedural (understanding how to undertake action – supported by theories such as the model of responsible environmental action); (3) effectiveness (understanding the effects of different actions – supported by models such as the theory of reasoned action); and (4) social knowledge (understanding the motives and intentions of others – supported by theories such as community-based social markets) (ibid.). They then establish four key competencies required for ESD, namely: (1) systems thinking and an understanding of interconnectedness (which should 'avoid "assembly-line" fragmentation of subjects and oversimplification of issues as simply right/wrong or true/false'); (2) long-term, foresighted thinking (which should 'avoid "one-size fits all" solutions in visioning activities'); (3) stakeholder engagement and group collaboration (which should 'avoid evaluating students solely based on individual activities and outcomes'); and (4) action-orientation and change-agent skills (which should 'avoid informational learning solely based on declarative knowledge') (Frisk and Larson, 2011, n.p.). These competencies intersect those reported by Didham and Ofei-Manu (2015).

Chineme et al. (2019) combined the key domains of knowledge suggested by Frisk and Larson (2011) with Kolb's ELT (Kolb, 1984; Kolb and Kolb, 2009) in order to approach a solar Power Hub project in a remote area in Africa within the science program in sustainable energy development at the University of Manitoba, Canada. They matched (1) procedural knowledge with reflecting; (2) effectiveness knowledge with experiencing; (3) social knowledge with acting; and (4) declarative knowledge with thinking (Chineme et al., 2019). Through this combination, they were able to assess the four competencies suggested by Frisk and Larson (2011) as well as propose two additional ones: (1) empathy and understanding of different worldviews and relationships; and (2) critical thinking and decision-making capacity within complexity. The work reviewed can lead us to synthesize an overall framework that localizes ELT for ESD. Through this framework, new programs and projects can move away from the generalized applications of ELT and focus on building the sustainability competencies presented. Such a framework could be used to understand the ability of educational activities in building the collective capacity for transformative action (summarized in Table 28.1).

Table 28.1   Framework for sustainability-focused experiential learning aiming for building capacity for transformative action

Components of the Learning Cycle	Sustainability Domains of Knowledge
Concrete experiences (experiencing)	Social knowledge
Reflective observation (observing)	Procedural knowledge
Abstract conceptualization (thinking)	Declarative knowledge
Active experimentation (applying)	Effectiveness knowledge

Which should lead to six competences:
(1) Systems thinking and an understanding of interconnectedness
(2) Long-term and foresighted thinking
(3) Stakeholder engagement and group collaboration
(4) Action-orientation and change-agent skills
(5) Empathy and understanding of different worldviews and relationships
(6) Critical thinking and decision-making capacity within complexity

Sources: Authors' compilation based on the work of Chineme et al. (2019); Frisk and Larson (2011); Kolb (1984); Kolb and Kolb (2009).

2.3   Food as a Medium for Knowledge Development

Food is a basic human right that was recognized in the 1948 Universal Declaration of Human Rights. In the UN 2030 Agenda, food is the theme that links and infiltrates all the SDGs – and the food system's connection to environmental, social, economic, and cultural sustainability is clearly visible (Gupta and Vegelin, 2016; Le Blanc, 2015; Nilsson et al., 2018; United Nations, 2015). Beyond the transformations needed to shift our current food system into a sustainable path, food is also a very versatile medium. Researchers, community development practitioners and institutions have pointed to the multipurpose and multilayer roles of food and its ability to be used as a medium for raising awareness and building capacity around sustainability issues.

Jennifer Brady (2011) critiques the formal and scientific approach to food and eating as the object of inquiry. Instead, she proposes, building on Heldke's (1988) work, that food and eating can become an inquiry: 'Cooking as inquiry builds on the existing foundation of food scholarship by offering a methodological approach that understands food not simply as an object of study, but makes food-making the means of garnering understanding about food, identity, and the body' (Brady, 2011, p. 323). She further clarifies that food making 'requires us to attend with our eyes, ears, noses, mouths, and hands and draws on the knowledge we hold in our bodies' (p. 326).

The notion of cooking together has been studied previously within the collective kitchen format. In a study in Canada, Engler-Stringer and Berenbaum (2005) found that there are mainly three types of community kitchens: (1) collective kitchens; (2) cooking classes; and (3) communal meal programs. The authors also found that the kitchens are generally driven by the needs of their participants and are specifically responding to socioeconomic, demographic, geographic and nutritional needs (ibid.). The collective kitchens also presented the groups' interlinked goals, including (1) food security-focused objectives (providing access to food knowledge and food processing spaces); (2) poverty-focused objectives (providing access to high-quality food and meals); and (3) empowerment-focused objectives (enabling control over food, providing confidence and community development) (ibid.). The authors also highlighted the community leadership capacity some collective kitchens could provide to their participants (ibid.). This is specifically important in the context of sustainability education since training people to become mentors and coaches can multiply the positive outcomes (Sommer and Strong, 2016). Isaku and Iba (2015, p. 2) expand these objectives and propose that 'CoCooking' should be viewed beyond the health, economic and skill-development objectives and that people could and should cook together 'for the pure joy of it' (ibid.). They propose what they name 'Creative CoCooking patterns' to help create engaged and fun experiences in collective cooking environments and highlight that such activities could have the following benefits: (1) acquisition of cooking techniques; (2) building teamwork; and (3) nurturing creativity (ibid.).

Within the context of Canada and other developed countries, the idea of collective cooking might be a solution to other systemic problems within society. In a study of the preference of university students, Conti et al. (2018) found that unhealthy food options are at the top of the list of preferences. In a report by Meal Exchange Canada, which investigates food security on university campuses, two in five students reported having experienced food insecurity, with cost barriers being the underlying reason for such insecurity (Silverthorn, 2016). When studying why university students find it hard to make sustainable dietary choices, Maher and Burkhart (2017) reported a number of barriers, including lack of knowledge, lack of reason or motivation to change, poor availability and access, lack of preparation and intention, and concerns regarding adequacy of dietary intake. However, by engaging students in sustainable dietary challenges based on the experiential learning model, the authors observed that students were able to overcome these barriers and reported positive behavioural changes (ibid.).

In the face of some of the cultural divisions today, researchers have also explored the use of food activities as a means to create a more cohesive community. This approach is important in order to address the food insecurity related to the access and availability of ethically relevant foods. For example, on Canadian campuses, almost one-third of the students experienced limited access to traditional and cultural foods (Silverthorn, 2016). Tsuji et al. (2018) were able to show that university students who engaged in multicultural cooking classes were able to develop their cultural competency. Their findings also echo the work of Chen et al. (2014) who found that students who were engaged in home cooking activities that involved different ethnic ingredients increased their familiarity, appreciation, and consumption of such ingredients. They also showed that this multi-cultural exposure improved their uptake of healthier and more sustainable foods such as vegetables that are more locally grown.

The review of literature highlights how food, and specifically food transformation, can be an appropriate mean of inquiry within the experiential learning model. Additionally, the available research proposes that food transformation activities can help deliver the six key sustainability competencies presented in Table 28.1. Additionally, collective food transformation projects on university campuses can help address some of the main barriers to transformative action around food, including lack of food literacy and knowledge, lack of access to food and culturally relevant food, lack of skill, lack of preparation, and lack of motivation.

3.   SEASON JARS – SUSTAINABILITY THROUGH FOOD PRESERVATION

3.1   Context – Concordia University and its Alternative Food Movement

Starting in the 1970s, the operation of food services in North American universities transition from a model that combined different non-exclusive independent providers with collective cooking spaces (such as industrial kitchens open for university community). University campuses are converted into a restricted corporate food system, where the control is increasingly centralized (Bennell, 2008). Today, a limited number of large corporations provide food services in most North American universities and colleges (these include Chartwells,[1] Sodexo[2] and Aramark[3]). Following this international trend, Concordia University signed its first exclusivity food services contract with Sodexo-Marriott (now Sodexo) in 2000, to service residence students (Concordia Food Coalition [CFC], 2013). CFC reported that resident students were required to adhere to an exclusive meal plan as a requirement for residence (ibid.). Since then, Concordia University food services' exclusive contracts have passed from Sodexo, to Chartwells, to Aramark (ibid.). In many cases, the contracts signed between universities and these corporations exempted them from university-specific strategies such as environmental policies or sustainability goals. Additionally, student cultural representation and food literacy can also be negatively affected by the narrow food options provided by exclusive providers. In this context, the Concordia University community developed a diverse sustainability movement driven by student initiatives. The Concordia Food Groups Research Project (CFG), led by Erik Chevrier and Kim Gagnon, is a project that aims to co-create food sovereignty at Concordia. CFG mapped the food-related student-run initiatives at the university and documented the reasons and underlying motives for the creation of such initiatives. They stated that one of the main reported reasons for the creation of initiatives is to fill the gaps left by the corporate-run cafeterias on campus. Figure 28.1 presents a map of the alternative food movement at Concordia University. In this 2018 snapshot, the student initiatives are categorized based on their approach and role in the food production cycle. Within this map, Season Jars appears in the categories of (1) food production; (2) food processing; and (3) educational activities. While the cross-listing of the initiative offers a glimpse at its multifaceted activities, this chapter proposes that Season Jars' approach mobilizes food as a means for ESD.

3.2   An Overview of Season Jars' Activities

Since the launch of the project in 2015, Season Jars has experimented with different approaches to ESD using food as a methodological medium. The research-creation project has specifically aimed at experimenting with the modes and mediums by which food can be used to generate, disseminate and duplicate sustainability knowledge. Beyond the food presentation workshops, which will be the focus of this chapter, Season Jars takes part in art exhibits, conferences and other academic activities, as well as pop-up workshops within and beyond Concordia University. Figure 28.2 presents a visual map of the project's activities and Figure 28.3 presents the project's brand. While interdisciplinarity is at the core of the project, all the participant-focused activities aim to provide a

Snap-Shot of the Student-Run Food System at Concordia
NOVEMBER 2018

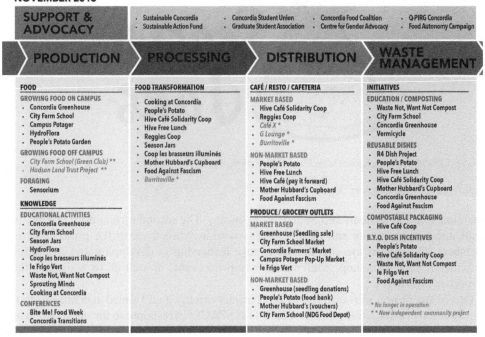

SUPPORT & ADVOCACY	· Sustainable Concordia · Sustainable Action Fund	· Concordia Student Union · Graduate Student Association	· Concordia Food Coalition · Centre for Gender Advocacy	· Q-PIRG Concordia · Food Autonomy Campaign

PRODUCTION	PROCESSING	DISTRIBUTION	WASTE MANAGEMENT
FOOD GROWING FOOD ON CAMPUS · Concordia Greenhouse · City Farm School · Campus Potager · HydroFlora · People's Potato Garden GROWING FOOD OFF CAMPUS · City Farm School (Green Club) ** · Hudson Land Trust Project ** FORAGING · Sensorium **KNOWLEDGE** EDUCATIONAL ACTIVITIES · Concordia Greenhouse · City Farm School · Season Jars · HydroFlora · Coop les brasseurs illuminés · le Frigo Vert · Waste Not, Want Not Compost · Sprouting Minds · Cooking at Concordia CONFERENCES · Bite Me! Food Week · Concordia Transitions	**FOOD TRANSFORMATION** · Cooking at Concordia · People's Potato · Hive Café Solidarity Coop · Hive Free Lunch · Reggies Coop · Season Jars · Coop les brasseurs illuminés · Mother Hubbard's Cupboard · Food Against Fascism · Burritoville *	**CAFÉ / RESTO / CAFETERIA** MARKET BASED · Hive Café Solidarity Coop · Reggies Coop · Café X * · G Lounge * · Burritoville * NON-MARKET BASED · People's Potato · Hive Free Lunch · Hive Café (pay it forward) · Mother Hubbard's Cupboard · Food Against Fascism **PRODUCE / GROCERY OUTLETS** MARKET BASED · Greenhouse (Seedling sale) · City Farm School Market · Concordia Farmers' Market · Campus Potager Pop-Up Market · le Frigo Vert NON-MARKET BASED · Greenhouse (seedling donations) · People's Potato (food bank) · Mother Hubbard's (vouchers) · City Farm School (NDG Food Depot)	**INITIATIVES** EDUCATION / COMPOSTING · Waste Not, Want Not Compost · City Farm School · Concordia Greenhouse · Vermicycle REUSABLE DISHES · R4 Dish Project · People's Potato · Hive Free Lunch · Hive Café Solidarity Coop · Mother Hubbard's Cupboard · Concordia Greenhouse · Food Against Fascism COMPOSTABLE PACKAGING · Hive Café Coop B.Y.O. DISH INCENTIVES · People's Potato · Hive Café Solidarity Coop · Waste Not, Want Not Compost · le Frigo Vert · Food Against Fascism * No longer in operation * * Now independent community project

Source: © Erik Chevrier and Kim Gagnon (Food Groups, 2019).

Figure 28.1 *Map of the student-run food organizations on Concordia University's campus*

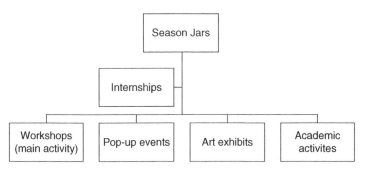

Figure 28.2 *A visual map of Season Jars' activities*

cross-disciplinary, intercultural and engaging experience that is embedded in the ELT. In the next paragraphs, some noteworthy activities will be briefly overviewed.

Season Jars offers the Concordia community opportunities to get involved with the project organization through two types of internships. The first option, which was developed in collaboration with Concordia faculty members, consists of academic integrated internships (as a requirement for course credits) for courses such as Sociology of Food,

Source: Brand design by l.goub; https://www.lgoub.com/.

Figure 28.3   Season Jars' logo

Sustainable Food Systems and Solidarity Economy. The second format does not involve academic course credits and entails interns working directly with the project's active members. The interns are encouraged to take leadership in developing and facilitating activities (i.e., a workshop, conference or pop-up event) as well as to assist in other project-related tasks.

One of the project's art exhibits, titled 'The jars can say it all'[4] aimed at creating a ludic and interactive installation at Concordia's 4TH SPACE[5] in response to the question – what is food? Aimed at mobilizing food literacy and food preservation knowledge, a physical structure formed a pathway built of shelves loaded with more than 50 Mason jars of different sizes, containing fresh and preserved food, as well as live edible plants. Walking in this space, viewers encountered themes that included seasons, people, processes, smells, tools, outcomes, evolution and the role of food in our lives. The installation aimed at questioning mainstream food narratives, at creating a space for new narratives to emerge, and to bring participants to explore and decipher stories about food. To promote future reflection and knowledge application, recipes were displayed on leaflets that visitors could bring home. Figure 28.4 presents a picture from the installation in November 2018.

Season Jars has been invited to academic events and engaged participants in several sustainability issues such as waste management, education, agriculture, community development, visualization of a Canadian national school lunch program and others. Season Jars' pop-up events share the same framework as the Seasonal Workshops series (overviewed in the next section). However, they are generally offered outside Concordia and are focused on creating ephemeral food experiences where space in the city is shared with other community organizations. This has allowed the project to interact with different sustainability initiatives around the city and to attract an intergenerational and intercultural audience to the Concordia workshops.

3.3   The Food Preservation Workshops

The Seasonal Workshops series is the main activity offered by Season Jars, and its approach to ESD is the focus of this chapter. The series is divided by seasons (i.e., summer, fall, spring and winter) in order to help the participants reconnect their food habits with nature cycles

Note: Setup at Concordia University's 4TH SPACE, November 2018.

Figure 28.4 'The jars can say it all' – Season Jars' interactive installation

through the use of seasonal ingredients and recipes. Season Jars' workshop participants comprise students (45 percent), university staff and faculty (35 percent), and the larger surrounding community (20 percent). Most workshops involve people with different cultural backgrounds and belonging to different age groups. On the community engagement aspect, it was observed that 30 percent of first-time participants return for different workshops at least a second time, and 5 percent become frequent participants. Through the course of the four years, more than five participants have facilitated their own workshops through Season Jars or through other community organizations. Additionally, more than ten students decided to volunteer in the project based on their engagement with Season Jars. Figure 28.5 shows a picture taken during a Japanese pickling workshop in late fall 2017.

The workshops consist of four main activities: (1) theoretical and recipe presentation; (2) collective kitchen; (3) food experiences; and (4) reflections. The workshops start with an introduction of the history and cultural heritage of the food preservation method presented, its health benefits and the biochemistry at play. This is followed by the presentation of the recipe(s), which also include historical, cultural, scientific, and technical dimensions. The theoretical part is usually followed by a discussion (e.g., the socio-economic, environmental or food security implications of the specific technique or recipe) where participants are encouraged to exchange knowledge. This is followed by the

Figure 28.5   Japanese pickling workshop in late fall 2017

collective kitchen, where participants collaboratively apply their theoretical knowledge to transform local, organic, and seasonal produce into recipes to take home. A food-sharing experience (which is prepared by the organizers before the workshop) helps to conclude the workshop. During this experience, participants are encouraged to reflect and discuss how the newly acquired knowledge could be applied to their daily lives. In many cases, these reflections have led participants to propose recipes they are interested to learn, food and sustainability topics that they want to know more about, as well as possible workshops that they could lead based on family or personal recipes.

4.   UNDERSTANDING SEASON JARS THROUGH THE EXISTING FRAMEWORKS

4.1   Intersecting Season Jars' Workshops with ELT and ESD

Table 28.2 presents the intersection of Season Jars' activities with the four stages of ELT and the resultant sustainability knowledge domains proposed by Frisk and Larson (2011). Table 28.3 presents the intersection of the four activities of the workshop with the

Table 28.2   *Intersecting Season Jars' activities with the four experiential learning cycle domains and the resultant sustainability knowledge domains proposed*

Components of the Learning Cycle	Season Jars' Workshop Activities			
	Theoretical and recipe presentation	Collective kitchen	Food experiences	Reflections
Abstract conceptualization (thinking)	Declarative knowledge			
Active experimentation (applying)		Procedural knowledge + Social knowledge		
Concrete experiences (experiencing)			Procedural knowledge + Effectiveness knowledge + Social knowledge	
Reflective observation (observing)				Effectiveness knowledge + Social knowledge

Source: As proposed by Frisk and Larson (2011).

six competencies proposed by Chineme et al. (2019) as well as Frisk and Larson (2011). Table 28.2 indicates that, unlike Chineme et al. (2019), who matched each domain of the ELT with one specific domain of knowledge, the activities of Season Jars were seen to be cross-cutting multiple domains. Also, our observations indicate that the food experience part of the workshop has an influential role in bridging the procedural, effectiveness, and social knowledge domains. Additionally, Table 28.3 makes clear that each sustainability competence is addressed at least twice during each workshop. It is also clear that the reflections part of the workshop, which is its conclusion, has the capacity to address five of the six competencies.

The first part of the workshop consists of the theory and recipe presentation. Even before the event takes place, this domain starts when the organizers employ theoretical research to produce declarative knowledge in the form of a handout, which is then presented to participants in an instructional format to provide the conceptualization and the directions that will guide the experience. The interdisciplinary content of the presentation addresses the systems thinking competence. It also provides an understanding of interconnectedness, long-term and foresighted thinking, and builds the participants' empathy and understanding of different worldviews.

In the collective kitchen, the application of procedural knowledge intersects with social knowledge. The participants focus on learning procedures to safely preserve food;

Table 28.3   Intersecting Season Jars' activities with the six sustainability competencies

Sustainability Competencies	Workshop Activity			
	Theoretical and recipe presentation	Collective kitchen	Food experiences	Reflection discussion
(1) Systems thinking and an understanding of interconnectedness	✓		✓	
(2) Long-term and foresighted thinking	✓			✓
(3) Stakeholder engagement and group collaboration		✓	✓	✓
(4) Action-orientation and change-agent skills		✓		✓
(5) Empathy and understanding of different worldviews and relationships	✓		✓	✓
(6) Critical thinking and decision-making capacity within complexity		✓		✓

Sources: As proposed by Chineme et al. (2019) and Frisk and Larson (2011).

they also are given information about where the ingredients came from, to understand the social motivations behind the recipes. They are encouraged to apply their own past experiences in order to exert change to the procedures collectively or individually. This approach to collective cooking develops the participants' group collaboration, action-orientation and change-agent skills, and helps in building their decision-making capacity within complexity competences.

Food experiences interrelate procedural knowledge, effectiveness knowledge and social knowledge. In a conversational arrangement, participants recognize the effectiveness of different actions. They also have the opportunity to enquire for clarification on the procedural knowledge experimented. While food and intercultural ideas are being shared, participants engage in sensorial food experience where knowledge is held in their bodies. This mixed experience speaks to the understanding of interconnectedness, stakeholder engagement, empathy and understanding of different worldviews and relationship competences.

The reflections part interrelates effectiveness and social knowledge. To conclude, the workshop participants are asked to draw a connection between the experience and their own world and lives, reflecting on how to make the knowledge applicable. The reflection allows the participants to critically assess their experience and to decide how their new knowledge can be developed or help in the development of others. This addresses almost all the sustainability competences since the reflection is future driven and transformational focused rather than reflective on the specific knowledge acquired during the workshop.

4.2 Understanding the Roles of Participants and Organizers

In their chapter in the *SAGE Handbook*, Alice Kolb and David Kolb (2009) focus attention on the roles of educators across the four domains of the ELT – with the educator moving between subject expert (to help organize learners' reflection), evaluator (to set standards and help learners meet performance requirements), coach (to help learners apply knowledge), and facilitator (to help learners get in touch with their personal experience). While their chapter's focus on formal education in HEIs dictated the exploration of the educators' roles, in the context of co-learning and participatory learning environments, there is a space to investigate the roles of both educators (organizers) and learners (participants).

In order to understand the general methodology for Season Jars' workshops, these shifting roles have been specifically investigated. The aim was to explore the process that allows for shifts in the roles of educators and learners within the same workshop. Such shifts enable the participants to build capacity and future expertise. By juxtaposing the roles played by both parties, the workshop's specific approach can be clearly visualized in Figure 28.6. In the first phases, the participants are seen to be learners and the expert knowledge (relating to the theory, science, history, and culture) is being conveyed to them by the organizers. However, as the workshop progresses to the collective kitchen, the participants' role evolves to include sharing their knowledge and experiences about

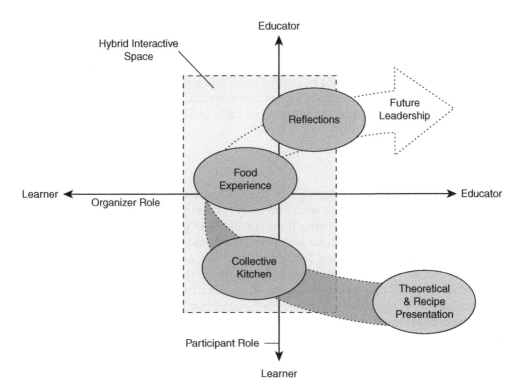

Figure 28.6 The shifting roles between organizers and participants within the workshops

the subject matter. This, in turn, sets the space for the collective food experiences and the reflections to naturally emerge as a participatory and co-created process challenging the linearity of other more traditional workshop approaches.

4.3   Making Dynamic Space(s) for Sustainability

The dialectics shown in Figure 28.6 between the workshop organizers and the participants provide a space for a dynamic learning experience. The shifting roles between organizers and participants allow for the activities to address multiple sustainability knowledge domains and competencies simultaneously. This, in turn, can accelerate the participants' move towards action – as seen in the cases where participants returned to learn in more workshops, to be involved as interns, or even to lead their own workshops. This organization would empower a participant to take on future leadership roles, such as organizing future workshops, mobilizing other members of the community, or personally combining the experiences with their own fields of study. On the other hand, the workshop is also a possibility for the organizers to move towards new future leadership roles, such as developing new materials based on the collective reflections and exploring new means to disseminate the knowledge created in the workshops (such as in exhibitions or academic publications).

The workshops create what we defined as a 'hybrid learning space'. In this intermediate space, there are continuous changes and shifts in the roles between educators and learners. Such shifts can allow participants to recognize themselves as 'contributory experts' (Collins and Evans, 2007; Trépos, 1996) – at the same level as the organizers – in a specific subject matter during the workshop experience. The intersections presented in Tables 28.2 and 28.3, which are built on the foundation of food scholarship as a medium for ESD, present the effectiveness of Season Jars' workshop approach. It could be said that while the participants' knowledge might be limited when it comes to food preservation and/or workshop facilitation, the sustainability competencies are, in fact, the specific expertise they build during the workshop (as proposed in Table 28.3).

5.   CONCLUSION

This research aimed at understanding how collective and student-led activities can support the creation of sustainability spaces on university campuses. The research provided an overview of the literature pertaining to sustainability on university campuses, experiential learning and food as medium for sustainability knowledge development. By focusing on the workshop model of Season Jars, the chapter uses auto-ethnographic methods to confront the frameworks and models available in the literature with a real-life example. The findings revealed that the creative application of ELT and ESD can help strengthen the sustainability competencies of participants, accelerate the uptake of transformative action, and most importantly overcome the knowledge-to-action gap reported in the literature.

Conducting this research has given project members an opportunity to contextualize and assess Season Jars' approach to sustainability education and to provide a deeper understanding of the project's alignment with existing frameworks. The organizer's self-reflection about the outcomes for the people involved can assist in intersectional discussions about the recognition of roles, spaces and agency that can be wielded by individuals within a community. The dynamic role shifting presented in this experience has shown agent-action empowerment features that can promote social and physical occupation of existing spaces for the creation of sustainability hubs. The systematic documentation helped explore the role that the project's activities play in capacity building for transformative action. The project's innovative ESD framework can be adopted in other university communities in order to help close the current knowledge–action gap.

To further propel transformative actions for sustainability on universities campus, Season Jars will also seek to document and understand further the role of faculty collaboration experiences in the capacity-building model. This might require investigating the outcomes of co-created internships and developing frameworks to understand how academic courses can better integrate experiential learning in ESD using food transformation as the medium. Instead of aiming at structuring and normalizing approaches to sustainability on campuses, future research should focus on understanding the dynamics at play in active student- or community-led projects. In addition to making social spaces (such as activities and projects) and physical spaces (such as meeting rooms or sustainability research offices), Season Jars' workshop model highlighted that activating the transformation towards the 'sustainable university' requires exploring hybrid learning spaces that are dynamic, adaptive, inclusive. and exploratory.

NOTES

1. See https://www.schoollunchorder.ca/. Accessed November 2019.
2. See https://ca.sodexo.com/home.html. Accessed November 2019.
3. See https://www.aramark.ca/. Accessed November 2019.
4. 'Season Jars food preservation project'. Accessed November 2019 at https://www.whatisfoodexhibit.com/copy-of-project-6.
5. 'Virtual 4TH SPACE'. Accessed November 2019 at https://www.concordia.ca/next-gen/4th-space.html.

REFERENCES

Bennell, S. 2008. Going local for a change: towards a community food security approach to farm-to-university development at Concordia University, Montreal, Quebec. Master's thesis, Concordia University.

Brady, Jennifer. 2011. 'Cooking as inquiry: a method to stir up prevailing ways of knowing food, body, and identity.' *International Journal of Qualitative Methods*, 10 (4), 321–34.

Burns, Heather and Weston Miller. 2012. 'The Learning Gardens Laboratory: teaching sustainability and developing sustainable food systems through unique partnerships.' *Journal of Agriculture, Food Systems, and Community Development*, 2 (3), 69–78.

Chen, Qiong, Keiko Goto and Cindy Wolff et al. 2014. 'Cooking up diversity: impact of a multicomponent, multicultural, experiential intervention on food and cooking behaviors among elementary-school students from low-income ethnically diverse families.' *Appetite*, 80, 114–22.

Chineme, Atinuke, Irene Herremans and Stace Wills. 2019. 'Building leadership competencies for the SDGs through community/university experiential learning.' *Journal of Sustainability Research*, 1 (2), Article e190028.

Collins, Harry and Robert Evans. 2007. *Rethinking Expertise*. Chicago, IL: The University of Chicago Press.

Concordia Food Coalition (CFC). 2013. *A Guide to Concordia's Food System: Current Operations & Future Directions*. Accessed November 2019 at http://concordiafoodgroups.ca/wp-content/uploads/2018/05/A--Guide-to-Concordias-Food-System-2013.pdf.

Conti, Cecilia, Annamaria Costa and Claudia Maria Balzaretti et al. 2018. 'Survey on food preferences of university students: from tradition to new food customs?', *Agriculture*, 8 (10), 1–12.

Coyne, Richard. 2005. 'Wicked problems revisited.' *Design Studies*, 26 (1), 5–17.

Didham, Robert J. and Paul Ofei-Manu. 2015. 'The role of education in the sustainable development agenda: empowering a learning society for sustainability through quality education.' In Institute for Global Environmental Strategies (IGES), *Achieving the Sustainable Development Goals: From Agenda to Action* (pp. 94–129). Kanagawa, Japan: Institute for Global Environmental Strategies.

Engler-Stringer, Rachel and Shawna Berenbaum. 2005. 'Collective kitchens in Canada: a review of the literature.' *Canadian Journal of Dietetic Practice and Research*, 66 (4), 246–51.

Food Groups. 2019. Concordia Food Groups Research Project. Archived by Erik Chevrier and Kim Gagnon. Accessed November 2019 at http://concordiafoodgroups.ca/the-project/.

Frisk, Erin and Kelli L. Larson. 2011. 'Educating for sustainability: competencies & practices for transformative action.' *Journal of Sustainability Education*, 2. Accessed 26 February 2021 at http://www.jsedimensions.org/wordpress/wp-content/uploads/2011/03/FriskLarson2011.pdf.

Goubran, Sherif. 2019. 'On the role of construction in achieving the SDGs.' *Journal of Sustainability Research*, 1 (2), 1–52.

Goubran, Sherif, Gilbert Emond and Carmela Cucuzzella. 2017. 'Understanding regional sustainability in the built environment.' Paper presented at the 2nd ARTEM Organisational Creativity and Sustainability International Conference, Nancy, France.

Gupta, Joyeeta and Courtney Vegelin. 2016. 'Sustainable Development Goals and inclusive development.' *International Environmental Agreements: Politics, Law and Economics*, 16 (3), 433–48.

Heldke, Lisa. 1988. 'Recipes for theory making.' *Hypatia*, 3 (2), 15–30.

Ingram, Mrill. 2012. 'Sculpting solutions: art–science collaborations in sustainability.' *Environment: Science and Policy for Sustainable Development*, 54 (4), 24–34.

Isaku, Taichi and Takashi Iba. 2015. 'Creative CoCooking patterns: a pattern language for creative collaborative cooking.' *EuroPloP '15: Proceedings of the 20th European Conference on Pattern Languages of Programs*, pp. 1–17.

Kolb, David A. 1984. *Experiential Learning: Experience as the Source of Learning and Development*. Upper Saddle River, NJ: Prentice-Hall Inc.

Kolb, Alice Y. and David A. Kolb. 2009. 'Experiential learning theory: a dynamic, holistic approach to management learning, education and development.' In Steve J. Armstrong and Cynthia V. Fukami (eds), *The SAGE Handbook of Management Learning, Education and Development* (pp. 42–68). London: SAGE Publications.

Le Blanc, David. 2015. 'Towards integration at last? The Sustainable Development Goals as a network of targets.' *DESA Working Paper No. 41*, ST/ESA/2015/DWP/141.

Maher, Judith and Sarah Burkhart. 2017. 'Experiential learning for engaging nutrition undergraduates with sustainability.' *International Journal of Sustainability in Higher Education*, 18 (7), 1108–22.

Nilsson, Måns, Elinor Chisholm and David Griggs et al. 2018. 'Mapping interactions between the Sustainable Development Goals: lessons learned and ways forward.' *Sustainability Science*, 13 (6), 1489–503.

Rittel, Horst W.J. and Melvin M. Webber. 1973. 'Dilemmas in a general theory of planning.' *Policy Sciences*, 4, 155–69.

Rosentrater, Kurt and Brianna Burke. 2017. 'University students and sustainability. Part 1: Attitudes, perceptions, and habits.' *Journal of Sustainability Education*, 16. Accessed 26 February 2021 at http://www.susted.com/wordpress/wp-content/uploads/2018/01/Rosentrater-Burke-JSE-General-Fall-2017-PDF.pdf.

Rowe, Debra. 2007. 'Education for a sustainable future.' *Science*, 317 (5836), 323–4.

Silverthorn, Drew. 2016. *Hungry for Knowledge: Assessing the Prevalence of Student Food Insecurity on Five Canadian Campuses*. Toronto, ON: Meal Exchange.

Sommer, Doris and Pauline Strong. 2016. 'Theory follows from practice: lessons from the field.' *University of Toronto Quarterly*, 85 (4), 67–81.

Sonetti, Giulia, Patrizia Lombardi and Lorenzo Chelleri. 2016. 'True green and sustainable university campuses? Toward a clusters approach.' *Sustainability*, 8 (1), 1–23.

Trépos, Jean-Yves. 1996. *Que sais-je? La sociologie de l'expertise*. Paris: Presses Universitaires de France.

Tsuji, Natsuko, Kasuen Mauldin, Angela Clinton and Cassie Barmore. 2018. 'Effect of multicultural cooking classes on cultural competency of university students.' *Journal of Cultural Diversity*, 25 (4), 136–41.

United Nations. 2015. *Transforming Our World: The 2030 Agenda for Sustainable Development*. New York: UN.

Washington-Ottombre, Camille and Siiri Bigalke. 2018. 'An aggregated and dynamic analysis of innovations in campus sustainability.' *International Journal of Sustainability in Higher Education*, 19 (2), 353–75.

29. Taday's agrofestive calendar – Ecuador: a methodology for creating a sustainability experience with a dialogue of knowledge approach

María Fernanda Acosta Altamirano,
Verónica Gabriela Tacuri Albarracín and
Erika Gabriela Araujo Pérez

1. INTRODUCTION: CONSTRUCTING A SUSTAINABLE METHODOLOGY

This chapter presents the results of the project entitled 'Ancestral knowledge and social and technological innovation of farmers, relatives of community farmers in Cañar, for the intercultural and inter-scientific dialogue, in the conceptual framework of the ecology of knowledge and the new pedagogical model' of the National University of Education (UNAE) in Ecuador. It aims to revitalize ancestral wisdom and knowledge in order to encourage social innovation. Furthermore, it also aims to produce educational materials and actions. All this is focused on the perspective of intercultural recognition, knowledge exchange and a dialogue among epistemes.

This project was carried out in the parish of San Andrés de Taday. In this parish, it is vital that its knowledge and traditions are shared with other communities. The purpose of this movement is to help revitalize the local knowledge and therefore strengthen the identity of the local people. The aim was to investigate and understand the agricultural and festive calendar based on the communitarian workshops that are focused on participatory action research (Fals Borda, 2008). *Chacareros* or *chacareras*[1] use this calendar to structure their family agroforestry systems, better known as *chakras*.[2] The *chakra* system derives from Andean knowledge and perceives the practice of farming through the Kichwa[3] vision of life. This approach is based on the logic of sustainability as the agricultural activity is aligned and balanced with the needs of the environment.

The main purpose of this chapter is to explore and gather information regarding the agricultural and festival calendar of Taday. This methodology acknowledges that the oral culture comprises certain practices that are part of the Andean cosmovision, or worldview. Stories and tales from the oral culture expose the social memory and identity of a place.

The methodology used was participatory action research (PAR, or IAP in Spanish). PAR generates collective processes in which the results of the research are the constant dialogue between the scholars and the community. In this kind of research, the community does not take a passive role but is the central actor in both scenarios – as part of the community and as part of the research team. From this logic, PAR generates results that are immediately given back to the community in order to break with academic extractivism[4] and ensure a more participative role in the community. In PAR, the community and the scholars share their experiences and expertise to create a participative process. This project aims to generate ideas for change and social emancipation in the development of the research.

First, this chapter will show the dimensions of sustainability that were present in the application of the agricultural and festive calendar and, second, will go into depth about this calendar. Finally, it will explain the methodology of the gathering of information on Taday's agricultural and festive calendar.

2.   SUSTAINABILITY AND THE AGRICULTURAL AND FESTIVE CALENDAR

Sustainability is related to economic, sociocultural and environmental harmony. However, despite the relevance of this concept, this is not a conscious activity. In other words, the process of sustainability of resources at a global level is not very efficient, which compromises the level and quality of life of future generations. In this sense, if the problems are analyzed from this perspective, the solutions will be centered in the whole ensemble of relations that are produced around the natural resources. Solutions need to be based on an understanding of the basic needs of the population – from extraction to transformation, distribution, access, consumption and waste production.

With respect to socioeconomic sustainability, the levels of inequality in the Ecuadorian population have increased in the last two decades. Poverty has not reduced as expected as it has not been possible to halt the loss of biodiversity and the degradation of the land; improve access to sustainable water, both in terms of quality and quantity; guarantee food security and encourage a sustainable way to farm and a responsible way to fish; value environmental services; build an economy of low-carbon consumption; and reduce poverty and social inequality, among others (Carabias, 2013).

The Impact of Development and Sustainability Interruption

Worldwide, the population is overwhelmed because of the economical, sociocultural and environmental crisis, so the issue of sustainable development is on hold. This has led to a limited number of resources with regard to sustainable development. As a result, this has made it more complicated to develop a model of sustainability to solve this complex crisis.

Globalization and technology are two of the biggest revolutions of this era and they have created previously unconceivable opportunities for the development of society. However, these have also favored overconsumption and have increased the abuse of natural resources. This is why, despite the research, it has been said that humanity has paid a high price for the existence of the planet and its species. This means that some biophysical limits have been broken – the same limits that have preserved the environment and civilization for millions of years. In an evaluation of the ecosystems over the millennia, it is estimated that 15 out of 24 of the most important environmental services have exceeded their sustainability (Carabias, 2013), including mitigation of greenhouse gas emissions, conservation of biodiversity and protection of water resources.

For this reason, if people do not reduce their overconsumption of natural resources, Carabias (2013) predicted that by 2050 this problem will worsen due to the world's popula-

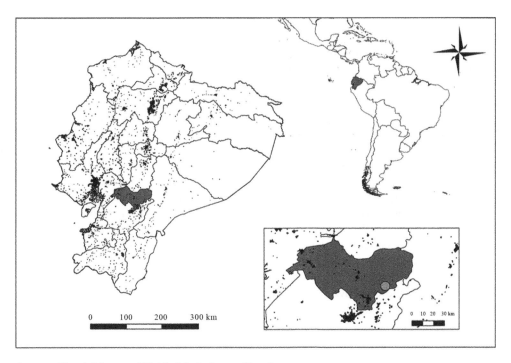

Source: Google Maps, modified by María Acosta Altamirano.

Figure 29.1 *Right: location of Ecuador in Latin America; left: geographical location of the province of Cañar; inset: geographical location of San Andrés de Taday parish*

tion increasing by around about 3 billion inhabitants who will need more food, water, raw materials and energy. To this must be added approximately 1.4 billion people who currently live in extreme poverty and who don't have access to water (ibid.). The situation will become critical.

Settlers in the parish of San Andrés de Taday, located in Cañar province (Figure 29.1), preserve the Andean traditions and culture from their origins to the present. They are and were *chacarero/chacarera* cultures. They are also dedicated to the production of a diverse combination of native plants and animals (polyculture) on each of the *chakras*, each of which has its own knowledge about raising plants and animals (knowledge that is transmitted from the *Taytas*[5]). It has always been, and always will be, their main activity and source of economic support, which makes this situation economically, socially and environmentally sustainable. Ancestral knowledge that has been passed down from antiquity to the present includes culture, agricultural knowledge and caring for the environment. These elements have preserved the balance of the ecological systems and subsystems.

One of the components of environmental sustainability is the compatibility of activities with the preservation of biodiversity and ecosystems, and also with an analysis of the impact of these activities on the environment. The latter determines whether they are positive or negative for environmental sustainability, whether they are positive for the present and future and focus on ecological harmony by using friendly and green technology.

To promote the management and use of natural resources, a compilation of knowledge and ancestral traditions is captured in the parish's agrofestive calendar (Figure 29.2). This includes the polyculture of corn, sowing dates, lunar phases, native varieties, production of traditional food (chicken soup, potatoes with roasted guinea pig and *chicha de jora*[6]) as the primary basis of the culture of the eastern communities of Cañar province. All these activities found within the backdrop of traditional polyculture ensure that these traditions have become sustainable to keep the ecosystems, culture and economy stable.

To address the additional demands of future increases in population, it is necessary to duplicate food production and also triple the percentage of water access. This means that under the current situation, it is not possible in biophysical terms (Carabias, 2013). It must be mentioned, however, that Ecuador is considered one of the richest countries in terms of biodiversity and ecosystems worldwide. As a result of its privileged geographical position and the presence of Andes mountains, there is a wide diversity of forests and microclimate. The fact that Ecuador has an immense variety of ecological zones and natural resources has allowed the population to cater to the basic needs not only of Ecuadorians but also worldwide.

In the National Development Plan, the *Plan Nacional del Buen Vivir 2013-2017 de Ecuador*, one of the objectives is to 'guarantee the rights of nature and promote the environmental, territorial and global sustainability'. Considering that one of the biggest advantages of this country is its biodiversity, it is vital to understand how to make the most of it through its conservation and sustainable use. For this reason, Ecuador is the first Latin American country to adopt the strong indicators of sustainability included in national planification. Additionally, Ecuador also estimates its ecological footprint and biocapacity, supported by official data (Ministerio del Ambiente, 2015). These indicators include an objective to measure sustainability called 'Gap between ecological footprint and biocapacity', as the country must ensure that it does not surpass the ecological limits that have been set as objectives to avoid an ecological deficit. To do this, an inter-institutional committee will be created to analyze, formulate, articulate and implement the policies that promote the management and use of natural resources, the development of productive activities and the adoption of measures to reduce the ecological footprint and preserve biocapacity. In doing so, it aims to prevent an ecological overshoot (ibid.).

While it is true that the concept of sustainability comes from the western world, it also makes sense in the Andean worldview that understands it as *alli kawsay*, a concept from Kichwa that means 'good living'. This breaks the anthropocentric paradigm and understands humankind as a living and sacred being in Nature. In this sense, this chapter is also a dialogue of knowledge in which the concepts of *alli kawsay* and sustainability are discussed within different epistemes and with a common goal.

3.   THE AGROFESTIVE CALENDAR IN THE ANDEAN COMMUNITY

Throughout history, ancestral and agronomic knowledge from communities has resulted in the creation of a calendar (as guidance) to optimize daily activities. These kinds of calendars are the source of the culture and history of the whole population of the community. They entwine with the knowledge of nature so that that settlers can observe,

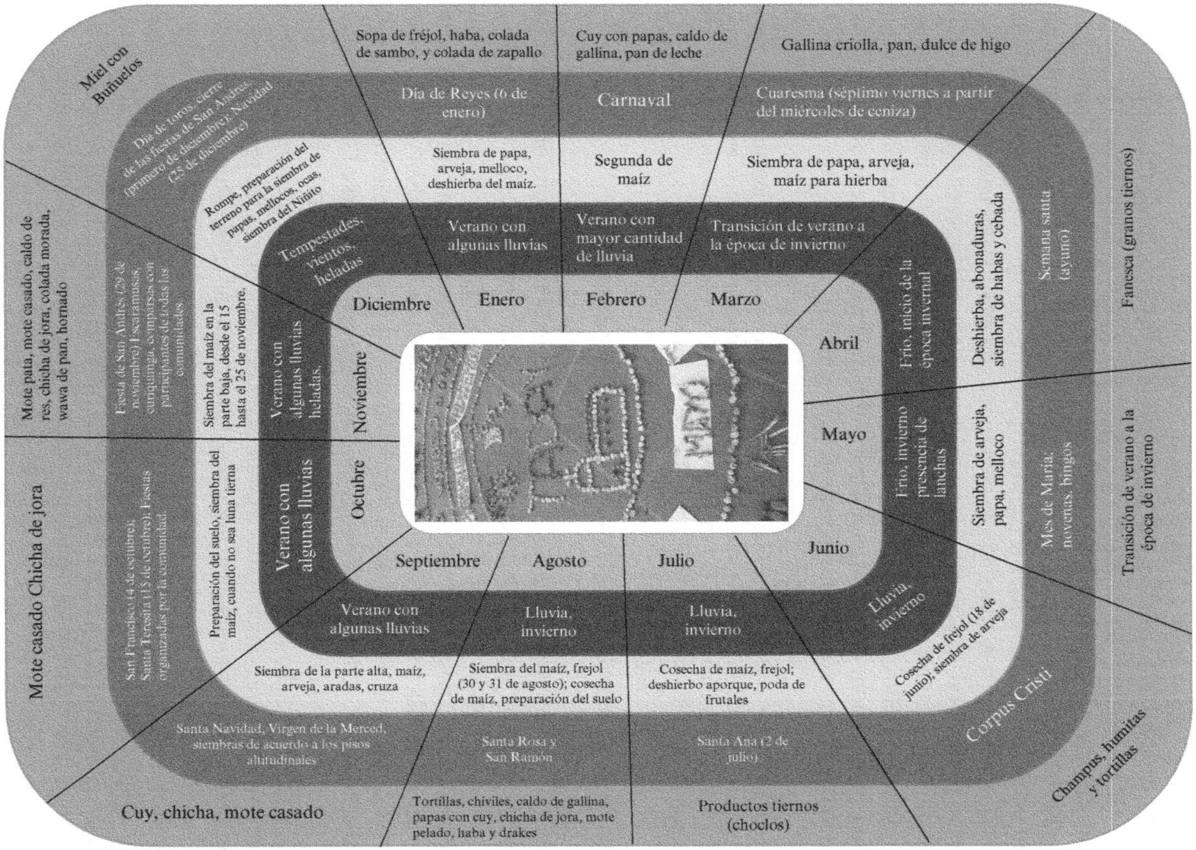

Source: Modification by Verónica Tacuri Albarracín.

Figure 29.2 Taday's agrofestive calendar

understand and interpret the signs of nature to prepare for the production of their land. In this sense, this process is developed according to the rhythms and cycles of the natural environment.

The local communities have ensured that the ancestral knowledge is integrated and passed down through generations. This is why agrofestive calendars are 'cyclic experiences that show the activities that take place in each farming stage, exposing the cosmovision of every farmer to nurture the diversity of crop; taking into consideration the songs, rituals and festivities of each moment' (Proyecto Andino de Tecnologías Campesinas [PRATEC], 2009, p. 57). In other words, these activities are closely linked with the natural environment and the cosmos, which the peasants internalize in agricultural labor from the sowing and the crops. Every activity has its own space and rite – transcendental processes that contribute to the food security of the population of the settlement.

Therefore, it is a collective nurturing that allows to the community to be, feel and act from the universe of nature and in doing so, make decisions around agriculture, raising animals, food preparation, ancestral medicine and handicrafts. These processes, along with the Andean cosmovision, create the agrofestive calendar:

> It is called agrofestive calendar because the Andean communities live nurturing the farm [*chakra*], at the same time this farm nurtures them, and this mutual nurturing is a celebration. A celebration that every moment is shared collectively with the community and with Mother Earth [*Pachamama*].[7] (PRATEC, 2009, p. 57)

The Importance of Time and the Cycles of the Agrofestive Calendar

There is a pairing of time and space that is related to periods and seasons of the year. In the calendar, the most important stages that regulate the dynamic cycle of each ritual are highlighted, mainly summer and winter. These cyclic periods represent stages of production and agricultural activities that are developed according to each month through the year. In this respect, Guilcamaigua and Chancusig (2008) stated that 'when we talk about the agrofestive calendar in the indigenous communities and peasant communities, we talk about the events, space, tempo of the land [*pacha*] entwined and marked for the cyclic walking of the sun in a lapse of time known as the year' (p. 8). There is an integrality of knowledge related to the activities of the community members, stemming from the climatic events of each era, which leads to established periods such as the rainy season or corn-growing time. As a consequence, the time of the calendar allows the community to know and find the most favorable day to hold celebrations, family or community reunions and to sow or harvest. In other words, it is a way to honor the land, or as Guilcamaigua and Chancusig state (2008): 'the peasant calendar is a living farmer network that is made for the families, nature and what is sacred' (p. 9). In this respect, there are unexpected moments of interaction that at the same time will transmit the ancestral knowledge and wisdom to the new generations.

In this sense, the agrofestive calendar is closely related to the farm. This is a substantial element of the Andean cosmovision because it resignifies creation, caring and life. In this cultural space, the Andeans became guardians, protectors of nature, crops, stars and people close to them. It is important to mention that 'the farm, understood as something else than an agricultural space is a scene of nurture because of the diversity of forms of life that converse to contribute to the regeneration of themselves' (Villares and Villares, 2012, p. 26). This is why the calendar includes an infinity of forms such as animals, divinities and ceremonies, among others.

The Agrofestive Calendar of the Sierra Region

The agrofestive calendar in this region of Ecuador is linked with the agro-ecological processes established in the country that include a diversity of ecosystems and ancestral culture. One of these systems is the Andean farm or *chakra*, largely worked in the Kichwa indigenous communities of the Andean Highlands (Ecuador, Bolivia, Peru). This process includes the management of a diversity of climate zones and their adaptation through the awareness of the land and its elements. It has a system of seed production that allows the growing of crops and raising of animals. At the same time, it is expressed in the agrofestive calendar. Its validity and permanence can be seen in the festival of Inti Raymi where the *chakra* is assumed as a space of ancestral agricultural practice (Intriago and Gortaire, 2016).

Special Features of the Elaboration of the Agrofestive Calendar

The first fundamental element is cohabitation of the natural and cultural environment, knowing how to relate harmoniously with the environment to discover the time, space, activities, rituals and moments that guarantee the food security of the whole community. In general, agrofestive calendars are characterized by their cyclic experiences that are linked to a variety of crops, stages and rituals and therefore are created from the knowledge and testimonies of the community, farmers and ranchers. Villares Aysabucha and Villares Aysabucha (2012) state that the agrofestive calendar must have:

- climatic periods;
- months of the year;
- chakra activities;
- agricultural activities;
- rituals and festivities of the community;
- cyclical direction of time and agro-astronomy systems.

4.   THE APPROACHES AND THE GATHERING OF INFORMATION: FROM ORALITY TO THE STRENGTHENING OF LOCAL KNOWLEDGE

The main approach in this investigation is aligned with participatory action research (PAR). This is a methodology that draws on the work of Fals Borda. Borda questions the role of academia, value neutrality and research independence. He says that, from the beginning, a political positioning must exist, and it is necessary to 'formalize alternative procedures of research and action focused on regional and local concerns that required political, educative and cultural emancipatory processes' (Fals Borda, 2008, p. 2). He is opposed to the commercialization or materialization of human phenomena that occur in 'the traditional way of doing research and also in the developmental policies' (ibid.). This vindicates the need to reassess the relationship between the 'scholar' and the 'object of study', as it takes into account the need to recognize the subject as social actor in a symmetrical relationship and in equality with the scholar within their condition as human beings. Therefore, the work done in this project is based on participative workshops with the community, in which verbal information was collected on the knowledge of these practices.

A commonality that this research has with PAR is the need to generate knowledge that can be given back to the community and, in doing so, encourages actions of transformation in society and breaks with the 'academic extractivism' that is centered only in the production of academic papers and the recognition of the scholar. In this sense, the information collected in the workshops was used by the local government to create a leaflet about the calendar and also to share the information around the parish in written form – knowledge that was previously was only found in the memories of the ancient people.

The Gathering of Information Processes

The UNAE is a university interested in approaches through dialogue among different kinds of knowledge in which there is an interaction between the positivist epistemes and those that come from ancestral knowledge. This is a way to build the community of the university from a point of view of sustainability and in concordance with the cultural diversity of Ecuador. In this context, in the first stage of this research, the family members from 23 *chakras* (from a total of 25 – 23 family farms and two from educative institutions) who used an agroecological approach in accordance with the ancestral knowledge, were called to three workshops that were run in Taday with the objective of systematically understanding that local knowledge. A team of researchers from the project followed this process.[8] The objective of these three workshops was to generate a process of revitalization of local ancestral knowledge.

The first workshop took place on 2 May 2017. The participants were divided into three groups to work on two elements: (1) knowledge about the use of cultural beliefs with respect to celestial bodies such as *inti, killa, kuyllur, allpa, tamia, wayra, kuychi* (these names are taken from Kichwa and they mean sun, moon, stars, earth, rain, wind, rainbow); (2) important dates based on the agricultural activities through the agricultural year. In the first workshop, weather, natural phenomena and agricultural activities were identified as key themes. These relations are periodical as these agricultural cycles are ruled by environmental changes.

The second workshop was carried out on 6 June 2017. The participants of this meeting were the same as those in the first workshop. The purpose of this second stage was to follow up and expand further on the work done in the first workshop. The results of this meeting was to collect information per month:

- weather particularities (weather, celestial bodies and nature phenomena);
- current agricultural activity of the cycle (activity, main crop and associative crops);
- current traditional celebrations of each month;
- current food from both daily meals and celebrations.

This process shows that all the activities in Taday are articulated with agricultural practices due to the fact that the traditional festivities are celebrated in sowing season, with the main focus being gratitude for the success of the harvest. These celebrations are a demonstration of cultural syncretism that fuses Catholic festivities and ancestral beliefs that are also linked with the land. Food choices are also dependent on agriculture – for example, in times of harvesting the traditional dishes will be made with fresh ingredients. On the other hand, during the rest of the year, these dishes will comprise dry grains or flour as the main ingredients.

The final workshop was on 28 September 2017. The result of this meeting was to collect information about the cycle of plants, reproduction of animals, cultivation techniques and varieties of products, as well as types of land and its uses. This information helped to understand the direct relationship between the land, animals and plants. One of the important findings of this workshop was the finding that animals and plants are part of an ecosystem that is ruled by land cycles and natural phenomena.

In summary, the research processes used in this project that included the participation not only of the scholars but also of the community is an important contribution to consolidating traditional knowledge. The effort to collect this information that was part of the orality of the community and write a document that can be shared and socialized is a way to revitalize the memory of these practices within the parish. Through the agrofestive calendar, the community understands the processes better and the relation between culture and land. From the cosmovision of the culture of Kichwa communities, the farm is an agricultural space with a holistic and integral dimension:

> It is a territory in which the Andean ecosophy is practiced. It is the space where life is recreated and conjugates the ability and creativity of the *runa*[9] with the productive capacity of the land – *runa* is the sower and grower and the *Pachamama* is the producer – it is a duality. (Rosero, Aguilar and Duchi, 2017, p. 59)

In this, the representations of the world in which the earth is more than land are entwined and transmitted. It is the *Pachamama*, the Mother Earth. This perception generates a relationship that is more respectful and more harmonious with nature, present in the Andean ecosophy.

5. CONCLUSIONS

This work of the UNAE in San Andrés de Taday parish describes a process that aims to revitalize ancestral knowledge of the community. The information gathering has been done through the collaboration and participation of scholars and members of the community. The results of this research have transformed oral practices that are part of the memory of Taday into written language. This leaflet is currently used for educational purposes in Vicente Rocafuerte School and Andrés Guritave high school where the students, scholars, teachers and families make vegetable patches for educational purposes. This material is also used for the families that participate to remember the agricultural periods, festivity dates and gastronomy, among others.

This agrofestive calendar that regulates the *chakra* is part of the memory and the ancestral cosmovision of the Andean communities. This calendar is a reference to the organization of time and shows the perception of time and space related to the sacred. The *Pachamama* is not only land as an element of nature, but also Mother Earth, an alive and sacred being. From this understanding of reality, sustainability is always present due to the community of Taday reproducing the ancestral knowledge of agriculture. This represents their harmonious relation with the earth. Most of the crops of Taday are produced without using any agricultural chemicals. These are not monocultures focused on productivity; on the contrary, they are produced in family *chakras* with polyculture that preserves the idea of association of plants and the preservation of the crops that are part of ancestral knowledge.

NOTES

1. *Literally*, farmers, male (*chacareros*) or female (*chacareras*), who are dedicated to agricultural work in the *chakras* (see note 2).
2. An traditional agroforestry production system with integral and holistic dimensions of Andean origins.
3. Indigenous peoples of Ecuador and also the name of the language of these peoples.
4. To use research information in order to publish and not to give it back to the community.
5. *Tayta* means father in Kichwa. It refers to a person full of wisdom and knowledge.
6. Drink of macerated corn – corn beer.
7. Concept taken from Kichwa that describes 'mother or earth world'.
8. Research team: Erika Gabriela Araujo Pérez, Gerardo Valdez, Josefina Aguilar, Fernando Rosero, María Fernanda Acosta Altamirano and Antonio Duchi.
9. *Runa*: human being in Kichwa.

REFERENCES

Carabias, J. (2013). 'La sustentabilidad ambiental: un reto para el desarrollo'. *Oikos*. Accessed October 2019 at http://web.ecologia.unam.mx/oikos3.0/index.php/todos-los-numeros/articulos-anteriores/76-sustentabilidad-ambiental.
Fals Borda, O. (2008). 'Orígenes universales y retos actuales de la IAP (investigación acción participativa)'. *Peripecias*, No. 110.
Guilcamaigua, D. and Chancusig, E. (2008). *El calendario agrofestivo: una propuesta metodológica para el diálogo de saberes*. Quito: HEIFER ECUADOR.
Intriago, R. and Gortaire, R. (2016). 'Agroecología en el Ecuador. Proceso histórico, logros y desafíos'. *Agroecología*, No. 11, 95–103.
Ministerio del Ambiente. (2015). 'Ecuador: un país que toma decisiones hacia la sustentabilidad para prevenir el sobregiro ecológico'. Accessed October 2019 at http://www.ambiente.gob.ec/ecuador-un-pais-que-toma-decisiones-hacia-la-sustentabilidad-para-prevenir-el-sobregiro-ecologico/.
Proyecto Andino de Tecnologías Campesinas (PRATEC) (2009). *Calendario agrofestivo en comunidades andino-amazónicas y escuela*. Lima: PRATEC.
Rosero, F., Aguilar, J. and Duchi, A. (2017). 'La huerta UNAE, un espacio pedagógico innovador'. *Mamakuna*, No. 6.
Villares Aysabucha, M.O. and Villares Aysabucha, E.O. (2012). El proceso de educación ambiental a través del calendario agrofestivo andino como estrategia de respeto a los saberes y conocimientos ancestrales en la comunidad de Apatug San Pablo. Thesis, Escuela Superior Politécnica de Chimborazo.

30. Free online spaces for learning and awareness in the sustainability field: the Universidade da Coruña (Spain) project

María Alló, Carmen Gago-Cortés, Ángeles Longarela-Ares and Estefanía Mourelle

1. THE ROLE OF EDUCATION IN SUSTAINABILITY

Over the last decades, many organizations have warned of the serious deterioration that the Earth's ecosystems suffer due to human activity. World population is increasing, but natural resources are limited. The production model has begun to be called into question, especially after different Earth Summits in the 1970s. Therefore, raising concern and awareness about this problem becomes a major global question, as well as becoming responsible for what we do in the present and what will be the legacy for future generations. This necessarily involves a change of individual and collective attitudes in order to stop the problem, as societies must learn to live together following sustainable principles (United Nations Educational, Scientific and Cultural Organization [UNESCO], 2013). It is within this framework that education becomes a major actor.

Education promotes the acquisition of competencies, abilities and skills, and is also a mechanism for knowledge absorption; education improves absorptive capacity, which is the ability to recognize the value of new external information, to assimilate it, and to apply it (Cohen and Levinthal, 1990). This fact would lead to the change of attitude already mentioned and to the development of actions in a sustainable environment. Moreover, education becomes one of the main ways to make the problem visible, apart from trying to correct it.

The positive effects of education can be observed in all areas around us. Importantly, education plays a central role in economic well-being, as well as increasing the human capital inherent in the labour force of a country (Hanushek and Wößmann, 2010). Promoting education has a clear positive effect on poverty reduction and economic growth. In this sense, the effects of education on economic development and growth have been widely studied (Marquez-Ramos and Mourelle, 2019). Moreover, education has a positive impact on health and social equity, as well as on civic participation and political stability (Didham and Ofei-Manu, 2015). According to Carneiro (1996, p. 202), 'education systems are a source of human capital (Becker), cultural capital (Bourdieu), and social capital (Putnam)'.

Furthermore, education is a key factor for implementing sustainable human development because of the positive benefits that can be derived from achieving the development goals (Didham and Ofei-Manu, 2015). Lutz, Muttarak and Striessnig (2014) state that investment in education can be more effective than investment in physical capital (for example, infrastructure) particularly in the long run; with regard to sustainable consumption, a better education leads to a better understanding of the consequences of our lifestyle and daily routines.

In addition, education promotes the development of critical thinking and cooperative work, which helps in analysing lifestyle practices, detecting deviations or problems, and identifying sustainable solutions (Didham, 2015). The Education for All (EFA) *Global Monitoring Report* (Global Education Monitoring Team, 2015, p. 294) points out that 'education will be the lynchpin of a sustainable development agenda whose success relies on individuals, throughout their lifetime, acquiring relevant knowledge and developing positive attitudes to address global challenges'.

United Nations Agenda 21 identifies the paths to sustainability, which include research and technology transfer, sustainable agriculture and forestry, sustainable production and consumption, and education, among others. But a crucial fact should be noted: education, on its own, cannot guide us to a more sustainable world, but without education for sustainability the goal will not be reached. To this end, UNESCO created the Education for Sustainable Development (ESD) programme. According to the UN Decade of Education for Sustainable Development, the main aim is to incorporate the principles, values and practices of sustainable development in the fields of education and learning, encouraging the creation of a more sustainable society at present and for the future; the idea is to reshape the educational systems in order to address the social, economic and environmental dimensions of sustainable development (Lenglet, Fadeeva and Mochizuki, 2010) by teaching students to examine relevant information, to think critically and to develop practices and applied actions (Wiek, Withycombe and Redman, 2011).

At this point is should be highlighted that although the objective of a sustainable development is global, it involves individuals, local and regional institutions, and national governments. Local and regional stakeholders must face the challenges of sustainability, and it is at this level where education and, particularly, tertiary education comes into play. Regarding higher education, this is the so-called 'third mission' of the universities.

The traditional missions of universities are teaching and research. However, as societies progress, and the generation and dissemination of knowledge become more important, there is an increasing interest in a new mission of the universities – higher education institutions (HEIs) are expected to extend knowledge beyond their own environments in order to contribute to regional evolution in economic, social and cultural terms (Trippl, Sinozic and Lawton Smith, 2015). The third mission is somehow related to the triple helix concept, which entails the relationship between university, industry and government (Stanford University, 2018). Moreover, there is a quadruple helix, accounting for any fourth relevant entity like innovation, internationalization and others (Leydesdorff, 2012).

More recently, universities are becoming more responsible in terms of their contribution to society, as they are expected to be active participants in their socioeconomic environments. In this respect, HEIs are including sustainable development actions in their systems and curricula (Leal Filho et al., 2019), as well as formulating policy statements and developing initiatives like the Green Campus programmes. As a fundamental issue, universities should incorporate sustainable development in the decision-making process of the professionals they are creating. These initiatives and actions enrich the communities around the universities so that they becoming involved in the decision-making process of their respective local and regional communities in the economic, social and environmental dimensions (Katiliūtė, Daunorienė and Katkutė, 2014); this role is emphasized in national and international policy frameworks (Zilahy and Huisingh, 2009).

In spite of the previous comments, it can be observed that education for sustainability skills are seldom fully integrated into HEIs curricula (Cebrián, 2017; Velazquez, Munguia and Sanchez, 2005); in general, the nature and the empirical application of the third mission have not been completely conceptualized (Molas-Gallart and Castro-Martínez, 2007). Following Peer and Stoeglehner (2013), universities must carry out two essential actions if they want to become more engaged at regional level: on the one hand, adaptation of education programmes to local and regional needs; and, on the other hand, leadership or collaboration with the surrounding communities in terms of research (i.e., to exchange knowledge). The cornerstone is to reach the stage of visibility of the universities' actions in the context of where they are located – that is, going beyond the inclusion of sustainability in curricula, teaching or research. In short, education is one of the main pillars for achieving sustainable development. It will make it possible to turn learners into agents of change through the promotion of sustainable development, raising awareness and giving visibility to the problems.

At this point we must bear in mind that the society in which we live, the current context of globalization and network society (Castells, 2010), is characterized by the speed of change and rapidly changing scenarios. The transformation of society is also mirrored in education, which must adapt to changing needs and changing learners (Lai, 2011). In this respect, we are witnessing the growth of non-traditional types of learning, from blended learning to learning based on any number of technological resources. As Deming, Goldin and Katz (2012) note, online education is the fastest-growing segment in higher education.

At present, there is a co-existence of two sorts of education: traditional and virtual. According to Veletsianos and Kimmons (2012, p. 167), the use of virtual and social media for educational purposes can 'foster the development of more equitable, effective, efficient, and transparent scholarly and educational processes'; in addition, the use of digital technology generates societal benefits by 'broadening access to education and scholarship for the common good' (Veletsianos and Kimmons, 2016, p. 1).

One type of education offered by virtual platforms are massive open online courses (MOOCs). These web-based courses have recently experienced a considerable increase, with positive results. As proof of their success, several accredited institutions already accept credits gained through virtual MOOC education. Further analysis and reflections on the MOOC phenomenon can be found in Mazoue (2013), Fischer (2014) and Calonge and Shah (2016).

This kind of distance education allows for sharing knowledge with a wider audience than in the traditional scenario (Greenhow, Robelia and Hughes, 2009). Moreover, it combines two key aspects: raising concern about sustainability and the speed of change in technology. This is one of the foundations of the MOOC on Sustainability in the Era of Big Data (hereinafter, SEBD) that we developed at the Universidade da Coruña, which is the purpose of this chapter. HEIs should accommodate, to the extent possible, the dramatic transformation of the society and its demands, as well as becoming an active part of their socioeconomic environments. The MOOC project to be presented in this chapter is a first attempt at our university at bringing education closer to society through the development of technological advances. By developing the MOOC, we are exploring a new teaching-learning process with the main aims of meeting societal needs, extending knowledge and developing competences and skills beyond face-to-face classes. Hence, the project will serve as a preliminary experience to understand the future of education (in the medium to long term) and to detect the effectiveness of this innovative methodology in raising awareness and knowledge about sustainable development (in the short term). In addition, it might serve as an example for researchers in both fields of higher education and sustainable development.

Some main characteristics of MOOCs are discussed in more detail in Section 2. In Section 3 we talk about the SEBD MOOC project, presenting the process and background, the course structure and the methodology of the chapter, while Section 4 presents the case study and the main results. Section 5 draws a series of conclusions.

2.   CHARACTERISTICS OF MOOCs

According to Sachs (2013, p. 2), 'global, free, online teaching about sustainable development can help to propel global solutions'. On the one hand, knowledge about sustainable development can be extended to a large number of people through MOOCs; the more informed people are, the more they are able to tackle the challenges of sustainable development, helping to solve problems like climate change, equal access to education and employment, or energy poverty. On the other hand, MOOCs are also important in order to achieve the UN 2030 Agenda's Sustainable Development Goal 4: quality education (McGreal, 2017). These courses can be used as a way to provide equitable access to knowledge and learning, opening up education to a large number of students. However, MOOCs that want to be useful in achieving these objectives must look at two issues: improving the quality of their pedagogical characteristics and overcoming their barriers. Some of these barriers are the low completion rates of MOOCs and the low-quality lecture formats, due to the fact that they do not promote equitable and non-discriminatory access.

One of the first concerns of MOOC promoters is the design of support and guidance procedures adapted to a massive audience. Typically, peer assistance is offered. In addition, collaborative discussion tools are appropriate to support group-based activity and assessment. The development of an appropriate evaluation system is one of the big challenges that all MOOCs have to deal with. Frequently, MOOCs do not offer support structures to the student, limiting the evaluation to automatic marking (Burd, 2015). In this sense, two pedagogical approaches emerged. (1) cMOOCs: the connectivist MOOCs follow the connectivism theory of learning networks that are developed informally. The aim is to promote collaborative learning through open-source learning platforms. The pedagogical model is peer-based learning. Social media applications become essential in this type of MOOCs because they allow participants to create and comment pedagogical materials (Kaplan, 2016). (2) xMOOCs: the content-based MOOCs are grounded on a more behaviourist approach. The content of these ones is delivered by paced sessions of video and examined by online testing. These are based on traditional lecture formats and can include online forums in order to engage participants, but these connections are not essential to the course (ibid.).

Another important decision that higher education institutions will need to make is what platform they can use in order to extend the MOOC to a wider audience. There are several international providers of MOOCs, like edX, Coursera or Udacity. The latter has a different model by which the students define the pace of learning, allowing them to start the course when desired. However, this reduces the opportunities of using collaborative tools and does not facilitate forming cohorts of learners (Burd, 2015).

A common problem related to MOOCs is the low completion rate. While registration rates are high, only a small number of participants complete the MOOC in a successful manner. Previous experiences with a combination of a celebrity professor (Sebastian Thrun – Udacity CEO), a cutting-edge corporation (Google), and a subject related to artificial intelligence (driverless car), have provided great registration results (160 000 students), but only 28 000 of them completed the course (17.5 per cent completion rate). However, this figure can be considered a good rate compared to other MOOCs with a 5 per cent completion rate. In the cited case, good results were influenced by Sebastian Thrun, who offered to hand in the top students' CVs to tech companies like Google (ibid.).

There are several business motivations for offering MOOCs. Among these, the following would seem to be particularly noteworthy: charging for certificates, linking students with potential employers and charging for supplementary services (ibid.). Due to low completion rates, MOOC providers that want to get revenues by charging for certificates must consider that a minimum of 100 000 students registered is necessary to make a profit and the average enrolment per MOOC is around 50 000 students. MOOC providers can also make the most of linking successful students to potential employers. The chief operating officer at Udacity, David Stavens, showed that the head-hunters in Silicon Valley often get paid finder's fees of around $15 000 per match.

A few institutions are using MOOCs both for public consumption and for credit for students. This allows students to complete their programmes more quickly and can be a way of decreasing the cost of state education. For example, San José State University has started to work with edX using its MOOCs in the context of a blended course to support traditional face-to-face teaching.

Finally, MOOCs can also be interesting for gaining access to potential students for postgraduate programmes, using 'Big Data' or data analytics. The institutions have the opportunity to increase the awareness of their brand at a national and international level through high-quality MOOCs. In the same way, the research community can improve awareness of research accomplishments, achieving more citations.

3. THE SEBD PROJECT

3.1 Background

The SEBD MOOC emerged in 2018 as an initiative of several professors, members of the Green Campus Environmental Committee from the Faculty of Economics and Business (Universidade da Coruña), in collaboration with the University Centre for Training and Educational Innovation (CUFIE) from the same educational institution. The main drivers for the creation of this kind of project have been, first, the urgent need to raise awareness among the population on the matter of the environment and sustainability as well as increasing the visibility of this problem; and second, to provide free access to basic knowledge on sustainability and the Big Data application to this area, with the aim of reaching the largest possible audience.

Regarding the provider's motivations, owing to the low number of registered students that requested the certificate (costing 40 euros) and to the fact that a high percentage of these profits goes to the Miríadax platform (see below), there are no economic reasons behind the SEBD MOOC. The costs of developing the MOOC and filming the video-tutorials have been significantly higher than the economic profits. Some authors compare the effort derived from the realization of a MOOC with producing a film (Kaplan, 2016), with costs ranging from 30 000 to 300 000 dollars. In addition, as pointed out earlier, there are no agreements with companies that need to incorporate talent in the SEBD MOOC, and there are no postgraduate programmes in the Universidade da Coruña related to the content in order to attract potential registrations. Therefore, the main provider's motivation for the creation and launch of the SEBD MOOC is the promoters' own involvement in the dissemination of this type of knowledge, in order to favour a more sustainable development, and to expand the number of people through whom the knowledge acquired in the field of research can be accessed, creating new contacts and making known the work carried out at the Universidade da Coruña (as part of its social mission). This aim is consistent with the work of Kalman (2014), who shows that MOOCs constitute an alternative way to fulfil this mission.

Once the initial idea and the objectives were defined, the teaching staff presented the proposal and a basic guide about its structure to the first public call for MOOCs in the Universidade da Coruña. Thus, it was a pioneer project at our university. The project was finally selected from various proposals also submitted. After recording the classes and giving it adequate advertisement, the course was finally released in June 2019 – specifically, it lasted from 17 June to 14 July. The SEBD was intended to be a space for sustainability, born in the university, open to a wide audience and specifically geared toward people who are not specialists in the field. As in Drake, O'Hara and Seeman (2015), while developing the MOOC proposal, several pedagogical and technological ideas were considered. The methods and format that the course followed were designed focusing on several aspects: involving students in the teaching-learning process; making the current problem visible and raising public awareness; developing knowledge about sustainability and Big Data; and enhancing the digital skills of the students. Keeping these aspects in mind, we determined the course format, the pedagogical approaches and the questionnaires.

The MOOC was developed under Miríadax, the first platform of Ibero-American MOOCs, with more than 6 million students enrolled and more than 100 educational partners. It promotes open knowledge in the field of higher education and has an international presence in countries of Central America, South America, along with Spain and Portugal, but also in the US, France, Italy and India (Miríadax, 2019). Platforms like Miríadax are open to an international and diverse audience, which allows greater dissemination, greater exchange of opinions and does not imply time constraints for students, who can carry out autonomous and self-regulated learning (SRL) with the support of audiovisual content and the teaching team guide.

3.2   Course Structure

The course had a temporary plan of four weeks, with a module for each of the first three weeks and a final challenge for the last week of the course. Starting at the same time allows students to use collaborative tools: the online forums available in Miríadax and the Twitter social network. Using both tools, the students share their knowledge and advances in the course, making the educational experience more constructive and enriching for teachers and students. In turn, by being trained in an online environment, new media technologies make it much easier to bring stories to life with animated short films (Andrews, Hull and Donahue, 2009; Jenkins and Deuze, 2006), as well as expanding the students' digital skills.

The three first modules have the same structure: short and concise videos with the presentation of the content of the course (around ten minutes per video), supporting documents with the content, a brief online test of six questions and a challenge related to the corresponding content. The students must pass the tests for the completion of the course and to obtain their certificate.

The three basic pillars of sustainability were considered, modules on environmental sustainability, social sustainability and economic sustainability, so that the course offered a global, broad and interrelated vision of the various sustainable development objectives involved, and, in turn, it was thought to offer a vision of the usefulness of Big Data in the aforementioned fields. The content was specified, analysing the main problems of each area in detail, especially the ecosystem assessment in the environmental field, education, housing, employment and health system policies in the social field, and economic inequality, sustainable production and consumption models in the economic field.

Subsequently, we looked for real examples of cases and projects that showed the usefulness and relevance of new technologies in collecting and analysing data in the areas under study. This can make it plausible that the proper use of Big Data and information management can mean great advances and great support in the search for sustainable development. Students can also expand their training with content prepared from data supported by government reports, scientific articles and various sources of information for free (Kalman, 2014). The variety of materials and content allows the development of knowledge about sustainability and Big Data with the support of experts in the related subjects.

We designed the course to include all the content in a dystopic story to engage the students and make the SEBD MOOC more attractive. The story was created based on a futuristic version of the real city of A Coruna in 2050: a city named Nova Crunia. The narrative introduces a population that is suffering the consequences of various environmental problems (such as rising sea levels or pollution), social problems (lack of access to basic services as education, health or employment, for example), and economic issues (such as rising poverty rates and irresponsible consumption and production). This population is organized into three clans: ocean, forest and grotto, and each clan has a hero. The student can find out which clan has the highest affinity by means of a test. The application of this system is supposed to reinforce the level of belonging and commitment of the students, since they play a role in the story – which promotes emotional engagement and entertainment – and carry out a mission throughout the course: to help the heroes complete various challenges in order to reduce the negative impacts on Nova Crunia and in the real world.

3.3 Methodology

The objective of our study is to show the usefulness of MOOCs as tools for the dissemination of knowledge about sustainability to a large number of people and as tools for measuring the degree of awareness of the participants. With this goal in mind, the case of the SEBD MOOC has been analysed in depth with the aim of serving as a reference for future educational activities in the field of higher education. The case study is used by authors such as Chatterjee and Nath (2014), Iniesto, Rodrigo and Moreira Teixeira (2014), Abbas and Singh (2014) or Drake et al. (2015) to analyse MOOCs projects. We divided the SEBD MOOC study case into two phases, as follows.

Phase 1: approach and course methodologies

We present and comment on the strategies designed and implemented in our course to guarantee that the key points and characteristics of this type of educational tools are preserved and improved through the combination of different pedagogical and educational methods.

We focus on some aspects commented on above, such as providing equitable access to knowledge and learning; opening education up to a large number of students; promoting collaborative learning; improving the quality of their pedagogical characteristics and overcoming barriers such as the low completion rates of MOOCs and the low-quality lecture formats; designing support and guidance procedures adapted to a massive audience; offering peer assistance, collaborative discussion tools and an appropriate evaluation system.

To promote collaborative learning and improve the active participation of the students in the teaching-learning process we combine two pedagogical approaches, the content-based MOOC and the connectivist MOOC (Kaplan, 2016), which allow the improvement of self-regulated learning and peer-based learning.

In order to train the community in education for sustainability, involve students and strengthen or foster their awareness and commitment, a methodology based on gamification, challenge-based learning (CBL) and storytelling technique was implemented (Andrews et al., 2009; Carrera and Ramírez-Hernández, 2018; Teixes, 2014; Vaibhav and Gupta, 2014).

Phase 2: Level of success and questionnaire results

We observe the number of enrolled people and the completion rate as a reference to determine if the course has reached a wide audience and to evaluate the level of success of the SEBD MOOC. Due to the fact that the enrolled students can have different socio-economic characteristics, it was a challenge to hold their attention, to prevent them from dropping out of the course and to ensure that they understood its content. Gamification, CBL and storytelling can help to engage the students and to reduce the possibility that they leave the course, which, combined with Big Data, can help to reach a wider audience.

We have also analysed how the participants perceived the course and how their motivation and learning were affected by the educational strategies applied through two online questionnaires, also useful in measuring the student's degree of commitment to sustainability. The questions were based on the studies carried out by authors such as Gomera Martínez, Villamandos de la Torre and Vaquero Abellán (2012) and Abbas and Singh (2014).

The first questionnaire had as its main goal to discover the reasons for taking part in the course, and previous experiences with MOOCs were also asked about. In addition, a set of questions dealing with the issue of environmental, social and economic problems was included in order to analyse their level of awareness regarding sustainable development. Finally, this first questionnaire also included some sociodemographic questions to identify the profile of the students involved. The second questionnaire was designed to study participants' opinions on the design of the course, to know which aspects were more positively assessed and what kind of material provided to them was perceived as useful. The students were asked for their opinion on the technical aspects of the course, the pace of learning, the duration of the videos, the presentation videos with the story of the clans, the theoretical documents, the final questionnaires of the modules, the general assessment of the course and how they see the management of the platform, among other aspects. The data analysis from the questionnaires was carried out through descriptive statistical techniques.

4. SEBD MOOC CASE STUDY

4.1 Approach and Course Methodologies

The SEBD MOOC combines two pedagogical approaches, the content-based MOOC and the connectivist MOOC, through a mandatory evaluation system and another that is voluntary (Kaplan, 2016), that allows for improved self-regulated learning and peer-based learning.

The mandatory system is based on xMOOCs, including short videos and support material for each topic, with online tests that return the correct answer to check if the students have been successful (Carrera and Ramírez-Hernández, 2018). In this way, students can organize their study time and self-assess the knowledge acquired through the available tests (ibid.), which allows the use of SRL and peer-based learning models. These methods are combined with the objective that the students reach a degree of autonomy that allows them to reflect on their own learning process (Zimmerman, 1998). Moreover, the students' SRL skills are important in an online environment because learners must plan, manage and control their learning activities in order to complete the MOOC successfully (Vilkova, 2019; Wang, Shannon and Ross, 2013).

The voluntary assessment has been carried out through online forums and Twitter, promoting collaborative and peer-based learning according to the cMOOCs perspective. In this case, the members of the teaching team guide were assigned as moderators in order to maintain the quality of the course and the reputation of the institution (Burd, 2015), focusing on facilitating interactions (Kaplan, 2016).

In order to make the current environmental, social and economic problem visible, raise awareness and commitment and involve students in the care of the environment, we have considered gamification, CBL and storytelling techniques. These methods allow an increase in the students' knowledge in the subject and the training of the community in education for sustainability in a fun way and with an attractive presentation that captures their attention.

Gamification is based on the use of game mechanics, aesthetics and recreational thinking to attract people, motivate actions, promote learning and solve problems in an attractive and dynamic way (Teixes, 2014). This methodology contributes to the retention of the enrolled students throughout the course and increases their engagement (Vaibhav and Gupta, 2014). CBL is a pedagogical approach that actively involves the student in a real context to solve a problematic situation that is linked to their environment (Carrera and Ramírez-Hernández, 2018). Regarding storytelling, we have seen that a combination of fables and real-life examples, as a method for teaching key principles of a discipline, helping to build analytical skills in students and being an information means, is strongly used today in education and training of all types (Andrews et al., 2009).

The purpose of using storytelling as a teaching-learning tool is to engage the learner through context in order to provide a simulated experience. Moreover, for all participants' profiles the completion of a gamification challenge can favour higher final test scores on the content of the course and improves students' performance in online teaching (Mena et al., 2018).

As Andrews et al. (2009) claim, the four major instructional methods that are organized around a story structure are case-based, scenario-based, narrative-based and problem-based instruction. For the SEBD MOOC, a story was created based on a dystopian world, named Nova Crunia, a futuristic version of the real city of A Coruna in 2050. A combination of narrative-based and scenario-based instructional methods was chosen due to the fact that the problem is fixed but the learner is positioned, at the same time, within the narrator's context (Nova Crunia) and in an interactive and real-time experience (A Coruna or the student's city) that allows for a variety of solution paths (Andrews et al., 2009; Cobley, 2001; Salas et al., 2006). This combination attempts to appeal to emotions, as well as recounting facts and events (Andrews et al., 2009; Martin, 1986). Case-based instruction could also be applied as a method because several cases of sustainable projects and initiatives are shown to the students. Nevertheless, although the problems shown and their solutions are found, in the SEBD MOOC the learner is not positioned as an outside observer relative to these specific situations; thus, the learner is an active agent with influence and a role in his or her environment, beyond identifying risks and proposing recommendations (Andrews et al., 2009).

Four challenges were raised and the students had to provide a solution. The students are motivated by a reward: to acquire new knowledge to solve the challenges, to help their clan and their environment, and to complete the course. When facing problems within a given context, students have to look for solutions and interact with other students to comment on their proposals, so they subsequently learn better than when they passively participate in structured activities (Carrera and Ramírez-Hernández, 2018). This is possible because the sharing of each one's personal vision on the issues discussed generates debate, which allows students to improve their ability to appreciate the complexity of the issues related to sustainability and develop skills such as critical thinking and reflection on information in public media (Janssen, Claesson and Lindqvist, 2016). Taking advantage of Big Data tools to favour more sustainable and efficient actions contributes to reaching a wider audience and generating more exchange of opinions, because we are combining two issues of great relevance and current interest.

By proposing challenges related to the story but applicable in the real world (scenario-based) more respectful acts are publicized and the students become actively involved in the care and protection of the environment. There are challenges such as sharing environmental news, taking photographs of impoverished areas that show the contrast with lower quality of life areas, or taking photographs that show habits of responsible consumption and production. In addition, the final challenge invites the students to propose a solution to achieve a more sustainable and egalitarian society and help the hero of his or her clan to create a more sustainable Nova Crunia (narrative-based). As it is observed, they become part of the story.

4.2 Level of Success and Questionnaire Results

In this section we provide some figures regarding the SEBD MOOC itself, as well as the results of the different questionnaires conducted. The course achieved a total of 1318 enrolled students: 736 of them started the course and 377 completed it. The result is a completion rate of almost 29 per cent, which can be considered a successful result on the basis of the above. In this case, the MOOC has neither been supported by a large corporation, nor have the students been offered additional advantages. Therefore, these results may be due to the free content of the course, in which advanced Big Data tools are placed at the service of ecosystem preservation and sustainable socio-economic development. That MOOCs provide access free high-level content is their main attraction (Kalman, 2014).

With regard to the results obtained from the questionnaires, the first one was completed by 70 students, with 41 per cent female participants and an average age of 42 years old. Considering the level of studies attained, more than 74 per cent confirmed having university studies. In addition, around 68 per cent of the sample confirmed they were working, 17 per cent were students, 11 per cent were unemployed and 4 per cent were retired. In addition, 45 per cent of participants live in Europe, 41 per cent in South America, 9 per cent in North America and approximately 5 per cent in Central America.

When analysing the reasons why they decided to participate in this MOOC, 86 per cent of the sample answered that they made the decision (first) because it is a 'topic that interests me', followed by 8 per cent who stated a desire 'to expand my knowledge', 5 per cent because 'it's a free course' and 1 per cent 'because they have recommended it to me'.

Regarding the level of experience in this kind of online education, for 17 per cent of the sample it was the first time they had taken part in MOOCs. The rest of the sample had previous experience; specifically, about 56 per cent had taken part in one to five courses, 9 per cent in five to ten courses and around 15 per cent affirmed to have participated in more than ten MOOCs. Therefore, on average, participants had moderate experience with this type of innovative education. When asked about how they knew about this MOOC, more than half of the sample stated that it was through the Internet.

The following relates to their opinions about what are the main entities responsible for the current problems when talking about sustainable development. Table 30.1 shows that individuals perceive that climate change and pollution are linked to society in general. Nevertheless, in the case of inequality (both social and economic) and energy poverty, both governments and politicians are held responsible.

In addition, more than 90 per cent of the respondents agreed with the idea that their countries should take action to fight against the above-mentioned problems independently of the actions of the rest of the countries. When asked about what kind of measures should be implemented in order to fight against climate change and pollution, more than half of the sample commented on the importance of investment in innovation and development. In contrast, when talking about social or economic inequality, as in the case

Table 30.1   Responsibility for the different problems

	Climate Change (%)	Social Inequality (%)	Economic Inequality (%)	Pollution	Energy Poverty (%)
Government and politicians	5.19	*58.44*	*59.74*	1.30	*62.34*
Industry	24.68	2.60	10.39	18.18	14.29
Society in general	*57.14*	33.77	24.68	*59.74*	14.29
NGOs			1.30		3.90
Myself	5.19	2.60		10.39	2.60
Those affected	7.79	2.60	3.90	10.39	2.60

Note: The highest percentages are in italics.

of energy poverty, the most mentioned measures were economic incentives (both taxes and subsidies).

The second questionnaire was developed with the aim of knowing the perception of the students after finishing the course. Thus, only 43 students decided to voluntarily take part in the questionnaire. First, we asked about what kind of tools had been more successful in improving their level of learning. In this respect, around 21 per cent commented that the documents presented on video; 2 per cent the documents presented on video and the practical activities; 24 per cent the documents on video together with the extra material shared with students to improve their sources of information; 9 per cent documents on video, extra material and the conduction of practical activities; 4 per cent the material on video, extra material, practical activities and the evaluation questionnaire; and, finally, 15 per cent all the material together with the activities proposed in forums. Thus, it seems that the development of videos becomes an important and attractive tool to share and spread knowledge.

In addition, when asked about the specific level of satisfaction with the material shared in videos and the theoretical documents, Table 30.2 shows the evaluation through a Likert scale of 1–5 (where 1 represents the lowest score and 5 represents the highest one); the results emphasize that videos and documents with theory are positively perceived by students.

We also asked the participants about the content they most appreciated. Regarding this aspect, around 70 per cent of the participants affirmed that the information was well organized, followed by the simplicity and ease of use of materials (over 13 per cent); the clear presentation of the videos (over 11 per cent); the attractiveness of the visuals, graphics and font type employed (4 per cent); and the flawless functioning of the platform (2 per cent). When asked about the learning pace, approximately 85 per cent commented that it was excellent and regarding the length of the videos they stated that it was adequate (more than 79 per cent of the sample).

To evaluate the level of learning, we included several questions to know their opinion about the evaluation questionnaires. We found that 75.5 per cent commented that they were adequate; 21 per cent found that they were enough but dense; and 4 per cent answered 'insufficient'. After that, we asked about the perceived level of the course, find-

Table 30.2   *Evaluation of the satisfaction with the material shared with students*

	Videos (%)	Theoretical Information (%)
1	–	1.89
2	5.66	5.66
3	9.43	11.32
4	*43.40*	*32.08*
5	*41.51*	*49.06*

Note: The highest percentages are in italics.

ing that over 77 per cent answered that it was adequate; 19 per cent that it was quite easy; and 4 per cent that it was a little difficult. Regarding the use of forums, around 49 per cent affirmed that they have used the forums a little; 40 per cent nothing; 10 per cent enough; while only 11 per cent stated that they used them a lot. Finally, when asking about the overall appreciation of the course, 97 per cent of the sample commented that they have learned about the subject under study.

5.   CONCLUSIONS

The main way to face the new environmental challenges in the world necessarily involves awareness raising and the fostering of a culture of sustainability at a grassroots level. Education becomes a fundamental tool in meeting this aim. On the one hand, it allows the acquisition of a clear vision of the consequences deriving from non-sustainable lifestyles, promoting the modification of this behaviour. On the other hand, it permits the demonstration of the most suitable behaviour for attaining the preservation of the entire ecosystem.

The next question is: how will this relevant knowledge reach people? Many educational institutions are incorporating sustainability into their school curricula, but there is a need for more specific training about this topic that reaches not only students but any interested person. This can be done through a MOOC. These types of courses have demonstrated their capability of reaching people from a wide range of countries and across a similarly wide age range. Moreover, knowledge is freely available. A computer with an Internet connection is necessary, but public institutions usually provide this basic service free of charge in spaces such as public libraries. In this way, the hurdle of access for those lacking resources could be overcome, becoming a more equitable way of educating. Furthermore, the forums of this type of courses that are used to foster cooperative learning can promote solidarity and mutual support within the course. It should also be added that the involvement of HEIs with these projects is critical to ensuring the standard of quality of such knowledge, making it accessible to all those people interested. Thus, these projects are part of social responsibility for these institutions.

The main objective of this study is to show the usefulness of MOOCs as a tool for the dissemination of knowledge about sustainability to a large number of people and as a tool for measuring the degree of awareness of the participants. For this, the case of the

SEBD MOOC has been analysed in depth, to serve as a reference for future educational activities of HEIs in this field. The main motivation for the launch of the SEBD MOOC is the promoters' own involvement in the dissemination of this type of knowledge, in order to favour more sustainable development. In fact, this course forms part of the Green Campus actions of the Faculty of Economics and Business (Universidade da Coruña). This innovative approach allows us to reach a wider audience, taking advantage of Big Data in order to favour more sustainable and efficient actions. Storytelling has also been used to transport participants to a dystopian future, in which society suffers the consequences of climate change and extreme socio-economic inequality, giving them the opportunity to design measures to try to avoid it; that is, the students take an active role in the teaching-learning process, implementing different pedagogical methods to make their experience more attractive.

To discover if the SEBD MOOC has served to meet the objective of disseminating sustainability knowledge to a wide audience, the number of people that started the course and the completion rate have been taken as a reference. In this case, it has reached 736 people in its first edition. This number by far exceeds the audience of on-site courses, although it can be improved in subsequent editions. In addition, the completion rate of almost 29 per cent can be considered a successful result. The age range of the participants has been mixed, with an average of 42 years old, and the countries of origin are not only European, but also South, Central and North American. In order to verify the level of awareness of the participants about the importance of carrying out sustainable measures and to know what the SEBD MOOC has provided them with, participants have been asked to complete some questionnaires.

By carrying out these questionnaires, some conclusions are emphasized. On the one hand, it seems that people interested in topics related to sustainable development and online education are middle-aged people, with university-level qualifications. Moreover, when referring to environmental problems, results seem to show that people feel responsible for them. Nevertheless, when talking about inequalities, it has been argued that politicians and governments are the main culprits. Another important conclusion is that people feel that governments should act and try to promote sustainable development in dealing with problems like climate change, pollution, social and economic inequalities or energy poverty. On the other hand, about the organization of this MOOC, it is important to highlight that students respond positively to the use of videos together with theoretical material and mention the importance of a well-organized course. In contrast, it seems that the use of forums is not seen as an important issue in following this course. This aspect should be further improved in order to promote greater collaborative learning among participants since, as mentioned above, these forums can also become inclusive spaces. In general, participants agree with the idea that they have learned. The completion of these questionnaires reveals the positive assessment of this kind of education given by the participants.

One limitation of this study is the confirmation of the effectiveness of the course with only the information of the first edition. Thus, it becomes necessary to oversee the following editions in order to confirm (or not) the results of the first edition. Another limitation is that, at this stage, the course is only available on a platform aimed primarily at Spanish-speaking countries. Having an English version would help to reach a wider audience, as there is a large number of English-speaking countries. This aspect is also taken into account for the next editions.

The main conclusions we have derived from developing this course are coherent with other studies claiming that the advantages of making use of innovative tools are to engage the students and the impact on the development of digital abilities and skills, in addition to the learning acquired on sustainability (Carrera and Ramírez-Hernández, 2018). The SEBD MOOC experience encourages the development of similar initiatives to raise concern and knowledge by means of innovative tools.

REFERENCES

Abbas, M.Y. and Singh, R. (2014). A survey of environmental awareness, attitude, and participation amongst university students: a case study. *International Journal of Science and Research*, 3(5), 1755–60.

Andrews, D.H., Hull, T.D. and Donahue, J.A. (2009). Storytelling as an instructional method: definitions and research questions. *Interdisciplinary Journal of Problem-Based Learning*, 3(2), Article 3.

Burd, E.L. (2015). Exploring business models for MOOCs in higher education. *Innovative Higher Education*, 40(1), 37–49.

Calonge, D.S. and Shah, M.A. (2016). MOOCs, graduate skills gaps, and employability: a qualitative systematic review of the literature. *The International Review of Research in Open and Distributed Learning*, 17(5), 67–90.

Carneiro, R. (1996). Revitalizing the community spirit: a glimpse of the socializing role of the school in the next century. In UNESCO (ed.), *Learning: The Treasure Within* (pp. 201–4). Paris: UNESCO.

Carrera, J. and Ramírez-Hernández, D. (2018). Innovative education in MOOC for sustainability: learnings and motivations. *Sustainability*, 10(9), 1–18.

Castells, M. (2010). *The Information Age: Economy, Society and Culture*. Oxford: Wiley-Blackwell.

Cebrián, G. (2017). A collaborative action research project towards embedding ESD within the higher education curriculum. *International Journal of Sustainability in Higher Education*, 18(6), 857–76.

Chatterjee, P. and Nath, A. (2014). Massive open online courses (MOOCs) in education – a case study in Indian context and vision to ubiquitous learning. Paper presented at the 2014 IEEE International Conference on MOOC, Innovation and Technology in Education (MITE). Accessed 4 November 2020 at https://ieeexplore.ieee.org/document/7020237.

Cobley, P. (2001). *Narrative*. New York: Routledge.

Cohen, W.M. and Levinthal, D.A. (1990). Absorptive capacity: a new perspective on learning and innovation. *Administrative Science Quarterly*, 35(1), 128–52.

Deming, D.J., Goldin, C. and Katz, L.F. (2012). The for-profit postsecondary school sector: nimble critters or agile predators? *Journal of Economic Perspectives*, 26(1), 139–64.

Didham, R.J. (2015). Pathways to sustainable lifestyles global stocktaking report [Published draft]. Accessed 4 November 2020 at https://iges.or.jp/en/pub/pathways-sustainable-lifestyles-global.

Didham, R.J. and Ofei-Manu, P. (2015). The role of education in the sustainable development agenda: empowering a learning society for sustainability through quality education. In M. Bengtsson, S. Hoiberg Olsen and E. Zusman (eds), *Achieving the Sustainable Development Goals: From Agenda to Action* (pp. 95–133). Kanagawa, Japan: Institute for Global Environmental Strategies (IGES).

Drake, J.R., O'Hara, M. and Seeman, E. (2015). Five principles for MOOC design: with a case study. *Journal of Information Technology Education: Innovations in Practice*, 14, 125–43.

Fischer, G. (2014). Beyond hype and underestimation: identifying research challenges for the future of MOOCs. *Distance Education*, 35(2), 149–58.

Global Education Monitoring Team (2015). *Education for All 2000–2015: Achievements and Challenges*. Accessed 4 November 2020 at https://unesdoc.unesco.org/ark:/48223/pf0000232205.

Gomera Martínez, A., Villamandos de la Torre, F. and Vaquero Abellán, M. (2012). Medición y categorización de la conciencia ambiental del alumnado universitario: contribución de la universidad a su fortalecimiento. *Profesorado, Revista de Curriculum y Formación del Profesorado*, 16(2), May–August.

Greenhow, C., Robelia, B. and Hughes, J.E. (2009). Learning, teaching, and scholarship in a digital age: Web 2.0 and classroom research: what path should we take now? *Educational Researcher*, 38(4), 246–59.

Hanushek, E.A. and Wößmann, L. (2010). Education and economic growth. In P. Peterson, E. Baker and B. McGaw (eds), *International Encyclopedia of Education* (3rd edition, pp. 245–52). Oxford: Academic Press.

Iniesto, F., Rodrigo, C. and Moreira Teixeira, A. (2014). Accessibility analysis in MOOC platforms. A case study: UNED COMA and UAbiMOOC. Paper presented at the V Congreso Internacional sobre Calidad y Accesibilidad de la Formación Virtual.

Janssen, M., Claesson, A.N. and Lindqvist, M. (2016). Design and early development of a MOOC on 'Sustainability in everyday life': role of the teachers. In W. Leal Filho and S. Nesbit (eds), *New Developments in Engineering Education for Sustainable Development* (pp. 113–23). Cham, Switzerland: Springer.

Jenkins, H. and Deuze, M. (2006). *Convergence Culture: Where Old and New Media Collide*. New York: New York University Press.

Kalman, Y.M. (2014). A race to the bottom: MOOCs and higher education business models. *Open Learning*, 29(1), 5–14.

Kaplan, A.M. (2016). Higher education and the digital revolution: about MOOCs, SPOCs, social media, and the cookie monster. *Business Horizons*, 59(4), 441–50.

Katiliūtė, E., Daunorienė, A. and Katkutė, J. (2014). Communicating the sustainability issues in higher education institutions World Wide Webs. *Procedia – Social and Behavioral Sciences*, 156, 106–10.

Lai, K. (2011). Digital technology and the culture of teaching and learning in higher education. *Australasian Journal of Educational Technology*, 27(8), 1291–303.

Leal Filho, W., Vargas, V.R. and Salvia, A.L. et al. (2019). The role of higher education institutions in sustainability initiatives at the local level. *Journal of Cleaner Production*, 233, 1004–15.

Lenglet, F., Fadeeva, Z. and Mochizuki, Y. (2010). ESD promises and challenges: increasing its relevance. *Global Environment Research*, 14(2), 93–100.

Leydesdorff, L. (2012). The triple helix, quadruple helix, . . . , and an *N*-tuple of helices: explanatory models for analyzing the knowledge-based economy? *Journal of the Knowledge Economy*, 3(1), 25–35.

Lutz, W., Muttarak, R. and Striessnig, E. (2014). Universal education is key to enhanced climate adaptation. *Science*, 346(6213), 1061–2.

Marquez-Ramos, L. and Mourelle, E. (2019). Education and economic growth: an empirical analysis of nonlinearities. *Applied Economic Analysis*, 27(79), 21–45.

Martin, W. (1986). *Recent Theories of Narrative*. New York: Cornell University Press.

Mazoue, J.G. (2013, 28 January). The MOOC model: challenging traditional education. *EDUCAUSE Review*. Accessed 4 November 2020 at https://er.educause.edu/articles/2013/1/the-mooc-model-challenging-traditional-education.

McGreal, R. (2017). Special report on the role of open educational resources in supporting the Sustainable Development Goal 4: quality education challenges and opportunities. *The International Review of Research in Open and Distributed Learning*, 18(7).

Mena, J.J., Rincón-Flores, E.G., Ramírez, R. and Ramírez-Montoya, M.S. (2018). The use of gamification as a teaching methodology in a MOOC about the strategic energy reform in México. In T. Di Mascio T., P. Vittorini and R. Gennari et al. (eds), *Methodologies and Intelligent Systems for Technology Enhanced Learning, 8th International Conference*. Cham, Switzerland: Springer.

Miríadax. (2019). Nuestro números. Accessed 4 November 2020 at https://miriadax.net/nuestros-numeros.

Molas-Gallart, J. and Castro-Martínez, E. (2007). Ambiguity and conflict in the development of 'Third Mission' indicators. *Research Evaluation*, 16(4), 321–30.

Peer, V. and Stoeglehner, G. (2013). Universities as change agents for sustainability – framing the role of knowledge transfer and generation in regional development processes. *Journal of Cleaner Production*, 44, 85–95.

Sachs, J.D. (2013). *The Age of Sustainable Development*. New York: Columbia University Press.

Salas, E., Wilson, K.A., Priest, H.A. and Guthrie, J.W. (2006). Design, delivery, and evaluation of training systems. In G. Salvendy (ed.), *Handbook of Human Factors and Ergonomics* (pp. 472–512). New York: John Wiley & Sons.

Stanford University. (2018). The triple helix concept. Accessed 3 January 2021 at http://www.triplehelixconference.org/th/9/the-triple-helix-concept.html.

Teixes, F. (2014). *Gamificación: fundamentos y aplicaciones*. Barcelona: Editorial UOC.

Trippl, M., Sinozic, T. and Lawton Smith, H. (2015). The role of universities in regional development: conceptual models and policy institutions in the UK, Sweden and Austria. *European Planning Studies*, 23(9), 1722–40.

United Nations Educational, Scientific and Cultural Organization (UNESCO). (2013). Education for sustainable development. Accessed 4 November 2020 at https://en.unesco.org/themes/education-sustainable-development.

Vaibhav, A. and Gupta, P. (2014). Gamification of MOOCs for increasing user engagement. Paper presented at the 2014 IEEE International Conference on MOOC, Innovation and Technology in Education (MITE). Accessed 4 November 2020 at https://ieeexplore.ieee.org/document/7020290.

Velazquez, L., Munguia, N. and Sanchez, M. (2005). Deterring sustainability in higher education institutions: an appraisal of the factors which influence sustainability in higher education institutions. *International Journal of Sustainability in Higher Education*, 6(4), 383–91.

Veletsianos, G. and Kimmons, R. (2012). Assumptions and challenges of open scholarship. *The International Review of Research in Open and Distributed Learning*, 13(4), 166–89.

Veletsianos, G. and Kimmons, R. (2016). Scholars in an increasingly open and digital world: how do education professors and students use Twitter? *The Internet and Higher Education*, 30, 1–10.

Vilkova, K. (2019). Self-regulated learning and successful MOOC completion. *Proceedings of EMOOCs 2019: Work in Progress of the Research, Experience and Business Track*. Accessed 4 November 2020 at http://ceur-ws. org/Vol-2356/research_short12.pdf.

Wang, C., Shannon, D.M. and Ross, M.E. (2013). Students' characteristics, self-regulated learning, technology self-efficacy, and course outcomes in online learning. *Distance Education*, 34(3), 302–23.

Wiek, A., Withycombe, L. and Redman, C.L. (2011). Key competencies in sustainability: a reference framework for academic program development. *Sustainability Science*, 6(2), 203–18.

Zilahy, G. and Huisingh, D. (2009). The roles of academia in regional sustainability initiatives. *Journal of Cleaner Production*, 17(12), 1057–66.

Zimmerman, B.J. (1998). Academic studying and the development of personal skill: a self-regulatory perspective. *Educational Psychologist*, 33(2–3), 73–86.

31. Sustainability in the workplace and the theory of planned behaviour: norms and identity predict environmentally friendly intentions

Dennis Nigbur, Ana Fernández, Sharon Coen, Anke Franz and Ian Hocking

1. INTRODUCTION: A SOCIAL-PSYCHOLOGICAL PERSPECTIVE ON SUSTAINABILITY

People's actions are central to more environmentally sustainable practice. For pro-environmental legislation and interventions to be effective, they must be adopted and enacted by people. A comprehensive analysis of how sustainability can be taught will therefore benefit from a social-psychological perspective on what informs sustainability-related intentions and behaviours. In this chapter, we review some relevant literature from social psychology, including thoughts about classic incentive schemes and their limitations (e.g., Dwyer et al., 1993), insights about the functioning of injunctive and descriptive social norms (e.g., Cialdini, 2003), social identity and self-categorisation (Tajfel and Turner, 1979; Turner et al., 1987), moral disengagement (Bandura, 2007), self-identity (Stryker and Burke, 2000) and the theory of planned behaviour (Ajzen, 1991). We then report a study testing the latter theory in the context of environmental sustainability in the workplace, at a British university.

1.1 Behavioural Interventions

Early attempts to examine the link between psychology and pro-environmental actions took the form of simple behavioural experiments, in which people – often college or university students – were exposed to some kind of intervention and the impact on behaviour was measured (for reviews, see Dwyer et al., 1993; Hornik et al., 1995; Schultz, Oskamp and Mainieri, 1995). Some manipulated the antecedents of sustainability-related behaviour – for example, reducing littering by making waste bins more attractive and easier to find (Geller, Brasted and Mann, 1979) or placing dedicated paper recycling containers in university offices (Humphrey et al., 1977). Others manipulated the consequences of behaviour – for example, using raffle incentives to increase recycling of drink containers (Luyben and Cummings, 1982) or paper (Couch, Garber and Karpus, 1978). Both approaches are generally effective, but differ in important practical aspects, with environmental design usually easier and cheaper to maintain than reward schemes (Dwyer et al., 1993). Reward incentives seem to be vulnerable because their effects are often limited to the particular behaviour that is being rewarded, and to the duration of the intervention – presumably because they appeal to extrinsic, rather than intrinsic, motivation (see Hornik et al., 1995). In an emblematic example of this limitation, one attempt to promote paper recycling at a school by means of a reward for each visit to the recycling facility succeeded in increasing participation rates, but not the overall amount of paper recycled (Hamad et al., 1980). The authors speculate that this may have been because the reward was given even if just one sheet of waste paper was delivered.

Consequently, other interventions have tried to mobilize intrinsic motivation. The display of information about recyclable materials in close proximity to recycling containers caused an increase in recycling on a university campus (Austin et al., 1993). Asking for a commitment to recycle more was associated with more recycled paper in a retirement home and a college (Wang and Katzev, 1990). And published feedback on the volume of recyclables collected was effective in increasing the recycling of paper (Katzev and Mishima, 1992) and aluminium cans (Larson, Houlihan and Goernert, 1995) in educational settings. Comparative feedback telling people how much energy they used relative to their neighbours reduced household energy consumption in the United States (Allcott, 2011). These methods explicitly set pro-environmental expectations (i.e., norms) and tie them to a particular social group or physical location. In fact, some approaches do both. One study (Siero et al., 1996) successfully promoted energy saving in an industrial setting by creating a competition between two units about who would, collectively, conserve more energy, and giving comparative feedback about this effort. In residential settings, meanwhile, strategies involving a 'block leader' (essentially a neighbour who continually encourages others to act sustainably) have yielded considerable success in increasing participation in kerbside waste recycling schemes in the neighbourhood (Burn, 1991; Hopper and Nielsen, 1991). These findings show that sustainability-related behaviours can be motivated effectively by mobilizing social norms.

1.2 Injunctive and Descriptive Social Norms

Research on littering by Cialdini and colleagues (Cialdini, 2003; Cialdini, Kallgren and Reno, 1991; Cialdini, Reno and Kallgren, 1990; Reno, Cialdini and Kallgren, 1993) makes a particularly clear connection between spaces, social norms and sustainable behaviour. This work suggests that social norms can be usefully subdivided into injunctive norms (an expectation emanating from a group or society) and descriptive norms (the observed or inferred behaviour of others, usually tied to a physical setting). In a series of field experiments, Cialdini and colleagues showed what happens when injunctive and descriptive norms are or are not in alignment.

A typical example (Reno et al., 1993, Study 1) involved observing motorists returning to their parked cars to find an unsolicited leaflet stuck under the windscreen wipers. Without any appropriate waste receptacles nearby, drivers could either litter the leaflet or take it into their cars. The relative frequency of these actions depended on how the experimenters had manipulated the situation to highlight relevant social norms: few people littered when they had just seen a passer-by (actually an actor working for the experimenters) pick up a fast-food bag from the ground, thus drawing attention to an injunctive norm against littering. Similarly, few people littered when they had just seen the actor drop a piece of litter but the car park was otherwise clean (a descriptive norm against littering). On the other hand, littering rates were higher when the actor had just dropped litter in an already littered environment (thus drawing attention to a descriptive norm in favour of littering) or just walked by without dropping or picking up any litter. In other words, littering rates were reduced when injunctive or descriptive norms against littering were highlighted. Generally, people seem to act according to the norm that is focal, or salient, at the time (Cialdini et al., 1990). This means that pro-environmental injunctive norms emanating from wider society may be weakened if they are less focal than contradictory descriptive norms – for example in a workplace or education environment where many people drive in rather than walk, cycle, or use public transport. Aligning descriptive and injunctive norms is likely to have the most beneficial effects (see Cialdini, 2003), and teaching on sustainability is well advised to pay attention to this.

1.3   Social Identity and Self-categorisation

Social psychology can also make sense of how different – and potentially contradictory – social norms can be associated with different group memberships. The norms of the workplace or place of learning may be entirely different from those of the family, neighbourhood, or nation. According to social identity theory (Tajfel and Turner, 1979), this is because group memberships are important aspects of a person's identity, and the contents of group identity – including its norms – matter to the individual who identifies with the group. The notion that a person may regard themselves as belonging to different groups in different situations is elaborated in self-categorization theory (Turner et al., 1987). The contextual determinants of self-categorization are not important for present purposes (for a summary, see Turner et al., 1994). What is crucial is the ability of self-categorizations or group identifications to create a great deal of normative influence to act in ways that satisfy group norms (Oakes, Haslam and Turner, 1998; Turner, Wetherell and Hogg, 1989). These processes are likely to have played a role in the aforementioned intervention studies that mobilized social group memberships and contexts towards increased pro-environmental efforts (e.g., Siero et al., 1996).

Endeavours to make places of learning more sustainable would therefore benefit from targeting groups that already exist there, rather than appealing to people individually. If groups such as student unions and societies, work teams and departments make sustainability part of their everyday practice and existence, they will exert influence on existing and new group members. Sustainability manifestos such as the one created by Sheffield Students' Union[1] in the UK are therefore valuable as a visible group commitment to a pro-environmental norm. Teaching sustainability effectively may mean appealing to existing group memberships and making clear that sustainability matters to these groups.

1.4   Moral Disengagement

Inconsistent social norms may not be the only reason why many people fail to act sustainably in spite of clear societal messages. It has been suggested that immoral behaviour can be facilitated by moral disengagement, originally to understand terrorism (Bandura, 1990) but more recently in relation to environmental behaviour (Bandura, 2007). According to this theory, people may dissociate themselves from normative pressures to act sustainably by making justifications using other social or moral norms – for example, about individual freedom or economic growth; by making exonerative comparisons with others who are less environmentally friendly; by using euphemistic language to describe unsustainable activity; by placing blame on others, such as legislators; by disputing or understating the impact of their behaviour; or by discounting the value or relevance of the entities affected by their behaviour – for example, small farms replaced by intensive 'biofuel' cultivation.

Moral disengagement strategies in relation to anthropogenic climate change were identified in an analysis of online comments to British newspaper articles (Woods, Coen and Fernández, 2018). Similar rhetoric, which could be interpreted as specific instances of moral disengagement, has also been found in attempts to denigrate climate scientists and climate science, thus delegitimizing pro-environmental initiatives (Jaspal, Nerlich and Koteyko, 2013), and in political speeches pitting 'common sense', jobs and economic development against the 'ideology' of climate targets (Kurz, Augoustinos and Crabb, 2010). Moral disengagement thus appears to be a promising interpretative framework for social-psychological analyses of sustainability-related action and inaction, although its relationships with other relevant approaches discussed here remain poorly understood. Teaching about sustainability could encourage learners to identify moral disengagement in examples of environmentally irresponsible action and relate it to the other social-psychological concepts introduced here.

1.5   The Theory of Planned Behaviour and Self-identity

Education about sustainability must go beyond the transmission of relevant information: knowledge about sustainability does not automatically lead to sustainable actions (Ellen, 1994), and campaigns to promote sustainability therefore cannot rely just on information and publicity (Uzzell, 2018). A more general social-psychological phenomenon is that the correspondence between attitudes and behaviour is often significant, but far from perfect (Kraus, 1995; Wicker, 1969). The theory of planned behaviour (TPB; Ajzen, 1991) tries to explain the attitude–behaviour discrepancy by suggesting that intentions, not attitudes, are the most proximal predictor of intentional behaviour. These intentions, in turn, are informed by attitudes but also by perceived control (the sense that the actor is capable of the behaviour and the environment offers the opportunity) and the subjective norm (the actor's sense of being expected to perform the behaviour). Consequently, behaviour may not correspond to a person's attitudes if there are contradictory normative pressures and/or the person does not feel capable of acting in line with attitudes. This links with the interventions discussed above: for example, perceived control over littering may be increased by prominent and convenient bins, and the subjective norm for energy saving may be increased by feedback about energy use.

The TPB is a widely supported theory (for reviews, see Armitage and Conner, 2001; Conner and Armitage, 1998). In the sustainability area, it has been shown to predict intentions and behaviours linked to household waste recycling (Aguilar-Luzón et al., 2012; Knussen et al., 2004), college paper recycling (Cheung, Chan and Wong, 1999), travel to university (Bamberg, Ajzen and Schmidt, 2003), students' sustainability-related behaviours from water and energy conservation to double-sided printing (de Leeuw et al., 2015), and workplace behaviours such as using video conferencing (Greaves, Zibarras and Stride, 2013). The evidence is less clear about depot-based recycling of specialist waste, where other factors may be particularly impactful (Rhodes et al., 2015).

Suggestions exist to extend the TPB by adding a self-identity construct (Rise, Sheeran and Hukkelberg, 2010; Sparks and Shepherd, 1992). Self-identity (Stryker, 1987; Stryker and Burke, 2000) is from a different tradition than social identity (Tajfel and Turner, 1979) and arguably more about individuals than groups. Its focus is on the roles that people adopt as part of their identities, and the consequences of this. Most importantly for present purposes, roles make role-congruent behaviours feel rewarding (see Burke and Stets, 2009): for example, when someone becomes a parent, they will be intrinsically motivated to perform the behaviours that make them a good parent (and not those that make them the opposite). Similarly, someone for whom sustainability and environmentally friendly habits are 'just part of who I am' will receive pleasure from performing the behaviours associated with that identification. Commitment to role-congruent behaviour (see the commitment interventions outlined above) is built into the adoption of a self-identity. Although self-identity has not yet become an official part of the TPB, its addition has usually worked well (Rise et al., 2010; Sparks, 2000).

Sustainability-related self-identity has been included in TPB studies on household waste recycling. An Australian study with 143 residents (Terry, Hogg and White, 1999) showed that the intention to recycle was predicted by attitudes towards recycling, perceived control over recycling, self-identity as a recycler, and the group norm for recycling among friends and peers (but only for those who strongly identified with the group). Self-reported behaviour, in turn, was predicted by intention and past behaviour. Similar findings were obtained in the United Kingdom (Nigbur, Lyons and Uzzell, 2010), where two studies involving over 700 households showed intentions to be predicted by attitudes, personal norms and perceived control as well as self-identity and a sense of responsibility for recycling. Behaviour was predicted by intentions as proposed by the TPB, but also by self-identity as a recycler and a favourable descriptive neighbourhood norm (i.e., the observation that most neighbours set out their recycling boxes). These findings demonstrate that the TPB and self-identity can predict household waste recycling. But there is a scarcity of research on other sustainability-related behaviours, especially in workplace settings (see Whitmarsh, Haggar and Thomas, 2018).

1.6   The Present Study

A sustainability initiative at our university offered an opportunity to test the TPB (plus self-identity) in the prediction of various sustainability-related behaviours performed by university staff. We expected, from the research reported above, that intentions to act sustainably would be predicted by attitudes, subjective norm, perceived control and self-identity. As usual for TPB studies, questionnaires were used to measure the relevant variables. The data collection reported here happened before a series of sustainability-related interventions under the Green Impact[2] scheme and was therefore unaffected by them. A second phase to assess the effects of the interventions is not reported here because not enough participants responded to both surveys.

2.   METHOD

An online questionnaire was created, approved by a formal ethics review, and deployed using the Qualtrics online survey platform. All staff members at Canterbury Christ Church University (CCCU) in the UK were invited to take part, and 118 of them completed this first survey. The sample included 77 women and 41 men. The youngest participant was 21 years old, the oldest 67 (median age = 47 years, mean age = 44.65). There was a very wide range in length of service at CCCU, from two months to over 33 years. There were 35 members of academic staff, 76 members of staff in non-academic posts, and seven whose jobs could not be unambiguously categorized. It was not expected that these demographic details would systematically affect the measures, and the distributions did not offer adequate statistical power for analysis. This information therefore just serves to describe the sample characteristics.

The survey started with questions about demographics and employment. It then measured the psychological variables using quantitative rating scales, where participants indicated their level of agreement with a written statement on a five-point scale ranging from 'totally disagree' to 'totally agree', 'unlikely' to 'likely', or similar.[3] Sustainability-related attitudes, subjective norms, perceived control, self-identity and intentions were measured using four items each. One of these four items was always about waste recycling (e.g., 'Recycling paper and other materials is entirely under my own control'), one about energy saving (e.g., 'I don't really think it's necessary to switch off currently unused appliances', reverse-scored), one about transport choices (e.g., 'I am not the type of person who would try to use environmentally friendly transport', reverse-scored), and one about water saving (e.g., 'People who are important to me would agree that water should be conserved'). Due to clerical error, the self-identity items included two about energy saving and none about water saving. All four items were used to calculate self-identity scores for the overall analysis, but a separate analysis for water saving became impossible.

Internal reliabilities of multi-item scales were assessed using Cronbach's alpha. Subjective norm ($\alpha = 0.82$) and self-identity ($\alpha = 0.73$) had good internal reliability, intentions were borderline ($\alpha = 0.65$), perceived control ($\alpha = 0.52$) and attitudes ($\alpha = 0.45$) were rather poor. Probably, the four items in each of the scales did not always correlate well because they concerned four different behaviours. For example, someone who feels in control of recycling in the workplace will not necessarily feel in control of energy saving too. Taking this into account, we decided to run one overall analysis to test our hypotheses, and then a set of exploratory analyses for each behaviour separately.

3.   RESULTS

For the overall analysis, composite scores for sustainability-related attitudes, subjective norms, perceived control, self-identity and intentions were calculated as the mean of the four items in each scale. These variables were all in favour of sustainable action, and positively correlated. Table 31.1 contains means, standard deviations and bivariate correlations.

First, we performed a multiple linear regression analysis with sustainability intentions as the outcome and sustainability-related attitudes, subjective norms and perceived control as predictors. This yielded a significant model: $R^2 = 0.35$, $F(3, 114) = 20.06$, $p < 0.001$. In a second step, self-identity was added to test whether it explained additional variance. It did: $R^2 = 0.46$, $F(1, 113) = 23.87$, $p < 0.001$. Subjective norms emerged as a significant predictor in the final model (standardized $\beta = 0.17$, $p = 0.05$), whereas attitudes narrowly ($\beta = 0.16$, $p = 0.07$) and perceived control clearly ($\beta = 0.08$, $p = 0.34$) missed significance. Self-identity was a highly significant predictor ($\beta = 0.43$, $p < 0.001$).

Table 31.1　Scale means, standard deviations and bivariate correlations (Pearson's correlation coefficient)

	Mean	SD	Attitude	Subjective Norm	Perceived Control	Self-identity	Intention
Attitude	4.33	0.53	1				
Subjective norm	4.00	0.83	0.49	1			
Perceived control	3.93	0.66	0.38	0.39	1		
Self-identity	3.56	0.75	0.53	0.49	0.42	1	
Intention	3.94	0.71	0.50	0.49	0.38	0.63	1

Note:　All correlations are significant at $p < 0.001$ (two-tailed).

3.1　Additional Analyses

Because measures of attitudes, subjective norms, perceived control, self-identity and intentions were available for recycling, energy saving and transport choices (but not for water saving as explained above), we ran additional analyses for each of these behaviours separately. The procedure was always the same as for the main analysis: a hierarchical multiple regression analysis with intention as the outcome; attitude, subjective norm and perceived control as predictors in the first step; and self-identity added as a predictor in the second step. This, of course, means that each variable is measured by just one item, which makes an internal reliability analysis obsolete but limits comparability across behaviours because of differences in item phrasing.

For the overall very positive intentions to recycle ($M = 4.53, s = 0.60$), the first step was significant ($R^2 = 0.27, F(3, 114) = 13.71, p < 0.001$) but the model was improved by the second step ($R^2 = 0.36, F(1, 113) = 17.48, p < 0.001$). In the final model, attitude towards recycling ($M = 4.68, s = 0.61, \beta = 0.21, p = 0.01$) significantly predicted intention, as did the subjective norm ($M = 4.33, s = 0.85, \beta = 0.24, p < 0.01$). Perceived control was not a significant predictor ($M = 3.82, s = 1.11, \beta = -0.04, p = 0.57$). Self-identity was highly significant ($M = 3.72, s = 1.11, \beta = 0.35, p < 0.001$).

For the also rather positive energy-saving intentions ($M = 4.43, s = 0.75$), the first step again explained a highly significant amount of variance ($R^2 = 0.42, F(3, 113) = 27.02, p < 0.001$) but the second step improved prediction ($R^2 = 0.49, F(1, 112) = 17.00, p < 0.001$). This time, attitude ($M = 4.32, s = 1.00, \beta = 0.39, p < 0.001$) and perceived control ($M = 4.56, s = 0.69, \beta = 0.24, p < 0.01$) were significant, but the subjective norm was not ($M = 4.12, s = 0.94, \beta = 0.07, p = 0.30$). Self-identity was a significant addition ($M = 3.97, s = 0.77, \beta = 0.30, p < 0.001$).[4]

For intentions to use sustainable transport, which were somewhat lower and more variable ($M = 3.39, s = 1.34$), the first step was significant ($R^2 = 0.39, F(3, 114) = 24.07, p < 0.001$) but the second step improved the model ($R^2 = 0.41, F(1, 113) = 4.36, p = 0.04$). In the final model, attitude was not significant ($M = 4.00, s = 0.93, \beta = 0.06, p = 0.46$), but subjective norm ($M = 3.29, s = 1.35, \beta = 0.31, p < 0.001$) and perceived control

($M = 3.21$, $s = 1.35$, $\beta = 0.33$, $p < 0.001$) were. Self-identity was again significant ($M = 3.68$, $s = 1.07$, $\beta = 0.17$, $p = 0.04$).

4. DISCUSSION

In all our analyses, the regression models including attitudes, subjective norms and perceived control as predictors explained highly significant amounts of variance in sustainability-related intentions. The TPB (Ajzen, 1991) was thus supported, although we were unable to include a measure of behaviour and could therefore only test the part of the TPB that predicts intentions. The addition of self-identity was also supported, explaining a significant amount of additional variance in the overall analysis and all additional analyses about individual behaviours. In fact, self-identity is the only predictor that was significant in all analyses. Our study adds to those that have successfully used the TPB and self-identity to predict sustainable behaviour (Nigbur et al., 2010; Terry et al., 1999), notably in a university rather than a residential setting and on other behaviours in addition to waste recycling.

Unexpectedly, attitudes and perceived control were not significant predictors in the overall analysis (although attitudes were close). This may be because of differences between sustainable behaviours causing poor correlations between them and thus the poor internal scale reliability observed here. But it may also be due to some particular characteristics of the workplace and/or the university, where norms and identity may be especially important. People work as part of a team with concomitant social norms (see Turner et al., 1989), spend every working day in the role of team member with role-congruent behaviour attached (see Burke and Stets, 2009), and are also exposed to influential descriptive norms (see Cialdini et al., 1990) in the campus setting. Although similar influences exist at home, the larger scale and more formal character of a university may have made a difference to our results. Being in a particular space and belonging to a particular group in a particular role will influence a person's sustainability-related actions.

Our additional analyses suggest that different behaviours (or, rather, just the intentions to perform them) may be predicted by different variables in the TPB. This is not a problem for the theory, which does not claim that every predictor must be equally influential to all behaviours (see Ajzen, 1991). But it does mean that interventions targeting particular behaviours should benefit from targeting particularly influential predictors. For example, intentions to travel to campus by sustainable means were not predicted by our participants' (very positive) attitudes towards sustainable transport, but predicted in some magnitude by perceived control. A closer look at why some people feel more in control than others – speculatively, perhaps something to do with the availability of public transport – may be instructive here. On the other hand, attitudes strongly predicted energy-saving intentions, perhaps because behaviours such as turning off lights and computers when leaving are comparatively private (Uzzell, 2018) and therefore determined to a greater extent by someone's personal attitude. Education towards sustainability thus has (at least) attitudes, norms, perceived control and self-identity as potential targets, and could potentially be tailored to local circumstances if particularly strong or weak predictors of sustainable intentions and behaviour are known or could be determined.

In addition to the flaws already mentioned, a limitation to our study is that only two of the questionnaire items used for the analysis reported here explicitly mentioned the workplace (e.g., 'I will recycle at work wherever possible in the future'). Although these questions were surrounded by instructions, items not used in the present analysis, and the wider context of the Green Impact scheme, which should all have made clear that the study was about sustainability at the university, it is possible that participants' home and personal lives may have influenced their questionnaire responses – in the case of transport choices, which highlighted the commute between home and work, inevitably so. This makes no difference to the conclusions drawn here, but more explicit specification might have improved the predictive power of the regression models (see Ajzen, 1991). A more general limitation affecting all attempts to investigate sustainability at an individual level of analysis is that they tempt readers to overlook the wider conditions. We do not intend to suggest that individual actions and their predictors are the best or only key to protecting the environment, or that education about sustainability should focus exclusively on them. If offices and teaching spaces with insufficient natural light or fresh air make artificial illumination or air conditioning necessary (Uzzell, 2018), or if frequent travel by unsustainable means is a prerequisite for job success, campaigns should target these systems and conditions rather than the individuals who try their best to function under them.

By replicating some of the findings from previous studies on the TPB, self-identity and sustainability (Nigbur et al., 2010; Terry et al., 1999), our university-based study points towards the potential of mobilizing norms and identity towards more environmentally sustainable practice. Teaching about sustainability need not limit itself to the communication of knowledge or the cultivation of positive individual attitudes. Even if the physical environment already affords opportunities to be environmentally friendly, teaching can promote a social environment that expects sustainable behaviour and makes sustainability a part of each member's role and self-concept – an integral part of who we are.

NOTES

1. 'Student manifesto for a sustainable University of Sheffield'. Accessed 24 April 2020 at https://issuu.com/sheffieldstudentsunion/docs/studentmanifesto_illustrated_final.
2. 'About Green Impact'. Accessed 24 April 2020 at https://sustainability.nus.org.uk/green-impact/about.
3. The survey contained several measures (moral disengagement, knowledge of local facilities, barriers and facilitators of sustainable behaviour, identification with CCCU) that were ultimately excluded for conceptual or statistical reasons. They are mentioned in this note for the sake of transparency; some exploratory analyses have been presented elsewhere (Nigbur et al., 2012).
4. This analysis includes one case fewer because a multivariate outlier was identified and excluded to prevent a disproportionate influence on the model. Running the analysis with the outlier included yielded different statistics, but the same conclusions about statistical significance.

REFERENCES

Aguilar-Luzón, M. del C., García-Martínez, J.M.Á., Calvo-Salguero, A. and Salinas, J.M. (2012). Comparative study between the theory of planned behavior and the value–belief–norm model regarding the environment, on Spanish housewives' recycling behavior. *Journal of Applied Social Psychology*, 42(11), 2797–833.
Ajzen, I. (1991). The theory of planned behavior. *Organizational Behavior and Human Decision Processes*, 50(2), 179–211.

Allcott, H. (2011). Social norms and energy conservation. *Journal of Public Economics*, 95(9), 1082–95.

Armitage, C.J. and Conner, M. (2001). Efficacy of the theory of planned behaviour: a meta-analytic review. *British Journal of Social Psychology*, 40(4), 471–99.

Austin, J., Hatfield, D.B., Grindle, A.C. and Bailey, J.S. (1993). Increasing recycling in office environments: the effects of specific, informative cues. *Journal of Applied Behavior Analysis*, 26(2), 247–53.

Bamberg, S., Ajzen, I. and Schmidt, P. (2003). Choice of travel mode in the theory of planned behavior: the roles of past behavior, habit, and reasoned action. *Basic and Applied Social Psychology*, 25(3), 175–87.

Bandura, A. (1990). Mechanisms of moral disengagement. In W. Reich (ed.), *Origins of Terrorism: Psychologies, Ideologies, Theologies, States of Mind* (pp. 161–91). Cambridge, UK: Cambridge University Press.

Bandura, A. (2007). Impeding ecological sustainability through selective moral disengagement. *International Journal of Innovation and Sustainable Development*, 2(1), 8–35.

Burke, P.J. and Stets, J.E. (2009). *Identity Theory*. New York: Oxford University Press.

Burn, S.M. (1991). Social psychology and the stimulation of recycling behaviors: the block leader approach. *Journal of Applied Social Psychology*, 21(8), 611–29.

Cheung, S.F., Chan, D.K.-S. and Wong, Z.S.-Y. (1999). Reexamining the theory of planned behavior in understanding wastepaper recycling. *Environment and Behavior*, 31(5), 587–612.

Cialdini, R.B. (2003). Crafting normative messages to protect the environment. *Current Directions in Psychological Science*, 12(4), 105–9.

Cialdini, R.B., Kallgren, C.A. and Reno, R.R. (1991). A focus theory of normative conduct: as theoretical refinement and re-evaluation of the role of norms in human behavior. In M.P. Zanna (ed.), *Advances in Experimental Social Psychology* (Vol. 24, pp. 201–34). San Diego, CA: Academic Press.

Cialdini, R.B., Reno, R.R. and Kallgren, C.A. (1990). A focus theory of normative conduct: recycling the concept of norms to reduce littering in public places. *Journal of Personality and Social Psychology*, 58(6), 1015–26.

Conner, M. and Armitage, C.J. (1998). Extending the theory of planned behavior: a review and avenues for further research. *Journal of Applied Social Psychology*, 28(15), 1429–64.

Couch, J.V., Garber, T. and Karpus, L. (1978). Response maintenance and paper recycling. *Journal of Environmental Systems*, 8, 127–37.

de Leeuw, A., Valois, P., Ajzen, I. and Schmidt, P. (2015). Using the theory of planned behavior to identify key beliefs underlying pro-environmental behavior in high-school students: implications for educational interventions. *Journal of Environmental Psychology*, 42, 128–38.

Dwyer, W.O., Leeming, F.C. and Cobern, M.K. et al. (1993). Critical review of behavioral interventions to preserve the environment: research since 1980. *Environment and Behavior*, 25(5), 275–321.

Ellen, P.S. (1994). Do we know what we need to know? Objective and subjective knowledge effects on pro-ecological behaviors. *Journal of Business Research*, 30(1), 43–52.

Geller, E.S., Brasted, W.S. and Mann, M.F. (1979). Waste receptacle designs as interventions for litter control. *Journal of Environmental Systems*, 9(2), 145–60.

Greaves, M., Zibarras, L.D. and Stride, C. (2013). Using the theory of planned behavior to explore environmental behavioral intentions in the workplace. *Journal of Environmental Psychology*, 34, 109–20.

Hamad, C.D., Bettinger, R., Cooper, D. and Semb, G. (1980). Using behavioral procedures to establish an elementary school paper recycling program. *Journal of Environmental Systems*, 10(2), 149–56.

Hopper, J.R. and Nielsen, J.M. (1991). Recycling as altruistic behavior: normative and behavioral strategies to expand participation in a community recycling program. *Environment and Behavior*, 23(2), 195–220.

Hornik, J., Cherian, J., Madansky, M. and Narayana, C. (1995). Determinants of recycling behavior: a synthesis of research results. *The Journal of Socio-Economics*, 24(1), 105–27.

Humphrey, C.R., Bord, R.J., Hammond, M.M. and Mann, S.H. (1977). Attitudes and conditions for cooperation in a paper recycling program. *Environment and Behavior*, 9(1), 107–24.

Jaspal, R., Nerlich, B. and Koteyko, N. (2013). Contesting science by appealing to its norms: readers discuss climate science in the *Daily Mail*. *Science Communication*, 35(3), 383–410.

Katzev, R. and Mishima, H.R. (1992). The use of posted feedback to promote recycling. *Psychological Reports*, 71(1), 259–64.

Knussen, C., Yule, F., MacKenzie, J. and Wells, M. (2004). An analysis of intentions to recycle household waste: the roles of past behaviour, perceived habit, and perceived lack of facilities. *Journal of Environmental Psychology*, 24(2), 237–46.

Kraus, S.J. (1995). Attitudes and the prediction of behavior: a meta-analysis of the empirical literature. *Personality and Social Psychology Bulletin*, 21(1), 58–75.

Kurz, T., Augoustinos, M. and Crabb, S. (2010). Contesting the 'national interest' and maintaining 'our lifestyle': a discursive analysis of political rhetoric around climate change. *British Journal of Social Psychology*, 49(3), 601–25.

Larson, M.E., Houlihan, D. and Goernert, P.N. (1995). Brief report: effects of informational feedback on aluminum can recycling. *Behavioral Interventions*, 10(2), 111–17.

Luyben, P.D. and Cummings, S. (1982). Motivating beverage container recycling on a college campus. *Journal of Environmental Systems*, 11(3), 235–45.

Nigbur, D., Coen, S., Fernández, A., Franz, A. and Hocking, I. (2012). The theory of planned behaviour, self-identity, and moral disengagement: what predicts sustainability at work? Presentation at the BPS Social Psychology Section Conference, University of St Andrews, 21 August.

Nigbur, D., Lyons, E. and Uzzell, D. (2010). Attitudes, norms, identity and environmental behaviour: using an expanded theory of planned behaviour to predict participation in a kerbside recycling programme. *British Journal of Social Psychology*, 49(2), 259–84.

Oakes, P., Haslam, S.A. and Turner, J.C. (1998). The role of prototypicality in group influence and cohesion: contextual variation in the graded structure of social categories. In S. Worchel, J.F. Morales, D. Páez and J.-C. Deschamps (eds), *Social Identity: International Perspectives* (pp. 75–92). Thousand Oaks, CA: SAGE.

Reno, R.R., Cialdini, R.B. and Kallgren, C.A. (1993). The transsituational influence of social norms. *Journal of Personality and Social Psychology*, 64(1), 104–12.

Rhodes, R.E., Beauchamp, M.R. and Conner, M. et al. (2015). Prediction of depot-based specialty recycling behavior using an extended theory of planned behavior. *Environment and Behavior*, 47(9), 1001–23.

Rise, J., Sheeran, P. and Hukkelberg, S. (2010). The role of self-identity in the theory of planned behavior: a meta-analysis. *Journal of Applied Social Psychology*, 40(5), 1085–105.

Schultz, P.W., Oskamp, S. and Mainieri, T. (1995). Who recycles and when? A review of personal and situational factors. *Journal of Environmental Psychology*, 15(2), 105–21.

Siero, F.W., Bakker, A.B., Dekker, G.B. and Van Den Burg, M.T.C. (1996). Changing organizational energy consumption behaviour through comparative feedback. *Journal of Environmental Psychology*, 16(3), 235–46.

Sparks, P. (2000). Subjective expected utility-based attitude–behavior models: the utility of self-identity. In D.J. Terry and M.A. Hogg (eds), *Attitudes, Behavior, and Social Context: The Role of Norms and Group Membership* (pp. 31–46). Abingdon: Routledge.

Sparks, P. and Shepherd, R. (1992). Self-identity and the theory of planned behavior: assessing the role of identification with 'green consumerism'. *Social Psychology Quarterly*, 55(4), 388–99.

Stryker, S. (1987). Identity theory: developments and extensions. In K. Yardley and T. Honess (eds), *Self and Identity: Psychosocial Perspectives* (pp. 89–103). New York: John Wiley & Sons.

Stryker, S. and Burke, P.J. (2000). The past, present, and future of an identity theory. *Social Psychology Quarterly*, 63(4), 284–97.

Tajfel, H. and Turner, J.C. (1979). An integrative theory of intergroup conflict. In W.G. Austin and S. Worchel (eds), *The Social Psychology of Intergroup Relations* (pp. 33–47). Monterey, CA: Brooks/Cole.

Terry, D.J., Hogg, M.A. and White, K.M. (1999). The theory of planned behaviour: self-identity, social identity and group norms. *British Journal of Social Psychology*, 38(3), 225–44.

Turner, J.C., Hogg, M.A. and Oakes, P.J. et al. (1987). *Rediscovering the Social Group: A Self-categorization Theory*. Oxford: Wiley-Blackwell.

Turner, J.C., Oakes, P.J., Haslam, S.A. and McGarty, C. (1994). Self and collective: cognition and social context. *Personality and Social Psychology Bulletin*, 20(5), 454–63.

Turner, J.C., Wetherell, M.S. and Hogg, M.A. (1989). Referent informational influence and group polarization. *British Journal of Social Psychology*, 28(2), 135–47.

Uzzell, D. (2018). Changing behaviour: energy consumption [Briefing]. British Psychological Society. Accessed 24 April 2020 at https://www.bps.org.uk/news-and-policy/changing-behaviour-energy-consumption.

Wang, T.H. and Katzev, R.D. (1990). Group commitment and resource conservation: two field experiments on promoting recycling. *Journal of Applied Social Psychology*, 20(4), 265–75.

Whitmarsh, L.E., Haggar, P. and Thomas, M. (2018). Waste reduction behaviors at home, at work, and on holiday: what influences behavioral consistency across contexts? *Frontiers in Psychology*, 9, Article 2447. https://doi.org/10.3389/fpsyg.2018.02447.

Wicker, A.W. (1969). Attitudes versus actions: the relationship of verbal and overt behavioral responses to attitude objects. *Journal of Social Issues*, 25(4), 41–78.

Woods, R., Coen, S. and Fernández, A. (2018). Moral (dis)engagement with anthropogenic climate change in online comments on newspaper articles. *Journal of Community and Applied Social Psychology*, 28(4), 244–57.

32. Challenges in sustainability teaching
Walter Leal Filho

BACKGROUND: BARRIERS TO SUSTAINABILITY TEACHING

Sustainability learning and teaching have become more prominent and essential in recent times due to the various environmental crises and depletion of resources (Eagle et al., 2019). However, there are many challenges and barriers to implementing successful sustainable teaching (Leal Filho et al., 2017).

The main barriers to implementing sustainability teaching are related to financial constraints, lack of knowledge, attitudes towards sustainable living, and problems in developing coherent curriculums (Ralph and Stubbs, 2014). Other major challenges include institutional priorities and external pressures, including the redirection of campus funds to more prioritised problems (Blanco-Portela et al., 2017).

With regard to financial resources, there is a lack of incentives in directing capital towards sustainability learning, as opposed to other initiatives (Blanco-Portela et al., 2017; Chukwu, Chinyelugo and Eze, 2017), especially those whose yields are more visible (e.g., marketing). This discrepancy is mainly driven by the lack of awareness and sometimes institutional knowledge of the need for sustainability teaching. In higher education institutions, there are several interdisciplinary issues that prevent the development of a holistic approach towards sustainability learning (Blanco-Portela et al., 2017). Such problems are often attributed to poor management and lack of leadership within the university. Stronger departments are more resistant to change and sometimes prevent other departments from successfully implementing sustainable education practices and teaching methods (Blanco-Portela et al., 2017; Dmochowski et al., 2016; Sammalisto, Sundström and Holm, 2015).

Furthermore, institutional frameworks are often designed without prioritising sustainability and environmental consciousness. This hinders the design of strategies and policies towards implementing sustainability at higher education institutions. Furthermore, some universities do not have sustainable policies in their mission statements, thereby reducing the pressure to implement such teaching practices in their curriculum. In addition, a lack of institutional frameworks often prevents the acquisition of external funding for such programmes, initiatives and strategies because they are not aligned with the university's mission statement (Blanco-Portela et al., 2017).

Pressures to pursue or implement sustainable development practices are sometimes created by external stakeholders, but often these have only specific aims in mind. Since these predominantly focus on university operations or on research, this diminishes the need for focusing on sustainability teaching. The lack of pressure is also driven by education models that do not conform to local needs, as well as the lack of awareness about environmental issues and the need for effective solutions to environmental problems (ibid.), which may be better handled under a sustainability perspective.

Another major challenge seen in sustainability teaching is the lack of interest from the public and important stakeholders. People often lack information about environmental crises as well as the climate change problems seen around the world (Abubakar, Al-Shihri and Ahmed, 2016; Blanco-Portela et al., 2017). Furthermore, some cultural barriers exist, as some cultures prevent people from implementing change. They often believe that change is unnecessary, or that will it interfere with their cultural norms and practices (Blanco-Portela et al., 2017).

At educational institutions, staff often lack the academic training to educate others about sustainability practices. In other instances, academic staff who are properly trained feel that they are not adequately compensated for their efforts and therefore move away from sustainable teaching, thus preventing the successful implementation of sustainability in higher education (Blanco-Portela et al., 2017; Crosling et al., 2020).

Many educational institutions have adopted sustainability teaching initiatives. However, this is insufficient as not all members of society have access to such education. Therefore, there is a major need to introduce place-based and community-based education programmes, to ensure that the local community has equal opportunities with regard to sustainability education. This could be implemented by higher education institutions that have the resources and funds to facilitate pre-service, in-service and project-based learning, as well as regionally oriented education programmes to ensure that people are equipped for the increasing socio-ecological problems. This approach would create a method of transformative learning that allows people to develop sustainable solutions that can assist local communities (Hensley, 2017).

Sustainability development education and teaching has been described as a transformative learning process. Learners often require time to adapt to transformational learning, which poses many challenges to educators, including learners' emotional and mental stress, and the resulting ethical considerations that need to be accounted for. Therefore, educators must make sure that resources are used to guarantee that the learners' mental capacity is considered to allow for quality assurance. The transformative learning process requires cooperation on a transdisciplinary level, ensuring that all frameworks are consolidated and that learners' mental health is taken care of (Förster, Zimmermann and Mader, 2019).

A recent study summarised some barriers identified by students that prevent the successful implementation of sustainability education. The major barriers included a lack of interest in sustainability as well as time constraints. Furthermore, they found no correlation between sustainability teaching and their chosen major. This makes it difficult to ensure proper sustainability teaching. In addition to this, many students found that it may clash with their well-established goals. They also stated that they noticed a lack of preparation by their educational institution, as well as insufficient motivation and awareness created by the professors (Pompeii et al., 2019).

However, faculty and students were able to identify solutions to problems, including the development of awareness-raising campaigns and the provision of the necessary incentives to both staff and students. Another suggestion was to develop links between major subjects and sustainable education as well as links toward future careers, thus helping in the promotion of sustainability teaching. In addition, more interdisciplinary action was suggested for courses that may be developed for all faculties to contribute to. In another instance, students suggested methods to obtain funding to develop new modules for education (ibid.).

Additionally, several government policies inhibit sustainability teaching and delay the process of sustainability education. Governments have the responsibility of promoting sustainability teaching through transparent programmes. Furthermore, they are expected to help in the funding of such initiatives for the betterment of their country. However, this is not always being carried out. The lack of government regulation – and commitment – often discourages stakeholders from engaging in sustainability teaching. Furthermore, this causes local communities to lose interest in such processes due to lack of communication from the government, which they trust (Blanco-Portela et al., 2017).

In addition to the lack of governmental awareness, many disciplines fail to share the responsibility of creating successful educational programmes. By combining the resources, funding and expertise from local governments, community, health and education sectors, many countries may be able to implement sustainability teaching despite the obvious challenges. Environment and education ministries can, for instance, connect both the formal and non-formal sectors through sustainability teaching, as a tool to pursue environmental conservation. However, in many countries, this responsibility is not always taken seriously, thereby hindering the implementation of sustainability teaching as part of the educational process (Blanco-Portela et al., 2017; Shiel et al., 2016).

THE WAY AHEAD

Moving forward, there are some tools and methods that can be deployed in order to further the cause of sustainable development teaching. Some of them are summarised in Table 32.1.

In addition, the use of techniques to foster the more active participation of learners

Table 32.1 Some elements that may support sustainability teaching

Element	Reasoning
Appropriate teaching methods	Raises interest of students and facilitates the learning process
Students' engagement in teaching	Fosters greater participation
Variety of methods	Caters for learning under different settings
Combination of theory and practice	Offers a balanced view and demonstrates why some contents are useful in real life
Contextualisation	Helps students to better understand what sustainability means in a concrete setting (e.g., sustainable consumption)
Balanced global–local focus	Helps to show how international issues and developments may influence global ones, and vice versa
Gathering of feedback	Supports teaching efforts by obtaining information from learners during the semester, as opposed to doing so at the end of the term
Adequate evaluation procedures	Helps to measure learning more holistically than traditional exams may do

---

BOX 32.1   ACTIVATED TEACHING

Activated teaching refers to an approach whereby passive, teacher-to-students-centred learning is replaced by students–teachers and students–students interactions. It can involve, for instance, a project-based learning or a problem-based learning approach where students build the skills as they perform specific tasks (e.g., reading, discussing, interactions or individual research tasks) in an interactive way, as opposed to conventional ('I teach, you listen') lectures.

---

may also help. Box 32.1, for instance, describes 'activated learning', a tool that is being increasingly used in educational systems round the world.

This book has shown many examples of strategies, teaching methods and tools that have been successful in overcoming the many challenges outlined in this concluding chapter.

CONCLUSIONS

The pursuit of sustainable development teaching is a complex task and one characterised by many logistical and economic barriers. There are, however, many ways to overcome these barriers. Choosing the right approach is likely to yield the expected benefits. While it is well known that sustainability teaching may contribute to the learning process and can assist in fostering the skills required to allow learners to better understand the economic, political and social issues that are connected with environmental ones, it is not being as widely practised as it should be. This trend needs to change to unlock the transformative power of sustainability teaching as a tool to inform and better engage learners, and hence enable them make a positive effect on their own lives, both personal and professional.

REFERENCES

Abubakar, I.R., Al-Shihri, F.S. and Ahmed, S.M. (2016). Students' assessment of campus sustainability at the University of Dammam, Saudi Arabia. *Sustainability*, 8(1), 59.

Blanco-Portela, N., Benayas, J., Pertierra, L.R. and Lozano, R. (2017). Towards the integration of sustainability in higher education institutions: a review of drivers of and barriers to organisational change and their comparison against those found of companies. *Journal of Cleaner Production*, 166, 563–78.

Chukwu, L.C., Chinyelugo, A.F. and Eze, S. (2017). Financing university education for sustainable development in Nigeria: issues and challenges. *Journal of Education and Practice*, 8(1), 61–5.

Crosling, G., Atherton, G. and Shuib, M. et al. (2020). The teaching of sustainability in higher education: improving environmental resilience in Malaysia. In E. Sengupta, P. Blessinger and T.S. Yamin (eds), *Introduction to Sustainable Development Leadership and Strategies in Higher Education. Innovations in Higher Education Teaching and Learning Volume 22* (pp. 17–38). Bingley, UK: Emerald Publishing Limited.

Dmochowski, J.E., Garofalo, D. and Fisher, S. et al. (2016). Integrating sustainability across the university curriculum. *International Journal of Sustainability in Higher Education*, 17(5), 652–70.

Eagle, L., McCarthy, B. and Hay, R. et al. (2019). Stakeholder perceptions of the importance and effects of sustainability education. In G. Eweje and R.J. Bathurst (eds), *Clean, Green and Responsible?* (pp. 65–86). Cham, Switzerland: Springer.

Förster, R., Zimmermann, A.B. and Mader, C. (2019). Transformative teaching in higher education for sustainable development: facing the challenges. *GAIA – Ecological Perspectives for Science and Society*, 28(3), 324–6.

Hensley, N. (2017, 24 March). The future of sustainability in higher education. *Journal of Sustainability Education.* Accessed 27 February 2021 at http://www.susted.com/wordpress/content/the-future-of-sustainability-in-higher-education_2017_03/.

Leal Filho, W., Wu, Y.-C.J. and Brandli, L.L. et al. (2017). Identifying and overcoming obstacles to the implementation of sustainable development at universities, *Journal of Integrative Environmental Sciences,* 14(1), 93–108.

Pompeii, B., Chiu, Y.-W. and Neill, D. et al. (2019). Identifying and overcoming barriers to integrating sustainability across the curriculum at a teaching-oriented university. *Sustainability,* 11(9), Article 2652.

Ralph, M. and Stubbs, W. (2014). Integrating environmental sustainability into universities. *Higher Education,* 67(1), 71–90.

Sammalisto, K., Sundström, A. and Holm, T. (2015). Implementation of sustainability in universities as perceived by faculty and staff – a model from a Swedish university. *Journal of Cleaner Production,* 106, 45–54.

Shiel, C., Leal Filho, W., do Paço, A. and Brandli, L. (2016). Evaluating the engagement of universities in capacity building for sustainable development in local communities. *Evaluation and Program Planning,* 54, 123–34.

Index

Printed and bound by CPI Group (UK) Ltd, Croydon, CR0 4YY

16/04/2025

14658390-0001